The Restoring Truth Series

Book One
The Elijah Calling
&

Book Two
Elijah vs Antichrist

by

Ken Mentell

Copyright © 2017 Ken Mentell

CreateSpace Independent Publishing Platform, North Charleston, SC

ISBN-13:
978-1985824614

ISBN-10:
1985824612

DEDICATION

May the Lord bless you and guard you–יְבָרֶכְךָ יְהֹוָה, וְיִשְׁמְרֶךָ
May the Lord shine His countenance toward you and be gracious to
you–יָאֵר יְהֹוָה פָּנָיו אֵלֶיךָ, וִיחֻנֶּךָּ
May the Lord lift up His countenance toward you and give you peace–
יִשָּׂא יְהֹוָה פָּנָיו אֵלֶיךָ, וְיָשֵׂם לְךָ שָׁלוֹם

Sh'ma Yis'ra'eil Adonai Eloheinu Adonai echad.
Hear, Israel, the Lord is our God, the Lord is One.

Exodus 3: 14, And God said unto Moses, I Am That I Am: and he said,
Thus shalt thou say unto the children of Israel, I Am hath sent me unto
you. 15 And God said moreover unto Moses, Thus shalt thou say unto the
children of Israel, the Lord God of your fathers, the God of Abraham, the
God of Isaac, and the God of Jacob, hath sent me unto you: this is my
name for ever, and this is my memorial unto all generations.

יד וַיֹּאמֶר אֱלֹהִים אֶל–מֹשֶׁה ,אֶהְיֶה אֲשֶׁר אֶהְיֶה ;וַיֹּאמֶר ,כֹּה
תֹאמַר לִבְנֵי יִשְׂרָאֵל ,אֶהְיֶה ,שְׁלָחַנִי אֲלֵיכֶם.
טו וַיֹּאמֶר עוֹד אֱלֹהִים אֶל–מֹשֶׁה ,כֹּה–תֹאמַר אֶל–בְּנֵי
יִשְׂרָאֵל ,יְהֹוָה אֱלֹהֵי אֲבֹתֵיכֶם אֱלֹהֵי אַבְרָהָם אֱלֹהֵי יִצְחָק וֵאלֹהֵי
יַעֲקֹב ,שְׁלָחַנִי אֲלֵיכֶם ;זֶה–שְׁמִי לְעֹלָם ,וְזֶה זִכְרִי לְדֹר דֹּר.

CONTENTS

RESTORING TRUTH SERIES

1 CO-EXISTENCE OR NON-EXISTENCE

Christianity is becoming irrelevant…culturally, socially, and morally. The modern liberal will tell you to "be nice", "be loving", "be accepting", "tone it down", or you just are not Christian. Many believers have bought this psychological ploy hook line and sinker. If you choose any other path than coexistence you will likely be chastised into non-existence…even by other Christians. It is now culturally acceptable for liberals to chastise and berate Christians for their beliefs and when they choose to respond they are told to be nice, be quiet, and don't challenge those who believe differently. As if this was the Godly and scriptural criteria for being Christian. Many believers today have forgotten that the apostles laid down their lives in sacrifice to tell people who disagreed with them about the Gospel! Not only that, they travelled thousands of miles into foreign territories, ruled by foreign powers to challenge the status quo about their beliefs. The modern Christian needs to be challenged. Be quiet and fit in? Is this what the Bible tells you? The modern Christian who likely has rarely cracked their bible will likely say… "yes…it's the way to be a good person and show the love of Christ." Shockingly the Apostle Paul, the Apostle of Grace, has a different answer.

> 2 Corinthians, 6:17, Wherefore come out from among them, and be ye separate, saith the Lord, and touch not the unclean thing; and I will receive you.

Paul is indicating very clearly to New Testament believers that there is something to "come out" from and something "unclean" to depart from. How does this jive with the modern Christian teaching that all things are clean, and all things are lawful?

What does the Christian believer do in their pursuit of holiness and truth? What are they to use for their moral and spiritual guide? The liberal of today will tell you that the measure for truth is "acceptance", but the Holy Bible has a much deeper code for holiness. God reached down into the affairs of man on more than once occasion…in fact on many occasions but only twice in history to date has He done so with miracles that shook nations and empires with the visible manifestation of His presence.

The Bible tells us that on both occasions Jesus Christ (Yeshua the Messiah) was present. The first time God manifested His glory to an entire nation called out of Egypt for the expressed goal of giving them His sanctified Law. He did it with awesome power, miraculous wonders, and fear inducing sound. The second time He did it with compassionate wonder, healing power, and resurrection life. Both times was for the purpose of expressing His never-ending grace and law. Both times to manifest His image and His name and to cast down false idols, images, and names. All of these terms can be synonymous for how God operates in manifesting His presence as the true God, true Image, and true name (person) vs. a false idol, broken image, or a name (person) that will not receive eternal life.

> 1 Samuel 24:21, Swear now therefore unto me by the Lord, that thou wilt not cut off my seed after me, and that thou wilt not destroy my name out of my father's house.

Just as every person comes under judgment, this judgment is personified by an evaluation of their seed, their name, and whether they will continue to exist (manifest) or come under judgment and be "cut off" from their "house". Just as every person manifests a name, so does God.

> "Like other Hebrew proper names, the name of God is more than a mere distinguishing title. It represents the Hebrew conception of the divine nature or character and of the relation of God to His people. It represents the Deity as He is known to His worshipers, and stands for all those attributes which He bears in relation to them and which are revealed to them through His activity on their behalf. A new manifestation of His interest or care may give rise to a new name. So, also, an old name may acquire new content and significance through new and varied experience of these sacred relations.

> It can readily be understood, therefore, how the divine name is often spoken of as equivalent to the divine presence or power or glory. In Ex. xxiii. 20-23 it is promised that Yhwh's angel will lead and give victory to His people, who must yield reverent obedience, for, the Lord says, "my name is in him." (Jewish Encyclopedia)

The Written Law of Moses is heavily focused on holiness and acceptable behavior before God. All of the ten commandments associate those approved behaviors vs. unapproved behaviors with proper worship of God vs. worshiping idols and fallen images.

When the Law was first given to Moses, God wrote it with His own hand with the expressed instruction that nothing should be added to it or taken away from it. This was called the Written Law of Moses. Over the centuries the Pharisees and Rabbinical teachers handed down their own Oral Traditions called the Oral Law. In time these Oral Traditions started to be treated the same as the Written Law and actually ended up becoming a burden and in some cases violated the Written Law.

The modern Christian has likely been taught that the law has been done away, but is that what the Old and New Testament scriptures actually say? Did the first century church actually stop keeping the Written Law of Moses? Or did they follow Yeshua's instruction regarding the Written Law and His criticism of the Pharisees' Rabbinical Oral Law? In our zeal to accept the gift of grace have we in our haste thrown out the biblically mandated Written Law that Yeshua said would never pass away?

Matthew 5:18, For verily I say unto you, Till heaven and earth pass, one jot or one tittle shall in no wise pass from the law, till all be fulfilled.

Can Christianity exist without God's law? Can grace exist without God's law? What need for grace…if there is no law? Is the measure of truth for the Christian love without conditions? Love without holiness? What was the measure of truth and what did the Apostles and first century Christians use to determine holiness vs. coexistence? Can the modern Christian dismiss this issue as unimportant and irrelevant? Let's check what the scriptures say…and then decide.

Believers need to remember this fundamental point of those who tell them to Co-exist. They in reality are being told to hide the manifestation of the seed of the Kingdom of God. They can believe what they want and worship as they desire, but that must not interfere with the social order. Freedom of religion has disappeared in the name of "freedom of worship". Their beliefs are forced to be hidden in the name of Co-existence and their beliefs hidden into non-existence. Those who fail to do so will be labeled, unloving, radical, judgmental, arrogant, and critical of others. Knowing this what does the Bible tell the believer to do? We cannot escape the fundamental truth of the scriptures that there was once a nation that expressed saving faith in the blood of the lamb, was delivered from a people who told them to coexist and become their slaves. Once God delivered these people of faith, he didn't tell them to just fit in and make those nations around them feel good. He drew them out and manifested His name, His presence, His image, and His countenance, for the sole purpose of giving them His law, not so they could coexist, but so that they could be a light to the nations. The believer of today has the same burden as the believer 4,000 years ago, be saved by faith in the Lord and receive His law and manifest it. How will Christians respond? Will they accept the mandate of the state to worship only in your heart, while restrained from manifesting those beliefs in outward action? Or will they do what the Bible tells them to do and write the Law of God in the inward parts and manifest it in their outward actions (Jeremiah 31:33)?

The apostle James gives us a clear answer. "Yea, a man may say, Thou hast faith, and I have works: shew me thy faith without thy works, and I will shew thee my faith by my works. (James 2:18)

2 EVIDENCE FOR TRUTH

John 1: 17, For the law was given by Moses, but grace and truth came by Jesus. (KJV throughout)

What do the scriptures actually say about the Christian's need to keep the Written Law of Moses (the Torah)?   How does this grace and truth relate to the Law of Moses, if at all?

The Prophet Malachi gives a dire warning to the final generation before the return of the Messiah and that warning is centered on the need to return to scriptural truth. Yeshua (Hebrew for "Jesus" which will be used for the entirety of the book) and the Apostles reinforced this warning that the generations leading up to His return would be confused by darkness and strong delusion.

Why use the name Yeshua instead of Jesus?   The meaning of His name is significant to the purpose of His coming and the nature of His being. Understanding the original nature of both will bring clarity to the believer's understanding of the veracity of the scriptures and will give you the tools to defend your faith. So let's establish the connection between Jesus (Yeshua) and YHWH and how that relates to God's manifest presence from a scripturally provable standpoint. We will use the spelling of YHWH without vowels as the Hebrew written language does not use vowels. We would rather not devolve into debates over the proper pronunciation of the name. Suffice it to say that translations of the Bible using the word "LORD" is actually replacing the actual proper name of "YHWH". It is important to understand that YHWH is associated with God "manifesting" and was revealed to Israel and Moses while God manifested His presence to the world in the process of delivering Israel from Egypt to the Promised Land. He literally was rescuing Israel through "manifestation" and glory.

Yeshua (ישוע, with vowel pointing יֵשׁוּעַ–yēšūăʻ in Hebrew)[1] was a common alternative form of the name יְהוֹשֻׁעַ ("Yehoshuah"–Joshua) in later books of the Hebrew Bible and among Jews of the Second Temple period. The name corresponds to the Greek spelling Iesous, from which, through the Latin

Iesus, comes the English spelling Jesus. [2][3]... Yeshua in Hebrew is verbal derivative from "to rescue", "to deliver". [9] Its usage among the Jews of the Second Temple Period, the Biblical Aramaic/Hebrew name יֵשׁוּעַ Yeshua was common: the Hebrew Bible mentions several individuals with this name–while also using their full name Joshua. (Wikipedia)

YHWH is pronounced YEHOVA. The vowel pointing has been hidden by the Rabbis for millennia and passed down from Rabbi to student in sacred ceremonies once every seven years. The vowel pointing is hidden by the fact that YHWH inhabits Eternity.

Exodus 3:15, And God said moreover unto Moses, Thus shalt thou say unto the children of Israel, the LORD God of your fathers, the God of Abraham, the God of Isaac, and the God of Jacob, hath sent me unto you: <u>this is my name for ever</u>, and this is my memorial unto all generations.

When you pray be sure to pray in the name of Yeshua YEHOVA.

How did so many faithful followers of Yeshua become so entrenched in unscriptural beliefs, ideas, and paradigms that no longer bear the hallmark of Godly truth? Yeshua clarifies that all who seek to worship God should do so in "truth".

John 4: 24, God is a Spirit: and they that worship him must worship him in spirit and in truth.

He further clarifies that this is the sanctification process that every Christian must go through.

John 17: 17, Sanctify them through thy truth: thy word is truth.

Yeshua clarified that He came into the world to achieve the fundamental goal of bearing witness to the truth.

John 18: 37, Pilate therefore said unto him, Art thou a king then? Yeshua answered, Thou sayest that I am a king. To this end was I born, and for this cause came I into the world, that I should bear witness unto the truth. Every one that is of the truth heareth my voice. (All KJV usage of "Jesus" will be translated to His Hebrew name, Yeshua, throughout)

So Yeshua is making it very clear that a Christian is defined by seeking out and conforming themselves to truth. Those who do not refine the truth and knowingly hold on to deception and untruth are in danger of the judgment.

2 Thessalonians 2: 10, And with all deceivableness of unrighteousness in them that perish; because they received not the love of the truth, that they might be saved. 11 And for this cause God shall send them strong delusion, that they should believe a lie: 12 That they all might be damned who believed

not the truth, but had pleasure in unrighteousness. 13 But we are bound to give thanks alway to God for you, brethren beloved of the Lord, because God hath from the beginning chosen you to salvation through sanctification of the Spirit and belief of the truth:

As Christians how can we gauge if something is true or not? We are given the answer in the New Testament.

2 Timothy 2: 15, Study to shew thyself approved unto God, a workman that needeth not to be ashamed, rightly dividing the word of truth.

What is this "word of truth"? We know what it is not. It is not unscriptural stories that do not hold the patterns, images, and fractals of natural God designed truth.

2 Timothy 4: 4, And they shall turn away their ears from the truth, and shall be turned unto fables.

What is a fractal?

A fractal is a never-ending pattern. Fractals are infinitely complex patterns that are self-similar across different scales. They are created by repeating a simple process over and over in an ongoing feedback loop. Driven by recursion, fractals are images of dynamic systems – the pictures of Chaos. Geometrically, they exist in between our familiar dimensions. Fractal patterns are extremely familiar, since nature is full of fractals. For instance: trees, rivers, coastlines, mountains, clouds, seashells, hurricanes, etc. Abstract fractals – such as the Mandelbrot Set – can be generated by a computer calculating a simple equation over and over. (Fractalfoundation.org)

Just as God's primary goal in creating all things in Genesis 1 was to bring forth a creation in His image, pattern, and fractal, so also all of nature, math, and biblical patterns follow this same principal of self-replicating and self-similar patterns called fractals. The patterns you observe in nature, science, and math, you will see replicated in reproduction and in the scriptures. You can verify the accuracy of your beliefs by examining your scriptural paradigms against the fractals you observe in nature.

When we turn from the God inspired scriptural patterns, images, and fractals to terminology and definitions that are not scripturally accurate in type or meaning, the truth is then lost and corrupted by the terms, definitions, and ideas that go along with those incorrect images. This has been the history and methodology of the Church for nearly 2,000 years. Yeshua prophesied that this would occur and before His return would need to be corrected. So where do we find the images, patterns, and fractals that hold God inspired meaning?

2 Timothy 3: 15, And that from a child thou hast known the holy scriptures, which are able to make thee wise unto salvation through faith which is in Christ

Yeshua. 16 All scripture is given by inspiration of God, and is profitable for doctrine, for reproof, for correction, for instruction in righteousness:

The book of Timothy was written by Paul. At the time of its writing the only "scripture" that would have been recognized was the Written Torah and the Tanach (Torah (Teaching), Nevi'im (Prophets), and Ketuvim (Writings) otherwise known as the Old Testament). There is the Written Torah that was revealed to Moses at Mount Sinai, or the Pentateuch (Genesis, Exodus, Leviticus, Numbers, Deuteronomy) and the rabbis teach that there is also an Oral Law called the Oral Torah (oral tradition, the Tradition of the Elders, or the Tradition of Men). This Oral Law was claimed by the rabbis to have been given privately to Moses and was supposedly handed down orally from rabbi to rabbi.

Paul is endorsing that all New Testament believers use the Old Testament scriptures to validate accurate church doctrine, spiritual correction, and on how a Christian believer should conduct him/herself. He goes so far as to encourage faithful and diligent seekers of truth to check any supposed writing from the Apostles against the truth of the Old Testament to validate its truthfulness. We see two synagogues contrasted in the book of Acts by how they validated concepts that they were unfamiliar with.

Acts 17: 1, Now when they had passed through Amphipolis and Apollonia, they came to Thessalonica, where was a synagogue of the Jews: 2 And Paul, as his manner was, went in unto them, and three Sabbath days reasoned with them out of the scriptures, 3 Opening and alleging, that Christ must needs have suffered, and risen again from the dead; and that this Yeshua, whom I preach unto you, is Christ. 4 And some of them believed, and consorted with Paul and Silas; and of the devout Greeks a great multitude, and of the chief women not a few. 5 But the Jews which believed not, moved with envy, took unto them certain lewd fellows of the baser sort, and gathered a company, and set all the city on an uproar, and assaulted the house of Jason, and sought to bring them out to the people. 6 And when they found them not, they drew Jason and certain brethren unto the rulers of the city, crying, These that have turned the world upside down are come hither also; 7 Whom Jason hath received: and these all do contrary to the decrees of Caesar, saying that there is another king, one Yeshua. 8 And they troubled the people and the rulers of the city, when they heard these things. 9 And when they had taken security of Jason, and of the other, they let them go. 10 And the brethren immediately sent away Paul and Silas by night unto Berea: who coming thither went into the synagogue of the Jews. 11 These were more noble than those in Thessalonica, in that they received the word with all readiness of mind, and searched the scriptures daily, whether those things were so. 12 Therefore many of them believed; also of honourable women which were Greeks, and of men, not a few. 13 But when the Jews of Thessalonica had knowledge that the word of God was preached of Paul at Berea, they came thither also, and stirred up the people.

Paul testifies to two separate synagogues about how the scriptures in the Old Testament validated that Yeshua needed to die and rise again in His role as the

Messiah. Those who were nobler took the time to search out the "scriptures", which we have already identified as the Tanach (Torah (Teaching), Nevi'im (Prophets), and Ketuvim (Writings) otherwise known as the Old Testament), to prove if Paul's allegations were true or false. Those who were not noble, identified with a "baser sort", did not search out the scriptures to determine the veracity of Paul's allegations about Yeshua.

The writings of Paul and the Apostles have clearly identified that any Christian doctrine or teaching must be consistent with the Old Testament scriptures or it is not "...profitable for doctrine, for reproof, for correction, for instruction in righteousness. . ." (2 Timothy 3:16)

Since the Apostles used this methodology, so must the modern church. The only way to restore accurate scriptural imagery, patterns, and fractals is to use the scriptural terminology and contextual meaning provided from the scriptures themselves, without our own man–made terminology and definitions. Once we follow this methodology we will see more and more mysteries plainly and simply revealed, and many of the modern churches delusions scripturally cast down. Much like the parable of the talents, those who are "faithful" will gather more talents.

Matthew 25: 14, For the kingdom of heaven is as a man travelling into a far country, who called his own servants, and delivered unto them his goods. 15 And unto one he gave five talents, to another two, and to another one; to every man according to his several ability; and straightway took his journey. 16 Then he that had received the five talents went and traded with the same, and made them other five talents. 17 And likewise he that had received two, he also gained other two. 18 But he that had received one went and digged in the earth, and hid his Lord's money. 19 After a long time the Lord of those servants cometh, and reckoneth with them. 20 And so he that had received five talents came and brought other five talents, saying, Lord, thou deliveredst unto me five talents: behold, I have gained beside them five talents more. 21 His Lord said unto him, Well done, thou good and faithful servant: thou hast been faithful over a few things, I will make thee ruler over many things: enter thou into the joy of thy Lord. 22 He also that had received two talents came and said, Lord, thou deliveredst unto me two talents: behold, I have gained two other talents beside them. 23 His Lord said unto him, Well done, good and faithful servant; thou hast been faithful over a few things, I will make thee ruler over many things: enter thou into the joy of thy Lord. 24 Then he which had received the one talent came and said, Lord, I knew thee that thou art an hard man, reaping where thou hast not sown, and gathering where thou hast not strawed: 25 And I was afraid, and went and hid thy talent in the earth: lo, there thou hast that is thine. 26 His Lord answered and said unto him, Thou wicked and slothful servant, thou knewest that I reap where I sowed not, and gather where I have not strawed: 27 Thou oughtest therefore to have put my money to the exchangers, and then at my coming I should have received mine own with usury. 28 Take therefore the talent from him, and give it unto him which hath ten talents. 29 For unto every one that hath shall be given, and he shall have abundance: but from him that hath not shall be taken away even that which he hath. 30 And <u>cast ye the unprofitable servant into outer darkness</u>: there shall be weeping and gnashing of teeth.

Now on the surface this parable of the talents makes the Messiah look like a very harsh man and certainly not generous. He is expecting the servant to work. It would also appear to be capricious to hand over the unprofitable servant's talent to the one who gained 10 talents. Why not give them to the one who gained two talents? Wouldn't this be more generous to give a talent to one who had less than the others?

Let's think about the parable of the talents in another way. Every place you see the word "talent", replace it with the word "truth". Once you do this you get to the root of what our purpose is here on earth and how it is God's natural order to give more truth to the one who seeks out and finds the most truth. Take note of how the "unprofitable servant" is associated with being cast into "outer darkness".

John 3: 18, He that believeth on him is not condemned: but he that believeth not is condemned already, because he hath not believed in the name of the only begotten Son of God. 19 And this is the condemnation, that light is come into the world, and men loved darkness rather than light, because their deeds were evil. 20 For every one that doeth evil hateth the light, neither cometh to the light, lest his deeds should be reproved.

Those who are unprofitable are associated with darkness and rejection of light. By association this is the rejection of the Messiah for He is identified by light and truth!

- John 18: 2, Then spake Yeshua again unto them, saying, I am the light of the world: he that followeth me shall not walk in darkness, but shall have the light of life.
- John 14: 6, Yeshua saith unto him, I am the way, the truth, and the life: no man cometh unto the Father, but by me.

So where can we find the revealing of His light and truth? The same place the Apostles went to validate accurate apostolic teaching, the Written Torah and the Tanach (Torah (Teaching), Nevi'im (Prophets), and Ketuvim (Writings) otherwise known as the Old Testament). Who was the giver of these inspirational teachings?

1 Corinthians 10: 1, Moreover, brethren, I would not that ye should be ignorant, how that all our fathers were under the cloud, and all passed through the sea; 2 And were all baptized unto Moses in the cloud and in the sea; 3 And did all eat the same spiritual meat; 4 And did all drink the same spiritual drink: <u>for they drank of that spiritual rock that followed them: and that rock was Christ.</u> 5 But with many of them God was not well pleased: for they were overthrown in the wilderness.

The Apostle Paul clarifies that it was the Messiah Yeshua who was leading Israel through the wilderness and manifesting the presence of God through His giving of the Law of Moses, the spiritual meat, which Paul is referring to.

> John 14: 15, If ye love me, keep my commandments. 16 And I will pray the Father, and he shall give you another Comforter, that he may abide with you for ever; 17 Even the Spirit of truth; whom the world cannot receive, because it seeth him not, neither knoweth him: but ye know him; for he dwelleth with you, and shall be in you. 18 I will not leave you comfortless: I will come to you. 19 Yet a little while, and the world seeth me no more; but ye see me: because I live, ye shall live also. 20 At that day ye shall know that I am in my Father, and ye in me, and I in you. 21 He that hath my commandments, and keepeth them, he it is that loveth me: and he that loveth me shall be loved of my Father, and I will love him, and will manifest myself to him. 22 Judas saith unto him, not Iscariot, Lord, how is it that thou wilt manifest thyself unto us, and not unto the world? 23 Yeshua answered and said unto him, If a man love me, he will keep my words: and my Father will love him, and we will come unto him, and make our abode with him. 24 He that loveth me not keepeth not my sayings: and the word which ye hear is not mine, but the Father's which sent me.

The writer of Hebrews takes the time to chastise followers of Yeshua that they are not more mature, failing to advance into the more meaningful things (meat) of Christ and instead still being consumed by simple things (milk).

> Hebrews 5: 11, Of whom we have many things to say, and hard to be uttered, seeing ye are dull of hearing. 12 For when for the time ye ought to be teachers, ye have need that one teach you again which be the first principles of the oracles of God; and are become such as have need of milk, and not of strong meat. 13 For every one that useth milk is unskilful in the word of righteousness: for he is a babe. 14 But strong meat belongeth to them that are of full age, even those who by reason of use have their senses exercised to discern both good and evil.

We see that their ability to hear is associated with what they are capable of eating. He is clear in saying that by now they should have moved from milk to meat. From Paul's early comments we can see that this "meat" is associated with the "spiritual meat" of 1 Corinthians 10:3 that was provided by Christ to Israel in the Wilderness, the Law of Moses.

If "law versus grace" is true then we need to understand why the Pre–incarnate Christ is feeding Israel the "Law of Moses". As we progress you will see that these associations are not accidental and tell us much more than what we might glean from a casual review of the scriptures. We need to be focused, searching, and having a state of mind of "open ears" as opposed to ears that "are dull of hearing". (Matthew 11:15)

In order to restore accurate doctrinal paradigms, imagery, meaning, patterns, and fractals we need to use the same source the Apostles did. We will be able to validate the truth of these concepts by following the scriptural patterns. These same patterns repeat themselves over and over again in the scriptures, in nature, and in the lives of those recorded in the scriptures. We will be able to check our math, just the same as if you were literally checking your arithmetic by working the equation backwards. If the pattern and the fractal does not hold up when checked from every angle, then it is likely not a scripturally supported belief and needs to be removed.

Knowing that we must depend upon scriptural context we will use extensive and copious amounts of scriptures to establish the scriptural patterns. If you are not prepared for an intensive analysis of scriptural review, you likely will not have the attention span to discover the mysteries that are hidden only for certain people. It requires the diligence of the believer to move from milk to meat.

Matthew 13: 10, And the disciples came, and said unto him, Why speakest thou unto them in parables? 11 He answered and said unto them, Because it is given unto you to know the mysteries of the kingdom of heaven, but to them it is not given. 12 For whosoever hath, to him shall be given, and he shall have more abundance: but whosoever hath not, from him shall be taken away even that he hath. 13 Therefore speak I to them in parables: because they seeing see not; and hearing they hear not, neither do they understand. 14 And in them is fulfilled the prophecy of Esaias, which saith, By hearing ye shall hear, and shall not understand; and seeing ye shall see, and shall not perceive: 15 For this people's heart is waxed gross, and their ears are dull of hearing, and their eyes they have closed; lest at any time they should see with their eyes and hear with their ears, and should understand with their heart, and should be converted, and I should heal them. 16 But blessed are your eyes, for they see: and your ears, for they hear. 17 For verily I say unto you, That many prophets and righteous men have desired to see those things which ye see, and have not seen them; and to hear those things which ye hear, and have not heard them.

Did you see how Matthew 13 reinforced the conclusion that we drew about the parable of the talents from Matthew 25? Yeshua uses the same phraseology linking the parable of the talents to His explanation of who the mysteries of the Kingdom are given to and why He insisted on talking in parables.

Matthew 25: 28, Take therefore the talent from him, and give it unto him which hath ten talents. 29 For unto every one that hath shall be given, and he shall have abundance: but from him that hath not shall be taken away even that which he hath.

Now compare it to Yeshua's explanation of why He spoke in parables from Matthew 13.

Matthew 13: 12, For whosoever hath, to him shall be given, and he shall have more abundance: but whosoever hath not, from him shall be taken away even that he hath.

Notice how they use the same phraseology and are almost word for word the same? Are you beginning to understand that there are no careless scriptures and that there is willful intention and patterns in what is written? So when you match up the parable of the talents with Yeshua's explanation of why He speaks in parables you can clearly see that a "talent" is a "hidden truth"!

After having read Frank Turek and Norman Geisler's book, "I Don't Have Enough faith to Be an Atheist", I decided to contact their ministry to see if they would be willing to apply their logical methodology for tackling Atheism/Evolution to the issue of "Grace versus Law".

I highly recommend their book and their methodology. Evidently they are more interested in scriptural truth than maintaining un–scriptural beliefs. At the very least that would be our hope.

In their book they tackle several pivotal questions that Christians need to think about when they assess the scriptural accuracy of their beliefs.

- What is truth?
- So what? Who cares about truth?
- How is truth known?
- The opposite of truth is false.
- Can you afford to be agnostic (not–knowing)?
- Should Christians be logical?
- The either–or proposition.
- The both–and logic.
- Truth versus Tolerance

The authors sum it up best on page 54 of their book, "Finally, in order to find truth, one must be ready to give up those subjective preferences in favor of objective facts. And facts are best discovered through logic, evidence, and science."

We are faced with the hard question, "Does it matter what Christians believe?" Many Christians will say, "We are saved by grace, it does not matter what you believe". The fundamental question is, "Is that statement scripturally true? Or must we be tolerant? "

Turek and Geisler comment on this religious Pluralism on page 46, "Tolerance now means that you're supposed to accept every belief as true!" The authors go on to explain that the Christian faith does not teach Christians to endorse this viewpoint, but to pursue truth.

We are confronted with the pivotal question, "Do the teachings of Yeshua have more authority than our own beliefs about what we think the Apostle Paul is teaching?"

As Turek and Geisler list on pages 37 and 38, we will examine our modern Christian beliefs versus the truths evident in the scriptures. We need to remember the following from "I Do not Have Enough faith to Be an Atheist":

- "Truth is discovered, not invented."
- "Truth is unchanging even though our beliefs about truth change."
- "Beliefs cannot change a fact, no matter how sincerely they are held."
- "Truth is not affected by the attitude of the one professing it."
- "All truths are absolute truths."

The issue is really simple. If you are a Christian you are only interested in the truth, and not any single opinion that conflicts with the truth. If you find that you are not interested in scriptural truth, can you still claim to be a Christian?

2 Thessalonians 2: 10, And with all deceivableness of unrighteousness in them that perish; because <u>they received not the love of the truth, that they might be saved.</u>

Let us examine what the scriptures say related to what Yeshua, the Apostles, and the first Century believers said and did in regard to grace and Law (Law of Moses). It would appear, as Christians, we cannot afford to be agnostic about grace and Law. Let us logically examine the factual testimony and historical record of the first century believers and determine what they believed about this topic and if they actually implemented those beliefs in their actions. Of course this means we must check our beliefs for the facts.

This book began with an exchange of truth with some of Turek and Geisler's representatives on their book, "I Don't Have Enough faith to Be an Atheist". I wanted to determine if they could use their same apologetics skills on a couple of un–scriptural points they brought up in their book. The challenge was to see if they could consistently apply their evidence analysis methodology for evaluating truth on a topic that they might not find as appealing as Atheism/Evolution versus Creationism. Despite disagreeing on this topic I highly respect their methodology and their intention of turning people to God.

CAN YOU HANDLE DOCUMENTED HISTORICAL FACT AND THE SCRIPTURAL TRUTH?

Frank Turek and Norman Geisler,

I wanted to thank you for your book, "I Don't Have Enough faith to Be an Atheist". I enjoyed the logical arguments and your methodology for examining Atheism and Christianity. I've bought several copies for friends and family. However, I have found some factual and logical errors in your later chapters that pre–suppose what the early church observed. Some of those statements clearly contradict the scriptures. I'd love to examine these with you using your logic formula and see if you are as open to using this tool on your own assumptions about grace and law that contradict the Old and New Testament scriptures.

In summary, I found the following errors in "I Don't Have Enough Faith to be an Atheist":

1. That the Apostles abandoned being Jewish. Page 234
2. That first century believers in Yeshua abandoned the 7th day Sabbath and began observing it on the first day of the week. Page 234, 290–291, 319
3. That the Law of Moses is no longer binding. Page 234, 291
4. That the Apostles and the Church abandoned strict Monotheism. Page 291
5. The animal sacrifice system is replaced. Page 290
6. That the Apostles abandoned circumcision. Page 234
7. And stopped observing the priestly system. Page 234

My question to you is simple. Can you handle the truth? What do the scriptures actually document? You might be surprised. Christians (Jews & Gentiles) were being taught by Paul and the Apostles every 7th day Sabbath in the synagogue.

Acts 13: 42, And when the <u>Jews were gone out of the synagogue</u>, the <u>Gentiles besought that these words might be preached to them the next</u> <u>Sabbath</u>. 43 Now when the congregation was broken up, many of the Jews and religious proselytes followed Paul and Barnabas: who, speaking to them, persuaded them to continue in the grace of God.

Notice they did not ask to be taught the very next Sunday. The word Sabbath or Shabbat is a technical term for the 7th day Sabbath, not the first day of the week. And because Christians were observing the 7th day Sabbath, they took collections for Paul and those in Jerusalem on the first day of the week. Why on the first day of the week? This collection was considered work and was not appropriate conduct for the 7th day Sabbath rest.

1 Corinthians 16: 2, Upon the first day of the week let every one of you lay by him in store, as God hath prospered him, that there be no gatherings when I come.

Paul wanted all the collecting to have been completed before he arrived and done on an appropriate day for labor, the first day of the week, and not on the 7th day Sabbath. Let's also not miss the fact that new Christian converts were instructed to learn the Law of Moses. Where? In the synagogue.

Acts 13: 14, But when they departed from Perga, they came to Antioch in Pisidia, and <u>went into the synagogue on the Sabbath day</u>, and sat down. 15 And <u>after the reading of the law and the prophets</u> the rulers of the synagogue sent unto them, saying, Ye men and brethren, if ye have any word of exhortation for the people, say on. 16 Then Paul stood up, and beckoning with his hand said, <u>Men of Israel, and ye that fear God</u>, give audience.

The Torah of Moses was not abandoned by followers of Yeshua. They went to the synagogues every Sabbath to learn the Written Torah of Moses and this is where Paul, the Apostles, and Yeshua went to teach the people. The Apostles even commanded that new converts start with a few simple Torah commands and then go to the synagogue and learn the rest of the things they ought to do. This happened every 7th day of the week after Yeshua's resurrection.

Acts 15: 20, But that we write unto them, that they abstain from pollutions of idols, and from fornication, and from things strangled, and from blood. <u>21</u> <u>For Moses of old time hath in every city them that preach him, being read in</u> <u>the synagogues every Sabbath day</u>. 22 Then pleased it the Apostles and elders with the whole church, to send chosen men of their own company to Antioch with Paul and Barnabas; namely, Judas surnamed Barsabas and Silas, chief men among the brethren:

So if this is factually the case, what was it that Yeshua, Paul and the Apostles were arguing against? Which Law? Was it the same Written Law of Moses (the Written Torah) that Yeshua said would remain until the heavens and earth pass away? Or was it the Oral Torah (The Oral Law or Traditions of the rabbis)? (Matthew 5: 17–18, Matthew 15: 1–3, Romans 3: 31)

It is clear that Yeshua, Paul, and the Apostles taught people to keep the Written Torah of Moses and that they need not observe all the extra traditions of the rabbis, the Oral Torah. Yeshua elaborates on what He has a problem with and He makes it clear His problem is not with the Written Law of Moses, the Torah.

Matthew 15: 3, But he answered and said unto them, Why do ye also transgress the commandment of God by your tradition?

Yeshua states very clearly that His problem is with the Oral Tradition or Oral Law of the rabbis that causes people to violate the Written Law of Moses. Logically Yeshua is making it very plain that He wants His followers to not violate the Written Law of Moses, and any tradition that causes a believer to violate the Written Law of Moses is not worthy to be followed or observed.

The Pharisees try and turn the argument by mislabeling their own traditions as "the Law" that people should be observing. Yeshua corrects their mis-understanding.

Matthew 15: 1, Then came to Jesus scribes and Pharisees, which were of Jerusalem, saying, 2 Why do thy disciples transgress the tradition of the elders? for they wash not their hands when they eat bread. 3 But he answered and said unto them, Why do ye also transgress the commandment of God by your tradition? 4 For God commanded, saying, Honour thy father and mother: and, He that curseth father or mother, let him die the death. 5 But ye say, Whosoever shall say to his father or his mother, It is a gift, by whatsoever thou mightest be profited by me; 6 And honour not his father or his mother, he shall be free. Thus have ye made the commandment of God of none effect by your tradition. 7 Ye hypocrites, well did Esaias prophesy of you, saying, 8 This people draweth nigh unto me with their mouth, and honoureth me with their lips; but their heart is far from me. 9 But in vain they do worship me, teaching for doctrines the commandments of men.

Yeshua brings great clarity to the issue: the Pharisees are attempting to teach their own traditions (Oral Torah) as being doctrines of the Written Torah of Moses, when in reality they are only their own man–made traditions, which cause people to violate the actual doctrines of the Written Torah of Moses.

Logically, Yeshua has maintained the sanctity of the Law of Moses, and clarified the act of subversion by the Pharisees who replaced the Written Law of Moses with their own man–made traditions which cause people to violate the Law that Yeshua expects them to observe and keep. He further quotes Isaiah 29:13 indicating that such efforts are full of vanity and cause separation between man and God. This is no small indictment!

This presents a logic problem for those who maintain that Yeshua is fulfilling the Law so that He could then turn around and do away with the Law upon His death and resurrection. To suggest that God, manifest in the flesh, is intentionally chastising Pharisees for violating the Law of Moses via their own Oral Torah, only to shortly thereafter do away with the Written Law of Moses because He fulfilled it for us, boggles the logical mind. Not only does this "logic" contradict the facts of scripture, it brings into question the integrity of the Son of God. Instead of trying to defend such a proposition, let us instead defend the scriptural facts. We can then evaluate which paradigm becomes a unified and scripturally accurate paradigm and which is lacking in scriptural merit. Malachi prophesies that right before the day of the Lord, we had one charge to fulfill.

Malachi 4: 1, For, behold, the day cometh, that shall burn as an oven; and all the proud, yea, and all that do wickedly, shall be stubble: and the day that cometh shall burn them up, saith the Lord of hosts, that it shall leave them neither root nor branch. 2 But unto you that fear my name shall the sun of righteousness arise with healing in his wings; and ye shall go forth, and grow up as calves of the stall. 3 And ye shall tread down the wicked; for they shall be ashes under the soles of your feet in the day that I shall do this, saith the Lord of hosts. 4 Remember ye the law of Moses my servant, which I commanded unto him in Horeb for all Israel, with the statutes and judgments. 5 Behold, I will send you Elijah the prophet before the coming of the great and dreadful day of the Lord:

Can it be any clearer? Why would God promise to send Elijah, right before the day of the Lord, with the commission to get His people to "remember the Law of Moses", if it was the same law that was abandoned? Let's use some of that logic here. Perhaps, if the facts are consistent, it is our paradigm that is wrong. So if we wish to gloss over these facts, let's ask one more question. If the sacrificial system had been abandoned by first century followers of Yeshua, why did Paul, after being saved by Yeshua, go to the temple to offer a sacrifice?

Acts 21: 26, Then Paul took the men, and the next day purifying himself with them entered into the temple, to signify the accomplishment of the days of purification, until that an offering should be offered for every one of them.

Furthermore there were many Levitical Priests that served in the temple even after the death and resurrection of Yeshua.

Acts 6:7, And the word of God increased; and the number of the disciples multiplied in Jerusalem greatly; and a great company of the priests were obedient to the faith.

This would pose a logical contradiction for those who say that the Levitical Priesthood, duties, and Law were abolished after the resurrection of Yeshua. It would appear that we need to examine this further later in the book.

THE ONENESS OF GOD IN THE NEW TESTAMENT:
Now let's tackle one more scriptural fact. The Old and the New Testament did not abandon strict monotheism. Christian believers maintained the same beliefs about that oneness of God that the Torah and the Shema teach.

Deuteronomy 6: 4, Hear, O Israel: The Lord our God is one Lord:

Deuteronomy 6:4 is known as the Shema. It is the cornerstone doctrine of the Jewish faith. We see the same affirmation made by Yeshua and the Apostles!
- Mark 12: 29, And <u>Yeshua answered him</u>, The first of all the commandments is, <u>Hear, O Israel; The Lord our God is one Lord</u>: 30 And thou shalt love the Lord thy God with all thy heart, and with all thy soul, and with all thy mind, and with all thy strength: this is the first commandment. 31 And the second is like, namely this, Thou shalt love thy neighbour as thyself. There is none other commandment greater than these. 32 And the scribe said unto him, Well, Master, thou hast said the truth: for <u>there is one God; and there is none other but he</u>: 33 And to love him with all the heart, and with all the understanding, and with all the soul, and with all the strength, and to love his neighbour as himself, is more than all whole burnt offerings and sacrifices. 34 And when <u>Yeshua</u> saw that he answered discreetly, <u>he said unto him, Thou art not far from the kingdom of God</u>. And no man after that durst ask him any question.
- Romans 3: 30, Seeing <u>it is one God</u>, which shall justify the circumcision by faith, and uncircumcision through faith.
- 1 Corinthians 8: 4, As concerning therefore the eating of those things that are offered in sacrifice unto idols, we know that an idol is nothing in the world, and <u>that there is none other God but one.</u>
- 1 Corinthians 8: 6, But to us there <u>is but one God</u>, the Father, of whom are all things, and we in him; and one Lord Yeshua, by whom are all things, and we by him.
- Galatians 3: 20, Now a mediator is not a mediator of one, <u>but God is one</u>.
- Ephesians 4: 6, <u>One God and Father of all</u>, who is above all, and through all, and in you all.
- 1 Timothy 2: 5, For <u>there is one God</u>, and one mediator between God and men, the man Christ Yeshua;
- James 2: 19, Thou believest that <u>there is one God; thou doest well</u>: the devils also believe, and tremble.

The New Testament repeatedly affirms a strict singularity of one God, not a modified version of monotheism. That being the case, the facts are clear, so perhaps once again it is our paradigm that is the problem.

I John 4: 12, <u>No man hath seen God at any time</u>. If we love one another, <u>God dwelleth in us</u>, and his love is perfected in us.

But we have seen Yeshua. It would appear on the surface that the scriptures are contradicting themselves. Perhaps there are other scriptures that will elaborate on the nature of the Messiah.

2 Corinthians 2: 9, For <u>in him dwelleth all the fulness of the Godhead bodily</u>.

So within Yeshua is God. Perhaps we have been asking the wrong questions about the oneness of God.

2 Corinthians 4: 4, In whom the god of this world hath blinded the minds of them which believe not, lest the light of the glorious Gospel of Christ, <u>who is the image of God</u>, should shine unto them.

Yeshua is the image of God. Paul is using very specific terminology here.

Colossians 1: 14, <u>In whom we have redemption</u> through his blood, even the forgiveness of sins: 15 <u>Who is the image of the invisible God</u>, the firstborn of every creature:

Yeshua, who is visible, is the manifestation of the invisible God. We will see how this relates to the manifestation of the name of God later on in this book.

John 10: 30, <u>I and my Father are one</u>.

So factually we are left with one conclusion, that there is only one God and Yeshua is the manifestation of His presence, literally the Image of God. John also states very clear that Yeshua is the Word and God.

John 1: 1, In the beginning was the Word, and the Word was with God, and <u>the Word was God</u>.... 14 And the <u>Word was made flesh</u>, and dwelt among us, (and we beheld his glory, the glory as of the only begotten of the Father,) full of grace and truth.

Is John here describing a trinity, duality or a singularity? The problem many Christians run into when trying to conceive of the oneness of God and the Deity of the Messiah is that we are using the wrong paradigm. Let's try and adjust the paradigm by asking some simple questions.

Matthew 28: 19, Go ye therefore, and teach all nations, baptizing them in the name of the Father, and of the Son, and of the Holy Ghost:

A cursory reading of this verse leaves many believers with the idea that there are three names that believers are baptized into. What does it really say? There is one name that believers are baptized into. It does not say "names", it says singular, "name". This singular name is the same for Father, Son, and Holy Spirit. It is not presenting a trinity, but as Yeshua has already indicated, a singular unity, hence one name; "I and my Father are one." If Yeshua is standing and talking with you, who would you say you are talking to, the Son or the Father?

John 8: 25, Then said they unto him, <u>Who art thou</u>? And Yeshua saith unto them, Even the same that I said unto you from the beginning. 26 I have many things to say and to judge of you: but he that sent me is true; and <u>I speak to the world those things which I have heard of him.</u> 27 They understood not that he <u>spake to them of the Father</u>. 28 Then said Yeshua unto them, When ye have lifted up the Son of man, then shall <u>ye know that I am he</u>, and that <u>I do nothing of myself; but as my Father hath taught me, I speak these things</u>. 29 And he that sent me is with me: the <u>Father hath not left me alone</u>; for I do always those things that please him.

Instead of counting containers let's think about the issue as it relates to consciousness. Based upon the factual information of John 8: 25–29, if Yeshua is standing and talking with you, who would you say you are talking to, the Son or the Father?

Yeshua's own testimony is that you are talking to the Father, not to a separate consciousness. How do we know this? Yeshua says, "I speak to the world those things which I have heard of him" and "I do nothing of myself; but as my Father hath taught me, I speak these things". Yeshua only mediates what the Father says and does, and He communicates nothing that is not from the Father. So Yeshua's testimony that He and the Father are one is true (John 10: 30 and 17: 11)!

God is one, not two or three. So when you examine John 1, try not to think of God and the Word as you would with containers, but think of God and the Word as water.

John 1: 1, In the beginning was the Word, and the Word was with God, and the Word was God...14 And the Word was made flesh, and dwelt among us, (and we beheld his glory, the glory as of the only begotten of the Father,) full of grace and truth.

Keep in mind how Yeshua is depicted in Luke 4:1 as "...being full of the Holy Spirit". The scriptures are replete with examples of how God's spirit is "poured" out like water.

- 1 Samuel 1:15, And Hannah answered and said, No, my lord, I am a woman of a sorrowful spirit: I have drunk neither wine nor strong drink, but have <u>poured out my soul</u> before the Lord.
- Proverbs 1:23, Turn you at my reproof: behold, I will <u>pour out my spirit unto you</u>, I will make known my words unto you.
- Ezekiel 39:29, Neither will I hide my face any more from them: <u>for I have poured out my spirit upon the house of Israel</u>, saith the Lord God.
- Joel 2:28, And it shall come to pass afterward, <u>that I will pour out my spirit upon all flesh</u>; and your sons and your daughters shall prophesy, your old men shall dream dreams, your young men shall see visions:
- Joel 2:29, And also upon the servants and upon the handmaids in those

days will I pour out my spirit.

- Acts 2:17, And it shall come to pass in the last days, saith God, I will pour out of my Spirit upon all flesh: and your sons and your daughters shall prophesy, and your young men shall see visions, and your old men shall dream dreams:
- Acts 2:18, And on my servants and on my handmaidens I will pour out in those days of my Spirit; and they shall prophesy:

If you take a pitcher of water and pour it into a glass, is the water still water? Yes. Is the water in the glass one with the water in the pitcher? They are one in nature only manifest in two containers now. Are they separated? Only via the containers, in all other respects they are one. The water in the glass was with the water in the pitcher in the beginning, the water in the glass was the water in the pitcher in the beginning. The water in the pitcher is now manifest in the glass for all men to see.

Scripturally God is one just as the water is one. Yeshua himself confesses that he neither speaks nor does anything that the Father does not do. So in regard to consciousness, if you are speaking with Yeshua and He is standing in front of you, you are talking with the Father, not a separate consciousness. "I do nothing of myself" (John 8:28).

THE TEACHING OF THE OLD TESTAMENT AFFIRMS THE TRUTH OF THE NEW TESTAMENT:

If all scripture is indeed God inspired and the Christian believer cannot reconcile his/her beliefs to the entirety of scripture (old and new) then clearly it is not the scriptures that are in error, it is the believer's paradigm that does not account for the validity of all scripture that is actually in error.

2 Timothy 3: 16, All scripture is given by inspiration of God, and is profitable for doctrine, for reproof, for correction, for instruction in righteousness:

The New Testament affirms the same as the Old, that "The Lord our God is one Lord" (Deuteronomy 6: 4). So if all these statements are scripturally and factually accurate (inspired by God), perhaps our paradigm is wrong and the Law of Moses is not done away, but this same Written Law of Moses is merely under a new administration of grace and mercy.

In fact you will see this fractal of condemnation and death versus grace and abundant mercy presented at both givings of the Law of Moses in the book of Exodus. What is present in both accounts? "The same words", i.e. the same Written Law. Exodus 20 highlights the giving of the Law of Moses under the administration of Death (the flesh), and Exodus 34 shows the second giving of the Law of Moses under grace and abundant mercy (the spirit and resurrection life). This second writing of the Law of Moses happens with the presentation of the manifest Name of the Lord (YHWH). So instead of having an Old and New Testament, in reality you have The Torah of Sin and Death and the Torah of Resurrection Life presented as a pattern and a fractal. Paul reinforces this knowledge.

Romans 8: 2, For the <u>law of the Spirit of life</u> in Christ Yeshua hath made me free from <u>the law of sin and death</u>.

We have already proven that the scriptures say that the rabbinical traditions (the Oral Torah) were burdensome and were not required for Christians to obey. But what about the Written Torah, the Law of Moses? Are we no longer under the Law of Moses? Notice the Law of Moses is not abandoned for no law, it is abandoned for a new administration of the Torah (the Law of Moses). Is this statement scripturally true?

2 Corinthians 3: 6, Who also hath made us able ministers of the new testament; not of the letter, but of the spirit: for the letter killeth, but the spirit giveth life. 7 But <u>if the ministration of death, written and engraven in stones</u>, was glorious, so that the children of Israel could not stedfastly behold the face of Moses for the glory of his countenance; which glory was to be done away: 8 How shall not the ministration of the spirit be rather glorious? 9 For <u>if the ministration of condemnation be glory, much more doth the ministration of righteousness</u> exceed in glory.

Notice the "ministration" is associated with what is engraved in stones. This is a direct reference to the Written Law of Moses. So the glory of the prior administration relates to the Law of Moses and logically the new administration should also be associated with the law and the covenant as the administrations are presented in direct contrast to one another. We are not seeing imagery of the Law being done away, where first it is there and then it is removed. We are seeing imagery of the same Law being presented with an old and a new administration of the same "stones" and what is "engraved" upon them.

Paul contrasts these ministrations: Flesh versus sprit, death versus resurrection life, condemnation versus grace and mercy. So if the Law of Moses is done away, why do the Apostles keep telling us it is the Law of Moses that identifies sin?

1 John 3: 4, Whosoever committeth sin transgresseth also the law (Anomia): for <u>sin is the transgression of the law (Anomia)</u>.

The New Testament writers still use the Written Law of Moses to identify what sin is. They are not using Roman law, or a self-interpreted moral law. How do we know this? They identify the source of the Law they are using to identify sin.

2 Timothy 3: 16, All scripture (Torah, Writings, & Prophets) is given by inspiration of God, and is profitable for doctrine, for reproof, for correction, for instruction in righteousness:

How do we know that he is referring to the Written Torah, Writings, and Prophets?

Acts 17: 11, These were more noble than those in Thessalonica, in that they received the word with all readiness of mind, and <u>searched the scriptures daily, whether those things were so</u>.

Logically the new potential believers were checking the apostolic writings against the God inspired Torah, Writings, and the Prophets. They would not be checking Paul's letters against his other letters as this would provide no objectivity for a measure of truth. They needed to validate his teachings against an independent and reliable source. The apostolic writings did not have mass distribution at this point in church history, so they would not be evaluating new apostolic writings against other apostolic writings.

So if the Apostles are still using the Law of Moses, the Written Torah, to validate proper conduct and accurate teaching, what should that tell us about what Christianity should be doing today? Modern teachers say that the Law is written on our hearts now, but not then.

Hebrews 8: 6, But now hath he obtained a <u>more excellent ministry,</u> by how much also he is the <u>mediator of a better covenant</u>, which <u>was established upon better promises</u>. 7 For if that first covenant had been faultless, then should no place have been sought for the second. 8 For <u>finding fault with them</u>, he saith, Behold, the days come, saith the Lord, when I will <u>make a new covenant</u> with the house of Israel and with the house of Judah: 9 Not <u>according to the covenant</u> that I made with their fathers in the day when I took them by the hand to lead them out of the land of Egypt; because they continued not in my covenant, and I regarded them not, saith the Lord. 10 For this is the covenant that I will make with the house of Israel after those days, saith the Lord; <u>I will put my laws into their mind, and write them in their hearts</u>: and I will be to them a God, and they shall be to me a people: 11 And they shall not teach every man his neighbour, and every man his brother, saying, Know the Lord: for all shall know me, from the least to the greatest. 12 <u>For I will be merciful to their unrighteousness</u>, and their sins and their iniquities will I remember no more. 13 In that he saith, A new covenant, he hath made the first old. Now that which decayeth and waxeth old is ready to vanish away.

What does it say is "new"? It is a new administration (mediation), with the principal change being that the same laws are put upon our hearts instead of being written on stone tablets. Why? It was not on our hearts before and caused sin to abound.

The hallmark of this new administration is grace, abundant mercy and life. The old covenant had hallmarks of sin, death, and condemnation. Does Hebrews say, "I will make different laws and put them on your hearts"? No. It says it is the same, "my law" (Hebrews 8:10). We see this clearly illustrated in Exodus 34 and the second giving of the Torah under this new administration of grace and mercy. Take careful note of which laws are now written on our hearts.

Exodus 34: 1, And the Lord said unto Moses, Hew thee two tablets of stone <u>like unto the first</u>: and <u>I will write upon these tablets the words that were</u>

in the first tablets, which thou brakest... 4 And he hewed two tablets of stone like unto the first; and Moses rose up early in the morning, and went up unto mount Sinai, as the Lord had commanded him, and took in his hand the two tablets of stone. 5 And the Lord descended in the cloud, and stood with him there, and proclaimed the Name of the Lord. 6 And the Lord passed by before him, and proclaimed, The Lord, The Lord God, merciful and gracious, longsuffering, and abundant in goodness and truth, 7 Keeping mercy for thousands, forgiving iniquity and transgression and sin, and that will by no means clear the guilty; visiting the iniquity of the fathers upon the children, and upon the children's children, unto the third and to the fourth generation. 8 And Moses made haste, and bowed his head toward the earth, and worshipped.

Did you catch that? This is the same imagery of "writing the Law of God on our hearts" that is used to validate the New Testament by the modern church. The external law is now written internally. But notice it says, "the words that were in the first tablets", these are the same commandments, not different words. Not better commandments. This dual giving of the Law of Moses is presenting the fractal of death and resurrection, flesh and spirit, condemnation and mercy, and two administrations. It shows the progression from the Law of Sin and Death to the law of resurrection life. Both stone tablets from Exodus 20 and Exodus 34 have the same words and the same commandments written upon them. For the follower of Yeshua, there is no escaping this crucial imagery and terminology of those same words.

So if this is the same imagery that the Christian church uses to justify the validity of the "new" covenant, then why are they not fulfilling the complete pattern of the imagery presented? "The same words" or the same commandments? After all what changed was the administration and the location of those "same words", not the actual words themselves. Do we then get to pick and choose which "words" to obey? Can I ask a question? Are you keeping the 4th commandment?

Exodus 20: 8, Remember the Sabbath day, to keep it holy. 9 Six days shalt thou labour, and do all thy work: 10 But the seventh day is the Sabbath of the Lord thy God: in it thou shalt not do any work, thou, nor thy son, nor thy daughter, thy manservant, nor thy maidservant, nor thy cattle, nor thy stranger that is within thy gates: 11 For in six days the Lord made heaven and earth, the sea, and all that in them is, and rested the seventh day: wherefore the Lord blessed the Sabbath day, and hallowed it.

After all the 7th day Sabbath is a part of the "same words" that were re–written on the second set of tablets, which the Christian church presents as the same laws and imagery that the believer should have written on their hearts. Can you really fulfill something in your heart and not manifest it in your flesh? The study of the patterns, images, and fractals that we will bring out of the scriptures will leave you with an inescapable conclusion. Because of the scriptures consistent patterns, thematic connections, and repeating imagery you will be faced with an obvious and necessary choice!

LEAVE MY PARADIGM ALONE...
Let's call this a starting point. I cannot begin to tell you the meaning of all the Law of Moses, you could not absorb it all in one sitting. Maybe this is why the Apostles instruct new believers in Acts 15 to start with just a few things while they go to the synagogue on the actual 7th day Sabbath to learn the Written Law of Moses.

The Apostles are incredibly clear that there should be absolutely no difference between how any believers observe the truth that the Messiah gave to the redeemed. They were all to observe in the exact same way. Gentiles and Jews in the first century were worshiping God by doing the very same things. To maintain that Jews were keeping the Torah and worshiping Christ, while Gentiles were not keeping the Torah and worshiping Christ, is contradicted by the facts of scripture.

> Acts 15: 9, And put no difference between us and them, purifying their hearts by faith.

Where the Apostles say to not bother the Gentiles, they are referencing the Oral Torah of the rabbis, that Yeshua said was an unreasonable burden and did not need to be observed.
- Acts 15: 10, Now therefore why tempt ye God, <u>to put a yoke upon the neck of the disciples, which neither our fathers nor we were able to bear</u>?
- Acts 15: 19, Wherefore my sentence is, <u>that we trouble not them</u>, which from among the Gentiles are turned to God:

How do we know the Apostles are referring only to the Rabbinical Oral Torah (Traditions of men)? Let's check the issue out thematically. What does Yeshua say?

> Matthew 23: 2, Saying the <u>scribes and the Pharisees</u> sit in Moses' seat: 3 All therefore whatsoever they bid you observe, that observe and do; but do not ye after their works: for they say, and do not. 4 For <u>they bind heavy burdens and grievous to be borne, and lay them on men's shoulders;</u> but they themselves will not move them with one of their fingers.

Both the Apostles and Yeshua describe the Rabbinical Oral Torah as a "burden" that is "borne" that causes "trouble". The Pharisees were saying that new believers must both be circumcised <u>and</u> keep the Torah of Moses before having fellowship with other believers. They were requiring that believers follow the Written Torah and their Rabbinical Oral Torah which would have required circumcision before fellowshipping with other proselytes <u>while</u> learning the Written Law of Moses.

> Pharisee, "The Pharisee ("separatist") party emerged largely out of the group of scribes and sages. Their name comes from the Hebrew and Aramaic parush or parushi, which means "one who is separated." It may refer to their separation from Gentiles, sources of ritual impurity or from irreligious Jews.

[14] The Pharisees, among other Jewish sects, were active from the middle of the second century B. C. E. until the destruction of the Temple in 70 C. E." (Wikipedia)

Yeshua and the Apostles clarified that the Rabbinical Oral Torah were extra burdens that were not required of believers in Yeshua. The Apostles in Acts 15 are talking about the Oral Torah not being required, not the Written Torah, as the Apostles address this issue in Acts 15:21, saying new believers should learn the Written Torah (the Law of Moses) every 7th day Sabbath in the Synagogue with other believers in Yeshua. We will delve into this more later. For added clarity, the Apostles go on to give some basic requirements for new believers while they learn the Written Torah of Moses in the Synagogue.

Acts 15: 19, Wherefore my sentence is, that we trouble not them, which from among the Gentiles are turned to God: 20 But that we write unto them, that they abstain from pollutions of idols, and from fornication, and from things strangled, and from blood. 21 For Moses of old time hath in every city them that preach him, being read in the synagogues every Sabbath day.

So, you have a factual and logical choice. Will you shut up your ears because I have shocked your paradigm? You may say, "You did not finish the quote from Hebrews 8: 13, "In that he saith, A new covenant, he hath made the first old. Now that which decayeth and waxeth old is ready to vanish away."

Most of Christianity will tell you it is the Law that was passing away. But factually and scripturally that is not accurate. So what is passing away? The flesh, the administration of condemnation, the Torah of Sin and Death. The Law is not passing away, the flesh is.

1 Corinthians 15: 50, Now this I say, brethren, that flesh and blood cannot inherit the kingdom of God; neither doth corruption inherit incorruption.

That being the case, what then shall we do?

Romans 6: 15, What then? shall we sin, because we are not under the law, but under grace? God forbid.

The modern church has presupposed the argument is "Grace versus Law". You will not find that anywhere in the scriptures. The scripturally accurate argument is, "which administration of the Law of Moses are you under? "Condemnation or grace"?

Romans 3: 31, Do we then make void the law through faith? God forbid: yea, we establish the law.

Does this mean we are not to observe the Law of Moses? No, it means we are not under the administration of sin and death, condemnation, and the flesh. We are under the administration of grace, mercy and those "same words".

The Law of Moses (death) is resurrected to the Law of Christ (resurrection life). So instead of falsely presupposing Old and New Testament, the accurate scriptural presentation is Torah of Sin and Death and Torah of Resurrection Life. You could also call it Old Covenant and Resurrected Covenant. The Law of Moses, the Messiah, and the redeemed all fulfill the same fractal of death and resurrection.

- Hebrews 8: 13, In that he saith, A new covenant, he hath made the first old. Now that which decayeth and waxeth old is ready to vanish away.
- 2 Corinthians 5: 17, Therefore if any man be in Christ, he is a new creature: old things are passed away; behold, all things are become new.

Notice both the redeemed believer and the law (covenant) have the same associations of "old" and "new" and "passing/vanish away". So to contend that the law (covenant) words are done away is to also say that the consciousness of the resurrected believer is also done away. So what is the benefit of being resurrected if you are not "still you" in consciousness and memory?

Just as the believer is presented as the "old" and "new" man before death and after resurrection, so also is the covenant and the Law of Moses. It is both "old" and "new". It fulfills the same fractal of death and resurrection as the Messiah and the believer. But just as the believer is the same "person" that is subject to corruption and then incorruption, so also is the Law of Moses. It is the same "words" or covenant, with a new administration. To say it is no longer the same "covenant" because it is new, is to say that the same "person" is no longer the same person because he/she is "new" in resurrection life. We see evidence of this in the prophecies that discuss the time after Yeshua's second coming.

Zechariah 14: 16, And it shall come to pass, that every one that is left of all the nations which came against Jerusalem shall even go up from year to year to worship the King, the Lord of hosts, and to keep the feast of tabernacles. 17 And it shall be, that whoso will not come up of all the families of the earth unto Jerusalem to worship the King, the Lord of hosts, even upon them shall be no rain.

"Old" Testament Holy Days will be observed by "everyone", not just Israel, after the return of Yeshua. Maybe it is time to fix our paradigm and heed the end-time warning of Malachi that before the day of the Lord…God will send Elijah with a message for believers to "remember ye the law of Moses my servant" (Malachi 4:1-5). Shockingly Yeshua reinforced this truth by telling His disciples, "…Elias truly shall first come, and restore all things. (Matthew 17:11)

Malachi 4: 1, For, behold, the day cometh, that shall burn as an oven; and all the proud, yea, and all that do wickedly, shall be stubble: and the day that cometh shall burn them up, saith the Lord of hosts, that it shall leave them neither root nor branch. 2 But unto you that fear my name shall the sun of righteousness arise with healing in his wings; and ye shall go forth, and grow up as calves of the stall…4 Remember ye the law of Moses my servant, which I commanded unto him in Horeb for all Israel, with the statutes and judgments. 5

Behold, <u>I will send you Elijah the prophet before the coming of the great and dreadful day of the Lord</u>:

3 THE FLESH WILL MANIFEST THE HEART...

L et's take the time to examine commonly held beliefs about "law vs. grace" and evaluate how they are commonly presented by the modern believer. Then we can take the time to scripturally evaluate their factual, historical, and logical merit. Just as we are to put on the mind of Christ those who seek to become mature in Christ should exhibit strong logic and flexibility to the documented facts of history and scripture.

Thomas Henry Huxley, known as Darwin's bulldog, for his belief in Darwin's theory of Evolution has three of the best quotes to keep in mind as we go through this exercise. Amazingly an Atheist is following the Apostle Paul's instruction…and likely never even realized it.

"Sit down before fact as a little child, be prepared to give up every preconceived notion, follow humbly wherever and to whatever abysses nature leads, or you shall learn nothing"

"The great tragedy of Science: the slaying of a beautiful hypothesis by an ugly fact"

"The deepest sin of the human mind is to believe things without evidence" (Thomas Henry Huxley)

It just goes to show that those, whether Evolutionist or Christian, who profess adamant belief and scientific thinking, can be blind to the facts because of their paradigm. Surprisingly Huxley is giving people the same advice as the apostle Paul. Paul tells believers in Christ that the mature and stable in faith conduct themselves…"who by reason of use have their senses exercised to discern both good and evil"(Hebrews 5:14). Huxley and the apostle Paul are giving the same methodology for determining truth, we are to use our senses to observe the natural patterns and fractals manifested in the universe to help us to discover which patterns repeat over and over again as self-replicating and self-similar patterns. These self-similar patterns are fractals. They occur in math and they occur in nature. Just as God intended to replicate His fractal (image) in man, all of creation bears the hallmarks of His self-replicating patterns. If you have a hard time validating the truth of scriptures all you need to do is look for the same self-similar and self-replicating patterns in the Bible that you find in nature. This is the reason why the giving of the Law of Moses was so heavily focused on patterns, truth, and accurate images and the absolute mandate to reject false images, called idols.

The scriptures can be treated like a mathematical function where you can check your theology front to back...and then back again. If your theology and paradigm do not conform to natural patterns and fractals then there are very good odds that you have an unscriptural paradigm that is keeping you from advancing to greater truth, just like in the Parable of the Talents.

As well intended and dedicated as Huxley was...claiming to diligently follow the patterns of nature, he became blinded to what actually is scientifically and factually found in nature. If he had radically followed those patterns he would have discovered the flaws in his paradigm and adapted to factual evidence. The question we as modern Christians face is...could we be making the same mistake as Huxley...well intended, dedicated to truth, claiming to follow a rigorous system for identifying facts...but all the while failing to actually follow the methodology and validating our beliefs by comparing them to God's creation and image. If we cannot reconcile and unify all of the scriptures then likely we have a flaw in our paradigm. Let's go back and analyze the proposition of "Grace vs. Law" and determine its scriptural, factual, and historical validity.

PRO "GRACE VERSUS LAW" POSITIONS:
Here are some common positions that believers in "Grace versus Law" will argue. Please take note of whether their points are focused on scriptural facts.

1. First century believers who had started out in the Spirit mistakenly had come to believe that one could not be Christian unless one applied the Law of Moses—specifically, the law requiring circumcision. Paul taught that the servants of Christ were to obey the Law of Moses by walking in the Spirit, not by attempting to obey the letter.

- Galatians 5: 2, Behold, I Paul say unto you, that if ye be circumcised, Christ shall profit you nothing. 3 For I testify again to every man that is circumcised, that he is a debtor to do the whole law. 4 Christ is become of no effect unto you, whosoever of you are justified by the law; ye are fallen from grace.

- Romans 8: 3, For what the law could not do, in that it was weak through the flesh, God sending his own Son in the likeness of sinful flesh, and for sin, condemned sin in the flesh: 4 That the righteousness of the law might be fulfilled in us, who walk not after the flesh, but after the Spirit.

2. Peter did not obey Moses and is corrected for hypocrisy for insisting on obedience to Moses.

3. The Law of Moses is not what we need to obey.

4. Coming under the law will severe you from Christ.

5. The Messiah finds fault with the Law of Moses. What Yeshua aims to accomplish goes beyond what was written in the Law of Moses.

6. Believers should not practice the Law of Moses as written but walk in the Spirit. We do not need to know perfectly what the Law says; we need simply to obey the Spirit.

7. The modern church is not commanded to practice as the first century church. The book of Acts is a narrative, not a book of rules. So what if they met on Saturday rather than Sunday?

8. The Messiah brought in a new way, of the Spirit, that the Jews did not have until they were baptized into the Christ. It is in the Spirit, not in obedience to the letter of Moses' Law, that we encounter the risen Christ.

9. We are not going to knuckle under to Judaizers and become 1st century Jews. As Hebrews says, what we have in the Messiah is better. I hope that you come to see the error of your obsession.

For better or worse these are the kind of arguments and criticisms, from one group or another, that you will face if you follow Yeshua. The crucial question is are these Pro "Grace versus Law" statements factually true and scripturally accurate? Let's examine the evidence!

REBUTTAL; PRO GRACE & LAW
THE FLESH WILL MANIFEST THE HEART...SEED THEN FLESH
If the arguments regarding circumcision are scripturally accurate, then it would be damnable for Paul to do anything that would bring him or others under the law. Perhaps Paul's actions can bring clarity to the issue of circumcision and believers in Yeshua.

Acts 16: 2, Which was well reported of by the brethren that were at Lystra and Iconium. 3 Him would <u>Paul have to go forth with him; and took and circumcised him because of the Jews which were in those quarters</u>: for they knew all that his father was a Greek. 4 And as they went through the cities, they delivered them the <u>decrees for to keep, that were ordained of the Apostles and elders</u> which were at Jerusalem.

Now if these pro "Grace versus Law" arguments are correct, whatever justification Paul uses to circumcise a believer is not only reprehensible, but places himself and the believer under the law and hence damnation as these arguments state, "You have been severed from the Christ". Perhaps the pre-supposition of "Grace versus Law" is incorrect.

Furthermore, the church label of Judaizer is not only non-scriptural, it pre-supposes the argument of "Grace versus Law" instead of "Written Torah versus Oral Torah" or "law of sin and death versus law of resurrection life", both of which actually have scriptural and factual merit. We must carefully examine the scriptural facts to determine which proposition has basis in the actual historical record.

We must not worry about the personal criticism of what proponents of "Grace versus Law" think our motives are, yet it would appear that they would rather dismiss us by those means rather than deal with the scriptural facts themselves. That should serve as a warning to those who claim to follow Christ but refuse to follow what is actually written in both Testaments. We will not prejudge them for that though. We all begin with our pre–conceptions.

If we study Galatians further we will see that circumcision is not nullified, it is reinforced. The Apostle Paul goes on to elaborate the necessity of circumcision and how circumcision of the flesh is nothing if the heart is uncircumcised. The heart always precedes the flesh, in circumcision and in sin.

> Romans 2: 25, <u>For circumcision verily profiteth, if thou keep the law: but if thou be a breaker of the law, thy circumcision is made uncircumcision</u>. 26 Therefore if the uncircumcision keep the righteousness of the law, shall not his uncircumcision be counted for circumcision? 27 And shall not uncircumcision which is by nature, if it fulfil the law, judge thee, who by the letter and circumcision dost transgress the law? 28 For he is not a Jew, which is one outwardly; neither is that circumcision, which is outward in the flesh: 29 <u>But he is a Jew, which is one inwardly; and circumcision is that of the heart, in the spirit, and not in the letter; whose praise is not of men, but of God.</u>

Paul is showing us the pattern of redemption provided by the Messiah. He restores first that which is within (the heart and spirit), then that which is without (the body) in resurrection. We see the example of seed then manifestation (fruit).

The principal lesson is observed in the first circumcision of the "father" of the faith, Abraham. We aspire to be the spiritual seed of this father of the faith. This is the same father that Malachi is talking about in "turning the hearts of the children to the fathers (of the faith)".

> Malachi 4: 5, Behold, I will send you Elijah the prophet before the coming of the great and dreadful day of the Lord: 6 And <u>he shall turn</u> the heart of the fathers to the children, and <u>the heart of the children to their fathers</u>, lest I come and smite the earth with a curse.

This pinnacle of the faith, who was established not by works, but by faith, just as we are, still took the sign (fleshly symbol) of circumcision. The key issue is not if he took the symbol, but when he took the symbol.

> Romans 4: 11, And <u>he received the sign of circumcision, a seal of the righteousness of the faith which he had yet being uncircumcised</u>: that he might be the father of all them that believe, though they be not circumcised; that righteousness might be imputed unto them also:

Is it not peculiar that the one person who is labeled as the father of those who have "faith" is himself circumcised, yet those who claim to be his spiritual seed claim that they do not need to be circumcised? Would not the father serve as a pattern for those who claim to follow in his "faith"? After all he is described as being righteous because of his faith and not for his works, but he himself still insisted on being circumcised! What really counts?

1 Corinthians 7: 19, Circumcision is nothing, and uncircumcision is nothing, <u>but the keeping of the commandments of God</u>.

What are these commandments? The Written Law of Moses. The apostle of grace tells the believer in no uncertain terms that what counts is keeping the commandments. How are we able to do this? By the operation of Christ.

Colossians 2: 11, In whom also <u>ye are circumcised with the circumcision made without hands,</u> in putting off the body of the sins of the flesh by the circumcision of Christ:

Circumcision is still important, so important it is done by Christ. The question is, are you better than Abraham? Faith precedes works, the heart precedes action. The presupposition that the Apostles did not practice circumcision is not scriptural. However, the issue is not "if" circumcision, the issue is "when". The early church did not use circumcision as a pre–requirement for fellowship of Gentile believers with Jewish believers. Early believers who were Pharisees demanded that this be the entry point for new Gentile believers in the church.

1 Corinthians 7: 18, Is any man called being circumcised? let him not become uncircumcised. Is any called in uncircumcision? let him not be circumcised.

Paul emphasizes what the real issue is, the state of the believer's heart.

1 Corinthians 7: 19, Circumcision is nothing, and uncircumcision is nothing, but the keeping of the commandments of God.

Notice how he directs the believer back to the Law of Moses and the need to obey the Written Law, not to be hypocrites by being circumcised and not acting circumcised. The meaning of circumcision was the invocation of a sign of acceptance of the Law of Moses. Being circumcised and not keeping the Law of Moses invalidates the sign and holds it in contempt. Paul talks about his goal in the Gospel to the Gentiles.

Romans 15: 7, Wherefore receive ye one another, as Christ also received us to the glory of God. 8 Now I say that <u>Jesus Christ was a minister of the circumcision for the truth of God, to confirm the promises made unto the fathers</u>: 9 And that the Gentiles might glorify God for his mercy; as it is written, For this cause I will confess to thee among the Gentiles, and sing unto thy name. 10 And again he saith, Rejoice, ye Gentiles, with his people. 11 And again, Praise the Lord, all ye Gentiles; and laud him, all ye people. 12 And again, Esaias saith, There shall be a root of Jesse, and he that shall rise to reign over the Gentiles; in him shall the Gentiles trust. 13 Now the God of hope fill you with all joy and peace in believing, that ye may abound in hope, through the power of the Holy Ghost. 14 And I myself also am persuaded of you, my brethren, that ye also are full of goodness, filled with all knowledge, able also to admonish one another. 15 Nevertheless, brethren, I have written the more boldly unto you in some sort, as putting you in mind, because of the grace that is given to me of God, 16 That <u>I should be the minister of Jesus Christ to the Gentiles,</u> ministering the Gospel of God, that the offering up of the Gentiles might be acceptable, being sanctified by the Holy Ghost. 17 I have therefore whereof I may glory through Jesus Christ in those things which pertain to God. 18 For I will not dare to speak of any of those things which Christ hath not wrought by me, <u>to make the Gentiles obedient, by word and deed,</u> 19 Through mighty signs and wonders, by the power of the Spirit of God; so that from Jerusalem, and round about unto Illyricum, I have fully preached the Gospel of Christ.

Notice that Yeshua's goal is the same as stated in Malachi to "turn the hearts of the children to the fathers" and "confirm the promises of the fathers" that were guaranteed by that first circumcision of Abraham. Yeshua is described as a "minister <u>of</u> the circumcision" and not as a minister <u>to</u> the circumcision (the Jews only). He is the minister of that original covenant of faith, which provides that great salvation for the Jews and the Gentiles. The goal for those Gentiles by Christ was to make them obedient in word and deed. Obedient to what? The Written Law of Moses. Why was Yeshua the "minister of the circumcision"? Because He confirmed the promises of the covenant through the power of an everlasting life: resurrection. Circumcision is a prophetic type of the work of the Messiah through resurrection, putting off the fleshly body and being resurrected in the spirit. We are first a natural body, then a spiritual body.

Hebrews 7: 16, Who is made, not after the law of a carnal commandment, but after the power of an endless life.

As the minister of the circumcision, it is by His work and not ours that we are justified.

Galatians 5: 2, Behold, I Paul say unto you, that if ye be circumcised, Christ shall profit you nothing. 3 For I testify again to every man that is circumcised, that he is a debtor to do the whole law. 4 Christ is become of no effect unto you, whosoever of you are justified by the law; ye are fallen from grace. 5 For we through the Spirit wait for the hope of righteousness by faith. 6 For in Jesus Christ neither circumcision availeth any thing, nor uncircumcision; but faith which worketh by love.

Once again he is reinforcing that the physical act of circumcision is not what will remedy our state under the penalty of the law. Christ as the fulfiller of the promises of the covenant of the circumcision is the only one that can do that and it must occur within us.

Romans 2: 28, For he is not a Jew, which is one outwardly; neither is that circumcision, which is outward in the flesh: 29 But he is a Jew, which is one inwardly; and circumcision is that of the heart, in the spirit, and not in the letter; whose praise is not of men, but of God.

Abraham's redemption occurred first in his heart while his flesh was yet unclean and uncircumcised. This is the same progression of events of the believer in Yeshua.

Romans 7: 23, But I see another law in my members, warring against the law of my mind, and bringing me into captivity to the law of sin which is in my members. 24 O wretched man that I am! who shall deliver me from the body of this death? 25 I thank God through Jesus Christ our Lord. So then with the mind I myself serve the law of God; but with the flesh the law of sin.

This should remind us that just as Paul considered himself still unclean, he cherished what Christ had done for him within and the promise that someday his flesh would manifest that inward change. Paul confirms that the circumcision of Christ happens through resurrection.

Colossians 2: 10, And ye are complete in him, which is the head of all principality and power: 11 In whom also ye are circumcised with the circumcision made without hands, in putting off the body of the sins of the flesh by the circumcision of Christ: 12 Buried with him in baptism, wherein also ye are risen with him through the faith of the operation of God, who hath raised him from the dead. 13 And you, being dead in your sins and the uncircumcision of your flesh, hath he quickened together with him, having forgiven you all trespasses;

Fundamentally the circumcision of Christ is the death of our fleshly and fallen bodies and our ascension in resurrection life to the spirit in Christ. This is symbolized in the new womb and birth of the baptism (mikvah). Just as Christ died like a seed, so must we also take on the imagery of death and putting off of the fleshly body. The Messiah tells us to clean first the inward (spirit/heart) part of the cup then clean the outward (fleshly) part of the cup. Yeshua affirmed this understanding and how the Pharisees fundamentally failed to understand how to cleanse the cup. Their focus was outward and Yeshua's focus was inward.

Matthew 3: 8, Bring forth therefore fruits meet for repentance: 9 And think not to say within yourselves, We have Abraham to our father: for I say unto you, that God is able of these stones to raise up children unto Abraham. 10 And now also the axe is laid unto the root of the trees: therefore every tree which bringeth not forth good fruit is hewn down, and cast into the fire.

The Pharisees insisted that they were "saved" because of what Abraham did and because they were his descendants. Yeshua clarifies that it is not that physical seed that saves them, but the inward seed of faith that Abraham demonstrated and that we should also demonstrate. Once again his focus is inward to outward, not outward to inward.

Matthew 23: 26, Thou blind Pharisee, cleanse first that which is within the cup and platter, that the outside of them may be clean also.

It is those who cannot see who focus upon the outward instead of the inward. This is also why that which is "without" or on the outside is depicted as being in a state of death and corruption and the Kingdom of God is pictured as being alive "within". That is why we move from death to life, outward to inward. This may bring new meaning to Yeshua's statement of letting the "dead bury the dead".

Luke 9: 59, And he said unto another, Follow me. But he said, Lord, suffer me first to go and bury my father. 60 Jesus said unto him, Let the dead bury their dead: but go thou and preach the kingdom of God.

Those who inherit the Kingdom of God must abandon the flesh, for "flesh and blood cannot inherit the Kingdom of God" (1 Corinthians 15: 50).

Galatians 6: 12, As many as desire to make a fair shew in the flesh, they constrain you to be circumcised; only lest they should suffer persecution for the cross of Christ. 13 For neither they themselves who are circumcised keep the law; but desire to have you circumcised, that they may glory in your flesh. 14 But God forbid that I should glory, save in the cross of our Lord Jesus Christ, by whom the world is crucified unto me, and I unto the world. 15 For in Christ Jesus neither circumcision availeth any thing, nor uncircumcision, but a new creature.

Once again Paul points out that the issue here is the hypocrisy of those who would force circumcision on others while they themselves violate the Law of Moses. Their inward man is still defiled yet they are worried about the state of the outward man. He clarifies that what causes us to succeed is not the state of our current outward man– we will become a "new creature" in resurrection life which happens only through the work of the Messiah and not by our own effort. He affirms that he is crucified to this world, the flesh, and that this occurred not by his circumcision, but by the cross of Christ.

1 Corinthians 15: 46, Howbeit that was not first which is spiritual, but that which is natural; and afterward that which is spiritual. 47 The first man is of the earth, earthy; the second man is the Lord from heaven. 48 As is the earthy, such are they also that are earthy: and as is the heavenly, such are they also that are heavenly. 49 And as we have borne the image of the earthy, we shall also bear the image of the heavenly. 50 Now this I say, brethren, that flesh and blood cannot inherit the kingdom of God; neither doth corruption inherit incorruption. 51 Behold, I shew you a mystery; We shall not all sleep, but we shall all be changed, 52 In a moment, in the twinkling of an eye, at the last trump: for the trumpet shall sound, and the dead shall be raised incorruptible, and we shall be changed. 53 For this corruptible must put on incorruption, and

this mortal must put on immortality. 54 So when this corruptible shall have put on incorruption, and this mortal shall have put on immortality, then shall be brought to pass the saying that is written, Death is swallowed up in victory.

Circumcision shows the removal of the outer flesh, which is the same pattern for our redemption. The pattern is always the same, death and resurrection, seed then manifestation (fruit), carnal then spiritual. Just as Abraham manifested inward faith while his flesh was still uncircumcised, so also does the believer in Yeshua–inwardly cleansed while outwardly unclean and uncircumcised. This is why Paul keeps redirecting people from circumcision to evaluating their inward hearts.

The pattern is always the same:
• Abraham having inward faith while being uncircumcised in his flesh.
• The believer in Yeshua with the seed of Christ planted within his/her heart, while the flesh is still corrupt and unlawful.
• The resurrection proceeds from flesh to spirit

Some would say that Paul is saying that they should never change their state and perhaps that is the case. It certainly is not a mandatory requirement as he says "let", not "must" or "should". So Paul has some explaining to do, because he is documented circumcising a believer when supposedly he should not be "severing people from Christ".

Additionally, Peter initially compromised with the Pharisaical believers by refusing to eat with the Gentile believers because of the Pharisees Oral Torah (Tradition of the rabbis). Acts 15 illustrates that the Pharisees demanded that new believers in Yeshua keep both the Oral Torah (immediate circumcision for new believers) and the Written Torah.

This separation of Jews and Gentiles while eating was not a Written Torah requirement, it was purely a rabbinic tradition. The early church had both Gentiles and Jews, some of which were Pharisees; who insisted that the church go above and beyond the Written Torah and keep the Oral Traditions as well. The Oral Torah demanded that they keep separate from the uncircumcised. Paul rightfully corrected Peter on the matter of not eating with the Gentile believers.

By refusing to eat with them, Peter was indicating that Gentile believers in Yeshua were unclean and not fit to abide in the Body of Christ. This is why Peter had to clarify, once corrected, that what God has called clean, man should not call unclean. The Jerusalem council decreed that believers need not observe the Oral Torah (traditions of the rabbis), but that new Gentile believers did need to learn the Written Law of Moses in the synagogue where it was taught every 7th day Sabbath (Acts 15: 21).

Again, there is no disagreement that the salvation act has nothing to do with our merit or qualification. But all those who are made clean, by the facts of scripture, kept the 7th day Sabbath, learned the Law of Moses in the synagogue, and kept the Written Torah.

Peter was not wavering between keeping and not keeping the Written Law of Moses. He was wavering between keeping the Oral Traditions (Oral Torah) of the rabbis and not keeping them. The Pharisaic believers were saying that everyone should be keeping the Traditions of the rabbis <u>and</u> the Written Torah of Moses.

This is the same battle Paul was fighting in his letters to the churches. This is also the same battle that Yeshua had with the Pharisees (Matthew 15:1–9). Pharisees who were not believers in Yeshua were teaching Gentile believers that they needed to keep the Oral Torah, not just the Written Torah.

We must address the argument that we do not have to keep the Written Torah just because the Apostles and the first century church did. This comment alone is frightening to contemplate because of the mental gymnastics required for a believer to say, "I am saved, I can remain as pagan as I wish to be". Thank God we do not live in a Christian nation of cannibals. Imagine the level of hypocrisy involved–a group of people claiming they are made clean but wallowing in the lowest carnality.

Romans 6: 1, What shall we say then? Shall we continue in sin, that grace may abound? 2 God forbid. How shall we, that are dead to sin, live any longer therein? 3 Know ye not, that so many of us as were baptized into Jesus Christ were baptized into his death?

Notice the associations of being dead to sin and being baptized into the death of Yeshua. Paul is teaching us that the grace of God severs (circumcises) us from the fleshly world. As for the spirit of the law versus the letter of the law, which requirement was stricter?

Matthew 5: 19, <u>Whosoever therefore shall break one of these least commandments</u>, and shall teach men so, he shall be called the least in the kingdom of heaven: but whosoever shall do and teach them, the same shall be called great in the kingdom of heaven. 20 For I say unto you, That except your righteousness shall exceed the righteousness of the scribes and Pharisees, ye shall in no case enter into the kingdom of heaven. 21 Ye have heard that it was said of them of old time, Thou shalt not kill; and whosoever shall kill shall be in danger of the judgment: 22 But I say unto you, That whosoever is angry with his brother without a cause shall be in danger of the judgment: and whosoever shall say to his brother, Raca, shall be in danger of the council: but whosoever shall say, Thou fool, shall be in danger of hell fire.

The pattern is clear that those under the grace of God through Yeshua become like Yeshua and dead to the flesh. Our spirit is made alive.

1 Corinthians 15: 22, For as in Adam all die, even so in Christ shall all be made alive.

The pattern of Adam is the flesh, and the pattern of Yeshua is the spirit.

1 Corinthians 15: 45, And so it is written, The first man Adam was made a living soul; the last Adam was made a quickening spirit.

What is more important? The spirit. Does this mean we can continue in sin? Does this mean we obey only in spirit and do not need to manifest that change of heart in our actions? No. That would be hypocritical.

This argument contradicts the fact that we should be doing as Yeshua said and avoiding hypocrisy. Keeping the Law in intent only, not in action is nothing but hypocritical. Most of the Church has done the opposite of Yeshua's admonition and voided the Law so that they might do whatever their conscience dictates, despite the teachings of Yeshua and the Apostles. This was a principal concern in the first century and they write about it.

2 Thessalonians 2: 7, For <u>the mystery of iniquity</u> doth already work: only he who now letteth will let, until he be taken out of the way.

Many in the first century church were already starting to use this grace as a license to be "Torahless" which is defined as iniquity.

1 Timothy 8: 8, But we know <u>that the law is good,</u> if a man use it lawfully; 9 Knowing this, that the law is not made for a righteous man, but for the lawless and disobedient, for the ungodly and for sinners, for unholy and profane, for murderers of fathers and murderers of mothers, for manslayers,

If we ascribe this law to the modern Christian's self–defined internal spiritual law and not to the Law of Moses, we need to explain why it is for the lawless and disobedient. They were not talking about the Roman law or some internal moral law. They were talking about the Written Torah of Moses. Paul is making it clear that the lawless man does not have an internal moral law that is keeping him obedient and hence needs an external law to keep him in check. The essential problem from start to finish is man's failure of internal law. This is what God is fixing. To suggest that you can keep the spirit of the law without keeping the letter of the law is a non–argument and without logic. You only manifest what you are.

James 1: 15, Then when lust hath conceived, it bringeth forth sin: and sin, when it is finished, bringeth forth death.

Furthermore let us keep in mind that the reason Paul had to correct Peter was that Peter was attempting to satisfy the Pharisees who insisted new believers must keep the Oral Law (the Traditions of the rabbis) which meant all new believers must be circumcised before eating with the Jews. Before even understanding their faith in a mature manner like Abraham, they had to start with circumcision instead of ending with it. Paul's alleged nullification of circumcision is not what the scriptures show. He is critiquing the hypocrisy of being circumcised without acting like one who is circumcised. This is the same critique that Yeshua had of the Pharisees. So Paul was not voiding the necessity of circumcision, but declaring that it should manifest a circumcised heart otherwise it is a useless symbol. But if it is a fulfillment of the heart, Paul says it is "profitable" for the believer in Yeshua.

Romans 2: 25, For circumcision verily profiteth, if thou keep the law: but if thou be a breaker of the law, thy circumcision is made uncircumcision.

Paul clarifies the necessity of the circumcision of the heart preceding the manifestation in the flesh.

> Romans 4: 7, Saying, Blessed are they whose iniquities are forgiven, and whose sins are covered. 8 Blessed is the man to whom the Lord will not impute sin. 9 Cometh this blessedness then upon the circumcision only, or upon the uncircumcision also? for we say that faith was reckoned to Abraham for righteousness. 10 How was it then reckoned? when he was in circumcision, or in uncircumcision? Not in circumcision, but in uncircumcision. 11 And he received the sign of circumcision, a seal of the righteousness of the faith which he had yet being uncircumcised: that he might be the father of all them that believe, though they be not circumcised; that righteousness might be imputed unto them also: 12 And the father of circumcision to them who are not of the circumcision only, but who also walk in the steps of that faith of our father Abraham, which he had being yet uncircumcised. 13 For the promise, that he should be the heir of the world, was not to Abraham, or to his seed, through the law, but through the righteousness of faith. 14 For if they which are of the law be heirs, faith is made void, and the promise made of none effect:

IS CIRCUMCISION OR HYPOCRISY "DONE AWAY"?

Notice Abraham had faith and righteousness established in his heart before he was circumcised and he manifested that faith when he was still uncircumcised. He is described as being the "father" and pattern of those who express faith while in uncircumcision. It is impossible to put the cart (circumcision) before the horse (faith in the heart) and still have faith developing a true work within the "inward man" only to then later manifest itself in an outward symbol. When you put the cart (circumcision) before the horse (faith) you end up with hypocrisy, which is an outward action that is not driven by an inward motivation.

Yeshua elaborates on these patterns. He talks about what sanctifies and what is sanctified. Remember the cart and the horse illustration from above. Yeshua says the Pharisees have it backwards, outward action sanctifying the inward man. Yeshua says the outward man is sanctified by the inward heart. Notice the contrasts of what makes something holy. The pattern is listed the same way each time, inward versus outward. The Pharisees believe the inward is sanctified by the outward. Yeshua says the outward is sanctified by the inward heart. Action (letter) without heart (spirit) is dead.

> Matthew 23: 16, Woe unto you, ye blind guides, which say, Whosoever shall swear by the temple, it is nothing; but whosoever shall swear by the gold of the temple, he is a debtor! 17 Ye fools and blind: <u>for whether is greater, the gold, or the temple that sanctifieth the gold?</u> 18 And, Whosoever shall <u>swear by the altar, it is nothing; but whosoever sweareth by the gift that is upon it,</u> he is guilty. 19 Ye fools and blind: for <u>whether is greater, the gift, or the altar that sanctifieth the gift?</u> 20 Whoso therefore <u>shall swear by the altar, sweareth by it, and by all things thereon.</u> 21 And whoso shall <u>swear by the temple, sweareth by it, and by him that dwelleth therein.</u> 22 And he <u>that shall swear by heaven,</u>

sweareth by the throne of God, and by him that sitteth thereon. 23 Woe unto you, scribes and Pharisees, hypocrites! for ye pay tithe of mint and anise and cummin, and have omitted the weightier matters of the law, judgment, mercy, and faith: these ought ye to have done, and not to leave the other undone. 24 Ye blind guides, which strain at a gnat, and swallow a camel. 25 Woe unto you, scribes and Pharisees, hypocrites! for ye make clean the outside of the cup and of the platter, but within they are full of extortion and excess. 26 Thou blind Pharisee, cleanse first that which is within the cup and platter, that the outside of them may be clean also. 27 Woe unto you, scribes and Pharisees, hypocrites! for ye are like unto whited sepulchres, which indeed appear beautiful outward, but are within full of dead men's bones, and of all uncleanness. 28 Even so ye also outwardly appear righteous unto men, but within ye are full of hypocrisy and iniquity. 29 Woe unto you, scribes and Pharisees, hypocrites! because ye build the tombs of the prophets, and garnish the sepulchres of the righteous, 30 And say, If we had been in the days of our fathers, we would not have been partakers with them in the blood of the prophets. 31 Wherefore ye be witnesses unto yourselves, that ye are the children of them which killed the prophets. 32 Fill ye up then the measure of your fathers. 33 Ye serpents, ye generation of vipers, how can ye escape the damnation of hell? 34 Wherefore, behold, I send unto you prophets, and wise men, and scribes: and some of them ye shall kill and crucify; and some of them shall ye scourge in your synagogues, and persecute them from city to city: 35 That upon you may come all the righteous blood shed upon the earth, from the blood of righteous Abel unto the blood of Zacharias son of Barachias, whom ye slew between the temple and the altar. 36 Verily I say unto you, All these things shall come upon this generation. 37 O Jerusalem, Jerusalem, thou that killest the prophets, and stonest them which are sent unto thee, how often would I have gathered thy children together, even as a hen gathereth her chickens under her wings, and ye would not! 38 Behold, your house is left unto you desolate. 39 For I say unto you, Ye shall not see me henceforth, till ye shall say, Blessed is he that cometh in the Name of the Lord.

In every example that which is holier sanctifies that which is made holy.

Let's look at the examples:
- What is more holy, the temple or the gold on the outside of the temple that is sanctified by the temple?
- What is more holy, the altar or the gift on the altar sanctified by the altar?
- What is more holy, swearing by the temple or by the one who sits (sanctifies) in the temple?
- Every time "that which sanctifies" is what they are told to focus upon. We are told to focus on that which is within.

We can clearly see the issue of Acts 15 is the same one that Yeshua dealt with in Matthew 23. The Pharisees want to put the cart (circumcision) before the horse (heart). Yeshua and the Apostles are making it clear, the heart and faith must come first while the outward man (vessel) is unclean and uncircumcised, and then the believer's flesh will manifest a pure and righteous heart full of faith in their flesh. So circumcision is not being done away, it is being put back within its proper order, heart then flesh.

Matthew 15: 9, But in vain they do worship me, teaching for doctrines the commandments of men. 10 And he called the multitude, and said unto them, Hear, and understand: 11 <u>Not that which goeth into the mouth defileth a man; but that which cometh out of the mouth, this defileth a man</u>. 12 Then came his disciples, and said unto him, <u>Knowest thou that the Pharisees were offended,</u> after they heard this saying? 13 But he answered and said, Every plant, which my heavenly Father hath not planted, shall be rooted up. 14 Let them alone: they be blind leaders of the blind. And if the blind lead the blind, both shall fall into the ditch. 15 Then answered Peter and said unto him, Declare unto us this parable. 16 And Jesus said, Are ye also yet without understanding? 17 Do not ye yet understand, that whatsoever entereth in at the mouth goeth into the belly, and is cast out into the draught? 18 <u>But those things which proceed out of the mouth come forth from the heart; and they defile the man. 19 For out of the heart proceed evil thoughts, murders, adulteries, fornications, thefts, false witness, blasphemies: 20 These are the things which defile a man: but to eat with unwashen hands defileth not a man.</u>

Their state of uncircumcision did not make these Gentile believer's unclean. Whether the believers flesh is circumcised or uncircumcised, if their hearts are full of defilement, lack of faith, and uncircumcision, the state of their outward fleshly circumcision means nothing. The inward state is first corrected while yet in "unbelief", turning that heart to a state of "belief". This is the horse before the cart, as it should be. All believers need to follow the same pattern as Abraham, seed then flesh (manifested fruit).

So the issue is not nullification of circumcision. It is an issue of proper order, heart before the flesh, inward before the outward, and seed before flesh. The Pharisees habitually had the order wrong, even after they became believers.

Jeremiah 4: 4, Circumcise yourselves to the Lord, and take away the foreskins of your heart, ye men of Judah and inhabitants of Jerusalem: lest my fury come forth like fire, and burn that none can quench it, because of the evil of your doings.

He reaffirms that the issue is not that those in covenant are uncircumcised, they are circumcised but not in their hearts.

Jeremiah 9: 26, Egypt, and Judah, and Edom, and the children of Ammon, and Moab, and all that are in the utmost corners, that dwell in the wilderness: for all these nations are uncircumcised, and all the house of Israel are uncircumcised in the heart.

This is not a call to abandon circumcision, it is a call to abandon hypocrisy, having an outward symbol that is not rooted in the faith of the heart. Notice

Joshua did not circumcise the second generation that came out of Egypt until 40 years later when they had ascended to the Promised land.

> Joshua 5: 1, And it came to pass, when all the kings of the Amorites, which were on the side of Jordan westward, and all the kings of the Canaanites, which were by the sea, heard that the Lord had dried up the waters of Jordan from before the children of Israel, until we were passed over, that their heart melted, neither was there spirit in them anymore, because of the children of Israel. 2 At that time the Lord said unto Joshua, Make thee sharp knives, and <u>circumcise again the children of Israel the second time</u>. 3 And Joshua made him sharp knives, and circumcised the children of Israel at the hill of the foreskins. 4 And this is the cause why Joshua did circumcise: All the people that came out of Egypt, that were males, even all the men of war, died in the wilderness by the way, after they came out of Egypt. 5 <u>Now all the people that came out were circumcised: but all the people that were born in the wilderness by the way as they came forth out of Egypt, them they had not circumcised</u>. 6 For the children of Israel walked forty years in the wilderness, till <u>all the people that were men of war, which came out of Egypt, were consumed, because they obeyed not the voice of the Lord</u>: unto whom the Lord sware that he would not shew them the land, which the Lord sware unto their fathers that he would give us, a land that floweth with milk and honey. 7 <u>And their children, whom he raised up in their stead, them Joshua circumcised</u>: for they were uncircumcised, because they had not circumcised them by the way. 8 And it came to pass, when they had done circumcising all the people, that they abode in their places in the camp, till they were whole. 9 And the Lord said unto Joshua, This day have I rolled away the reproach of Egypt from off you. Wherefore the name of the place is called Gilgal unto this day.

Notice the entire second generation that came out of Egypt was not circumcised, until they ascended to the Promised land. We will discuss the first and second generations of those who left Egypt and what their patterns signify for the flesh and the spirit, death and resurrection, and seed and manifestation. Try not to forget that the role of Joshua is "raising up the children in their stead". We will discuss what that means as it pertains to death and resurrection and why they had to be circumcised when they ascended.

Joshua clarifies why all the men of the first generation died in the wilderness that were circumcised, "because they obeyed not the voice of the Lord." They had a problem with hypocrisy. Do you see how the theme of circumcision, the state of the believer's heart, and the conduct that is manifested by those who are not driven first by faith of the heart? The first generation of Egypt were circumcised outwardly, but not inwardly. They said they would obey God, but they did not fulfill their word.

> Exodus 19: 8, And all the people answered together, and said, All that the Lord hath spoken we will do. And Moses returned the words of the people unto the Lord.

Joshua talks about it. Jeremiah talks about. Yeshua talks about it and so do the Apostles. The theme is always the same, faith before action. It is never "do away with circumcision". Every time Paul brings up circumcision it is not to rail on doing away with circumcision, it is to rail upon hypocrisy.

THE FALSE ACCUSATION-DID THE FIRST CENTURY CHURCH CIRCUMCISE?

In fact when Paul reports back to the Apostles in Jerusalem a false allegation is brought against him and he is asked to do something to prove it is false.

> Acts 21: 18, And the day following Paul went in with us unto James; and all the elders were present. 19 And when he had saluted them, he declared particularly what things God had wrought among the Gentiles by his ministry. 20 And when they heard it, they glorified the Lord, and said unto him, Thou seest, brother, how many thousands of Jews there are which believe; and they are all zealous of the law: 21 And they are informed of thee, that thou teachest all the Jews which are among the Gentiles to forsake Moses, saying that they ought not to circumcise their children, neither to walk after the customs. 22 What is it therefore? the multitude must needs come together: for they will hear that thou art come. 23 Do therefore this that we say to thee: We have four men which have a vow on them; 24 Them take, and purify thyself with them, and be at charges with them, that they may shave their heads: and all may know that those things, whereof they were informed concerning thee, are nothing; but that thou thyself also walkest orderly, and keepest the law. 25 As touching the Gentiles which believe, we have written and concluded that they observe no such thing, save only that they keep themselves from things offered to idols, and from blood, and from strangled, and from fornication. 26 Then Paul took the men, and the next day purifying himself with them entered into the temple, to signify the accomplishment of the days of purification, until that an offering should be offered for every one of them.

It must be noted that in the above scripture the section, "*that they observe no such thing, save only*" appears only in later manuscripts and the majority of translations actually omit this phrase as it is clear that the older manuscripts do not have this phrase in this scripture. Codex Bezae adds this phrase in the 5th Century. Ephraemi Rescriptus of the 5th Century also includes it. Codex Sinaiticus from the 4th Century does not include this phrase and neither does the Codex Vaticanus of the 4th Century. Codex Alexandrinus of the 5th Century also does not include the phrase, nor does P74 (Bodmer XVII) of the 7th Century. The NET, ESV, RSV, NRSV, NASB95, CJB, NIV, ISV, CSB, TEV, LEB, ASV 1901 all omit this phrase, while only the KJV, NKJV, Geneva, and Darby add it.

Those who added this phrase were attempting to tell the reader that the Gentile Churches were not following Paul's example of keeping the Torah and neither should Gentile believers of Yeshua. Whereas the Churches confirmed that they were following Paul's example of being saved by grace and being zealous for the Written Torah and keeping it. For those who insist that the KJV is infallible the context of the scriptures clarify that Paul and the Early Church were teaching the

Gentiles the same things as the Jews and that they all observed the same things. So, whether the added phrase is interpreted that Gentile believers were not following Paul's example of keeping the Written Torah or that this phrase is referencing what they were not observing…the false allegations of Paul teaching Gentile Churches to forsake the Torah of Moses…the conclusion is still the same. All believers including Gentiles are saved by Grace and then should be learning the Written Law of Moses and keeping it.

Notice the elders of the church state that they have confirmed the Apostle Paul is <u>not</u> teaching people to "not circumcise their children" and that the Apostles have taken the time to write to the Gentile churches to confirm what Paul has been instructing them, "As touching the Gentiles which believe, <u>we have written and concluded that they observe no such thing</u>."

What is the list of "no such thing(s)"?

- "thou teachest all the Jews which are among the Gentiles to forsake Moses"
- "saying that they ought not to circumcise their children, neither to walk after the customs"

The elders clearly establish the facts by writing to the Gentile churches. They confirm that Paul was walking according to the Written Law of Moses in regard to the teaching of circumcision. They confirm that he is not forsaking the Law of Moses and is in fact teaching others to observe the Written Law of Moses.

The elders also verified that Paul was teaching Gentile converts as instructed by the Jerusalem council in Acts 15. Then Paul goes to the temple to fulfill the ritual of purification and brings an offering for every one of them. He does this to prove that he "walkest orderly, and keepest the law…" The elders in Jerusalem were afraid that these rumors might be perceived as true and that is why they ask Paul to go the temple. "And all may know that those things, whereof they were informed concerning thee, <u>are nothing</u>; but that <u>thou thyself also walkest orderly, and keepest the law</u>".

This proves that the expectation of the leaders of the church was that all believers learn and keep the Written Law of Moses (the Written Torah) and that these false allegations about not circumcising their children were unfounded and untrue.

The modern church's positon that nobody should be circumcised is factually and scripturally untrue. At the very minimum we have evidence presented that at least Jewish believers in Yeshua were still expected to circumcise their children.

Historically, the Roman Catholic Church denounced religious circumcision for its members in the Cantate Domino, written during the 11th council of Florence in 1442. This decision was based on the belief that baptism had superseded circumcision. The Coptic Christians in Egypt and the Ethiopian Orthodox Christians— two of the oldest surviving forms of Christianity— retain many of the features of early Christianity, including male circumcision. (Wikipedia)

The prophets mention that the future fulfilled state of Jerusalem requires circumcision.

> Isaiah 52: 1, Awake, awake; put on thy strength, O Sion; put on thy beautiful garments, O Jerusalem, the holy city: for henceforth there shall no more come into thee the uncircumcised and the unclean.

If circumcision is done away, then there is certainly no need for the pregnant expectation that only the circumcised and clean come unto Jerusalem.

> Deuteronomy 30: 6, And the Lord thy <u>God will circumcise thine heart, and the heart of thy seed</u>, to love the Lord thy God with all thine heart, and with all thy soul, that thou mayest live. 7 And the Lord thy God will put all these curses upon thine enemies, and on them that hate thee, which persecuted thee. 8 And thou shalt return and obey the voice of the Lord, <u>and do all his commandments which I command thee this day</u>.

Notice the clear future expectation is that God will circumcise our hearts and we will "do all his commandments". Which commandments? Some internal moral law that is made up by the believer depending on what he wants? Moses actually says which law, "all his commandments which I command thee this day". These commandments are the Written Law of Moses. If both circumcision and the Written Law of Moses are done away, then there would be no future expectation by the prophets. Since physical circumcision is part of the Written Torah we also cannot divorce it from that future expectation.

> Leviticus 12: 2, Speak unto the children of Israel, saying, If a woman have conceived seed, and born a man child: then she shall be unclean seven days; according to the days of the separation for her infirmity shall she be unclean. 3 And in the eighth day the flesh of his foreskin shall be circumcised.

If Deuteronomy 30:6 were talking about the redeemed final state in the resurrection body, then it could be referring to the circumcision of the heart only. However, as verse 7 refers to God placing "these curses" on their "enemies", they must have physical flesh as would those who "return and obey the voice of the Lord". A real covenant has a real sign and God has clearly shown that His sign is circumcision.

The "no such things" of Acts 21:25 are allegations proven false in writing by the elders of the church. Paul proves them all to be untrue so that "all may know that those things, whereof they were informed concerning thee, are nothing".

Knowing this scriptural fact, what are we to do with the traditional view of Acts 15 that the Gentiles need not keep the Written Law of Moses? Peter, after being corrected by Paul, made it clear that we should not call unclean what God has cleansed by the operation of God, circumcision in Christ. The Apostles clarified that new believers had to do what the Written Torah commanded.

New believers had to:

- "abstain from pollutions of idols"
- "and from fornication"
- "and from things strangled"
- "and from blood" (Acts 15: 20).

If they did these things they could eat with Jewish believers while learning the Law of Moses in the synagogue. Otherwise they could not. This was the believers starting point. It did not absolve them from the responsibility of learning and doing the other things required of them. This was word for word exactly what the Written Torah required as a starting point for God fearers in the Torah of Moses.

In regard to divorce, the allegation that Yeshua was criticizing the Law of Moses for permitting divorce is not scripturally accurate. He was criticizing the people for the same reason that God needed to give a new covenant, the hardness of our hearts. There was no problem with the laws, it was with the heart.

Hebrews 8: 7, For if that first covenant had been faultless, then should no place have been sought for the second. 8 For finding fault with them, he saith, Behold, the days come, saith the Lord, when I will make a new covenant with the house of Israel and with the house of Judah: 9 Not according to the covenant that I made with their fathers in the day when I took them by the hand to lead them out of the land of Egypt; because they continued not in my covenant, and I regarded them not, saith the Lord. 10 For this is the covenant that I will make with the house of Israel after those days, saith the Lord; I will put my laws into their mind, and write them in their hearts: and I will be to them a God, and they shall be to me a people:

Notice the remedy is not to void our keeping of the Law of Moses, the remedy is to put the same laws into our hearts. Instead of using the scriptures as a compass, many spiritualize it all away and proceed in pagan practices that the Apostles did not observe and in fact warned of in their writings. This illustrates the blind spot that even well intentioned believers have to actual truth and fact when it contradicts what they want.

Further study is required on Paul's continual contrasting of the flesh and the spirit, death and resurrection, law of sin and death versus the law of resurrection life, being under the law versus free from law, as well as the letter versus the spirit. These are all fractals of death and resurrection. Paul simplifies this issue.

Romans 7: 5, For when we were in the flesh, the motions of sins, which were by the law, did work in our members to bring forth fruit unto death. 6 But now we are delivered from the law, that being dead wherein we were held; that we should serve in newness of spirit, and not in the oldness of the letter. 7 What shall we say then? Is the law sin? God forbid. Nay, I had not known sin, but by the law: for I had not known lust, except the law had said, Thou shalt not covet.

Notice how Paul compares the flesh with sin under the law and our needed deliverance from the bondage of the flesh, sin, and the condemnation of the law. And once delivered from that judgment we appear in the Spirit, by the resurrection, to keep the law in the spirit, free from the flesh, free from condemnation, and free from death. Paul explains further.

1 Corinthians 15: 42 <u>So also is the resurrection of the dead</u>. It is <u>sown in corruption; it is raised in incorruption</u>: 43 It is sown in dishonour; it is raised in glory: it is sown in weakness; it is raised in power: 44 It is sown a natural body; it is raised a spiritual body. There is a natural body, and there is a spiritual body. 45 And so it is written, The first man Adam was made a living soul; the last Adam was made a quickening spirit. 46 <u>Howbeit that was not first which is spiritual, but that which is natural; and afterward that which is spiritual</u>. 47 The first man is of the earth, earthy; the second man is the Lord from heaven. 48 As is the earthy, such are they also that are earthy: and as is the heavenly, such are they also that are heavenly. 49 And as we have borne the image of the earthy, we shall also bear the image of the heavenly. 50 Now this I say, brethren, that <u>flesh and blood cannot inherit the kingdom of God; neither doth corruption inherit incorruption</u>. 51 Behold, I shew you a mystery; We shall not all sleep, but we shall all be changed, 52 In a moment, in the twinkling of an eye, at the last trump: for the trumpet shall sound, and the dead shall be raised incorruptible, and we shall be changed. 53 For <u>this corruptible must put on incorruption</u>, and this mortal must put on immortality. 54 So when this corruptible shall have put on incorruption, and this mortal shall have put on immortality, then shall be brought to pass the saying that is written, Death is swallowed up in victory. 55 O death, where is thy sting? O grave, where is thy victory? 56 <u>The sting of death is sin; and the strength of sin is the law</u>. 57 But thanks be to God, which giveth us the victory through our Lord Yeshua.

Do you see how the Law of Moses does not change and is not destroyed or done away? What is changed? We are changed. The administration of condemnation and death passes away to the new administration of grace and resurrection life.

So the central issue is the entry point to eating, dwelling, and worshiping with the Jews. The Pharisees were demanding circumcision as the starting point and that it must occur right away.

"At this time it was that two great men, who were under the jurisdiction of the king [Agrippa] came to me out of the region of Trachonius, bringing their horses and their arms, and carrying with them their money also; and <u>when the Jews would force them to be circumcised, if they would stay among them</u>, I would not permit them to have any force put upon them, but said to them, "Every one ought to worship God according to his own conscience, and not to be constrained by force; and that these men, who had fled to us for protection, ought not to be so treated as to repent of their coming hither. " And when I had pacified the multitude, I provided for the men that were come to us whatsoever it was they wanted, according to their usual way of living, and that in great plenty also. " (The Life of Flavius Josephus 23/111)

This was the same thing that the Pharisees were doing in the early church to Gentile believers. The Jerusalem council of Acts 15 clarified that new Gentile believers need not be circumcised upon believing in Yeshua, but that they should follow the basic requirements for fellowship with Jewish believers. The Pharisees found this offensive and as a result continually sent rabbis to the Gentile churches telling them that they must be circumcised.

Galatians 5: 1, Stand fast therefore in the liberty wherewith Christ hath made us free, and be not entangled again with the yoke of bondage. 2 Behold, I Paul say unto you, that if ye be circumcised, Christ shall profit you nothing. 3 For I testify again to every man that is circumcised, that he is a debtor to do the whole law. 4 Christ is become of no effect unto you, whosoever of you are justified by the law; ye are fallen from grace. 5 <u>For we through the Spirit wait for the hope of righteousness by faith. 6 For in Jesus Christ neither circumcision availeth any thing, nor uncircumcision; but faith which worketh by love.</u> 7 Ye did run well; who did hinder you that ye should not obey the truth? 8 This persuasion cometh not of him that calleth you. 9 A little leaven leaveneth the whole lump. 10 I have confidence in you through the Lord, that ye will be none otherwise minded: but he that troubleth you shall bear his judgment, whosoever he be. 11 And I, brethren, <u>if I yet preach circumcision, why do I yet suffer persecution</u>? then is the offence of the cross ceased. 12 I would they were even cut off which trouble you.

Paul is writing to a Gentile church that is beset by Jewish Pharisees that keep demanding that they be circumcised, not because they are believers in Yeshua, but because they are attending the synagogue and learning the Law of Moses. Paul emphasizes that, like Abraham, we are to "wait for the hope" for the work of Christ to be complete in the removal of the fleshly body in the resurrection, of which baptism (mikvah) is a symbol.

Because Paul was teaching what the Jerusalem Council dictated, the non–believing Pharisees continually assaulted him and the Gentile believers for not being immediately circumcised.

Acts 17: 2, And Paul, as his manner was, <u>went in unto them, and three Sabbath days</u> reasoned with them <u>out of the scriptures</u>, 3 Opening and alleging, that Christ must needs have suffered, and risen again from the dead; and that this Jesus, whom I preach unto you, is Christ. 4 And some of them believed, <u>and consorted with Paul and Silas; and of the devout Greeks</u> a great multitude, and of the chief women not a few. 5 But the Jews which believed not, moved with envy, took unto them certain lewd fellows of the baser sort, and gathered a company, and set all the city on an uproar, and assaulted the house of Jason, and sought to bring them out to the people. 6 And when they found them not, they drew Jason and certain brethren unto the rulers of the city, crying, These that have turned the world upside down are come hither also; 7 Whom Jason hath received: and these all do contrary to the decrees of Caesar, saying that there is another king, one Jesus. 8 And they troubled the people and the rulers of the city, when they heard these things.

WHAT WAS PAUL REALLY TEACHING?

The baser sort refused to prove if what Paul was testifying about Yeshua's work as the "messenger of the circumcision" was true or not as cited from the Old Testament scriptures. Instead of proving or disproving it, they persecuted him for teaching the work of the Messiah, which is the circumcision and removal of the flesh in resurrection life.

What have we confirmed?

- New Gentile believers had to immediately:
    - "abstain from pollutions of idols"
    - "and from fornication"
    - "and from things strangled"
    - "and from blood" (Acts 15: 20).

- Jewish and Gentile believers could remain in whatever state of circumcision or uncircumcision that they were in as the "messenger of the circumcision" who is Christ had done the work of making man clean in order to fellowship with God and one another.

- Paul was teaching the Written Torah (Law of Moses) to Jews and Gentiles. We know this because un–believing Pharisees kept telling believing Gentiles in the synagogue that they needed to be circumcised.

- The elders of the church in Jerusalem confirmed all of the above facts in writing by contacting the Gentile believers to establish what was true and what was false. They affirm that the accusations were false and instructed Paul to go to the temple, purify himself according to the Law of Moses with a sacrifice made for himself. Paul did so.

- These allegations are proven false:
    - "thou teachest all the Jews which are among the Gentiles to forsake Moses"
    - "saying that they ought not to circumcise their children, neither to walk after the customs"

- Logically this means that Paul was teaching Gentiles to keep the Law of Moses, but not according to the demands of the Oral Torah of the Pharisees. It also means that Paul was teaching the Jewish believers to circumcise their children and to walk according to Moses.

- Circumcision is an image of resurrection that can only be performed ultimately by the resurrected Messiah.

- Paul as a believer in Yeshua was perfectly fine with the elders' request that he go to the temple and offer a sacrifice, even though Christ is our sacrifice.
    - 1 Corinthians 5: 7, Purge out therefore the old leaven, that ye may be a new lump, as ye are unleavened. For even Christ our Passover is sacrificed for us:

To say that circumcision was done away by the early church is inaccurate and ignores the scriptures that show God's expectation that people be circumcised when they return to the Lord (Deuteronomy 30: 6).

The directive is not "do not circumcise". More accurately it is "circumcise your hearts" and "do not be a hypocrite". This circumcision can only be performed by the Messiah as He enters into the heart of the believer like a seed and writes His commandments upon the heart. Paul confirms this truth.

1 Corinthians 7: 19, Circumcision is nothing, and uncircumcision is nothing, but the keeping of the commandments of God.

These commandments are the Written Law of Moses that new Gentile believers were learning in the synagogue on the 7th day Sabbath with Jewish believers.

2 Corinthians 3: 12, Seeing then that we have such hope, we use great plainness of speech: 13 And not as Moses, which put a veil over his face, that the children of Israel could not stedfastly look to the end of that which is abolished: 14 But their minds were blinded: for until this day remaineth the same vail untaken away in the reading of the Old Testament; which vail is done away in Christ. 15 But even unto this day, when Moses is read, the vail is upon their heart. 16 Nevertheless when it shall turn to the Lord, the vail shall be taken away.

The circumcision is the work of the Messiah removing the veil (hardened covering) that blinds the hearts and minds when reading the Law of Moses.

Isaiah 63: 17, O Lord, why hast thou made us to err from thy ways, and hardened our heart from thy fear? Return for thy servants' sake, the tribes of thine inheritance. 18 The people of thy holiness have possessed it but a little while: our adversaries have trodden down thy sanctuary.

This straying and blinding is done on purpose by God.

John 12: 40, He hath blinded their eyes, and hardened their heart; that they should not see with their eyes, nor understand with their heart, and be converted, and I should heal them.

Instead of establishing our own righteousness, it is established by God in Christ in our hearts. The "it" of 2 Corinthians 3: 16 ("when it shall turn to the Lord") is Israel (Judah), who are still blinded by God until they return to the Messiah, the administrator of the Resurrected Covenant, the Law of Moses with grace and abundant mercy (Exodus 34). The problem is with the heart and the ability to see and hear. This is the seed that needs to be circumcised.

Romans 11: 25, For I would not, brethren, that ye should be ignorant of this mystery, lest ye should be wise in your own conceits; that blindness in part is happened to Israel, until the fulness of the Gentiles be come in.

Through God's willful intent Israel has been blinded until the Gentiles come in.

Matthew 23: 37, O Jerusalem, Jerusalem, thou that killest the prophets, and stonest them which are sent unto thee, how often would I have gathered thy children together, even as a hen gathereth her chickens under her wings, and ye would not! 38 Behold, your house is left unto you desolate. 39 For I say unto you, Ye shall not see me henceforth, till ye shall say, <u>Blessed is he that cometh in the Name of the Lord</u>.

The only cure begins within the heart. This work can only be done by Yeshua the Messiah. Once Judah and Israel turn to the Messiah Yeshua, the removal of the veil by "circumcision of the Messiah" will be completed. What does that mean? The resurrection of the dead.

It is quite likely that first century Christians followed the same pattern as Abraham and did not immediately get circumcised when they first believed. It was not required by the church that you "do not circumcise". Otherwise Paul would not have circumcised a Gentile believer in Yeshua as we see in Acts 16.

Acts 16: 3, Him would Paul have to go forth with him; and took and circumcised him because of the Jews which were in those quarters: for they knew all that his father was a Greek.

Seeing that this circumcision occurred immediately after the Jerusalem council of Acts 15 where they declared how to handle Gentile Converts, we have two options. We can assume that Paul ignored the edict of the council, which we know is untrue from witness statements made in writing to the elders in Jerusalem and by Paul's own statements and actions in Acts 21: 19–27. Or we can suppose that he had a clearer understanding of what was affirmed in Acts 15 than the modern church currently agrees with or understands. Paul clarifies that the focus of circumcision is on the Messiah and His work on the heart.

Galatians 5: 6, For <u>in Jesus Christ neither circumcision availeth any thing, nor uncircumcision; but faith which worketh by love</u>. 7 Ye did run well; who did hinder you that ye should not obey the truth? 8 This persuasion cometh not of him that calleth you. 9 A little leaven leaveneth the whole lump. 10 I have confidence in you through the Lord, that ye will be none otherwise minded: but he that troubleth you shall bear his judgment, whosoever he be. 11 And I, brethren, <u>if I yet preach circumcision, why do I yet suffer persecution? then is the offence of the cross ceased</u>.

We cannot get around the clarity of Paul in regard to the work of Christ and the offense of the cross.

Galatians 5: 2, Behold, I Paul say unto you, that if ye be circumcised, Christ shall profit you nothing.

The Apostles, like Christ, are all focused on one central issue in all of their writings: the state of the believer's heart. They are fulfilling the same image, pattern, and fractal as Yeshua, the "seed of the Kingdom of God". Perhaps this explains the necessity of focusing on the heart–new believers were having their hearts circumcised while the offense of the "cross" remained as the outward man was uncircumcised. Why was this offensive? It was a work that the Pharisees and the rabbis could not do themselves.

THE FRACTAL OF DEATH THEN RESURRECTION OR SEED THEN MANIFESTED FRUIT

We saw how the law has not passed away and while it is the circumcision of the heart that matters, the sign that points to that inward transformation is still required by the Lord. The sign of the flesh points to the workings of the spirit. We are not better than our father of the faith, Abraham who was also circumcised after he believed. Now we will look at the fruit of Israel and the pattern of the flesh and spirit in the death and resurrection of Israel in the fullness of the Gentiles. Once the fullness of the Gentiles occurs . . .

Romans 11: 12, Now if the fall of them be the riches of the world, and the diminishing of them the riches of the Gentiles; how much more their fulness? 13 For I speak to you Gentiles, inasmuch as I am the apostle of the Gentiles, I magnify mine office: 14 If by any means I may provoke to emulation them which are my flesh, and might save some of them. 15 For if the casting away of them be the reconciling of the world, what shall the receiving of them be, but life from the dead?

Notice how Israel is fulfilling the imagery of the "casting away" of the seed. They are fulfilling the imagery of a seed death, just like the Messiah, and just like mankind in this current corruptible state. We see Israel performing the same fractal as the seed in death. They are cast away as a seed for the planting of the Gentiles. So while they appear with the same imagery as the Messiah, cast away, dead, and unseen, they like the Messiah appear in restoration, growth, and manifested resurrection. We see this same imagery in the death of the firstborn that leave Egypt (death, seed) and the ascension (resurrection, manifested fruit) of the second generation that came out of Egypt to the Promised land. This pattern also fulfills itself in Judah (death, seed) and the Gentiles (resurrection, manifested fruit).

Once the fullness of the Gentiles occurs, Israel and Judah turn to Yeshua the new administrator of the Resurrected Covenant (the Law of Moses). They have their sight restored and appear in resurrection life. The veil that was upon their hearts is removed by the "operation of Christ" and their understanding and their sight is restored.

The Gentiles and Israel are fulfilling the imagery of the covenant and the Messiah: death and resurrection. This is why we see resurrection at the same time as we see the fullness of the Gentiles and the turning of the Jews to Yeshua the Messiah. The pattern is always the same, flesh then spirit, carnal than spiritual, corruptible then incorruptible, death then life, seed then manifestation (fruit).

Romans 6: 5, For if we have been planted together in the likeness of his death, we shall be also in the likeness of his resurrection:

So why the delay of the Kingdom of God? Follow the imagery of the seed! The patterns of nature are replicated in the patterns of the scriptures. Those same patterns underlie our fundamental reality as it relates to death and resurrection. Just as a seed manifests a fruit, so also does the natural body manifest a resurrected spiritual body. So as man's current state is portrayed as corrupt and full of death we should examine the God designed nature of seeds to understand the process and workings of our current corruptible state. Just as a seed is dormant and buried in the earth, so also is the natural and corrupt body to await resurrection. The process of seed germination will give us great insight into the reasons, nature and timing of resurrection. Paul teaches the seed and fruit pattern over and over again.

Conditions have to be just right for the seed to break forth from its seed coat and sometimes that takes years, decades, centuries, even thousands of years. Temperature, freezing, thawing, drying, or even being eaten will affect if and when that seed coat is shed and the seed takes on water to then germinate and produce fruit. I suggest you do a simple study on seed germination and you will see the simple natural patterns that God repeatedly operates upon. Those same patterns will be repeated in us and all creation.

Some seeds have a water gap to prevent immediate germination. When this gap closes it is a sign of maturity and that it is ready to receive water and start reproduction. A part of this is that the seed shed its hard outer shell just like circumcision. Some seeds have growth regulators that are chemical in nature and actually need to be washed out just like in baptism, before it can start to germinate. Some are affected by temperature and some by light. The season has to be right for the seed to have time to grow and produce fruit. In its very nature the seed is programed to respond to its environment to begin reproduction and bring forth manifested life. It goes from a state of hiddenness like being in the womb to a state of manifestation like a fruit.

A dormant seed is one that is unable to germinate in a specified period of time under a combination of environmental factors that are normally suitable for the germination of the non–dormant seed. [1] Dormancy is a mechanism to prevent germination during unsuitable ecological conditions, when the probability of seedling survival is low. [2] True dormancy or innate dormancy is caused by conditions within the seed that prevent germination under normally ideal conditions. <u>Dormancy that is caused by an impermeable seed coat is known as physical dormancy</u>. Physical dormancy is the result of impermeable layer(s) that develops during maturation and drying of the seed or fruit. [7] This impermeable layer prevents the seed from taking up water or gases. As a result, the seed is prevented from germinating until dormancy is broken. In natural systems, <u>physical dormancy is broken by several factors including high temperatures, fluctuating temperatures, fire, freezing/thawing</u>, drying or passage through the digestive tracts of animals. [8] Generally, physical dormancy is the result of one or more palisade layers in the fruit or seed coat. These layers are lignified with malphigian cells tightly packed together and impregnated with water–repellent. [11] In the Anacardiaceae and Nelumbonaceae families the seed coat is not well developed. Therefore, palisade layers in the fruit perform the functional role of preventing water uptake . While physical dormancy is a common feature, several species in these families do not have physical dormancy or produce non–dormant seeds. [9]Specialised structures, which function as a "water–gap", are associated with the impermeable layers of the seed to prevent the uptake of water. [9] The water–gap is closed at seed maturity and is opened in response to the appropriate environmental signal. [11] Breaking physical dormancy involves the disruption of these specialised structures within the seed, and acts as an environmental signal detector for germination. [9] For example, legume (Fabaceae) seeds become permeable after the thin–walled cells of lens (water–gap structure}. [11] Following disrupted pulls apart to allow water entry into the seed. In nature, the seed coats of physically dormant seeds are thought to become water permeable over time through repeated heating and cooling over many months–years in the soil seedbank. [7] Mechanical dormancy occurs when seed coats or other coverings are too hard to allow the embryo to expand during germination. [16] In the past this mechanism of dormancy was ascribed to a number of species that have been found to have endogenous factors for their dormancy instead. These endogenous facts include physiologically dormancy cased by low embryo growth potential [17] Includes growth regulators etc., that are present in the coverings around the embryo. They may be leached out of the tissues by washing or soaking the seed, or deactivated by other means. Other chemicals that prevent germination are washed out of the seeds by rainwater or snow melt. Physiological dormancy prevents embryo growth and seed germination until chemical changes occur. [3] These chemicals include inhibitors that often retard embryo growth to the point where it is not strong enough to break through the seed coat or other tissues. In some seeds physiological dormancy is indicated when scarification increases germination. [18] Physiological dormancy is broken when inhibiting chemicals are broken down or are no longer produced by the seed; often by a period of cool moist conditions, normally below (+4C) 39F, or in the case of many species in Ranunculaceae and a few others,(−5C) 24F. Abscisic acid is usually the growth inhibitor in seeds and its production can be affected by light. Therefore, the timing of the mechanisms that breaks physical dormancy is critical and must be tuned to environmental cues. This maximises the chances for germination occurring in conditions where the plant will successfully germinate, establish and eventually reproduce. [9] Compounding this problem is that the same seed that is dormant for one reason at a given point may be dormant for another reason at a later point. Some seeds fluctuate from periods of dormancy to non dormancy, and despite the fact that a dormant seed appears to be static or inert, in reality they are still receiving and responding to environmental cues. One important function of most seeds is delayed germination, which allows time for dispersal and prevents germination of all the seeds at the same time. The staggering of germination safeguards some seeds and seedlings from suffering damage or death from short periods of bad weather or from transient herbivores; it also allows some seeds to germinate when competition from other plants for light and water might be less intense. Another form of delayed seed germination is <u>seed quiescence,</u> which is different than true seed dormancy and occurs when a seed fails to germinate <u>because the external environmental conditions are too dry or warm or cold for germination.</u> [3] Many species of plants have seeds that delay germination for many months or years, and some seeds can remain in the soil seed bank for more than 50 years before germination. <u>Some seeds have a very long viability period, and the oldest documented germinating seed was nearly 2000 years</u> old based on radiocarbon dating. (Wikipedia)

There are several reasons for the seed to be delayed from producing fruit:
- Dormancy that is caused by an impermeable seed coat
- Some seeds have a water gap that is closed at maturity
- Some seeds have a coat that requires scarification (circumcision) to allow water into the seed
- Some seeds need to be washed to remove chemicals that prevent germination
- Some seeds are designed to delay germination until a suitable environment shows itself in light and water
- Some seeds are delayed in germination to prevent competition with other plants

All of these reasons are the same imagery we see in Jewish and Gentile believers in regards to circumcision, baptism (mikvah), and why there is a delay in the manifestation of the Kingdom of God. The right season needs to present itself to move from seed to manifested fruit.

WAITING FOR GOD'S SEASON
Just as Yeshua was planting the "seed of the Kingdom" and fulfilling the natural God given fractal of a seed death appropriate to His season, so are we. We are awaiting the latter rain to bring the seed to fruit.

Jeremiah 3: 2, Lift up thine eyes unto the high places, and see where thou hast not been lien with. In the ways hast thou sat for them, as the Arabian in the wilderness; and thou hast polluted the land with thy whoredoms and with thy wickedness. 3 Therefore the showers have been withholden, and there hath been no latter rain; and thou hadst a whore's forehead, thou refusedst to be ashamed.

The promise of His coming is as "rain".

Hosea 6: 3, Then shall we know, if we follow on to know the Lord: his going forth is prepared as the morning; and <u>he shall come unto us as the rain,</u> as the latter and former rain unto the earth.

And the timing of that rain is according to its appropriate season.
- Joel 2: 23, Be glad then, ye children of Sion, and rejoice in the Lord your God: for he hath given you the former rain moderately, and he will cause to come down for you the rain, the former rain, and the latter rain in the first month.
- Zechariah 10: 1, Ask ye of the Lord rain in the time of the latter rain; so the Lord shall make bright clouds, and give them showers of rain, to every one grass in the field.

We are admonished to be good husbandman and sow the seed and await the rain.

James 5: 7, Be patient therefore, brethren, unto the coming of the Lord. Behold, the husbandman waiteth for the precious fruit of the earth, and hath long patience for it, until he receive the early and latter rain.

We can clearly see that the patterns and fractals of nature tell us why there has been a delay in the Kingdom of God. We are fulfilling the seed portion of the fractal of "seed then manifestation". The hallmarks of the seed are burial, death, and hiddenness, just like the first generation that left Egypt.
Currently the Jews reject Yeshua because He did not immediately return the scattered tribes of Israel and reunite the Kingdom of God. Unfortunately they were blind to the "seasons" of God.

Mark 4: 23, If any man have ears to hear, let him hear. 24 And he said unto them, Take heed what ye hear: with what measure ye mete, it shall be measured to you: and unto you that hear shall more be given. 25 For he that hath, to him shall be given: and he that hath not, from him shall be taken even that which he hath. 26 And he said, So is the kingdom of God, as if a man should cast seed into the ground; 27 And should sleep, and rise night and day, and the seed should spring and grow up, he knoweth not how. 28 For the earth bringeth forth fruit of herself; first the blade, then the ear, after that the full corn in the ear. 29 But when the fruit is brought forth, immediately he putteth in the sickle, because the harvest is come. 30 And he said, Whereunto shall we liken the kingdom of God? or with what comparison shall we compare it? 31 It is like a grain of mustard seed, which, when it is sown in the earth, is less than all the seeds that be in the earth: 32 But when it is sown, it groweth up, and becometh greater than all herbs, and shooteth out great branches; so that the fowls of the air may lodge under the shadow of it.

We who are now in His image are fulfilling the same pattern and awaiting the fullness (fruitfulness) that precedes the restoring of Israel and Judah.

Acts 1: 6, When they therefore were come together, they asked of him, saying, Lord, wilt thou at this time restore again the kingdom to Israel? 7 And he said unto them, It is not for you to know the times or the seasons, which the Father hath put in his own power. 8 But ye shall receive power, after that the Holy Ghost is come upon you: and ye shall be witnesses unto me both in Jerusalem, and in all Judaea, and in Samaria, and unto the uttermost part of the earth.

Like the need for circumcision of the outer coat of the seed, we must have the seed of our hearts circumcised by the "Messiah of the Circumcision" so that He may write His commandments on our hearts, in order that we might "bear fruit".

- Romans 2: 29, But he is a Jew, which is one inwardly; and circumcision is that of the heart, in the spirit, and not in the letter; whose praise is not of men, but of God.
- Romans 15: 8, Now I say that Jesus Christ was a minister of the circumcision for the truth of God, to confirm the promises made unto the fathers:

A person who has been cleansed by the blood of Yeshua has the Torah written on his/her hearts and does it, not just in spirit but in literal manifested action. The redeemed have received the Holy Spirit. The early rain is symbolized by only part of the discipleship being present for the receiving of the Holy Spirit after Christ's resurrection. We await a latter rain where all are present and redemption has fully come. Notice the sign of the Son of Man in connection with the re–gathering and redemption of Israel and their companions in Diaspora.

Matthew 24: 29, Immediately after the tribulation of those days shall the sun be darkened, and the moon shall not give her light, and the stars shall fall from heaven, and the powers of the heavens shall be shaken: 30 And then shall appear the sign of the Son of man in heaven: and then shall all the tribes of the earth mourn, and they shall see the Son of man coming in the clouds of heaven with power and great glory. 31 And he shall send his angels with a great sound of a trumpet, <u>and they shall gather together his elect</u> from the four winds, from one end of heaven to the other.

GRAFTED INTO ISRAEL OR "INTO THE LORD"
Just as God uses the seed and fruit pattern of nature to describe His redemptive work in the earth, he also uses another natural pattern of horticulture for improving the fruit of a tree: Grafting.

Romans 11:24, For if thou wert cut out of the olive tree which is wild by nature, and wert grafted <u>contrary to nature</u> into a good olive tree: how much more shall these, which be the natural branches, be grafted into their own olive tree?

The redeemed are grafted or baptized into the image of Yeshua. This is symbolized by being grafted into the Tree of Life. The term modern science uses for a branch that is grafted into a tree is "Scion" (phonetically sounds similar to "Sion"). It is the same as becoming one flesh with Yeshua. His flesh, His branch, makes it possible for those of us in exile from God to be grafted back into the covenant with YHWH.

Grafting is a method of plant propagation widely used in horticulture, where the tissues of one plant are encouraged to fuse with those of another. It is most commonly used for the propagation of trees and shrubs grown commercially. (Wikipedia)

There are so many scriptures that point to the term "Sion" and "bringing back from captivity", "re–gathering of His people", "remembering His people", and "bearing fruit" that they cannot all be mentioned. Yeshua is our salvation. Yeshua is our Scion (Sion). We are grafted into Him (the Tree of life).

Zechariah 6: 12, And speak unto him, saying, Thus speaketh the Lord of hosts, saying, Behold the man whose name is The Branch; and he shall grow up out of his place, and he shall build the temple of the Lord: 13 Even he shall build the temple of the Lord; and he shall bear the glory, and shall sit and rule upon his throne; and he shall be a priest upon his throne: and the counsel of peace shall be between them both.

Just as the Messiah is depicted as "the branch", Yeshua explained how He was the vine into which believers were joined and maintained their lives (John 15:1-10).

In most cases, one plant is selected for its roots and this is called the stock or rootstock. The other plant is selected for its stems, leaves, flowers, or fruits and is called the scion or cion. [1] The scion contains the desired genes to be duplicated in future production by the stock/scion plant. (Wikipedia)

In grafting one tree is selected for its good traits or its roots and the other tree is selected for its other traits, like leaves or fruit. The scion contains the best genetics and the goal is to replicate its DNA in the characteristics of the other tree. Notice how the purpose of the scion is to replicate the "genes" or the seed that need to be passed on to the rest of the branches. This is exactly what the Messiah does for those needing salvation.

Isaiah 11: 1, And there shall come forth a rod out of the stem of Jesse, and a Branch shall grow out of his roots: 2 And the spirit of the Lord shall rest upon him, the spirit of wisdom and understanding, the spirit of counsel and might, the spirit of knowledge and of the fear of the Lord; ... 10 And in that day there shall be a root of Jesse, which shall stand for an ensign of the people; to it shall the Gentiles seek: and his rest shall be glorious. 11 And it shall come to pass in that day, that the Lord shall set his hand again the second time to recover the remnant of his people, which shall be left, from Assyria, and from Egypt, and from Pathros, and from Cush, and from Elam, and from Shinar, and from Hamath, and from the islands of the sea. 12 And he shall set up an ensign for the nations, and shall assemble the outcasts of Israel, and gather together the dispersed of Judah from the four corners of the earth. 13 The envy also of Ephraim shall depart, and the adversaries of Judah shall be cut off: Ephraim shall not envy Judah, and Judah shall not vex Ephraim.

This is the other "fold" that Yeshua was describing to His disciples.

John 10: 16, And other sheep I have, which are not of this fold: them also I must bring, and they shall hear my voice; and there shall be one fold, and one shepherd.

The fulfillment of the reunification of the Kingdom of God was the chief concern of Yeshua's disciples after His resurrection.

Acts 1: 6, When they therefore were come together, they asked of him, saying, Lord, wilt thou at this time restore again the kingdom to Israel? 7 And he said unto them, It is not for you to know the times or the seasons, which the Father hath put in his own power.

Yeshua's reply is that it will occur in its appropriate season and fractal and that right now we need to fulfill the fractal of the seed hidden in death, just like Israel wandering in the wilderness.

Luke 9:23, And he said to them all, If any man will come after me, let him deny himself, and take up his cross daily, and follow me.

This imagery of death of taking up your own cross is associated with not following your own will but doing the will of the Father and sowing the seed of the Kingdom of God (Matthew 13:19). The seed by nature is associated with burial and death...only to await manifested fruit in resurrection life. This pattern of seed and fruit is none other that death and resurrection.

1 Corinthians 3:7, So then neither is he that planteth any thing, neither he that watereth; but God that giveth the increase.

God keeps using the patterns and fractals of nature to show us what is going to occur in the end times and why it must be according to its "season". In the end–time we are no longer dealing with seeds, but with branches.

Ezekiel 37: 15, The word of the Lord came again unto me, saying, 16 Moreover, thou son of man, take thee one stick, and write upon it, For Judah, and for the children of Israel his companions: then take another stick, and write upon it, For Joseph, the stick of Ephraim and for all the house of Israel his companions: 17 And join them one to another into one stick; and they shall become one in thine hand. 18 And when the children of thy people shall speak unto thee, saying, Wilt thou not shew us what thou meanest by these? 19 Say unto them, Thus saith the Lord God; Behold, I will take the stick of Joseph, which is in the hand of Ephraim, and the tribes of Israel his fellows, and will put them with him, even with the stick of Judah, and make them one stick, and they shall be one in mine hand. 20 And the sticks whereon thou writest shall be in thine hand before their eyes. 21 And say unto them, Thus saith the Lord God; Behold, I will take the children of Israel from among the heathen, whither they be gone, and will gather them on every side, and bring them into their own land: 22 And I will make them one nation in the land upon the mountains of Israel; and one king shall be king to them all: and they shall be no more two nations, neither shall they be divided into two kingdoms any more at all. 23 Neither shall they defile themselves any more with their idols, nor with their detestable things, nor with any of their transgressions: but I will save them out of all their dwellingplaces, wherein they have sinned, and will cleanse them: so shall they be my people, and I will be their God. 24 And David my servant shall be king over them; and they all shall have one shepherd: they shall also walk in my judgments, and observe my statutes, and do them.

With great clarity the scriptures show the grafting of two branches together in the "Hand of the Lord", the Messiah. One branch (stick) is not grafted into the other, both are grafted into "mine hand" (also see Exodus 32:11, Deuteronomy 4:34, 5:15). This is an allusion to the Messiah. We see the restoration of Israel and the Jews when their blindness is healed and the two branches (Judah & Ephraim) are united in Yeshua's hand.

- Psalm 14: 5, There were they in great fear: for God is in the generation of the righteous. 6 Ye have shamed the counsel of the poor, because the Lord is his refuge. 7 Oh that the salvation of Israel were come out of Sion! when the Lord bringeth back the captivity of his people, Jacob shall rejoice, and Israel shall be glad.

- Psalm 9: 10, And they that know thy name will put their trust in thee: for thou, Lord, hast not forsaken them that seek thee. 11 Sing praises to the Lord, which dwelleth in Sion: declare among the people his doings. 12 When he maketh inquisition for blood, he remembereth them: he forgetteth not the cry of the humble. 13 Have mercy upon me, O Lord; consider my trouble which I suffer of them that hate me, thou that liftest me up from the gates of death:

Sion is repeatedly mentioned in connection with the redemption of all Israel and the return from Diaspora, which is a picture of resurrection and manifested fruit from a state of death and exile (seed). There are so many scriptures relating to Sion and redemption a topical study is recommended to cover them all.

Micah 4: 1, But in the last days it shall come to pass, that the mountain of the house of the Lord shall be established in the top of the mountains, and it shall be exalted above the hills; and people shall flow unto it. 2 And many nations shall come, and say, Come, and let us go up to the mountain of the Lord, and to the house of the God of Jacob; and he will teach us of his ways, and we will walk in his paths: for the law shall go forth of Sion, and the word of the Lord from Jerusalem.

God appeals to us, who dwell with the daughter of Babylon, to deliver ourselves. Many nations will be joined to God in that day and He will dwell in Sion.

> Zechariah 2: 6, Ho, ho, come forth, and flee from the land of the north, saith the Lord: for I have spread you abroad as the four winds of the heaven, saith the Lord. 7 <u>Deliver thyself, O Sion,</u> that dwellest with the daughter of Babylon. 8 For thus saith the Lord of hosts; After the glory hath he sent me unto the nations which spoiled you: for he that toucheth you toucheth the apple of his eye. 9 For, behold, I will shake mine hand upon them, and they shall be a spoil to their servants: and ye shall know that the Lord of hosts hath sent me. 10 Sing and rejoice, O daughter of Sion: for, lo, I come, and I will dwell in the midst of thee, saith the Lord. 11 And <u>many nations shall be joined to the Lord in that day,</u> and shall be my people: and I will dwell in the midst of thee, and thou shalt know that the Lord of hosts hath sent me unto thee. 12 And the Lord shall inherit Judah his portion in the holy land, and shall choose Jerusalem again. 13 Be silent, O all flesh, before the Lord: for he is raised up out of his holy habitation.

Over and over the scriptures are very specific that we are "joined to the Lord" and this is the salvific act. Not once do the scriptures say to be "joined or grafted into Israel". Israel is the consequential state, not the initiating act of salvation. To say we are "grafted into Israel" is unscriptural and the result of a lack of theological discipline. Zechariah is very clear that the goal is to "be joined to the Lord in the day".

This hearkens back to God being one with Yeshua, and us becoming one with Yeshua. We are all one, one tree producing good fruit. We again cannot escape God's future expectation that His Law, the one that He gave Moses, will "go forth from Sion" to "many nations" (Gentiles).

The end–times are always associated with God going out to gather His lost sheep and to restore the unity of the Kingdom of God. This is the very purpose of the Messiah.

> John 8: 14, Now Caiaphas was he, which gave counsel to the Jews, that it was expedient that one man should die for the people.

Yeshua fulfilled this very prophecy. Why? To unify two sheep folds into one.

> John 10: 16, And other sheep I have, which are not of this fold: them also I must bring, and they shall hear my voice; and there shall be one fold, and one shepherd.

The role of the Messiah is to unite the Kingdom of God in its due season.

> Ezekiel 34: 11, For thus saith the Lord GOD; Behold, <u>I, even I, will both search my sheep, and seek them out.</u> 12 As a shepherd seeketh out his flock in the day that he is among his sheep that are scattered; so will I seek out my sheep, <u>and will deliver them out of all places where they have been scattered</u>

<u>in the cloudy and dark day</u>. 13 And I will bring them out from the people, and gather them from the countries, and will bring them to their own land, and feed them upon the mountains of Israel by the rivers, and in all the inhabited places of the country.

The darkening of the sun is repeatedly used as a sign in connection with the re–gathering and resurrection of those to be re–attached to the Tree of Life. It was a sign to Israel when they were redeemed from Egypt, it was a sign of the coming of Yeshua when He died on the cross, and it is a sign for the final redemption of Israel and their companions from Babylon and the Diaspora (exile).

Zechariah 8: 22, Yea, many people and strong nations shall come to seek the Lord of hosts in Jerusalem, and to pray before the Lord. 23 Thus saith the Lord of hosts; In those days it shall come to pass, that ten men shall take hold out of all languages of the nations, even shall take hold of the skirt of him that is a Jew, saying, We will go with you: for we have heard that God is with you.

Notice there are still ten tribes in Diaspora and they are speaking all languages of the nations. We will grab hold of the Tallit (prayer shawl) and the fringes of his garment (Tzizit) of him that is a Jew declaring we have heard "God is with you". The Tzizit are a reminder to keep the Torah. Keep in mind Yeshua is Jewish, kept the Written Torah of Moses, kept the Feasts of the Lord, and wore a prayer shawl with Tzizit. So the believer is "grafted in to the Lord" as the Apostle Paul teaches.

Romans 11: 16, I For if the firstfruit be holy, the lump is also holy: and if the root be holy, so are the branches. 17 And if some of the branches be broken off, and thou, being a wild olive tree, wert grafted in among them, and with them partakest of the root and fatness of the olive tree;

Paul is clear that believers are grafted in "among the others" and our branches will bear the same fruit as the other branches, not a different fruit. Many incorrectly assume that means the believer is grafted into Israel. Paul confirms this is not the case as Judah/Israel's branches are broken off and need to be grafted back in just like the Gentiles through "faith" in the Messiah. He told the Gentiles in Rome that he wanted to "provoke to emulation them which are [his Jewish] flesh," that he "might save some of them., and that even though "some of the branches be broken off," and they, "being a wild olive tree, wert grafted in among them, and with them," God's desire was that "the full number of the Gentiles . . . come in" (Rom. 11:14, 17, 25).

Romans 11: 10, Let their eyes be darkened, that they may not see, and bow down their back alway. 11 I say then, Have they stumbled that they should fall? God forbid: but rather through their fall salvation is come unto the Gentiles, for to provoke them to jealousy. 12 Now if the fall of them be the riches of the world, and the diminishing of them the riches of the Gentiles; how much more their fulness? 13 For I speak to you Gentiles, inasmuch as I am the apostle of the Gentiles, I magnify mine office: 14 If by any means <u>I may provoke to emulation them which are my flesh, and might save some of them</u>. 15 For if the casting away of them be the reconciling of the world, what shall the receiving of them be, but life from the dead? For if the firstfruit be holy, the lump is also holy: and if the root be holy, so are the branches. 17 And <u>if some of the branches be broken off, and thou, being a wild olive tree, wert grafted in among them, and with them</u> partakest of the root and fatness of the olive tree; 18 Boast not against the branches. But if thou boast, thou bearest not the root, but the root thee. 19 Thou wilt say then, The branches were broken off, that I might be grafted in.

Notice it says grafted in "among them", it does not say "grafted into them". So if the olive tree is not Israel, what is the olive tree we are joined to? You cannot graft a wild branch into a branch that has been cut off from the tree. Paul has already clarified that the branch of Judah/Israel is cut off from the tree and he desires to "save some" of his brethren.

Isaiah 56: 3, Neither let the son of the stranger, that hath joined himself to the Lord, speak, saying, The Lord hath utterly separated me from his people: neither let the eunuch say, Behold, I am a dry tree.

The scriptures are clear that all branches are grafted and joined "to the Lord", the Messiah Yeshua. Former branches that are cut off from the covenant with the Messiah can be grafted back into Him once they express faith in His name.
- Zechariah 2: 11, And many nations shall be joined to the Lord in that day, and shall be my people: and I will dwell in the midst of thee, and thou shalt know that the Lord of hosts hath sent me unto thee.
- Matthew 23: 39, For I say unto you, Ye shall not see me henceforth, till ye shall say, Blessed is he that cometh in the Name of the Lord.

The imagery is plain, we are the branches and we are grafted into the Messiah.

1 Corinthians 8: 6, But to us there is but one God, the Father, of whom are all things, and we in him; and one Lord Jesus Christ, by whom are all things, and we by him.

Paul clarifies that this "fullness" we have been talking about happens in Christ.

Ephesians 1: 10, That in the dispensation of the fulness of times he might gather together in one all things in Christ, both which are in heaven, and which are on earth; even in him:

He leaves absolutely no ambiguity.

Ephesians 2: 15, Having abolished in his flesh the enmity, even the law of commandments contained in ordinances; for to make <u>in himself</u> of twain one new man, so making peace;

We will go into a very deep review of Ephesians 2:15 proving the reality that this one new man is Yeshua and not Israel. This does not deny the future reality of the reunification of the 12 tribes of Israel, which will happen "in the Lord".

We have already established that the Lord, the Messiah Yeshua, is our spirit (male), and we are His body (female). You would not join one female to another female to create a unified and ascended completed male. The completed male can only present himself when he is unified in the marriage chamber with his female. So you would never join a female (branches) to another female (Israel). You would join a female (branches) to her male husband (the root) the Messiah Yeshua. It is thereby that the redeemed gain the name of Israel as they are in covenant with the Holy One of Israel.

> Isaiah 11: 1, And there shall come forth a rod out of the stem of Jesse, and a <u>Branch shall grow out of his roots</u>: 2 And the spirit of the Lord shall rest upon him, the spirit of wisdom and understanding, the spirit of counsel and might, the spirit of knowledge and of the fear of the Lord; 3 And shall make him of quick understanding in the fear of the Lord: and he shall not judge after the sight of his eyes, neither reprove after the hearing of his ears:

It is only when the unity between the Messiah and Israel occurs that her femaleness turns into an ascended male because the female takes on the identity of her husband as His name is placed upon her. This is why you see the redeemed as "sons of God" and not daughters.

> Numbers 6: 26, The Lord lift up his countenance upon thee, and give thee peace. 27 And they shall put my name upon the children of Israel, and I will bless them.

Those who were in covenant with the Messiah via faith in His name, forsook the covenant and had their branches cut off. Their branches can be grafted back "into the Lord" by faith in His name just as ours are grafted "into the Lord". The Messiah is the manifest Name of the Lord.

> Jeremiah 11: 15, What hath my beloved to do in mine house, seeing she hath wrought lewdness with many, and the holy flesh is passed from thee? when thou doest evil, then thou rejoicest. 16 The Lord called thy name, A green olive tree, fair, and of goodly fruit: with the noise of a great tumult he hath kindled fire upon it, and the branches of it are broken. 17 For the Lord of hosts, that planted thee, hath pronounced evil against thee, for the evil of the house of Israel and of the house of Judah, which they have done against themselves to provoke me to anger in offering incense unto Baal.

The grafting process is clear and simple and happens through the Lord. The covenant is with the Lord and we receive our identity as Israel from being grafted into the Name of the Lord. The Messiah is the manifest Name of YHWH (Exodus

34: 5–8).

  • Exodus 23: 21, Beware of him, and obey his voice, provoke him not; for he will not pardon your transgressions: for my name is in him.

  • Acts 3: 12, And when Peter saw it, he answered unto the people, Ye men of Israel, why marvel ye at this? or why look ye so earnestly on us, as though by our own power or holiness we had made this man to walk? 13 The God of Abraham, and of Isaac, and of Jacob, the God of our fathers, hath glorified his Son Jesus; whom ye delivered up, and denied him in the presence of Pilate, when he was determined to let him go. 14 <u>But ye denied the Holy One</u> and the Just, and desired a murderer to be granted unto you; 15 And killed the Prince of life, whom God hath raised from the dead; <u>whereof we are witnesses. 16 And his name through faith in his name hath made this man strong</u>, whom ye see and know: yea, the faith which is by him hath given him this perfect soundness in the presence of you all.

We will examine further the nature of the Messiah as the manifest Name of YHWH and how the fractal of male and female is a divine presentation of the restoration of Israel, mankind, the world, and the universe to God.

  Isaiah 61: 10, I will greatly rejoice in the Lord, my soul shall be joyful in my God; for he hath clothed me with the garments of salvation, he hath covered me with the robe of righteousness, as a bridegroom decketh himself with ornaments, and as a bride adorneth herself with her jewels.

Notice how the salvific act is associated with a "covering" provided by God to the redeemed and is pictured by the union of male and female in marriage.

  Isaiah 62: 5, For as a young man marrieth a virgin, so shall thy sons marry thee: and as the bridegroom rejoiceth over the bride, so shall thy God rejoice over thee.

Yeshua confirms this pattern.

  Matthew 9: 15, And Jesus said unto them, Can the children of the bridechamber mourn, as long as the bridegroom is with them? but the days will come, when the bridegroom shall be taken from them, and then shall they fast.

He identifies Himself as the (male) bridegroom and those that He is with (Israel/Judah) as the (female) bride's chamber. The second coming of the Messiah is again typified by the sexual union in marriage of male and female.

  Matthew 25: 1, Then shall the kingdom of heaven be likened unto ten virgins, which took their lamps, and went forth to meet the bridegroom… 10 And while they went to buy, the bridegroom came; and they that were ready went in with him to the marriage: and the door was shut.

The divine male (the Messiah) is waiting for the preparation of the bride (female).

> Revelation 21: 9, And there came unto me one of the seven angels which had the seven vials full of the seven last plagues, and talked with me, saying, Come hither, I will shew thee the bride, the Lamb's wife.

As Israel is sanctified by the Name of the Lord, the Messiah, so also is the bride by her husband. This sanctification is associated with blind eyes being opened and occurring "in" the Messiah Yeshua.

> Acts 26: 18, To open their eyes, and to turn them from darkness to light, and from the power of Satan unto God, that they may receive forgiveness of sins, and inheritance among them which are <u>sanctified by faith that is in me</u>.

God tells us very clearly what He is expecting from His bride.

> Jeremiah 31: 31, Behold, the days come, saith the Lord, that I will make a new covenant with the house of Israel, and with the house of Judah: 32 Not according to the covenant that I made with their fathers in the day that I took them by the hand to bring them out of the land of Egypt; which my covenant they brake, <u>although I was an husband unto them</u>, saith the Lord: 33 But <u>this shall be the covenant that I will make with the house of Israel</u>; After those days, saith the Lord, <u>I will put my law in their inward parts, and write it in their hearts</u>; and will be their God, and they shall be my people.

He is expecting His bride to have His Law, the same Law of Moses (with the new administration of Yeshua in grace and abundant mercy) written on her inward parts and in her heart. This is how we are made clean by our husband, the Messiah Yeshua.

> 1 Corinthians 7: 14, For the unbelieving husband is sanctified by the wife, and the unbelieving wife is sanctified by the husband: else were your children unclean; but now are they holy.

We are sanctified by faith in His name, being joined to our husband, the Messiah Yeshua, the manifest Name of the Lord (YHWH). This is why we are not baptized or grafted into Israel. Those who are "joined to the Lord" or "grafted into the Lord" (the Messiah) receive His name and manifest themselves as Israel. The Messiah is the seed of the Kingdom of God and Israel is the manifestation of that seed.

> Galatians 3: 27, For as many of you as have been baptized into Christ have put on Christ.

This is the only name and image that can save. We are not baptized into Israel, those who are baptized into Christ are Israel and manifest the seed of the Messiah and bring forth great fruit.

1 Corinthians 1: 12, Now this I say, that every one of you saith, I am of Paul; and I of Apollos; and I of Cephas; and I of Christ. 13 <u>Is Christ divided?</u> was Paul crucified for you? or were ye baptized in the name of Paul? 14 I thank God that I baptized none of you, but Crispus and Gaius; 15 Lest any should say that I had baptized in mine own name.

Those who have "put on Christ" and are "baptized into Christ" received His name. This is why there is only one name under heaven whereby we must be saved.

- Philippians 2: 8, And being found in fashion as a man, he humbled himself, and became obedient unto death, even the death of the cross. 9 Wherefore God also hath highly exalted him, and given him a name which is above every name: 10 That at the name of Jesus every knee should bow, of things in heaven, and things in earth, and things under the earth;
- Romans 10: 13, For whosoever shall call upon the Name of the Lord shall be saved.

This is the name that provides our cleansing.

1 Corinthians 6: 11, And such were some of you: but ye are washed, but ye are sanctified, but ye are justified in the Name of the Lord Jesus, and by the Spirit of our God.

How does this cleansing occur? Remember Adam and Eve were originally created in the image of God, and through sin that image was broken. That image needs to be restored and that is the work of the promised seed, the Messiah (Genesis 3: 15).

Hebrews 1: 3, Who being the brightness of his glory, and <u>the express image of his person,</u> and upholding all things by the word of his power, when he had by himself purged our sins, sat down on the right hand of the Majesty on high: 4 Being made so much better than the angels, as he hath by inheritance <u>obtained a more excellent name</u> than they. 5 For unto which of the angels said he at any time, Thou art my Son, this day have I begotten thee?

It is through the essential nature of the Messiah being the image of God and our literal joining with Him that provides our cleansing, our name, and our covering. The Messiah Yeshua gives His image to us.

Romans 8: 29, For whom he did foreknow, he also did predestinate to be conformed to the image of his Son, that he might be the firstborn among many brethren.

4 THE IMAGE OF GOD

Genesis 1: 26, And God said, Let us make man in our image, after our likeness: and let them have dominion over the fish of the sea, and over the fowl of the air, and over the cattle, and over all the earth, and over every creeping thing that creepeth upon the earth. 27 So God created man in his own image, in the image of God created he him; male and female created he them. 28 And God blessed them, and God said unto them, Be fruitful, and multiply, and replenish the earth, and subdue it: and have dominion over the fish of the sea, and over the fowl of the air, and over every living thing that moveth upon the earth.

How important is it to God that we be in His image? It means everything. Without it there is no relationship. The Torah and the New Testament start and end with the importance of the image of God in man. The end–time battle centers on the image God and the image of the Beast, the Mark of God and the Mark of the Beast.

Revelation 14: 11, And the smoke of their torment ascendeth up for ever and ever: and they have no rest day nor night, who worship the beast and his image, and whosoever receiveth the mark of his name.

Those who worship God receive His mark.

Ezekiel 9: 4, And the Lord said unto him, Go through the midst of the city, through the midst of Jerusalem, and set a mark upon the foreheads of the men that sigh and that cry for all the abominations that be done in the midst thereof.

A critical issue before the return of the Messiah will be which image we conform to, His or that of the Beast. Paul talks about the importance of what image we conform to and the necessity of not changing the glory of the incorruptible God into an image made like fallen man and beasts.

Romans 1: 22, Professing themselves to be wise, they became fools, 23 And changed the glory of the uncorruptible God into an image made like to corruptible man, and to birds, and fourfooted beasts, and creeping things. 24 Wherefore God also gave them up to uncleanness through the lusts of their own hearts, to dishonour their own bodies between themselves:

Eve took of the fruit of the Tree of the Knowledge of Good and Evil in the pursuit of wisdom and knowledge, for the purpose of opening of the eyes to see, and to become as a god. But little did Eve know what the serpent was really tempting her with. Notice God's warning not to eat of this tree.

Genesis 2: 17, But of the Tree of the Knowledge of Good and Evil, thou shalt not eat of it: for in the day that thou eatest thereof thou shalt surely die.

The serpent offers a lie to entice Eve to eat in spite of God's warning.

Genesis 3: 5, For God doth know that in the day ye eat thereof, then your eyes shall be opened, and ye shall be as gods, knowing good and evil. 6 And when the woman saw that the tree was good for food, and that it was pleasant to the eyes, and a tree to be desired to make one wise, she took of the fruit thereof, and did eat, and gave also unto her husband with her; and he did eat.

God was clear in His instruction to Adam and Eve that in the day that they eat thereof, they would die. Why would they die and need to be separated from the source of life? What kind of God would curse man in this way? Or was it something else? God knew the terrible fate that awaited man now that his flesh had fallen. If Adam and Eve took of the Fruit of the Tree of Life, they would forever be an enslaved man in this corrupted fallen flesh.

Genesis 3: 22, And the Lord God said, Behold, the man is become as one of us, to know good and evil: and now, lest he put forth his hand, and take also of the Tree of Life, and eat, and live for ever: 23 Therefore the Lord God sent him forth from the garden of Eden, to till the ground from whence he was taken.

God needed to provide a way for fallen man to get back to the Tree of Life, but without a broken image and a fallen flesh. What flesh could do it? Surely not animal flesh.

Hebrews 10: 3, But in those sacrifices there is a remembrance again made of sins every year. 4 For it is not possible that the blood of bulls and of goats should take away sins. 5 Wherefore when he cometh into the world, he saith, Sacrifice and offering thou wouldest not, but a body hast thou prepared me:

Clearly the book of Hebrews is showing us that animal flesh cannot redeem us.

It can point us to the true redeemer, Yeshua, but by itself cannot provide the needed value for the redemptive equation. Verse 4 clearly explains what flesh could provide the value for the redemptive equation, Yeshua's body and flesh as the image of God.

Hebrews 10: 10, By the which will we are sanctified through the offering of the body of Jesus Christ once for all. 11 And every priest standeth daily ministering and offering oftentimes the same sacrifices, which can never take away sins: 12 But this man, after he had offered one sacrifice for sins for ever, sat down on the right hand of God;

We are sanctified though Yeshua's body. God is being so detailed and specific, but we have glossed over the clarity of the truth for 2,000 years. Bulls and goats cannot cover our sin. The sin is in our flesh, it is corrupted and subject to death. Only Yeshua's body can cover our sins. He has provided the way back into the Holy of Holies and fellowship with God. Why is it so important that our sins be "covered"? Adam and Eve were covered with flesh after they sinned. The marks of sin and its penalties were born in their flesh and their seed. They needed a way back to an incorruptible image of God.

Hebrews 10: 20, By a new and living way, which he hath consecrated for us, through the veil, that is to say, his flesh; 21 And having an high priest over the house of God; 22 Let us draw near with a true heart in full assurance of faith, having our hearts sprinkled from an evil conscience, and our bodies washed with pure water.

He is the way, the truth, and the life. There is no other way back to God. Why? We must have His image, His flesh, His body, His blood. The veil that was His flesh was rent and torn so that we may enter.

Luke 23: 44, And it was about the sixth hour, and there was a darkness over all the earth until the ninth hour. 45 And the sun was darkened, and the veil of the temple was rent in the midst. 46 And when Yeshua had cried with a loud voice, he said, Father, into thy hands I commend my spirit: and having said thus, he gave up the ghost.

We see the clear connection of the veil of the temple to the flesh of the Messiah and how it provides entry into the Holy of Holies. Paul clarifies how this relates to the reading of the Law of Moses and the inability to understand because of the "vail" that covers our hearts. What is the remedy? The Messiah (the seed) begins His work in the heart.

II Corinthians 3: 12, Seeing then that we have such hope, we use great plainness of speech: 13 And not as Moses, which put a veil over his face, that the children of Israel could not stedfastly look to the end of that which is abolished: 14 But their minds were blinded: for until this day remaineth the same vail untaken away in the reading of the Old Testament; which vail is done away in Christ. 15 But even unto this day, when Moses is read, the vail is upon their heart. 16 Nevertheless when it shall turn to the Lord, the vail shall be taken away. 17 Now the Lord is that Spirit: and where the Spirit of the Lord is, there is liberty. 18 But we all, with open face beholding as in a glass the glory of the Lord, are changed into the same image from glory to glory, even as by the Spirit of the Lord.

Moses needs to cover the glory he receives from being in the presence of God with a veil so that others may look upon Him. This is a sampling of what an uncorrupted body would be like, full of glory and powerful. Verse 16 is plainly saying that when it comes to Yeshua, the vail will be taken away and we can openly view the glory of God. Corrupted flesh is replaced with incorruptible, earthy with heavenly, death with life. The veil of the heart is circumcised, along with the veil of the mind, which results in our being able to see and discern spiritual things. This new and living way is through Yeshua's uncorrupted flesh.

Hebrews 10: 19, Having therefore, brethren, boldness to enter into the holiest by the blood of Jesus, 20 By a new and living way, which he hath consecrated for us, through the veil, that is to say, his flesh; 21 And having an high priest over the house of God;

There is no way we can approach God without Yeshua's flesh and body.

John 14: 5, Thomas saith unto him, Lord, we know not whither thou goest; and how can we know the way? 6 Jesus saith unto him, I am the way, the truth, and the life: no man cometh unto the Father, but by me. 7 If ye had known me, ye should have known my Father also: and from henceforth ye know him, and have seen him.

What is this image that is being restored through Yeshua's flesh? We cannot approach without His image, without His body, and without His blood. II Corinthians 3 talked about the need to have this veil of the heart and mind circumcised.

Deuteronomy 30: 5, He will bring you to the land that belonged to your fathers, and you will take possession of it. He will make you more prosperous and numerous than your fathers. 6 The Lord your God will circumcise your hearts and the hearts of your descendants, so that you may love him with all your heart and with all your soul, and live. 7 The Lord your God will put all these curses on your enemies who hate and persecute you.

After Israel's sin of worshiping an image of a beast, a graven image (the golden calf, Exodus 32:4,10), God talks about destroying Israel and starting anew with Moses. After Moses' intercession, God writes His covenant again and promises to place it in their hearts.

Deuteronomy 30: 10, If thou shalt hearken unto the voice of the Lord thy

God, to keep his commandments and his statutes which are written in this book of the law, and if thou turn unto the Lord thy God with all thine heart, and with all thy soul.

This required the circumcision of the heart for the accomplishment of this promise. His Torah would be placed in our hearts.

Hebrews 8: 7, For if that first covenant had been faultless, then should no place have been sought for the second. 8 For finding fault with them, he saith, Behold, the days come, saith the Lord, when I will make a new covenant with the house of Israel and with the house of Judah: 9 Not according to the covenant that I made with their fathers in the day when I took them by the hand to lead them out of the land of Egypt; because they continued not in my covenant, and I regarded them not, saith the Lord. 10 For this is the covenant that I will make with the house of Israel after those days, saith the Lord; I will put my laws into their mind, and write them in their hearts: and I will be to them a God, and they shall be to me a people:

The problem was not with the Torah or the covenant, the problem was with our hearts. So let's flash back to the giving of the ten commandments. As Moses is receiving personal instruction on behalf of the people of Israel, the people at the foot of the mountain begin to worship a graven or false image. Is this coincidence? What is the significance of man worshiping a false or graven image?

Joel 2: 12, Therefore also now, saith the Lord, turn ye even to me with all your heart, and with fasting, and with weeping, and with mourning: 13 And rend your heart, and not your garments, and turn unto the Lord your God: for he is gracious and merciful, slow to anger, and of great kindness, and repenteth him of the evil. 14 Who knoweth if he will return and repent, and leave a blessing behind him; even a meat offering and a drink offering unto the Lord your God?

Just as our hearts should be circumcised, the Temple veil was rent, as was Yeshua's flesh. Our hearts need to return to the covenant and to the Law of Moses. By doing this we can regain God's image in our lives. Let's look at the ten commandments. The full chapter is included as we need to see the context of what God is communicating to Israel. Are these only commandments or something more? These are expressions of the image of God.

He is working to restore His image in man. When man was in the Garden of Eden before he fell, Adam and Eve could hear the voice of God and communicate with Him. By the time of the Exodus man's flesh had fallen so far that He could no longer bear to hear the voice of God (Exodus 20:19).

God's purpose to redeem Israel out of Egypt was to reveal Himself to these people and restore His image to them so that He could dwell with them. So these are not commands we fulfill without thought, these are expressions of who God is and how we need to be like Him so that we may come into fellowship with Him. This makes it possible for God to dwell with us. The whole chapter is dealing with

God's image throwing down false images and the fruit of false images.

Exodus 20: 1, And God spake all these words, saying, 2 I am the Lord thy God, which have brought thee out of the land of Egypt, out of the house of bondage. 3 <u>Thou shalt have no other gods before me.</u> <u>4 Thou shalt not make unto thee any graven image, or any likeness of any thing that is in heaven above, or that is in the earth beneath, or that is in the water under the earth.</u> 5 Thou shalt not bow down thyself to them, nor serve them: for I the Lord thy God am a jealous God, visiting the iniquity of the fathers upon the children unto the third and fourth generation of them that hate me; 6 And shewing mercy unto thousands of them that love me, and keep my commandments. 7 Thou shalt not take the Name of the Lord thy God in vain; for the Lord will not hold him guiltless that taketh his name in vain. 8 Remember the Sabbath day, to keep it holy. 9 Six days shalt thou labour, and do all thy work: 10 But the seventh day is the Sabbath of the Lord thy God: in it thou shalt not do any work, thou, nor thy son, nor thy daughter, thy manservant, nor thy maidservant, nor thy cattle, nor thy stranger that is within thy gates: 11 For in six days the Lord made heaven and earth, the sea, and all that in them is, and rested the seventh day: wherefore the Lord blessed the Sabbath day, and hallowed it. 12 Honour thy father and thy mother: that thy days may be long upon the land which the Lord thy God giveth thee. 13 Thou shalt not kill. 14 Thou shalt not commit adultery. 15 Thou shalt not steal. 16 Thou shalt not bear false witness against thy neighbour. 17 Thou shalt not covet thy neighbour's house, thou shalt not covet thy neighbour's wife, nor his manservant, nor his maidservant, nor his ox, nor his ass, nor any thing that is thy neighbour's. 18 And all the people saw the thunderings, and the lightnings, and the noise of the trumpet, and the mountain smoking: and when the people saw it, they removed, and stood afar off. 19 And they said unto Moses, <u>Speak thou with us, and we will hear: but let not God speak with us, lest we die</u>. 20 And Moses said unto the people, Fear not: for God is come to prove you, and that his fear may be before your faces, that ye sin not. 21 And the people stood afar off, and Moses drew near unto the thick darkness where God was. 22 And the Lord said unto Moses, Thus thou shalt say unto the children of Israel, Ye have seen that I have talked with you from heaven. 23 <u>Ye shall not make with me gods of silver, neither shall ye make unto you gods of gold</u>. 24 An altar of earth thou shalt make unto me, and shalt sacrifice thereon thy burnt offerings, and thy peace offerings, thy sheep, and thine oxen: in all places where I record my name I will come unto thee, and I will bless thee. 25 And if thou wilt make me an altar of stone, thou shalt not build it of hewn stone: for if thou lift up thy tool upon it, thou hast polluted it. 26 Neither shalt thou go up by steps unto mine altar, <u>that thy nakedness be not discovered thereon.</u>

Exodus 20 is the restoration of the image of God in fallen man. When Adam and Eve broke covenant with God and made covenant with the Serpent in the Garden, they broke the image of God. They realized they were naked and needed to be covered. It is not happenstance that the ten Utterances begin with the holiness of God and not taking any false image. This is why the Apostle Paul states that "death reigned from Adam to Moses" and that Adam was "the figure (image) of him that was to come" (Romans 5:14). Why had death reigned only until Moses? It is because he was pre-figuring the coming of the Image of God, the Messiah as the manifest Name of YHWH (Deuteronomy 18:15, 18-19, Exodus 23:21) the one who would restore our broken images back to being conformed to the Image of God (Romans 8:29).

Romans 1: 22, Professing themselves to be wise, they became fools, 23 And changed the glory of the uncorruptible God into an image made like to corruptible man, and to birds, and fourfooted beasts, and creeping things. 24 Wherefore God also gave them up to uncleanness through the lusts of their own hearts, to dishonour their own bodies between themselves:

Because they broke the image of God in their flesh, it became corrupted, fallen, sinful, and subject to death. No longer could they bear fruit in God's image or His seed.

Genesis 5: 1, This is the book of the generations of Adam. In the day that God created man, in the likeness of God made he him; 2 Male and female created he them; and blessed them, and called their name Adam, in the day when they were created. 3 And Adam lived an hundred and thirty years, and begat a son in his own likeness, and after his image; and called his name Seth:

Adam and Eve now bore children in their own fallen image and likeness, no longer able to bear the seed of God. A great gulf now separated man from His maker. How could it be repaired? Man needed to be born again with incorruptible flesh with the image of God restored.

God needed to come in uncorrupted flesh and be glorified before all the people to provide a way for us to be made clean. He became our baptism (mikvah) into His body and incorruptible flesh. It is the way to restoration, the way to redemption, the way of life, the way back to the garden and fellowship with God.

The two Trees presented to Adam and Eve are two seeds that, when consumed, combine with our flesh. To take of the Tree of Life is to be in covenant with God and taking on His flesh, His seed, and His life. To take of the Tree of Knowledge of Good and Evil is to covenant with Satan, to take on corrupted flesh, his seed, and his death. Notice that it was not only the nature of our flesh that was changed and cursed, but also the serpent's nature.

This theme of two seeds continues down to Cain and Abel and the two types of sacrifices that they made, Abel made a sacrifice that was acceptable to God and Cain made a sacrifice that was not acceptable to God. Abel's sacrifice was of clean animal flesh and it was found acceptable to God. Cain's offering was of the fruit of the field and it was not acceptable to God. Why? God is not careless in His judgments. It is because of what the sacrifice pictures and the restoration that has to be done to our flesh. Any imitation is just that, an imitation that will not fix the problem of the curse of our flesh.

Genesis 4: 3, And in process of time it came to pass, that Cain brought of the fruit of the ground an offering unto the Lord. 4 And Abel, he also brought of the firstlings of his flock and of the fat thereof. And the Lord had respect unto Abel and to his offering: 5 But unto Cain and to his offering he had not respect. And Cain was very wroth, and his countenance fell. 6 And the Lord said unto Cain, Why art thou wroth? and why is thy countenance fallen? 7 If thou doest well, shalt thou not be accepted? and if thou doest not well, sin lieth at the door. And unto thee shall be his desire, and thou shalt rule over him.

We cannot randomly select how we will be redeemed and restored to our original state, our original flesh (image), and our original relationship with God. We must explicitly follow the instruction of God or our end will be the same as Aaron's sons when we approach the throne of God.

Leviticus 10: 1, And Nadab and Abihu, the sons of Aaron, took either of them his censer, and put fire therein, and put incense thereon, and offered strange fire before the Lord, which he commanded them not. 2 And there went out fire from the Lord, and devoured them, and they died before the Lord. 3 Then Moses said unto Aaron, This is it that the Lord spake, saying, I will be sanctified in them that come nigh me, and before all the people I will be glorified. And Aaron held his peace.

God is explicitly clear that Nadab and Abihu did something that He did not command them, and this resulted in the rejection of their presence in the Holy of Holies. In all of the other instruction, the scripture repeatedly says that the lesson for us is clear, we cannot make up our way to return to God. We must do as He has instructed. Nor can we mix part of what God instructs with things we would like to do. A clear example of this is when Moses went to the mountain to receive the instruction of God, and the people chose to worship an image in a way that is not in obedience to what God instructs.

Exodus 32: 30, And it came to pass on the morrow, that Moses said unto the people, Ye have sinned a great sin: and now I will go up unto the Lord; peradventure I shall make an atonement for your sin. 31 And Moses returned unto the Lord, and said, Oh, this people have sinned a great sin, and have made them Gods of gold. 32 Yet now, if thou wilt forgive their sin—; and if not, blot me, I pray thee, out of thy book which thou hast written. 33 And the Lord said unto Moses, Whosoever hath sinned against me, him will I blot out of my book. 34 Therefore now go, lead the people unto the place of which I have spoken unto thee: behold, mine Angel shall go before thee: nevertheless in the day when I visit I will visit their sin upon them. 35 And the Lord plagued the people, because they made the calf, which Aaron made.

In contrast, when Israel follows God's instructions exactly in all the work of preparation for correct worship, they are blessed.

Exodus 39: 42, According to all that the Lord commanded Moses, so the children of Israel made all the work. 43 And Moses did look upon all the work, and, behold, <u>they had done it as the Lord had commanded</u>, even so had they done it: and Moses blessed them.

Christianity has randomly syncretized with pagan religions, adhering somewhat to the Written Law of Moses and somewhat to pagan practices. We must come out of those half–truths into the full light of God's revealed word, the Torah. Clinging to half–truths has kept us from realizing the reality of our circumstance and our need for redemption. Paul understood our situation, as he pleaded to be released from "this body of death". Paul exhorts us to remember that the purpose of the redemption of our bodies is to restore our relationship to God. All the preparations of the people, the priests, the tabernacle, the baptism (mikvah), and the sacrifices were so that God could dwell with His people.

Romans 12: 1, I beseech you therefore, brethren, by the mercies of God, that ye <u>present your bodies a living sacrifice, holy, acceptable unto God</u>, which is your reasonable service. 2 And be not conformed to this world: but <u>be ye transformed by the renewing of your mind</u>, that ye may prove what is that good, and acceptable, and perfect, will of God. 3 For I say, through the grace given unto me, to every man that is among you, not to think of himself more highly than he ought to think; but to think soberly, according as God hath dealt to every man the measure of faith.

Redemption lies in being conformed to the image of God while our fall continues by being "conformed to this world" in our corrupt flesh.

I Corinthians 6: 14, And God hath both raised up the Lord, and will also raise up us by his own power. 15 Know ye not that your bodies are the members of Christ? shall I then take the members of Christ, and make them the members of an harlot? God forbid. 16 What? know ye not that he which is joined to an harlot is one body? for two, saith he, shall be one flesh.

Our bodies are to become members of Yeshua the Messiah. If our flesh becomes a member of Yeshua's flesh via the baptism (mikvah) and partaking of His Heavenly sacrifice, His body and flesh, we cannot turn around and desecrate this tabernacle by joining His flesh, our redeemed flesh, in fornication with a harlot. This is absolutely forbidden by God. We cannot mix truth with lies or God's truth with pagan beliefs and conduct. We as the redeemed female must remain one flesh with our ascended male, Yeshua.

I Corinthians 6: 18, Flee fornication. Every sin that a man doeth is without the body; but he that committeth fornication sinneth against his own body. 19 What? know ye not that <u>your body is the temple of the Holy Ghost which is in you</u>, which ye have of God, and ye are not your own? 20 For ye are bought with a price: therefore glorify God in your body, and in your spirit, which are God's.

We are no longer our own, we are our husband's, Yeshua, the last Adam. The Bride of Yeshua is the last Eve. We cannot adulterate our flesh or His by joining it with another in forbidden sexual relations. The temple of God must remain clean and uncorrupted.

I Corinthians 15: 44, It is sown a natural body; it is raised a spiritual body. There is a natural body, and there is a spiritual body. 45 And so it is written, The first man Adam was made a living soul; the last Adam was made a quickening spirit. 46 Howbeit that was not first which is spiritual, but that which is natural; and afterward that which is spiritual.

That is why the sin of Balaam (improper sexual relations) is forbidden to Israel. It causes our downfall. It brings about the joining of our flesh with foreign gods and idols instead of the rectification of our fallen state.

Revelations 2: 14, But I have a few things against thee, because thou hast there them that hold the doctrine of Balaam, who taught Balac to cast a stumblingblock before the children of Israel, to eat things sacrificed unto idols, and to commit fornication.

The stumbling block of eating flesh sacrificed to idols (graven images) and committing fornication as a part of worship are all tied to the religious practice of becoming one flesh, through eating or sexual activity, with the divine. God clearly shows us how our flesh is to be redeemed. If we attempt to redeem our fallen flesh through our own ideas or practices, the result is death.

Hebrews 1: 2, Hath in these last days <u>spoken unto us by his Son</u>, whom he hath appointed heir of all things, by whom also he made the worlds; 3 Who being the brightness of his glory, <u>and the express image of his person</u>, and upholding all things by the word of his power, when he had by himself purged our sins, sat down on the right hand of the Majesty on high: 4 Being made so much better than the angels, as he hath by inheritance obtained a more excellent name than they.

We need to be one flesh with the Messiah, having our image conformed to His image, and being "one flesh" with Him.

Colossians 2:8, Beware lest any man spoil you through philosophy and vain deceit, after the tradition of men, after the rudiments of the world, and not after Christ. 9 For in him dwelleth all the fulness of the Godhead bodily. 10 And <u>ye are complete in him</u>, which is the head of all principality and power:

We are to be conformed to the image of God's son. By doing this we have life because we share in His flesh, His life, and are justified and glorified by Him. We must be one with Him as He is one with the Father.

Romans 8: 28, And we know that all things work together for good to them that love God, to them who are the called according to his purpose. 29 For whom he did foreknow, <u>he also did predestinate to be conformed to the image of his Son</u>, that he might be the firstborn among many brethren. 30 Moreover whom he did predestinate, them he also called: and whom he called, them he also justified: and whom he justified, them he also glorified.

God was glorified before all the people in Yeshua and through our becoming one with Him. We ought to act according to our calling. What does it mean to pray in Yeshua's name? Israel did not pray in the name of Aaron, the High Priest who enters the Holy of Holies. The patriarchs repeatedly called on the Name of the Lord, the one sitting on the mercy seat. This should tell us something.

John 16: 25, These things have I spoken unto you in proverbs: but the time cometh, when I shall no more speak unto you in proverbs, but I shall shew you plainly of the Father. 26 At that day ye shall ask in my name: and I say not unto you, that I will pray the Father for you: 27 For the Father himself loveth you, because ye have loved me, and have believed that I came out from God.

This is why there is only way to salvation. This is why we cannot syncretize beliefs between Torah and other religions. This is why we cannot accept any other savior.

Acts 4: 11, This is the stone which was set at nought of you builders, which is become the head of the corner. 12 <u>Neither is there salvation in any other: for there is none other name under heaven given among men, whereby we must be saved</u>. 13 Now when they saw the boldness of Peter and John, and perceived that they were unlearned and ignorant men, they marvelled; and they took knowledge of them, that they had been with Jesus.

That is why we cannot proclaim brotherhood with any other faith. There is no other name under heaven whereby men can be saved because no one else has incorruptible flesh and blood...the perfect Image of God. To reject that name is to reject the very means of redemption. Christians have taken the redemptive work of Yeshua too figuratively and have failed to accept Yeshua's very own testimony that He is the only way to have our flesh redeemed so that we might take part of the Tree of Life and live forever. Those who claim to be Christian yet say that all religions are valid and that there are many paths to God are in reality stating an idea that is not scripturally founded and blatantly contradicts Yeshua's own statements that He is the "way the truth and the life" and that "no man cometh unto the Father, but by me" (John 14:6).

Paul reiterates that the pattern of male and female unity in marriage is the pattern of the redeemed and the redeemer. The female needs the covering of the male.

1 Corinthians 11: 3, But I would have you know, <u>that the head of every man is Christ; and the head of the woman is the man; and the head of Christ is God</u>. Every man praying or prophesying, having his head covered, dishonoureth his

head. 5 But every woman that prayeth or prophesieth with her head uncovered dishonoureth her head: for that is even all one as if she were shaven. 6 For if the woman be not covered, let her also be shorn: but if it be a shame for a woman to be shorn or shaven, let her be covered. 7 For a man indeed ought not to cover his head, forasmuch as he is the image and glory of God: but the woman is the glory of the man. 8 For the man is not of the woman: but the woman of the man. 9 Neither was the man created for the woman; but the woman for the man. 10 For this cause ought the woman to have power on her head because of the angels. 11 Nevertheless <u>neither is the man without the woman, neither the woman without the man, in the Lord</u>.

Notice how the female joining with the male in marriage is a pattern of the Messiah and the church. The church is the redeemed and needs a covering and a head, which is her male, the Messiah Yeshua. We see this same imagery in Boaz and Ruth.

Ruth 3: 9, And he said, Who art thou? And she answered, I am Ruth thine handmaid: spread therefore thy skirt over thine handmaid; for thou art a near kinsman.

This joining of the male and the female as a covering and a covered is a fulfillment of the pattern of the redeemed spirit and the body.

Ephesians 5: 22, Wives, submit yourselves unto your own husbands, as unto the Lord. 23 For the husband is the head of the wife, <u>even as Christ is the head of the church: and he is the saviour of the body</u>. 24 Therefore as the church is subject unto Christ, so let the wives be to their own husbands in every thing. 25 Husbands, love your wives, even as Christ also loved the church, and gave himself for it; 26 That he might sanctify and cleanse it with the washing of water by the word, 27 That he might present it to himself a glorious church, not having spot, or wrinkle, or any such thing; but that it should be holy and without blemish. 28 So ought <u>men to love their wives as their own bodies</u>. He that loveth his wife loveth himself. 29 For <u>no man ever yet hated his own flesh</u>; but nourisheth and cherisheth it, even as the Lord the church: 30 For we are members of his body, of his flesh, and of his bones. 31 For this cause shall a man leave his father and mother, and shall be joined unto his wife, and they two shall be one flesh. 32 This is a great mystery: <u>but I speak concerning Christ and the church</u>.

The female is typified as the body of Christ and Yeshua is typified as the head of the body, the spirit and the mind.

Philippians 2: 5, Let this mind be in you, which was also in Christ Jesus:

The restored joining of the resurrected body with the circumcised heart and mind is the pattern of the redeeming by the male of the female in the marriage union. Division is turned into the singularity of the unity of faith.

Matthew 10: 32, Whosoever therefore shall confess me before men, him will I confess also before my Father which is in heaven. 33 But whosoever shall deny me before men, him will I also deny before my Father which is in heaven. 34 Think not that I am come to send peace on earth: I came not to send peace, but a sword.

If Yeshua denies us before the Father it means we are not one with His flesh and therefore means we will not be able to stand in the presence of God.

I John 4: 14, And we have seen and do testify that the Father sent the Son to be the Saviour of the world. 15 Whosoever shall confess that Jesus is the Son of God, God dwelleth in him, and he in God. 16 And we have known and believed the love that God hath to us. God is love; and he that dwelleth in love dwelleth in God, and God in him.

Our testimony must reflect Yeshua's testimony, that God sent Yeshua to be the saviour of the World. How does He save the world? By God dwelling in Yeshua and Yeshua in God, whereby we dwell in Yeshua and Yeshua in us. Adam fell and was separated from God. Yeshua came to literally redeem Adam's seed so his seed can once again dwell with God and have His image. This is salvation. If we forsake the name of that salvation, there is no other way, flesh, or seed, by which man can be saved to live in the presence of God. Denial of the Savior can only be cured by having the love of Messiah. Peter set the example.

Mark 14: 71, But he began to curse and to swear, saying, I know not this man of whom ye speak. 72 And the second time the cock crew. And Peter called to mind the word that Jesus said unto him, Before the cock crow twice, thou shalt deny me thrice. And when he thought thereon, he wept.

Just as Peter denied the name of His salvation three times, he had to remedy his chance for salvation through love of the Messiah.

John 21: 14, This is now the third time that Jesus shewed himself to his disciples, after that he was risen from the dead. 15 So when they had dined, Jesus saith to Simon Peter, Simon, son of Jonas, lovest thou me more than these? He saith unto him, Yea, Lord; thou knowest that I love thee. He saith unto him, Feed my lambs. 16 He saith to him again the second time, Simon, son of Jonas, lovest thou me? He saith unto him, Yea, Lord; thou knowest that I love thee. He saith unto him, Feed my sheep. 17 He saith unto him the third time, Simon, son of Jonas, lovest thou me? Peter was grieved because he said unto him the third time, Lovest thou me? And he said unto him, Lord, thou knowest all things; thou knowest that I love thee. Jesus saith unto him, Feed my sheep.

For each time Peter denied the name of his literal salvation, he had to rectify that denial through a declaration of love for Yeshua. He did this three times after

Yeshua was resurrected. Each time that declaration of love was met with the expectation from the Messiah, "Feed my Sheep". Being joined to our husband the Messiah Yeshua is to bear His name and His image. Just as in a loving relationship of husband and wife, the wife is conforming herself to the image of her husband, she is taking on the role of her husband and doing the things that He is actively involved in. His name is placed upon her and she is covered by his garment (image).

In the case of the Messiah, that role focuses on sowing seed, feeding the flock, and preaching the gospel. Taking His name upon us enjoins upon the believer the sacred responsibility to partake in His sacrifice and work by telling others about His work, His name, and His image. How their broken images, broken names, and fallen state can be redeemed through the only promised seed and name that can deliver.

Romans 12: 1, I beseech you therefore, brethren, by the mercies of God, that ye present your bodies a living sacrifice, holy, acceptable unto God, which is your reasonable service. 2 And be not conformed to this world: but be ye transformed by the renewing of your mind, that ye may prove what is that good, and acceptable, and perfect, will of God. 3 For I say, through the grace given unto me, to every man that is among you, not to think of himself more highly than he ought to think; but to think soberly, according as God hath dealt to every man the measure of faith. 4 For as we have many members in one body, and all members have not the same office: 5 So we, being many, are one body in Christ, and every one members one of another.

The goal is to be one with the Messiah, the manifest Name of the Lord.

Romans 8: 29, For whom he did foreknow, he also did predestinate to be conformed to the image of his Son, that he might be the firstborn among many brethren.

Being "joined to the Lord" we are one flesh with Him and receive His covering and as His wife, we have His name.

Romans 12: 22, And be not conformed to this world: but be ye transformed by the renewing of your mind, that ye may prove what is that good, and acceptable, and perfect, will of God.

Having been redeemed, Yeshua is circumcising our hearts and restoring His image to our hearts and minds. He has been hidden so that we might manifest His image.

Scripturally Correct Patterns:
Pre-fall:
- Man is in the Image of God
- God and man dwell in unity
- Man believes God and abides in faith

Post-Fall:

- Man is no longer in the image of God & has a broken image
- Man has been separated from God
- Man does not believe God and abides in unbelief

Redemption:

- Man is warned not to worship images before God
- The unity of male and female in marriage is depicted as a holy singularity "one flesh" (Genesis 2:24)
    - Male is depicted as the head (mind) of the female (manifestation)
    - The Messiah is depicted as the head (mind of Christ) to the redeemed female (bodily believer)
    - The Messiah is the image of God and we are redeemed by being conformed to His image. How does this occur? Through the renewing of our "minds" (Romans 12:2)

Symbols:

- Messiah: The Image of God, the Mind of God, the Divine Male, Shekinah Glory, covering (male) , and the Promised Seed
- Believer: The restored image of God, the bodily presence of the Messiah, those of the Bride chamber, mountain/tabernacle/temple, covered (female), and good ground.

5 THEY RECEIVED NOT THE LOVE OF THE TRUTH, THAT THEY MIGHT BE SAVED

I f keeping the Written Torah were scripturally true…would you believe it? This is a simple logic question. If you are unwilling to do what is true, even if it is confirmed to be factual and therefore truth, the issue is not about truth, but about what you want. "And blessed is he, whosoever shall not be offended in me." (Luke 7: 23).

It may be difficult for those who say they love Yeshua, to find out that they have not followed His commandments, and the result is confusion, denial, and anger. It can be shocking to find out that you really do not love Him, you just loved Him if you could remain the way you were.

Those who go beyond their feelings and strive after scriptural truth achieve an admirable goal. Most Christians will not do it. Clearly those that do this have the mind of Christ and will follow Him wherever He leads.

It must be shocking to think, "I'm doing exactly what Christ wants me to do", only to find out that those things are contrary to His very sayings and of the very Apostles He selected. Christ's own disciples found themselves at this very nexus point and many of them abandoned Him.

John 6: 60, Many therefore of his disciples, when they had heard this, said, This is an hard saying; who can hear it? 61 When Yeshua knew in himself that his disciples murmured at it, he said unto them, Doth this offend you? 62 What and if ye shall see the Son of man ascend up where he was before? 63 It is the spirit that quickeneth; the flesh profiteth nothing: the words that I speak unto you, they are spirit, and they are life. 64 But there are some of you that believe not. For Yeshua knew from the beginning who they were that believed not, and who should betray him. 65 And he said, Therefore said I unto you, that no man can come unto me, except it were given unto him of my Father. 66 From that time many of his disciples went back, and walked no more with him. 67 Then said Yeshua unto the twelve, Will ye also go away?

My question is simple. Will you follow the whole truth of scripture or will you refuse to hear it and also go away? Many of you are still confused by this issue of law and grace. You are not alone. This was also a common problem right after Yeshua was resurrected.

2 Peter 3: 15, And account that the longsuffering of our Lord is salvation; even as our beloved brother Paul also according to the wisdom given unto him hath written unto you; 16 As also in all his epistles, speaking in them of these things; in which are some things hard to be understood, which they that are unlearned and unstable wrest, as they do also the other scriptures, unto their own destruction. 17 Ye therefore, beloved, seeing ye know these things before, beware lest ye also, being led away with the error of the wicked, fall from your own stedfastness. 18 But grow in grace, and in the knowledge of our Lord and Saviour Yeshua. To him be glory both now and for ever. Amen.

So what is the error of the wicked? They believe that they can be Torahless and do whatever they want because they are under grace. Many first century Christians were twisting what Paul said about grace and the Written Torah (Law of Moses) to their own destruction. What was the outcome of their Torahlessness (lawlessness)? Wickedness and destruction. Peter cautions others to learn from their error, "beware"…do not be led away into the lawlessness (Torahlessness) of the wicked. He edifies them to continue learning and growing in the knowledge of Yeshua. How are we to do this? By keeping the scriptures, the Written Torah, the Writings, and the Prophets, along with the writings of the Apostles.

2 Timothy 3: 16, All scripture is given by inspiration of God, and is profitable for doctrine, for reproof, for correction, for instruction in righteousness:

He was not talking about some arbitrary internal moral law. He was talking about the literal Written Law of Moses (Torah). Is this too psychologically offensive to your sensibilities? If it is you should ask yourself, "If what he is saying about grace, so that you can then learn and keep the Written Torah, is scripturally true and accurate would I believe it and do it?"

If not, maybe you are fooling yourself about really loving Yeshua. So if this this is scripturally correct, you have the choice of being, as Peter described as, "unlearned in the truth and unstable" or to grow in truth! Which will it be?

It is hard to imagine how emotionally conflicted the believer could be, especially if he/she has a degree in Theology and has spent decades following Christ, to then find out that he/she has not done all that is needed. But, does that preclude you from continuing to grow in the knowledge of Yeshua? Peter was humble enough to be corrected by Paul when Peter was personally taught by Christ. Will you follow his example? Christ loves you…do you really love Him? Does this scriptural truth offend you?

2 Thessalonians 2:10, And with all deceivableness of unrighteousness in

them that perish; because <u>they received not the love of the truth, that they might be saved</u>.

Let's ask a logic question. Does someone who is deceived know that they are deceived? The greater guilt occurs when the deception turns into willful self–deception. Once awareness occurs the unlearned turn into the unstable. How so? They refuse to reconcile all of the facts of all of the scriptures and instead pick and choose snippets that favor their opinion. But we all know as good scientists, you need to adjust your theory and your paradigm to accommodate all, not just some of the facts.

Please do not be offended by this statement. This is the central issue of our age, people would rather reject the truth instead of reconciling all truth with their actions. That is why the truth is naturally linked to the sanctification process of those who wish to abide in Yeshua.

2 Thessalonians 2: 13, But we are bound to give thanks alway to God for you, brethren beloved of the Lord, because God hath from the beginning chosen you to <u>salvation through sanctification of the Spirit and belief of the truth</u>:

Will you abide in Christ? Will you abide in the truth? Will you continue in the sanctification process? Or will you also go away?

6 LAW VS GRACE OR WRITTEN LAW VS ORAL LAW? YESHUA AND PAUL GIVE THE SAME ANSWER...

Let's continue digging through the pro "Grace versus Law" positions to give them a full vetting and determine how accurate those arguments really are.

PRO "GRACE VERSUS LAW" POSITIONS:

1. Here is a short excerpt that Dr. Geisler wrote in 1992 in his book, "When Critics Ask: A Popular Handbook on Bible Difficulties":

Per Exodus 20: 8–11—Why do Christians worship on Sunday when the commandment sets apart Saturday as the day of worship?

Problem: This commandment states that the seventh day of the week, Saturday, is the day which the Lord selected as the day of rest and worship. However, in the NT the Christian church began to worship and rest on the first day of the week, Sunday. Aren't Christians violating the Sabbath commandment by worshiping on the first day of the week rather than the seventh day?

Solution: First, the basis for the command to observe the Sabbath, as stated in Exodus 20: 11, is that God rested on the seventh day after six days of work, and that God blessed the seventh day and sanctified it. The Sabbath day was instituted as a day of rest and worship. The people of God were to follow God's example in His pattern of work and rest. However, as Jesus said in correcting the distorted view of the Pharisees, "The Sabbath was made for man, and not man for the Sabbath" (Mark 2: 27). The point which Jesus made is that the Sabbath was not instituted to enslave people, but to benefit them. The spirit of Sabbath observance is continued in the NT observance of rest and worship on the first day of the week.

Second, it must be remembered that, according to Colossians 2: 17, the Sabbath was "a shadow of things to come, but the substance is of Christ". The Sabbath observance was associated with redemption in Deuteronomy 5: 15 where Moses stated, "Remember that you were a slave in the land of Egypt, and that the Lord your God brought you out from there by a mighty hand and by an outstretched arm; therefore the Lord your God commanded you to keep the Sabbath day". The Sabbath was a shadow of the redemption which would be provided in Christ. It symbolized the rest from our works and an entrance into the rest of God provided by His finished work.

Finally, although the moral principles expressed in the commandments are reaffirmed in the NT, the command to set Saturday apart as a day of rest and worship is the only commandment not repeated. There are very good reasons for this.

- New Testament believers are not under the OT Law (Romans 6: 14; Galatians 3: 24–25).

- By His resurrection on the first day of the week (Matthew 28: 1)

- His continued appearances on succeeding Sundays (John 20: 26), and the descent of the Holy Spirit on Sunday (Acts 2: 1), the early church was given the pattern of Sunday worship. This they did regularly (Acts 20: 7; 1 Corinthians 16: 2).

- Sunday worship was further hallowed by our Lord who appeared to John in that last great vision on the Lord's day (Revelation 1: 10).

It is for these reasons that Christians worship on Sunday, rather than on the Jewish Sabbath. ("When Critics Ask: A Popular Handbook on Bible Difficulties" by Dr. Norman Geisler)

2. The Apostle Paul says to Colossae and Rome that we should not get hung up on Seventh versus first or second or third or fourth or fifth or sixth days of the week as holy.

- Colossians 2: 16, "Therefore do not let anyone judge you with respect to food or drink, or in the matter of a feast, new moon, or Sabbath days–17 these are only the shadow of the things to come, but the reality is Christ!"

- Romans 14: 1, "Him that is weak in the faith receive ye, but not to doubtful disputations. 2 For one believeth that he may eat all things: another, who is weak, eateth herbs. 3 Let not him that eateth despise him that eateth not; and let not him which eateth not judge him that eateth: for God hath received him. 4 Who art thou that judgest another man's servant? to his own master he standeth or falleth. Yea, he shall be holden up: for God is able to make him stand. 5 One man esteemeth one day above another: another esteemeth every day alike. Let every man be fully persuaded in his own mind. 6 He that regardeth the day, regardeth it unto the Lord;

and he that regardeth not the day, to the Lord he doth not regard it. He that eateth, eateth to the Lord, for he giveth God thanks; and he that eateth not, to the Lord he eateth not, and giveth God thanks."

Therefore we must not pass judgment on one another, but rather determine never to place an obstacle or a trap before a brother or sister.

3.   So from a strictly biblical standpoint, it's actually morally wrong for Seventh day Adventists to judge First day Adventists and wrong for First day Adventists to judge Seventh day Adventists on matters of which days we hold holy.

4.   From a historical standpoint, there was a general shift from seventh day to first day by the time of the second century—easily 200 years before Constantine put his unhelpful mark on it all.   And this shift was not just among the Gentile Christians.

5.   The Lord's day—which is understood to be the first day of the week, they did not call it Sunday. They called the first day the Lord's day.   And why shouldn't they? That's the day he conquered death and rose from the dead.

6.   Ignatius, a Gentile Christian, writing in the second century, also said of the Jewish Christians, "If then they who walked in ancient customs came to a new hope, no longer living for the Sabbath, but for the Lord's day, on which also our life sprang up through Him and His death. "

7.   Justin, a Gentile Christian who also wrote in the second century, writing around AD 150, wrote, "On the day called Sunday all [believers] who live in the cities or in the countryside gather together at one place, and the memoirs of the Apostles or the writings of the Prophets are read, as long as time permits." Sunday is the day on which we all hold our common assembly, because it is the first day on which God, having transformed the darkness and matter, created the world. And Jesus our Savior on the same day rose from the dead.

8.   Ignatius and Justin are not trying to change Sabbatarian's into "Sundatarians". They're reporting the facts.   It was a common practice to meet on First–day in the early Christian communities. And why? Was it because they were worshipping the sun god?

REBUTTAL: PRO GRACE & LAW
LAW VERSUS GRACE OR WRITTEN LAW VERSUS ORAL LAW? YESHUA AND PAUL GIVE THE SAME ANSWER...
Truly if the 7th day Sabbath is fulfilled in Yeshua and we do not have to keep it, you have to wonder why "all flesh" is keeping the 7th day Sabbath in the Millennium.

Isaiah 66: 22, For as the new heavens and the new earth, which I will make, shall remain before me, saith the Lord, so shall your seed and your name remain. 23 And it shall come to pass, that from one new moon to another, and from one Sabbath to another, shall all flesh come to worship before me, saith the Lord.

It would seem inescapable that once again God has a future expectation that "all flesh" will keep the 7th day Sabbath. Even the sanctuary will follow this same pattern.

Ezekiel 46: 1, Thus saith the Lord God; The gate of the inner court that looketh toward the east shall be shut the six working days; but on the Sabbath it shall be opened, and in the day of the new moon it shall be opened.

Please take note that is not on the first day of the week, Sunday. If the pattern you suggest is correct, it would be true, past, present and in the future. Is the work of Yeshua undone after His return? Or could it be that the assumption that, "Christ fulfilled the Law and that means we do not have to keep it", is incorrect? Is it scripturally factual? Is it logical?

So we know in the Old Testament believers kept the 7th day Sabbath. We know in the New Testament Yeshua and all believers (Jews and Gentiles) kept the 7th day Sabbath. Acts affirms that the Apostles taught new believers in the synagogues on the 7th day Sabbath. It also confirms that offerings for Jerusalem were collected on the first day of the week at Paul's (Apostle to the Gentiles) direction, as this collection was a violation of the 7th day Sabbath, since it was work and is forbidden on the Sabbath. New believing Gentiles when hearing Paul teach entreated him to teach them again. When?

Acts 13: 42, And when the Jews were gone out of the synagogue, the Gentiles besought that these words might be preached to them the next Sabbath.

Notice they did not ask him to teach the next "first day of the week" or the next Sunday. They asked for him to teach the "next Sabbath". The Sabbath is a technical Jewish term for the day of rest that occurs after 6 days of labor on the 7th day (Exodus 20: 8–11)

Acts 13: 44, And the next Sabbath day came almost the whole city together to hear the word of God.

Please notice these are Gentiles being taught by Paul on the 7th day Sabbath in the synagogues. Only poor scholarship would assume that the offering directed by Paul was during their regular worship.

The assumption that all days are holy presupposes that Gentiles are being told by Judaizers that they need to keep the 7th day Sabbath, instead of the historical and scripturally factual account. Pharisees were telling Gentile believers, who were properly keeping the 7th day Sabbath that they also needed to keep the other days that the Rabbinical Oral Torah requires in addition to the Written Torah. The Oral

Torah of the rabbis had excessive and enslaving requirements beyond the Written Torah–this was the slavery and bondage that Yeshua was clarifying was unnecessary and hence that the "Sabbath was made for man and not man for the Sabbath". A careful reading of this scripture will show that the context is the Pharisees criticizing the disciples for not keeping their rabbinic tradition related to the Sabbath day.

Mark 3: 23, 23 And it came to pass, that <u>he went through the corn fields on the Sabbath day; and his disciples began, as they went, to pluck the ears of corn</u>. 24 And the Pharisees said unto him, <u>Behold, why do they on the Sabbath day that which is not lawful</u>? 25 And he said unto them, Have ye never read what David did, when he had need, and was an hungred, he, and they that were with him? 26 How he went into the house of God in the days of Abiathar the high priest, and did eat the shewbread, which is not lawful to eat but for the priests, and gave also to them which were with him? 27 And he said unto them, The Sabbath was made for man, and not man for the Sabbath: 28 Therefore the Son of man is Lord also of the Sabbath.

The context of Yeshua's rebuke is that they once again were putting their oral tradition before the Written Law of Moses. The issue is not "Grace versus Law", the context proves the issue is Written Law of Moses versus Oral Law of the rabbis.

The presupposition that Colossians is telling Christians not to keep the Sabbath or Holy Days is scripturally inaccurate. The scriptures confirm that Pharisees were telling new believers and observers of the Written Torah that they needed to also follow the rabbinical Oral Torah that caused these days to become a burden. Yeshua, the Apostles, and Paul all dealt with this very same issue.

Matthew 15: 3, But he answered and said unto them, Why do <u>ye also transgress the commandment of God by your tradition</u>?

This seems to be really important to Yeshua. What about Paul? Does he feel the same way? In Colossians Paul deals with these rabbinical Oral Traditions, the "Commandments of men", not the "Commandments of God".

Colossians 2: 8, Beware lest any man spoil you through philosophy and vain deceit, <u>after the tradition of men</u>, after the rudiments of the world, and not after Christ. 9 For in him dwelleth all the fulness of the Godhead bodily. 10 And ye are complete in him, which is the head of all principality and power: 11 In whom also ye are circumcised with the circumcision made without hands, in putting off the body of the sins of the flesh by the circumcision of Christ: 12 Buried with him in baptism, wherein also ye are risen with him through the faith of the operation of God, who hath raised him from the dead. 13 And you, being dead in your sins and the uncircumcision of your flesh, hath he quickened together with him, having forgiven you all trespasses; 14 Blotting out the handwriting of ordinances that was against us, which was contrary to us, and took it out of the way, nailing it to his cross; 15 And having spoiled principalities and powers, he made a shew of them openly, triumphing over them in it. 16 Let no man therefore judge you in meat, or in drink, or in respect of an holyday, or of the new moon, or of the Sabbath days: 17 Which are a shadow of things to come; but the body is of Christ. 18 Let no man beguile you of your reward in a voluntary humility and worshipping of angels, intruding into those things which he hath not seen, vainly puffed up by his fleshly mind, 19 And not holding the Head, from which all the body by joints and bands having nourishment ministered, and knit together, increaseth with the increase of God. 20 Wherefore if ye be dead with Christ from the rudiments of the world, why, as though living in the world, are ye subject to ordinances, 21 (Touch not; taste not; handle not; 22 Which all are to perish with the using;) <u>after the commandments and doctrines of men</u>?

The context of Colossians 2 is correcting believers from following these Pharisaical Oral Traditions that violate the Written Torah. Paul starts and ends Colossians 2 with the "traditions of men" and "commandments and doctrines of men". This is the same issue Peter was dealing with when the Pharisaic believers were demanding that new believers first be circumcised before eating with Jews. This was an Oral Torah rabbinical tradition and not a requirement of the Written Torah. Remember the goal of a Christian is to become a "Jew, which is one inwardly" (Romans 2:29). The essential inward nature is an expression of faith which results in God's marking of the individual with His Law. Abraham manifested faith by his works by offering Isaac (James 2:21). Israel after expressing faith by putting the blood of the lamb on the lintels of their doors in Egypt, then manifested this faith in their being brought of Egypt to the wilderness to receive the Law of Moses, given to him by God. There can be no expression of faith without God's measure of righteousness...otherwise known as His written Law. Unfortunately rabbinical oral traditions kept creating extra burdens above and beyond God's written law.

These same rabbinical traditions often required extra holy days to be observed around the actual holy days prescribed in the Written Torah to avoid violating the Sabbath or holy day. An example of this is the Feast of Trumpets (Rosh Hashanah/Yom Teruah) where the Pharisees observe two days instead of one day.

Another example of the Oral Torah is observance of Glat Kosher, which is an Oral Torah requirement, where you cannot use the same dishes for milk and meat. These are not Written Torah requirements. The Written Torah requirement regarding kosher is strictly clean and unclean meats, and how the animal is killed. Paul is telling new believers not to worry about these extra traditions that are not a part of the Written Torah.

You have a simple logical and factual issue. What is the context of what Paul is writing about? 1. Paul is telling new believers they do not need to learn the Law of Moses (Written)...or 2. Paul is telling them the same thing that Yeshua and the Apostles told them, that they do not need to observe the rabbinical Oral Law?

Unfortunately many "Grace versus Law" proponents have presupposed that the context is the former and not the latter. By doing so, you cannot reconcile the scriptures that show Peter telling the church that new Gentile believers should learn the Law of Moses in the Synagogue and why Paul carries out this message by teaching Gentile believers in the synagogue.

Acts 15: 20, But that we write unto them, that they abstain from pollutions of idols, and from fornication, and from things strangled, and from blood. 21 For Moses of old time hath in every city them that preach him, being read in the synagogues every Sabbath day.

This was an issue of where do Gentiles begin, not where they end. The Pharisees wanted new believers circumcised before eating with Jewish believers. The Apostles concluded that they should begin in the same place as God fearers did in the Written Torah. That is why they started new believers with a few simple requirements, which would allow them to be taught in the synagogues on the 7th day Sabbath with other believers.

There is not even one instance of rest and worship in the New Testament scriptures on the first day of the week. The assumption that Christ was resurrected on the first day of the week (Matthew 28:1) is because that's when the tomb was found empty presupposes that He could not have been raised on the 7th day Sabbath. It is far more likely that Christ was risen on the 7th day Sabbath, which is the fulfilment of the original 7th day Sabbath, where God brought forth His very own image in Adam and Eve. Since the work of the "promised seed" is to restore that fallen and broken image, it is far more likely that He would have been raised on the day crowning the creation when God rested. As you will see in Genesis 5, Adam no longer produced God's image. He needed a promised seed to fix his image (Genesis 3: 15).

Genesis 5: 1, This is the book of the generations of Adam. In the day that God created man, in the likeness of God made he him; 2 Male and female created he them; and blessed them, and called their name Adam, in the day when they were created. 3 And Adam lived an hundred and thirty years, and begat a son in his own likeness, and after his image; and called his name Seth:

Notice Adam is not able to reproduce God's image due to his sin. This was the reason for the last Adam, Christ, the promised seed who is literally the image of God.

- Colossians 1: 15, Who is the image of the invisible God, the firstborn of every creature:
- 1 Corinthians 15: 45, And so it is written, the first man Adam was made a living soul; the last Adam was made a quickening spirit.

This resurrection of the literal image of God (the Messiah) occurred in the same pattern as the first image, on the 7th day Sabbath. We should not presuppose facts where really there are assumptions. The empty tomb was found and the resurrected Christ is seen on the first day, but it does not mean that He was resurrected on the first day of the week.

We also cannot assume that disciples were now commemorating the first day of the week to worship. The scriptures simply do not bear out this conclusion. John 20: 26 is clearly not a Sunday as 8 days from the first day of the week is not another

Sunday. Notice what John says in verse 19.

John 20: 19, Then <u>the same day at evening, being the first day of the week,</u> when the doors were shut where the disciples were assembled for fear of the Jews, came Jesus and stood in the midst, and saith unto them, Peace be unto you.

Verse 19 is clearly the first day after the resurrection when the risen Lord is observed by the disciples. The disciples gather again 8 days later.

John 20: 26, And <u>after eight days</u> again his disciples were within, and Thomas with them: then came Jesus, the doors being shut, and stood in the midst, and said, Peace be unto you.

Counting 8 days from this day, does not bring you to another Sunday. The assumption that we are not under the Law of Moses (per Romans 6:14, Galatians 3:24–25) is an unsupported presupposition that the Law is done away, while the scriptures clearly present the death and resurrection fractal of the Messiah, the Torah, and the world.

The term "under the law" refers to the administration of sin and death that the Torah was originally given under, as we see in Exodus 20. In Exodus 34, under Yeshua's administration of grace and abundant mercy, the same commandments were given a second time as the Torah of Resurrection Life! This alone leaves the modern Christian without excuse, as they have recited that the Law is put in our hearts, not some new law, but the very same law.

Exodus 34: 1, And the Lord said unto Moses, Hew thee two tablets of stone like unto the first: and <u>I will write upon these tablets the words that were in the first tablets,</u> which thou brakest.

We will address whether Yeshua consecrated Sunday as the new Sabbath day with His appearances in a later chapter. If you take the time to study the facts, you will wonder why anyone would attempt to make that allegation. We will find that nothing changed in regard to the 7th day Sabbath observance, just like the two sets of tablets with the same words written upon both!

7 THE ENEMY OF TRUTH IS ILLOGICAL AND UN–FACTUAL PRE–SUPPOSITION...

Here are some arguments with the following unscriptural presuppositions:

      1. That Christians began to worship and rest on the first day of the week.

Answer: The scriptures clearly illustrate that this is an un–factual statement in the first century.

      2. The spirit of Sabbath observance is continued in the New Testament observance of rest and worship on the first day of the week.

Answer: The scriptures clearly illustrate that this is an un–factual statement. The scriptures affirm that worship and rest occurred on the 7th day Sabbath in the synagogue and the work of collection for Jerusalem occurred on the first day of the week.

      3. The point which Jesus made is that the Sabbath was not instituted to enslave people and you do not have to keep it on any given day.

Answer: This is an incorrect presupposition and is scripturally un–factual. Yeshua was combating Rabbinical Oral Traditions. The Oral Law put extra requirements above and beyond the Written Torah in regard to keeping the 7th day Sabbath, and it was these extra Oral Traditions that Yeshua stated were not needed to be observed as they conflict with the Written Law of Moses. These are the same issues the Apostles and Paul dealt with on a continual basis and are documented for our benefit.

      4. The Sabbath symbolized the rest from our labors and an entrance into the rest of God provided by His finished work. Hence, we do not have to keep it.

Answer: The assumption is that Yeshua saved us so that we could now work on the 7th day Sabbath. Why? "Because the true meaning of the 7th day Sabbath is that Christ worked for us, so now we can work." This does not make any logical sense. Keep in mind that labor was one of the curses of the sin of Adam and Eve. The original blessing of the 7th day Sabbath was cessation from work.

> Genesis 2: 1, Thus the heavens and the earth were finished, and all the host of them. 2 And on the seventh day God ended his work which he had made; and he rested on the seventh day from all his work which he had made. 3 And God blessed the seventh day, and sanctified it: because that in it he had rested from all his work which God created and made.

The peace of that holy rest was broken by Adam and Eve's sin. Rest ceased and the curse of labor began. The promise and seal of the redemptive work that God was bringing about for our restoration to the Garden of Eden was the gift of a cessation of labor on the 7th day Sabbath. It was a taste of what was to come.

To say that Yeshua's work allows us to rest in Him and "work" on the 7th day Sabbath simply does not follow the patterns and the fractals of the scriptures. Proponents of this idea would have you embrace "the curse" and call it "a blessing". Being allowed to work because you are freed from the penalty of labor is not exactly logical or scriptural.

> Genesis 2: 17, And unto Adam he said, Because thou hast hearkened unto the voice of thy wife, and hast eaten of the tree, of which I commanded thee, saying, Thou shalt not eat of it: cursed is the ground for thy sake; in sorrow shalt thou eat of it all the days of thy life; 18 Thorns also and thistles shall it bring forth to thee; and thou shalt eat the herb of the field; 19 In the sweat of thy face shalt thou eat bread, till thou return unto the ground; for out of it wast thou taken: for dust thou art, and unto dust shalt thou return. 20 And Adam called his wife's name Eve; because she was the mother of all living. 21 Unto Adam also and to his wife did the Lord God make coats of skins, and clothed them. 22 And the Lord God said, Behold, the man is become as one of us, to know good and evil: and now, lest he put forth his hand, and take also of the Tree of Life, and eat, and live for ever: 23 Therefore the Lord God sent him forth from the garden of Eden, to till the ground from whence he was taken. 24 So he drove out the man; and he placed at the east of the garden of Eden Cherubims, and a flaming sword which turned every way, to keep the way of the Tree of Life.

Scripturally, the Sabbath being fulfilled in Christ focuses on the actual work of the 7th day, bringing forth the image of God. The modern Christian has abandoned logic and the scriptures so that they can present a Messiah who keeps the Law for them, so that they might "...continue in sin, that grace may abound..." (Romans 6:1).

Labor is the curse of those who sin, and the "rest" of the 7th day Sabbath is the delight and freedom of those under grace and without sin. Why would the modern Christian insist on indulging a paradigm that conflicts with the truth revealed by God in Genesis 3? "Jesus fulfilled the Sabbath for me, so I do not have to..." they claim. The gift of the 7th day Sabbath and not having to work is called a burden by the modern Christian!

Isaiah 5:20, Woe unto them that call evil good, and good evil; that put darkness for light, and light for darkness; that put bitter for sweet, and sweet for bitter!

Grace is not about allowing the believer to continue to labor under the curse, because the Messiah fulfilled the Law so that we don't have to. The Messiah came to free us from the curse. He did not come to fulfill the Law for us, so that we can remain under the curse. He came to free us from our cursed and broken image and to give us His "whole" image. This gift took place on the first 7th day Sabbath.

- Broken image—Our current fallen state (labor & sweat—death)
- Whole image—Provided by the Messiah to restore us from our fallen image (rest & no sweat—resurrection life).

Notice nothing that God created in days 1–6 had flesh (image) as yet. This was the work of the 7th day.

Genesis 2: 5, And every plant of the field before it was in the earth, and every herb of the field before it grew: for the Lord God had not caused it to rain upon the earth, and there was not a man to till the ground.

This is how the 7th day Sabbath is fulfilled in Yeshua. He is the last Adam and the image of God. We need His seed to have our broken image restored.

5. The descent of the Holy Spirit happened on Sunday.
Answer: According to the Jewish count of fifty (counting the omer), Pentecost (Shavuot) does not happen on a Sunday, it happens on Sivan 6, which can be any day of the week. The account of Acts 2 is of actual Jews counting the actual Pentecost, which would have begun with the Feast of First Fruits and concluded on Sivan 6 (50 day count). This is another great example of modern Christians taking a pagan observance and applying it to the scriptures, instead of applying scriptural facts to the modern Christian observance.

6. Sunday worship was further hallowed by our Lord who appeared to John in the last great vision on the Lord's day in Revelation 1:10.
Answer: It is an unscriptural assumption that this refers to a Sunday. The book of Revelation is about the revealing of the true image of God, on the Lord's day. Malachi talks about the Lord's day.

Malachi 4: 1, For, behold, the day cometh, that shall burn as an oven; and all the proud, yea, and all that do wickedly, shall be stubble: and the day that cometh shall burn them up, saith the Lord of hosts, that it shall leave them neither root nor branch. 2 But unto you that fear my name shall the sun of righteousness arise with healing in his wings; and ye shall go forth, and grow up as calves of the stall. 3 And ye shall tread down the wicked; for they shall be ashes under the soles of your feet in the day that I shall do this, saith the Lord of hosts. 4 <u>Remember ye the law of Moses my servant</u>, which I commanded unto him in Horeb for all Israel, with the statutes and judgments. 5 Behold, <u>I will send you Elijah the prophet before the coming of the great and dreadful day of the Lord</u>: 6 And he shall turn the heart of the fathers to the children, and the heart of the children to their fathers, lest I come and smite the earth with a curse.

Let's clarify who these "fathers" are. They are the "fathers" of faith.

Micah 7: 20, Thou wilt perform the truth to Jacob, and the mercy to Abraham, <u>which thou hast sworn unto our fathers</u> from the days of old.

He is talking about Abraham, Isaac, and Jacob. The urgent agenda of Elijah right before the return of Yeshua is to return believers to the faith of Abraham, Isaac, and Jacob. This suggests that believers (those who fear the Name of the Lord, the Messiah) right before Yeshua's second coming, (The Day of the Lord), will have strayed so far from true and scripturally accurate paradigms that unless this "return" occurs God will strike the entire earth with a curse!

In regard to the quotes from Ignatius and Justin, the writings of the Apostles have sufficient accurate testimony of what they and Gentile believers did and how the Apostles were already dealing with a spirit of Torahlessness. No doubt it had grown worse by the time of Ignatius and Justin.

Notice that the pattern of the 7th day Sabbath is true in the past, in the first century after Christ's death and resurrection, and in the future…. so why is not true now? Perhaps it is and you have an incorrect paradigm.

We need to follow a logical methodology on this issue. We cannot make the same logical errors as the Atheists and Evolutionists, pertaining to "Grace versus Law". Picking and choosing the facts we like and ignoring the facts that we do not like will only lead to an uninformed and inaccurate conclusion. We must instead reconcile all of the scriptures.

8 "FOR THEY ARE NOT ALL ISRAEL, WHICH ARE OF ISRAEL"...SO WHAT ARE YOU? (ROMANS 9:6)

P RO "GRACE VERSUS LAW" POSITIONS:
      1. Arguments for the Sabbath day changing to Sunday are very compelling.

    2. In the 4th century, the church formally declared that the Sabbath be moved to Sunday.

    3. The Sabbath will continue into the world to come (Isa. 66: 22–23) but we do not need to observe it now.

    4. The 7th day Sabbath was given as a sign between Israel and God.

Exodus 31: 16, Wherefore the children of Israel shall keep the Sabbath, to observe the Sabbath throughout their generations, for a perpetual covenant. 17 It is a sign between me and the children of Israel for ever: for in six days the Lord made heaven and earth, and on the seventh day he rested, and was refreshed.

    5. God did not call any other nation to observe the Sabbath though he did open the door for Gentiles to be part of the covenant with Israel.

Isaiah 56: 4, For thus saith the Lord unto the eunuchs that keep my sabbaths, and choose the things that please me, and take hold of my covenant; 5 Even unto them will I give in mine house and within my walls a place and a name better than of sons and of daughters: I will give them an everlasting name, that shall not be cut off. 6 Also the sons of the stranger, that join themselves to the Lord, to serve him, and to love the Name of the Lord, to be his servants, every one that keepeth the Sabbath from polluting it, and taketh hold of my covenant; 7 Even them will I bring to my holy mountain, and make them joyful in my house of prayer: their burnt offerings and their sacrifices shall be accepted upon mine altar; for mine house shall be called an house of prayer for all people.

6.   In the New Testament, believers are never called or required to observe the 7th day Sabbath.

- Both in Colossians 2:16–17 and Romans 14:5–8, Paul makes it clear that Gentiles are not required to observe a specific day as set apart. And in those contexts, we are not to pass judgment on them based on their observance or non–observance of the Sabbath or any other holy day.
- Colossians 2: 16, Let no man therefore judge you in meat, or in drink, or in respect of an holyday, or of the new moon, or of the Sabbath days: 17 Which are a shadow of things to come; but the body is of Christ.
- Romans 14: 5, One man esteemeth one day above another: another esteemeth every day alike. Let every man be fully persuaded in his own mind. 6 He that regardeth the day, regardeth it unto the Lord; and he that regardeth not the day, to the Lord he doth not regard it. He that eateth, eateth to the Lord, for he giveth God thanks; and he that eateth not, to the Lord he eateth not, and giveth God thanks. 7 For none of us liveth to himself, and no man dieth to himself. 8 For whether we live, we live unto the Lord; and whether we die, we die unto the Lord: whether we live therefore, or die, we are the Lord's.

7.   Our ultimate rest is now found in Jesus and not a specific day.

8.   Observers of the Torah are taking their viewpoint from scriptures that are out of context.

9.   Israel and the church are separate. This is supported by the conflicts documented in Paul's writing. If we look at Paul's letters, it is not difficult to pull out what on the surface appear to be directly opposing views.

- o   Galatians 3: 10, For as many as are of the works of the law are under the curse: for it is written, Cursed is every one that continueth not in all things which are written in the book of the law to do them.
- o   Galatians 3: 11, But that no man is justified by the law in the sight of God, it is evident: for, The just shall live by faith.
- o   Galatians 6: 15, For in Christ Jesus neither circumcision availeth any thing, nor uncircumcision, but a new creature.
- o   Romans 3: 20, Therefore by the deeds of the law there shall no flesh be justified in his sight: for by the law is the knowledge of sin.
- o   Romans 9:31, But Israel, which followed after the law

of righteousness, hath not attained to the law of righteousness.

    o   Corinthians 3: 14, But their minds were blinded: for until this day remaineth the same vail untaken away in the reading of the Old Testament; which vail is done away in Christ. 15 But even unto this day, when Moses is read, the vail is upon their heart.

    o   Romans 9: 4, Who are Israelites; to whom pertaineth the adoption, and the glory, and the covenants, and the giving of the law, and the service of God, and the promises;

    o   Romans 11: 1, I say then, Hath God cast away his people? God forbid. For I also am an Israelite, of the seed of Abraham, of the tribe of Benjamin.

    o   Romans 11: 26, And so all Israel shall be saved: as it is written, There shall come out of Sion the Deliverer, and shall turn away ungodliness from Jacob:

    o   Galatians 3: 21, Is the law then against the promises of God? God forbid: for if there had been a law given which could have given life, verily righteousness should have been by the law.

10. The entire thrust of the NT is that our life and identity is found in the Messiah. For Jewish believers, if they want to keep the Torah as part of their covenantal responsibility, so be it.

REBUTTAL: PRO GRACE & LAW
"FOR THEY ARE NOT ALL ISRAEL, WHICH ARE OF ISRAEL"...SO WHAT ARE YOU? (ROMANS 9:6)
The essential question is, are there are two ways for believers in Christ, one for Jewish Christians and another for Gentile Christians? Is the Church separate from Israel? Are there two ways of salvation?

1 Corinthians 1: 12, Now this I say, that every one of you saith, I am of Paul; and I of Apollos; and I of Cephas; and I of Christ. 13 Is Christ divided? was Paul crucified for you? or were ye baptized in the name of Paul? 14 I thank God that I baptized none of you, but Crispus and Gaius;

Paul appears to be saying that there is only one way of salvation and both Jews and Gentiles become baptized into "one body" and they are all doing the same things.

1 Corinthians 12: 13, For by one Spirit are we all baptized into one body, whether we be Jews or Gentiles, whether we be bond or free; and have been all made to drink into one Spirit.

The scriptures are clear that both the Jews and the Gentiles were observing the same commandments, and the principal issue was how to introduce new unlearned Gentile converts into learning the true way. The Pharisees had a very detailed set of requirements (Oral Torah) that they expected God fearers (Gentile converts) to adhere to that were above and beyond the requirements of the Written Law of Moses.

God Fearer, A God–fearer or Godfearer was a member of a class of non–Jewish (Gentile) sympathizers to Second Temple Judaism mentioned in the Christian New Testament and other contemporary sources such as synagogue inscriptions in Diaspora Hellenistic Judaism. The concept has precedents in the proselytes of the Hebrew Bible. In the Hebrew Bible, there is some recognition of non–Jewish monotheistic worship as being directed toward the same God. This forms the category of yirei Hashem ("יראי השם," meaning "Fearers of the Name", "the Name" being a Jewish euphemism for the Tetragrammaton, cf. Psalm 115: 11). (Wikipedia)

Ger Toshav, Ger toshav (Hebrew: גר תושב ger "foreigner" + toshav "resident"), is a term used in Judaism to refer to a Gentile who is a "resident alien", that is, one who lives in a Jewish state and has certain protections under Jewish law, and is considered[1] a righteous Gentile (Hebrew: חסיד אומות העולם chassid umot ha–olam "pious among the nations")...The Amora'im who produced the Talmud set out three requirements for a conversion to Judaism (Keritot 8b), which must be witnessed and affirmed by a beth din hedyot rabbinical court composed of three Jewish males above the age of thirteen (they do not need to be rabbis): [original research?]

- Circumcision (Brit milah or hatafat dam brit) for men[4]
- Immersion (tevilah) in a ritual bath (mikveh) for both men and women[4]
- Offering a certain sacrifice (korban) in the Temple (the Beit Hamikdash)–this requirement is deferred while the Temple does not exist until such time as it may be rebuilt.

The consensus of halakhic authorities also requires a convert to understand and accept the duties of the classical Jewish law. This is not stated explicitly in the Talmud, but was inferred by subsequent commentators. [22]

After confirming that all these requirements have been met, the beth din issues a "Certificate of Conversion" (Shtar Giur), certifying that the person is now a Jew. (Wikipedia)

Considering the fact that Yeshua circumcised the hearts of believers who then took the name of the Messiah by faith in "the baptism (mikvah) of His death" (Romans 6:3) and that He served as our sacrifice, all of these requirements were clearly fulfilled in the simple steps that Yeshua laid out for new converts, Jew and Gentile. We cannot escape the fact that these requirements were for the intent of joining the covenant to "understand and accept the duties of the classical Jewish law", and then "certifying that the person is now a Jew".

Please keep in mind that God fearers in the first century would not be allowed to continue in the synagogue if they were violating the 7th day Sabbath. As we have already confirmed, Jewish and Gentile believers were learning the Law of Moses every 7th day Sabbath.

Acts 15: 21, For Moses of old time hath in every city them that preach him, being read in the synagogues every Sabbath day.

This would confirm the fact that all first century believers were indeed keeping the 7th day Sabbath. This is also the case with eating unclean meats and meats offered to idols. The Jews were so adamant about new believers doing these things that Peter and the Jerusalem council had to issue a ruling to make sure all new believers met the requirements.

Acts 15: 29, That ye abstain from meats offered to idols, and from blood, and from things strangled, and from fornication: from which if ye keep yourselves, ye shall do well. Fare ye well.

Furthermore, we need to address the issue of whether the church is a separate entity from Israel. It is a presupposition to say that the church was born on Pentecost (Shavuot) or that the church was separate from Israel from that date on.

WHO IS ISRAEL?

The scriptures make it clear that those of faith are "Israel". How is Romans 11 interpreted by most Christians? They say that the believer is grafted into either Israel or Judah. They assume that the tree is Judah or Israel because the branches are grafted into a tree that is natural to them. But is this what Romans 11 is saying?

Let's look closer at the whole chapter and make sure we are properly interpreting the symbols of the imagery and metaphor that is given. Some Messianic teachers claim that if you analyze a metaphor too much it will simply break down. This is especially true of a metaphor where the symbols are given incorrect meanings. Let's analyze what Romans 11 is saying and then review it in light of Romans 2.

Romans 11: 1, I say then, <u>Hath God cast away his people? God forbid</u>. For I also am an Israelite, of the seed of Abraham, of the tribe of Benjamin. 2 God hath not cast away his people which he foreknew. Wot ye not what the scripture saith of Elias? how he maketh intercession to God against Israel saying, 3 Lord, they have killed thy prophets, and digged down thine altars; and I am left alone, and they seek my life. 4 But what saith the answer of God unto him? I have reserved to myself seven thousand men, who have not bowed the knee to the image of Baal. 5 Even so then <u>at this present time also there is a remnant according to the election of grace. 6 And if by grace, then is it no more of works</u>: otherwise grace is no more grace. But if it be of works, then it is no more grace: otherwise work is no more work. 7 What then? <u>Israel hath not obtained that which he seeketh for; but the election hath obtained it</u>, and the rest were blinded. 8 (According as it is written, God hath given them the spirit of slumber, eyes that they should not see, and ears that they should not hear;) unto this day. 9 And David saith, Let their table be made a snare, and a trap, and a stumblingblock, and a recompence unto them: 10 Let their eyes be darkened, that they may not see, and bow down their back alway. 11 I say then, Have they stumbled that they should fall? God forbid: but rather through their fall salvation is come unto the Gentiles, for to provoke them to jealousy. 12 Now if the fall of them be the riches of the world, and the diminishing of them the riches of the Gentiles; how much more their fulness? 13 For I speak to you Gentiles, inasmuch as I am the apostle of the Gentiles, I magnify mine office: 14 If by any means I may provoke to emulation them which are my flesh, and might save some of them. 15 For if the casting away of them be the reconciling of the world, what shall the receiving of them be, but life from the dead? 16 For if the firstfruit be holy, the lump is also holy: and if the root be holy, so are the branches. 17 And if some of the branches be broken off, and thou, being a wild olive tree, wert grafted in among them, and with them partakest of the root and fatness of the olive tree; 18 Boast not against the branches. But if thou boast, thou bearest not the root, but the root thee. 19 Thou wilt say then, The branches were broken off, that I might be grafted in. 20 Well; because of unbelief they were broken off, and thou standest by faith. Be not highminded, but fear: 21 For if God spared not the natural branches, take heed lest he also spare not thee. 22 Behold therefore the goodness and severity of God: on them which fell, severity; but toward thee, goodness, if thou continue in his goodness: otherwise thou also shalt be cut off. 23 And they also, if they abide not still in unbelief, shall be grafted in: for God is able to graft them in again. 24 For if thou wert cut out of the olive tree which is wild by nature, and wert grafted contrary to nature into a good olive tree: how much more shall these, which be the natural branches, be grafted into their own olive tree? 25 For I would not, brethren, that ye should be ignorant of this mystery, lest ye should be wise in your own conceits; that blindness in part is happened to Israel, until the fulness of the Gentiles be come in. 26 And so all Israel shall be saved: as it is written, There shall come out of Sion the Deliverer, and shall turn away ungodliness from Jacob: 27 For this is my covenant unto them, when I shall take away their sins. 28 As concerning the Gospel, they are enemies for your sakes: but as touching the election, they are beloved for the father's sakes. 29 For the gifts and calling of God are without repentance. 30 For as ye in times past have not believed God, yet have now obtained mercy through their unbelief: 31 Even so have these also now not believed, that through your mercy they also may obtain mercy. 32 For God hath concluded them all in unbelief, that he might have mercy upon all. 33 O the depth of the riches both of the wisdom and knowledge of God! how unsearchable are his judgments, and his ways past finding out! 34 For who hath known the mind of the Lord? or who hath been his counsellor? 35 Or who hath first given to him, and it shall be recompensed unto him again? 36 For of him, and through him, and to him, are all things: to whom be glory for ever. Amen.

It is easy to see why people would assume this tree is Israel or Judah. But the scripture is plain and clear that this tree is the covenant of faith in the Messiah Yeshua, the manifest Name of YHWH. There is no other name under heaven whereby we must be saved. What confuses many believers is the fact that the tree is identified as "natural" to the Jews. Hence many claim that Christians are grafted into Israel.

But a careful reading of Romans 11 and Romans 2 will show that the commonality between the Jews and the tree that should be natural to them is not their fleshly genetic link to Abraham, Isaac, and Jacob. The link is the expression of faith in the "Angel of the Lord (YHWH)" (Genesis 48:6), that Abraham, Isaac, and Jacob expressed saving faith in.

We will go into a clear explanation on two of the root names of God, El and YHWH, and will clarify the thematic relationship between these two root names and why each is used purposefully and specifically relating to seed and manifestation (flesh). For the remainder of the book we will use the terms God, El, YHWH as appropriate to the original Hebrew and dispense with the replacement term of "Lord".

Tetragrammaton, The tetragrammaton (from Greek τετραγράμματον, meaning "(consisting of) four letters")[1][2] is the Hebrew theonym יהוה, commonly transliterated into Latin letters as YHWH. It is one of the names of the national God of Israel used in the Hebrew Bible. [3][4][5]While YHWH is the most common transliteration of the tetragrammaton in English academic studies, the alternatives YHVH, JHVH and JHWH are also used. [6][7]Although "Yahweh" is favored by most Hebrew scholars and is widely accepted as the pronunciation of the tetragrammaton, Jehovah is still used in some translations of the Bible. The Samaritans understood the pronunciation to be iabe. Some patristic sources give evidence for a Greek pronunciation iaō. [8]Religiously observant Jews are forbidden to pronounce the name of God, and when reading the Torah they use the word Adonai ("Lord"). [8] The name may be derived from a verb that means "to be, to exist". (Wikipedia)

Tetragrammaton, "the rabbis forbade the Utterance of the Tetragrammaton, to guard against desecration of the Sacred Name; but such an ordinance could not have been effectual unless it had met with popular approval. The reasons assigned by Lagarde ("Psalterium Hicronymi," p. 155) and Halévy ("Recherches Bibliques," i. 65 et seq.) are untenable, and are refuted by Jacob (l. c. pp. 172, 174), who believes that the Divine Name was not pronounced lest it should be desecrated by the heathen. The true name of God was uttered only during worship in the Temple, in which the people were alone; and in the course of the services on the day of Atonement the high priest pronounced the Sacred Name ten times (Tosef. , Yoma, ii. 2; Yoma 39b). This was done as late as the last years of the Temple (Yer. Yoma 40a, 67). If such was the purpose, the means were ineffectual, since the pronunciation of the Tetragrammaton was known not only in Jewish, but also in non–Jewish circles centuries after the destruction of the Temple, as is clear from the interdictions against uttering it (Sanh. x. 1; Tosef. , Sanh. xii. 9; Sifre Zuṭa, in Yalḳ. , Gen. 711; 'Ab. Zarah 18a; Midr. Teh. to Ps. xci. , end). " (Jewish Encyclopedia)

Because the focus of this book is to establish scripturally correct images and definitions we cannot escape the need for the original terminology that was used by the authors of the scriptures. To avoid confusion we will use the full spelling of the names of God cited, even though, for the sake of our brothers the Jews, we would be happy to use L—d instead of Lord, G—d instead of God, Y—H instead of YHWH. However for clarity we will use the full spelling to avoid any confusion on the part of the reader. As we have seen, the clear testimony of Yeshua and the Apostles is that we need not keep the Oral Torah of the rabbis, of which their edict to not write or say the name of God is one of those unnecessary burdens that we need not bear.

Again, a careful reading of Romans 11 and Romans 2 will show that the commonality between the Jews and the tree that should be natural to them is not their fleshly genetic link to Abraham, Isaac, and Jacob. The link is the expression of faith in the "Angel of the Lord (YHWH)", that Abraham expressed saving faith in.

- Genesis 48: 15, And he blessed Joseph, and said, God, before whom my fathers Abraham and Isaac did walk, the God which fed me all my life long unto this day, 16 The <u>Angel which redeemed me from all evil</u>, bless the lads; and let my name be named on them, and the name of my fathers Abraham and Isaac; and let them grow into a multitude in the midst of the earth.

- Galatians 3: 5, He therefore that ministereth to you the Spirit, and worketh miracles among you, doeth he it by the works of the law, <u>or by the hearing of faith</u>? 6 <u>Even as Abraham believed God, and it was accounted to him for righteousness</u>. 7 Know ye therefore that they which are of faith, the same are the children of Abraham.

THE TREE OF FAITH

An examination of Romans 11 in light of Romans 2 makes this issue of "faith" the central claim of being "natural" to Abraham. Let's now examine Romans 2 as this will help clarify the imagery of Romans 11. Are you saved by your flesh or are you saved by faith? Can you claim salvation by genetic heritage and live hypocritically towards the faith that provided deliverance to the one who originated the "tree"? Notice again the central issue is flesh versus spirit, and hypocrisy versus genuine faith and obedience.

Romans 2: 1, Therefore thou art inexcusable, O man, whosoever thou art that judgest: for wherein thou judgest another, thou condemnest thyself; for thou that judgest doest the same things. 2 But we are sure that the judgment of God is according to truth against them which commit such things. 3 And thinkest thou this, O man, that judgest them which do such things, and doest the same, that thou shalt escape the judgment of God? 4 Or despisest thou the riches of his goodness and forbearance and longsuffering; not knowing that the goodness of God leadeth thee to repentance? 5 But after thy hardness and impenitent heart treasurest up unto thyself wrath against the day of wrath and revelation of the righteous judgment of God: 6 Who will render to every man according to his deeds: 7 To them who by patient continuance in well doing seek for glory and honour and immortality, eternal life: 8 But unto them that are contentious, and do not obey the truth, but obey unrighteousness, indignation and wrath, 9 Tribulation and anguish, upon every soul of man that doeth evil, of the Jew first, and also of the Gentile; 10 But <u>glory, honour, and peace, to every man that worketh good</u>, to the Jew first, and also to the Gentile: 11 For there is no respect of persons with God. 12 <u>For as many as have sinned without law shall also perish without law: and as many as have sinned in the law shall be judged by the law</u>; 13 (For not the hearers of the law are just before God, but the doers of the law shall be justified. 14 For <u>when the Gentiles, which have not the law, do by nature the things contained in the law, these, having not the law, are a law unto themselves</u>: 15 Which <u>shew the work of the law written in their hearts</u>, their conscience also bearing witness, and their thoughts the mean while accusing or else excusing one another;)16 In the day when God shall judge the secrets of men by Yeshua according to my Gospel. 17 Behold, thou art called a Jew, and restest in the law, and makest thy boast of God, 18 And knowest his will, and approvest the things that are more excellent, being instructed out of the law; 19 And art confident that thou thyself art a guide of the blind, a light of them which are in darkness, 20 An instructor of the foolish, a teacher of babes, which hast the form of knowledge and of the truth in the law. 21 <u>Thou therefore which teachest another, teachest thou not thyself? thou that preachest a man should not steal, dost thou steal</u>? 22 Thou that sayest a man should not commit adultery, dost thou commit adultery? thou that abhorrest idols, dost thou commit sacrilege? 23 Thou that makest thy boast of the law, through breaking the law dishonourest thou God? 24 For the name of God is blasphemed among the Gentiles through you, as it is written. 25 For <u>circumcision verily profiteth, if thou keep the law: but if thou be a breaker of the law, thy circumcision is made uncircumcision. 26 Therefore if the uncircumcision keep the righteousness of the law, shall not his uncircumcision be counted for circumcision</u>? 27 And shall not uncircumcision which is by nature, if it fulfil the law, judge thee, who by the letter and circumcision dost transgress the law? 28 For <u>he is not a Jew, which is one outwardly; neither is that circumcision, which is outward in the flesh: 29 But he is a Jew, which is one inwardly; and circumcision is that of the heart, in the spirit, and not in the letter</u>; whose praise is not of men, but of God.

Paul is clarifying what really counts to make you a descendant of Abraham and be "grafted into the tree of faith". As usual he is contrasting the flesh versus the spirit, and faith versus unbelief. He is making it clear what makes one of the tree is "faith". Once that seed of faith is established in the heart, it will then manifest itself in righteous conduct which is obedience to the Law of Moses.

Flesh Versus Spirit based on Romans 2 & 11		
Flesh	Spirit	What Counts?
Not all Israel act like Israel	Not all Gentiles act like Gentiles	How you act
Not all circumcised act circumcised	Not all uncircumcised act uncircumcised	Your true state will manifest itself

Flesh Versus Spirt based on Romans 2 & 11		
Flesh	**Spirit**	**What Counts?**
Circumcision of the heart is what counts	Circumcision of the spirit is what counts	True circumcision of the heart & spirit
Try to establish your own righteousness by works and fail	God establishes your righteousness by faith in His manifest Name, the Messiah	Key question is how are you established/saved
Moses and the works of the law leaves you under condemnation and death	Abraham and the law of faith leaves you under grace (no condemnation) and resurrected life	What leaves you free of condemnation? Law of faith only.
Boasting would suggest you have done some work to become worthy. Hence your branch is doing the work for the root (by carrying it) instead of the root carrying the branch.	Not boasting would suggest worthiness comes by faith in the manifest Name of YHWH, the Messiah through faith in His name. Hence the root is properly carrying the branch (you).	Faith is without boasting. You did NOTHING of worth. The work is the Messiah's. The work of the root, faith, is the strength of the branch!
Israel is condemned for trying to establish their own righteousness without faith in the manifest Name of YHWH, the Messiah Yeshua. Hence their branch is cut off for lack of faith.	The Gentiles are established and grafted into the tree by faith in the manifest Name of YHWH, Yeshua the Messiah. They are not trying to establish their own righteousness, they have accepted the righteousness of the Messiah.	You are established only, Jew or Gentile, by faith in His manifest Name, Yeshua Adonai YHWH.
Israel/Judah's branch is cut out of the tree for lack of faith in the	Gentiles' branch is grafted into the tree for faith in the Messiah.	Your branch is in or out according to your faith.

Flesh Versus Spirt based on Romans 2 & 11		
Flesh	Spirit	What Counts?
Messiah.		
Israel is the branch that is natural to the tree. What makes it natural to the tree? This is the pivotal issue!	Gentiles are a wild olive branch which are grafted in because of faith in the Messiah.	Natural or unnatural, what makes the Tzion (graft) is faith.
What is the root of the tree? The Covenant of faith, the same one that Abraham was accounted as righteous for believing in his redeemer, the Messiah.	This tree is identified as not being… Israel and Judah. They are only grafted back in when they exhibit the natural faith of their father Abraham. It should be natural for them to exhibit the same faith that Abraham did!	What makes Israel natural to this tree? It was their father Abraham that established this covenant of faith with His redeemer the manifest Name of YHWH, the Messiah!

Just as Jacob having prevailed with God through faith, God changes Jacob's name to Israel and Israel seeks after the blessing of God's name.

Genesis 32:27, And he said unto him, What is thy name? And he said, Jacob. 28 And he said, Thy name shall be called no more Jacob, but Israel: for as a prince hast thou power with God and with men, and hast prevailed. 29 And Jacob asked him, and said, Tell me, I pray thee, thy name. And he said, Wherefore is it that thou dost ask after my name? And he blessed him there.

Paul clearly illustrates that the goal is to have true faith in the Messiah Yeshua in order to be "in" the tree. The church members are illustrated as being "in the faith" and "having Christ" and as such exhibiting that which is natural to the tree…faith just like Jacob.

1 Corinthians 10:32, Give none offence, neither to the Jews, nor to the Gentiles, nor to the church of God:

Paul is clarifying to the Corinthians that there are three separate groups; Jews (who have not expressed faith in the Messiah), Gentiles (who have not expressed faith in the Messiah), and the Church (a remnant previously from both groups who have now expressed faith in Yeshua the Messiah, Romans 9:27, 11:5, 7). As such

Jews and Gentiles are not in the tree because they have not expressed that which is natural to the tree or the fathers of the faith (Abraham, Isaac, and Jacob/Israel). We are not grafted into Judah or Israel, we are grafted into Yeshua the Messiah.

It is easy to see why people would assume this tree is Israel or Judah. But the scripture is plain and clear that this tree is the covenant of faith in the Messiah Yeshua, the manifest Name of YHWH. There is none other name under heaven whereby we must be saved.

Yeshua (ישוע, with vowel pointing יֵשׁוּעַ–yēšūăʿ in Hebrew)[1] was a common alternative form of the name יְהוֹשֻׁעַ ("Yehoshuah"–Joshua) in later books of the Hebrew Bible and among Jews of the Second Temple period. The name corresponds to the Greek spelling Iesous, from which, through the Latin Iesus, comes the English spelling Jesus. [2][3]… Yeshua in Hebrew is verbal derivative from "to rescue", "to deliver". [9] The name Yehoshua has the form of a compound of "Yeho–" and "shua": Yeho– יְהוֹ is another form of יהו Yahu, a theophoric element standing for the name of God יהוה (the Tetragrammaton YHWH, sometimes transcribed into English as Yahweh or Jehovah), and שׁוּעַ shuaʿ is a noun meaning "a cry for help", "a saving cry",[12][13][14] that is to say, a shout given when in need of rescue. Together, the name would then literally mean, "YHWH (Yahu) is a saving–cry," that is to say, shout to YHWH [God] when in need of help. Another explanation for the name Yehoshua is that it comes from the root ישע yod–shin–ʿayin, meaning "to deliver, save, or rescue". According to the Book of Numbers verse 13: 16, the name of Joshua son of Nun was originally Hosheaʿ הוֹשֵׁעַ, and the name "Yehoshuaʿ" יְהוֹשֻׁעַ is usually spelled the same but with a yod added at the beginning. "Hosheaʿ" certainly comes from the root ישע, "yasha", yod–shin–ʿayin (in the Hifʿil form the yod becomes a waw), and not from the word שׁוע shuaʿ (Jewish Encyclopedia[15]) although ultimately both roots appear to be related. (Wikipedia)

THE MANIFEST NAME OF YHWH: THE MESSIAH

We see the manifestation of the Name of God, YHWH, at the second giving of the Torah with "grace and abundant mercy" in Exodus 34.

Exodus 34: 5, And the Lord descended in the cloud, and stood with him there, and proclaimed the Name of the Lord. 6 And the Lord passed by before him, and proclaimed, The Lord, The Lord God, merciful and gracious, longsuffering, and abundant in goodness and truth,

We will explore the significance of this event on the redeemed, and why "the Name of the Lord (YHWH)" is presented by God to Moses at the second giving of the Law of Moses (the Written Torah). We will also see why this event changes the countenance of Moses to a glorified form. This event is a picture of the resurrection portion of the fractal of death (seed) and then resurrection (manifestation).

Fundamentally we need to clarify the nexus point of the salvific act. Why would we be grafted into Israel's branches when Yeshua Himself stated that their house is left desolate (Luke 13:35)? He says that they will remain desolate until they declare "Blessed is he that cometh in the Name of the Lord" (Matthew 23:39). Paul affirms this fact by declaring that their branches are cut off for unbelief. Paul testifies, we are grafted into Yeshua, the manifest Name of the Lord (YHWH), not Israel! Isaiah clarifies this issue.

Isaiah 56: 3, Neither let the son of the stranger, <u>that hath joined himself to the Lord</u>, speak, saying, The Lord hath utterly separated me from his people: neither let the eunuch say, <u>Behold, I am a dry tree</u>.

All of scripture affirms that we are redeemed and joined to the Lord (YHWH). In fact the prophets depict the Messiah as the "branch". Yeshua makes the answer quite plain.

John 15: 1, <u>I am the true vine</u>, and my Father is the husbandman. 2 <u>Every branch in me</u> that beareth not fruit he taketh away: and <u>every branch</u> that beareth fruit, he purgeth it, that it may bring forth more fruit. 3 Now ye are clean through the word which I have spoken unto you. 4 <u>Abide in me, and I in you. As the branch</u> cannot bear fruit of itself, except it abide in the vine; no more can ye, <u>except ye abide in me</u>. 5 <u>I am the vine, ye are the branches: He that abideth in me, and I in him</u>, the same bringeth forth much fruit: for without me ye can do nothing. 6 <u>If a man abide not in me, he is cast forth as a branch, and is withered; and men gather them, and cast them into the fire</u>, and they are burned. 7 <u>If ye abide in me</u>, and my words abide in you, ye shall ask what ye will, and it shall be done unto you.

Notice:
- Who is the vine, Israel or Yeshua? Yeshua
- Who is your branch attached to, Israel or Yeshua? Yeshua
- Who do you abide in, Israel or Yeshua? Yeshua

These are Yeshua's own words. We need to adhere to answers that have scriptural foundation and integrity. To say anything otherwise is only displaying theological carelessness.
- Isaiah 11: 1, And there <u>shall come forth a rod out of the stem of Jesse, and a Branch shall grow out of his roots</u>:
- Jeremiah 23: 5, Behold, the days come, saith the Lord, that <u>I will raise unto David a righteous Branch,</u> and a King shall reign and prosper, and shall execute judgment and justice in the earth.
- Jeremiah 33: 15, In those days, and at that time, <u>will I cause the Branch of righteousness to grow up unto David</u>; and he shall execute judgment and righteousness in the land.
- Zechariah 3: 8, Hear now, O Joshua the high priest, thou, and thy fellows that sit before thee: for they are men wondered at: for, <u>behold, I will bring forth my servant the Branch</u>.
- Zechariah 6: 12, And speak unto him, saying, Thus speaketh the Lord of

hosts, saying, <u>Behold the man whose name is The Branch; and he shall grow up out of his place, and he shall build the temple of the Lord</u>:

None of the above scriptures describe the branch of salvation as Israel but as the Messiah providing redemption for Israel. All of these scriptures and Yeshua's own testimony confirm that we are to be grafted into the Lord (YHWH), and as a consequence of that covenant of faith and belief in His name we are saved, not by any work or worth of our own.

Being joined to the Messiah Yeshua, we become "the commonwealth of Israel" (Ephesians 2:12). We will explore further why there is absolutely no pass on accepting the work of Yeshua, even for those who keep the Torah, and consequently why there is only one name under heaven by which we must be saved, for both Jews and Gentiles. The mystery related to this issue focuses upon the two administrations of death and resurrection.

Acts 4: 11, This is the stone which was set at nought of you builders, which is become the head of the corner. 12 <u>Neither is there salvation in any other: for there is none other name under heaven given among men, whereby we must be saved</u>. 13 Now when they saw the boldness of Peter and John, and perceived that they were unlearned and ignorant men, they marvelled; and they took knowledge of them, that they had been with Yeshua.

You must be grafted into the Messiah Yeshua, the manifest Name of YHWH, in order to be saved. It does not matter if you are Jew or Gentile, bond or free, at home or abroad (Galatians 3:28, Colossians 3:11). The salvific act does not depend upon your ability to keep the Torah. Keeping the Torah will not save you, it will leave you under condemnation and death without the resurrected manifest Name of YHWH, the Messiah Yeshua, the administrator of the Resurrected Covenant (Torah). Once you have the Messiah and are grafted into Him, you are then of the commonwealth of Israel.

Ephesians 2: 8, For <u>by grace are ye saved through faith; and that not of yourselves</u>: it is the gift of God: 9 Not of works, lest any man should boast. 10 For we are his workmanship, <u>created in Christ Yeshua</u> unto good works, which God hath before ordained that we should walk in them. 11 Wherefore remember, that ye being in time past Gentiles in the flesh, who are called Uncircumcision by that which is called the Circumcision in the flesh made by hands; 12 That <u>at that time ye were without Christ, being aliens from the commonwealth of Israel</u>, and strangers from the covenants of promise, having no hope, and without God in the world: 13 But now in Christ Yeshua ye who sometimes were far off are made nigh by the blood of Christ. 14 For he is our peace, who hath made both one, and hath broken down the middle wall of partition between us; 15 Having abolished in his flesh the enmity, even the law of commandments contained in ordinances; for <u>to make in himself of twain one new man</u>, so making peace; 16 And that he might reconcile both <u>unto God in one body</u> by the cross, having slain the enmity thereby:

Many have incorrectly stated that this one new man is Israel or Judah or the joining of both. If you look more closely you will see that it is through the redemption of the Messiah that we (both Jews and Gentiles) become a part of His body, the commonwealth of Israel. Without the Messiah, there is no commonwealth of Israel and there is no peace between man and God.

The enmity that is slain is not between the two houses of Israel, although they will surely be joined together in the Messiah Yeshua. The enmity that is slain is between God and us, because of our violations of the covenant and our lack of faith in His provision of the manifest Name of YHWH to become our righteousness through faith.

Notice those who are strangers to the commonwealth of Israel and the covenants of promise are "without the Messiah". This is what makes you either a part of the commonwealth of Israel or apart from it. Being without the Messiah makes you strangers from God.

> Ephesians 2: 12, That <u>at that time ye were without Christ, being aliens from the commonwealth of Israel</u>, and strangers from the covenants of promise, having no hope, and without God in the world: 13 But now in Christ Yeshua ye who sometimes were far off are made nigh by the blood of Christ.

It is not the Torah that makes you of the commonwealth of Israel, it is having the Messiah via faith in His manifest Name, YHWH. We can see this tree is all about faith in the manifest Name of YHWH, the Messiah Yeshua. He bears the branches, the branches do not bear Him by their own works or worth. We also see Paul addressing this very same issue with the Corinthians.

> 1 Corinthians 13: 1, And I, brethren, could not speak unto you as unto spiritual, but as unto carnal, even as unto babes in Christ. 2 I have fed you with milk, and not with meat: for hitherto ye were not able to bear it, neither yet now are ye able. 3 For ye are yet carnal: for whereas there is among you envying, and strife, and divisions, are ye not carnal, and walk as men? 4 For while one saith, I am of Paul; and another, I am of Apollos; are ye not carnal? 5 Who then is Paul, and who is Apollos, <u>but ministers by whom ye believed</u>, even as the Lord gave to every man? 6 I have planted, Apollos watered; but God gave the increase. 7 So then neither is he that planteth any thing, neither he that watereth; but God that giveth the increase. 8 Now he that planteth and he that watereth are one: and every man shall receive his own reward according to his own labour. 9 For we are labourers together with God: ye are God's husbandry, ye are God's building. 10 According to the grace of God which is given unto me, as a wise masterbuilder, I have laid the foundation, and another buildeth thereon. But let every man take heed how he buildeth thereupon. 11 <u>For other foundation can no man lay than that is laid, which is Yeshua.</u>

Notice how Paul focuses upon the imagery and fractals of nature. He says he is involved in the season of planting seeds, fulfilling the imagery of death, burial, and hiddenness.

Mark 4: 25, For he that hath, to him shall be given: and he that hath not, from him shall be taken even that which he hath. 26 And he said, So is the kingdom of God, as if a man should cast seed into the ground; 27 And should sleep, and rise night and day, and the seed should spring and grow up, he knoweth not how.

The prophets and Apostles stated that later there would be a season of "latter rain", "harvest", and "revelation" (manifestation). Yeshua said God would restore the Kingdom of God in its due "season". As we have already pointed out, the work of the Messiah and the seed He is sowing starts first in the heart of faith.

Luke 17: 20, And when he was demanded of the Pharisees, when the kingdom of God should come, he answered them and said, The kingdom of God cometh not with observation: 21 Neither shall they say, Lo here! or, lo there! for, behold, the kingdom of God is within you.

Once this seed has taken root it will manifest itself in the end at the appropriate season.

Acts 1: 6, When they therefore were come together, they asked of him, saying, Lord, wilt thou at this time restore again the kingdom to Israel? 7 And he said unto them, It is not for you to know the times or the seasons, which the Father hath put in his own power.

Paul is clear, redemption comes only by the manifest Name of YHWH, the Messiah Yeshua. It does not matter who taught you or who baptized you. Paul did not save you. You were not baptized into Israel. You were baptized into the manifest Name of YHWH, Yeshua the Messiah!

1 Corinthians 1: 12, Now this I say, that every one of you saith, I am of Paul; and I of Apollos; and I of Cephas; and I of Christ. 13 <u>Is Christ divided? was Paul crucified for you? or were ye baptized in the name of Paul</u>? 14 I thank God that I baptized none of you, but Crispus and Gaius; 15 Lest any should say that I had baptized in mine own name. 16 And I baptized also the household of Stephanas: besides, I know not whether I baptized any other. 17 For Christ sent me not to baptize, but to preach the Gospel: not with wisdom of words, lest the cross of Christ should be made of none effect. 18 For the preaching of the cross is to them that perish foolishness; but unto us which are saved it is the power of God. 19 For it is written, I will destroy the wisdom of the wise, and will bring to nothing the understanding of the prudent. 20 Where is the wise? where is the scribe? where is the disputer of this world? hath not God made foolish the wisdom of this world? 21 For after that in the wisdom of God the world by wisdom knew not God, it pleased God by the foolishness of preaching to save them that believe. 22 For the Jews require a sign, and the Greeks seek after wisdom: 23 But <u>we preach Christ crucified</u>, unto the Jews a stumblingblock, and unto the Greeks foolishness; 24 But unto them which are called, both Jews and Greeks, Christ the power of God, and the wisdom of

God.

It is this crucifixion tree that the manifest Name of YHWH, Yeshua the Messiah, was affixed to that pictures the engrafting of the believer into the covenant of faith. We should conform our image to His image.

On that first Pentecost you do not see the birth of the church, you see the fulfillment of the manifestation of the image of God in the Apostles. The imagery presented is the union of male (Spirit of the Messiah) and female (the bodily believer). It is manifested in the Shekinah Glory (Pillar of cloud & fire that led Israel in the wilderness, Exodus 13:21) dwelling upon new tabernacles and giving them the Utterance of God.

> Acts 2: 1, And when the day of Pentecost was fully come, they were all with one accord in one place. 2 And suddenly there came a sound from heaven as of a rushing mighty wind, and it filled all the house where they were sitting. 3 And there appeared unto them cloven tongues like as of fire, and it sat upon each of them. 4 And they were all filled with the Holy Ghost, and began to speak with other tongues, as the Spirit gave them Utterance. 5 And there were dwelling at Jerusalem Jews, devout men, out of every nation under heaven. 6 Now when this was noised abroad, the multitude came together, and were confounded, because that every man heard them speak in his own language.

Those of faith are Israel. We are not grafted into Israel, we are grafted into the Messiah. We are in complete agreement that you are not justified by keeping the Written Torah. We are justified by Yeshua. Once you believe, you should have the same question on your lips as the Jews who killed Christ. "Men and brethren what shall we do" (Acts 2:37–38)?

The example of Yeshua and the Apostles is to begin to learn the Written Torah. As Israel you should have the sign of the Covenant, the 7th day Sabbath. In regard to the contention that there is no New Testament command to keep the 7th day Sabbath, such a statement is scripturally and factually incorrect. This is a prophetic warning for the end–times from the lips of Yeshua.

> Matthew 24: 20, But pray ye that your flight be not in the winter, <u>neither on the Sabbath day</u>:

And as our final rest is in Yeshua, we should do as He did all His life, and rest on the 7th day Sabbath. As to justification, the Law will not save you, which is the work of the Messiah. Once you are saved you should keep His commandments.

> John 15: 10, <u>If ye keep my commandments, ye shall abide in my love</u>; even as I have kept my Father's commandments, and abide in his love.

After all it was Yeshua that spoke from Mt. Sinai. We see Him in the wilderness.

> 1 Corinthians 10: 3, And did all eat the same spiritual meat; 4 And did all

drink the same spiritual drink: for <u>they drank of that spiritual rock that followed them: and that rock was Christ</u>. 5 But with <u>many of them God was not well pleased</u>: for they were overthrown in the wilderness.

We see the Messiah (the manifest Name of YHWH) administrating the Resurrected Covenant in prophetic type at the giving of the second set of tablets after Israel had broken the first covenant by their worship of the golden calf.

Exodus 34: And the Lord said unto Moses, Hew thee two tablets of stone <u>like unto the first: and I will write upon these tablets the words that were in the first tablets</u>, which thou brakest. 2 And be ready in the morning, and come up in the morning unto mount Sinai, and present thyself there to me in the top of the mount. 3 And no man shall come up with thee, neither let any man be seen throughout all the mount; neither let the flocks nor herds feed before that mount. 4 And he hewed two tablets of stone like unto the first; and Moses rose up early in the morning, and went up unto mount Sinai, as the Lord had commanded him, and took in his hand the two tablets of stone. 5 And the <u>Lord descended in the cloud, and stood with him there, and proclaimed the Name of the Lord</u>. 6 And <u>the Lord passed by before him, and proclaimed, The Lord, The Lord God, merciful and gracious, longsuffering, and abundant in goodness and truth, 7 Keeping mercy</u> for thousands, forgiving iniquity and transgression and sin, and that will by no means clear the guilty; visiting the iniquity of the fathers upon the children, and upon the children's children, unto the third and to the fourth generation. 8 And Moses made haste, and bowed his head toward the earth, <u>and worshipped</u>.

This was none other than Yeshua presented as the Name of the Lord (YHWH) administering the New/Resurrected Covenant with grace and abundant mercy. The sign of that covenant is the same today as it was then, as it will be in the Millennium. Paul knew this to be true.

Acts 18: 4, And he reasoned in the synagogue <u>every Sabbath</u>, and persuaded the <u>Jews and the Greeks.</u>

Do not be confused into thinking there are two ways for the one body. There is only one way, and one law. There is only one new administrator for Jews and Gentiles. There is no pass on accepting the new administrator.

9 CAN GENTILE BELIEVERS MURDER, STEAL, LIE, & COMMIT ADULTERY AND STILL BE CHRISTIANS? THEY CAN IF YOU BELIEVE ACTS 15 ONLY HAS 4 BASIC REQUIREMENTS FOR GENTILE BELIEVERS...

PRO "GRACE VERSUS LAW" POSITIONS:

    1. Romans 11 is not relevant to "Grace versus Law".

    2. Even if first century Christians were keeping the 7th day Sabbath in the New Testament, there is no binding command on Gentiles anywhere in the New Testament to keep the 7th day Sabbath.

    3. If Christians that meet on Sundays are in sin, God will convict them. If they are in sin, many more would have been more convicted about this issue by now. Good Christians can disagree.

    4. In Acts 15, there are 4 prohibitions that correspond to the four requirements to the alien who sojourns in your/their midst in Leviticus 17–18.
They are:

        • Things sacrificed to idols which is seen in Leviticus 17: 7–9, 2

        • Blood (i. e., eating blood) as seen in Leviticus 17: 10, 12, 3

        • Things strangled (i. e., meat which has not been strangled in such a way as to drain the blood from it) are prohibited by implication in Leviticus 17: 13, 4)

        • Sexual immorality which is seen in Leviticus 18: 26 and covers all prohibited forms of sexual practice in Leviticus 18: 6–

23

- Gentile members of the messianic people of God are to refrain from these moral impurities.

5. There is nothing about Gentiles needing to keep the 7th day Sabbath in Acts 15. Anyone that says there is, is reading into the text something that does not exist.

6. Since they are members of the messianic people as Gentiles by faith in Yeshua, they do not have to be circumcised and keep other aspects of the Torah in order to be morally pure, just keep specific prohibitions of the Torah against the above mentioned four polluting practices.

7. This was done in order that they wouldn't be suspected of idolatry and immorality which would impede fellowship between Jews and Gentiles in the church.

REBUTTAL; PRO GRACE & LAW
FALSE ALLEGATIONS BROUGHT IN A COURT OF LAW AGAINST PAUL THE APOSTLE…
If you accept that Acts 15 is all that Gentile believers have to do in order to be a true follower of Yeshua, then you need to be prepared to allow justified Gentile Christians to murder, steal, commit adultery, and lie, because they are not listed as requirements in Acts 15.

The context of Acts 15 is clearly the rejection of Pharisaic Oral Torah requirements added to the Law of Moses. Pharisaic Judaism required converts to observe both the Written Law of Moses and the Oral Torah of the rabbis. The apostles were teaching only the Written Torah of Moses and were rejecting the Pharisees' demand that new converts keep both. These basic rules for new believers were never intended to replace the Law of Moses—the Apostles were happy to have new believers learn it in the synagogues every Sabbath. (Acts 15: 21)

Please also remember that these same Pharisees brought false accusations against Paul in a court of law, saying that he was teaching against the Law of Moses. Notice these false allegations that were brought against Paul were un-provable.

Acts 25: 6, And when he had tarried among them more than ten days, he went down unto Caesarea; and the next day <u>sitting on the judgment seat</u> commanded Paul to be brought. 7 And when he was come, the Jews which came down from Jerusalem stood round about, <u>and laid many and grievous complaints against Paul, which they could not prove.</u> 8 While he answered for himself, <u>Neither against the law of the Jews,</u> neither against the temple, nor yet against Caesar, have I offended any thing at all.

Notice these Pharisees falsely accused Paul of teaching the people to violate the Law of Moses. What was the outcome? They could not prove their allegations.

This is an actual historical record from a documented court case proving that Paul did not teach anyone (Jew or Gentile) to violate the Written Law of Moses. The Apostle Paul goes so far as to publicly state that in regard to all of these charges, "Neither against the law of the Jews, neither against the temple, nor yet against Caesar, have I offended any thing at all." He pleads complete innocence of these false charges. Logically we affirm what he is actually teaching by his own testimony. We see there are false allegations brought up earlier in Acts.

> Acts 21: 27, And when the seven days were almost ended, the Jews which were of Asia, when they saw him in the temple, stirred up all the people, and laid hands on him, 28 Crying out, Men of Israel, help: <u>This is the man, that teacheth all men every where against the people, and the law, and this place</u>: and further brought Greeks also into the temple, and hath polluted this holy place. 29 (For they had seen before with him in the city Trophimus an Ephesian, whom they supposed that Paul had brought into the temple.)

These were the same charges that could not be proven in Acts 25. They were alleging the same thing that "Grace versus Law" proponents claim, that Paul was teaching "everyone", Jew and Gentile, that they do not need to keep the Written Law of Moses. They were unable to prove their claims and Paul flatly denied those false allegations in a court of law. This court case is historically documented for our benefit. To deny the facts of this eye–witness testimony is damning for those who would claim to pursue truth, logic, and scientific method.

Again, we have factual history from a documented court case of the chief priests and the elders falsely claiming that Paul was teaching "everyone" to violate the Written Law of Moses. What does that mean? Paul was not teaching anyone to violate the Written Law of Moses. It was a false and untrue allegation that they could not prove or bring one witness to support and Paul flatly denied the allegation!

How do we read Acts 15 then? The Pharisaic believers wanted new Gentile believers in Yeshua to convert to Rabbinic Judaism and keep both the Written Torah of Moses and the Oral Traditions of the rabbis (which Yeshua taught against) before sitting and eating with the Jews. How do we know this? The principal requirement mentioned in Acts 15 is circumcision and that is the entry requirement to make a proselyte for Rabbinic Jews.

The central question of Acts 15 is, "should Gentile believers in Yeshua keep only the Written Law of Moses or additionally the Oral Torah of the rabbis".

The answer from factual history proves that Paul taught all people to observe the Written Law of Moses. We also know that the allegation that Paul was teaching believers to violate the Written Law of Moses was indeed false…then…and now.

Logically we also know that the few restrictions for new believers are not the sum total of what was required of them, as additional restrictions on adultery, murder, theft, and lying, are detailed in other apostolic writings, the Written Law of Moses, and the Tanach (Old Testament). To state that all a Gentile believer needs to do is listed in Acts 15 clearly contradicts the Old and New Testament scriptures. Knowing that your allegation that "the Law is done away" is proven false, by history, by scripture, and by logic, do you really love Yeshua?

10 FACTUAL BURDEN OF PROOF IN A COURT OF LAW...

P RO GRACE & LAW: REBUTTAL CONTINUED...
FACTUAL BURDEN OF PROOF IN A COURT OF LAW...
Let's discuss burden of proof. It is no longer on those who are
saved by grace, follow the scriptures, and keep the Written Torah of
Moses. The burden of proof is on those who are lawless and disregard the
testimony of historical fact and the scriptural record.

1. Yeshua said the Written Torah of Moses would not pass away so long as
heaven and earth remain.

Matthew 5: 17, <u>Think not that I am come to destroy the law, or the
prophets</u>: I am not come to destroy, but to fulfil. 18 For verily I say unto you,
<u>Till heaven and earth pass, one jot or one tittle shall in no wise pass from the
law</u>, till all be fulfilled. 19 <u>Whosoever therefore shall break one of these least
commandments, and shall teach men so</u>, he shall be called the least in the
kingdom of heaven: but whosoever shall do and teach them, the same shall be
called great in the kingdom of heaven.

Yeshua is not discussing some internal moral law, He is talking about the
Written Torah of Moses. Instead of following Yeshua's divinely spoken words,
many Christians adhere to misinterpretation of Paul over the word of the Son of
God. Logically the Son of God has more authority than Paul. Believers need to
reconcile that simple fact. Heaven and earth have not passed away.

2. Yeshua, the Apostles, and Paul all fought the Rabbinic Oral Traditions
that the Pharisees were trying to make new believers observe. This is clearly

and frequently historically documented.

Mark 7: 4, And when they come from the market, <u>except they wash, they eat not. And many other things there be, which they have received to hold, as the washing of cups, and pots, brasen vessels, and of tablets.</u> 5 Then the <u>Pharisees and scribes asked him, Why walk not thy disciples according to the tradition of the elders,</u> but eat bread with unwashen hands? 6 He answered and said unto them, Well hath Esaias prophesied of you hypocrites, as it is written, This people honoureth me with their lips, but their heart is far from me.

Paul confirms that his former opinion, before being saved by Yeshua, was the same as the Pharisees in regard to the Oral Torah. He is not talking about the "Commandments of God", he is talking about the "traditions of men".

Galatians 1: 14, And profited in the Jews' religion above many my equals in mine own nation, <u>being more exceedingly zealous of the traditions of my fathers.</u>

Both Yeshua and Paul are in complete agreement. They are both against the Oral Law of the Pharisees. So if Paul is in clear agreement with Yeshua on the Oral Traditions, why would he logically not be in complete agreement with Yeshua on the Written Torah of Moses? He is and he confirms it.

Romans 3: 31, Do we then make void the law through faith? God forbid: yea, we establish the law.

Paul is clarifying the simple fact that we are justified, saved, and redeemed through no act of our own, but purely by faith in Yeshua's sacrifice. Having clarified how we are saved, he goes on to clarify what we are to do once we are saved: "establish the Law (Written Torah of Moses)".

3. We have historical documented court cases proving the Pharisees falsely accused Paul of teaching others to violate the Law of Moses.

Acts 21: 27, And when the seven days were almost ended, the Jews which were of Asia, when they saw him in the temple, stirred up all the people, and laid hands on him, 28 Crying out, Men of Israel, help: This is the man, that teacheth all men every where against the people, and the law, and this place: and further brought Greeks also into the temple, and hath polluted this holy place. 29 (For they had seen before with him in the city Trophimus an Ephesian, whom they supposed that Paul had brought into the temple.)

The Pharisees repeatedly bring the same false charge against Paul and repeatedly they cannot provide any proof of any of those allegations. Furthermore, Paul vehemently rejects those false allegations.

Acts 25: 6, And when he had tarried among them more than ten days, he went down unto Caesarea; and the next day <u>sitting on the judgment seat</u> commanded Paul to be brought. 7 And when he was come, the Jews which came down from Jerusalem stood round about, <u>and laid many and grievous complaints against Paul, which they could not prove</u>. 8 While he answered for himself, <u>Neither against the law of the Jews</u>, neither against the temple, nor yet against Caesar, <u>have I offended any thing at all</u>.

4. We have clear historical documented eye–witness proof that Jewish and Gentile believers observed the 7th day Sabbath in the synagogue as one unified body.
- Acts 18: 4, And he reasoned in the synagogue <u>every Sabbath</u>, and persuaded the <u>Jews and the Greeks</u>.
- Acts 13: 42, And when the Jews were gone out of the synagogue, the Gentiles besought that these words might be preached to them <u>the next Sabbath</u>.
- Acts 13: 44, And the <u>next Sabbath day</u> came almost the whole city together to <u>hear the word of God</u>.

5. We have clear New Testament proof that Yeshua had the expectation that His followers would be observing the 7th day Sabbath.

Matthew 24: 20, But pray ye that your flight be not in the winter, <u>neither on the Sabbath day</u>:

6. We have clear prophetic testimony that the 7th day Sabbath will be observed by "all flesh", not just Jews, in the Millennium.
- Isaiah 66: 22, For as the new heavens and the new earth, which I will make, shall remain before me, saith the Lord, so shall your seed and your name remain. 23 And it shall come to pass, that from one new moon to another, and from one <u>Sabbath to another, shall all flesh come to worship before me</u>, saith the Lord.
- Ezekiel 46: 1, Thus saith the Lord God; The gate of the inner court that looketh toward the east <u>shall be shut the six working days; but on the Sabbath it shall be opened</u>, and in the day of the new moon it shall be opened.

7. We have contextual factual documented proof that the central issue of the Jerusalem council was whether new believers needed to be circumcised before eating with Jewish believers and beginning to learn the Written Law of Moses. The issue in question is whether new Gentile believers needed to convert to Rabbinic Judaism <u>and</u> keep the Oral Torah (Traditions of the rabbis) and the Written Torah or just keep the Written Torah. Yeshua had already made His position on this issue clear.

Matthew 15: 3, But he answered and said unto them, Why do <u>ye also transgress the commandment of God by your tradition</u>?

This seems to be really important to Yeshua. What about Paul? Does he feel the same way?

> Colossians 2: 8, Beware lest any man spoil you through philosophy and vain deceit, <u>after the tradition of men</u>, after the rudiments of the world, and not after Christ. 9 For in him dwelleth all the fulness of the Godhead bodily. 10 And ye are complete in him, which is the head of all principality and power: 11 In whom also ye are circumcised with the circumcision made without hands, in putting off the body of the sins of the flesh by the circumcision of Christ: 12 Buried with him in baptism, wherein also ye are risen with him through the faith of the operation of God, who hath raised him from the dead. 13 And you, being dead in your sins and the uncircumcision of your flesh, hath he quickened together with him, having forgiven you all trespasses; 14 Blotting out the handwriting of ordinances that was against us, which was contrary to us, and took it out of the way, nailing it to his cross; 15 And having spoiled principalities and powers, he made a shew of them openly, triumphing over them in it. 16 Let no man therefore judge you in meat, or in drink, or in respect of an holyday, or of the new moon, or of the Sabbath days: 17 Which are a shadow of things to come; but the body is of Christ. 18 Let no man beguile you of your reward in a voluntary humility and worshipping of angels, intruding into those things which he hath not seen, vainly puffed up by his fleshly mind, 19 And not holding the Head, from which all the body by joints and bands having nourishment ministered, and knit together, increaseth with the increase of God. 20 Wherefore if ye be dead with Christ from the rudiments of the world, why, as though living in the world, are ye subject to ordinances, 21 (Touch not; taste not; handle not; 22 Which all are to perish with the using;) <u>after the commandments and doctrines of men</u>?

The context of Colossians 2 is correcting believers from following these Pharisaical Oral Traditions that violate the Written Torah. Paul starts and ends Colossians 2 with the "traditions of men" and "commandments and doctrines of men". Notice how Yeshua contrasts the "tradition of men" with the "commandment of God". They are not the same thing.

> Mark 7: 8, For laying aside the commandment of God, ye hold the tradition of men, as the washing of pots and cups: and many other such like things ye do.

This is the same issue Peter was dealing with when the Pharisees were demanding that new believers first be circumcised before eating with Jews. This was an Oral Torah rabbinical tradition and not a requirement of the Written Torah. To say that they are the same thing is nothing but theological carelessness.

> 8. We have confirmed there are not two ways of salvation for Christians and that the Body of Christ is not divided. Jewish and Gentile believers were to be doing the same things.

1 Corinthians 1: 12, Now this I say, that every one of you saith, I am of Paul; and I of Apollos; and I of Cephas; and I of Christ. 13 Is Christ divided? Was Paul crucified for you? or were ye baptized in the name of Paul? 14 I thank God that I baptized none of you, but Crispus and Gaius;

Paul would again appear to be saying that there is only one way.

- 1 Corinthians 12: 13, For by one Spirit are we all baptized into one body, whether we be Jews or Gentiles, whether we be bond or free; and have been all made to drink into one Spirit.
- Galatians 3: 28, There is neither Jew nor Greek, there is neither bond nor free, there is neither male nor female: for ye are all one in Christ Yeshua.

9. We have confirmed that the New Testament teaches that those of faith are Israel, the church was not born on Pentecost, and it was not a separate entity from Israel. Those who are Israel should bear the sign of the covenant of Israel, the 7th day Sabbath.

Ephesians 2: 12, That at that time ye were without Christ, being aliens from the commonwealth of Israel, and strangers from the covenants of promise, having no hope, and without God in the world: 13 But now in Christ Yeshua ye who sometimes were far off are made nigh by the blood of Christ.

God gave His own signet to confirm who His Israel is.

Exodus 31: 13, Speak thou also unto the children of Israel, saying, Verily my sabbaths ye shall keep: for it is a sign between me and you throughout your generations; that ye may know that I am the Lord that doth sanctify you.

What is the sign of the covenant between God and His redeemed?
"My sabbaths ye shall keep: for it is a sign between me and you"

How long should this signet confirm who God's people (Israel) were?
"Throughout your generations".

Why do we keep the sign?
"That ye may know that I am the Lord that doth sanctify you."

If prior to being "saved" you were not Israel and Ephesians 2:12 clarifies that because you are now "with Christ" then you are no longer a stranger to the "covenant of promise" and you are now a member of the "commonwealth of Israel", so then you should bear the sign as well.

10. We have confirmed that it was Yeshua that gave those very same commandments at Mt. Sinai.

1 Corinthians 10: 3, And did all eat the same spiritual meat; 4 And did all drink the same spiritual drink: for they drank of that spiritual rock that followed

them: and that rock was Christ. 5 But with many of them God was not well pleased: for they were overthrown in the wilderness.

We also see Yeshua administering the Resurrected Covenant in type at the giving of the second set of tablets after Israel had broken the first covenant by their worship of the golden calf.

Exodus 34: 1, And the Lord said unto Moses, Hew thee two tablets of stone like unto the first: and I will write upon these tablets the words that were in the first tablets, which thou brakest. 2 And be ready in the morning, and come up in the morning unto mount Sinai, and present thyself there to me in the top of the mount. 3 And no man shall come up with thee, neither let any man be seen throughout all the mount; neither let the flocks nor herds feed before that mount. 4 And he hewed two tablets of stone like unto the first; and Moses rose up early in the morning, and went up unto mount Sinai, as the Lord had commanded him, and took in his hand the two tablets of stone. 5 And the Lord descended in the cloud, and stood with him there, and proclaimed the Name of the Lord. 6 And the Lord passed by before him, and proclaimed, The Lord, The Lord God, merciful and gracious, longsuffering, and abundant in goodness and truth, 7 Keeping mercy for thousands, forgiving iniquity and transgression and sin, and that will by no means clear the guilty; visiting the iniquity of the fathers upon the children, and upon the children's children, unto the third and to the fourth generation. 8 And Moses made haste, and bowed his head toward the earth, and worshipped.

This was none other than Yeshua presented as the Name of the Lord administering the New/Resurrected Covenant.

11. We have confirmed that it is Yeshua's own expectation that we keep those very same commandments. It is so important to Him that He verbally instructs His followers to keep them.

John 15: 10, If ye keep my commandments, ye shall abide in my love; even as I have kept my Father's commandments, and abide in his love.

To assume that Yeshua kept His Father's commandments but then gives us a pass on keeping them is unscriptural and illogical. What is the future for those who are willfully ignorant of the truth of the scriptures?

Romans 1: 21, Because that, when they knew God, they glorified him not as God, neither were thankful; but became vain in their imaginations, and their foolish heart was darkened. 22 Professing themselves to be wise, they became fools,

A lack of faith in God leads to a darkening of the heart. This leads to lawlessness and selfishness.

1 Corinthians 15: 32, If after the manner of men I have fought with beasts at Ephesus, what advantageth it me, if the dead rise not? let us eat and drink; for to morrow we die. 33 Be not deceived: evil communications corrupt good manners. 34 Awake to righteousness, and sin not; for some have not the knowledge of God: I speak this to your shame.

Unfortunately this corrupt lack of faith will manifest itself in the last days in a complete failure of people to obey God.

2 Timothy 3: 1, This know also, that in the last days perilous times shall come. 2 For men shall be lovers of their own selves, covetous, boasters, proud, blasphemers, disobedient to parents, unthankful, unholy, 3 Without natural affection, trucebreakers, false accusers, incontinent, fierce, despisers of those that are good, 4 Traitors, heady, highminded, lovers of pleasures more than lovers of God; 5 Having a form of godliness, but denying the power thereof: from such turn away. 6 For of this sort are they which creep into houses, and lead captive silly women laden with sins, led away with divers lusts, 7 Ever learning, and never able to come to the knowledge of the truth. 8 Now as Jannes and Jambres withstood Moses, so do these also resist the truth: men of corrupt minds, reprobate concerning the faith. 9 But they shall proceed no further: for their folly shall be manifest unto all men, as their's also was.

Those that deny the patterns and fractals that God designed in all things will become foolish and unlearned. Refusal to see and hear the truth that He is continually speaking in His manifest images and creation leads to darkness.

Romans 1: 19, Because that which may be known of God is manifest in them; for God hath shewed it unto them. 20 For the invisible things of him from the creation of the world are clearly seen, being understood by the things that are made, even his eternal power and Godhead; so that they are without excuse: 21 Because that, when they knew God, they glorified him not as God, neither were thankful; but became vain in their imaginations, and their foolish heart was darkened.

All we need to do is follow the images, patterns, and fractals presented by God and His designed meanings. If we do so, we will grow in wisdom and we will be "full of light". If we refuse to do so, we will have hearts and minds that are willfully darkened. Check the patterns, follow their meanings, and prove it for yourself.

Matthew 6: 22, The light of the body is the eye: if therefore thine eye be single, thy whole body shall be full of light. But if thine eye be evil, thy whole body shall be full of darkness. If therefore the light that is in thee be darkness, how great is that darkness!

Will you "proceed further" as one who embraces the natural patterns of "truth" or be one of those Yeshua mentioned, "the least in the kingdom"?

Truth:
trooTH/noun
The quality or state of being true.
"he had to accept the truth of her accusation"
synonyms: veracity, truthfulness, verity, sincerity, candor, honesty;
antonyms: dishonesty, falseness
That which is true or in accordance with fact or reality.
noun: the truth
"tell me the truth"
synonyms: what actually happened, the case, so; More
A fact or belief that is accepted as true.
plural noun: truths
"the emergence of scientific truths"
synonyms: fact, verity, certainty, certitude; More

Matthew 5: 17, <u>Think not that I am come to destroy the law</u>, or the prophets: I am not come to destroy, but to fulfil. 18 For verily I say unto you, <u>Till heaven and earth pass, one jot or one tittle shall in no wise pass from the law</u>, till all be fulfilled. 19 <u>Whosoever therefore shall break one of these least commandments, and shall teach men so, he shall be called the least in the kingdom of heaven</u>: but whosoever shall do and teach them, the same shall be called great in the kingdom of heaven.

Keep in mind, this is Yeshua, the Son of God, talking. What will you do? The burden of proof is upon you. Most "Grace versus Law" presentations on this topic suffer from the following fatal flaws.

- The "Grace versus Law" paradigm of factual events in the first century is scripturally and factually inaccurate.
- The "Grace versus Law" paradigm that Paul is more authoritative than Yeshua is fatally flawed.
- The "Grace versus Law" paradigm that Paul and Peter are telling people not to observe the Written Law of Moses is factually incorrect.
- The "Grace versus Law" paradigm disregards historical legal documents and eye–witness testimony showing a bias away from facts and towards "what you want".
- The "Grace versus Law" paradigm suffers from poor education of the Law of Moses and rabbinical Oral Torah which prevents accurate understanding of the issues of the first century church.
- The "Grace versus Law" paradigm has a willful disregard of clear instructions from Yeshua, the Apostles, and Paul that the Written Torah is not

done away and needs to be established by all believers.

- o Luke 16: 17, And it is easier for heaven and earth to pass, than one tittle of the law to fail.
- o Acts 13: 14, but when they departed from Perga, they came to Antioch in Pisidia, <u>and went into the synagogue on the Sabbath day</u>, and sat down. 15 And <u>after the reading of the law</u> and the prophets the rulers of the synagogue sent unto them, saying, Ye men and brethren, if ye have any word of exhortation for the people, say on. 16 Then Paul stood up, and beckoning with his hand said, <u>Men of Israel, and ye that fear God</u>, give audience.

12. The central issue of Acts 15 is if new believers must keep both the Law of Moses and the Oral Torah of the rabbis which required new believers to be circumcised immediately.

Acts 15: 5, But there rose up certain of the sect of the Pharisees which believed, saying, That it was needful to circumcise them, <u>and</u> to command them to keep the law of Moses.

The Apostles confirm they gave no such commandment that new believers must do both.

Acts 15: 24, Forasmuch as we have heard, that certain which went out from us have troubled you with words, subverting your souls, saying, Ye must be circumcised, <u>and</u> keep the law: to whom we gave no such commandment:

The issue is clear, they are clarifying there is no need for new converts to do both, this does not logically preclude new converts from doing one, keeping the Law of Moses. These same teachers in all their other writings affirm that new believers need to keep the Written Law of Moses. The Jerusalem council affirms in Acts 15 with clarity that new believers need to only do one of these items, keep and learn the Law of Moses.

Acts 15: 21, For Moses of old time hath in every city them that preach him, being read in the synagogues every Sabbath day.

So let's use the scientific method. If you are not interested in using objectivity and a logical methodology on issues that you may have a biased, incorrect, unscriptural, and historically un-factual understanding of, you may never come to the point of acknowledging truth that you currently disagree with. Now if you truly love Yeshua and truth, none of this should offend you. You will want to prove what the truth is and not "what you want".

11 WHAT DO YOU DO WHEN YOU DO NOT LIKE THE TRUTH...OR THE FACTS?

Typically this kind of healthy debate will devolve quickly into accusations like:

- Your belief betrays an unhealthy obsession.
- I am going to address your claims, in the hope that you might wake up from your very serious confusion.
- You are a Judaizer.
- No, we are not going to knuckle under to Judaizers and become 1st century Jews.
- I hope that you come to see the error of your obsession.
- I would think that if they are in sin, many more would have been more convicted about this issue by now.

Please do not take these comments personally, just stick to the documented history, the scriptural facts, and a logical methodology that reconciles all of the scriptures, not just the ones you favor.

As we have seen, the scriptures are very clear and precise in their accuracy. Unfortunately for many scripturally un–educated they are confusing because they appear to be making conflicting statements. Things become quite clear once you remove the incorrect paradigm of "law versus grace" and replace it with the scripturally accurate paradigm of "saved by grace and follow Yeshua by keeping the Written Torah". This means that like Yeshua we reject the conflicting Oral Torah of the rabbis and modern oral traditions that are not biblical.

I say scripturally un–educated because most of these debates will likely be with those who have doctorates in their specific brand of oral tradition, but may have little actual study of the written scriptures. This is not much different from the time of Yeshua. The pattern is the same, truth is in the wilderness crying out against the establishment of "un–truths". We are left with this end time warning that precedes the literal day of the Lord and the return of Yeshua.

Malachi 4: 1, For, behold, the day cometh, that shall burn as an oven; and all the proud, yea, and all that do wickedly, shall be stubble: and the day that cometh shall burn them up, saith the Lord of hosts, that it shall leave them neither root nor branch. 2 But unto you that fear my name shall the sun of righteousness arise with healing in his wings; and ye shall go forth, and grow up as calves of the stall. 3 And ye shall tread down the wicked; for they shall be ashes under the soles of your feet in the day that I shall do this, saith the Lord of hosts. 4 Remember ye the law of Moses my servant, which I commanded unto him in Horeb for all Israel, with the statutes and judgments. 5 Behold, I will send you Elijah the prophet before the coming of the great and dreadful day of the Lord: 6 And he shall turn the heart of the fathers to the children, and the heart of the children to their fathers, lest I come and smite the earth with a curse.

Notice:
- This is right before the day of the Lord.
- The message is to those who fear His name, the Messiah.
- In that day those who fear His name should remember the Written Law of Moses with the statues and judgments.
- God will send Elijah at this time to perform this function.
- If this does not occur, the Lord will curse the earth.

We are left with a choice. Yeshua literally meant what He said or He did not.

Matthew 5: 17, Think not that I am come to destroy the law, or the prophets: I am not come to destroy, but to fulfil. 18 For verily I say unto you, Till heaven and earth pass, one jot or one tittle shall in no wise pass from the law, till all be fulfilled. 19 Whosoever therefore shall break one of these least commandments, and shall teach men so, he shall be called the least in the kingdom of heaven: but whosoever shall do and teach them, the same shall be called great in the kingdom of heaven.

Notice:
- Yeshua issues several warnings to His followers.
- The Written Torah (Law of Moses) is not done away, and all is fulfilled when heaven and earth pass away, not before. The book of Revelation actually talks about this event. (Revelation 21:1)
- Those who break the Written Torah of Moses and teach others to do so are the least in the Kingdom.
- Those who keep them and teach others to keep them are the greatest in the Kingdom.
- One group is less favored than the other.
  - Daniel 12: 2, And many of them that sleep in the dust of the

earth shall awake, some to everlasting life, and some to shame and everlasting contempt.

- Yeshua begins this section with the warning, "Think not". Obviously He knew this would be an issue for His followers.

Again, we are left with a choice. Yeshua literally meant what He said and we are misunderstanding Paul or Paul is a hypocrite claiming grace but then keeping the Law of Moses. If we believe that Paul taught grace and that believers do not need to follow Yeshua's words, we have to wonder why the scriptures documented the following facts.

Paul did all of the following <u>after</u> he was saved by Yeshua:
- He kept the 7th day Sabbath with Jews and Gentiles in the Synagogue.
- He kept the Holy Days with Jews and Gentiles.
- He went to the Temple to make a sacrifice.
- He circumcised a fellow believer in Yeshua.
- He proved allegations that he was teaching Jews and Gentiles against the Written Torah of Moses to be false in a court of law.
- He consented with Peter at the Jerusalem council that the Pharisaical Oral Torah requirement of immediate circumcision for new believers was not necessary, but that Gentiles should learn the Written Law of Moses in the synagogues with other believers in Yeshua.
- He wrote to a Gentile (not a Jewish) church when he said, "Do we then make void the law through faith? God forbid: yea, we establish the law" (Romans 3:31). In His own words, Paul clarified that even though he was saved and justified by grace, he established the Law of Moses and so should all believers in Yeshua.
- He repeatedly clarified that the Oral Torah of the rabbis was not required for Christians, but that all believers should be keeping the Written Torah of Moses.

Romans 3: 22, Even <u>the righteousness of God which is by faith of Yeshua</u> unto all and upon all them that believe: for there is no difference: 23 For all have sinned, and come short of the glory of God; 24 Being <u>justified freely by his grace through the redemption that is in Christ Yeshua</u>: 25 Whom <u>God hath set forth to be a propitiation through faith in his blood</u>, to declare his righteousness for the remission of sins that are past, through the forbearance of God; 26 To <u>declare, I say, at this time his righteousness</u>: that he might be just, and the <u>justifier of him which believeth in Yeshua. 27 Where is boasting then? It is excluded. By what law? of works? Nay: but by the law of faith</u>. 28 Therefore we conclude that a <u>man is justified by faith without the deeds of the law</u>. 29 Is he the God of the Jews only? is he not also of the Gentiles? Yes, of the Gentiles also: 30 Seeing it is one God, which shall justify the circumcision by faith, and uncircumcision through faith. 31 <u>Do we then make void the law through faith? God forbid: yea, we establish the law</u>.

Paul is so clear in his writing. He is contrasting the Law of Works versus the Law of Faith and how righteousness is imparted to those needing to be freed from sin and death. How does this occur through the Torah of faith? The Torah (Commandments) are not made void by our faith, they are established in our hearts by our faith in Yeshua.

That being the case, is this a message <u>to the Jews</u>, showing them that they still need to keep the Written Torah? No.

Who is this message to?

This message is "…<u>unto all and upon all them that believe: for there is no difference</u>: For all have sinned, and come short of the glory of God;" (Romans 3:22–23).

We are justified by faith and not by works. The message is clear that <u>both</u> Jews and Gentiles should be keeping the Written Law (Torah) of Moses once they have been justified!

"Men and brethren what then shall we do"?

Acts 2: 36, Therefore let all the house of Israel know assuredly, that God hath made the same Jesus, whom ye have crucified, both Lord and Christ. 37 Now when they heard this, they were pricked in their heart, and said unto Peter and to the rest of the Apostles, Men and brethren, what shall we do? 38 Then Peter said unto them, <u>Repent</u>, and be baptized every one of you in the name of Jesus Christ for the remission of sins, and ye shall receive the gift of the Holy Ghost.

Paul is writing to Romans (Gentiles) telling them to establish the Written Torah of Moses. Are you? Paul spends a great deal of time and detail on specifically what law he is discussing and it is not an arbitrary self-made internal moral law. He describes a law that does exactly what it was meant to do, cause sin and death to abound. The Messiah, the Torah, and the world all fulfill the same fractal of death and resurrection: First "Law of Sin and Death", then "Law of Resurrection Life".

As Frank Turek and Norman Geisler said, "I Don't Have Enough faith to be an Atheist":

- "Truth is unchanging even though our beliefs about truth change."
- "Beliefs cannot change a fact, no matter how sincerely they are held."
- "Truth is not affected by the attitude of the one professing it."
- "All truths are absolute truths."

12 OLD & NEW COVENANT OR DEAD AND RESURRECTED COVENANT?

Is it Old & New Covenant...or Dead and Resurrected Covenant? What does Paul Teach? How can the facts be so well documented and clear, yet Christianity has such a divided opinion on the truth? Perhaps it is not the facts that are the problem, but our paradigm.

We need to clear up some common misunderstandings about the concepts of an old and a new covenant. The Apostle Paul goes into great detail clarifying how we should view both covenants.

We will see this prophetic pattern with the Israelites that were saved from Egypt. The first generation is associated with death and the second generation is associated with resurrected and ascended life. This first generation is associated with the Messiah and the second generation is associated with the image of the resurrected Messiah and the Resurrected Covenant.

Do you realize Paul's testimony centers around the resurrection of the dead? What have we been overlooking in regard to his testimony about the Resurrected Covenant? The prophetic image, pattern, and fractal shows that the Messiah is resurrected, the world is resurrected, and the covenant is resurrected! Life is given to all stones!

By the conclusion of this study we will understand why Moses and Elijah appear with Yeshua on the Mount of Transfiguration and then disappear! We will also see the prophetic tie between the shattered tablets of stone that the covenant was written upon and our divine purpose. God is raising up rocks to the glory of His manifested name!

> Matthew 3: 9, And think not to say within yourselves, We have Abraham to our father: for I say unto you, that God is able of these stones to raise up children unto Abraham.

Then we will examine how the Countenance of God is associated with the removal of the first covenant (the Written Torah of Moses) which was initially coupled with death and judgment, and then is joined with resurrection of the covenant (the Written Torah of Moses) under the administration of the Messiah via grace and abundant mercy. We will do a close examination behind the veil of Moses and evaluate what these images mean prophetically in regard to the Messiah.

SCRIPTURAL PATTERNS & FRACTALS:
The Apostle Paul teaches that we can learn about the hidden wisdom of God if we only pay attention to His images, patterns, and fractals that appear in the natural world.

Romans 1: 19, Because that which may be known of God is manifest in them; for God hath shewed it unto them. 20 For the invisible things of him from the creation of the world are clearly seen, being understood by the things that are made, even his eternal power and Godhead; so that they are without excuse:

All we need to do is pay attention to what we see, hear, and observe to become wise in the hidden things of God.

Hebrews 5: 11, Of whom we have many things to say, and hard to be uttered, seeing ye are dull of hearing. 12 For when for the time ye ought to be teachers, ye have need that one teach you again which be the first principles of the oracles of God; and are become such as have need of milk, and not of strong meat. 13 For every one that useth milk is unskilful in the word of righteousness: for he is a babe. 14 But strong meat belongeth to them that are of full age, even those who by reason of use have their senses exercised to discern both good and evil.

Are the things (manifest images) of nature happenstance or are they all by interconnected design? The answer will be self-evident. A mystery is only hidden so long as we cannot see the pattern, image, and fractal. Once we see the pattern we will understand how it's parts are interconnected and what they mean. The mystery is then revealed to us. This is why God is so aggrieved by those who do not hear.

Matthew 13: 11, He answered and said unto them, Because it is given unto you to know the mysteries of the kingdom of heaven, but to them it is not given. 12 For whosoever hath, to him shall be given, and he shall have more abundance: but whosoever hath not, from him shall be taken away even that he hath. 13 Therefore speak I to them in parables: because they seeing see not; and hearing they hear not, neither do they understand. 14 And in them is fulfilled the prophecy of Esaias, which saith, By hearing ye shall hear, and shall not understand; and seeing ye shall see, and shall not perceive: 15 For this people's heart is waxed gross, and their ears are dull of hearing, and their eyes they have closed; lest at any time they should see with their eyes and hear with their ears, and should understand with their heart, and should be converted, and I should heal them. 16 But blessed are your eyes, for they see: and your ears, for they hear. 17 For verily I say unto you, That many prophets and righteous men have desired to see those things which ye see, and have not seen them; and to hear those things which ye hear, and have not heard them.

What is a parable? It is a story of imagery that presents hidden meaning only to those who have senses that are refined and mature. They may glean the hidden truth that is reserved for those who have a heart that is ready. Be sure to take note of how this is connected to the prophecy of Elijah and having "eyes to see and ears to hear".

We are about to discover the wonder of the resurrection. This study will show the repeating image, pattern, and fractal of death and resurrection and clarify whether or not the New Testament is different from the Old Testament.

We will find this repeating image in the scriptures.

- The Messiah is resurrected.
- The people are resurrected.
- The covenant is resurrected.

The pattern and image repeats itself showing the glory of God manifested. Most Christians agree that the breaking of the tablets given by God at Mt. Sinai shows the annulling of the first covenant due to the people's disobedience. Subsequently God required a new set of tablets, which are representative of our hearts under the new covenant. We might question, what is written on the new set of tablets?

Exodus 34: 1, And the Lord said unto Moses, Hew thee <u>two tablets of stone like unto the first: and I will write upon these tablets the words that were in the first tablets, which thou brakest.</u>

The very same covenant and the very same words that were on the first set of tablets are written on the new set of tablets. The only changes were 1) the location, stone versus our hearts and 2) the administrator, the manifested Name of the Lord, YHWH.

The first covenant is under the administration of condemnation and judgment (death), the second set of tablets is under righteousness and grace/mercy (resurrected life). The new administrator is Yeshua (the Name of YHWH made manifest and declared). We will examine the scriptural facts to determine if these statements are true.

We also need to reconcile another issue. Modern Christianity's testimony is that the Law of Moses (called the Torah—the first 5 books of the Old Testament) is done away and that we do not need to keep it. Yeshua clarifies His position on the Torah (the Written Law of Moses). He says, the Law of Moses (the Written Torah) is <u>not</u> done away.

Matthew 5: 17, <u>Think not that I am come to destroy the law, or the prophets: I am not come to destroy, but to fulfil.</u> 18 For verily I say unto you,

Till heaven and earth pass, one jot or one tittle shall in no wise pass from the law, till all be fulfilled. 19 Whosoever therefore shall break one of these least commandments, and shall teach men so, he shall be called the least in the kingdom of heaven: but whosoever shall do and teach them, the same shall be called great in the kingdom of heaven.

Notice Yeshua is talking about the ultimate purpose for His coming and the final act of crucifixion and resurrection. Any attempt to lump this statement into just "fulfilling law" while He was "under law" so that His final act could do away with the Law of Moses simply holds no logical water.

IF THEY HEAR NOT MOSES…
Yeshua also taught that the testimony of Moses and the prophets was a sufficient witness to provide salvation to the people. If they did not listen to Moses and the prophets, they would not listen to Yeshua, someone who rose from the dead.

> Luke 16: 19, There was a certain rich man, which was clothed in purple and fine linen, and fared sumptuously every day: 20 And there was a certain beggar named Lazarus, which was laid at his gate, full of sores, 21 And desiring to be fed with the crumbs which fell from the rich man's table: moreover the dogs came and licked his sores. 22 And it came to pass, that the beggar died, and was carried by the angels into Abraham's bosom: the rich man also died, and was buried; 23 And in hell he lift up his eyes, being in torments, and seeth Abraham afar off, and Lazarus in his bosom. 24 And he cried and said, Father Abraham, have mercy on me, and send Lazarus, that he may dip the tip of his finger in water, and cool my tongue; for I am tormented in this flame. 25 But Abraham said, Son, remember that thou in thy lifetime receivedst thy good things, and likewise Lazarus evil things: but now he is comforted, and thou art tormented. 26 And beside all this, between us and you there is a great gulf fixed: so that they which would pass from hence to you cannot; neither can they pass to us, that would come from thence. 27 Then he said, I pray thee therefore, father, that thou wouldest send him to my father's house: 28 For I have five brethren; that he may testify unto them, lest they also come into this place of torment. 29 Abraham saith unto him, They have Moses and the prophets; let them hear them. 30 And he said, Nay, father Abraham: but if one went unto them from the dead, they will repent. 31 And he said unto him, If they hear not Moses and the prophets, neither will they be persuaded, though one rose from the dead.

Yeshua says via this parable that the Law of Moses and the Old Testament prophets are sufficient testimony for salvation. But, the Written Law of Moses states that His covenant people are not to listen to anyone who teaches people not to keep the Torah. How do we reconcile this paradox if modern Christianity's teaching that the Law of Moses is done away is accurate? The Law of Moses says that those who turn away from the Torah are cursed.

- Deuteronomy 29: 18, Lest there should be among you man, or woman, or family, or tribe, <u>whose heart turneth away this day from the Lord our God</u>, to go and serve the gods of these nations; lest there should be among you a root that beareth gall and wormwood; …21 And the Lord shall separate him unto evil out of all the tribes of Israel, <u>according to all the curses of the covenant that are written in this book of the law</u>: (See also Deuteronomy 28:15, 45,)

- Deuteronomy 13: 1, <u>If there arise among you a prophet</u>, or a dreamer of dreams, and giveth thee a sign or a wonder, 2 And the sign or the wonder come to pass, whereof he spake unto thee, saying, <u>Let us go after other gods, which thou hast not known, and let us serve them</u>; 3 Thou shalt not hearken unto the words of that prophet, or that dreamer of dreams: for the Lord your God proveth you, to know whether ye love the Lord your God with all your heart and with all your soul. 4 <u>Ye shall walk after the Lord your God, and fear him, and keep his commandments, and obey his voice</u>, and ye shall serve him, and cleave unto him. 5 And <u>that prophet, or that dreamer of dreams, shall be put to death</u>; because he hath spoken to turn you away from the Lord your God, which brought you out of the land of Egypt, and redeemed you out of the house of bondage, to thrust thee out of the way which the Lord thy God commanded thee to walk in. So shalt thou put the evil away from the midst of thee.

Yeshua must support the Law of Moses since He said via a parable that Moses (symbolic of the Torah) and the Prophets (symbolic of the call to repent and return to the Torah) are sufficient testimony for salvation. Moses told the people to ignore those who do not teach obedience to the Torah. What does this mean?

Keep in mind it was the manifest Name of YHWH who gave the Torah to Israel. So Moses, YHWH, and Yeshua must always agree. If we cannot reconcile this apparent paradox then we are still confused over "Grace versus Law" (Torah). Either Yeshua supports the Torah, or by His own words He has condemned Himself by saying that Moses and the Prophets are sufficient testimony for salvation.

Many people hold inaccurate and unscriptural doctrines because they are not taught what Paul was actually saying. Paul's teaching is consistent with Yeshua's testimony. They both state that the "traditions of men/the rabbis" (the Oral Torah) are not required of a believer in order to be saved. Paul also clarifies that it is the "handwriting of ordinances or writ of transgressions", which show our violations of the Torah, that is taken care of by the work of the crucifixion. It is the writ of our transgressions of the Torah that is nailed to the cross and is covered with the blood of the Messiah.

Colossians 2: 13, And you, being dead in your sins and the uncircumcision of your flesh, hath he quickened together with him, having forgiven you all trespasses; 14 Blotting out the handwriting of ordinances that was against us, which was contrary to us, and took it out of the way, nailing it to his cross; 15 And having spoiled principalities and powers, he made a shew of them openly, triumphing over them in it.

Again, this is a document showing our violations of the Law of Moses. This document nailed to the cross is not the covenant itself. Many Christians are simply not educated about the ongoing argument between the Jewish rabbis over whether only the Written Torah is required, or whether the Oral Torah (rabbinic traditions) is also required.

Orthodox rabbis, also known as Pharisees, teach that both the Written and the Oral Torah, (called the Traditions of men) are required to satisfy God and the terms of the covenant. You find these rabbis in conflict with Yeshua throughout the Gospels over this very issue. Yeshua is consistent and clear in response to their rabbinical Oral Law.

> Matthew 15: 8, This people draweth nigh unto me with their mouth, and honoureth me with their lips; but their heart is far from me. 9 But in vain they do worship me, teaching for doctrines the commandments of men.

Yeshua is clear, the Written Torah is required, and the Oral Torah (commandments of men) is not required.

WRITTEN TORAH VERSUS ORAL TORAH (TRADITIONS OF THE RABBIS):
The traditions of the rabbis (traditions of the elders, otherwise known as the Talmud, the Mishnah, or as the Takanot, Minhag, Halakha, or Ma'aseh) are not required to be in conformance with the covenant (meaning you would be without sin). Paul reaffirms Yeshua's declarations throughout the Gospels that the Oral Torah is not required for a believer.

> Colossians 2: 7, Rooted and built up in him, and stablished in the faith, as ye have been taught, abounding therein with thanksgiving. 8 Beware lest any man spoil you through philosophy and vain deceit, after the tradition of men, after the rudiments of the world, and not after Christ. 9 For in him dwelleth all the fulness of the Godhead bodily.

Paul is clearly saying that the Oral Torah is not required. Paul is not talking about the Written Torah (the Law of Moses). There is a clear and distinct difference between the Written Torah that Yeshua and the Apostles taught us to observe and the Oral Torah or the traditions of men that Yeshua and the Apostles rejected.

This is the historical context of the debate that was ongoing in the lives of first century Christians. It was not a debate of whether to keep the Law of Moses (the Written Torah). The teaching of grace without following the Written Torah was labeled as iniquity and lawlessness by the Apostles. This was clearly understood to be the mystery of iniquity or lawlessness (torahlessness).

> 2 Thessalonians 2: 7, For the mystery of iniquity doth already work: only he who now letteth will let until he be taken out of the way.

Notice in Colossians 2 that Paul talks about the problem of the traditions of men (the Oral Torah of the rabbis). He then addresses the Christian doctrine of the nature of the Messiah, saying that the Messiah is the fullness of the Godhead bodily. The Pharisees called this teaching blasphemy, which caused the death of many Christians including Christ Himself over this very pivotal issue. Paul clarifies that the administrator of the covenant, the Messiah, is literally the Countenance of YHWH. The central issue of the annulling of the covenant is thematically focused on the countenance of Moses and the veil that covered his face and their hearts. Remember Moses is a prophetic type of the Messiah. Paul goes on to clarify what has been done away.

THE LAW IS THE SAME, THE ADMINISTRATION OF IT HAS CHANGED:

2 Corinthians 3: 7, But if the ministration of death, written and engraven in stones, was glorious, so that the children of Israel could not stedfastly behold the face of Moses for the glory of his countenance; which glory was to be done away:

It was the administration of condemnation and judgment (called the ministration of death) that results in death for the covenant breaker, that was done away. The covenant, which is called the Law, the Written Torah, or the Law of Moses, was not done away. The people were not done away. The Utterances that were written on the stone tablets were not done away. Paul goes on to clarify the change of the administration from the flesh and death (condemnation) to the spirit and life (righteousness).

What changed?

The administration turned to the Resurrected Covenant and to the resurrected administrator, Yeshua.

2 Corinthians 3: 8, How shall not the ministration of the spirit be rather glorious? 9 For if the ministration of condemnation be glory, much more doth the ministration of righteousness exceed in glory. 10 For even that which was made glorious had no glory in this respect, by reason of the glory that excelleth. 11 For if that which is done away was glorious, much more that which remaineth is glorious. 12 Seeing then that we have such hope, we use great plainness of speech: 13 And not as Moses, which put a veil over his face, that the children of Israel could not stedfastly look to the end (telos) of that which is abolished: 14 But their minds were blinded: for until this day remaineth the same vail untaken away in the reading of the Old Testament; which vail is done away in Christ. 15 But even unto this day, when Moses is read, the vail is upon their heart. 16 Nevertheless when it shall turn to the Lord, the vail shall be taken away. 17 Now the Lord is that Spirit: and where the Spirit of the Lord is, there is liberty. 18 But we all, with open face beholding as in a glass the glory of the Lord, are changed into the same image from glory to glory, even as by the Spirit of the Lord.

What was abolished by this new administration of Yeshua? The enmity of God against sinful man. (Ephesians 2:15) and death (2 Timothy 1:10). It is the administrator of the Resurrected Covenant, typified by the glorified countenance of Moses, which the people are not able to view because the veil covers his glorified countenance. This is a prophetic picture of the coming of the manifest Name of YHWH, the Messiah, as the Countenance of God and the administrator of the Resurrected Covenant. This glorified righteousness, provided by the Countenance of YHWH, the manifest Name of the Lord (YHWH), is the end (telos-Strong's #G5056, the end to which all things relate, the aim, purpose) or embodiment of His grace that transcribes His righteousness upon us via faith in His name. This is why Paul takes so much time associating the glorified countenance of Moses with the people's inability to view the fulfillment of the promises of YHWH.

Romans 10: 1, Brethren, my heart's desire and prayer to God for Israel is, that they might be saved. 2 For I bear them record that they have a zeal of God, but not according to knowledge. 3 For they being ignorant of God's righteousness, and going about to establish their own righteousness, <u>have not submitted themselves unto the righteousness of God. 4 For Christ is the end (telos) of the law for righteousness to every one that believeth.</u>

Again, our righteousness under the Resurrected Covenant is not by our works but by the administrator of the Resurrected Covenant, the glorified Countenance of YHWH, the manifested Name of the Lord (YHWH), whom they could not behold because a veil was over His countenance and over their hearts. We do not do the writing, Yeshua does! The end and fulfillment of the promises was not a dead law written on a dead stone that brings death and condemnation. That death and condemnation was ended, and a resurrected administrator is writing a resurrected Law of Moses on resurrected hearts, all of which are alive. That which is dead has ended, that which is made alive went into effect when the Covenant turned over to the new administrator. Judgment is replaced with grace, death is replaced with resurrected life. Remember this is not an end as in something done away. This is an end as in a prophetic completion or fulfillment. Yeshua is the manifest presence of the Name of YHWH, the administrator of the Resurrected Covenant. The scriptural pattern is showing us death and resurrection, not old and new.

2 Corinthians 3: 15, But even unto this day, when Moses is read, the vail is upon their heart. 16 Nevertheless <u>when it shall turn to the Lord, the vail shall be taken away.</u>

Notice the patterns from the scriptures we have already read:
- The administration of the flesh is abolished and replaced by the spirit.
- The administration of death is replaced with a glorious countenance of the Messiah not covered by a fleshly garment that is symbolic of corrupted life. It is replaced with resurrected life.
- The veil that covered the glorified countenance of Moses is taken away so that we can behold the image of YHWH, the countenance of the Father, the image of God, the Messiah Yeshua.

13 THE REVEALING OF THE COUNTENANCE OF GOD

A cts 2: 28, Thou hast made known to me the ways of life; thou shalt make me full of joy with thy countenance.

Paul affirms the nature of the Messiah and how God dwells within Him.

Colossians 2: 8, Beware lest any man spoil you through philosophy and vain deceit, after the tradition of men, after the rudiments of the world, and not after Christ. 9 For in him dwelleth all the fulness of the Godhead bodily. 10 And ye are complete in him, which is the head of all principality and power:

Being the "fullness of the Godhead bodily", Paul further clarifies that the Messiah is the image of God.

2 Corinthians 4: 3, But if our Gospel be hid, it is hid to them that are lost: 4 In whom the god of this world hath blinded the minds of them which believe not, lest the light of the glorious Gospel of Christ, who is the image of God, should shine unto them. 5 For we preach not ourselves, but Christ Jesus the Lord; and ourselves your servants for Jesus' sake. 6 For God, who commanded the light to shine out of darkness, hath shined in our hearts, to give the light of the knowledge of the glory of God in the face of Jesus Christ. 7 But we have this treasure in earthen vessels, that the excellency of the power may be of God, and not of us.

Notice how the Messiah is being emphasized as the image of God and how the "glory of God" is directly associated with the "face" (countenance) of Yeshua. We saw the prophetic template for the Messiah in Moses. He was the forerunner or shadow type of the Messiah. So we should be able to see patterns and imagery in the life of Moses that matches up with Yeshua.

Deuteronomy 18: 15, The Lord thy God will raise up unto thee a Prophet from the midst of thee, of thy brethren, like unto me; unto him ye shall hearken;

After the second giving of the Torah the central imagery focuses around the glorified countenance of Moses and the initial reaction of Israel of fear and withdrawal then to restored faith and drawing near. Paul speaks of this in regard to its prophetic meaning related to the Messiah.

2 Corinthians 3: 7, But if the ministration of death, written and engraven in stones, was glorious, so that the children of Israel could not stedfastly behold the face of Moses for the glory of his countenance; which glory was to be done away:

Take notice of how the inability of the people to see is associated with the glory of Moses' administration, which needed to be replaced with a new and more glorious one that provides sight.

Exodus 34: 29, And it came to pass, when Moses came down from mount Sinai with the two tablets of testimony in Moses' hand, when he came down from the mount, that Moses wist not that the skin of his face shone while he talked with him. 30 And when Aaron and all the children of Israel saw Moses, behold, the skin of his face shone; and they were afraid to come nigh him. 31 And Moses called unto them; and Aaron and all the rulers of the congregation returned unto him: and Moses talked with them. 32 And afterward all the children of Israel came nigh: and he gave them in commandment all that the Lord had spoken with him in mount Sinai. 33 And till Moses had done speaking with them, he put a vail on his face. 34 But when Moses went in before the Lord to speak with him, he took the vail off, until he came out. And he came out, and spake unto the children of Israel that which he was commanded. 35 And the children of Israel _: and Moses put the vail upon his face again, until he went in to speak with him.

The hiding of the countenance and image of God, the Messiah Yeshua, is done away. Notice the veil is done away in Christ. That happens when the administration of the covenant turns to the Messiah and the veil of blindness is taken away. That which is dead has ended, that which is made alive goes into effect when the Covenant turns over to the new administrator.

Judgment is replaced with grace, Death is replaced with resurrected life. Remember this is not an end as in something done away. This is an end as in a prophetic completion or fulfillment. Yeshua is the manifest presence of the Name of YHWH, the administrator of the Resurrected Covenant.

2 Corinthians 3: 15, But even unto this day, when Moses is read, the vail is upon their heart. 16 Nevertheless when it shall turn to the Lord, the vail shall be taken away.

Remember the imagery that was presented earlier about the work of the Messiah beginning first in hiddenness and death while He circumcises the seed of our hearts in preparation for writing His laws on our hearts. He is literally transcribing His image upon ours. He is replacing our fallen image and countenance with His. Can we prove this from the patterns, images, and fractals of the Bible? Absolutely.

The Messiah is revealed in the fractal of death like a seed and then resurrection like a manifested fruit. Yeshua had to bear the imagery of both to fulfill His divine role. The Countenance of God, the Messiah, is then revealed and manifested for all to see. This prophetic pattern is scriptural and comes straight from the Written Law of Moses.

> Deuteronomy 18: 17, And the Lord said unto me, They have well spoken that which they have spoken. 18 I will raise them up a Prophet from among their brethren, like unto thee, and will put my words in his mouth; and he shall speak unto them all that I shall command him. 19 And it shall come to pass, that whosoever will not hearken unto my words which he shall speak in my name, I will require it of him.

Remember Moses is a prophetic pattern of the Messiah. One is an image of the other. Let's quickly examine the chiastic structure found in chapter 18.

Deuteronomy 18:
15 The Lord thy <u>God will raise up</u> unto thee a Prophet from the midst of thee, of thy brethren, <u>like unto me</u>; unto him ye shall hearken;

16 According to all that thou desiredst of the Lord thy God in Horeb in the day of the assembly, saying, Let me not <u>hear again the voice of the Lord my God</u>, neither let me <u>see this great fire</u> any more, that I die not. 17 And the Lord said unto me, <u>They have well spoken</u> that which they have spoken.

18 <u>I will raise them up a Prophet</u> from among their brethren, <u>like unto thee</u>, and will <u>put my words in his mouth</u>; and <u>he shall speak unto them all that I shall command him</u>.

Notice that the prophet to come, the Messiah, will be "like Moses" and make it possible for the people to "hear the voice of God" and to "see God's great fire". The Messiah (prophet like unto Moses) will have God's Utterance and will speak everything that God commands Him. This fact alone should give those who claim that Yeshua has no interest in the Law of Moses or our adherence to the original Utterances (the Ten Commandments) great pause. What is God's goal in sending this "prophet"? So that the people might "hear again the voice of the Lord my God" as they did at the giving of the Ten Commandments. This association of hearing the voice of God in the Messiah with the original Ten Commandments is not happenstance.

2 Corinthians 3: 7, But if the ministration of death, written and engraven in stones, was glorious, so that the children of Israel could not stedfastly behold the face of Moses for the glory of his countenance; which glory was to be done away: 8 How shall not the ministration of the spirit be rather glorious? 9 For if the ministration of condemnation be glory, much more doth the ministration of righteousness exceed in glory.

Two Administrations		
Administrator	Moses	Yeshua
Nature	Flesh	Spirit
Glory	Glorious	More Glorious
State	Death	Resurrection life
Countenance	Covered with a Veil	Uncovered
Face	Closed	Open
Mirror	Dim	Lighted
Baptized Into	Moses	Yeshua
Emotional State	Judgment	Grace & Mercy
Consequence	Condemnation	Forgiveness
Result	Death	Resurrection
Image	Earthy	Heavenly
Location of Commandments	Tablets of Stone	Heart
Hearing & Seeing	Dull	Clear
Heart	Waxed Gross	Circumcised

Notice Paul's comment that the administration of the flesh changes, with the turning over to the revealed Countenance of YHWH, the Messiah, to the administration of the Holy Spirit (Ruach Hakodesh). We can then behold Him via an open countenance as in a mirror, having our images changed to conform to that of the Countenance of YHWH, the Messiah Yeshua.

2 Corinthians 3: 17, Now the Lord is that Spirit: and where the Spirit of the Lord is, there is liberty. 18 But we all, with open face beholding as in a glass the glory of the Lord, are changed into the same image from glory to glory, even as by the Spirit of the Lord.

Paul keeps directing us to the countenance of the Messiah and relating it to Moses' glorified countenance. Paul is showing us how Yeshua is that "prophet like unto me (Moses)". The goal of changing the countenance from Moses to Yeshua centers on changing our fallen image to the glorious image of His Son. Just as the current administration of Moses (the flesh) is glorious (death), it must pass to the administration of Yeshua (the Spirit) which is more glorious (resurrection life).

Romans 8: 28, And we know that all things work together for good to them that love God, to them who are the called according to his purpose. 29 For whom he did foreknow, <u>he also did predestinate to be conformed to the image of his Son</u>, that he might be the firstborn among many brethren. 30 Moreover whom he did predestinate, them he also called: and whom he called, them he also justified: and whom he justified, them he also glorified.

This uncovered countenance or image of the Messiah is then transcribed on to us. There are wonderful truths to this mystery within the Aaronic blessing which describes the transcribing of the Countenance of God, which is the Messiah, upon the believer. This scripture clarifies what was wrong with the first covenant, the Law of Moses.

Hebrews 8: 6, But now hath he obtained a more excellent ministry, by how much also he is the mediator of a better covenant, which was <u>established upon better promises</u>. 7 For if that first covenant had been faultless, then should no place have been sought for the second. 8 <u>For finding fault with them</u>, he saith, Behold, the days come, saith the Lord, when I will make a new covenant with the house of Israel and with the house of Judah:

The fault was not with the words or the Utterances of the covenant, the Written Law of Moses, the Torah. The fault was with the people violating the covenant, "finding fault with them". That is why the words of the second set of tablets (the renewed or Resurrected Covenant) are the same as the first set of tablets (the original covenant—the Torah).

What changed?
- The location, the heart versus stone
- The administration, grace versus judgment/condemnation
- The administrator (the Name of YHWH manifested—the Countenance of YHWH)

If God is consistent we should also follow the imagery that was presented at the giving of the covenant, the Law/Torah. We need to understand the significance of the dual giving of the Torah and its implications upon followers of Yeshua. To discover the answer we must follow the patterns, images, and fractals presented to us by God.

1 Corinthians 10: 4, And did all drink the same spiritual drink: for they drank of that spiritual rock that followed them: and <u>that rock was Christ</u>. 5 But with many of them God was not well pleased: for they were overthrown in the wilderness. 6 Now these things were our examples, to the intent we should not lust after evil things, as they also lusted.

THE DEATH AND RESURRECTION OF THE TABLETS OF THE LAW:
To put it plainly, one covenant is made in the image of the other. Should this surprise us having learned the fractal of death and resurrection? Let's look at the imagery of the stone tablets that the covenant were written upon. The old was broken, crushed and buried underneath the mount, which ultimately caused the death of the first generation as they died in the wilderness. The first tablets of stone are carved out by God at the top of the mountain and are given to Moses.

Exodus 24: 12, And the Lord said unto Moses, Come up to me into the mount, and be there: and I will give thee tablets of stone, and a law, and commandments which I have written; that thou mayest teach them.

The first set of tablets, carved out at the top of the mountain by God and were engraved by His finger.

Exodus 31: 19, And he gave unto Moses, when he had made an end of communing with him upon mount Sinai, two tablets of testimony, tablets of stone, written with the finger of God.

Those tablets were broken by Moses when he found the people of Israel worshipping the golden calf at the base of the mountain. This was the breaking of the covenant.

Exodus 32: 19, And it came to pass, as soon as he came nigh unto the camp, that he saw the calf, and the dancing: and Moses' anger waxed hot, and he cast the tablets out of his hands, and brake them beneath the mount.

God commanded Moses to carve out a new set of tablets at the base of the mountain and bring them up to the top of the mountain. God could then re-write the same Utterances on the second set of tablets. This is the renewal or resurrection of the covenant, the Law of Moses.

Exodus 34: 1, And the Lord said unto Moses, Hew thee two tablets of stone like unto the first: and I will write upon these tablets the words that were in the first tablets, which thou brakest.

The Resurrected Covenant was now established with better promises and were to be copied on to tablets that were not directly carved out by the Hand of God, but were carved out by Moses in the valley, and were then brought with him when he ascended the mountain when the covenant was resurrected.

Exodus 34: 4, And he hewed two tablets of stone like unto the first; and Moses rose up early in the morning, and went up unto mount Sinai, as the Lord had commanded him, and took in his hand the two tablets of stone.

The New Covenant—the Law of Moses, the Torah, was resurrected in the image of the old with the presentation of the manifested Name of YHWH, the Messiah. We have already reviewed this in Exodus 34. Both tablets of stone (first and second giving) had the same words (Utterances) written upon them. They were both written by God.

This second set of stone tablets are written via the Utterance (Word) of God, the manifest Name of YHWH, the Messiah, in grace and abundant mercy. Moses is fulfilling the fractal of the death and resurrection of the Law of Moses. That which Moses is in type is prophetic of and fulfilled by the Messiah.

We can now better understand the ministry of Paul and the significance of why he was put on trial. He was sent to re–gather the gentiles and the northern ten tribes of Israel (which are also called Gentiles), who are in diaspora (exile). His testimony is centered on Yeshua the Messiah and His death and resurrection.

As the Messiah was broken and buried in the ground like a seed, so was the first covenant which bore the administration of judgment and condemnation (death). This is prophetically pictured by the breaking of the first set of tablets given at Mt. Sinai, the death of the first generation of Israel that departed Egypt, and God's refusal to allow Moses to ascend to the Promised land.

> Exodus 34: 1, And the Lord said unto Moses, <u>Hew thee two tablets of stone like unto the first: and I will write upon these tablets the words that were in the first tablets, which thou brakest.</u>

When the Messiah was resurrected so was the image of the first covenant (the Law of Moses) but the Law of Moses was now based upon better promises and with a new location, our hearts. Notice the Utterances and the words are the same on both sets of tablets! When Paul testified about resurrection he was not only talking about the Messiah or His followers. He was also talking about the Law of Moses with its new administrator, Yeshua the Messiah.

> Acts 23: 6, But when Paul perceived that the one part were Sadducees, and the other Pharisees, he cried out in the council, Men and brethren, I am a Pharisee, the son of a Pharisee: <u>of the hope and resurrection of the dead I am called in question</u>. 7 And when he had so said, there arose a dissension between the Pharisees and the Sadducees: and the multitude was divided.

The multitude was divided because the Sadducees did not believe in resurrection, while the Pharisees did. Because of the resurrection of the Messiah and the Covenant (the Written Torah), Paul was working to re–gather those who were viewed as unclean and exiled (dead). Among these are the Torah breakers from the dispersed northern ten tribes of Israel. But keep in mind Judah is also under the Resurrected Covenant (Torah) and its new administrator. There is no pass on the administrator, even if you think you have the covenant/Torah!

The Torah will not save you, the new administrator is the only way to be saved. So those who say they have Yeshua but do not keep the Written Law of Moses are still under condemnation, as are those from the house of Judah that say they keep the Written Law of Moses but have rejected its resurrected administrator, the Messiah Yeshua. If you do not have the administrator of grace and abundant mercy (resurrection life) then you are still under the old administration of condemnation and death even if you are keeping the Torah.

Exodus 34: 5, And the Lord descended in the cloud, and stood with him there, and proclaimed the Name of the Lord. 6 And the Lord passed by before him, and proclaimed, The Lord, The Lord God, merciful and gracious, longsuffering, and abundant in goodness and truth, 7 Keeping mercy for thousands, forgiving iniquity and transgression and sin, and that will by no means clear the guilty; visiting the iniquity of the fathers upon the children, and upon the children's children, unto the third and to the fourth generation. 8 And Moses made haste, and bowed his head toward the earth, and worshipped.

Keep in mind there is only one pattern of redemption, the way of life. The Messiah is resurrected, the Written Torah of Moses is resurrected, and the people that are in covenant with YHWH via the new administrator, the Messiah Yeshua, are resurrected. Ultimately the whole manifest universe is resurrected.

Revelation 21: 1, And I saw a new heaven and a new earth: for the first heaven and the first earth were passed away; and there was no more sea.

Peter confirms this understanding.

2 Peter 3: 12, Looking for and hasting unto the coming of the day of God, wherein the heavens being on fire shall be dissolved, and the elements shall melt with fervent heat? 13 Nevertheless we, according to his promise, look for new heavens and a new earth, wherein dwelleth righteousness.

This prophetic pattern or fractal replicates itself in all aspects of the covenant. Like the law, it brings forth first death, then resurrected life. Like the Messiah, who was broken for our iniquities and then is resurrected to eternal life. Like the believer who must first die and then be brought forth to glory through his/her individual resurrection, passing from death to life, from corruption to incorruption, from condemnation to grace. There is only one way of salvation in the scriptures no matter how far you go back or forward! Seeing that Moses is prophetic of Yeshua and Yeshua is "like unto Moses" what are the lawful implications that we need to consider?

Exodus 12: 49, One law shall be to him that is homeborn, and unto the stranger that sojourneth among you. 50 Thus did all the children of Israel; as the Lord commanded Moses and Aaron, so did they.

Again there is only one pattern of redemption, salvation, and glorification. None are exempt. None can save themselves. There is only one Written Torah of Moses, which is our covenant with God.

1 Corinthians 12: 12, For as the body is one, and hath many members, and all the members of that one body, being many, are one body: so also is Christ.

13 For by one Spirit are <u>we all baptized into one body, whether we be Jews or Gentiles, whether we be bond or free; and have been all made to drink into one Spirit</u>. 14 For the body is not one member, but many.

Can it be any clearer? There is only one way, one body, one spirit, one baptism...for Jews and Gentiles. Let's be extra clear. We are not grafted into Judah or Israel. Yeshua the Messiah is the tree that both Jews and Gentiles are grafted into. If you are not grafted into the new administrator, you are not associated with resurrected life and are "under the law" and the penalty of that administration, death.

There is one body, one spirit, one resurrected Law of Moses, and one resurrected administrator, Yeshua the Messiah! Jew or Gentile, bond or free, at home or in exile you need to come under the new administration of "grace and abundant mercy" of the Law of Moses. Two are made one in the administrator of the Resurrected Covenant, Yeshua the Messiah. This was Yeshua and the Apostles' testimony. You have to twist and pervert scripture to make it say anything else.

PRESENTATION OF THE NEW ADMINISTRATOR, THE MESSIAH:
The Written Law of Moses brought forth first condemnation fulfilling its God given fractal of death, then it brought forth life under the new administrator, the manifest Name of YHWH. We see the presence of the new administrator at the second giving of the tablets, with the manifest presence of the Name of the Lord. Take notice how the manifestation of the new administrator is connected with seeing the glory of God and the desire of Moses to behold His countenance.

Exodus 33: 13, Now therefore, I pray thee, if I have <u>found grace in thy sight, shew me now thy way</u>, that I may know thee, that I may find grace in thy sight: and <u>consider that this nation is thy people</u>. 14 And he said, <u>My presence shall go with thee</u>, and I will give thee rest. 15 And he said unto him<u>, If thy presence go not with me, carry us not up hence. 16 For wherein shall it be known here that I and thy people have found grace in thy sight? is it not in that thou goest with us</u>? so shall we be separated, I and thy people, from all the people that are upon the face of the earth. 17 And the Lord said unto Moses, I will do this thing also that thou hast spoken: for thou hast found grace in my sight, and I know thee by name. 18 And he said, I beseech thee, <u>shew me thy glory</u>. 19 And he said, <u>I will make all my goodness pass before thee, and I will proclaim the Name of the Lord before thee; and will be gracious to whom I will be gracious, and will shew mercy on whom I will shew mercy</u>. 20 And he said, Thou <u>canst not see my face</u>: for there shall no man see me, and live. 21 And the Lord said, Behold, there is a place by me, and thou shalt stand upon a rock: 22 And it shall come to pass, <u>while my glory passeth by</u>, that I will put thee in a clift of the rock, and will cover thee with my hand while I pass by: 23 And I will take away mine hand, and thou shalt <u>see my back parts: but my face shall not be seen</u>.

Notice all of the thematic patterns related to the resurrection of the

Covenant, the Law of Moses.

- Grace is given.
- Confirmation of receiving God's grace is that His presence goes up with you.
- The believer is known to God by name.
- The Name of the Lord is proclaimed, declared, and made manifest before the believer.
- The glory and goodness (grace) of God passes before the believer and he will have the desire to see the Countenance of God.
- The believer will be able to behold the back–parts (end) of God.

What do we see at the resurrection of the Law of Moses?

- The presentation of the new administrator of the Law of Moses
- The presence of God is manifested as:
  - The Name of YHWH
  - The Countenance of God
  - The grace and goodness of YHWH
  - The way

All of these are manifested to Moses immediately following the presentation of the Resurrected Covenant, the Written Law of Moses, which are the same Utterance as the first covenant.

Exodus 34: 1, And the Lord said unto Moses, <u>Hew thee two tablets of stone like unto the first: and I will write upon these tablets the words that were in the first tablets</u>, which thou brakest. 2 And be ready in the morning, and come up in the morning unto mount Sinai, and present thyself there to me in the top of the mount. 3 And no man shall come up with thee, neither let any man be seen throughout all the mount; neither let the flocks nor herds feed before that mount. 4 And <u>he hewed two tablets of stone like unto the first; and Moses rose up early in the morning, and went up unto mount Sinai, as the Lord had commanded him, and took in his hand the two tablets of stone</u>. 5 And the Lord descended in the cloud, and stood with him there, <u>and proclaimed the Name of the Lord</u>. 6 And the <u>Lord passed by before him, and proclaimed, The Lord, The Lord God, merciful and gracious, longsuffering, and abundant in goodness and truth,</u> 7 Keeping mercy for thousands, forgiving iniquity and transgression and sin, and that will by no means clear the guilty; visiting the iniquity of the fathers upon the children, and upon the children's children, unto the third and to the fourth generation. 8 And Moses made haste, and bowed his head toward the earth, and worshipped. 9 And he said, If now I have found grace in thy sight, O Lord, let my Lord, I pray thee, go among us; for it is a stiffnecked people; and pardon our iniquity and our sin, and take us for thine inheritance. 10 And he said, Behold, I make a covenant: before all thy people I will do marvels, such as have not been done in all the earth, nor in any nation: and all the people among which thou art shall see the work of the Lord: for it is a terrible thing that I will do with thee.

Notice the following patterns:

- The fractal or prophetic pattern of the resurrection of the Utterances that were written on the first set of tablets.
- The fractal of the ascension of the tablets (prophetic of our hearts) carved out by Moses at the base of the mountain.
- The fractal of the presentation of the manifestation of the declared Name of YHWH who is associated with grace, the Messiah, and the Countenance of YHWH.
- The fractal of Moses worshiping the manifest declared Name of YHWH (the Messiah), the new administrator of the Resurrected Covenant.
- The resurrected Law of Moses appears immediately with the glorified manifest Name of YHWH, the Messiah promising to do marvels before the people of the covenant.

This is the resurrection that Paul was preaching to Judah, the Gentiles and to dispersed Israel. He was not just talking about the resurrection of the Messiah or our resurrection. He was also talking about the resurrection of the covenant for all of Israel and the reunification of all the tribes of Israel and Judah. Unfortunately there were many rabbis, Pharisees, and Sadducees that disapproved of this message of resurrection. They thought those exiled Israelites were still unclean, dead, and should remain in exile.

They refused to acknowledge the administrator of the Resurrected Covenant, the manifest and declared Name of YHWH, the Countenance of YHWH, the Messiah Yeshua. They remained under the old administrator of the flesh and death. Subsequently that administration of condemnation under the law brought them death and judgment. They did not become grafted into the manifest Name of YHWH, the fullness of God bodily, the Messiah Yeshua, and become covenanted with resurrected life and the resurrected Torah. They did not understand that the same Utterances as the first covenant need to be written in our hearts and not on stone.

> Acts 21: 27, And when the seven days were almost ended, the Jews which were of Asia, when they saw him in the temple, stirred up all the people, and laid hands on him, 28 Crying out, Men of Israel, help: This is the man, that teacheth all men every where against the people, and the law, and this place: and further brought Greeks also into the temple, and hath polluted this holy place. 29 (For they had seen before with him in the city Trophimus an Ephesians, whom they supposed that Paul had brought into the temple.)

It was because of this outreach to the exiled ten tribes that Paul was brought up on charges of stirring up the people. Paul made it clear that the central issue for his trial was the resurrection of the dead, as it pertained to his testimony regarding:

- The breaking, death, burial, and resurrection of Yeshua the Messiah to life

- The death and resurrection of the Written Torah (the Law of Moses)
- The Resurrected Covenant and the resurrection of the exiles of Israel (from their violation of the Torah), now being under the administration of grace as provided by the testator, administrator, and mediator of the covenant (Torah), the resurrected Messiah Yeshua

Ephesians 2: 4, But God, who is rich in mercy, for his great love wherewith he loved us, 5 Even when we were dead in sins, hath quickened us together with Christ, (by grace ye are saved;) 6 And hath raised us up together, and made us sit together in heavenly places in Christ Yeshua:

We see the pattern of the Messiah in the tablets of the old and new covenant that the "same words" are written upon.

14 DEATH & RESURRECTION OF THE COVENANT (THE LAW OF MOSES)

L et's look at the patterns of the giving of the Torah and its resurrection. They are self–explanatory and can easily be found in the Bible. Instead of going into a lot of explanation, here is an outline of the patterns.

DEATH & RESURRECTION OF THE LAW OF MOSES FRACTAL:
- **First Giving of the Torah:**   Tablets of stone were carved by the hand of God.

- **Resurrection of the Torah:**   Tablets of stone were carved by the hand of Moses.

- **First Giving of the Torah:**   Tablets of stone were already at the top of the mountain.

- **Resurrection of the Torah:**   Tablets of stone ascended with Moses.

- **First Giving of the Torah:**   Tablets of stone were carved with the ten Utterances of the Covenant.

- **Resurrection of the Torah:**   Tablets of stone were carved with the same ten Utterances of the covenant.

- **First Giving of the Torah:**   Tablets of stone were written upon with the finger of God.

- **Resurrection of the Torah:**   Tablets were written upon with the declaration of the Name of YHWH.

- **First Giving of the Torah:** Tablets of stone were written in accordance with judgment and condemnation for violators.

Exodus 32: 33, And the Lord said unto Moses, Whosoever hath sinned against me, him will I blot out of my book.

- **Resurrection of the Torah:** Tablets of stone were written in accordance with "merciful and gracious, longsuffering, and abundant in goodness and truth".

Exodus 34: 6, And the Lord passed by before him, and proclaimed, The Lord, The Lord God, merciful and gracious, longsuffering, and abundant in goodness and truth,

This declaration to Moses was done along with the assignment of the administrator of the Resurrected Covenant, the manifestation of the Name of the Lord (YHWH).

- **First Giving of the Torah:** Tablets of stone are broken.

Exodus 32: 19, And it came to pass, as soon as he came nigh unto the camp, that he saw the calf, and the dancing: and Moses' anger waxed hot, and he cast the tablets out of his hands, and brake them beneath the mount.

The tablets of stone are left broken beneath the mountain.

- **Resurrection of the Torah:** The second set of tablets of stone are placed within the Ark of the Testimony which abides within the Holy of Holies and leads the people as they journey.

- **First Giving of the Torah:** Moses has no change of countenance at the first giving of the covenant.

- **Resurrection of the Torah:** Moses' countenance is changed at the resurrection of the covenant. When he descends the mountain, his countenance is covered by a veil and the people are afraid of his glory. The people withdraw from him and then return to him. This image of exile and redemption (drawing near) repeats.

Exodus 34: 30, And when Aaron and all the children of Israel saw Moses, behold, the skin of his face shone; and they were afraid to come nigh him. 31 And Moses called unto them; and Aaron and all the rulers of the congregation returned unto him: and Moses talked with them.

Notice the passing of the image of the manifest Name of YHWH to Moses' countenance. Being unable to directly observe the Countenance of God, it is transcribed on to the countenance of Moses, so that all can behold the glory and manifestation of the presence (fullness) of God. This event happens in thematic connection with the "rock", the "hand" of YHWH, and His manifest Name.

Concurrent with the giving and accepting of the covenant, we see the same continuing patterns, images, and fractals. **We see the giving of the Utterance of God to the people.** The first time Israel pleaded for it to stop, fearing death if it continued. The second time we see the Word become flesh (John 1: 1–14).

> Exodus 20: 18, And all the people saw the thunderings, and the lightnings, and the noise of the trumpet, and the mountain smoking: and when the people saw it, they removed, and stood afar off. 19 And they said unto Moses, Speak thou with us, and we will hear: but let not God speak with us, lest we die. 20 And Moses said unto the people, Fear not: for God is come to prove you, and that his fear may be before your faces, that ye sin not.

We see the dual exact image of the Messiah: one (Moses) with condemnation and judgment (flesh & death) and the other (Yeshua) with grace and abundant mercy (spirit & resurrected life).

We see the dual exact image of the two covenants (the Torah) with the same words. The only changes are that the administration of condemnation is done away with the first set of tablets of stone, replaced by the new administrator who is the presence of the manifested Name of the Lord (YHWH).

The location where the stone tablets are obtained from changes. The first time the stone tablets are provided by God on the top of the mountain (associated with a seed that must descend, die and be planted in the ground). The second time the stone tablets are carved out by Moses in the valley and ascend with him to receive the "same words" by the new administrator, the manifested Name of YHWH, the Messiah Yeshua (associated with grace and resurrected life, spirit, fruit, and manifestation).

The final location of the broken tablets is underneath the mountain (buried in death), whereas the final location of the resurrected tablets are in the Ark of the Testimony in the Holy of Holies (in the presence of life and the heart and mind of the believer).

THE MESSIAH & THE LAW FULFILLING THE SAME SCRIPTURAL PATTERNS & FRACTALS:

Let's remember the patterns of the Messiah and the covenant and how they are in the image of one another.

- **Messiah:** First coming of the Messiah ends in death.

- **Covenant:** First cutting of the Law of Moses ends in death. The first generation dies in the wilderness.

- **Meaning:** The first comings are associated with the seed. They bear the hallmarks of judgment, condemnation, death, and hiddenness. The resurrection of the Messiah ends in eternal life. The second cutting of the Law of Moses ends in life. The second generation of Israel in the wilderness ascends to the Promised land, which is a picture of resurrected and ascended life (spirit). The resurrection of the administrator of the covenant and the covenant itself (Torah) ends in life (resurrection) for those who are under judgment and are exiles.

- **Messiah:** The first coming of the Messiah is from heaven.

- **Covenant:** First tablets of stone are cut from the top of the mountain by the hand of God.

- **Meaning:** The Messiah and the Covenant (Torah) descended from God via His Utterance (John 1: 1–18). Aside from a literal second coming of the Messiah, we also see a second coming of the Messiah within the hearts of His covenant people.

Acts 1: 11, Which also said, Ye men of Galilee, why stand ye gazing up into heaven? this same Jesus, which is taken up from you into heaven, shall so come in like manner as ye have seen him go into heaven.

Here we see Yeshua's literal return and on Pentecost (Shavuot) we see His return in the hearts of His followers.

Acts 2: 2, And suddenly there came a sound from heaven as of a rushing mighty wind, and it filled all the house where they were sitting. 3 And there appeared unto them cloven tongues like as of fire, and it sat upon each of them. 4 And they were all filled with the Holy Ghost, and began to speak with other tongues, as the Spirit gave them Utterance.

Notice the connections to the first givings of the Torah and how the event on Pentecost (Shavuot) after Yeshua's resurrection has the same hallmarks of the "fire of God" and the "Utterance of God" as already discussed.

The second tablets of stone are cut by Moses at God's Utterance (instruction) while he is in the valley under the shadow of the mountain. These tablets need to ascend into the presence of the declared and manifest Name of YHWH.

Romans 8: 8, So then they that are in the flesh cannot please God. 9 But ye are not in the flesh, but in the Spirit, if so be that the Spirit of God dwell in you. Now if any man have not the Spirit of Christ, he is none of his. 10 And if Christ be in you, the body is dead because of sin; but the Spirit is life because of righteousness.

Notice there is no distinction between Jew and Gentile. Both must have the Messiah Yeshua engrafted. Paul is exact in his wording as he says, "any man", not "any Jew" nor "any Gentile".

What saves that "any man"? The Spirit of Christ.

Remember the Jewish branch was also cut off and the Gentiles were engrafted into the tree of faith in the manifest Name of YHWH, the new administrator. All branches need to be engrafted into the Messiah Yeshua.

Romans 11: 13, For I speak to you Gentiles, inasmuch as I am the apostle of the Gentiles, I magnify mine office: 14 If by any means I may provoke to emulation them which are my flesh, and might save some of them. 15 For if the casting away of them be the reconciling of the world, what shall the receiving of them be, but life from the dead? 16 For if the firstfruit be holy, the lump is also holy: and if the root be holy, so are the branches. 17 And if some of the branches be broken off, and thou, being a wild olive tree, wert grafted in among them, and with them partakest of the root and fatness of the olive tree; 18 Boast not against the branches. But if thou boast, thou bearest not the root, but the root thee. 19 Thou wilt say then, The branches were broken off, that I might be grafted in. 20 Well; because of unbelief they were broken off, and thou standest by faith. Be not highminded, but fear: 21 For if God spared not the natural branches, take heed lest he also spare not thee. 22 Behold therefore the goodness and severity of God: on them which fell, severity; but toward thee, goodness, if thou continue in his goodness: otherwise thou also shalt be cut off. 23 And they also, if they abide not still in unbelief, shall be grafted in: for God is able to graft them in again.

The scripture is clear that we are not grafted into Judah or Israel. We are all (Jews and Gentiles) grafted in via belief in the administrator of the Resurrected Covenant, the Messiah Yeshua, the manifest Name of YHWH. There is no other way. Paul is so clear, saying they were "broken off" from the tree of faith and can be grafted in again once they express faith in the Messiah Yeshua. Notice Paul does not say you are grafted into them, but that you "with them" (if they express faith) partake of the same root, the Messiah, the one we are both grafted into.

- **Messiah:** The first generation of Israel that left Egypt dies in the wilderness just as the testator (Moses) of the covenant does. Moses is not permitted to ascend to the Promised land. Yeshua dies at His first coming fulfilling the imagery of a seed planted in death, exile, and the wilderness of the manifest universe.

- **Covenant:** The second generation of Israel in the wilderness ascends up out of a place of death, "a place of no seed" (Numbers 20: 5), to a place of ascended and resurrected life (Israel), just as their testator (Joshua) does.

- **Meaning:** Joshua is in the image of Moses.

Joshua 1: 7, Only be thou strong and very courageous, that thou mayest observe to do according to all the law, which Moses my servant commanded thee: turn not from it to the right hand or to the left, that thou mayest prosper withersoever thou goest. 8 This book of the law shall not depart out of thy mouth; but thou shalt meditate therein day and night, that thou mayest observe to do according to all that is written therein: for then thou shalt make thy way prosperous, and then thou shalt have good success. 9 Have not I commanded thee? Be strong and of a good courage; be not afraid, neither be thou dismayed: for the Lord thy God is with thee whithersoever thou goest. . . . 17 According as we hearkened unto Moses in all things, so will we hearken unto thee: only the Lord thy God be with thee, as he was with Moses.

We cannot escape the fact that the one who is raised up in the prophetic type or image of Moses is given his charter as the new administrator, like Moses, and is directed to keep the Law of Moses. The implications for the modern Christian in regard to the Law of Moses and these repeating fractals of death and resurrection are inescapable.

- **Messiah:** The Messiah is the seed, broken and planted in the ground just as John says.

John 12: 23, And Yeshua answered them, saying, The hour is come, that the Son of man should be glorified. 24 Verily, verily, I say unto you, Except a corn of wheat fall into the ground and die, it abideth alone: but if it die, it bringeth forth much fruit.

- **Covenant:** The image (copy) made by the Messiah (seed) is His flesh and body (fruit). The first generation saved from Egypt is a picture of the Messiah and the second generation that ascends to the land of Israel is the image of the seed, the flesh and body of the Messiah (the fruit of their seed).

- **Meaning:** The fractal of a seed death (burial) and then the ascension of the fruit of that seed is an image or picture of resurrection life.

1 Corinthians 15: 37, And that which thou sowest, thou sowest not that body that shall be, but bare grain, it may chance of wheat, or of some other grain: 38 But God giveth it a body as it hath pleased him, and to every seed his own body. 39 All flesh is not the same flesh: but there is one kind of flesh of men, another flesh of beasts, another of fishes, and another of birds.

Paul affirms the concept that everybody has a seed. As with nature we all must go through the same pattern of a seed death and then an ascended (resurrected) fruit.

Ephesians 5: 29, For no man ever yet hated his own flesh; but nourisheth and cherisheth it, even as the Lord the church: 30 For we are members of his body, of his flesh, and of his bones. 31 For this cause shall a man leave his father and mother, and shall be joined unto his wife, and they two shall be one flesh.

Believers are depicted as the body and flesh of the Messiah. Yeshua being the spirit (male), we are His body (female). We will be joined just as a man and wife are united in the marriage bed. As a husband places his name upon the wife and she becomes one flesh with her husband, so it is with our redemption. He covers us with His garment and transfers His image on to us.

Ephesians 3: 5, Which in other ages was not made known unto the sons of men, as it is now revealed unto his holy Apostles and prophets by the Spirit; 6 That the Gentiles should be fellowheirs, and of the same body, and partakers of his promise in Christ by the Gospel: 7 Whereof I was made a minister, according to the gift of the grace of God given unto me by the effectual working of his power.

Just as the Messiah is replicating His image in us, making us His body and flesh (seed of the Kingdom of YHWH), He is replicating the image of the covenant (the Torah) by resurrecting it from the broken state of death due to our iniquities. He makes it a new and lively image, resurrected, and embodied in our fleshly hearts.

Ephesians 5: 29, For no man ever yet hated his own flesh; but nourisheth and cherisheth it, even as the Lord the church: 30 For we are members of his body, of his flesh, and of his bones. 31 For this cause shall a man leave his father.

Notice how Paul is associating the male with the Messiah. He identifies the female as being associated with the body.

Ephesians 5: 23, For the husband is the head of the wife, even as Christ is the head of the church: and he is the saviour of the body.

By this we know that the male is associated with the spirit, as the Messiah is a "quickening spirit" and the head of the church, as he describes the male being the head of the female.

1 Corinthians 15: 45, And so it is written, The first man Adam was made a living soul; the last Adam was made a quickening spirit.

If we follow the pattern, image, and fractal we find that the spirit is associated with the seed that must bear the image of burial and death (condemnation and judgment), so that it may break forth in resurrection life when unified in the bridal chamber with his female wife. The female is then depicted as fruit that ascends in unity with her head in resurrection life (grace and mercy). This is the fulfillment of the "promised seed" of Genesis 3: 15–16.

THE MESSIAH, THE IMAGE OF GOD:
1 Peter 1: 2, Elect according to the foreknowledge of God the Father, through sanctification of the Spirit, unto obedience and sprinkling of the blood

of Yeshua: grace unto you, and peace, be multiplied. 3 Blessed be the God and Father of our Lord Yeshua, which according to his abundant mercy hath begotten us again <u>unto a lively hope by the resurrection of Yeshua from the dead</u>, 4 To an inheritance incorruptible, and undefiled, and that fadeth not away, reserved in heaven for you,

Being conformed to the image of God through the work of the death and resurrection of the Messiah, we become the temples of the living Father, the God who we cannot see and live.

1 Peter 2: 4, <u>To whom coming, as unto a living stone, disallowed indeed of men, but chosen of God</u>, and precious, 5 <u>Ye also, as lively stones, are built up a spiritual house</u>, an holy priesthood, to offer up spiritual sacrifices, acceptable to God by Yeshua. 6 Wherefore also it is contained in the scripture, Behold, I lay in Sion a chief corner stone, elect, precious: and he that believeth on him shall not be confounded.

Again the scripture is clear for both Jews and Gentiles, our belief on the new administrator of the Resurrected Covenant is required for our reconciliation to God the Father. There are no exceptions. We cannot establish our own righteousness. We are dependent upon the manifest Name of YHWH to exercise grace and transcribe His image upon us. This is salvation.

Romans 10: 1, Brethren, my heart's desire and prayer to God for Israel is, that they might be saved. 2 For I bear them record that they have a zeal of God, but not according to knowledge. 3 For they being ignorant of God's righteousness, and going about to establish their own righteousness, have not submitted themselves unto the righteousness of God. 4 For Christ is the end of the law for righteousness to every one that believeth. 5 For Moses describeth the righteousness which is of the law, That the man which doeth those things shall live by them. 6 But the righteousness which is of faith speaketh on this wise, Say not in thine heart, Who shall ascend into heaven? (that is, to bring Christ down from above :) 7 Or, Who shall descend into the deep? (that is, to bring up Christ again from the dead.) 8 But what saith it? The word is nigh thee, even in thy mouth, and <u>in thy heart: that is, the word of faith</u>, which we preach; 9 That <u>if thou shalt confess with thy mouth the Lord Yeshua, and shalt believe in thine heart that God hath raised him from the dead, thou shalt be saved</u>. 10 For with the heart man believeth unto righteousness; and with the mouth confession is made unto salvation. 11 For the scripture saith, Whosoever believeth on him shall not be ashamed. 12 For there is no difference between the Jew and the Greek: for the same Lord over all is rich unto all that call upon him. 13 For whosoever shall call upon the Name of the Lord shall be saved.

The Messiah is the manifest Name of the Lord, otherwise known as YHWH. He is the administrator of the Resurrected Covenant (the Law of Moses), which bears the hallmarks of grace and faith.

Trying to establish your own righteousness by keeping the Torah (Law of Moses) without faith in the new administrator, the manifest Name of YHWH, will only result in your judgment and condemnation. It does not matter if you are a Jew or Gentile. There are no exceptions or exemptions.

You are either under the Torah of death or you are under the Torah of resurrected life. In order to be in covenant under the resurrected terms you must acknowledge the Lord, the manifest Name of YHWH, the Messiah Yeshua. His sign of the covenant is resurrection. If He was not resurrected from the dead, then He is not the manifest Name of YHWH.

Some would misapply Romans 10 saying "Israel" is used here as only the exiled ten tribes of Israel and that the Jews have no need of the Messiah as they try to observe the Torah. The context of the scripture is extremely clear. The people of Israel who need to be redeemed are those going about trying to establish their own righteousness without acknowledging belief in the resurrected Lord and administrator of the resurrected Torah, the Messiah Yeshua. Again keeping the Torah will not save you. It leaves you under condemnation and death without the new administrator. This is its purpose, to condemn the flesh.

It is belief in the administrator of the Resurrected Covenant and His transcription of His righteousness upon us that saves us. It then behooves us to keep the resurrected Law of Moses as it has now been transcribed on to our fleshly hearts through the work of the new administrator, Yeshua the Messiah. Notice Paul is exceptionally clear.

> Romans 10: 11, <u>Whosoever believeth on him shall not be ashamed. 12 For there is no difference between the Jew and the Greek: for the same Lord over all is rich unto all that call upon him</u>.

The "whosoevers" refer to both Jew and Greek, both are required to acknowledge the administrator of the Resurrected Covenant in order to be saved. It is not happenstance that Paul is clarifying that it does not matter if you are Jew or Greek when it comes to belief in the manifest Name of YHWH, the Messiah Yeshua. Without doing so, you are not saved and are "under the Law" of condemnation and death. Paul started out this whole section of scripture discussing those who seek to save themselves by keeping the Torah and how they still need to be saved! Why? Because they cannot "establish their own righteousness".

> Romans 10: 1, Brethren, my heart's desire and prayer to God <u>for Israel is, that they might be saved</u>. 2 For I bear them record that <u>they have a zeal of God, but not according to knowledge</u>. 3 For they being ignorant of God's righteousness, and <u>going about to establish their own righteousness, have not submitted themselves unto the righteousness of God</u>.

This is talking about the Jews who rejected the new administrator of the Resurrected Covenant. The Gentiles were not going about trying to establish their own righteousness. They were not even trying to keep the Written Torah. Righteousness is defined as conformance with the Law of Moses.

Let's be clear, there is no new testament or covenant per say. There is a resurrected and renewed covenant. There is a resurrected Messiah. There is a resurrected image, the body of the Messiah comprised of those who are predestined by the calling of the Father.

Just as the Messiah's image is replicated, so also is the image of the covenant (the Torah), from a broken stone to lively stones, from an administration of condemnation and death to an administration of grace and resurrected life. Let's not miss the connection between the change in the covenant and the recognition of the fullness of the Godhead bodily.

Colossians 2: 5, beholding your order, and the stedfastness of your faith in Christ. 6 As ye have therefore received Christ Yeshua the Lord, so walk ye in him: 7 Rooted and built up in him, and stablished in the faith, as ye have been taught, abounding therein with thanksgiving. 8 Beware lest any man spoil you through philosophy and vain deceit, after the tradition of men, after the rudiments of the world, and not after Christ. 9 For in him dwelleth all the fulness of the Godhead bodily. 10 And ye are complete in him, which is the head of all principality and power: 11 In whom also ye are circumcised with the circumcision made without hands, in putting off the body of the sins of the flesh by the circumcision of Christ: 12 Buried with him in baptism, wherein also ye are risen with him through the faith of the operation of God, who hath raised him from the dead. 13 And you, being dead in your sins and the uncircumcision of your flesh, hath he quickened together with him, having forgiven you all trespasses;

THE MESSIAH IS THE COUNTENANCE OF GOD:

The work of the Messiah is to transcribe His countenance (righteousness) on to our countenance. Why? We are not able to transcribe it ourselves. We cannot establish our own righteousness. The Aaronic benediction is in reality a prophecy of the work of Yeshua.

Numbers 6: 25, The Lord make his face shine upon thee, and be gracious unto thee: 26 The Lord lift up his countenance upon thee, and give thee peace. 27 And they shall put my name upon the children of Israel, and I will bless them.

We see this prophetic pattern of rewriting at the engraving of the Resurrected Covenant when the second set of tablets are brought down to Israel by Moses. Notice Moses is changed by his encounter with the manifest Name of YHWH while on the mountain.

Exodus 34: 28, And he was there with the Lord forty days and forty nights; he did neither eat bread, nor drink water. And he wrote upon the tablets the words of the covenant, the ten commandments. 29 And it came to pass, when Moses came down from mount Sinai with the two tablets of testimony in Moses' hand, when he came down from the mount, that Moses wist not that the skin of his face shone while he talked with him. 30 And when Aaron and all the children of Israel <u>saw Moses, behold, the skin of his face shone; and they</u> <u>were afraid to come nigh him</u>.

Remember this is at the engraving of the second set of tablets. Also remember that Moses foreshadows the "prophet" that would come that would be "like unto Moses". This is the manifest Name of YHWH, the Messiah Yeshua, the administrator of the Resurrected Covenant. He is also known as the Utterance (Word) of God.

Notice the similarities of Moses' glorified countenance with Yeshua's glorification. The people of Israel are afraid to come nigh to Yeshua, just as they were afraid to come nigh to Moses with a glorified countenance. The words that were written are the words and Utterance of the covenant. They were the terms of the covenant. They are expressions of the image of God. Because of Israel's fear of Moses' glorified countenance, he had to cover his face with a veil.

Exodus 34: 31, And Moses called unto them; <u>and Aaron and all the rulers</u> <u>of the congregation returned unto him</u>: and Moses talked with them. 32 And <u>afterward all the children of Israel came nigh</u>: and he gave them in commandment all that the Lord had spoken with him in mount Sinai. 33 And <u>till Moses had done speaking with them, he put a vail on his face</u>. 34 But when Moses went in before the Lord to speak with him, he took the vail off, until he came out. And he came out, and spake unto the children of Israel that which he was commanded. 35 And the children of Israel <u>saw the face of Moses,</u> <u>that the skin of Moses' face shone: and Moses put the vail upon his face again,</u> <u>until he went in to speak with him</u>.

Coinciding with the removal of the veil from the glorified countenance of Moses (who is a prophetic image/type of the Messiah) we see the glorification and resurrection of the covenant with grace and life to those stones that are made in the Messiah's image.

Failing to recognize the Countenance of YHWH, the manifest Name of YHWH, the Messiah Yeshua, leads to God intervening so that His name might be openly declared, sanctified, and glorified in the eyes of the people.

Numbers 20: 8, Take the rod, and gather thou the assembly together, thou, and Aaron thy brother, and speak ye unto the rock <u>before their eyes</u>; and it shall give forth his water, and thou shalt bring forth to them water out of the rock: so thou shalt give the congregation and their beasts drink. 9 And Moses took the rod from before the Lord, as he commanded him. 10 And Moses and Aaron gathered the congregation together before the rock, and he said unto them, Hear now, ye rebels; must we fetch you water out of this rock? 11 And Moses lifted up his hand, and with his rod he smote the rock twice: and the water came out abundantly, and the congregation drank, and their beasts also. 12 And the <u>Lord spake unto Moses and Aaron, Because ye believed me not, to</u> <u>sanctify me in the eyes of the children of Israel</u>, therefore ye shall not bring this congregation into the land which I have given them.

Mankind's great failure is refusal to acknowledge "He who comes in the Name of the Lord", the manifest Name of YHWH, the Messiah Yeshua, who is the administrator of the Resurrected Covenant. Our second great failure is not doing as the manifest Name of YHWH has commanded, which is to keep the resurrected Law of Moses because of our faith in its new administrator, Yeshua.

Luke 19: 37, And when he was come nigh, even now at the descent of the mount of Olives, the whole multitude of the disciples began to rejoice and praise God with a loud voice for all the mighty works that they had seen; 38 Saying, Blessed be the King that cometh in the Name of the Lord: peace in heaven, and glory in the highest. 39 And some of the Pharisees from among the multitude said unto him, Master, rebuke thy disciples. 40 And he answered and said unto them, I tell you that, if these should hold their peace, the stones would immediately cry out. 41 And when he was come near, he beheld the city, and wept over it, 42 Saying, If thou hadst known, even thou, at least in this thy day, the things which belong unto thy peace! but now they are hid from thine eyes.

Notice that unless the anointed King is praised as coming in the Name of YHWH, God would allow the stones to come alive and cry out the declaration of His name (the Messiah), who is the presence of the Godhead bodily, the Countenance of YHWH.

Remember the first set of broken tablets, left beneath the mountain, which are broken, dead, and planted in the ground like a seed. The same Utterances (commandments) are proclaimed and engraved upon the new tablets (our hearts) with a new administrator (the manifest Name of YHWH, the Messiah). He is the administrator of better promises and the resurrected Law of Moses (the covenant) written in a better place, our hearts.

As we have already seen in earlier chapters, Moses is associated with being a prophetic type of the Messiah Yeshua and Elijah is associated with the coming of the Name of YHWH being glorified in the peoples' presence.

The Ruach Hakodesh (Holy Spirit) comes from the wilderness (a picture of exile) proclaiming the coming of the countenance of the King, the Messiah, and is responsible for preparing the way of YHWH, teaching repentance and to return to the resurrected Law of Moses as when it was given at Mt. Sinai.

Matthew 3: 1, In those days came John the Baptist, preaching in the wilderness of Judaea, 2 And saying, Repent ye: for the kingdom of heaven is at hand. 3 For this is he that was spoken of by the prophet Esaias, saying, The voice of one crying in the wilderness, Prepare ye the way of the Lord, make his paths straight.

15 REPENT & RETURN TO WHAT?

Acts 2: 38, Then Peter said unto them, Repent, and be baptized every one of you in the name of Jesus Christ for the remission of sins, and ye shall receive the gift of the Holy Ghost.

Repent, In Biblical Hebrew, the idea of repentance is represented by two verbs: שוב shuv (to return) and נחם nicham (to feel sorrow). In the New Testament, the word translated as 'repentance' is the Greek word μετάνοια (metanoia), "after/behind one's mind", which is a compound word of the preposition 'meta' (after, with), and the verb 'noeo' (to perceive, to think, the result of perceiving or observing). In this compound word the preposition combines the two meanings of time and change, which may be denoted by 'after' and 'different'; so that the whole compound means: 'to think differently after'. Metanoia is therefore primarily an after–thought, different from the former thought; a change of mind accompanied by regret and change of conduct, "change of mind and heart", or, "change of consciousness". (Wikipedia)

Repent means to "return" to the former ways (the covenant/the Law of Moses).

1 John 3: 3, And every man that hath this hope in him purifieth himself, even as he is pure. 4 <u>Whosoever committeth sin transgresseth also the law: for sin is the transgression of the law. 5 And ye know that he was manifested to take away our sins</u>; and in him is no sin.

This law as stated in 1 John is the same as ever. It is the Written Torah of Moses. It is not Roman law. It is not some self–determined moral law that leads many professing believers down a path of self–deception and indulgence of iniquity that clearly contradict the scriptures of the Bible.

It is not the Oral Torah (traditions of the rabbis). It certainly is not many of the oral traditions of modern Christian churches. It is the Torah of Moses given by YHWH at Mt. Sinai. Yeshua stated that he would guide the people how to repent and that Elijah would again "first come" and lead the people to return to the Torah of Moses as it was given at Mt. Sinai.

> Matthew 17: 10, And his disciples asked him, saying, <u>Why then say the scribes that Elias must first come?</u> 11And Yeshua answered and said unto them, <u>Elias truly shall first come, and restore all things.</u> 12 But I say unto you, That Elias is come already, and they knew him not, but have done unto him whatsoever they listed. Likewise shall also the Son of man suffer of them.

What is it that this end–time Elijah is supposed to restore the people to? The Resurrected Covenant (the Written Torah) of YHWH. This event is prophesied to immediately precede the end–time coming of the administrator of the Resurrected Covenant, the Messiah Yeshua, the manifest Name of YHWH. Blessed be He who comes in the Name of the Lord (YHWH).

> Malachi 4: 3, And ye shall tread down the wicked; for they shall be ashes under the soles of your feet in the day that I shall do this, saith the Lord of hosts. 4 <u>Remember ye the law of Moses my servant, which I commanded unto him in Horeb for all Israel, with the statutes and judgments. 5 Behold, I will send you Elijah the prophet before the coming of the great and dreadful day of the Lord</u>:

The end–time message is clear. We are to declare for the people of God to repent and return to the Resurrected Covenant, the Torah of Moses. Not the Oral Torah, not the Roman law, not a self–defined and self–indulgent moral law. The scripture is unequivocal; we are to return to the Torah of Moses with the statutes and judgments as it was given at Mt. Horeb (This is the same mountain as Mt. Sinai). Remember this scripture from Malachi is within the context of the end-time "day of the Lord". It is an end–time fulfillment.

Notice it does not direct us to repent and return to the traditions of men, the Oral Torah, pagan traditions, or unscriptural church doctrine. It is very specific. We are to return to the Torah of Moses, as it was when it was given in Mt. Horeb (also known as Mt. Sinai) to the entire nation of Israel, with the statues and judgments! There is no room for doubt that this is referring to the Written Torah, which is called the Law of Moses by Malachi.

Now let us be clear. The Written Torah is the foreshadow image of the "end" or "fulfillment" of the Torah, the Messiah, the Countenance of YHWII. Like Moses' veiled and glorified countenance, this image of YHWH was covered by a veil which kept the people from seeing the glorification, end, fulfillment, or the embodiment of the countenance of the Name of the Lord (YHWH) as the Messiah. He is the administrator of the Resurrected Covenant (Torah) with better promises, "grace and mercy".

This new administrator is the resurrected Messiah Yeshua, the manifest Name of YHWH. Because of the death and resurrection fractal that is fulfilled by the Law of Moses, its new administrator had to fulfill that same fractal of death and resurrection. It is by fulfilling this pattern that He is qualified to serve as the mediator between God and man in the Holy of Holies. Israel fulfilled the same fractal of the death of a seed by having their understanding darkened as they could not behold that glorified countenance due to the veil over their hearts. Just as they fulfilled that portion of the fractal they will also bear the second part of the pattern, resurrection.

Keep in mind the original Written Torah is only a foreshadow image of the fullness of YHWH written on dead stones. It was dead and could not show the full image of God, which is life manifested. Only something that was moving and living, the Messiah, could show forth the fullness of the Godhead bodily (resurrected life) which is the true image of God.

Colossians 2: 16, Let no man therefore judge you in meat, or in drink, or in respect of an holyday, or of the new moon, or of the Sabbath days: 17 Which are a shadow of things to come; but the body is of Christ.

Hence the first Written Torah showed death, no movement, no life, and was symbolically covered by a veil of flesh. There was no glorification of Moses' countenance at the first engraving of the tablets in Exodus 20. His countenance was only glorified with the proclamation of the manifest Name of YHWH in Exodus 34 at the second giving of the Law.

SEED & FRUIT, DEATH & RESURRECTION:
We've learned that the Resurrected Covenant (the Torah of Life) is embodied, living, moving, and shows the full glory of God before the people and "in their eyes" (Numbers 27:14). As the administrator (the Messiah) of the Resurrected Covenant died and rose again to life, so also does the Resurrected Covenant, the Written Torah of YHWH.

Both the administrator and the covenant show the image and fractal of a seed death and ascension to resurrected life like an ascended fruit. Moses pictures the seed death in the wilderness. Elijah, the one who leads the call of repentance to return to the Resurrected Covenant, the Law of Moses, pictures the manifestation of the image of YHWH, the resurrected ascension of fruit and a whole and restored image full of life (promised seed of the woman-Genesis 3:15). That is why you see the transfiguration of Moses and Elijah with Yeshua. Both parts of the fractal need to be present in order to behold the glorified Countenance of God (the Messiah).

Mark 9: 1, And he said unto them, Verily I say unto you, That there be some of them that stand here, which shall not taste of death, till they have seen the kingdom of God come with power. 2 And after six days Yeshua taketh with him Peter, and James, and John, and leadeth them up into an high mountain apart by themselves: and he was transfigured before them. 3 And his raiment became shining, exceeding white as snow; so as no fuller on earth can white them. 4 And there appeared unto them Elias with Moses: and they were talking with Yeshua. 5 And Peter answered and said to Yeshua, Master, it is good for us to be here: and let us make three tabernacles; one for thee, and one for Moses, and one for Elias. 6 For he wist not what to say; for they were sore afraid. 7 And there was a cloud that overshadowed them: and a voice came out of the cloud, saying, This is my beloved Son: hear him. 8 And suddenly, when they had looked round about, they saw no man any more, save Yeshua only with themselves. 9 And as they came down from the mountain, he charged them that they should tell no man what things they had seen, till the Son of man were risen from the dead. 10 And they kept that saying with themselves, questioning one with another what the rising from the dead should mean. 11 And they asked him, saying, Why say the scribes that Elias must first come? 12 And he answered and told them, Elias verily cometh first, and restoreth all things; and how it is written of the Son of man, that he must suffer many things, and be set at nought. 13 But I say unto you, That Elias is indeed come, and they have done unto him whatsoever they listed, as it is written of him.

Notice the connections:

• Just like Moses and Elijah at Mt. Horeb (also known as Mt. Sinai) they ascend a mountain. Both Elijah and Moses go to the same mountain to hear the "voice of God" (1 Kings 19:8–12 and Exodus 20 & 34).

• Both Moses (an image of the original covenant–Torah that brought death) and Elijah (an image of the Resurrected Covenant–Torah) appear with the glorified Countenance of YHWH, the Messiah (the manifested Name of the Lord (YHWH).

• The Utterance (Word) of YHWH manifests Himself in a glorified state (like the manifest Name of YHWH in Exodus 34 and Moses' glorified countenance) and the Father declares that they should make a tabernacle for His Son, the Messiah Yeshua, by "hearing Him".

• They are told to not verbally repeat or replicate the image (by giving testimony) of the work of the manifested Countenance of YHWH, the Messiah Yeshua, until after He had risen from the dead and fulfilled the imagery of the Law of Moses in death and then in resurrection.

• This is why the question is asked why "Elijah must first come" and "restore all things" occurs with the event of the transfiguration and the imagery of the resurrection of the Messiah and the Covenant of God.

• Romans 8: 2 now has added clarity.

   •   Romans 8: 2, For the law of the Spirit of life in Christ Jesus hath made me free from the law of sin and death.

• It is the joining of the imagery of the "law of sin and death" (flesh–Moses) with Elijah (spirit–"law of the spirit"), that is associated with the imagery of the restoration of the stones for the altar of YHWH (1 Kings 18:31–33) and the proclamation for the people to return to the Torah of Moses as it was given at Mt. Horeb/Mt. Sinai. Together these are a picture of death and resurrection and glorification of the Messiah, the Countenance of YHWH. Both Moses and Elijah appear with the glorified Countenance of YHWH, who is the manifest presence of the Name of YHWH, Yeshua. It is after the Utterance by the Father that Yeshua is declared to be the administrator of the

Resurrected Covenant, "This is my beloved Son: hear him" (Mark 9:7).

- Both Moses and Elijah disappear and only the glorified Messiah Yeshua remains with the believer.
- All those involved in the covenant will bear the same imagery, death then resurrection, flesh then spirit, seed then manifested fruit.
- The administrator of the covenant is resurrected. Moses, Elijah, and Yeshua are all prophetic types of death and glorification.
- The tablets (stones) of the covenant are resurrected. The same Utterances are transcribed from one stone to another by the administrator of the covenant, the manifest and declared Name of YHWH.
- The covenant is resurrected; the Written Torah is kept, lost, and restored.
- The condemned participants are exiled, lost, and dead and then found, returned, and resurrected (Ezekiel 37).
- That which is written the first time brings death. It is written on a dead stone. It is not moving or alive. That which is written the second time brings resurrected life, it is moving and alive. It is written in our hearts (Jeremiah 31:33, Hebrews 8:10, Hebrews 10:16).
- On both the tablets of stone and our hearts are written the "same words" (Exodus 34:1).
- **Are Yeshua and the Torah the same thing?** No, that which is written on stone is a foreshadow image of that which is alive, the Messiah, who is the end, the goal, the fulfillment, the fullness of the Godhead bodily. He is literally our righteousness. We cannot establish our own righteousness.

Will keeping the Written Torah save you? No.

Romans 9: 9, For I was alive without the law once: but <u>when the commandment came, sin revived, and I died</u>. 10 And <u>the commandment, which was ordained to life, I found to be unto death</u>. 11 For sin, taking occasion by the commandment, deceived me, and by it slew me.

This covenant, the Written Torah, under the administration of judgment brought condemnation and death to the flesh. This is what it was meant to do. It was fulfilling the fractal of the death of our flesh. We are all guilty under sin, which is the transgression of the Law of Moses. We are not saved by keeping the Torah; we are saved by the new administration of grace and its resurrected administrator, the Countenance of YHWH, the Messiah Yeshua.

Romans 8: 1, <u>There is therefore now no condemnation to them which are in Christ Yeshua</u>, who walk not after the flesh, but after the Spirit. 2 For the <u>law of the Spirit of life in Christ Yeshua hath made me free from the law of sin and death</u>. 3 For <u>what the law could not do, in that it was weak through the flesh, God sending his own Son in the likeness of sinful flesh, and for sin, condemned sin in the flesh:</u>

The Law of Moses brought death and judgment, but now the Resurrected Covenant and its resurrected administrator, the Name of YHWH, the Messiah, is administered with grace and mercy which brings resurrected life via His righteousness. It is not an administration of the flesh. It is fulfilling its fractal of resurrection life (ascended fruit) of the spirit.

Ephesians 2: 1, And you hath he quickened, who were dead in trespasses and sins; 2 Wherein in time past ye walked according to the course of this world, according to the prince of the power of the air, the spirit that now worketh in the children of disobedience: 3 Among whom also we all had our conversation in times past in the lusts of our flesh, fulfilling the desires of the flesh and of the mind; and were by nature the children of wrath, even as others. 4 But God, who is rich in mercy, for his great love wherewith he loved us, 5 Even when we were dead in sins, hath quickened us together with Christ, (by grace ye are saved;) 6 And hath raised us up together, and made us sit together in heavenly places in Christ Yeshua: 7 That in the ages to come he might shew the exceeding riches of his grace in his kindness toward us through Christ Yeshua. 8 For by grace are ye saved through faith; and that not of yourselves: it is the gift of God: 9 Not of works, lest any man should boast. 10 For we are his workmanship, created in Christ Yeshua unto good works, which God hath before ordained that we should walk in them. 11 Wherefore remember, that ye being in time past Gentiles in the flesh, who are called Uncircumcision by that which is called the Circumcision in the flesh made by hands; 12 That at that time ye were without Christ, being aliens from the commonwealth of Israel, and strangers from the covenants of promise, having no hope, and without God in the world: 13 But now in Christ Yeshua ye who sometimes were far off are made nigh by the blood of Christ. 14 For he is our peace, who hath made both one, and hath broken down the middle wall of partition between us; 15 Having abolished in his flesh the enmity, even the law of commandments contained in ordinances; for to make in himself of twain one new man, so making peace; 16 And that he might reconcile both unto God in one body by the cross, having slain the enmity thereby: 17 And came and preached peace to you which were afar off, and to them that were nigh. 18 For through him we both have access by one Spirit unto the Father. 19 Now therefore ye are no more strangers and foreigners, but fellowcitizens with the saints, and of the household of God; 20 And are built upon the foundation of the Apostles and prophets, Yeshua himself being the chief corner stone;

Notice what the exiles and uncircumcised were without that made them strangers to the commonwealth of Israel. They were without the Messiah Yeshua. It was not the lack of the Torah that made them strangers. It was the lack of the resurrected administrator of the Resurrected Covenant that made them strangers. Anyone can be identified with the commonwealth of Israel, if they have the resurrected administrator, the Messiah Yeshua. Notice he did not say it was the lack of the Torah that kept them from being identified as a part of the commonwealth of Israel. Why is that?

Romans 10: 3, For they being ignorant of God's righteousness, and going about to establish their own righteousness, have not submitted themselves unto the righteousness of God.

Even Judah who had the Written Torah and were trying to "establish their own righteousness" thereby were not a part of the commonwealth of Israel because they were still under the tablets associated with death and judgment and the administration of condemnation and death of the flesh. Hence their rejection of faith in the new administrator, the Messiah Yeshua has resulted in their branches being cut off from the covenant of faith despite their having the Law of Moses. They needed to identify with and accept the administrator of the Resurrected Covenant (Law of Moses) under "grace and abundant mercy (spirit)", the resurrected Messiah Yeshua, in order to be in the commonwealth of Israel.

GRAFTED INTO THE MESSIAH...NOT ISRAEL:
The Bible bears out this simple truth. We are not grafted into Judah or Israel. The commonwealth of Israel is identified by the presence of the manifest Name of YHWH, the new administrator of the covenant, the resurrected Messiah Yeshua. It is His work that abolishes the law of death, the first set of tablets, which identify sin and cause judgment and death via the flesh. It is through the Messiah's flesh that He resurrects the tablets, the same Utterances (words), the Law of Moses, this time with grace, mercy, and resurrected life (which is Spirit) and places those same laws within our hearts. The conflict between the Torah and our hearts is now gone. We are not freed from the Law of Moses, we are freed from disobedience.

Ephesians 2: 2, Wherein in time past ye walked according to the course of this world, according to the prince of the power of the air, the spirit that now worketh in the children of disobedience:

It is this state of disobedience that causes God to separate Himself from His people. This is the middle wall of partition that is caused by the violation of the terms of the covenant. Notice Paul is talking about how we who are without the Messiah Yeshua are in exile from God and are separated from God. This "middle wall of partition" of Ephesians 2:14 is not talking about the separation between Judah and the northern ten tribes of Israel (also called Ephraim), nor between Jews and Gentiles, although they fulfill the same pattern of separation as God and His people.
Notice the Gospel of the Messiah is preached to both those that are "far off" and to those that are "near". Both are separated from God and need the middle wall of partition, which separates us from God, to be brought down. Both need the Gospel preached to them so that they might be saved. This is the work of the manifest Name of YHWH. The wall went up between us and God because of our sin and violation of the covenant. When the wall of separation goes up we are without God in the world, Jews and Gentiles alike.

Galatians 3: 22, But the scripture hath concluded all under sin, that the promise by faith of Jesus Christ might be given to them that believe.

The two, God and man, are made one in Yeshua's resurrected flesh and image because he is administrating the Resurrected Covenant based upon grace and mercy. This is the covenant of promise (Ephesians 2:12).

Remember God's goal is to be glorified in the eyes and the presence of His people (Numbers 27:14). We can only behold His image and countenance through the divine union of the glorified and resurrected countenance; the literal end and fulfillment, or embodiment of the manifest Name of YHWH. His image and countenance is transcribed on to ours.

Yeshua slays the enmity of the two and makes them one with a resurrected heart. It is the enmity and separation between God and man that is abolished, which is caused by our transgression of the covenant of God.

> Ephesians 4: 23, And be renewed in the spirit of your mind; 24 And that ye put on the new man, which after God is created in righteousness and true holiness. 25 Wherefore putting away lying, speak every man truth with his neighbour: for we are members one of another.

Yeshua the Messiah made it possible for us to put on the image of the new man, which is after the pattern and image of God, righteous, holy, and without sin. There is then no transgression and therefore no enmity between us and God. We become temples that God can dwell within. There is no separation and we then have the embodiment of God in the world. Through Yeshua's work, God is made manifest in the world and His name is declared to all nations. Immanuel has greater meaning to us now.

> Immanuel-Hebrew עִמָּנוּאֵל meaning, "God with us" (Wikipedia)

The Torah is no longer written on stone but on fleshly tablets. The focus is no longer on uncircumcised flesh but on resurrected spirit, which is a picture of removing the flesh and being circumcised. We then have access to that Spirit of Messiah that gives us access to God. The image of the Messiah is passed on to His people and Immanuel, which means God with us, becomes a manifest reality.

> Matthew 1: 23, Behold, a virgin shall be with child, and shall bring forth a son, and they shall call his name Emmanuel, which being interpreted is, God with us.

How does this happen? Is it through Israel? Are we baptized into Israel or into a better name? Yeshua the Messiah is the better name that we need to put on. He is the image of God, the redeemer. The redeemed are called Israel. The male (spirit) is the Messiah. The female (flesh) is the redeemed. We need to join with Him and ascend as a resurrected fruit.

> Colossians 3: 9, Lie not one to another, seeing that ye have put off the old man with his deeds; 10 And have put on the new man, which is renewed in knowledge after the image of him that created him: 11 Where there is neither

Greek nor Jew, circumcision nor uncircumcision, Barbarian, Scythian, bond nor free: <u>but Christ is all, and in all.</u>

Those who think that these scriptures are only talking about the re–unification of Israel are sadly mistaken. The goal above is clear. Israel and Judah are not only to be reconciled with one another, the ultimate goal is for all things to be reconciled to God.

We see that the believer receives a new name, the name of her husband, the manifest Name of YHWH, who is known as the Angel of YHWH and the Messiah Yeshua. He is prophesied by Moses as the Countenance of God. Can we prove this pattern and fractal in other places in the Torah? Let's turn our hearts to the "fathers" as we have been admonished by Malachi and Yeshua.

> Genesis 32: 1, And Jacob went on his way, and the angels of God met him…22 And he rose up that night, and took his two wives, and his two womenservants, and his eleven sons, and passed over the ford Jabbok. 23 And he took them, and sent them over the brook, and sent over that he had. 24 And Jacob was left alone; and there wrestled a man with him until the breaking of the day. 25 And when he saw that he prevailed not against him, he touched the hollow of his thigh; and the hollow of Jacob's thigh was out of joint, as he wrestled with him. 26 And he said, Let me go, for the day breaketh. And he said, I will not let thee go, except thou bless me. 27 And he said unto him, What is thy name? And he said, Jacob. 28 And he said, Thy name shall be called no more Jacob, but Israel: for as a prince hast thou power with God and with men, and hast prevailed. 29 And Jacob asked him, and said, Tell me, I pray thee, thy name. And he said, Wherefore is it that thou dost ask after my name? And he blessed him there. 30 And Jacob called the name of the place Peniel: for I have seen God face to face, and my life is preserved.

In conjunction with the "redeemed" wrestling with the "redeemer" we see the following patterns.
- The Angel of YHWH meets him/her.
- The redeemed does not let go until he/she receives a blessing.
- The name of the redeemed is changed by the Angel of YHWH.
- The redeemed seeks to know the name of the redeemer.
- The redeemed sees God "face to face" or countenance to countenance.
- The redeemed's life is preserved.

The repeating imagery of the manifestation of the Name of YHWH and the Countenance of God happens in conjunction with the redemption of the believer and God's saving work. The prophetic implications of the Aaronic Benediction should have all the more meaning to us.

> Numbers 6: 25, The Lord make his face shine upon thee, and be gracious unto thee: 26 The Lord lift up his countenance upon thee, and give thee peace. 27 And they shall put my name upon the children of Israel, and I will bless them.

16 TRUE RECONCILIATION...BETWEEN GOD AND MAN

Who needs to be reconciled?

Ephesians 2: 16, And that he might <u>reconcile both unto God in one body</u> by the cross, <u>having slain the enmity thereby</u>:

What is the goal?
...Reconcile BOTH unto God. . . It is not the near and far that are the ultimate reconciliation. Both need reconciliation to God.

Romans 5: 10, For if, when we were enemies, we were reconciled to God by the death of his Son, much more, being reconciled, we shall be saved by his life.

The ultimate goal is the restoration of the Garden of Eden and the relationship that all the creation had with God.

2 Corinthians 5: 18, And all things are of <u>God, who hath reconciled us to himself by Jesus Christ</u>, and hath given to us the ministry of reconciliation; 19 To wit, that God was in Christ, <u>reconciling the world unto himself</u>, not imputing their trespasses unto them; and hath committed unto us the word of reconciliation. 20 Now then we are ambassadors for Christ, as though God did beseech you by us: we pray you in Christ's stead, <u>be ye reconciled to God</u>. 21 For he hath made him to be sin for us, who knew no sin; that we might be made the righteousness of God in him.

How is this accomplished?
"...in one body by the cross. . . " This is not Israel's or Judah's body, this is the body of the manifest Name of YHWH, the Messiah Yeshua.

Whose enmity is slain?

"God in one body". Our spirit is in conflict with God's spirit. The conflict between our hearts and the Torah is done away via the Spirit of the Messiah. Notice Ephesians 2 is talking about the conflicting spirits that operate in the heart and mind of man separated from God.

> Ephesians 2: 1, And you hath he quickened, who were dead in trespasses and sins; 2 Wherein in time past ye walked according to the course of this world, according to the prince of the power of the air, the spirit that now worketh in the children of disobedience:

This spirit cannot keep the Torah and is therefore subject to condemnation, enmity, and death. It must die and be replaced with the Spirit of the Messiah so that this separation and enmity from God can end and man can have God manifest in the world.

The enmity is brought about because we violate the Torah and then become subject to death. That being the case, we must die and be buried with Yeshua, like the breaking of the original tablets, so that we might be resurrected with Him and the Resurrected Covenant, no longer subject to the flesh, but to the Ruach Hakodesh (Holy Spirit), which we receive through the Messiah Yeshua.

The Torah is no longer written on stone but on fleshly tablets. The focus is no longer on uncircumcised flesh but on resurrected spirit, which is a picture of removing the flesh and being circumcised. We then have access to that Spirit of Messiah that gives us access to God. The image of the Messiah is then passed on to His people and Immanuel, which means God with us, becomes a manifest reality.

So what does this mean in the end–times? Embrace the administrator of the Resurrected Covenant. Yeshua is the image of God and you need to be grafted into Him for your salvation thereby obtaining grace and mercy. Follow the leading of the Spirit of the Messiah and return to the Law of Moses as it was given at Mt. Horeb with the statutes and ordinances. The prophet Ezekiel sums this up perfectly in an end–time prophecy.

> Ezekiel 11: 18, And they shall come thither, and they shall take away all the detestable things thereof and all the abominations thereof from thence. 19 And I will give them one heart, and I will put a new spirit within you; and I will take the stony heart out of their flesh, and will give them an heart of flesh: 20 That they may walk in my statutes, and keep mine ordinances, and do them: and they shall be my people, and I will be their God.

Notice the specific outcome is that they "walk in my statutes, and keep mine ordinances, and do them". This is not some arbitrary and capricious self–defined internal moral law that is in conflict with the truth of the scriptures.

Does this mean you can just do what your heart says to do because you are a good person? Can you define your own moral law? Does this mean the Torah (Law of Moses) is done away? Ezekiel is clear we are to follow God's statutes and His ordinances, not ours. The Law of Moses is resurrected! This is the way we are commanded to walk.

Romans 3: 19, Now we know that what things soever the law saith, it saith to them who are under the law: that every mouth may be stopped, and all the world may become guilty before God. 20 Therefore by the deeds of the law there shall no flesh be justified in his sight: for by the law is the knowledge of sin. 21 But now the righteousness of God without the law is manifested, being witnessed by the law and the prophets; 22 Even the righteousness of God which is by faith of Yeshua unto all and upon all them that believe: for there is no difference: 23 For all have sinned, and come short of the glory of God; 24 Being justified freely by his grace through the redemption that is in Christ Yeshua: 25 Whom God hath set forth to be a propitiation through faith in his blood, to declare his righteousness for the remission of sins that are past, through the forbearance of God; 26 To declare, I say, at this time his righteousness: that he might be just, and the justifier of him which believeth in Yeshua. 27 Where is boasting then? It is excluded. By what law? of works? Nay: but by the law of faith. 28 Therefore we conclude that a man is justified by faith without the deeds of the law. 29 Is he the God of the Jews only? is he not also of the Gentiles? Yes, of the Gentiles also: 30 Seeing it is one God, which shall justify the circumcision by faith, and uncircumcision through faith. 31 Do we then make void the law through faith? God forbid: yea, we establish the law.

What identifies sin?
The Law of Moses, the Written Torah, the Covenant.

What makes us righteous?
The righteousness of God "by faith of Yeshua" the Messiah, the administrator of the Resurrected Covenant.

Being in violation of the Torah/Covenant, how are we reconciled to God?
By His grace through the redemption that is in Yeshua the Messiah, through faith in His blood.

Does our righteousness or faithful observance of the Torah save us? No.
God's righteousness saves us through belief on the administrator of the Resurrected Covenant, the resurrected and manifest Name of YHWH, the Messiah Yeshua.

Are there two ways of reconciliation with God, one for those who keep the Torah and one for those who do not? No. There is only one way, the Law of faith—the Resurrected Covenant.

Does this Law of faith nullify our keeping the Torah?
No. We establish the Torah and the Covenant for both those that are near and far.

This law that is established is the Resurrected Covenant (the Law of Moses), the one based on better promises, placed in a better location (our hearts), and administered by the Countenance of YHWH, the Resurrected Messiah. This is the same promise of faith that delivered Abraham.

> Romans 4: 20, <u>He staggered not at the promise of God through unbelief; but was strong in faith,</u> giving glory to God; 21 And being fully persuaded that, <u>what he had promised, he was able also to perform.</u> 22 And therefore <u>it was imputed to him for righteousness.</u> 23 Now it was not written for his sake alone, that it was imputed to him; 24 But for us also, <u>to whom it shall be imputed, if we believe on him that raised up Yeshua our Lord from the dead; 25 Who was delivered for our offences, and was raised again for our justification.</u>

We know the following:
- We are not saved by keeping the Torah.
- We are saved by faith in God (YHWH) and His Countenance (the Messiah), the administrator of the Resurrected Covenant.
- The Torah brings death and judgment through condemnation of sin under the old administration of the flesh.
- The Resurrected Covenant (the Law of Moses) brings life though grace and faith in the work of the redeemer, the new administrator of the Resurrected Covenant. He is the manifest Name of YHWH (Angel of YHWH).
- The Torah brought judgment on the flesh, and the Resurrected Covenant (the Torah) brings life to the spirit.
- We are to return to the Resurrected Covenant, the Law of Moses, administered by Yeshua the Messiah under grace and mercy.
- We are to have faith in the administrator of the Resurrected Covenant to write it on our hearts.
    - o Philippians 1: 6, Being confident of this very thing, that he which hath begun a good work in you will perform it until the day of Yeshua:
- Moses and Elijah are prophetic types of the Countenance of YHWH, the Messiah. Moses pictures the first cutting of the covenant, the Law of Moses, which is associated with judgment and death (flesh). Elijah is prophetic of the second cutting of the Resurrected Covenant though Yeshua, which is associated with the glorified countenance and ascended life (spirit).

17 PROPHETIC SCRIPTURAL PATTERNS & FRACTALS

L et's examine the prophetic patterns and images that we find in the lives of Moses, Elijah, and Yeshua. They will provide insight into the nature of the universe and the means of redemption for all creation. These biblical patterns and fractals will provide great perception into whether modern church doctrine is on or off track. Just as you can check your math division by working backwards through the equation, you can do the same thing with the patterns and fractals (images) of God. "As above so below".

- Exodus 25: 8, And let them make me a sanctuary; that I may dwell among them. 9 According to all that I shew thee, <u>after the pattern of the tabernacle, and the pattern of all the instruments thereof</u>, even so shall ye make it.

- Exodus 25: 40, And <u>look that thou make them after their pattern</u>, which was shewed thee in the mount.

- Hebrews 8: 5, <u>Who serve unto the example and shadow of heavenly things</u>, as Moses was admonished of God when he was about to make the tabernacle: for, See, saith he, that thou make all things according to the pattern shewed to thee in the mount.

- Hebrews 9: 23, It was therefore necessary <u>that the patterns of things in the heavens</u> should be purified with these; but the heavenly things themselves with better sacrifices than these.

- 1 Corinthians 15: 49, And as <u>we have borne the image of the earthy</u>, we shall also <u>bear the image of the heavenly</u>.

We also see clearly that the things manifested on earth are after the pattern and image (fractal) of the heavenly.

Genesis 1: 26, And <u>God said, Let us make man in our image, after our likeness</u>: and let them have dominion over the fish of the sea, and over the fowl of the air, and over the cattle, and over all the earth, and over every creeping thing that creepeth upon the earth. 27 So <u>God created man in his own image, in</u>

the image of God created he him; male and female created he them.

God also clarified that all creatures would manifest after their particular kind (pattern).

Genesis 1: 24, And God said, Let the earth bring forth the living creature after his kind, cattle, and creeping thing, and beast of the earth after his kind: and it was so. 25 And God made the beast of the earth after his kind, and cattle after their kind, and every thing that creepeth upon the earth after his kind: and God saw that it was good.

We see here the biblical pattern of a creation (manifestation) occurring according to its heavenly pattern and kind. The Apostle Paul confirms this scriptural paradigm. He shows us the pattern of death and burial (seed) and resurrection (body or manifestation). The body results from its own particular seed. Paul affirms the necessity of death so that all things might live according to the spirit. It begins below and ascends above. It starts in corruption and ends in incorruption. It moves from weakness to strength and from dishonor to glory.

1 Corinthians 15: 35, But some man will say, How are the dead raised up? and with what body do they come? 36 Thou fool, that which thou sowest is not quickened, except it die: 37 And that which thou sowest, thou sowest not that body that shall be, but bare grain, it may chance of wheat, or of some other grain: 38 But God giveth it a body as it hath pleased him, and to every seed his own body. 39 All flesh is not the same flesh: but there is one kind of flesh of men, another flesh of beasts, another of fishes, and another of birds. 40 There are also celestial bodies, and bodies terrestrial: but the glory of the celestial is one, and the glory of the terrestrial is another. 41 There is one glory of the sun, and another glory of the moon, and another glory of the stars: for one star differeth from another star in glory. 42 So also is the resurrection of the dead. It is sown in corruption; it is raised in incorruption: 43 It is sown in dishonour; it is raised in glory: it is sown in weakness; it is raised in power: 44 It is sown a natural body; it is raised a spiritual body. There is a natural body, and there is a spiritual body. 45 And so it is written, The first man Adam was made a living soul; the last Adam was made a quickening spirit. 46 Howbeit that was not first which is spiritual, but that which is natural; and afterward that which is spiritual. 47 The first man is of the earth, earthy; the second man is the Lord from heaven. 48 As is the earthy, such are they also that are earthy: and as is the heavenly, such are they also that are heavenly. 49 And as we have borne the image of the earthy, we shall also bear the image of the heavenly. 50 Now this I say, brethren, that flesh and blood cannot inherit the kingdom of God; neither doth corruption inherit incorruption. 51 Behold, I shew you a mystery; We shall not all sleep, but we shall all be changed, 52 In a moment, in the twinkling of an eye, at the last trump: for the trumpet shall sound, and the dead shall be raised incorruptible, and we shall be changed. 53 For this corruptible must put on incorruption, and this mortal must put on immortality. 54 So when this corruptible shall have put on incorruption, and this mortal shall have put on

immortality, then shall be brought to pass the saying that is written, Death is swallowed up in victory. 55 O death, where is thy sting? O grave, where is thy victory?

Paul clarifies that flesh and blood is incapable of inheriting the Kingdom of God and the necessity of our death so that we might be raised a spiritual body in strength, glory, and power. That is why we are left with the comfort of, "O death, where is thy sting? O grave, where is thy victory? " (1 Corinthians 15:55)

Let's examine the biblical fractals that we find related to Moses (death), Elijah (resurrection life), and Yeshua who is the fulfillment of death and resurrection life. We should begin to understand why both Moses and Elijah appear with Yeshua on the Mount of Transfiguration and then disappear!

We will examine the patterns and images in brevity. The pattern is either easily observed or it is not. No amount of grand explanation can make the pattern more self–evident.

Prophetic Pattern: Stones

Moses: The breaking and making of the two sets of tablets of stone. (Exodus 32:19 & 34:1)

Elijah: The restoring the altar stones of YHWH and teaching the way of return from false worship.

1 Kings 18:30, And Elijah said unto all the people, Come near unto me. And all the people came near unto him. And he repaired the altar of the Lord that was broken down.

Yeshua: The Messiah is the manifest presence of the Countenance of YHWH, in death and life. The Cornerstone is first rejected and then made chief cornerstone. He is the writer of the covenant and He is the fire (glory) of God (the Shekinah) upon the altar of God (us). Just as He is the head of the body, he is also the head (chief cornerstone) of the altar.

Matthew 21: 42, Jesus saith unto them, Did ye never read in the scriptures, The stone which the builders rejected, the same is become the head of the corner: this is the Lord's doing, and it is marvellous in our eyes?

Prophetic Pattern: Ascending & Descending

Moses: Moses ascends and descends the mountain and enters the cloud (Shekinah Glory) on the mount (Exodus 19:16, 34:5 , Deuteronomy 4:11, 5:22)

Elijah: Elijah ascends into the Shekinah via the whirlwind (pillar of cloud by day) (Exodus 13: 21).

Yeshua: The manifest presence of the Glory of YHWH is the administrator of the Resurrected Covenant, the Messiah. We see this in the transfiguration when Yeshua and the disciples ascend up a mountain (Matthew 17:5) where the Shekinah

Glory overshadows Him and the Father declares "this is my beloved Son, hear Him", and at Yeshua's ascension after His resurrection (Acts 1: 9–11) where He ascends into the Shekinah Glory.

> Acts 1: 9, And when he had spoken these things, while they beheld, he was taken up; and a cloud received him out of their sight.

Prophetic Pattern: Breaking Stones

Moses: The first tablets of stone are carved from the top of the mountain and then are broken beneath the mountain, which is a picture of death.

Elijah: Elijah is judging the profane priests who teach false worship and false traditions of men. He is declaring the need to repent and return to the Law of Moses. The people need to ascend with Elijah by uniting the broken stones into the altar, which is a picture of ascension and resurrection life and returning to the Law of Moses.

Yeshua: The breaking of the stones is a picture of the rejection and death of the Messiah. Just as the tablets are broken and buried under the mountain, so also is the Messiah (buried like a seed), by taking on the transgressions of the covenant. "He is wounded for our transgressions" (Isaiah 53:5). The Messiah pays this penalty to provide the grace for the repentant to ascend with the resurrected administrator of the Resurrected Covenant.

> Acts 4: 10, Be it known unto you all, and to all the people of Israel, that by the name of Jesus Christ of Nazareth, whom ye crucified, whom God raised from the dead, even by him doth this man stand here before you whole. 11 This is the stone which was set at nought of you builders, which is become the head of the corner. 12 Neither is there salvation in any other: for there is none other name under heaven given among men, whereby we must be saved.

The Messiah is the stone that is broken for us. He is fulfilling the same pattern as the tablets of stone that the Law of Moses were written upon.

> Isaiah 53: 5, But he was wounded for our transgressions, he was bruised for our iniquities: the chastisement of our peace was upon him; and with his stripes we are healed.

Just as we take on the image of the Messiah, we fulfill the same fractal of being crushed.
- Matthew 21: 44, And whosoever shall fall on this stone shall be broken: but on whomsoever it shall fall, it will grind him to powder.
- Romans 6: 4, Therefore we are buried with him by baptism into death: that like as Christ was raised up from the dead by the glory of the Father, even so we also should walk in newness of life.
- 1 Corinthians 11: 23, For I have received of the Lord that which also I delivered unto you, that the Lord Jesus the same night in which he was betrayed

took bread: 24 And when he had given thanks, he brake it, and said, Take, eat: this is my body, which is broken for you: this do in remembrance of me.

Prophetic Pattern: Restoring Stones

Moses: Moses is instructed by God to carve the new set of stone tablets down in the valley and to carry them up the mountain, causing them to ascend to the top of the mountain, for inscription by the manifest Name of YHWH (Exodus 34).

Elijah: Elijah is gathering the stones of the altar to the top of Mt. Carmel and restoring the Torah of Moses to the lawless (exiles).

> 1 Kings 18: 17, And it came to pass, when Ahab saw Elijah, that Ahab said unto him, Art thou he that troubleth Israel? 18 And he answered, I have not troubled Israel; but thou, and thy father's house, in that ye have forsaken the commandments of the Lord, and thou hast followed Baalim. 19 Now therefore send, and gather to me all Israel unto mount Carmel, and the prophets of Baal four hundred and fifty, and the prophets of the groves four hundred, which eat at Jezebel's table. 20 So Ahab sent unto all the children of Israel, and gathered the prophets together unto mount Carmel.

Yeshua: The resurrected administrator writes the Resurrected Covenant (Law of Moses) in the hearts of those who have faith in the Messiah. It is an administration of the Spirit.

- Luke 20: 17, And he beheld them, and said, What is this then that is written, The stone which the builders rejected, the same is become the head of the corner?
- Hebrew 10: 15, Whereof the Holy Ghost also is a witness to us: for after that he had said before, 16 This is the covenant that I will make with them after those days, saith the Lord, I will put my laws into their hearts, and in their minds will I write them; 17 And their sins and iniquities will I remember no more.

Prophetic Pattern: Glorification & the Countenance

Moses: Moses' countenance is glorified and covered.

> Exodus 34:28, 28 And he was there with the Lord forty days and forty nights; he did neither eat bread, nor drink water. And he wrote upon the tables the words of the covenant, the ten commandments. 29 And it came to pass, when Moses came down from mount Sinai with the two tables of testimony in Moses' hand, when he came down from the mount, that Moses wist not that the skin of his face shone while he talked with him. 30 And when Aaron and all the children of Israel saw Moses, behold, the skin of his face shone; and they were afraid to come nigh him. 31 And Moses called unto them; and Aaron and all the rulers of the congregation returned unto him: and Moses talked with them.

Elijah: Elijah is taken up into the Shekinah with imagery of the transfer of his countenance to a "garment" that is later transferred to Elisha.

- 1 Kings 19: 13, And it was so, when <u>Elijah heard it, that he wrapped his face in his mantle</u>, and went out, and stood in the entering in of the cave. And, behold, there came a voice unto him, and said, What doest thou here, Elijah?... 19 So he departed thence, and found Elisha the son of Shaphat, who was plowing with twelve yoke of oxen before him, and he with the twelfth: and Elijah passed by him, and <u>cast his mantle upon him</u>.
- 2 Kings 2: 1, And it came to pass, when <u>the Lord would take up Elijah into heaven by a whirlwind</u>, that Elijah went with Elisha from Gilgal.

Yeshua: Yeshua is the actual Countenance of YHWH (Matthew 28:3). Moses, who was prophetic of Yeshua, covered his glorified countenance when he descended the mountain before the people. When he goes back into the presence of God (the Shekinah–the cloud) he removes the garment from his glorified countenance.

Prophetic Pattern: Covering Garment

Moses: The garment is typified by the veil that covers Moses glorified countenance via its donning and removal depending upon if Moses is with the people or with God.

Elijah: Elijah passes his covering garment (with his countenance) which is called his "mantle", on to Elisha. Elijah's image (countenance wrapped in his mantle) is passed onto one who will double his miracles.

Yeshua: The believer participates in the death of Yeshua's flesh and blood (the garment of the manifest Name of YHWH) and His resurrection with a glorified body. This is the passing on of the image of God, the Countenance of God, on to His body, the ascended manifestation (the second generation). This second generation are the redeemed that ascend to the Promised land with Joshua and are prophetic of the believer redeemed by Christ, passing from death to life, and from the flesh to the spirit.

- 1 Corinthians 11: 23, For I have received of the Lord that which also I delivered unto you, that the Lord Jesus the same night in which he was betrayed took bread: 24 And when he had given thanks, he brake it, and said, Take, eat: this is my body, which is broken for you: this do in remembrance of me. 25 After the same manner also he took the cup, when he had supped, saying, this cup is the new testament in my blood: this do ye, as oft as ye drink it, in remembrance of me. 26 For as often as ye eat this bread, and drink this cup, ye do shew the Lord's death till he come.
- 2 Kings 2: 11, And it came to pass, as they still went on, and talked, that, behold, there appeared a chariot of fire, and horses of fire, and parted them both asunder; and Elijah went up by a whirlwind into heaven. 12 And Elisha saw it, and he cried, My father, my father, the chariot of Israel, and the horsemen thereof. And he saw him no more: and he took hold of his own clothes, and rent them in two pieces. 13 <u>He took up also the mantle of Elijah that fell from him</u>, and went back, and stood by the bank of Jordan; 14 And <u>he</u>

took the mantle of Elijah that fell from him, and smote the waters, and said, Where is the Lord God of Elijah? and when he also had smitten the waters, they parted hither and thither: and Elisha went over. 15 And when the sons of the prophets which were to view at Jericho saw him, they said, The spirit of Elijah doth rest on Elisha. And they came to meet him, and bowed themselves to the ground before him.

- John 7: 37, In the last day, that great day of the feast, Jesus stood and cried, saying, If any man thirst, let him come unto me, and drink. 38 He that believeth on me, as the scripture hath said, out of his belly shall flow rivers of living water. 39 (But this spake he of the Spirit, which they that believe on him should receive: for the Holy Ghost was not yet given; because that Jesus was not yet glorified.)

- Luke 24: 49, And, behold, I send the promise of my Father upon you: but tarry ye in the city of Jerusalem, until ye be endued with power from on high. 50 And he led them out as far as to Bethany, and he lifted up his hands, and blessed them.

- Acts 2: 38, Then Peter said unto them, Repent, and be baptized every one of you in the name of Jesus Christ for the remission of sins, and ye shall receive the gift of the Holy Ghost. 39 For the promise is unto you, and to your children, and to all that are afar off, even as many as the Lord our God shall call.

Prophetic Pattern: Scattering of the People

Moses: All of the people are afraid of the glorified countenance of Moses and move afar off.

Exodus 34: 29, And it came to pass, when Moses came down from mount Sinai with the two tablets of testimony in Moses' hand, when he came down from the mount, that Moses wist not that the skin of his face shone while he talked with him. 30 And when Aaron and all the children of Israel saw Moses, behold, the skin of his face shone; and they were afraid to come nigh him. 31 And Moses called unto them; and Aaron and all the rulers of the congregation returned unto him: and Moses talked with them.

Elijah: Elijah is working to gather those who are "afar off" from God, those who are profane and without God in the world. Those who have a spirit of disobedience are being cleansed and through the Messiah receive His Holy Spirit. Through the sin of Adam all of creation is "far off" from God.

Mark 1: 14, Now after that John was put in prison, Jesus came into Galilee, preaching the Gospel of the kingdom of God, 15 And saying, The time is fulfilled, and the kingdom of God is at hand: repent ye, and believe the Gospel.

Yeshua: The work of the Messiah is to save the nation and those scattered abroad from perishing.

John 11: 49, And one of them, named Caiaphas, being the high priest that same year, said unto them, Ye know nothing at all, 50 Nor consider that it is expedient for us, that one man should die for the people, and that the whole nation perish not. 51 And this spake he not of himself: but being high priest that year, he prophesied that Yeshua should die for that nation; 52 And not for that nation only, but that also he should gather together in one the children of God that were scattered abroad.

Prophetic Pattern: Return & Repentance of the People
Moses: The people return near to Moses once he speaks to them after descending from the mountain.

> Exodus 34: 29, And it came to pass, when Moses came down from mount Sinai with the two tablets of testimony in Moses' hand, when he came down from the mount, that Moses wist not that the skin of his face shone while he talked with him. 30 And when Aaron and all the children of Israel saw Moses, behold, the skin of his face shone; and <u>they were afraid to come nigh him. 31 And Moses called unto them; and Aaron and all the rulers of the congregation returned unto him</u>: and Moses talked with them. 32 And afterward all the children of Israel came nigh: and he gave them in commandment all that the Lord had spoken with him in mount Sinai. 33 And till Moses had done speaking with them, he put a vail on his face. 34 But when Moses went in before the Lord to speak with him, he took the vail off, until he came out. And he came out, and spake unto the children of Israel that which he was commanded. 35 And the children of Israel saw the face of Moses, that the skin of Moses' face shone: and Moses put the vail upon his face again, until he went in to speak with him.

Elijah: Elijah goes to the same mountain as Moses (Mt. Sinai which is also called Mt. Horeb) until the voice of YHWH speaks to him in the "still small voice". Elijah with his restored spirit, goes to anoint Elisha and transfer his garment and mantle of authority to him. It is through this "voice" of God that repentance is called for. The pivotal question is asked, "What is the Lord in"? He is in the "still small voice" otherwise known as the Utterance and the Word of God.

> 1 Kings 19: 11, And he said, Go forth, and stand upon the mount before the Lord. And, behold, the Lord passed by, and a great and strong wind rent the mountains, and brake in pieces the rocks before the Lord; but the Lord was not in the wind: and after the wind an earthquake; but the Lord was not in the earthquake: 12 And after the earthquake a fire; but the Lord was not in the fire: and after the fire a still small voice. 13 And it was so, when Elijah heard it, that he wrapped his face in his mantle, and went out, and stood in the entering in of the cave. And, behold, there came a voice unto him, and said, What doest thou here, Elijah?

Yeshua: In the Messiah we see the presentation of the Word of God calling all of creation to repentance. The Messiah is the combination of the glorified Countenance of God and the Utterance of God, otherwise known as the "fullness of the Godhead bodily".

John 1: 1, In the beginning was the Word, and the Word was with God, and the Word was God. 2 The same was in the beginning with God. 3 All things were made by him; and without him was not any thing made that was made. 4 In him was life; and the life was the light of men. 5 And the light shineth in darkness; and the darkness comprehended it not. 6 There was a man sent from God, whose name was John. 7 The same came for a witness, to bear witness of the light, that all men through him might believe. 8 He was not that light, but was sent to bear witness of that light. 9 That was the true light, which lighteth every man that cometh into the world. 10 He was in the world, and the world was made by him, and the world knew him not. 11 He came unto his own, and his own received him not. 12 But as many as received him, to them gave he power to become the sons of God, even to them that believe on his name: 13 Which were born, not of blood, nor of the will of the flesh, nor of the will of man, but of God. 14 And the Word was made flesh, and dwelt among us, (and we beheld his glory, the glory as of the only begotten of the Father,) full of grace and truth. 15 John bare witness of him, and cried, saying, This was he of whom I spake, He that cometh after me is preferred before me: for he was before me. 16 And of his fulness have all we received, and grace for grace. 17 For the law was given by Moses, but grace and truth came by Yeshua. 18 No man hath seen God at any time, the only begotten Son, which is in the bosom of the Father, he hath declared him.

How does God manifest His "fullness"? By declaring and manifesting the Name of YHWH with grace and abundant mercy (Exodus 34: 5–7). This manifest Name is the Messiah Yeshua.

Hebrews 1: 3, Who being the brightness of his glory, and the express image of his person, and upholding all things by the word of his power, when he had by himself purged our sins, sat down on the right hand of the Majesty on high: 4 Being made so much better than the angels, as he hath by inheritance obtained a more excellent name than they. 5 For unto which of the angels said he at any time, Thou art my Son, this day have I begotten thee? And again, I will be to him a Father, and he shall be to me a Son?

The work of the manifest Name of YHWH is passing on His image to the redeemed.

___

Prophetic Pattern: The Body of the Redeemer
Moses: Moses' body is buried in the wilderness and is subject to a dispute of angels.

Jude 1: 9, Yet Michael the archangel, when contending with the devil he disputed about the body of Moses, durst not bring against him a railing accusation, but said, The Lord rebuke thee.

Elijah: Elijah's body ascends alive into the Shekinah and is not found.

2 Kings 2: 16, And they said unto him, Behold now, there be with thy servants fifty strong men; let them go, we pray thee, and seek thy master: lest peradventure the Spirit of the Lord hath taken him up, and cast him upon some mountain, or into some valley. And he said, Ye shall not send. 17 And when they urged him till he was ashamed, he said, Send. They sent therefore fifty men; and they sought three days, but found him not.

Yeshua: The Countenance of YHWH, the Messiah's body, is subject to death, burial, dispute over the body, and resurrection and ascension into the Shekinah (Matthew 26:64, Mark 13:26, 16:19, Luke 24:51, Acts 1:9-11, 1 Thessalonians 4:17)

Prophetic Pattern: Disappearance of the Body
Moses: There is a dispute over Moses' body that was buried in the wilderness. The body could not be found.

Elijah: Elijah was not found when he went up into the whirlwind.

Yeshua: The Messiah's fleshly body cannot be located by those who killed Him. Yeshua ascended into heaven and is hidden.
- Luke 24: 3, And they entered in, and found not the body of the Lord Jesus.
- Matthew 28: 11, Now when they were going, behold, some of the watch came into the city, and shewed unto the chief priests all the things that were done. 12 And when they were assembled with the elders, and had taken counsel, they gave large money unto the soldiers, 13 Saying, Say ye, His disciples came by night, and stole him away while we slept.
- John 20: 17, Jesus saith unto her, Touch me not; for I am not yet ascended to my Father: but go to my brethren, and say unto them, I ascend unto my Father, and your Father; and to my God, and your God.
- John 3: 13, And no man hath ascended up to heaven, but he that came down from heaven, even the Son of man which is in heaven.
  - o Keep in mind the imagery of Elijah ascending into the whirlwind (Shekinah Glory) and not being found does not mean that he did not return. The imagery is presenting his literal ascent into the Shekinah Glory while ascending in the air (heaven) via a Chariot of Fire. (2 Chronicles 21:12)

Prophetic Pattern: Death & Resurrected Life
Moses: He is subject to death in the wilderness.

Elijah: He ascended to life via the whirlwind.

Yeshua: He submitted to death and resurrected to life literally.

Prophetic Pattern: Corruption & Incorruption

Moses: He is focused on fallen and corruptible flesh.

Elijah: He is focused on the ascension of spirit via the Ruach Hakodesh (Holy Spirit).

Yeshua: He is subject to the flesh and death and then resurrected to the Spirit.

Prophetic Pattern: Death of the Seed & Manifestation of the Fruit

Moses: His principal prophetic type is "seed", which must die and be buried. This is typified by Moses and the first generation of Israel dying in the wilderness.

Elijah: His principal prophetic type is "manifestation" (fruit) of the Presence of YHWH, the hearing of the Utterance of God, and the manifestation of the Countenance of YHWH, the Messiah.

Yeshua: Yeshua is a combination of the seed that must die and be planted in the ground so that many in His image may ascend and come to glory. Seed (Elohim) produces image/fruit (YHWH). We will examine this pattern later.

Prophetic Pattern: Rebellion & Repentance

Moses: The first generation of Israel called out of Egypt is in rebellion against God and dies in the wilderness.

- Numbers 14: 35, I the Lord have said, I will surely do it unto all this evil congregation, that are gathered together against me: in this wilderness they shall be consumed, and there they shall die.

- Numbers 26: 65, For the Lord had said of them, They shall surely die in the wilderness. And there was not left a man of them, save Caleb the son of Jephunneh, and Joshua the son of Nun.

Elijah: Israel is called to repentance, restoration and return to God and the Law of Moses.

1 Kings 18: 21, And Elijah came unto all the people, and said, How long halt ye between two opinions? if the Lord be God, follow him: but if Baal, then follow him. And the people answered him not a word.

Yeshua: God is reconciling the lawless (those afar off from God) through the restoration provided via the Countenance of YHWH, the manifestation of the Name of YHWH, the Messiah.

Prophetic Pattern: Judgment & Grace

Moses: Judgment and condemnation

Elijah: Grace and forgiveness

Yeshua: Judgment/condemnation (death) then grace (resurrection life)

Prophetic Pattern: Defilement & Purification

Moses: The work of purification is done for the exiles wandering in the wilderness. Moses via the Torah is teaching them how to purify themselves of a fallen and corruptible image.

Elijah: The work is done for the returning (repentant) exiles wandering without God in the world. Elijah is working to return the profane and idolatrous to the worship of YHWH via the Resurrected Torah.

Yeshua: Yeshua the Messiah makes two into one. God is able to dwell within man through the Spirit of the Messiah. God's countenance is glorified and transcribed via the image of the Messiah onto the believer.

Isaiah 7: 14, Therefore the Lord himself shall give you a sign; Behold, a virgin shall conceive, and bear a son, and shall call his name Immanuel.

We will discuss the concept of Immanuel meaning "God with us" in later chapters.

Prophetic Pattern: Manifestation of the Utterance (Word) of YHWH

Moses: Utterance of YHWH is made manifest before the people and in their eyes.

- Exodus 19: 7, And Moses came and called for the elders of the people, and laid <u>before their faces all these words</u> which the Lord commanded him.
  - o Do not miss the connection between the words being spoken before the "face" or "countenance" of the believer. This is not a casual reference but a purposeful one.
- Leviticus 10: 3, Then Moses said unto Aaron, This is it that the Lord spake, saying, <u>I will be sanctified in them</u> that come nigh me, and before all the people I will be glorified. And Aaron held his peace.
- Numbers 27: 14, For ye rebelled against my commandment in the desert of Zin, in the strife of the congregation, <u>to sanctify me at the water before their eyes</u>: that is the water of Meribah in Kadesh in the wilderness of Zin.

Elijah: The focus is upon hearing "the still small voice" of God. Elijah hears the voice of YHWH at Mt. Horeb. The critical question is "what is God in"?

1 Kings 19: 11, And he said, Go forth, and stand upon the mount before the Lord. And, behold, <u>the Lord passed by</u>, and a great and strong wind rent the mountains, and brake in pieces the rocks before the Lord; but the Lord was not in the wind: and after the wind an earthquake; but the Lord was not in the earthquake: 12 And after the earthquake a fire; <u>but the Lord was not in the fire:</u>

and after the fire a still small voice. 13 And it was so, when Elijah heard it, that he wrapped his face in his mantle, and went out, and stood in the entering in of the cave. And, behold, there came a voice unto him, and said, What doest thou here, Elijah? 14 And he said, I have been very jealous for the Lord God of hosts: because the children of Israel have forsaken thy covenant, thrown down thine altars, and slain thy prophets with the sword; and I, even I only, am left; and they seek my life, to take it away.

YHWH is in the "still small voice". Elijah is experiencing the same event that Moses went through when he pleaded with God to show him "your face" (countenance).

Exodus 33: 18, And he said, I beseech thee, shew me thy glory. 19 And he said, I will make all my goodness pass before thee, and I will proclaim the Name of the Lord before thee; and will be gracious to whom I will be gracious, and will shew mercy on whom I will shew mercy. 20 And he said, Thou canst not see my face: for there shall no man see me, and live. 21 And the Lord said, Behold, there is a place by me, and thou shalt stand upon a rock: 22 And it shall come to pass, while my glory passeth by, that I will put thee in a clift of the rock, and will cover thee with my hand while I pass by: 23 And I will take away mine hand, and thou shalt see my back parts: but my face shall not be seen.

Both Elijah and Moses have the Lord (the manifest Name of YHWH) pass before them and God's glory is presented to them. For Elijah "the Lord passed by" (1 Kings 19:11) and for Moses "I will make all my goodness pass before thee, and I will proclaim the Name of the Lord before thee." (Exodus 33:19). Because God's face cannot be seen, He manifests the Name of YHWH which is the image of God and the fullness of the Godhead bodily. The Messiah is literally the Countenance of God dwelling with man.

Yeshua: The Utterance (Word) is made flesh that He might make manifest the Name of YHWH before the people and in their eyes.
- John 12: 28, Father, glorify thy name. Then came there a voice from heaven, saying, I have both glorified it, and will glorify it again. "
- Those who have "ears to hear" will believe on the Messiah Yeshua and hear the Word of YHWH.
  - o   John 1: 12, But as many as received him, to them gave he power to become the sons of God, even to them that believe on his name:

Believing on the Word of God requires both the seed and the manifestation of hearing. It requires a willing heart and a willing teacher.
- Ezekiel 12: 2, Son of man, thou dwellest in the midst of a rebellious house, which have eyes to see, and see not; they have ears to hear, and hear not: for they are a rebellious house.
- Matthew 11: 14, And if ye will receive it, this is Elias, which was for to come. 15 He that hath ears to hear, let him hear.

- Mark 4: 22, For there is nothing hid, which shall not be manifested; neither was any thing kept secret, but that it should come abroad. 23 If any man have ears to hear, let him hear.
- Matthew 10: 7, And as ye go, preach, saying, The kingdom of heaven is at hand.
- Matthew 11: 5, The blind receive their sight, and the lame walk, the lepers are cleansed, and the deaf hear, the dead are raised up, and the poor have the Gospel preached to them.
- Mark 6: 12, And they went out, and preached that men should repent.
- Mark 16: 15, And he said unto them, Go ye into all the world, and preach the Gospel to every creature.
- Luke 4: 17, And there was delivered unto him the book of the prophet Esaias. And when he had opened the book, he found the place where it was written, 18 The Spirit of the Lord is upon me, because he hath anointed me to preach the Gospel to the poor; he hath sent me to heal the brokenhearted, to preach deliverance to the captives, and recovering of sight to the blind, to set at liberty them that are bruised, 19 To preach the acceptable year of the Lord.
- Luke 24: 47, And that repentance and remission of sins should be preached in his name among all nations, beginning at Jerusalem.
- Romans 10: 13, For whosoever shall call upon the Name of the Lord shall be saved. 14 How then shall they call on him in whom they have not believed? and how shall they believe in him of whom they have not heard? and how shall they hear without a preacher? 15 And how shall they preach, except they be sent? as it is written, How beautiful are the feet of them that preach the Gospel of peace, and bring glad tidings of good things! 16 But they have not all obeyed the Gospel. For Esaias saith, Lord, who hath believed our report? 17 So then faith cometh by hearing, and hearing by the word of God. 18 But I say, Have they not heard? Yes verily, their sound went into all the earth, and their words unto the ends of the world. 19 But I say, Did not Israel know? First Moses saith, I will provoke you to jealousy by them that are no people, and by a foolish nation I will anger you. 20 But Esaias is very bold, and saith, I was found of them that sought me not; I was made manifest unto them that asked not after me.

Prophetic Pattern: First generation equals sin and death (seed) & the second generation equals grace and resurrected life (manifested fruit)

Moses: The first generation called out of Egypt dies in the wilderness. It is a picture of a dead and buried seed like the Messiah. The testator and intercessor, Moses, also dies in the wilderness which is a picture of the flesh. The first generation and their intercessor bear the same image and pattern of a seed that requires burial, hiddenness, exile, and scattering.

Elijah: The second generation that left Egypt, is the ascended fruit of the seed (the first generation). They ascend to life in the Promised land, which is a picture of resurrection. Joshua as their new intercessor who is in the image of Moses ascends with them. Elijah as the intercessor ascends into heaven (the Whirlwind or the Shekinah Glory), which is a picture of the spirit. The second generation and their intercessor bear the same image and pattern of a fruit ascending in resurrection life and attachment to the Shekinah Glory.

Yeshua: We are called in Yeshua to both die to self (flesh) and to ascend to resurrection life (Spirit) in Yeshua the Messiah. We are cut into the Resurrection Covenant through the resurrected Messiah that we may have resurrection life!

Prophetic Pattern: First rock of Exodus 17 equals striking and death (seed). The second rock of Numbers 20 is the voice transcription (preaching the gospel and planting the seed of the Kingdom of God) of the image of God on to the believer (manifest fruit).

Moses: The key issue of Moses intercession is the continual rebellion and judgment of Israel under the Torah's first administration of condemnation and judgment. This is why the entire generation except Joshua and Caleb die in the wilderness.

With the first striking of the rock in conjunction with the Angel of YHWH (death) the key issue, is "is the Lord among us or not?"

- Exodus 17: 7, And he called the name of the place Massah, and Meribah, because of the chiding of the children of Israel, and because they tempted the Lord, saying, Is the Lord among us, or not?
- The first rock that is struck is prophetic of the Messiah descending from the Father in order to fulfill the imagery of a seed death. He descended just like the first tablets of the covenant and is broken and buried for our transgressions.
- Isaiah 53: 5, But he was wounded for our transgressions, he was bruised for our iniquities: the chastisement of our peace was upon him; and with his stripes we are healed.

Elijah: The key issue at the second striking of the rock is transmitting of the Countenance of YHWH to the rock of our hearts (the second generation). The key question is, "why are they in a place of no seed"?

Numbers 20: 5, And wherefore have ye made us to come up out of Egypt, to bring us in unto this evil place? it is no place of seed, or of figs, or of vines, or of pomegranates; neither is there any water to drink.

The second striking of the rock was done in violation of God's instructions by the administrator (Moses and Aaron) and should have been done via the Utterance (Word) of the administrator of the covenant. This is imagery presenting the transmission of life (seed, image, life) from the Utterance (the Word of YHWH) to those who have no life (seed) in themselves.

The Messiah is pictured as sowing the seed of the Kingdom of God because the place we are in, the manifest universe, is a wilderness of "no seed". It has a fallen and corrupt image. It no longer produces the seed and image of God.

Matthew 13: 24, Another parable put he forth unto them, saying, The kingdom of heaven is likened unto a man which sowed good seed in his field: 25 But while men slept, his enemy came and sowed tares among the wheat, and went his way. 26 But when the blade was sprung up, and brought forth fruit, then appeared the tares also. 27 So the servants of the householder came and said unto him, Sir, didst not thou sow good seed in thy field? from whence then hath it tares? 28 He said unto them, An enemy hath done this. The servants said unto him, Wilt thou then that we go and gather them up? 29 But he said, Nay; lest while ye gather up the tares, ye root up also the wheat with them. 30 Let both grow together until the harvest: and in the time of harvest I will say to the reapers, Gather ye together first the tares, and bind them in bundles to burn them: but gather the wheat into my barn.

We need the image of God (the good seed) restored to us. We are incapable of doing the writing ourselves, as is the administrator of the flesh which has become our enemy. This is why Yeshua had to come and set up a new and more glorious administration of the spirit.

The second rock that is struck is prophetic of those who need to be redeemed, which dies, then comes to life via Utterance of God. We were intended to live, but then descended like a seed and were struck with death until we received the transcribed image of YHWH via the Utterance of YHWH which made us alive again like a resurrected and ascended fruit. This is just like the second set of stone tablets that the covenant was written upon.

Yeshua: Yeshua the Messiah fulfills both events of the striking of the rock in the first generation (death) and the transcribing of the image of YHWH (life) to the second rock via the Utterance of God. The second stone pictures the resurrected and lively stone that brings forth the waters of life via the transcribed countenance of YHWH.

- John 7: 37, In the last day, that great day of the feast, Jesus stood and cried, saying, If any man thirst, let him come unto me, and drink. 38 He that believeth on me, as the scripture hath said, out of his belly shall flow rivers of living water.

- 1 Corinthians 10: 4, And did all drink the same spiritual drink: for they drank of that spiritual rock that followed them: and that rock was Christ.

Just as the Messiah produces living waters, His role is to transcribe His image upon us by the preaching of the Word, so that by faith in Him we can replicate His image and also bring forth "living waters". He is the first stone struck (death) and we are the second stone that bears the striking of death, but is brought to life by the Word of God. Remember burial of the dead seed brings forth a replicated image. We have no seed in ourselves, which is why we must have the seed of the Kingdom of God.

- Mark 4: 25, For he that hath, to him shall be given: and he that hath not, from him shall be taken even that which he hath. 26 And he said, <u>So is the kingdom of God, as if a man should cast seed into the ground;</u> 27 And should sleep, and rise night and day, and the seed should spring and grow up, he knoweth not how.

- 1 Corinthians 15: 42, So also is the resurrection of the dead. <u>It is sown in corruption; it is raised in incorruption: 43 It is sown in dishonour; it is raised in glory: it is sown in weakness; it is raised in power: 44 It is sown a natural body; it is raised a spiritual body.</u> There is a natural body, and there is a spiritual body. 45 And so it is written, The first man Adam was made a living soul; the last Adam was made a quickening spirit. <u>46 Howbeit that was not first which is spiritual, but that which is natural; and afterward that which is spiritual.</u> 47 The first man is of the earth, earthy; the second man is the Lord from heaven. 48 As is the earthy, such are they also that are earthy: and as is the heavenly, such are they also that are heavenly. 49 And <u>as we have borne the image of the earthy, we shall also bear the image of the heavenly.</u> 50 Now this I say, brethren, that flesh and blood cannot inherit the kingdom of God; neither doth corruption inherit incorruption. 51 Behold, I shew you a mystery; We shall not all sleep, but we shall all be changed, 52 In a moment, in the twinkling of an eye, at the last trump: for the trumpet shall sound, and the dead shall be raised incorruptible, and we shall be changed. 53 For this corruptible must put on incorruption, and this mortal must put on immortality. 54 So when this corruptible shall have put on incorruption, and this mortal shall have put on immortality, then shall be brought to pass the saying that is written, Death is swallowed up in victory. 55 O death, where is thy sting? O grave, where is thy victory?

First we must descend like a seed and then ascend like a resurrected fruit.

MOSES & ELIJAH; PROPHETIC PATTERNS & FRACTALS OF THE PROMISED MESSIAH:

Often Jews will reject the Messiah Yeshua for one reason. They claim that He did not regather the exiles and restore the Kingdom of Israel. For that reason they call Him a failed prophet. We must remember that Moses is a prophetic type of the Messiah. If we carry over the same logic that rabbinic Judaism has applied to Yeshua, then we must also disqualify Moses.

Moses would then qualify as a failed prophet and failed intercessor since he died in the wilderness and was not able to deliver the exiles of that first generation of Israel that left Egypt. They died in the wilderness. It took another intercessor to deliver them up to the Promised land. It was Joshua, someone who followed in the image of Moses, that delivered the people up to the land of Promise. Even though Moses administered the cutting of the first covenant (Torah), he did not deliver the people from the wilderness.

In accordance with the prophetic image presented by Moses, Yeshua died in the wilderness of the manifest universe. And following the prophetic pattern of accession as presented by Elijah, Yeshua was then resurrected so that He could cut the Resurrected Covenant (Torah) in our hearts.

He literally dwells within believers via the Ruach Hakodesh (Holy Spirit). It is this spirit that reconciles both into one as Ephesians 2 has already shown us. It is through the Messiah Yeshua's death and resurrection that the middle wall of partition between us and God has been torn down. It is the Messiah Yeshua's spirit that intercedes between our spirit and God, making us living stones and living temples of the presence of God.

Yeshua is the one that both Judah and the scattered ones are grafted into. We are not grafted into Israel. We are not grafted into Judah. Judah, Israel, and all scattered people need reconciliation to God through the work of the manifest Name of YHWH, Yeshua the Messiah, the Word of God. The two that are made one are us and God. This is the restoration of the image of God. This is the work of the Messiah. This is the redemption of man. This is Immanuel, God with man. This is the resurrection of the dead.

Ephesians 2: 1, And you hath he quickened, who were dead in trespasses and sins;

It is the enmity between us and God due to our transgression of the covenant that is done away through the work of the Messiah.

Ephesians 2: 16, And that he might reconcile both unto God in one body by the cross, having slain the enmity thereby: 17 And came and preached peace to you which were afar off, and to them that were nigh. 18 For through him we both have access by one Spirit unto the Father.

The Law of faith, the Resurrected Covenant, the Law of Moses is remembered and administered with the Utterance and manifestation of the Name of YHWH, Yeshua the Messiah. This process of redemption from exile in the wilderness took more than one generation. So if the prophetic type holds true, it is the one who is made in the image of Moses, Joshua, who delivers the people up to the land of Israel. Also it is the joint work of the end–time Elijah to restore the people of God via the Resurrected Covenant. Remember, the prophetic pattern is always the same, seed then flesh, hidden then revealed, death then resurrection.

Romans 8: 28, And we know that all things work together for good to them that love God, to them who are the called according to his purpose. 29 For whom he did foreknow, he also did predestinate to be conformed to the image of his Son, that he might be the firstborn among many brethren. 30 Moreover whom he did predestinate, them he also called: and whom he called, them he also justified: and whom he justified, them he also glorified.

If we conform to the image of YHWH, the Messiah, the Countenance of God, we will walk as He walked. Yeshua the Messiah, the manifest Name of YHWH administers the Law of Moses as it was given at Mt. Sinai (Mt. Horeb) with the statues and ordinances. As Malachi 4 instructs, this is a prophecy for the end–time day of the Lord.

Revelation 12: 17, And the dragon was wroth with the woman, and went to make war with the remnant of her seed, which keep the commandments of God, and have the testimony of Yeshua.

These "commandments of God" are the Written Law of Moses. Follow the resurrected administrator of the Resurrected Covenant and the image will repeat itself in you. You will be resurrected!

18 I'M CONFUSED...WHAT HAS CHANGED?

W hat has changed as it relates to the Resurrected Covenant (the Law of Moses)?
- The administration of death is gone and replaced with an administration of resurrection life.
- The administrator of death is done away and replaced with an administrator of resurrection life, Yeshua the Messiah, the manifest Name of the Lord (YHWH).
- The location of the Utterances written by YHWH is no longer on external rock but on fleshly hearts, which are brought forward in faith in YHWH and His administrator, mediator, and intercessor, Yeshua the Messiah (the Name of YHWH manifested).
- The administration of judgment and condemnation is done away and replaced with an administration of grace and abundant mercy.
- The mediator of this better covenant with better promises is the manifestation of the Name of YHWH, the Countenance of YHWH, the image of God, the resurrected Messiah Yeshua.

What has <u>NOT</u> changed as it relates to the Resurrected Covenant?
- The Utterances (words) are the same for the first covenant and the Resurrected Covenant.
- The writer of the Utterances (words) is the same, it is YHWH.
- The same people are engaged in the covenant, whether they be near or far (exiled), home born or sojourner, any "whosoever".
- Everyone must make the same choice to enter into the Resurrected Covenant, through faith in the Messiah Yeshua. It is available to all peoples everywhere, no matter who they are descended from.
  - o Exodus 12: 38, And a mixed multitude went up also with them; and flocks, and herds, even very much cattle.

- Romans 10: 12, For there is no difference between the Jew and the Greek: for the same Lord over all is rich unto all that call upon him. 13 For whosoever shall call upon the Name of the Lord shall be saved. 14 How then shall they call on him in whom they have not believed? and how shall they believe in him of whom they have not heard? and how shall they hear without a preacher?
- Exodus 12: 48, And when a stranger shall sojourn with thee, and will keep the Passover to the Lord, let all his males be circumcised, and then let him come near and keep it; and he shall be as one that is born in the land: for no uncircumcised person shall eat thereof. 49 <u>One law shall be to him that is homeborn, and unto the stranger that sojourneth among you</u>. 50 Thus did all the children of Israel; as the Lord commanded Moses and Aaron, so did they.)

If we follow the image of YHWH, the patterns of redemption are clear! There is a resurrected administrator of a Resurrected Covenant (the Written Torah of Moses) for a resurrected and redeemed people. God and man are made one.

The patterns and images of resurrection are set forth clearly in the scriptures:
- Seed then flesh
- Death then life
- Striking then Utterance
- Judgment then mercy
- Exiled then redeemed
- Wilderness then ascension
- Separation then unity
- Uncleanness then cleansing
- Hearing then testimony
- Divided then joined
- Female then unified male and female
- Shadow then reality
- Partial then completeness (Shalom, Wholeness, Goal, End)
- Broken then healed
- Hidden then revealed
- Descend then ascend
- Corruptible then incorruptible
- Flesh then spirit
- Death then resurrected life
- Darkness then light
- Iniquity then righteousness
- Weakness then power
- Dull of hearing then hearing
- Blind then seeing
- Light then manifested image,

- Covenant of death (Torah) then Covenant of Life (Resurrected Torah).

As scripture has proven, the very same covenant and the very same words that were on the first set of tablets are written on the new set of tablets. The only change was the location, stone versus our hearts and the administrator (the Messiah), the Name of the Lord, Yeshua Adonai YHWH.

The first covenant was under the administration of condemnation and judgment (death), the second set of tablets is under righteousness and mercy (resurrected life) and the Messiah Yeshua (the Name of YHWH is manifested before the people).

- The Messiah is resurrected.
- The people are resurrected.
- The covenant is resurrected.
- The universe is resurrected.

The pattern and image repeats itself showing the Glory of YHWH.

AM I DOING WHAT IS SCRIPTURALLY ACCURATE?
Let's examine the following religious groups by critical topic: Christian, Rabbinic Judaism, Messianic Jew, and Two–House Messianic.

1. **DO YOU KEEP THE WRITTEN TORAH, THE LAW OF MOSES?**

Yes, that is required no matter who you are, Jew or Gentile. The saved spirit that is in reconciliation with God's spirit through Yeshua the Messiah's redemptive work needs to remember the Law of Moses as Malachi 4 prophesied.

Malachi 4: 4, <u>Remember ye the law of Moses</u> my servant, which I commanded unto him in Horeb for all Israel, <u>with the statutes and judgments</u>. 5 Behold, <u>I will send you Elijah</u> the prophet before the coming of the great and dreadful day of the Lord: 6 And he shall turn the heart of the fathers to the children, and the heart of the children to their fathers, <u>lest I come and smite the earth with a curse</u>.

2. **DO YOU REQUIRE THE ORAL TORAH (RABBINICAL TRADITIONS) OBSERVANCE FOR REDEMPTION?**

The scriptures are replete with Yeshua, Paul, and the Apostles rejecting all forms of traditions of men, be they Rabbinic, Pagan, Christian, or otherwise that cause you to violate the "commandments of God", as a requirement for salvation. Furthermore those Messianic Jews and Two–House that teach you must keep the Oral Law are in conflict with Yeshua and His teachings.

- Matthew 15: 3, But he answered and said unto them, Why do ye also transgress the commandment of God by your tradition? . . .9 But in vain they do worship me, <u>teaching for doctrines the commandments of men</u>.

- Deuteronomy 4:2, <u>Ye shall not add unto the word which I command you</u>, neither shall ye diminish ought from it, that ye may keep the commandments of the Lord your God which I command you.
- Joshua 8:33, And all Israel, and their elders, and officers, and their judges, stood on this side the ark and on that side before the priests the Levites, which bare the ark of the covenant of the Lord, as well the stranger, as he that was born among them; half of them over against mount Gerizim, and half of them over against mount Ebal; as Moses the servant of the Lord had commanded before, that they should bless the people of Israel. 34 And afterward <u>he read all the words of the law, the blessings and cursings, according to all that is written in the book of the law</u>. 35 <u>There was not a word of all that Moses commanded, which Joshua read</u> not before all the congregation of Israel, with the women, and the little ones, and the strangers that were conversant among them.

3. DO YOU HOLD FAITH IN THE MANIFEST NAME OF THE LORD YHWH?

Having faith in the manifest Name of YHWH, Yeshua the Messiah is required no matter what group you are from.

- Matthew 23: 37, O Jerusalem, Jerusalem, thou that killest the prophets, and stonest them which are sent unto thee, how often would I have gathered thy children together, even as a hen gathereth her chickens under her wings, and ye would not! 38 Behold, your house is left unto you desolate. 39 For I say unto you, Ye shall not see me henceforth, <u>till ye shall say, Blessed is he that cometh in the Name of the Lord</u>.
- Acts 2: 20, The sun shall be turned into darkness, and the moon into blood, before the great and notable day of the Lord come: 21 And it shall come to pass, that <u>whosoever shall call on the Name of the Lord shall be saved</u>. 22 Ye men of Israel, hear these words; Yeshua of Nazareth, a man approved of God among you by miracles and wonders and signs, which God did by him in the midst of you, as ye yourselves also know:

Moses' example is clear at the cutting of the second set of tablets with the manifestation of the Name of YHWH declared as the administrator of the Resurrected Covenant. Moses immediately bowed and worshiped the manifest Name of YHWH when He was presented to him.

Exodus 34: 4, And <u>he hewed two tablets of stone like unto the first</u>; and Moses rose up early in the morning, and went up unto mount Sinai, as the Lord had commanded him, and took in his hand the two tablets of stone. 5 And the <u>Lord descended in the cloud, and stood with him there, and proclaimed the Name of the Lord. 6 And the Lord passed by before him, and proclaimed, The Lord, The Lord God, merciful and gracious,</u> longsuffering, and abundant in goodness and truth, 7 Keeping mercy for thousands, forgiving iniquity and transgression and sin, and that will by no means clear the guilty; visiting the iniquity of the fathers upon the children, and upon the children's children, unto the third and to the fourth generation. 8 And <u>Moses made haste, and bowed his head toward the earth, and worshipped</u>. 9 And he said, <u>If now I have found grace in thy sight, O Lord, let my Lord, I pray thee, go among us</u>; for it is a stiffnecked people; and pardon our iniquity and our sin, and take us for thine inheritance.

Yeshua is not the Torah. Yeshua is the manifest Name of YHWH, who is the administrator of the Resurrected Covenant, the Law of Moses. The Written Torah is only a shadow image of the end, reality, fulfillment, embodiment, and manifestation of the Name of YHWH, the Messiah.

4. DO YOU REQUIRE THE BELIEVER TO REJECT THE MANIFEST NAME OF THE LORD YHWH?
Rabbinic Jews require the convert to verbally swear and reject the Messiah Yeshua before a Beit Din (Rabbinical Court or Beth Din) and keep the traditions of men (Oral Law of the rabbis) in order to be in covenant with God. Yeshua is the administrator of the Resurrected Torah, the Written Law of Moses, as given at Mt. Sinai, so rejection of His redemptive work is contrary to the will of God.
Furthermore those Messianic Jews that teach that you must keep the Oral Law are in conflict with Yeshua and His teachings. Not all Messianic groups demand this, but some do.

Matthew 15: 9, But in vain they do worship me, teaching for doctrines the commandments of men.

5. DO YOU REQUIRE THE BELIEVER TO REJECT THE RESURRECTED TORAH (LAW OF MOSES AS GIVEN AT MT. SINAI):
Not all Rabbinic Jews and Messianic Jews believe the Law of Moses is for the entire world. In many cases Rabbinic Jews teach that the Written Torah of Moses is for Judah only and Gentiles are only allowed to keep a very small portion of the Written Torah, called the Noahide Laws. This is in direct conflict with the teachings of the Torah. There is one Torah for the home–born and the sojourner.

Exodus 12: 48, And when a stranger shall sojourn with thee, and will keep the Passover to the Lord, let all his males be circumcised, and then let him come near and keep it; and <u>he shall be as one that is born in the land</u>: for no uncircumcised person shall eat thereof. 49 <u>One law shall be to him that is homeborn, and unto the stranger that sojourneth among you</u>. 50 Thus did all the children of Israel; as the Lord commanded Moses and Aaron, so did they.

Modern Christianity requires that you reject the keeping of the Written Torah. This is in direct conflict with the Gospel of Yeshua the Messiah. Currently all sects are not aware of the Resurrected Torah and have made up their own moral law. The Messiah has made it clear what law His followers should be adhering to, the Law of Moses.

Matthew 5: 16, Let your light so shine before men, that they may see your good works, and glorify your Father which is in heaven. 17 <u>Think not that I am come to destroy the law, or the prophets: I am not come to destroy, but to fulfil</u>. 18 For verily I say unto you<u>, Till heaven and earth pass, one jot or one tittle shall in no wise pass from the law, till all be fulfilled</u>. 19 Whosoever therefore shall <u>break one of these least commandments, and shall teach men so, he shall be called the least in the kingdom of heaven</u>: but <u>whosoever shall do and teach them, the same shall be called great in the kingdom of heaven</u>. 20 For I say unto you, That except your righteousness shall exceed the righteousness of the scribes and Pharisees, ye shall in no case enter into the kingdom of heaven.

6. DO YOU RECOGNIZE THE MESSIAH AS THE IMAGE OF YHWH, THE PRESENCE OF THE GODHEAD BODILY?

Rabbinic Judaism and many Messianic assemblies reject the idea of the manifestation of God. Those Rabbinic and Messianic Jews that have not recognized Yeshua the Messiah as being the manifest Name of the Lord (YHWH) are in conflict with the clear teachings of the Torah and the testimony of the Apostles. Some Messianic assemblies try to affirm the Shema (the Oneness of God) by saying that Yeshua is the manifestation of the Torah instead of the scripturally accurate statements that Yeshua is the "fullness of the Godhead bodily", the "manifest Name of YHWH", and "the image of God". They do so because they cannot reconcile the scriptures with their incorrect paradigm regarding the nature of God. We will delve into this topic in a later chapter.

Christianity does acknowledge Yeshua as being the manifestation of the Name of YHWH, but have mistakenly tried to divide God into two or three entities. The Shema and the scriptures are clear. There is only one God, one spirit, and one name that the believer is baptized into.

Yeshua is the manifestation of the one God, one spirit, and one name on earth. He is the administrator of the Resurrected Torah, the Written Law of Moses as given at Mt. Sinai. Believers, after being saved by faith in His Name, must accept the Resurrected Torah, the Written Law of Moses as given at Mt. Sinai, and by doing so we will come out of lawlessness (iniquity) and be reconciled to God.

2 Thessalonians 2: 7, For the mystery of iniquity doth already work: only he who now letteth will let, until he be taken out of the way.

This mystery of iniquity is believing on Yeshua through grace and living torahlessly (lawless and being full of iniquity).

Matthew 7: 20, Wherefore by their fruits ye shall know them. 21 <u>Not every one that saith unto me, Lord, Lord, shall enter into the kingdom of heaven;</u> but he that doeth the will of my Father which is in heaven. 22 many will say to me in that day, Lord, Lord, have we not prophesied in thy name? and in thy name have cast out devils? and in thy name done many wonderful works? 23 <u>And then will I profess unto them, I never knew you: depart from me, ye that work iniquity</u>. 24 Therefore whosoever heareth these sayings of mine, and doeth them, I will liken him unto a wise man, which built his house upon a rock: 25 And the rain descended, and the floods came, and the winds blew, and beat upon that house; and it fell not: for it was founded upon a rock.

Remember the following about Yeshua's role as the administrator of the Resurrected Covenant as the manifest Name of YHWH.

1.   Malachi 4: 3, And ye shall tread down the wicked; for they shall be ashes under the soles of your feet in the day that I shall do this, saith the Lord of hosts. 4 <u>Remember ye the law of Moses my servant, which I commanded unto him in Horeb for all Israel</u>, with the statutes and judgments. 5 Behold, <u>I will send you Elijah the prophet before the coming of the great and dreadful day of the Lord</u>:

2.   God's expectation in the end time is that followers of Yeshua will "remember the Law of Moses". It is also His expectation that those who have rejected the Messiah Yeshua will repent and call upon His name.

Matthew 23: 38, Behold, your house is left unto you desolate. 39 For I say unto you, Ye shall not see me henceforth, <u>till ye shall say, Blessed is he that cometh in the Name of the Lord</u>.

This is how God glorified His name in the eyes and the presence of the people. Not just before them, but in them. It starts with the Messiah and is transferred to our hearts.

John 12: 27, Now is my soul troubled; and what shall I say? Father, save me from this hour: but <u>for this cause came I unto this hour</u>. 28 <u>Father, glorify thy name</u>. Then came there a voice from heaven, saying, <u>I have both glorified it, and will glorify it again</u>. 29 The people therefore, that stood by, and heard it, said that it thundered: others said, An angel spake to him.

The work of the Messiah is to reunite the two that are divided, God and man. It all begins with the manifestation of the Name of YHWH and results in the Resurrected Covenant being written in our hearts.

Exodus 34: 5, And <u>the Lord descended in the cloud, and stood with him there, and proclaimed the Name of the Lord</u>. 6 And the Lord passed by before him, <u>and proclaimed, The Lord, The Lord God, merciful</u> and gracious, longsuffering, and abundant in goodness and truth, 7 Keeping mercy for thousands, forgiving iniquity and transgression and sin, and that will by no means clear the guilty; visiting the iniquity of the fathers upon the children, and upon the children's children, unto the third and to the fourth generation. 8 And Moses made haste, and bowed his head toward the earth, and worshipped.

Just as the manifest Name of YHWH is declared to Moses, we see the fulfillment of the coming of His manifest Name in Luke.

Luke 2: 9, And, lo, the angel of the Lord came upon them, and the <u>glory of the Lord shone round about them</u>: and they were sore afraid. 10 And the angel said unto them, Fear not: for, behold, <u>I bring you good tidings of great joy, which shall be to all people</u>. 11 For unto you is born this day in the city of David a <u>Saviour, which is Christ the Lord</u>. 12 And this shall be a sign unto you; Ye shall find the babe wrapped in swaddling clothes, lying in a manger. 13 And suddenly there was with the angel a multitude of the heavenly host praising God, and saying, 14 <u>Glory to God in the highest, and on earth peace, good will toward men</u>.

Having established the fact that we cannot save ourselves and that we must be redeemed by the Messiah Yeshua, let's discuss the nature of our existence and what it means to be flesh and spirit.

19 PERFECTING THE SPIRIT; WHAT DO THE PATTERNS OF SCRIPTURE ACTUALLY SAY ABOUT THE DUALITY OF OUR EXISTENCE?

We have discussed the ultimate importance of being grafted into the Messiah and how there is no substitute for His redemptive work. In prior chapters we have clarified how we are grafted into the tree of the Messiah via faith in His name and that there is no other Tree of Life that we can be grafted into and be redeemed. We will continue to clarify the necessity of becoming one with the Messiah and what that means.

We have clarified how Romans 11 is talking about the Tree of Life we are grafted into and how that tree has often been misidentified as Israel, Judah or the Torah. Here is a brief recap of how Romans 11 clarifies that we are grafted into the Messiah Yeshua, the manifest Name of YHWH, via a singular and unwavering faith. We must take careful note of the patterns that are revealed in the scriptures and manifest reality (the manifest universe), for in these patterns the mysteries of God are revealed.

> Romans 1: 20, For the invisible things of him from the creation of the world are clearly seen, being understood by the things that are made, even his eternal power and Godhead; so that they are without excuse: 21 Because that, when they knew God, they glorified him not as God, neither were thankful; but became vain in their imaginations, and their foolish heart was darkened. 22 Professing themselves to be wise, they became fools, 23 And changed the glory of the uncorruptible God into an image made like to corruptible man, and to birds, and fourfooted beasts, and creeping things.

This redemption of our minds happens by the light of the Messiah, not by Israel or Judah. So how is it we have come to this conclusion that we are grafted into Israel or Judah? We will review Romans 11 in depth. But first let us not confuse the issue of who has redeemed us. It is the Messiah Yeshua, the manifest Name of YHWH! Let's pay particular note to how the tree from Romans 11 is associated with faith and deliverance. Remember, this tree imagery is associated with Genesis 3 and the two trees in the Garden of Eden. Adam and Eve, like us, were submitted to a test of being part of a tree or being exiled from a tree. This involved a test of their belief or lack thereof in the Word of God. God had already told them the consequences of being a part of each tree and because of their lack of faith, unbelief, they chose to become a part of and grafted into the Tree of the Knowledge of Good and Evil (duality).

How are we then delivered from this tree of duality? We must be grafted into the Tree of Life, Yeshua the Messiah, via faith in His name. Israel is walking out the same pattern as Adam and Eve. Adam and Eve, Israel, and all of creation are powerless to deliver themselves from exile.

Let's recap how this tree of Romans 11 is not Israel, Judah, or the Torah, and clarify how this Tree of Life has everything to do with the manifest Name of YHWH, the Messiah Yeshua, and deliverance by a singular faith in His name.

Furthermore, we need to address the issue of whether the church is a separate entity from Israel. It is a presupposition to say that the church was born on Pentecost or that the church was separate from Israel from that date on. Why is this issue so critical? Most of the church has rejected the Law of Moses contrary to Yeshua's plain statements that He did not come to do away with the Law of Moses.

Matthew 5: 17, Think not that I am come to destroy the law, or the prophets: I am not come to destroy, but to fulfil.

The scriptures make it clear that those of faith are "Israel". How is Romans 11 interpreted by most Christians? They say that the believer is grafted into either Israel or Judah. They assume that the tree is Judah or Israel because Judah's branches are grafted into a tree that is "natural" to them. But is this what Romans 11 is saying?

If you would like to review the whole chapter and make sure the symbols and metaphor are properly interpreted, please go back and re-read the full analysis in Chapter 8.

Let's analyze what Romans 11 is saying and then review it in light of Romans 2. Paul is clarifying what really counts as making you a descendant of Abraham and being "grafted into the tree of faith". As usual he is contrasting the flesh versus the spirit, and faith versus unbelief. He is making it clear that what makes one of the tree is "faith". Once that seed of faith is established in the heart, it will then manifest itself in righteous conduct, which is obedience to the Law of Moses.

Flesh Versus Spirt based on Romans 2 & 11		
Flesh	**Spirit**	**What Counts?**
Not all Israel act like Israel	Not all Gentiles act like Gentiles	How you act
Not all circumcised act circumcised	Not all uncircumcised act uncircumcised	Your true state will manifest itself
Circumcision of the heart is what counts.	Circumcision of the spirit is what counts	True circumcision of the heart & spirit
Try to establish your own righteousness by works and fail	God establishes your righteousness by faith in His manifest Name, the Messiah	Key question is how are you established/saved
Moses and the works of the law leaves you under condemnation and death	Abraham and the law of faith leaves you under grace (no condemnation) and resurrected life	What leaves you free of condemnation? Law of faith only.
Boasting would suggest you have done some work to become worthy. Hence your branch is doing the work for the root (by carrying it) instead of the root carrying the branch.	Not boasting would suggest worthiness comes by faith in the manifest Name of YHWH, the Messiah through faith in His name. Hence the root is properly carrying the branch (you).	Faith is without boasting. You did NOTHING of worth. The work is the Messiah's. The work of the root, faith, is the strength of the branch!
Israel is condemned for trying to establish their own righteousness without faith in the manifest Name of YHWH, the Messiah Yeshua. Hence their branch is cut off for	The Gentiles are established and grafted into the tree by faith in the manifest Name of YHWH, Yeshua the Messiah. They are not trying to establish their own righteousness, they have accepted the	You are established only, Jew or Gentile, by faith in His manifest Name, Yeshua Adonai YHWH.

Flesh Versus Spirt based on Romans 2 & 11		
Flesh	Spirit	What Counts?
lack of faith.	righteousness of the Messiah.	
Israel/Judah's branch is cut out of the tree for lack of faith in the Messiah.	Gentiles' branch is grafted into the tree for faith in the Messiah.	Your branch is in or out according to your faith.
Israel is the branch that is natural to the tree. What makes it natural to the tree? This is the pivotal issue!	Gentiles are a wild olive branch which are grafted in because of faith in the Messiah.	Natural or unnatural, what makes the Tzion (graft) is faith.
What is the root of the tree? The Covenant of faith, the same one that Abraham was accounted as righteous for believing in his redeemer, the Messiah.	This tree is identified as not being… Israel and Judah. They are only grafted back in when they exhibit the natural faith of their father Abraham. It should be natural for them to exhibit the same faith that Abraham did!	What makes Israel natural to this tree? It was their father Abraham that established this covenant of faith with His redeemer the manifest Name of YHWH, the Messiah!

It is easy to see why people would assume this tree is Israel or Judah. But the scripture is plain and clear that this tree is the covenant of faith in the Messiah Yeshua, the manifest Name of YHWH. There is none other name under heaven whereby we must be saved.

Fundamentally we need to make plain if we are grafted into branches that Yeshua himself stated are cut off for unbelief (Judah/Israel) or as Paul testifies, we are grafted into Yeshua. Isaiah clarifies this issue.

Isaiah 56: 3, Neither let the son of the stranger, that hath joined himself to the Lord, speak, saying, The Lord hath utterly separated me from his people: neither let the eunuch say, Behold, I am a dry tree.

All of scriptures affirm that we are redeemed and joined to the Lord. In fact the prophets depict the Messiah as the "branch". The Apostle John records the Messiah's own statements on this topic.

- John 15: 1, <u>I am the true vine</u>, and my Father is the husbandman. 2 <u>Every branch in me</u> that beareth not fruit he taketh away: and <u>every branch</u> that beareth fruit, he purgeth it, that it may bring forth more fruit. 3 Now ye are clean through the word which I have spoken unto you. 4 <u>Abide in me, and I in you. As the branch</u> cannot bear fruit of itself, except it abide in the vine; no more can ye, <u>except ye abide in me.</u> 5 <u>I am the vine, ye are the branches: He that abideth in me, and I in him,</u> the same bringeth forth much fruit: for without me ye can do nothing. 6 <u>If a man abide not in me, he is cast forth as a branch, and is withered; and men gather them, and cast them into the fire,</u> and they are burned. 7 <u>If ye abide in me,</u> and my words abide in you, ye shall ask what ye will, and it shall be done unto you.
- Isaiah 11: 1, And there <u>shall come forth a rod out of the stem of Jesse, and a Branch shall grow out of his roots</u>:
- Jeremiah 23: 5, Behold, the days come, saith the Lord, that <u>I will raise unto David a righteous Branch</u>, and a King shall reign and prosper, and shall execute judgment and justice in the earth.
- Jeremiah 33: 15, In those days, and at that time, <u>will I cause the Branch of righteousness to grow up unto David</u>; and he shall execute judgment and righteousness in the land.
- Zechariah 3: 8, Hear now, O Joshua the high priest, thou, and thy fellows that sit before thee: for they are men wondered at: for, <u>behold, I will bring forth my servant the Branch</u>.
- Zechariah 6: 12, And speak unto him, saying, Thus speaketh the Lord of hosts, saying, <u>Behold the man whose name is The Branch; and he shall grow up out of his place, and he shall build the temple of the Lord</u>:

All of these scriptures, including Yeshua's own testimony, confirm that we are to be grafted into the Lord and, as a consequence of that covenant of faith and belief in His name, we are saved and not by any work or worth of our own. Being joined to the Messiah Yeshua we are then of "the commonwealth of Israel". There is no pass on accepting the work of Yeshua, even for those who keep the Torah, and consequently why there is only one name under heaven by which we must be saved, for both Jew and Gentile. The mystery related to this issue focuses upon the two administrations of death (flesh) and resurrection (spirit).

Acts 4: 11, This is the stone which was set at nought of you builders, which is become the head of the corner. 12 <u>Neither is there salvation in any other: for there is none other name under heaven given among men, whereby we must be saved</u>. 13 Now when they saw the boldness of Peter and John, and perceived that they were unlearned and ignorant men, they marvelled; and they took knowledge of them, that they had been with Yeshua.

You must be grafted into the Messiah Yeshua, the manifest Name of YHWH, in order to be saved. It does not matter if you are Jew or Gentile, bond or free, at home or abroad. Even if you keep the Torah you still need to be under the new administration of grace and abundant mercy and the new administrator, Yeshua the Messiah. Why? Even with Torah keeping you still need a redeemer. Keeping the

Torah will not save you, it will leave you under condemnation and death without the redeemer, the resurrected manifest Name of YHWH, the Messiah Yeshua, the administrator of the Resurrected Covenant (Torah). Once you have the Messiah and are grafted into Him, you are then of the commonwealth of Israel and you should begin to learn the Torah. That moment of salvation does not come through any work or worth of yours, it is all made possible by the redeeming "seed of the woman" (Genesis 3: 15), the Countenance of YHWH, the manifest Name of YHWH, Yeshua the Messiah.

Knowing this we must now ask the question, "Why must we be grafted into a new tree and what does this mean?" Why does Paul spend so much time clarifying the destiny of the believer? And why does he constantly contrast the flesh with the spirit?

20 FLESH VERSUS THE SPIRIT

Notice how Paul continually contrasts the flesh and the spirit.

1 Corinthians 15: 49, And as we have borne the image of the earthy, we shall also bear the image of the heavenly. 50 Now this I say, brethren, that flesh and blood cannot inherit the kingdom of God; neither doth corruption inherit incorruption. 51 Behold, I shew you a mystery; We shall not all sleep, but we shall all be changed,

He does it again in Galatians.

Galatians 3: 2, This only would I learn of you, Received ye the Spirit by the works of the law, or by the hearing of faith? 3 Are ye so foolish? having begun in the Spirit, are ye now made perfect by the flesh?

Take notice of this repeating duality of our current existence (flesh and spirit) and the conflict that arises because of this duality: spirit fighting with the flesh.

HAGAR VERSUS SARAH:
We see this again in the allegory presented by Paul about Hagar and Sarah.

Galatians 4: 22, For it is written, that Abraham had two sons, the one by a bondmaid, the other by a freewoman. 23 But he who was of the bondwoman was born after the flesh; but he of the freewoman was by promise. 24 Which things are an allegory: for these are the two covenants; the one from the mount Sinai, which gendereth to bondage, which is Agar. 25 For this Agar is mount Sinai in Arabia, and answereth to Jerusalem which now is, and is in bondage with her children. 26 But Jerusalem which is above is free, which is the mother of us all. 27 For it is written, Rejoice, thou barren that bearest not; break forth and cry, thou that travailest not: for the desolate hath many more children than she which hath an husband. 28 Now we, brethren, as Isaac was, are the children of promise. 29 But as then he that was born after the flesh persecuted him that was born after the Spirit, even so it is now. 30 Nevertheless what saith the scripture?   Cast out the bondwoman and her son: for the son of the bondwoman shall not be heir with the son of the freewoman. 31 So then, brethren, we are not children of the bondwoman, but of the free.

Paul clarified, as we have already learned, that the covenant of Mt. Sinai is associated with the flesh and the Resurrected Covenant is associated with the "free woman" (the spirit). Paul then contrasts Isaac and Ishmael. Isaac is associated with the spirit and Ishmael is associated with the flesh. Remember how there was conflict between Isaac and Ishmael. One is typified as being free and the other is typified as being in bondage. Freedom and bondage cannot coexist, one state occurs with the absence of the other. They cannot be mixed together. Both seeds are mutually exclusive. To mix them together causes corruption.

Genesis 21: 7, And she said, Who would have said unto Abraham, that Sarah should have given children suck? for I have born him a son in his old age. 8 And the child grew, and was weaned: and Abraham made a great feast the same day that Isaac was weaned. 9 And Sarah saw the son of Hagar the Egyptian, which she had born unto Abraham, mocking. 10 Wherefore she said unto Abraham, Cast out this bondwoman and her son: for the son of this bondwoman shall not be heir with my son, even with Isaac. 11 And the thing was very grievous in Abraham's sight because of his son. 12 And God said unto Abraham, Let it not be grievous in thy sight because of the lad, and because of thy bondwoman; in all that Sarah hath said unto thee, hearken unto her voice; for in Isaac shall thy seed be called. 13 And also of the son of the bondwoman will I make a nation, because he is thy seed. 14 And Abraham rose up early in the morning, and took bread, and a bottle of water, and gave it unto Hagar, putting it on her shoulder, and the child, and sent her away: and she departed, and wandered in the wilderness of Beersheba. 15 And the water was spent in the bottle, and she cast the child under one of the shrubs. 16 And she went, and sat her down over against him a good way off, as it were a bow shot: for she said, Let me not see the death of the child. And she sat over against him, and lift up her voice, and wept. 17 And God heard the voice of the lad; and the angel of God called to Hagar out of heaven, and said unto her, What aileth thee, Hagar? fear not; for God hath heard the voice of the lad where he is. 18 Arise, lift up the lad, and hold him in thine hand; for I will make him a great nation. 19 And God opened her eyes, and she saw a well of water; and she went, and filled the bottle with water, and gave the lad drink. 20 And God was with the lad; and he grew, and dwelt in the wilderness, and became an archer.

The natural conflict is between the spirit and the flesh; the flesh desires to rise up above the spirit and mock it and eventually attempt to kill it. The only thing that saves the spirit is the intervention from above, which causes the flesh to be cast out into the wilderness. So Ishmael is just like Israel in the wilderness who had their covenant given to them at Mt. Sinai which is associated with the flesh and death.

Notice how Ishmael is cast under a shrub (tree) in the wilderness. Let's not lose sight of this tree imagery and the conflict between the two trees of Genesis 3. The

Tree of the Knowledge of Good and Evil is associated with the mixture of spirit and flesh and results in bondage. The Tree of the Life is associated with a singular spirit and results in freedom.

Many have mistakenly taken the scripture in Galatians 4 to mean that the Torah of Moses is done away. But this clear allegory relates how the spirit (Sarah) is conflicting with the flesh (Hagar).

Hagar is associated with Mt. Sinai and how the Torah of Sin and Death (Moses), as it was given the first time, related to the flesh and death (resulting in the shattering of the tablets) and the death of the first generation of Israel saved from Egypt. When the Torah is given the second time in Exodus 34 with the presence of the manifest Name of YHWH, it became a resurrected Torah of life and is then related to the spirit only with the manifestation of Moses' glorified countenance.

Ishmael (the flesh) is cast into the wilderness under a tree while Isaac ascends a mountain with Abraham and is offered (as a type) upon branches of a tree upon an altar. Isaac ascends with the tree carried upon his back, fulfilling very similar imagery of Yeshua the Messiah at His crucifixion.

> Genesis 22: 1, And it came to pass after these things, that God did tempt Abraham, and said unto him, Abraham: and he said, Behold, here I am. 2 And he said, Take now thy son, thine only son Isaac, whom thou lovest, and get thee into the land of Moriah; and offer him there for a burnt offering upon one of the mountains which I will tell thee of. 3 And Abraham rose up early in the morning, and saddled his ass, and took two of his young men with him, and Isaac his son, and <u>clave the wood for the burnt offering, and rose up, and went unto the place of which God had told him</u>. 4 Then on the third day Abraham lifted up his eyes, and saw the place afar off. 5 And Abraham said unto his young men, Abide ye here with the ass; and I and the lad will go yonder and worship, and come again to you. 6 And <u>Abraham took the wood of the burnt offering, and laid it upon Isaac his son;</u> and he took the fire in his hand, and a knife; and they went both of them together. 7 And Isaac spake unto Abraham his father, and said, My father: and he said, Here am I, my son. And he said, Behold the fire and the wood: but where is the lamb for a burnt offering? 8 And Abraham said, My son, God will provide himself a lamb for a burnt offering: so they went both of them together. 9 And they came to the place which God had told him of; and Abraham built an altar there, <u>and laid the wood in order, and bound Isaac his son, and laid him on the altar upon the wood</u>. 10 And Abraham stretched forth his hand, and took the knife to slay his son.

Ishmael (the flesh) was caused to descend into the wilderness and be cast under a tree (Tree of the Knowledge of Good and Evil). Isaac ascends the mountain and is raised upon the firewood (a Tree of Life). Yeshua, who is also a picture of the accession of the spirit, fulfils the same imagery as Isaac as He is caused to ascend the tree and be laid upon it.

> Acts 5: 29, Then Peter and the other Apostles answered and said, We ought to obey God rather than men. 30 The God of our fathers raised up Yeshua,

whom ye slew and hanged on a tree. 31 Him hath God exalted with his right hand to be a Prince and a Saviour, for to give repentance to Israel, and forgiveness of sins.

ESAU VERSUS JACOB:
We see repeating imagery of the spirit being separated from the flesh in the Torah. Notice the same pattern is fulfilled in Jacob and Esau. Notice the patterns. Rebekah has twins (duality) fighting within her. One will eventually serve the other. Do not forget that Jacob and Esau look alike with some exceptions. They are twins!

Genesis 25: 21, And Isaac intreated the Lord for his wife, because she was barren: and the Lord was intreated of him, and Rebekah his wife conceived. 22 And the children struggled together within her; and she said, If it be so, why am I thus? And she went to enquire of the Lord. 23 And the Lord said unto her, Two nations are in thy womb, and two manner of people shall be separated from thy bowels; and the one people shall be stronger than the other people; and the elder shall serve the younger. 24 And when her days to be delivered were fulfilled, behold, there were twins in her womb. 25 And the first came out red, all over like an hairy garment; and they called his name Esau. 26 And after that came his brother out, and his hand took hold on Esau's heel; and his name was called Jacob: and Isaac was threescore years old when she bare them. 27 And the boys grew: and Esau was a cunning hunter, a man of the field; and Jacob was a plain man, dwelling in tents. 28 And Isaac loved Esau, because he did eat of his venison: but Rebekah loved Jacob. 29 And Jacob sod pottage: and Esau came from the field, and he was faint: 30 And Esau said to Jacob, Feed me, I pray thee, with that same red pottage; for I am faint: therefore was his name called Edom. 31 And Jacob said, Sell me this day thy birthright. 32 And Esau said, Behold, I am at the point to die: and what profit shall this birthright do to me? 33 And Jacob said, Swear to me this day; and he sware unto him: and he sold his birthright unto Jacob. 34 Then Jacob gave Esau bread and pottage of lentiles; and he did eat and drink, and rose up, and went his way: thus Esau despised his birthright.

Once again, we have the duality of the spirit and the flesh in conflict. Esau is typified as the flesh and Jacob as the spirit. How do we know this? Notice again that all these dualities become a life and death conflict. Here are some patterns you should be starting to see.

Esau	Jacob
Flesh (identified by "hands" and garments smelling like the "field")	Spirit (identified by "voice")
Red	No mention of color
Covered with hair (like a garment)	Plain (smooth)
Lives in the wilderness (on the outside)	Lives within tents (on the inside)
Only cares about filling his belly (sells his birthright for food)	"Lives in tents" is associated with study (knowledge)
Despises his inheritance	Yearns for an inheritance
Firstborn	Second born
Hated by God (Romans 9: 12–14)	Loved by God (Romans 9: 12–14)
Weak (hungry/lacking faith and belief)	Strong in faith and belief

Let's not forget that these two are legitimate twins. They are born together and at the same time. They are in constant battle from the womb and throughout their lives, one is favored more than the other. In the end one is stronger and one will serve the other. Just as the firstborn is the flesh, the spirit is born at the same time, but second. The spirit is despised and lives within and yearns for its own inheritance. It can only obtain it by taking it from the firstborn and causing the flesh to serve him. The spirit lives within (tents/garments), the flesh lives without (wilderness). Also remember how Esau is associated with red (pottage/hair), just as Adam and Eve are associated with red earth (clay) from which they are made. Take notice of how the blessing of Esau (flesh) is passed on to Jacob (spirit). Jacob has to dress up within Esau's garments to actually receive the inheritance.

Genesis 27: 6, And Rebekah spake unto Jacob her son, saying, Behold, I heard thy father speak unto Esau thy brother, saying, 7 Bring me venison, and make me savoury meat, that I may eat, and bless thee before the Lord before my death. 8 Now therefore, my son, obey my voice according to that which I command thee. 9 Go now to the flock, and fetch me from thence two good kids of the goats; and I will make them savoury meat for thy father, such as he loveth: 10 And thou shalt bring it to thy father, that he may eat, and that he may bless thee before his death. 11 And Jacob said to Rebekah his mother, Behold, <u>Esau my brother is a hairy man, and I am a smooth man</u>: 12 My father peradventure will feel me, and <u>I shall seem to him as a deceiver; and I shall bring a curse upon me, and not a blessing</u>. 13 And his mother said unto him, <u>Upon me be thy curse, my son: only obey my voice</u>, and go fetch me them. 14 And he went, and fetched, and brought them to his mother: and his mother made savoury meat, such as his father loved. 15 And <u>Rebekah took goodly raiment of her eldest son Esau, which were with her in the house, and put them upon Jacob her younger son: 16 And she put the skins of the kids of the goats upon his hands, and upon the smooth of his neck</u>: 17 And she gave the savoury meat and the bread, which she had prepared, into the hand of her son Jacob. 18 And he came unto his father, and said, My father: and he said, Here am I; who art thou, my son? 19 And Jacob said unto his father, I am Esau thy firstborn; I have done according as thou badest me: arise, I pray thee, sit and eat of my venison, that thy soul may bless me. 20 And Isaac said unto his son, How is it that thou hast found it so quickly, my son? And he said, Because the Lord thy God brought it to me. 21 And Isaac said unto Jacob, Come near, I pray thee, <u>that I may feel thee, my son, whether thou be my very son Esau or not</u>. 22 And Jacob went near unto Isaac his father; and he felt him, and said, <u>The voice is Jacob's voice, but the hands are the hands of Esau</u>. 23 And he discerned him not, <u>because his hands were hairy, as his brother Esau's hands</u>: so he blessed him. 24 And he said, <u>Art thou my very son Esau? And he said, I am</u>. 25 And he said, Bring it near to me, and I will eat of my son's venison, that my soul may bless thee. And he brought it near to him, and he did eat: and he brought him wine and he drank. 26 And his father Isaac said unto him, Come near now, and kiss me, my son. 27 And he came near, and kissed him: and <u>he smelled the smell of his raiment, and blessed him, and said, See, the smell of my son is as the smell of a field</u> which the Lord hath blessed:

The inheritance of the spirit is obtained through living through the flesh of Esau. This duality of existence is the means to perfect the spirit. The continual contrasting of Esau and Jacob occurs throughout the story of their lives. Esau is described as being "without" or on the outside (wilderness or the field) and as a garment, whereas Jacob exists "within" as the spirit (like dwelling within a tent). This shows the spirit conflicting with the flesh and then being separated from the flesh in order to receive the blessing.

After Jacob's exile and return to the land, we see the very odd circumstances of Jacob separating his family into a duality (two companies) before meeting with his brother Esau, who had previously promised to kill him. Remember the imagery of the firstborn desiring to kill the second born (flesh trying to kill the spirit). This is the same replay of Cain (flesh) killing Abel (spirit).

Genesis 27: 39, And Isaac his father answered and said unto him, Behold, thy dwelling shall be the fatness of the earth, and of the dew of heaven from above; 40 And by thy sword shalt thou live, and shalt serve thy brother; and it shall come to pass when thou shalt have the dominion, that thou shalt break his yoke from off thy neck. 41 And Esau hated Jacob because of the blessing wherewith his father blessed him: and Esau said in his heart, The days of mourning for my father are at hand; then will I slay my brother Jacob.

We see the same conflict and basic themes in Cain (flesh) and Abel (spirit). Be sure to look for the falling of the "countenance" and its restoration if Cain does "well" in accordance with God's commandments.

Genesis 4: 3, And in process of time it came to pass, that Cain brought of the fruit of the ground an offering unto the Lord. 4 And Abel, he also brought of the firstlings of his flock and of the fat thereof. And the Lord had respect unto Abel and to his offering: 5 But unto Cain and to his offering he had not respect. And Cain was very wroth, and his countenance fell. 6 And the Lord said unto Cain, Why art thou wroth? and why is thy countenance fallen? 7 If thou doest well, shalt thou not be accepted? and if thou doest not well, sin lieth at the door. And unto thee shall be his desire, and thou shalt rule over him. 8 And Cain talked with Abel his brother: and it came to pass, when they were in the field, that Cain rose up against Abel his brother, and slew him. 9 And the Lord said unto Cain, Where is Abel thy brother? And he said, I know not: Am I my brother's keeper? 10 And he said, What hast thou done? the voice of thy brother's blood crieth unto me from the ground.

We see the most basic portrayal of the conflict between the spirit (Abel) and the flesh (Cain). Notice Cain is associated with an improper offering and a fallen countenance that needs to be restored. We have already discussed at great length the purpose and role of the Messiah is to restore the fallen countenance of man by writing His countenance upon ours. Also take notice of how Abel's voice is crying out from his blood from the ground, just as Jacob's voice is emphasized as coming from within Esau's garments when Isaac is identifying who his heir and blessing should be passed on to.

Genesis 27: 22, And Jacob went near unto Isaac his father; and he felt him, and said, The voice is Jacob's voice, but the hands are the hands of Esau. 23 And he discerned him not, because his hands were hairy, as his brother Esau's hands: so he blessed him.

Just as Esau dwelt in the wilderness, Cain is exiled to the wilderness. Just as Esau wanted to slay Jacob, Cain slays Abel. Also take note of how this conflict is determining who will rule, the flesh or the spirit.

Genesis 4: 7, If thou doest well, shalt thou not be accepted? and if thou doest not well, sin lieth at the door. And unto thee shall be his desire, and thou shalt rule over him.

TREE OF THE KNOWLEDGE OF GOOD & EVIL VERSUS THE TREE OF LIFE:

Cain and Abel have the same conflict that arises after Adam and Eve are cursed for partaking of the Tree of the Knowledge of Good and Evil, the tree of duality (mixed seed).

> Genesis 3: 16, Unto the woman he said, I will greatly multiply thy sorrow and thy conception; in sorrow thou shalt bring forth children; and <u>thy desire shall be to thy husband, and he shall rule over thee</u>. 17 And unto Adam he said, Because thou hast hearkened unto the voice of thy wife, and hast eaten of the tree, of which I commanded thee, saying, Thou shalt not eat of it: cursed is the ground for thy sake; in sorrow shalt thou eat of it all the days of thy life; 18 Thorns also and thistles shall it bring forth to thee; and thou shalt eat the herb of the field; 19 In the sweat of thy face shalt thou eat bread, till thou return unto the ground; for out of it wast thou taken: for dust thou art, and unto dust shalt thou return. 20 And Adam called his wife's name Eve; because she was the mother of all living. 21 <u>Unto Adam also and to his wife did the Lord God make coats of skins, and clothed them</u>. 22 And the Lord God said, Behold, the man is become as one of us, to know good and evil: and now, lest he put forth his hand, and take also of the Tree of Life, and eat, and live for ever: 23 Therefore the <u>Lord God sent him forth from the garden of Eden</u>, to till the ground from whence he was taken. 24 So he drove out the man; and he placed at the east of the garden of Eden Cherubims, and a flaming sword which turned every way, <u>to keep the way of the Tree of Life</u>.

Do you see how the statement of Cain and Abel is an exact repeat from Adam and Eve?

- Genesis 4: 7, "…And unto thee shall be his desire, and thou shalt rule over him."
- Genesis 3: 16, "… And thy desire shall be to thy husband, and he shall rule over thee."
- The conflict is to determine who will rule, the spirit or the flesh. The exact same terminology is used between Cain and Abel and between Adam and Eve. The same patterns keep repeating themselves. Why? They are universal patterns and fractals that are teaching a mystery!
  - A fallen countenance needing restoration
  - A power conflict between two (duality–mixed seed of flesh and spirit)
  - The need of clothing and garments due to sin (flesh)
  - Sending into exile (wilderness)–a physical and fallen (dual) reality
  - Prevention from being grafted into the Tree of Life (singularity)
  - Spirit living within flesh
  - Flesh desiring to kill the spirit
  - The firstborn (flesh) battling with the second born (spirit)
  - Battle of the twins for rulership

How did Jacob (spirit) solve the problem of Esau (flesh) wanting to kill him? He goes into exile (descend) and then returns (ascends). Just before entering the Promised land, his inheritance, he must conclude the battle with Esau.

Going to the Promised land is always an ascension in geographical elevation and spiritually. Leaving the Promised land and going into exile is a descending in geographical elevation and spiritually descending. Jacob's need to ascend again coincides with meeting the Angel of YHWH and seeing the Countenance of God.

> Genesis 32: 24, And Jacob was left alone; and there wrestled a man with him until the breaking of the day. 25 And when he saw that he prevailed not against him, he touched the hollow of his thigh; and the hollow of Jacob's thigh was out of joint, as he wrestled with him. 26 And he said, Let me go, for the day breaketh. And he said, I will not let thee go, except thou bless me. 27 And he said unto him, What is thy name? And he said, Jacob. 28 And he said, Thy name shall be called no more Jacob, but Israel: for as a prince hast thou power with God and with men, and hast prevailed. 29 And Jacob asked him, and said, <u>Tell me, I pray thee, thy name</u>. And he said, Wherefore is it that thou dost ask after my name? And he blessed him there. 30 And Jacob called the name of the place Peniel: for <u>I have seen God face to face</u>, and my life is preserved.

We have already discussed how this is the pattern of the redeemed. Faith is expressed in the manifest Name of YHWH (the Messiah), then the believer sees the Countenance of God (the Messiah) and receives a new name. The outcome is the life of the spirit (Jacob) is preserved. Then Jacob (spirit) goes out to meet Esau (flesh) with a new name (Genesis 32:24-30).

> Genesis 33: 33, And Jacob lifted up his eyes, and looked, and, behold, Esau came, and with him four hundred men. And he divided the children unto Leah, and unto Rachel, and unto the two handmaids. 2 And he put the handmaids and their children foremost, and Leah and her children after, and Rachel and Joseph hindermost. 3 And he passed over before them, and bowed himself to the ground seven times, until he came near to his brother. 4 And Esau ran to meet him, and embraced him, and fell on his neck, and kissed him: and they wept. 5 And he lifted up his eyes, and saw the women and the children; and said, Who are those with thee? And he said, The children which God hath graciously given thy servant. 6 Then the handmaidens came near, they and their children, and they bowed themselves. 7 And Leah also with her children came near, and bowed themselves: and after came Joseph near and Rachel, and they bowed themselves. 8 And he said, What meanest thou by all this drove which I met? And he said, These are to find grace in the sight of my Lord. 9 And Esau said, I have enough, my brother; keep that thou hast unto thyself. 10 And Jacob said, Nay, I pray thee, <u>if now I have found grace in thy sight, then receive my present at my hand: for therefore I have seen thy face, as though I had seen the face of God,</u> and thou wast pleased with me. 11 Take, I pray thee, my blessing that is brought to thee; because God hath dealt graciously with me, and because I have enough. And he urged him, and he took it. 12 And he said, Let us take our journey, and let us go, and I will go before thee. 13 And he said unto him,

My Lord knoweth that the children are tender, and the flocks and herds with young are with me: and if men should overdrive them one day, all the flock will die. 14 Let my Lord, I pray thee, pass over before his servant: and I will lead on softly, according as the cattle that goeth before me and the children be able to endure, until I come unto my Lord unto Seir.

We will not go into great detail as to the deep mysteries presented within this passage but will briefly detail the themes that show the ending of the conflict between the spirit (Jacob) and Esau (flesh). It fully relates to the change in countenance of Esau. Just as God focused on the change in Cain's countenance, how it was fallen and needed to be restored, so also was the case for Esau. This change of countenance came through the many gifts from Jacob (Spirit) to Esau (flesh) and the great humility shown by the spirit (Jacob). Notice the night before the meeting of the twins, Jacob experiences the battle of his life with the manifest Name of YHWH, the Countenance of God.

THE COUNTENANCE OF GOD (THE MESSIAH) AND THE PRESENTATION OF RESURRECTION LIFE:
We have discussed at length in prior chapters about the role of the Messiah as the restorer of the Countenance of God. The night before reconciling with Esau, Jacob needs to be blessed and see the Countenance of God. With this blessing, peace is assured between the flesh and the spirit. The fall of Adam and Eve resulted in the breaking of the Countenance of God (the image of God) and the promised seed (the Messiah, the Countenance of YHWH) is what restores that Countenance (image of God).
- First Adam is earthy (flesh) and a broken image of God
- Last Adam is spirit and restores the image of God

1 Corinthians 15: 45, And so it is written, The first man Adam was made a living soul; the last Adam was made a quickening spirit...47 The first man is of the earth, earthy; the second man is the Lord from heaven.

This can only be done by bringing peace (wholeness) between the flesh and the spirit. The duality of spirit and flesh (Tree of the Knowledge of Good and Evil) must be replaced with the singularity of the Tree of Life (spirit only). Jacob sees the Countenance of God the night before meeting Esau and then sees Esau's countenance changed the next day.

Genesis 33: 10, And Jacob said, Nay, I pray thee, if now I have found grace in thy sight, then receive my present at my hand: for therefore I have seen thy face, as though I had seen the face of God, and thou wast pleased with me. 11 Take, I pray thee, my blessing that is brought to thee; because God hath dealt graciously with me, and because I have enough.

The Countenance of God is transcribed on to Esau and this causes peace to occur between the twins. Notice that after peace has been established Esau (flesh) and Jacob (spirit) do not continue on together. They are separated and Jacob and his band proceed along at the pace of a child. We will not take the time to explain in great detail how circumcision portrays the act of separating the flesh from the seed of life. It reveals the promise of life (spirit). It also relates to why we are born dual in nature (spirit and flesh) and then need to become singular in nature (spirit) in the resurrection.

This is reflected in how Adam is divided into Adam (male) and Eve (female) and made a duality. This is why the male and female must be reunited via the marriage chamber and the two must become one flesh. Male and female become the ascended and unified male, a Son of God. Paul elaborates on this necessary change from the flesh to the spirit.

1 Corinthians 15: 35, But some man will say, How are the dead raised up? and with what body do they come? 36 Thou fool, that which thou sowest is not quickened, except it die: 37 And that which thou sowest, thou sowest not that body that shall be, but bare grain, it may chance of wheat, or of some other grain: 38 But God giveth it a body as it hath pleased him, and to every seed his own body. 39 All flesh is not the same flesh: but there is one kind of flesh of men, another flesh of beasts, another of fishes, and another of birds. 40 There are also celestial bodies, and bodies terrestrial: but the glory of the celestial is one, and the glory of the terrestrial is another. 41 There is one glory of the sun, and another glory of the moon, and another glory of the stars: for one star differeth from another star in glory. 42 So also is the resurrection of the dead. It is sown in corruption; it is raised in incorruption: 43 It is sown in dishonour; it is raised in glory: it is sown in weakness; it is raised in power: 44 It is sown a natural body; it is raised a spiritual body. There is a natural body, and there is a spiritual body. 45 And so it is written, The first man Adam was made a living soul; the last Adam was made a quickening spirit. 46 Howbeit that was not first which is spiritual, but that which is natural; and afterward that which is spiritual. 47 The first man is of the earth, earthy; the second man is the Lord from heaven. 48 As is the earthy, such are they also that are earthy: and as is the heavenly, such are they also that are heavenly. 49 And as we have borne the image of the earthy, we shall also bear the image of the heavenly. 50 Now this I say, brethren, that flesh and blood cannot inherit the kingdom of God; neither doth corruption inherit incorruption. 51 Behold, I shew you a mystery; We shall not all sleep, but we shall all be changed, 52 In a moment, in the twinkling of an eye, at the last trump: for the trumpet shall sound, and the dead shall be raised incorruptible, and we shall be changed. 53 For this corruptible must put on incorruption, and this mortal must put on immortality. 54 So when this corruptible shall have put on incorruption, and this mortal shall have put on immortality, then shall be brought to pass the saying that is written, Death is swallowed up in victory.

We clearly see that in the resurrection we will not have fleshly (fallen) bodies, but spiritual bodies. The spirit will be separated from the flesh and given an incorruptible tent to dwell within. The duality will cease and singularity of the Messiah will proceed. That is why we must be grafted into the Messiah Yeshua and His countenance. He is the Tree of Life that we must be grafted into.

The pattern of manifest reality starts with the corruption (mixing of seeds–spirit and flesh) and proceeds to incorruption (spirit only). It starts with the duality of the Tree of the Knowledge of Good and Evil (the spirit mixed with flesh) and proceeds with the engrafting of the new tree, the Tree of Life (spirit only), the Messiah Yeshua.

Genesis 2: 16, And the Lord God commanded the man, saying, Of every tree of the garden thou mayest freely eat: 17 But of the Tree of the Knowledge of Good and Evil, thou shalt not eat of it: for in the day that thou eatest thereof thou shalt surely die.

The Tree of the Knowledge of Good and Evil is the duality of spirit and flesh, good and evil. It results in death. We need to be grafted into the singularity of life, the spirit, Yeshua the Messiah, the Countenance of God.

Genesis 2: 9, And out of the ground made the Lord God to grow every tree that is pleasant to the sight, and good for food; the Tree of Life also in the midst of the garden, and the tree of knowledge of good and evil.

It is the Tree of Life that we must be grafted into, but the way is guarded so those that have already been grafted into the Tree of the Knowledge of Good and Evil cannot approach it.

Genesis 3: 24, So he drove out the man; and he placed at the east of the garden of Eden Cherubims, and a flaming sword which turned every way, to keep the way of the Tree of Life.

Those with a fallen countenance, a broken image, dual nature (flesh and spirit) cannot be grafted into the Tree of Life in our current (fallen) state.

1 Corinthians 15: 50, Now this I say, brethren, that flesh and blood cannot inherit the kingdom of God; neither doth corruption inherit incorruption.

We must be redeemed by the true of image of God, the Messiah Yeshua, the manifest Name of YHWH. He is the resurrection and the life.

John 11: 24, Martha saith unto him, I know that he shall rise again in the resurrection at the last day. 25 Yeshua said unto her, I am the resurrection, and the life: he that believeth in me, though he were dead, yet shall he live: 26 And whosoever liveth and believeth in me shall never die. Believest thou this?

We are grafted and rooted in Him. That is how we pass from death, corruption, and duality (spirit and flesh) to life (spirit).

Colossians 2: 2, For I would that ye knew what great conflict I have for you, and for them at Laodicea, and for as many as have not seen my face in the flesh; 2 That their hearts might be comforted, being knit together in love, and unto all riches of the full assurance of understanding, to the acknowledgement of the <u>mystery of God</u>, and of the Father, and of Christ; 3 In whom are hid all the treasures of wisdom and knowledge. 4 And this I say, lest any man should beguile you with enticing words. 5 For though I be <u>absent in the flesh, yet am I with you in the spirit</u>, joying and beholding your order, and the stedfastness of your faith in Christ. 6 As ye have therefore received Christ Yeshua the Lord, so walk ye in him: 7 <u>Rooted and built up in him</u>, and stablished in the faith, as ye have been taught, abounding therein with thanksgiving. 8 Beware lest any man spoil you through philosophy and vain deceit, after the tradition of men, after the rudiments of the world, and not after Christ. 9 For in him dwelleth all the fulness of the Godhead bodily. 10 And <u>ye are complete in him</u>, which is the head of all principality and power: 11 <u>In whom also ye are circumcised with the circumcision made without hands, in putting off the body of the sins of the flesh by the circumcision of Christ</u>: 12 Buried with him in baptism, wherein also ye are risen with him through the faith of the operation of God, who hath raised him from the dead. 13 And you, being dead in your sins and the uncircumcision of your flesh, hath he quickened together with him, having forgiven you all trespasses; 14 <u>Blotting out the handwriting of ordinances</u> that was against us, which was contrary to us, and took it out of the way, nailing it to his cross; 15 And having spoiled principalities and powers, he made a shew of them openly, triumphing over them in it. 16 Let no man therefore judge you in meat, or in drink, or in respect of an holyday, or of the new moon, or of the sabbath days: 17 Which are a shadow of things to come; <u>but the body is of Christ</u>.

Notice:

- Paul starts out this passage relating to the Colossians about their not seeing His countenance in the flesh. Remember what we learned above about the restoration of the countenance and how that relates to the work of the Messiah and the spirit.

- Our redemption comes through faith in the Messiah, the Tree of Life from Romans 11. This is not Israel, Judah, or the Torah, this is the Tree of Life.

- We are "rooted and grafted" into the Messiah Yeshua, the manifest Name of YHWH.

- We are made one, complete, whole in Yeshua.

- This results in the removal of the flesh by the circumcision of the Messiah's work.

- This causes the judgment and exile, because of our guilt, to be removed, "blotting out the handwriting of ordinances that was against us", giving us access to the Tree of Life, Yeshua the Messiah.

- We are made one with Yeshua the Messiah who has the fulness of the Godhead dwelling within Him.

- The mystery of God is turning the duality (flesh and spirit of the Tree of the Knowledge of Good and Evil) to the singularity of the Tree of Life (the Spirit). The corruption is circumcised and what remains is incorruption.

Ezekiel 11: 18, And they shall come thither, and they shall take away all the detestable things thereof and all the abominations thereof from thence. 19 And I will give them one heart, and I will put a new spirit within you; and I will take the stony heart out of their flesh, and will give them an heart of flesh: 20 That they may walk in my statutes, and keep mine ordinances, and do them: and they shall be my people, and I will be their God.

Yeshua continually emphasizes the inability of the flesh to complete the spirit.

Matthew 26: 41, Watch and pray, that ye enter not into temptation: the spirit indeed is willing, but the flesh is weak.

This is the duality of the Tree of the Knowledge of Good and Evil. The spirit is willing and good, the flesh is weak and evil.

John 6: 63, It is the spirit that quickeneth; the flesh profiteth nothing: the words that I speak unto you, they are spirit, and they are life.

There is a need for the separation of the flesh from the spirit. This is the second birth, the baptism, and the circumcision. We need to be living according to spirit.

Romans 8: 9, But ye are not in the flesh, but in the Spirit, if so be that the Spirit of God dwell in you. Now if any man have not the Spirit of Christ, he is none of his.

The goal is to leave the body of corruption, the flesh, and be born again into the spirit, to leave the duality of the Tree of the Knowledge of Good and Evil and to cling to the Tree of Life, the spirit only. Death is no longer a bad day, death is now the second birth.

Ecclesiastes 7: 1, A good name is better than precious ointment; and the day of death than the day of one's birth. 2 It is better to go to the house of mourning, than to go to the house of feasting: for that is the end of all men; and the living will lay it to his heart. 3 Sorrow is better than laughter: for by the sadness of the countenance the heart is made better.

Notice again how the healing of the countenance is restored by the sorrow of death, the departure from the duality of the spirit and the flesh (Tree of the Knowledge of Good and Evil) and the grafting of the believer into the singularity of the spirit (Tree of Life). Remember these patterns and take a new look at Moses' request that he would know God by name, have the presence of God, and obtain "rest" from the curse of "labor" that was placed upon Adam and Eve because of their sin. The final outcome is the desire to see the glory of God. This glorious countenance is then transcribed on to Moses' face.

Exodus 33: 12, And Moses said unto the Lord, See, thou sayest unto me,

Bring up this people: and thou hast not let me know whom thou wilt send with me. Yet thou hast said, <u>I know thee by name, and thou hast also found grace in my sight</u>. 13 Now therefore, I pray thee, if I have found grace in thy sight, shew me now thy way, that I may know thee, that I may find grace in thy sight: and consider that this nation is thy people. 14 And he said, <u>My presence shall go with thee</u>, and <u>I will give thee rest</u>. 15 And he said unto him, If thy presence go not with me, carry us not up hence. 16 For wherein shall it be known here that I and thy people have found grace in thy sight? is it not in that thou goest with us? so shall we be separated, I and thy people, from all the people that are upon the face of the earth. 17 And the Lord said unto Moses, I will do this thing also that thou hast spoken: for thou hast found grace in my sight, <u>and I know thee by name</u>. 18 And he said, I beseech thee, <u>shew me thy glory</u>. 19 And he said, I will make all my goodness pass before thee, and <u>I will proclaim the Name of the Lord before thee</u>; and will be gracious to whom I will be gracious, and will shew mercy on whom I will shew mercy. 20 And he said, <u>Thou canst not see my face: for there shall no man see me, and live</u>.

THE DUAL STATE OF CORRUPTION (FLESH & SPIRIT) VERSUS THE SINGULARITY OF RESURRECTION FAITH (SPIRIT):

Man in his current fallen (dual) state cannot behold the Countenance of God. This corrupted and fallen state must be changed to a singular state of the spirit so that Yeshua's countenance can be written upon ours.

The countenance is made better as Ecclesiastes 7 says by changing the covenant from death (duality–flesh and spirit) to resurrected life (singular–spirit only). We see this in the two givings of the Torah of Moses. The first time it is given under the administration of death and judgment (the flesh) and the second time it is given by the administration of abundant grace and mercy, resurrected life (the spirit).

Exodus 34: 1, And the Lord said unto Moses, <u>Hew thee two tablets of stone like unto the first</u>: and I will write upon these tablets the words that were in the first tablets, which thou brakest. 2 And be ready in the morning, and come up in the morning unto mount Sinai, and present thyself there to me in the top of the mount. 3 And no man shall come up with thee, neither let any man be seen throughout all the mount; neither let the flocks nor herds feed before that mount. 4 And he hewed two tablets of stone like unto the first; and Moses rose up early in the morning, and went up unto mount Sinai, as the Lord had commanded him, and took in his hand the two tablets of stone. 5 And the <u>Lord descended in the cloud, and stood with him there, and proclaimed the Name of the Lord. 6 And the Lord passed by before him, and proclaimed, The Lord, The Lord God, merciful and gracious, longsuffering, and abundant in goodness and truth, 7 Keeping mercy for thousands, forgiving iniquity and transgression and sin, and that will by no means clear the guilty;</u> visiting the iniquity of the fathers upon the children, and upon the children's children, unto the third and to the fourth generation. 8 And Moses made haste, and bowed his head toward the earth, and worshipped. 9 And he said, If now <u>I have found grace in thy sight</u>, O Lord, let my Lord, I pray thee, go among us; for it is a stiffnecked people; and pardon our iniquity and our sin, and take us for thine inheritance. 10 And he said, <u>Behold, I make a covenant: before all thy people I will do marvels</u>, such as have not been done in all the earth, nor in any nation: and all the people among which thou art shall see the work of the Lord: for it is a terrible thing that I will do with thee.

Once again we see the dual giving of the Torah. The first time the tablets are broken (like the flesh), and then the tablets are remade and caused to ascend the mountain with Moses for the re–Utterance of the same commandments. This time it is with grace and mercy assured. This is a picture of resurrection life (the spirit). The Utterances are the same for both sets of tablets.

When Moses descends the mountain with the new set of tablets that were written with grace and mercy and the manifest Name of YHWH presented to him we see a new wonder. Moses' countenance has been glorified by the work of the manifest Name of YHWH, the Messiah Yeshua.

> Exodus 34: 29, And it came to pass, when Moses came down from mount Sinai <u>with the two tablets of testimony in Moses' hand</u>, when he came down from the mount, that Moses wist not that <u>the skin of his face shone while he talked with him</u>. 30 And when Aaron and all the children of Israel saw Moses, behold, <u>the skin of his face shone</u>; and they were afraid to come nigh him. 31 And Moses called unto them; and Aaron and all the rulers of the congregation returned unto him: and Moses talked with them. 32 And afterward all the children of Israel came nigh: and he gave them in commandment all that the Lord had spoken with him in mount Sinai. 33 And till Moses had done speaking with them, <u>he put a vail on his face</u>. 34 But when Moses went in before the Lord to speak with him, he took the vail off, until he came out. And he came out, and spake unto the children of Israel that which he was commanded. 35 And the children of Israel <u>saw the face of Moses, that the skin of Moses' face shone: and Moses put the vail upon his face again, until he went in to speak with him.</u>

Once again we see the correction of the broken image of God and the duality of the Tree of the Knowledge of Good and Evil. There are two givings of the Torah, one according to death and judgment (flesh) and the second according to the spirit (resurrection, grace and mercy). The first giving of the Torah occurs with a sprinkling of blood (flesh).

> Exodus 24: 8, And Moses took the blood, and sprinkled it on the people, and said, Behold the blood of the covenant, which the Lord hath made with you concerning all these words.

The second giving of the Torah results in the glorification of the countenance of Moses. These events are all a prophetic type of our current fallen state and the promise of the resurrection. This is how the Torah is easily understood to be a Law (Torah) of Sin and Death–flesh, which is then resurrected into a Torah of Life–the Spirit. Both have the same Utterances. Only the second is uttered with the manifest presence of the Name of YHWH, the Messiah Yeshua.

Many Christians and Torah observant followers of Yeshua have mistakenly missed the dual imagery of the giving of the Torah and its significance as it relates to our fallen and dual existence of flesh and spirit. They do not understand the Apostle Paul because they still do not understand the imagery of the Torah. Many Christians mistakenly think Paul is saying that we are free from the Torah. Also many Messianics cannot understand how the Torah could have been both according to "sin and death" and then unto resurrected "life". Notice Paul prefaces his comments about the Torah with the clarification of the conflict between the flesh and the spirit. All of his comments must relate back to this basic duality and conflict.

Romans 8: 1, There is therefore now no condemnation to them which are in Christ Yeshua, who walk not after the flesh, but after the Spirit. 2 For the law of the Spirit of life in Christ Yeshua hath made me free from the law of sin and death. 3 For what the law could not do, in that it was weak through the flesh, God sending his own Son in the likeness of sinful flesh, and for sin, condemned sin in the flesh: 4 That the righteousness of the law might be fulfilled in us, who walk not after the flesh, but after the Spirit. 5 For they that are after the flesh do mind the things of the flesh; but they that are after the Spirit the things of the Spirit. 6 For to be carnally minded is death; but to be spiritually minded is life and peace. 7 Because the carnal mind is enmity against God: for it is not subject to the law of God, neither indeed can be. 8 So then they that are in the flesh cannot please God. 9 But ye are not in the flesh, but in the Spirit, if so be that the Spirit of God dwell in you. Now if any man have not the Spirit of Christ, he is none of his. 10 And if Christ be in you, the body is dead because of sin; but the Spirit is life because of righteousness. 11 But if the Spirit of him that raised up Yeshua from the dead dwell in you, he that raised up Christ from the dead shall also quicken your mortal bodies by his Spirit that dwelleth in you. 12 Therefore, brethren, we are debtors, not to the flesh, to live after the flesh. 13 For if ye live after the flesh, ye shall die: but if ye through the Spirit do mortify the deeds of the body, ye shall live. 14 For as many as are led by the Spirit of God, they are the sons of God.

Paul is extremely clear:
- The Torah was given the first time according to the duality of the Tree of the Knowledge of Good and Evil (spirit and flesh), sin and death (the flesh and blood)– (Exodus 24:8)
- When the Torah was given the second time it was according to the Tree of Life (singular and spirit)–(Exodus 34).
- We are to put off the flesh and mind the things of the spirit.
- We must leave the flesh (literally at death) in order to please God and leave the duality of sin and death behind.
- If you are in Christ your spirit is living and your flesh is dying.
- God will quicken your body and make it spirit after death.
- It is the flesh that we need to be delivered from.

Paul is not showing us being freed from the Law of Moses. He is showing us that we need to be freed from our fallen and dual state of flesh and spirit, which is incapable of keeping the Law.

21 WHAT HAVE WE LEARNED ABOUT THE LAW OF MOSES AND ITS EFFECT ON THE FLESH?

The Law of Moses does what it should, it condemns the flesh.

Romans 7: 7, What shall we say then? <u>Is the law sin? God forbid. Nay, I had not known sin, but by the law</u>: for I had not known lust, except the law had said, Thou shalt not covet. 8 But sin, taking occasion by the commandment, wrought in me all manner of concupiscence. For without the law sin was dead. 9 For I was alive without the law once: <u>but when the commandment came, sin revived, and I died</u>. 10 And the commandment, which was ordained to life, <u>I found to be unto death</u>. 11 For sin, taking occasion by the commandment, deceived me, and by it slew me. 12 Wherefore <u>the law is holy, and the commandment holy, and just, and good</u>. 13 Was then <u>that which is good made death unto me</u>? God forbid. But sin, that it might appear sin, working death in me by that which is good; that sin by the commandment might become exceeding sinful. 14 For <u>we know that the law is spiritual: but I am carnal, sold under sin. 15 For that which I do I allow not: for what I would, that do I not; but what I hate, that do I. 16 If then I do that which I would not, I consent unto the law that it is good</u>. 17 Now then it is no more I that do it, but sin that dwelleth in me. 18 For I know that in me (that is, in my flesh,) dwelleth no good thing: for to will is present with me; but how to perform that which is good I find not. 19 <u>For the good that I would I do not: but the evil which I would not, that I do. 20 Now if I do that I would not, it is no more I that do it, but sin that dwelleth in me</u>. 21 I find then a law, that, when I would do good, evil is present with me. 22 <u>For I delight in the law of God after the inward man</u>: 23 But I see another law in my members, warring against the law of my mind, and bringing me into captivity to the law of sin which is in my members. 24 O wretched man that I am! who shall deliver me from the body of this death?

25 I thank God through Yeshua our Lord. So then with the mind <u>I myself serve the law of God; but with the flesh the law of sin</u>.

Notice:

- The Torah of Moses defines what sin is and the Torah is holy and good.
- The Torah does what it should, it condemns the flesh because it is by nature the Tree of the Knowledge of Good and Evil (dual and corrupt).
- Paul presents man as a duality, the inward man having a law of God (of the mind-spirit) and his "members" (flesh) being under a law of sin.
- The Torah identifies sin and condemns the flesh as it should. The flesh is not meant to survive. The Torah is rightfully the Law of sin and death.
- The Torah is spiritual (of the mind) and condemns the carnal (flesh) as it should.
- Those who are subject to the dual nature (flesh and sprit) are powerless to deliver themselves.
- We sin because we are subject to the flesh. That will not change until we are delivered from the flesh and are made singular (spirit).
- Paul rightfully concludes his outward man (flesh) cannot keep the Torah, so he does what he can and delights in the Torah after the inward man (the spirit).
- Who can deliver us from the body of this death (flesh)? Yeshua the Messiah, the manifest Name of YHWH.
- We see the presence of two administrations, one that must pass away (the flesh) so that the new administration of the spirit can remain. This follows the same pattern as the dual givings of the Law of Moses.
- Just as with both administrations of the Torah, the commandments are the same, but one is under condemnation (death) and the other is under grace and mercy (resurrection life). Hence Paul asks, "Is the law sin?" He concludes, "the law is holy" and does what it is meant to do, "I found to be unto death" and "that which is good made death unto me".

Paul is saying that man, a duality of spirit and flesh, are under the same "commandments of God", which produces life to the spirit and death to the flesh. Why? Because the flesh is under the administration of "sin and death" and produces its natural outcome, "sin to abound". The "law of sin" is your carnal and fleshly desire to sin against the "commandments of God", the Law of Moses. He indicates the fleshly and carnal desire is man's fundamental problem and we need to be delivered from that which causes fleshly desire that conflicts with the "good" Law of Moses. He is clear that we need to be delivered from the flesh.

Romans 7: 13, Was then <u>that which is good made death unto me</u>? God forbid. But sin, that it might appear sin, working death in me by that which is good; that sin by the commandment might become exceeding sinful.

We cannot conclude as do many Messianics that this "law of sin" is just your carnal desire and not the Law of Moses. From the pattern presented we conclude:

- The first administration under judgment and condemnation causes sin to abound, just as it did for the first generation of Israel that left Egypt.
- The first administration of the Law of Moses brings death.
- The first administration is "good" as the Law of Moses does what it should, it condemns the flesh.
- The "law of sin" is the individual under the first administration of the Law of Moses, the flesh.

Paul is clarifying that it is those same "commandments of God", the Law of Moses, that are meant to be "good" and be "life" (Romans 7:13) to the individual while under the administration of condemnation and death does what it should, it condemns sin in the flesh. This administration passes from death to the new administration of resurrection life in the Messiah Yeshua. The flesh is destroyed and the spirit is saved.

1 Corinthians 5: 5, To deliver such an one unto Satan for the destruction of the flesh, that the spirit may be saved in the day of the Lord Jesus.

Knowing that we are in the battle of the duality of the Tree of the Knowledge of Good and Evil, the flesh versus the spirit, how do we proceed?

- **Do we forsake the Torah?** No, we delight in it.
- **Do we cling to the flesh?** No, we cling to the spirit.
- **Was there a fault with the covenant?** Yes, the people were under a curse, the Tree of the Knowledge of Good and Evil. We all are dual in nature, flesh and spirit. By nature it is not possible for us to keep the Torah (Law) of God successfully. Our tabernacle is flawed. We need a new tabernacle made by the Messiah Yeshua. We need a new body, singular in nature (spirit) and made in accordance with grace and mercy (resurrection life).

Hebrews 8: 2, A minister of the sanctuary, and of the true tabernacle, which the Lord pitched, and not man. 3 For every high priest is ordained to offer gifts and sacrifices: wherefore it is of necessity that this man have somewhat also to offer. 4 For if he were on earth, he should not be a priest, seeing that there are priests that offer gifts according to the law: 5 Who serve unto the example and shadow of heavenly things, as Moses was admonished of God when he was about to make the tabernacle: for, See, saith he, that thou make all things according to the pattern shewed to thee in the mount. 6 But now hath he obtained a more excellent ministry, by how much also he is the mediator of a better covenant, which was established upon better promises. 7 For if that first covenant had been faultless, then should no place have been sought for the second. 8 For finding fault with them, he saith, Behold, the days come, saith the Lord, when I will make a new covenant with the house of Israel and with the house of Judah: 9 Not according to the covenant that I made with their fathers in the day when I took them by the hand to lead them out of the land of Egypt; because they continued not in my covenant, and I regarded them not, saith the Lord. 10 For <u>this is the covenant that I will make with the house of Israel after those days, saith the Lord; I will put my laws into their mind, and write them in their hearts</u>: and I will be to them a God, and they shall be to me a people: 11 And they shall not teach every man his neighbour, and every man his brother, saying, Know the Lord: for all shall know me, from the least to the greatest. 12 For I will be merciful to their unrighteousness, and their sins and their iniquities will I remember no more. 13 In that he saith, <u>A new covenant, he hath made the first old. Now that which decayeth and waxeth old is ready to vanish away</u>.

Notice:
- The "first" covenant brought death to those led out of Egypt.
- The "first" covenant found "fault with them", their essential nature (their tabernacle).
- The "first" covenant under the administration of the flesh "which decayeth and waxeth old is ready to vanish away".
- The "better" covenant has "better promises".
- The "better" covenant is based upon, "I will put my laws into their mind, and write them in their hearts".
- The "better" covenant "will be merciful to their unrighteousness".
- The "better" covenant of the spirit is a true "heavenly tabernacle" and does not pass away.

Paul is contrasting the tabernacles that God dwells within, us. One was earthly and the other is heavenly. One brought death, the new brings life. One is passing away and one will remain forever.

What is the goal?   "I will be to them a God, and they shall be to me a people." (Hebrews 8:10)

WHAT IS DECAYING AND READY TO VANISH AWAY?
So what is old and decaying and ready to vanish away? The Torah? No, our fleshly bodies that are dual in nature (flesh and spirit) and subject to the Tree of the Knowledge of Good and Evil. We are corruption needing to put on incorruption (singularity–spirit). Yeshua is the minister of that new sanctuary. We are grafted into His tree, the Tree of Life. The flesh is vanishing away!

1 Corinthians 15: 50, Now this I say, brethren, that flesh and blood cannot inherit the kingdom of God; neither doth corruption inherit incorruption.

Hebrews 9 clarifies that it is the tabernacle that is passing away. This tabernacle is passing from the flesh to the spirit.

Hebrews 9: 6, Now when these things were thus ordained, the priests went always <u>into the first tabernacle</u>, accomplishing the service of God. 7 <u>But into</u>

the second went the high priest alone once every year, not without blood, which he offered for himself, and for the errors of the people: 8 The Holy Ghost this signifying, that <u>the way into the holiest of all was not yet made manifest, while as the first tabernacle was yet standing</u>: 9 Which was a figure for the time then present, in which were offered both gifts and sacrifices, that could not make him that did the service perfect, as <u>pertaining to the conscience</u>; 10 Which stood only in meats and drinks, and divers washings, and carnal ordinances, imposed on them until the time of reformation. 11 But <u>Christ being come an high priest of good things to come, by a greater and more perfect tabernacle, not made with hands</u>, that is to say, <u>not of this building</u>; 12 Neither by the blood of goats and calves, but by his own blood he entered in once into the holy place, having obtained eternal redemption for us. 13 For if the blood of bulls and of goats, and the ashes of an heifer sprinkling the unclean, <u>sanctifieth to the purifying of the flesh</u>: 14 How much more shall the blood of Christ, who through the eternal Spirit offered himself without spot to God, purge your conscience from dead works to serve the living God? 15 And for this cause <u>he is the mediator of the new testament, that by means of death, for the redemption of the transgressions that were under the first testament, they which are called might receive the promise of eternal inheritance</u>. 16 For where a testament is, there must also of necessity be the death of the testator.

Notice:

- There are really two tabernacles: the Holy Place (the body/flesh–"the first tabernacle") and the Holy of Holies (the mind–"the second tabernacle").
- The way into the Holy of Holies is not made manifest while the first tabernacle is "yet standing". The flesh "decayeth and waxeth old is ready to vanish away".
- Christ establishes a "new tabernacle" not made "with hands". The spirit is an eternal habitation for God.
  - o Ephesian 2: 22, In whom ye also are builded together for an habitation of God through the Spirit.
- The "new tabernacle" is not "of this building" (flesh).
- The earthly sacrifices were to "purify the flesh".
- The heavenly sacrifice (Yeshua's blood) is to purify the mind, "purge the conscience".

Once again the work of the Messiah begins hidden within the heart and mind of the redeemed, purifying and cleansing the inside of the cup before providing a new eternal and incorruptible sanctuary made of the spirit. Circumcision must begin within the heart and will then later be manifested in our actions.

It is the current tabernacle of the Tree of the Knowledge of Good and Evil (the flesh and spirit) that is passing away, to be replaced by a greater and more perfect tabernacle not made with hands, the Tree of Life (spirit). That greater and more perfect tabernacle, the spirit, is not "of this building" or dual nature. There is no need for the purification of the flesh in that more perfect tabernacle. Remember the concept of a tent or tabernacle is a type of the body in which God dwells. The new tabernacle is not of the flesh, it is of the spirit only. This provides new insight as to why Yeshua told Pilate, "My kingdom is not of this world."

> John 18: 36, Jesus answered, <u>My kingdom is not of this world</u>: if my kingdom were of this world, then would my servants fight, that I should not be delivered to the Jews: <u>but now is my kingdom not from hence</u>. 37 Pilate therefore said unto him, Art thou a king then? Jesus answered, Thou sayest that I am a king. To this end was I born, and for this cause came I into the world, that I should bear witness unto the truth. Every one that is of the truth heareth my voice.

We need to remember the continuing patterns of the conflict of the flesh and the spirit and how it underlies the reality of the manifest universe.

BIBLICAL PATTERNS OF THE DUALITY OF FLESH & SPIRIT:
Flesh: Eve (manifestation, body, tabernacle, covered)
Spirit: Adam (seed, mind, Shekinah Glory, covering)
Meaning: Eve is born out of Adam's body but falls through eating the fruit of the Tree of the Knowledge of Good and Evil. Redemption happens through the "seed of the woman" (the Messiah, the Countenance of God, the fulness of the Godhead bodily). Creation begins with "seed" then "manifestation". The fall resulted in a striving for power between the mind (Adam) and the body (Eve).

> Genesis 3: 16, Unto the woman he said, I will greatly multiply thy sorrow and thy conception; in sorrow thou shalt bring forth children; and thy desire shall be to thy husband, and he shall rule over thee.

Both the seed and the manifestation fell and need to be redeemed. How does this happen? We need a new "last Adam", the Messiah, to give His seed to the fallen woman. As we have already pointed out the male element is spirit and mind and the female element is the image of that mind and is a body. When sin comes into play the flesh (body) comes into conflict with the spirit (mind) and a battle ensues over who will rule. Whereas "under sin" the female and the flesh is always portrayed as the firstborn, in the original unfallen state, the spirit is born first (Colossians 1:15, 18).

Under the current administration of the flesh and death, the order of birth is inverted and the firstborn is the flesh while the second born is the spirit. Under the administration of the spirit and resurrection life, the male (Adam) is the firstborn and is spirit. The female (Eve) is then the second born and the manifestation of that mind and spirit.

> Romans 8: 29, For whom he did foreknow, he also did predestinate to be conformed to the image of his Son, that he might be the firstborn among many brethren.

Notice how all of the redeemed are depicted as "brethren". This is not happenstance as the "fallen woman" is joined to her ascended male and is no longer female but an ascended male, which is the unity of the male and the female in the marriage chamber. This is why the redeemed are not depicted as female, but as males.

John 1: 12, But as many as received him, to them gave he power to become the sons of God, even to them that believe on his name:

The redeemed are all, whether they currently be male or female in the flesh, then called "sons of God" and are depicted as male. While we are yet in this fallen state, the flesh, whether you be male or female, we are all depicted as fallen "female" that need to be purified so that we might re–enter the sanctuary.

Leviticus 15: 13, And when he that hath an issue is cleansed of his issue; then he shall number to himself seven days for his cleansing, and wash his clothes, and bathe his flesh in running water, and shall be clean. 14 And on the eighth day he shall take to him two turtledoves, or two young pigeons, and come before the Lord unto the door of the tabernacle of the congregation, and give them unto the priest: 15 And the priest shall offer them, the one for a sin offering, and the other for a burnt offering; and the priest shall make an atonement for him before the Lord for his issue.

This is the prophetic type that we are all fulfilling. This is also indicative of why Yeshua declares that there is no marrying in heaven as we see it now on earth, for we will have been joined in marriage to our "bridegroom", the ascended male.

Matthew 22: 30, For in the resurrection they neither marry, nor are given in marriage, but are as the angels of God in heaven.

Let's continue and see if the inverted pattern of flesh and spirit is a provable fractal from the scriptures.

Flesh: Firstborn
Spirit: Second born
Meaning: The firstborn does not inherit, only the second born inherits. (Examples: Isaac versus Ishmael, Jacob versus Esau, Joseph versus Reuben, Ephraim versus Manasseh, David versus Saul, Amnon versus Solomon, etc.)

Flesh: Cain
Spirit: Abel
Meaning: Flesh tries to kill the spirit.

Flesh: Lot
Spirit: Abraham
Meaning: Lot descends to Sodom, Abraham ascends the mountain.

Flesh: Hagar
Spirit: Sarah

Meaning: The spirit has difficulty bringing forth life and requires the intervention of the Angel of YHWH, the Messiah. The flesh is exiled to the wilderness.

Flesh: Ishmael
Spirit: Isaac
Meaning: The flesh holds the spirit in contempt, Ishmael is exiled to the wilderness under a tree, and Isaac ascends the mountain with the tree on the altar of God.

Flesh: Esau
Spirit: Jacob
Meaning: Esau dwells outside (flesh), while Jacob dwells inside (spirit). Jacob can only inherit through living inside of Esau, making peace with him and then parting from him. The Countenance is restored via the transference of the Countenance of God from the Angel of YHWH to Jacob and Esau. Esau is associated with red blood like a female who is menstruating and is covered with red hair all over like a covering garment. The female is also associated with her hair serving as her covering.

1 Corinthians 11: 1, Be ye followers of me, even as I also am of Christ. 2 Now I praise you, brethren, that ye remember me in all things, and keep the ordinances, as I delivered them to you. 3 But I would have you know, that the head of every man is Christ; and the head of the woman is the man; and the head of Christ is God. 4 Every man praying or prophesying, having his head covered, dishonoureth his head. 5 But every woman that prayeth or prophesieth with her head uncovered dishonoureth her head: for that is even all one as if she were shaven. 6 For if the woman be not covered, let her also be shorn: but if it be a shame for a woman to be shorn or shaven, let her be covered. 7 For a man indeed ought not to cover his head, forasmuch as he is the image and glory of God: but the woman is the glory of the man. 8 For the man is not of the woman: but the woman of the man. 9 Neither was the man created for the woman; but the woman for the man. 10 For this cause ought the woman to have power on her head because of the angels. 11 Nevertheless neither is the man without the woman, neither the woman without the man, in the Lord. 12 For as the woman is of the man, even so is the man also by the woman; but all things of God. 13 Judge in yourselves: is it comely that a woman pray unto God uncovered? 14 Doth not even nature itself teach you, that, if a man have long hair, it is a shame unto him? 15 But if a woman have long hair, it is a glory to her: for her hair is given her for a covering.

We can see by this that Esau is associated with the fallen flesh and being the "unclean woman" who needs to obtain a "covering". Paul states the female needs a "covering" and a "head", which she obtains from the male (Messiah) to remove her shame (fallen state). He associates hair with the female. Being shorn is typified as being without her covering (husband), the Messiah. Just as the female is the glory of the male, the redeemed female (us) is the glory of the male (the Messiah).

Just as the female is created for the male, we are created for the Messiah and become His glory (body). This body is to have His spirit (the mind of Christ).

1 Corinthians 2: 16, For who hath known the mind of the Lord, that he may instruct him? but we have the mind of Christ.

Jacob is associated with a voice (spirit) within Esau's garment. Jacob is indeed rightfully called "supplanter" as the role of the spirit is to inherit in the place of the flesh.

Genesis 27: 36, And he said, Is not he rightly named Jacob? for he hath supplanted me these two times: he took away my birthright; and, behold, now he hath taken away my blessing. And he said, Hast thou not reserved a blessing for me?

Flesh: Leah
Spirit: Rachel
Meaning: Leah is associated with sorrow (flesh). She was to be wed to Esau. Rachel is associated with beauty (spirit). Rachel is not able to conceive without the intervention of God. It is only after Leah brings forth a daughter that God remembers Rachel and gives her Joseph (a type of the Messiah).

Flesh: The other Children of Jacob
Spirit: Joseph (Redeemer)/Benjamin (Redeemed)
Meaning: Joseph is exiled to a land of images (descent to Egypt) for the goal of preserving life for the rest of the family. This redemption culminates with bringing Benjamin (who is dual in nature–"son of my sorrow"/"son of my right hand") to serve Joseph (the Messiah). The other brothers (flesh) hate Joseph (spirit) and fear him.

Flesh: Aaron/Miriam
Spirit: Moses
Meaning: Moses is made in the image of YHWH to deliver the people from bondage and to cleanse the garments of His people. Aaron and Miriam are a picture of the dual nature of the fallen universe. Moses is a picture of the Messiah who writes His countenance upon our fallen images. Aaron speaks only what Moses tells him to say. Aaron carries Moses' staff/branch (image). Miriam is a prophetess that has the Utterance of God. Aaron and Miriam speak against Moses and Miriam is turned leprous and is exiled from the camp for seven days for her contempt of Moses (spirit).

Flesh: First generation that left Egypt
Spirit: Second generation that left Egypt
Meaning: The first generation that left Egypt is associated with the flesh and death. The second generation that left Egypt is associated with the spirit and resurrected (ascended) life. The first generation wanted to keep the Torah and could not do it. They lacked faith and died, like the flesh in the wilderness of the

manifest universe. The second generation had faith and ascended to resurrected and ascended life (Promised land). The first giving of the Torah (flesh) results in shattered tablets, the second giving of the Torah (spirit) results in the ascension of new tablets engraved by the Utterance of the manifest Name of YHWH, Yeshua (Exodus 34) and results in a glorified countenance.

Flesh: Tree of the Knowledge of Good and Evil
Spirit: Tree of Life
Meaning: The tree of the Knowledge of Good and Evil is dual in nature (mix of spirit and flesh) and is subject to death. It is a duality and is corrupt. The Tree of Life is spirit, it is singular in nature and brings life. Those who are grafted into the Tree of the Knowledge of Good and Evil have shown a lack of faith and unbelief (duality). Those grafted into the Tree of Life have shown a singular faith (unity of the faith–Ephesians 4:13).

Flesh: Firstborn of Egypt
Spirit: Firstborn of Israel
Meaning: Israel needed to be delivered from the Egyptians because the bondage was very great. The Egyptians were killing the male children of Israel by drowning them in the water. This resulted in female children being left alive. This culminated with the conflict between judgment on the firstborn of Egypt and the sanctification of the firstborn of Israel.

- Exodus 1: 16, And he said, When ye do the office of a midwife to the Hebrew women, and see them upon the stools; if it be a son, then ye shall kill him: but if it be a daughter, then she shall live. 17 But the midwives feared God, and did not as the king of Egypt commanded them, but saved the men children alive.

- Exodus 13: 2, Sanctify unto me all the firstborn, whatsoever openeth the womb among the children of Israel, both of man and of beast: it is mine.

- Exodus 13: 5, And it came to pass, when Pharaoh would hardly let us go, that the Lord slew all the firstborn in the land of Egypt, both the firstborn of man, and the firstborn of beast: therefore I sacrifice to the Lord all that openeth the matrix, being males; but all the firstborn of my children I redeem.

Flesh: 3 (first coming in death)
Spirit: 7 (second coming in resurrection life)
Meaning: We see the same type of imagery with Job's children.

- Job has ten (3 daughters and 7 sons) children before God tests Job. They are all killed.

- Job has ten (3 daughters and 7 sons) children after God tests Job. They appear to have a "resurrection" imagery". He has 10 new children, the same number of male children and female children as before and "no women found as fair as the daughters of Job".

    - Job 1: 2, And there were born unto him seven sons and three daughters….18 While he was yet speaking, there came also another, and said, Thy sons and thy daughters were eating and drinking wine in their eldest brother's house: 19 And, behold, there came a great wind from the wilderness, and smote the four corners of the house, and it fell upon the young men, and they are dead; and I only am escaped alone to tell thee.

- Job 42: 12, So the Lord blessed the latter end of Job more than his beginning: for he had fourteen thousand sheep, and six thousand camels, and a thousand yoke of oxen, and a thousand she asses. 13 He had also seven sons and three daughters. 14 And he called the name of the first, Jemima; and the name of the second, Kezia; and the name of the third, Kerenhappuch. And in all the land were no women found so fair as the daughters of Job: and their father gave them inheritance among their brethren.

Flesh: Female
Spirit: Male
Meaning: The Torah depicts the female as unclean and needing to dip into the mikvah (baptism) to be able to enter the camp (Leviticus 12:2, 15:19, 25, 33, 18:19). This occurs through the union of the female and the heavenly male (redeemer). Just to clarify, all of creation is the fallen and unclean female needing to be cleansed and unified with her heavenly male (the promised seed–Messiah). The concept of being unclean is associated with death.

Numbers 19: 11, He that toucheth the dead body of any man shall be unclean seven days. 12 He shall purify himself with it on the third day, and on the seventh day he shall be clean: but if he purify not himself the third day, then the seventh day he shall not be clean. 13 Whosoever toucheth the dead body of any man that is dead, and purifieth not himself, defileth the tabernacle of the Lord; and that soul shall be cut off from Israel: because the water of separation was not sprinkled upon him, he shall be unclean; his uncleanness is yet upon him.

This is another reason why you are not grafted into Israel. Israel is female, you do not graft one female into another female. You graft a female with a male. We are joined to the Lord (the Messiah) in the baptism (mikvah) of death.

Romans 6: 3, Know ye not, that so many of us as were baptized into Jesus Christ were baptized into his death?

Flesh: Left
Spirit: Right
Meaning: The right side is depicted as the spirit and the left side is depicted as the flesh. That is why you see the Messiah depicted as the Right Hand of YHWH.

Acts 2: 32, This Jesus hath God raised up, whereof we all are witnesses. 33 Therefore being by the right hand of God exalted, and having received of the Father the promise of the Holy Ghost, he hath shed forth this, which ye now see and hear.

Flesh: Leavened Bread
Spirit: Unleavened Bread
Meaning: The Bread of Heaven, Yeshua the Messiah, is the Unleavened Bread we must consume.

- John 6: 51, I am the living bread which came down from heaven: if any man eat of this bread, he shall live for ever: and the bread that I will give is my flesh, which I will give for the life of the world.

- Mark 14: 12, And the first day of unleavened bread, when they killed the Passover, his disciples said unto him, Where wilt thou that we go and prepare that thou mayest eat the Passover?

- 1 Corinthians 5: 7, Purge out therefore the old leaven, that ye may be a new lump, as ye are unleavened. For even Christ our Passover is sacrificed for us:

- Mark 14: 22, And as they did eat, Jesus took bread, and blessed, and brake it, and gave to them, and said, Take, eat: this is my body. 23 And he took the cup, and when he had given thanks, he gave it to them: and they all drank of it. 24 And he said unto them, This is my blood of the new testament, which is shed for many.

Flesh: Falsity (mixture of truth and not truth)
Spirit: Truth
Meaning: Any mixture of truth with non–truth is a mixing of seed and becomes a lie.

John 4: 24, God is a Spirit: and <u>they that worship him must worship him in spirit and in truth</u>.

Put off the flesh and pursue the spirit by being grafted into the manifest Name of YHWH, Yeshua the Messiah, the Countenance of YHWH!

1 Corinthians 15: 55, O death, where is thy sting? O grave, where is thy victory?

We are not meant to remain here in the flesh. Our destiny lies upward. This deliverance is not through our works or worth, nor our zeal or ability to keep the Torah (Law). Yet, we manifest our faith by what we do and how we live.

James 2: 21, Was not Abraham our father justified by works, when he had offered Isaac his son upon the altar? 22 Seest thou how faith wrought with his works, and by works was faith made perfect? 23 And the scripture was fulfilled which saith, Abraham believed God, and it was imputed unto him for righteousness: and he was called the Friend of God.

THE SINGULARITY OF FAITH:
We must turn the duality of unbelief and lack of faith into the singularity of faith in the Messiah Yeshua.

Hebrews 12: 22, But ye are come unto mount Sion, and unto the city of the living God, the heavenly Jerusalem, and to an innumerable company of angels, 23 To the general assembly and church of the firstborn, which are written in heaven, and to God the Judge of all, <u>and to the spirits of just men made perfect,</u> 24 And to Yeshua the mediator of the new covenant, and to the blood of sprinkling, that speaketh better things than that of Abel. 25 See that ye refuse not him that speaketh. For if they escaped not who refused him that spake on earth, much more shall not we escape, if we turn away from him that speaketh from heaven: 26 Whose voice then shook the earth: but now he hath promised, saying, Yet once more I shake not the earth only, but also heaven. 27 And <u>this word, Yet once more, signifieth the removing of those things that are shaken, as of things that are made, that those things which cannot be shaken may remain.</u> 28 Wherefore we receiving a kingdom which cannot be moved, let us have grace, whereby we may serve God acceptably with reverence and godly fear: 29 For our God is a consuming fire.

The shaking is meant to cast down the flesh and cause it to pass away and separate from the spirit which cannot be shaken by unbelief.

Matthew 3: 11, I indeed baptize you with water unto repentance. but he that cometh after me is mightier than I, whose shoes I am not worthy to bear: he shall baptize you with the Holy Ghost, and with fire: 12 Whose fan is in his hand, and he will throughly purge his floor, and gather his wheat into the garner; but he will burn up the chaff with unquenchable fire.

Just as the wheat must be separated from the chaff, so must the spirit be separated from the flesh. Chaff is the outer husk that is circumcised from the seed. This happens first to the hardened heart, which is circumcised so that the seed of the Kingdom of God can be planted within and begin to grow and then it manifests itself in the removal and circumcision of the fleshly body, so that the spirit may live.

This is how the spirits of man are made perfect. We must pass from the duality of the Tree of the Knowledge of Good and Evil (flesh and spirit) and be grafted via faith in the manifest Name of YHWH, Yeshua the Messiah, the Tree of Life (the singular spirit). This circumcision is the second birth. Knowing this, Yeshua's words to Nicodemus gain tremendous clarity.

John 3: 3, Yeshua answered and said unto him, Verily, verily, I say unto thee, <u>Except a man be born again, he cannot see the kingdom of God.</u> 4 Nicodemus saith unto him, How can a man be born when he is old? can he enter the second time into his mother's womb, and be born? 5 Yeshua answered, Verily, verily, I say unto thee, <u>Except a man be born of water and of the Spirit, he cannot enter into the kingdom of God. 6 That which is born of the flesh is flesh; and that which is born of the Spirit is spirit.</u> 7 Marvel not that I said unto thee, Ye must be born again. 8 The wind bloweth where it listeth, and thou hearest the sound thereof, but canst not tell whence it cometh, and whither it goeth: so is every one that is born of the Spirit. 9 Nicodemus answered and said unto him, How can these things be? 10 Yeshua answered and said unto him, Art thou a master of Israel, and knowest not these things? 11 Verily, verily, I say unto thee, We speak that we do know, and testify that we have seen; and ye receive not our witness. 12 If I have told you earthly things, and ye believe not, how shall ye believe, if I tell you of heavenly things? 13 And no man hath ascended up to heaven, but he that came down from heaven, even the Son of man which is in heaven. 14 And as Moses lifted up the serpent in the wilderness, even so must the Son of man be lifted up: 15 That whosoever believeth in him should not perish, but have eternal life. 16 For God so loved the world, that he gave his only begotten Son, that whosoever believeth in him should not perish, but have everlasting life. 17 For God sent not his Son into the world to condemn the world; but that the world through him might be saved. 18 He that believeth on him is not condemned: but he that believeth not is condemned already, because he hath not believed in the name of the only begotten Son of God. 19 And this is the condemnation, that light is come into the world, and men loved darkness rather than light, because their deeds were evil. 20 For every one that doeth evil hateth the light, neither cometh to the light, lest his deeds should be reproved. 21 But he that doeth truth cometh to the light, that his deeds may be made manifest, that they are wrought in God.

It is through this belief on the manifest Name of YHWH, the seed of the woman, the Messiah Yeshua, that our fallen countenance is restored to the image of YHWH. Our duality (flesh and spirit) is made singularity (spirit and resurrected life). We are literally born again when we leave the flesh of these corrupted bodies.

1 Peter 1: 19, But with the precious blood of Christ, as of a lamb without blemish and without spot: 20 Who verily was foreordained before the foundation of the world, but was manifest in these last times for you, 21 Who by him do believe in God, that raised him up from the dead, and gave him glory; that your faith and hope might be in God. 22 Seeing ye have purified your souls in obeying the truth through the Spirit unto unfeigned love of the brethren, see that ye love one another with a pure heart fervently: 23 Being born again, not of corruptible seed, but of incorruptible, by the word of God, which liveth and abideth for ever. 24 For all flesh is as grass, and all the glory of man as the flower of grass. The grass withereth, and the flower thereof falleth away: 25 But the word of the Lord endureth for ever. And this is the word which by the Gospel is preached unto you.

What have we learned?
- We are redeemed by the precious blood of Yeshua the Messiah, the manifest Name of YHWH.
- With singular faith/belief (unwavering and undivided) "by Him" (Yeshua) we believe in God.
- We are to be born again of incorruptible seed and the corruptible seed (flesh) we currently have will be burned up like grass.
- This is the Gospel.
- Technically it would appear that we are conceived again in the womb of

the baptism.

- Our seed has joined with the Messiah's in a form of a seed death, so that it might grow in the womb and be born again when the flesh dies.

What seed are you sowing? Flesh or Spirit?

Galatians 6: 7, Be not deceived; God is not mocked: for whatsoever a man soweth, that shall he also reap. 8 For <u>he that soweth to his flesh shall of the flesh reap corruption; but he that soweth to the Spirit shall of the Spirit reap life everlasting</u>. 9 And let us not be weary in well doing: for in due season we shall reap, if we faint not.

If you are a Christian who thinks you do not need to keep the Written Torah of Moses, you need to accept the Messiah Yeshua as your Savior. Once you have done so, with the Spirit of the Messiah that is reconciled to God, you should do as Yeshua says and "keep my commandments" (John 14:15).   This is how our spirits are perfected while in the flesh.

Hebrew 12: 22, But ye are come unto mount Sion, and unto the city of the living God, the heavenly Jerusalem, and to an innumerable company of angels, 23 To the general assembly and church of the firstborn, which are written in heaven, and to God the Judge of all, <u>and to the spirits of just men made perfect,</u> 24 And to Jesus the mediator of the new covenant, and to the blood of sprinkling, that speaketh better things than that of Abel.

We are not saved by keeping the Torah, we are saved by the Messiah. However, that does not mean we have a license to sin.

Jude 1: 4, For there are certain men crept in unawares, who were before of old ordained to this condemnation, ungodly men, turning the grace of our God into lasciviousness, and denying the only Lord God, and our Lord Jesus Christ.

If you think you are saved by keeping the Torah or that the Messiah is the manifestation of the Torah then you are straying from the truth of the scriptures. He is the manifest presence of the Godhead bodily.

1 Timothy 3: 9, Holding the <u>mystery of the faith</u> in a pure conscience. 10 And let these also first be proved; then let them use the office of a deacon, being found blameless. 11 Even so must their wives be grave, not slanderers, sober, faithful in all things. 12 Let the deacons be the husbands of one wife, ruling their children and their own houses well. 13 For they that have used the office of a deacon well purchase to themselves a good degree, and <u>great boldness in the faith which is in Christ Yeshua</u>. 14 These things write I unto thee, hoping to come unto thee shortly: 15 But if I tarry long, that thou mayest know how thou oughtest to behave thyself in the house of God, which is the church of the living God, the pillar and ground of the truth. 16 And without controversy great is the mystery of godliness: <u>God was manifest in the flesh,</u>

justified in the Spirit, seen of angels, preached unto the Gentiles, believed on in the world, received up into glory.

THE DUALITY OF THE GIVING OF THE TORAH:

Yeshua is not the Torah in the flesh or the Living Torah. He is the manifest Name of YHWH. Remember at the first giving of the Torah, the manifest Name of YHWH is not present, but He is at the second giving of the Torah (Exodus 34) and Moses immediately bows and worships the manifest Name of YHWH. The first giving of the Torah is associated with death (flesh/blood) and the second giving of the Torah is associated with resurrected life and the Countenance of God (spirit), the Messiah. Remember the manifestation of our propitiation is manifested without the Law! Can we prove this?

Romans 3: 19, Now we know that what things soever the law saith, it saith to them who are under the law: that every mouth may be stopped, and all the world may become guilty before God. 20 Therefore by the deeds of the law there shall no flesh be justified in his sight: for by the law is the knowledge of sin. 21 But now the righteousness of God without the law is manifested, being witnessed by the law and the prophets; 22 Even the righteousness of God which is by faith of Yeshua unto all and upon all them that believe: for there is no difference: 23 For all have sinned, and come short of the glory of God; 24 Being justified freely by his grace through the redemption that is in Christ Yeshua: 25 Whom God hath set forth to be a propitiation through faith in his blood, to declare his righteousness for the remission of sins that are past, through the forbearance of God; 26 To declare, I say, at this time his righteousness: that he might be just, and the justifier of him which believeth in Yeshua.

The manifestation of God's righteousness, His Son, occurred without the Law (Torah). Yeshua, the Son of God, the manifest Name of YHWH, the righteousness of God, was manifested as a propitiation through faith in His blood, and not by the presence of the Torah. Notice Paul says, "But now the righteousness of God without the law is manifested" (Romans 3:21). There is no doubt, Yeshua is not the Torah made flesh or the living Torah or one with the Torah. He is the manifest Name of YHWH, the Countenance of God, and the administrator of the Resurrected Covenant! Paul further clarifies this very point in the book of Hebrews. He again contrasts the Messiah, the manifest Name of YHWH, with the Torah.

Hebrews 10: 1, For the law having a shadow of good things to come, and not the very image of the things, can never with those sacrifices which they offered year by year continually make the comers thereunto perfect. 2 For then would they not have ceased to be offered? because that the worshippers once purged should have had no more conscience of sins. 3 But in those sacrifices there is a remembrance again made of sins every year. 4 For it is not possible that the blood of bulls and of goats should take away sins. 5 Wherefore when he cometh into the world, he saith, Sacrifice and offering thou wouldest not,

<u>but a body hast thou prepared me</u>: 6 In burnt offerings and sacrifices for sin thou hast had no pleasure.

Unbelief and lack of faith results in the Tree of the Knowledge of Good and Evil (flesh and spirit–duality and death). Singular belief and faith results in the grafting into the Tree of Life, the manifest Name of YHWH, Yeshua the Messiah (Romans 11). We are literally joined or grafted into the Lord. We are not grafted into Israel, Judah, or the Torah.

Isaiah 56: 6, Also the sons of the stranger, <u>that join themselves to the Lord</u>, to serve him, and to love the Name of the Lord, to be his servants, every one that keepeth the sabbath from polluting it, and taketh hold of my covenant; 7 Even them will I bring to my holy mountain, and make them joyful in my house of prayer: their burnt offerings and their sacrifices shall be accepted upon mine altar; for mine house shall be called an house of prayer for all people. 8 The Lord God, which gathereth the outcasts of Israel saith, Yet will I gather others to him, beside those <u>that are gathered unto him</u>.

Rejoice in the faith once delivered. Now that we have established that we are saved by grace via faith in the manifest Name of YHWH and that we should be keeping the Written Law of Moses because the new administrator instructs us to "keep His commandments", let's move on to clarify why Yeshua is not the Torah, the living Torah, one with the Torah, or the Torah manifested. Often well intended new believers swing to the far side of the pendulum to new unscriptural oral traditions that are not supported by the scriptures or the testimony of the Apostles. Why do they do this? Their paradigm is still not fully corrected.

22 WHAT IS THE LAW OF SIN & DEATH?

Many Messianic and Hebrew Roots teachers have in their writings and in their teachings repeatedly made some of the statements listed in the table titled "Popular Hebrew Roots/Messianic Sayings That Are Scripturally Inaccurate". We will evaluate those statements and their scriptural accuracy. Error typically does not creep in through obvious heretical teaching. Typically it is some truth mixed with some un–truth. The quality of the teacher depends upon their conformance to the scriptural images presented and the meanings presented by the scriptures to those patterns and fractals. Undisciplined teachers often bring about inaccurate teaching, which can have serious consequences for the uneducated believer.

The author of this book is a Hebrew Roots believer and teacher who has followed Yeshua and the Written Torah since childhood…well over forty years. Please do not assume this is written by a new believer because of disagreement with some of these teachers and some of their teachings.

We need to evaluate if these frequent statements are scripturally sound and accurate, and if not, correct the source and question the source publically. If the teacher refuses to acknowledge error by correcting the teaching to conform to the scriptures, you should ask yourself why. This is exactly what the Bereans did.

Acts 17: 11, These were more noble than those in Thessalonica, in that they received the word with all readiness of mind, and searched the scriptures daily, whether those things were so.

It is never easy to hear things that you do not want to hear. Correction is rarely pleasant, unless your goal is truth.

Proverbs 3: 11, My son, despise not the chastening of the Lord; neither be weary of his correction:

Has the body of Christ lost their ability to correct themselves when they discover they have stepped off the path of truth?

> Exodus 34: 6, And the Lord passed by before him, and proclaimed, The Lord, The Lord God, merciful and gracious, longsuffering, and abundant in goodness <u>and truth</u>...

What is the future of those who forsake the truth?

> 2 Thessalonians 2:10, And with all deceivableness of unrighteousness in them that perish; because they received not the love of the truth, that they might be saved.

Whenever tackling holy and sacred ideas people often respond with a knee–jerk rejection due to how they feel. They respond with the same visceral emotion that they felt when someone first told them that Christmas was a pagan holiday (I would suggest the reader study what the Catholic Encyclopedia says about "Christmas" and its origins). They might say, "How can that be? My best feelings of joy and love of family and religion come from Christmas and Easter. What you are saying cannot be true."

They are thinking with their feelings and emotions and not with reason, facts, or truth. On the contrary, those who have come out of Sunday sabbath and pagan holidays often feel that they have arrived. They think that what got them to this point cannot be questioned or modified. "I have found the truth and no one can convince me otherwise."

Remember truth is continually pursued, it is not a singular destination. The believer can never say, "I have found the truth...and there is no more truth to discover". If you find yourself resistant to learning more, and proving the veracity of what you think you know, you might want to ask yourself if you are truly a follower of Yeshua.

> 2 Thessalonians 2: 14, But we are bound to give thanks alway to God for you, brethren beloved of the Lord, because God hath from the beginning chosen you to salvation <u>through sanctification of the Spirit and belief of the truth</u>:

In the pursuit of truth, it is often necessary to evaluate what we believe and whether those teachings are scripturally accurate. In the Messianic and Hebrew Roots Movement some are willing to go through this effort, and many are not. They would rather stick to their current paradigm regardless of what the scriptures say or acknowledge that their paradigm does not embrace all of the scriptures. Both Christians and Messianics suffer from the same problem to one degree or another. It is understandable since both groups are made up of people that handle truth only as they are able to see. Sometimes our feelings get in the way of wanting to see.

Several popular teachings and sayings are often recited in the Messianic and

Hebrew Roots Movement that need to be corrected and aligned to the scriptures.

Popular Hebrew Roots/Messianic Sayings That Are Scripturally Inaccurate:
Yeshua is the Torah in the flesh
Yeshua is the Torah
Yeshua is one with the Torah
The Torah was manifested
You must be grafted into Judah
You must be grafted into Israel
You must be grafted into the Torah
The tree of Romans 11 is Israel/Judah
"Under the Law" means being under the Oral Torah
"Works of the Law" means being under the Oral Torah
Sarah versus Hagar means being under the Oral Torah
The Middle Wall of Partition is the Oral Torah

I will affirm from the beginning so that there is no confusion, that; Yeshua is the Word of God, Paul is a true Apostle, Paul and Yeshua teach that we are saved by Yeshua, through grace and mercy and not by keeping the Torah, once saved by grace we are to walk the Written Torah, and we are not required to keep the Oral Torah (Traditions of the rabbis/Traditions of men) for salvation. Yet even with that declaration, the above list of popular sayings are still scripturally inaccurate and are leading people away from the revealed truth of scripture.

IS IT POSSIBLE THAT THE WRITTEN TORAH COULD BE THE LAW OF SIN & DEATH?

Let us first affirm that the Written Torah is still valid after being saved by Yeshua.

Matthew 5: 17, <u>Think not that I am come to destroy the law (Torah)</u>, or the prophets: I am not come to destroy, but to fulfil. 18 For verily I say unto you,

<u>Till heaven and earth pass, one jot or one tittle shall in no wise pass from the law (Torah)</u>, till all be fulfilled. 19 Whosoever therefore shall break one of these least commandments, and shall teach men so, he shall be called the least in the kingdom of heaven: but whosoever shall do and teach them, the same shall be called great in the kingdom of heaven.

Yeshua is giving a clear declaration that the commandments of the Written Law of Moses are still in effect until the "heavens and earth pass away". Clearly Yeshua has died and risen, and the heavens and earth are still here, so despite being saved by grace in Yeshua, we are to keep the Written Torah.

Yet, Yeshua makes it absolutely clear that though we are to keep and walk the Written Torah, we have no need to keep the Oral Torah (the Traditions of the rabbis also known as the Traditions of men or the Traditions of the Elders) in order to remain in the covenant with God.

Matthew 15: 1, Then came to Yeshua scribes and Pharisees, which were of Jerusalem, saying, 2 <u>Why do thy disciples transgress the tradition of the elders</u>? for they wash not their hands when they eat bread. 3 But he answered and said unto them, <u>Why do ye also transgress the commandment of God by your tradition</u>?

Paul also affirms that the Oral Torah is not required for salvation.

Colossians 2: 7, <u>Rooted and built up in him, and stablished in the faith</u>, as ye have been taught, abounding therein with thanksgiving. 8 Beware lest any man spoil you through philosophy and vain deceit, <u>after the tradition of men</u>, after the rudiments of the world, and not after Christ. 9 For in him dwelleth all the fulness of the Godhead bodily.

He confirms we are rooted and built up in him, Yeshua the Messiah, and not by the Oral Torah (traditions of men).

Galatians 1: 13, For ye have heard of my conversation in time past in the <u>Jews' religion</u>, how that beyond measure I persecuted the church of God, and wasted it: 14 And <u>profited in the Jews' religion</u> above many my equals in mine own nation, being more exceedingly <u>zealous of the traditions of my fathers</u>. 15 But when it pleased God, who separated me from my mother's womb, <u>and called me by his grace</u>,

Paul affirms that it was these Rabbinical Oral Traditions that caused him to persecute the body of Christ. He goes so far as to say that it was the "Jews' religion" and does not associate it with God. That being the case, many Christians think that Paul is teaching that we do not need to observe the Written Torah. They do so because they do not understand the first century rabbinical requirement that their Oral Traditions, which are not the Written Torah, must be observed to remain in covenant with God. They went so far as to persecute those who did not observe their Oral Laws and Traditions.

Paul further clarifies the matter and says that he abandoned those Rabbinic Oral Traditions when he was saved by Yeshua through grace and now establishes the Written Torah.

Romans 3: 22, Even <u>the righteousness of God which is by faith of Yeshua</u> unto all and upon all them that believe: for there is no difference: 23 For all have sinned, and come short of the glory of God; 24 Being <u>justified freely by his grace through the redemption that is in Christ Yeshua</u>: 25 Whom <u>God hath set forth to be a propitiation through faith in his blood</u>, to declare his righteousness for the remission of sins that are past, through the forbearance of God; 26 To <u>declare, I say, at this time his righteousness</u>: that he might be just, and the <u>justifier of him which believeth in Yeshua</u>. 27 <u>Where is boasting then? It is excluded. By what law? of works? Nay: but by the law of faith</u>. 28 Therefore we conclude that a <u>man is justified by faith without the deeds of the law</u>. 29 Is he the God of the Jews only? is he not also of the Gentiles? Yes, of the Gentiles also: 30 Seeing it is one God, which shall justify the circumcision by faith, and uncircumcision through faith. 31 <u>Do we then make void the law through faith? God forbid: yea, we establish the law.</u>

Notice how clear Paul is in his writing. He is contrasting the Law of Works versus the Law of faith and how righteousness is imparted to those needing to be freed from sin and death. How does this occur through the Torah of faith? The Torah (Commandments) are not made void by our faith, they are established by our faith in Yeshua.

Is this a message to the Jews, showing them that they still need to keep the Written Torah? No. This message is "…<u>unto all and upon all them that believe: for there is no difference</u>: For all have sinned, and come short of the glory of God;" (Romans 3:22–23). It is for all followers of Yeshua.

Paul is clarifying that all believers, Jews and Gentiles, should be establishing the Written Torah because they are saved by Yeshua. "Is he the God of the Jews only? is he not also of the Gentiles? Yes, of the Gentiles also: Seeing it is one God, which shall justify the circumcision by faith, and uncircumcision through faith." (Romans 3:29). Both Jews and Gentiles are now one and delivered by the same means, faith in Yeshua.

This point is so important to Paul that he is emphasizing that he is not talking about the religion of the Jews and their Oral Torah. He is talking about the deliverance of all mankind from death, Jews and Gentiles alike.

Romans 3: 9, What then? are we better than they? No, in no wise: for <u>we have before proved both Jews and Gentiles, that they are all under sin</u>; 10 As it is written, There is none righteous, no, not one: 11 There is none that understandeth, there is none that seeketh after God.

What Paul is talking about is salvation for all mankind, who are all under sin. He is therefore referencing the unity of mankind in our need for deliverance from sin and death. And once that deliverance is provided, we cannot boast, because we did nothing to qualify ourselves for deliverance. So we should rejoice in the righteousness provided by Yeshua the Messiah and establish the (written) Torah.

Paul is clarifying that even though the Jews had the Written Torah, they were not justified by it, because all it did was manifest their sin and cause their death. This did not make Israel any better than the Gentiles, who were also under sin and death, being without the Written Torah.

> Romans 5: 19, For as <u>by one man's disobedience many were made sinners</u>, so by the obedience of one shall many be made righteous. 20 Moreover <u>the law entered, that the offence might abound</u>. But where sin abounded, grace did much more abound: 21 That <u>as sin hath reigned unto death, even so might grace reign through righteousness</u> unto eternal life by Yeshua our Lord.

Once grace was provided to all mankind, we could not boast in the Torah, because it was not by our works of the Torah that provided our righteousness. By design, it caused our sin to abound. It became a Torah of Sin and Death.

> Romans 8: 1, There is therefore <u>now no condemnation to them which are in Christ Yeshua, who walk not after the flesh, but after the Spirit</u>. 2 For the law of the Spirit of life in Christ Yeshua hath made me <u>free from the law of sin and death</u>. 3 For <u>what the law could not do</u>, in that it was weak through the flesh, God sending his own Son in the likeness of sinful flesh, and for sin, condemned sin in the flesh:

How can the Torah become a Torah of Sin and Death? Is not this anathema to those who now, saved through Yeshua…establish the Law (Torah)? The Torah is life only, right? The Torah is light that only brings life, right? What do the scriptures actually say?

23 THE DEATH & RESURRECTION FRACTAL

Remember Paul is always contrasting the flesh with the spirit, death with resurrection life, the Torah of Sin and Death with the Torah of the Spirit of Christ. We need to remember these scriptural fractals.

Old Covenant	New Covenant
Torah of Sin and Death	Torah of Resurrection Life
Flesh	Spirit
Hagar	Sarah
Ishmael	Isaac
Sinai	Jerusalem
Moses	Yeshua
Torah	Resurrected Covenant
Letter	Spirit
Seed	Fruit
Death	Resurrection life
Ministration of condemnation	Ministration of grace & mercy
Law/Torah of works	Law/Torah of faith
Shadow	Image (manifestation)

Knowing the importance of these scriptural fractals, we gain new insight into Yeshua's great distress in the Garden of Gethsemane.

Luke 22: 42, Saying, Father, if thou be willing, remove this cup from me: nevertheless not my will, but thine, be done. 43 And there appeared an angel unto him from heaven, strengthening him. 44 And being in an agony he prayed more earnestly: and his sweat was as it were great drops of blood falling down to the ground.

Yeshua was appealing to the Father to please deliver the world through some other way. Yeshua clearly understood that in order to fulfill His fractal, he had to fulfill the same imagery of the seed, buried in death to await resurrection. He knew He had to fulfill the same imagery as the Torah: sin and death to await resurrection. This is why He also knew that the Father had no option, the fractal of death (sin) had to be fulfilled in Him, so that the fractal of resurrection life could also be fulfilled in him. This was the key to the kingdom in order for Yeshua to qualify to be the new administrator of the Resurrected Covenant (Torah of Resurrection Life).

2 Corinthians 3: 6, Who also hath made us able ministers of the new testament; not of the letter, but of the spirit: for the letter killeth, but the spirit giveth life. 7 But if the ministration of death, written and engraven in stones, was glorious, so that the children of Israel could not stedfastly behold the face of Moses for the glory of his countenance; which glory was to be done away: 8 How shall not the ministration of the spirit be rather glorious? 9 For if the ministration of condemnation be glory, much more doth the ministration of righteousness exceed in glory.

If Yeshua was to be the administrator of this Resurrected Covenant (Torah), then He had to bear the marks of that same fractal of death and resurrection. He was taking our sin and death upon himself so that He could provide His resurrection life and place it upon us. He had to show He was qualified through the power of resurrection life. If He could not prove it, then He could not qualify to be the new administrator.

Hebrews 7: 15, And it is yet far more evident: for that after the similitude of Melchisedec there ariseth another priest, Who is made, not after the law of a carnal commandment, but after the power of an endless life.

Now because Yeshua bears the same fractal hallmarks as the Torah of Sin and Death, many would like to say He is the Torah manifested. We will explain why that is not the case in great detail.

Before we go into this subject in detail we must finish dealing with how some Messianics came to the idea that the "works of the law" and being "under the law" came to be interpreted as being the Oral Torah. We have already affirmed that Paul says we have no need to keep the Oral Torah (the Traditions of the rabbis, the

Traditions of the Elders, otherwise known as the Talmud, the Mishnah, or as the Takanot, Minhag, Halakha, or Ma'aseh).

Many in the Hebrew Roots Movement have read Avi Ben Mordechai's Galatians Commentary and agree that the Bible is clear that the Oral Traditions (Oral Torah) are not required. Many others in the Messianic Community do not hold this same opinion, as they believe it is necessary to fulfill the Oral Torah to remain in covenant with God.

Paul has already addressed this issue and shown that he affirms the Written Torah. Paul was accused by the Jews that he was undermining the Torah, because he would not adhere to their Oral Laws and Traditions and also because of his insistence on teaching about the fractal of death and resurrection.

> Acts 21: 28, Crying out, Men of Israel, help: This is the man, <u>that teacheth all men every where against the people, and the law, and this place</u>: and further brought Greeks also into the temple, and hath polluted this holy place.

Paul responds to this accusation of teaching against the Law.

> Acts 21: 40, And when he had given him licence, Paul stood on the stairs, and beckoned with the hand unto the people. And when there was made a great silence, he spake unto them in the Hebrew tongue, saying... 22:3 I am verily a man which am a Jew, born in Tarsus, a city in Cilicia, yet brought up in this city at the feet of Gamaliel, and taught according to the <u>perfect manner of the law of the fathers</u>, and was zealous toward God, as ye all are this day.

Paul is confessing that he has kept the Written Torah in a perfect manner.

> Acts 23: 6, But when Paul perceived that the one part were Sadducees, and the other Pharisees, he cried out in the council, Men and brethren, I am a Pharisee, the son of a Pharisee: <u>of the hope and resurrection of the dead I am called in question.</u>

He then clarifies that he is being called into judgment, by the chief priests and their council, for declaring the resurrection, not only of the Messiah Yeshua, but of the Torah. By implication this means that the Law was a Torah of Sin and Death and then the same Commandments (Exodus 34:1) are resurrected by the administrator of resurrection life (Yeshua the Messiah). By inference, if that mediating work is effected by Yeshua's sacrifice, then the sacrifices of the Temple become of no effect. Hence, this is why the Jews were claiming that he was teaching "against the people, and the law, and this place".

> Hebrews 10: 11, And every priest standeth daily ministering and offering oftentimes the same sacrifices, <u>which can never take away sins</u>: 12 But this man, after <u>he had offered one sacrifice for sins for ever</u>, sat down on the right hand of God;

This one sacrifice of Yeshua made those of the Temple unnecessary in regards to justification. This was offensive to the chief priests.

> Hebrews 10: 1, For the law having a shadow of good things to come, and not the very image of the things, <u>can never with those sacrifices which they offered year by year continually make the comers thereunto perfect</u>.

The Jews viewed this as sacrilegious. Paul viewed this as the fulfillment of seed then fruit, death then resurrection life, Torah of Sin and Death then Torah of Resurrection Life. Paul again affirms that, even though saved by faith in Yeshua, he keeps the Written Torah.

> Acts 24: 14, But this I confess unto thee, that after the way which they call heresy, <u>so worship I the God of my fathers, believing all things which are written in the law and in the prophets</u>: 15 And have hope toward God, which they themselves also allow, that <u>there shall be a resurrection of the dead</u>, both of the just and unjust. 16 And herein do I exercise myself, to have always a conscience void to offence toward God, and toward men.

Again Paul is clarifying that he keeps the Written Torah and believes in the fractal of death and resurrection. He states this is the reason that he is called in judgment and not for causing sedition as he was accused.

> Acts 24: 21, Except it be for this one voice, that I cried standing among them, <u>Touching the resurrection of the dead I am called in question</u> by you this day.

That being the case they still found that Paul kept the Written Torah.

> Acts 25: 7, And when he was come, the Jews which came down from Jerusalem stood round about, and <u>laid many and grievous complaints against Paul, which they could not prove</u>. 8 While he answered for himself, <u>Neither against the law of the Jews, neither against the temple, nor yet against Caesar, have I offended any thing at all</u>.

Notice the false accusers could not prove that Paul was teaching against the Written Torah! Remember this was after Paul was saved by Yeshua, and he is still keeping the Written Torah. That being the case, every time Paul speaks, he brings up the death and resurrection fractal.

> Acts 26: 6, And now I stand and <u>am judged for the hope of the promise</u> made of God, unto our fathers: 7 Unto which promise our twelve tribes, instantly serving God day and night, hope to come. For which hope's sake, king Agrippa, I am accused of the Jews. 8 Why <u>should it be thought a thing incredible with you, that God should raise the dead</u>? 9 I verily thought with myself, that I ought to do many things contrary to the name of Yeshua of Nazareth.

If the chief priests and their council kept accusing Paul of violating the Torah, yet could not prove it, they likely are not openly stating to the Roman judges what the differences are between the Written Torah and the Rabbinical Oral Torah (Traditions of the rabbis/men). But Paul found it easy to prove that he was obedient to the Written Torah as given to the "fathers". The chief priests and their council appeared to be unable to prove otherwise.

Acts 26: 21, For these causes the Jews caught me in the temple, and went about to kill me. 22 Having therefore obtained help of God, I continue unto this day, witnessing both to small and great, saying none other things than those which the prophets and Moses did say should come: 23 That Christ should suffer, and that he should be the first that should rise from the dead, and should shew light unto the people, and to the Gentiles.

We have to wonder if the rabbis were offended by Paul teaching the death and resurrection fractal of the Torah, of men, and the Messiah. And saying that the Law/Torah (Moses) and the writings (prophets) all proclaim the death and resurrection fractal, first of the Messiah, then to follow…others.

Imagine all of the implications of Paul teaching the death and resurrection fractal on the priesthood, on the temple, on the sacrifices, and on the Torah. To accept those implications would mandate that the Torah of Moses was indeed a Torah of Sin and Death, that the temple would not abide, and that sacrifices would not make them justified before God. This realization should lead them to the following question.

Acts 2: 36, Therefore let all the house of Israel know assuredly, that God hath made the same Yeshua, whom ye have crucified, both Lord and Christ. 37 Now when they heard this, they were pricked in their heart, and said unto Peter and to the rest of the Apostles, Men and brethren, what shall we do? 38 Then Peter said unto them, Repent, and be baptized every one of you in the name of Yeshua for the remission of sins, and ye shall receive the gift of the Holy Ghost. 39 For the promise is unto you, and to your children, and to all that are afar off, even as many as the Lord our God shall call.

God has always desired to dwell within the temple of man. Our sin prevents that from happening. This can only occur through the work of the Messiah, circumcising the heart and preparing the mind and spirit of man.

1 Corinthians 6: 17, But he that is joined unto the Lord is one spirit. 18 Flee fornication. Every sin that a man doeth is without the body; but he that committeth fornication sinneth against his own body. 19 What? know ye not that your body is the temple of the Holy Ghost which is in you, which ye have of God, and ye are not your own? 20 For ye are bought with a price: therefore glorify God in your body, and in your spirit, which are God's.

Accepting the teaching of death and resurrection affirmed by the resurrection of Yeshua would seal their judgment under the Law (Torah of Moses) and require that they seek entry into the resurrected Torah via the faith in the new resurrected administrator, Yeshua the Messiah. Scripturally there is no pass on the new administrator for the Jews or the Gentiles. The works of the Written Torah could not justify them. Why? It was a Torah of Sin and Death, designed to bring condemnation on the flesh.

> Romans 3: 26, To declare, I say, at this time his righteousness: that he might be just, and the justifier of him which believeth in Yeshua. 27 Where is boasting then? It is excluded. By what law? of works? Nay: but by the law of faith. 28 Therefore we conclude that a man is justified by faith without the deeds of the law.

Time and again Paul is testifying on behalf of the Written Torah about the fractal of death and resurrection. It was the proponents of the Oral Torah that were trying to make it seem that Paul, though saved, was not keeping the Written Torah Commandments.

> Acts 6: 12, And they stirred up the people, and the elders, and the scribes, and came upon him, and caught him, and brought him to the council, 13 And set up false witnesses, which said, This man ceaseth not to speak blasphemous words against this holy place, and the law: 14 For we have heard him say, that this Yeshua of Nazareth shall destroy this place, and shall change the customs which Moses delivered us.

Notice their accusation against Paul is that he is not keeping the Torah and that he is teaching others to not keep the Written Torah. Why are they drawing this conclusion? Because Paul was clearly identifying the Torah of Moses, the Written Torah, with the Torah of Sin and Death.

This was an affront to the core of their beliefs, and rightfully so. What could they not see? That death and resurrection is the fractal of God and had to be fulfilled in the Commandments of God (the Written Torah), the administrations of the Written Torah, and their administrators.

TWO ADMINISTRATORS: DEATH (MOSES) & RESURRECTION (YESHUA):

This provides clear insight into why Moses could not be permitted to ascend to the Promised land and that another would have to prophetically fulfill his work. Moses had to fulfill the fractal of death and of the flesh.

> Exodus 31: 1, And Moses went and spake these words unto all Israel. 2 And he said unto them, I am an hundred and twenty years old this day; I can no more go out and come in: also the Lord hath said unto me, Thou shalt not go over this Jordan.

Moses needed to remain descended, in exile, in the wilderness, and fulfill the imagery and fractal of death, the flesh, condemnation and judgment, while another fulfilled the imagery of resurrection life. Moses is actually prophetic of the one to come; the Messiah.

Deuteronomy 18: 15, The <u>Lord thy God will raise up unto thee a Prophet</u> from the midst of thee, of thy brethren, <u>like unto me; unto him ye shall hearken;</u> 16 According to all that thou desiredst of the Lord thy God in Horeb in the day of the assembly, saying, Let me not hear again the voice of the Lord my God, neither let me see this great fire any more, that I die not. 17 And the Lord said unto me, They have well spoken that which they have spoken. 18 <u>I will raise them up a Prophet from among their brethren, like unto thee, and will put my words in his mouth;</u> and he shall speak unto them all that I shall command him.

This one who is like unto Moses would bear the fractal of resurrection life and of the spirit. This is the Messiah Yeshua, through whom we are sanctified. This is something Moses could not do, as he was a picture of sin and death, the flesh. God gives his judgment on Moses and says the reason he is not allowed to enter was because of his failure to sanctify God in the people.

Deuteronomy 32: 51, Because ye trespassed against me among the children of Israel at the waters of MeribahKadesh, in the wilderness of Zin; <u>because ye sanctified me not in the midst of the children of Israel.</u>

This was the essential failure of the Written Law (Torah) of Moses, not the Oral Torah. The Oral Torah is not even the focus here. The failure was Israel's willful disobedience to that Written Torah, which brought condemnation through their sin and death.

Ephesians 2: 2, Wherein in time past ye walked according to the course of this world, according to the prince of the power of the air, <u>the spirit that now worketh in the children of disobedience:</u>

It is this spirit that caused Israel to fail and the Covenant to be subjected to sin and death. This is also why they needed a new administrator, so they could receive a spirit of obedience to the Written Torah, turning it to a Torah of Resurrection Life.

Why was this confusing to the rabbinic leaders of Paul's time?

1 Peter 1: 1, Peter, an apostle of Yeshua, to the strangers scattered throughout Pontus, Galatia, Cappadocia, Asia, and Bithynia, 2 Elect according to the foreknowledge of God the Father, <u>through sanctification of the Spirit, unto obedience</u> and <u>sprinkling of the blood of Yeshua; grace</u> unto you, and peace, be multiplied. 3 Blessed be the God and Father of our Lord Yeshua, which <u>according to his abundant mercy hath begotten us again unto a lively hope by the resurrection</u> of Yeshua from the dead, 4 To an inheritance incorruptible, and undefiled, and that fadeth not away, reserved in heaven for

you, 5 <u>Who are kept by the power of God through faith unto salvation ready to be revealed in the last time</u>.

It was confusing because they did not understand the death and resurrection fractal. Also, it was confusing because the fullness of the fractal was not revealed until the "last time". Peter is affirming the centrality of the death and resurrection fractal message and its new administrator, Yeshua the Messiah. How did Yeshua qualify to be the administrator of the Resurrected Covenant (the Written Torah)?

Hebrews 7: 15, And it is yet far more evident: for that after the similitude of Melchisedec there ariseth another priest, 16 <u>Who is made</u>, not after the law of a carnal commandment, <u>but after the power of an endless life</u>. 17 For he testifieth, Thou art a priest for ever after the order of Melchisedec.

Yeshua qualified to be the new administrator by the power of a resurrection (endless) life. Remember Moses is the picture of the death (seed) fractal, and Yeshua is the picture of the resurrection (fruit) fractal.

Paul is examined time and again over this false accusation of not keeping the Written Torah and time and again he is found in conformance with Yeshua's instruction in Matthew 5:17, "Think not that I am come to destroy the law (Written Torah), or the prophets: I am not come to destroy, but to fulfil."

Paul agrees with Yeshua, walks just as Yeshua walks, according to the Written Torah. He did not come to destroy the Torah, but to resurrect it to new life in the inward man. This is how Yeshua fulfills the Law. He does not do away with it, He resurrects it within the believer's heart. The same commandments are on the second set of tablets that were on the first set of tablets. Those who say Yeshua fulfilled the Law so that we do not have to keep the Law clearly do not understand the work of the Messiah.

Exodus 34: 1, And the Lord said unto Moses, Hew thee two tablets of stone like unto the first: and I will <u>write upon these tablets the words that were in the first tablets</u>, which thou brakest.

Many modern Christians do an injustice to the scriptures by applying the truth of Yeshua's and the Apostle's teaching us to observe the Written Torah after we have been saved, to the scriptures about being "under the law" or the "works of the law" or the "Law of Sin and Death" and then say we do not have to keep the Torah.

Some Messianics do the scriptures an equal injustice by saying these same terms refer to the Oral Torah and why we don't have to keep the oral traditions of the rabbis. Notice how both groups uses these terms to refer to something that the biblical fractal does not support. There are plenty of scriptures clearly showing Yeshua and the Apostles teaching us to observe the Written Torah after we have been saved by Him alone. There are also many scriptures that show we need not observe the Oral Torah. These terms, "under the law" or the "works of the law" or the "Law of Sin and Death" are referring to neither the Oral Torah, nor to the abolishment of the Written Torah of Moses. These terms are referring to the death and resurrection fractal of the Torah of Moses and how it was once under the administration of death (flesh) and now it is under resurrection life (spirit).

Paul is so very clear that he is talking about the Written Torah by using the terms "under the law" or the "works of the law" or the "Law of Sin and Death". Both Yeshua and Paul in many other scriptures say the Oral Torah of the rabbis is not required. Unfortunately some have misapplied the terms "under the law" or the "works of the law" or the "Law of Sin and Death" as referring to the Oral Torah.

The scriptural fractal clearly indicates that these terms point to the Written Law of Moses under the administration of condemnation and death prior to the resurrection of those same words under the administration of the Messiah Yeshua via resurrection life.

It is especially an injustice to the scriptures when we evaluate those references from Paul, the Apostles, and Yeshua within the context of the centrality of the fractal of death and resurrection, which applies to the Torah, to men, to the Messiah, and to all creation. This is why Paul brings it up every single time he is testifying to the truth of the revelation of resurrection.

Paul affirms this singular truth:
- The Law of Moses is to be established by believers in Yeshua
- The Law of Moses has two administrations, one of sin and death and one of resurrection life.
- Both administrations have the same commandments.
- Each administration has its own administrator:
   o Sin and death (flesh)–Moses
   o Grace & abundant mercy and resurrection life (spirit)–Yeshua
- The Written Torah is required, the Oral Torah is not.
- The Law without the Messiah does what it should–it brings death to the flesh.
- The Law with the Messiah brings life to the spirit.

My apologies to Avi Ben Mordechai, but we need to more accurately explain the truth of the scriptures according to the imagery and fractals presented in them. Unfortunately, and no doubt well intended, Avi has applied the Oral Torah argument to a myriad of scriptures that are not talking about the Oral Torah, but are talking about the fractal of death (flesh) and resurrection (spirit), and the Written Law of Moses under each of those administrations.

Here are some examples:
- Hagar and Sarah
- Torah of Sin and Death and the Torah of Resurrection Life
- Conflict between the flesh and the resurrection spirit

We need to restore the concepts of being "under the law" and "works of the law" as referencing the Written Torah. Paul's central message is that we are unable to save ourselves, that we are "under a Torah of Sin and Death" and that the Law (Torah) referenced in the "works of the law" and "under the Law" is indeed the Written Torah.

Many Hebrew Roots teachers object to this statement because they say the Torah is life and light. That is true, the same commands written twice are light and life, but the first set of tablets are "under sin and death" as we see the sin of the golden calf and the shedding of blood at the first giving of the Law of Moses (Exodus 20, 32:4). This is the first administration of condemnation and judgment.

The second set of tablets are under resurrection life, grace and mercy as we see the manifestation of the Name of YHWH (Exodus 34). The first administration must die and the new administration of resurrection life must be enacted. Those who deny faith in that new administrator, Yeshua, are indeed still under the law (Written Torah) of Sin and Death and cannot pass to the Torah of Resurrection Life until they express faith in its administrator, Yeshua the Messiah. This is why there is only one way and one name by which we can all (Jew and Gentile) be saved.

> Acts 4: 12, Neither is there salvation in any other: for <u>there is none other name under heaven given among men, whereby we must be saved</u>.

Remember all Israel was baptized into Moses and Moses' name. This is the first administration. When Yeshua came, the administration changed and we must all be baptized into Him and His name.

- 1 Corinthians 10: 2, And were all <u>baptized unto Moses</u> in the cloud and in the sea;
- Matthew 3: 14, But John forbad him, saying, <u>I have need to be baptized of thee</u>, and comest thou to me?
- Matthew 3: 11, I indeed baptize you with water unto repentance. but he that cometh after me is mightier than I, whose shoes I am not worthy to bear: he shall baptize you with the Holy Ghost, and with fire:
- Matthew 20: 22, But Jesus answered and said, Ye know not what ye ask. Are ye able to drink of the cup that I shall drink of, <u>and to be baptized with the baptism that I am baptized with</u>? They say unto him, We are able.
- Mark 16:16, He that believeth and is baptized shall be saved; but he that believeth not shall be damned.
- Acts 2: 38, Then Peter said unto them, Repent, and <u>be baptized every one of you in the name of Jesus Christ </u>for the remission of sins, and ye shall receive the gift of the Holy Ghost.

John is puzzled by Yeshua's request to be baptized by John, but Yeshua knew He had to fulfill the fractal of death (old administration) before fulfilling the fractal of the Baptism of the Spirit that Yeshua would provide. But, as we have learned, that despite the glory of Moses' administration, it could not free the people from sin and death and was not qualified to save them due to their spirit of disobedience. This spirit kept them separated from God.

1 Corinthians 10: 5, But with many of them God was not well pleased: for they were overthrown in the wilderness.

There is not one way for the Jews and another way for the Gentiles. All must confess faith in the new administrator, or they are under the "Torah of Sin and Death" administration. All must confess faith, for they are unable to bring about works of the Torah to justify themselves.

Romans 3: 10, Seeing it is one God, which shall justify the circumcision by faith, and uncircumcision through faith.

How are we (Jew and Gentile) justified? By faith in Yeshua, the New administrator.

Galatians 3: 7, <u>Know ye therefore that they which are of faith</u>, the same are the children of Abraham. 8 And the scripture, foreseeing that God would <u>justify the heathen through faith</u>, preached before the Gospel unto Abraham, saying, In thee shall all nations be blessed. 9 So <u>then they which be of faith are blessed with faithful Abraham</u>.

Are Jews saved a different way than Gentiles? No, all must come through faith in Yeshua.

Romans 3: 1, What advantage then hath the Jew? or what profit is there of circumcision? 2 Much every way: chiefly, because that unto them were committed the oracles of God. 3 For what if some did not believe? <u>shall their unbelief make the faith of God without effect? 4 God forbid: yea, let God be true, but every man a liar;</u> as it is written, That thou mightest be justified in thy sayings, and mightest overcome when thou art judged.

The key issue is faith or lack thereof, from the start to end of the Bible. You cannot justify yourself or make yourself righteous. Avi Ben Mordechai suggests that Paul's letters were tampered with saying that the term "under the law" was added by Marcion.

"Greek: For as many as are of the works of the law are under the Curse... (Galatians 3: 10a)

Aramaic: For those who are servants (workers) of the law are still under a curse...

Marcion: For as many as are under the law are under the curse...

Gordon looked at this, then squarely looked at me, and said, here's a smoking gun. Works of, Greek ergon, was removed, permitting the text to imply that this thing called the Law of Moses is the real culprit; it was the curse!" (Galatians Commentary by Avi Ben Mordechai, page 252)

To clarify, we have a well–intended teacher, who, instead of adjusting his understanding of the scriptures, decides to edit out the scriptures (or translation) that do not agree with his paradigm. Some Hebrew Roots and Messianic teachers have chosen this path in order to avoid changing their paradigm to conform to the truth of the scriptures. Why did Avi do this? I assume it is because he did not see the death and resurrection fractal of the Messiah, the Torah, or their administrations.

We agree with Avi that in other locations of the scriptures, Yeshua, the Apostles, and Paul all affirm that we need not keep the Oral Torah. Unfortunately, this same brush is being applied to scriptures that are not discussing the Oral Torah. Why is this being done? We could not see what Paul saw, the fractal of death and resurrection. How can the Torah be a curse and still be light and life? It can, because it is fulfilling the same fractal as the Messiah, death and resurrection!

- Proverbs 6: 23, For the <u>commandment is a lamp; and the law is light;</u> and reproofs of instruction are the <u>way of life</u>:
- Proverbs 13: 4, The <u>law of the wise is a fountain of life</u>, to depart from the snares of death.

Both as statements are accurate, but we need to remember that God cannot be approached in the flesh no matter how good the light is.

Exodus 3: 1, Now Moses kept the flock of Jethro his father in law, the priest of Midian: and he led the flock to the backside of the desert, and came to the mountain of God, even to Horeb. 2 And the <u>angel of the Lord appeared unto him in a flame of fire</u> out of the midst of a bush: and he looked, and, behold, the <u>bush burned with fire</u>, and the bush was not consumed. 3 And Moses said, I will now turn aside, and see this great sight, why the bush is not burnt. 4 And when the Lord saw that he turned aside to see, <u>God called unto him out of the midst of the bush</u>, and said, Moses, Moses. And he said, Here am I. 5 And he said, <u>Draw not nigh hither</u>: put off thy shoes from off thy feet, for the place whereon thou standest is holy ground.

God's warning to Moses is clear, do not come any closer lest you die. Just as many Hebrew Roots teachers say the Torah is a light, a fire, and a lamp, these same things can bring fallen flesh to destruction. (Genesis 3:3, Leviticus 10:6–9, Numbers 18:2–3). To oversimplify the allusions of the Torah as only being light and life do an injustice to the scriptures and keep us from seeing the fractal of death and resurrection.

But because of the spirit of disobedience, the Torah (Law of Moses) continually brought the people death. They needed to be freed from that administration in order to have the hope of resurrection life.

Romans 7: 2, For the woman which hath an husband is bound by the law to her husband so long as he liveth; but if the husband be dead, <u>she is loosed from the law</u> of her husband.

Romans 7 illustrates the need of the woman to be loosed from the law of her current husband to be attached to the law of the new testator and administrator. Paul elaborates on the need for that new law because being under the law of the old testator brought only death.

Romans 7: 3, So then if, while her husband liveth, she be married to another man, she shall be called an adulteress: but if her husband be dead, <u>she is free from that law;</u> so that she is no adulteress, though she be married to another man. 4 Wherefore, my brethren, <u>ye also are become dead to the law by the body of Christ; that ye should be married to another, even to him who is raised from the dead,</u> that we should bring forth fruit unto God. 5 For <u>when we were in the flesh, the motions of sins, which were by the law, did work in our members to bring forth fruit unto death.</u>

Again Paul is contrasting the two administrations and showing how they brought out their respective fruit: death and resurrection. He is clearly saying that the fruit of the Law of Moses, the Written Torah, was death. There is no way around this scriptural fact.

Remember Paul is always presenting a duality in contrast.

Flesh	Spirit
Seed	Fruit
Death	Resurrection
Works of the Law (Written Torah)	Faith
Torah of Sin & Death	Torah of Resurrection Life
Under the Law (Written Torah) (Old administration)	Under grace (Law of Spirit) (New administration)
Glorious	More Glorious
Cannot Justify Self	Justified by God's Son
Carnal Mind	Mind of Christ

Who's fault was it that the Law of Moses brought forth the fruit of death?

Hebrews 8: 6, But now hath he obtained a more excellent ministry, by how much also <u>he is the mediator of a better covenant</u>, which was <u>established upon better promises</u>. 7 For <u>if that first covenant had been faultless</u>, then should no place have been sought for the second. 8 For <u>finding fault with them</u>, he saith, Behold, the days come, saith the Lord, when I will make a new covenant with the house of Israel and with the house of Judah: 9 Not according to the covenant that I made with their fathers in the day when I took them by the hand to lead them out of the land of Egypt; because <u>they continued not in my covenant,</u> and I regarded them not, saith the Lord. 10 For this is the covenant that I will make with the house of Israel after those days, saith the Lord; <u>I will put my laws into their mind, and write them in their hearts</u>: and I will be to them a God, and they shall be to me a people: 11 And they shall not teach every man his neighbour, and every man his brother, saying, Know the Lord: for all shall know me, from the least to the greatest. 12 For <u>I will be merciful to their unrighteousness,</u> and their sins and their iniquities will I remember no more.

The fault of the first covenant, the Written Torah of Moses, was their minds and their hearts. They have a spirit of disobedience that needs to be replaced with a new mediator.

24 THE ELIJAH CALLING

Yeshua was extremely clear that Elijah would come to restore all things before His return.

Matthew 17: 10, And his disciples asked him, saying, Why then say the scribes that Elias must first come? 11 And Yeshua answered and said unto them, <u>Elias (Elijah) truly shall first come, and restore all things</u>. 12 But I say unto you, That Elias is come already, and they knew him not, but have done unto him whatsoever they listed. Likewise shall also the Son of man suffer of them. 13 Then the disciples understood that he spake unto them of John the Baptist.

Yeshua is clarifying that John fulfilled the Elijah calling and this same Spirit of Elijah would come before the day of the Lord and fulfill the same ministry, restoration to the Torah of Moses under grace and abundant mercy via the administration of Yeshua the Messiah. We see the commission of those who come in the spirit of Elijah.

Luke 1: 13, But the angel said unto him, Fear not, Zacharias: for thy prayer is heard; and thy wife Elisabeth shall bear thee a son, and thou shalt call his name John. 14 And thou shalt have joy and gladness; and many shall rejoice at his birth. 15 For he shall be great in the sight of the Lord, and shall drink neither wine nor strong drink; and <u>he shall be filled with the Holy Ghost</u>, even from his mother's womb. 16 And <u>many of the children of Israel shall he turn to the Lord their God. 17 And he shall go before him in the spirit and power of Elias, to turn the hearts of the fathers to the children</u>, and the disobedient to the wisdom of the just; to make ready a people prepared for the Lord.

This turning of the children to the fathers is talking about the restoration of the future generations being restored to the faith of Abraham, Isaac, and Jacob: The Law of Moses under the administration of grace and mercy via the new administrator, Yeshua the Messiah. Malachi affirms this.

Malachi 4: 4, <u>Remember ye the law of Moses my servant</u>, which I commanded unto him in Horeb for all Israel, with the statutes and judgments. 5 Behold, I will send you Elijah the prophet before the coming of the great and dreadful day of the Lord: 6 And <u>he shall turn the heart of the fathers to the children, and the heart of the children to their fathers</u>, lest I come and smite the earth with a curse.

The book of Revelation also affirms this.
- Revelation 12: 17, And the dragon was wroth with the woman, and went to make war with the remnant of her seed, <u>which keep the commandments of God, and have the testimony of Yeshua</u>.
- Revelation 14: 12, Here is the patience of the saints: <u>here are they that keep the commandments of God, and the faith of Yeshua</u>.

There is only one question you need to answer…

"Do you have ears to hear?"
Zechariah 17: 11, But they refused to hearken, and pulled away the shoulder, and stopped their ears, that they should not hear.

"What kind of ground are you made of?"
Luke 8: 8, And other fell on good ground, and sprang up, and bare fruit an hundredfold. And when he had said these things, he cried, He that hath ears to hear, let him hear.

If you have ears to hear, repent and turn to the Lord, Yeshua, and begin to learn about the Written Law of Moses. There is only one way of salvation, Yeshua the Messiah, totally by grace and not by any work or righteousness of your own. Once you have received His sacrifice, learn to walk as He walked and keep His Law.

John 14: 15, <u>If ye love me, keep my commandments</u>. 16 And I will pray the Father, and he shall give you another Comforter, that he may abide with you for ever; 17 Even the Spirit of truth; whom the world cannot receive, because it seeth him not, neither knoweth him: but ye know him; for he dwelleth with you, and shall be in you. 18 I will not leave you comfortless: I will come to you. 19 Yet a little while, and the world seeth me no more; but ye see me: because I live, ye shall live also. 20 At that day ye shall know that I am in my Father, and ye in me, and I in you. 21 <u>He that hath my commandments, and keepeth them, he it is that loveth me</u>: and he that loveth me shall be loved of my Father, and <u>I will love him, and will manifest myself to him</u>.

Just as the Atheist/Evolutionist and the Creationist have the same facts, the same observable natural world to draw their conclusions from, so also does the Christian and those of other faiths. What sets these groups apart is the accuracy of their paradigm. If you insist on reading the scriptures and filtering its unrefined truth through your incorrect presumptions, then you will ensure that you never gain greater truth. The issue is not the available facts, but the quality of the eyesight and hearing observing those God given natural truths. The measure of a Christian is their love for the truth. So the greater we love the truth, the more in conformance with God's law (natural & otherwise) we become. This is what Paul refers to as the maturing of the senses. This is also God's and Yeshua's greatest criticism of the last Church given a letter of correction in the book of Revelation (manifestation).

> Revelation 3: 13, He that hath an ear, let him hear what the Spirit saith unto the churches.14 And unto the angel of the church of the Laodiceans write; These things saith the Amen, the faithful and true witness, the beginning of the creation of God;15 I know thy works, that thou art neither cold nor hot: I would thou wert cold or hot.16 So then because thou art lukewarm, and neither cold nor hot, I will spue thee out of my mouth.17 Because thou sayest, I am rich, and increased with goods, and have need of nothing; and knowest not that thou art wretched, and miserable, and poor, and blind, and naked:18 I counsel thee to buy of me gold tried in the fire, that thou mayest be rich; and white raiment, that thou mayest be clothed, and that the shame of thy nakedness do not appear; and anoint thine eyes with eyesalve, that thou mayest see.19 As many as I love, I rebuke and chasten: be zealous therefore, and repent.20 Behold, I stand at the door, and knock: if any man hear my voice, and open the door, I will come in to him, and will sup with him, and he with me.21 To him that overcometh will I grant to sit with me in my throne, even as I also overcame, and am set down with my Father in his throne.22 He that hath an ear, let him hear what the Spirit saith unto the churches.

Too often the modern Church has refused to listen and insisted that God conform to our image, instead of the believer conforming to the Image of His Son. We insist that we know better, that the truth of scripture is too uncompassionate, too rough, too divisive. Yet God is telling believers in Christ that in this generation, we are blind, naked, miserable, and poor. And the most telling fact is that He tells us we are not able to discern our own state of being. That our senses have become so corrupted that we can't even tell how much we are out of sync with the will of God. God gives us the remedy for this lowly estate. He says to anoint your eyes so that you can begin to see…because currently we are blind. Those who claim to know, have led the church into a wayward state without a covering garment.

This end time generation is deceived and corrupted with delusion. God gives a remedy. He says, stop being lukewarm, be zealous, and repent (return). Just as Yeshua is standing outside this supposed believer's house, He desires to come in and express God's love for these wayward people. What is preventing Him from entering? The willingness of the believer to open the door and welcome Him in. This requires the believer to acknowledge the power and authority of the true message of the Messiah Yeshua. This same pattern is completed every Passover in Jewish households, when the children of the house are sent to the door to open it and cry out for Elijah to come and feast with them.

The Jewish and Messianic Passover celebrates 5 cups of wine. These cups all relate back to God's promises to Moses and Israel when He brought them forth from Egypt.

> Exodus 6:2-8, And God spake unto Moses, and said unto him, I am the Lord:3 And I appeared unto Abraham, unto Isaac, and unto Jacob, by the name of God Almighty, but by my name Jehovah was I not known to them.4 And I have also established my covenant with them, to give them the land of Canaan, the land of their pilgrimage, wherein they were strangers.5 And I have also heard the groaning of the children of Israel, whom the Egyptians keep in bondage; and I have remembered my covenant.6 Wherefore say unto the children of Israel, I am the Lord, and <u>I will bring you out</u> from under the burdens of the Egyptians, and <u>I will rid you out of their bondage</u>, and <u>I will redeem you with a stretched out arm</u>, and with great judgments:7 And <u>I will take you to me for a people</u>, <u>and I will be to you a God</u>: and ye shall know that I am the Lord your God, which bringeth you out from under the burdens of the Egyptians.8 And <u>I will bring you in unto the land</u>, concerning the which I did swear to give it to Abraham, to Isaac, and to Jacob; and I will give it you for an heritage: I am the Lord.

The 5 Cups of Passover:

1. 1st Cup "I will bring you out"
2. 2nd Cup, "I will rid you out of their bondage"
3. 3rd Cup, "I will redeem you with a stretched out arm"
4. 4th Cup, "I will take you to me for a people"
5. 5th Cup, "I will bring you in unto the land"

The fifth cup is traditionally set out for Elijah and remains full and is not drunk. As Israel remains in exile today, they wait for the fulfillment of all the tribes of Israel to reunite and return to the Land of Promise. As of now only Judah has returned to the Land of Israel. These promises of redemption begin with the departure of Israel from Egypt and only conclude with their entry into the Land of Promise. This fifth cup is left for Elijah, for it is his future role to deliver the final restoration of all things.

Just as the child runs to the door on Passover evening and swings the door wide calling for Elijah to come in and sup with them, so also we are required to do the work of swinging the door wide open with the fervent call on our lips for repentance and restoration. This is our part to do and it cannot be done by someone else. We are participants in the end time redemption. Perhaps this is what Yeshua was referring to believers needing to "become as little children" (Matthew 18:3) in order to receive the Kingdom of God.

Just as Yeshua prophesied that Elijah would "truly shall first come, and restore all things" (Matthew 17:11) we must carefully determine what this scripture portends for the modern Christian and Jew. Many Christian churches would like to think that they are fully in conformance with the will of God and that they have no work to do in order to perfectly manifest the will of the Messiah. But if one takes the time to read Yeshua's own words, let alone the words to the Churches in the Book of Revelation (Manifestation), they will see that Yeshua the Messiah (Jesus the Christ) is repeatedly un-happy with the state of His Church.

- **Ephesus:** Revelation 2: 4, "Nevertheless <u>I have somewhat against thee, because thou hast left thy first love</u>. 5 Remember therefore from whence thou art fallen, and repent, and do the first works; or else I will come unto thee quickly, and will remove thy candlestick out of his place, except thou repent. 6 But this thou hast, that thou hatest the deeds of the Nicolaitanes, which I also hate."

- **Smyrna:** Revelation 2: 8, "8 And unto the angel of the church in Smyrna write; These things saith the first and the last, which was dead, and is alive;9 I know thy works, and tribulation, and poverty, (but thou art rich) and I know the blasphemy of them which say they are Jews, and are not, but are the synagogue of Satan.10 Fear none of those things which thou shalt suffer: behold, the devil shall cast some of you into prison, that ye may be tried; and ye shall have tribulation ten days: be thou faithful unto death, and I will give thee a crown of life.11 He that hath an ear, let him hear what the Spirit saith unto the churches; He that overcometh shall not be hurt of the second death."

- **Pergamos:** Revelation 2: 14, "But <u>I have a few things against thee</u>, because thou hast there them that hold the doctrine of Balaam, who taught Balac to cast a stumblingblock before the children of Israel, to eat things sacrificed unto idols, and to commit fornication.15 So hast thou also them that hold the doctrine of the Nicolaitanes, which thing I hate.16 Repent; or else I will come unto thee quickly, and will fight against them with the sword of my mouth."

- **Thyatira:** Revelation 2:20, "Notwithstanding <u>I have a few things against thee</u>, because thou sufferest that woman Jezebel, which calleth herself a prophetess, to teach and to seduce my servants to commit fornication, and to eat things sacrificed unto idols.21 And I gave her space to repent of her fornication; and she repented not.22 Behold, I will cast her into a bed, and them that commit adultery with her into great tribulation, except they repent of their deeds.23 And I will kill her children with death; and all the churches shall know that I am he which searcheth the reins and hearts: and I will give unto every one of you according to your works.

- **Sardis:** Revelation 3:2, "Be watchful, and <u>strengthen the things which remain, that are ready to die</u>: for I have not found thy works perfect before God.3 Remember therefore how thou hast received and heard, and <u>hold fast, and repent</u>. If therefore thou shalt not watch, I will come on thee as a thief, and thou shalt not know what hour I will come upon thee.4 Thou hast <u>a few names even in Sardis which have not defiled their garments;</u> and they shall walk with me in white: for they are worthy.

- **Philadelphia:** Revelation 3: 11, "Behold, I come quickly: hold that fast which thou hast, that no man take thy crown."

- **Laodicea:** Revelation 3:15, "I know thy works, <u>that thou art neither cold nor hot: I would thou wert cold or hot</u>.16 So then because thou art lukewarm, and neither cold nor hot, <u>I will spue thee out of my mouth</u>.17 Because thou sayest, I am rich, and increased with goods, and have need of nothing; <u>and knowest not that thou art wretched, and miserable, and poor, and blind, and naked</u>:18 I counsel thee to buy of me gold tried in the fire, that thou mayest be rich; and white raiment, that thou mayest be clothed, and that the shame of thy nakedness do not appear; and <u>anoint thine eyes with eyesalve, that thou mayest see</u>.19 As many as I love, I rebuke and chasten: <u>be zealous therefore, and repent</u>.20 <u>Behold, I stand at the door, and knock: if any man hear my voice, and open the door, I will come in to him, and will sup with him, and he with me.</u>

The description of the Churches by Yeshua certainly doesn't sound like the fluff of modern Christianity. He sounds like an expectant King who doesn't want His costly sacrifice to be wasted on the lazy.

Of these seven churches only Smyrna and Philadelphia have no criticism. The rest have the Messiah telling them to repent and that their very savior has something against them. The modern church must find this repugnant as they have more of a desire to make God in their image instead of coming into conformance with their own redeemer. And the grand finale of criticisms is set out against the last Church, Laodicea. The Messiah tells them that they are miserable, yet they think they are wonderful. The Messiah tells them they are blind and cannot see themselves for what they really are. This is a Church in desperate trouble with their own redeemer, to the point that Yeshua is telling them He is going to expel them from His own body.

What is the imagery that the Messiah presents to the Church of Laodicea to repair their desperate state? He presents the imagery of Elijah waiting outside the house on Passover evening. The same language that is used by the children at the door asking Elijah to enter into the house and sup with them is the same language Yeshua uses to the lukewarm Church of Laodicea, "...be zealous therefore, and repent. 20 Behold, <u>I stand at the door, and knock: if any man hear my voice, and open the door, I will come in to him, and will sup with him</u>, and he with me." (Revelation 3: 19-20)

Matthew 26:29, "But I say unto you, <u>I will not drink henceforth of this fruit of the vine, until that day when I drink it new with you in my Father's kingdom</u>. 30 And when they had sung an hymn, they went out into the mount of Olives."

Passover Seder

While the best-known explanation of why we welcome Elijah on Passover is his role as herald of the messianic age, this, in fact, is not his primary function at the seder, at least not when the tradition started. Back in the second century, when the sages were establishing the rituals of the seder, a disagreement arose as to whether there should be four or five cups of wine.

The custom of drinking multiple cups of wine derived from God's promises to the enslaved Israelites. Four promises follow one another in rapid succession within Exodus chapter six, verses six and seven: " I will free you...", "I will deliver you...", "I will redeem you...", "and I will take you to be My people." Then, after an intervening verse, a fifth promise appears: "I will bring you into the land...." Each cup of wine is a symbol of the joy we feel as beneficiaries of God's promises. But is the fifth promise connected to the prior four, or is it a separate promise? On this the rabbis could not agree. Some said there should be four cups in honor of four promises; others said five cups for five promises.

The Talmud uses the Aramaic word teku to indicate that the rabbis could not reach a decision on a matter under discussion. And so the decision as to the number of cups was left teku, but the Passover haggadah prescribes four cups for us to drink-possibly as a parallel to the four questions and the four sons. But just in case there really should be five, the writers of the haggadah called for an additional symbolic cup.

How did this symbolic fifth cup come to be known as "the cup of Elijah"? Ah, that takes us back to that word teku.

Nobody is certain of the derivation of teku (which, by the way, is also used in Israel today when a soccer match ends in a tie). It may derive from tekum, meaning "it will stand," i.e., "it will remain a question." A folk etymology, though, has it that teku is an acronym for " Tishbi yetaretz kushiot v-abayot- the Tishbite [i.e., Elijah] will answer all unresolved questions." According to this folk belief, the first thing Elijah will do after he returns to the Jewish people to proclaim the advent of the messianic age is to resolve all those questions of Jewish law that confounded the rabbis.

Later folk literature would often introduce Elijah as the savior in all-too-frequent situations when communities of Jews were in dire straits. Out of nowhere and often disguised, Elijah would appear and foil the wicked plot. Again, why Elijah? Because he was the hero who could call down miracles; he was the intimate of God who never died; and he was the intercessor who would zealously plead the cause of his people. And so, Jews continue to venerate him-at every meal, at the end of every Sabbath, at circumcisions, and, most famously, at our Passover Seders. (Rabbi Simeon J. Maslin, www.reformjudaism.org)

This presentation of the Elijah Cup is the acceptance of the believer of the Messiah into their own house (body & mind). It is up to every believer to repent, cleanse the house, and receive the honored guest. We can see how Yeshua fulfills the role of the Elijah in the administration of resurrection life and the resurrected covenant in the believer's heart. The restoration of all things promised by Yeshua begins like a seed in death then is fulfilled in the manifestation of resurrection life.

- Matthew 17:11, "And Jesus answered and said unto them, Elias truly shall first come, and restore all things…"

- Mark 9:10, "And they kept that saying with themselves, questioning one with another what the rising from the dead should mean. 11 And they asked him, saying, Why say the scribes that Elias must first come? 12 And he answered and told them, Elias verily cometh first, and restoreth all things; and how it is written of the Son of man, that he must suffer many things, and be set at nought. 13 But I say unto you, That Elias is indeed come, and they have done unto him whatsoever they listed, as it is written of him.

Notice how the Apostles question about Elijah is connected to being "raised from the dead" and how Yeshua' s response is about the "restoration of all things" is connected to His very own death…and then resurrection. As we have described already just as the pattern and fractal of seed then manifestation, so also is the pattern of Moses and Elijah, and also in John the Baptist and Yeshua the Son of God. In the seminal event of the Passover which was first invoked through Moses…we see the fulfillment and anticipation of Elijah at this same event…outside the house yearning to come in. Here…but not yet. Death and resurrection. Two administrations…one Passover…one Law…

We have seen the unmistakable patterns of death and resurrection, seed then manifestation, and how Yeshua is connected to the Elijah ministry. That being the case those who sit idly in their pews waiting for the minister, the pastor, and the priest to do the work of the Messiah for them are sadly disconnected from the truth of the Bible. Those who have joined with Yeshua, conform to His image, and fulfill the same patterns of redemption. Just as Yeshua went sowing the seed of the Kingdom, so also the Apostles and the Church fulfilled and fulfill this same imagery. If you are sitting in the pew waiting for someone else to do it for you…then you might be a Laodicean. Get up out of the pew and get to work and participate in the restoration of all things and "The Elijah Calling".

Malachi 4: 2, "But unto you that fear my name shall the Sun of righteousness arise with healing in his wings; and ye shall go forth, and grow up as calves of the stall.3 And ye shall tread down the wicked; for they shall be ashes under the soles of your feet in the day that I shall do this, saith the Lord of hosts.4 Remember ye the law of Moses my servant, which I commanded unto him in Horeb for all Israel, with the statutes and judgments.5 Behold, I will send you Elijah the prophet before the coming of the great and dreadful day of the Lord:6 And he shall turn the heart of the fathers to the children, and the heart of the children to their fathers, lest I come and smite the earth with a curse.

Those that have been confused by grace and law over the past 2,000 years should re-read the scriptures using the Biblical paradigm of "Grace & Law". The scriptures will become a unified whole. Those who fall asleep reading the Bible will find a new zeal, because the scriptures will now make sense and you will have the tools you need to go deeper into the hidden aspects of God's revealed word. Those who want to reach out to friends and family who have rejected the Bible for all the wrong reasons, will now have a toolbox of truth to answer the criticisms of flawed paradigms.

Those with friends and family that are Jewish, you will have a fresh perspective that your Jewish friends will find incontestable. Why? Because it is straight from the Torah. Jews love debating lawless Christians. Why? It's easy to do from the scriptures. Modern rabbis become very concerned when they see truly saved Christians walking the Written Torah. Why? Because it becomes an incontestable testimony of truth! It is easy to refute that which is lawless and unscriptural, but when a Christian has a lawful testimony and can show death and resurrection in the Torah, the history of Israel, the redemption from Egypt, in Moses and Elijah, then the modern Talmud observant rabbi is forced into a very uncomfortable position…listening and learning from a Christian.

The same thing happens when an evolutionist is confronted by a Christian who uses the patterns and fractals of nature to explain the observable universe in Biblical context. Evolutionists love to argue from un-factual positions, because Christians are easily won over by illogical and un-factual positions. What is the remedy? Make sure you learn the patterns of nature and how they replicate themselves in the Word of God. You will find the evolutionist back on the heels, reeling from scriptural arguments that make sense and reinforce the rules and observations of logic and nature. Christians have been denigrated for centuries for arguing from a perspective of "faith" as if that "faith" has no substance or verifiable truth.

When you take the fractals of nature, that you learned by your mature senses, and apply them to the Bible, you will see those truths replicated over and over again. They become self-verifiable. Just as you can check your math by working the equation backwards, you can do the same from natural patterns and biblical patterns. Those concepts that are un-truthful will weed themselves out because they won't replicate the pattern and fractals that God gave to all creation. Those patterns we will discuss in depth in Book 2 of the "Restoring Truth" series, "Elijah vs Antichrist"!

Don't believe me…believe the scriptures. Fulfill your Elijah Calling!

BOOK TWO OF THE RESTORING TRUTH SERIES

ELIJAH VS ANTICHRIST

THE END-TIME BATTLE

1 IMAGE OF GOD VS. THE IMAGE OF THE BEAST

No greater sorrow or curse has been muttered than that which God directed against His own creation. Because of it He is hated by many, feared by most, and sought after by the world's religions. Few dare to love the one who has leveled the single most fearsome specter against all creation.

> Genesis 2:17, But of the tree of the knowledge of good and evil, thou shalt not eat of it: for in the day that thou eatest thereof thou shalt surely die.

Adam and Eve in a perfect setting do the one thing that God warned them not to do. They were presented with an existential choice. We cannot assume that these two were gullible, foolish, unlearned children, but indeed they were the height of God's creation and set as King and Queen over all that God had made...and as such had wisdom and knowledge far surpassing anything modern man has attempted in the modern world. Adam was the height of all that God wanted to manifest.

> Genesis 1:26, And God said, Let us make man in our image, after our likeness:

In all of history and pre-history this is the first time that God had sought to bring forth His own image. This was something special and new. Once He had manifested Adam and then brought forth Eve out from Adam, He presented them with a choice between two destinies; The Tree of Life and the Tree of the Knowledge of Good and Evil. The consequences of that choice were at the centermost part of the Garden of Eden and as such carried central importance to their future. Each of these trees carry greater meaning than just the simple choice to obey or disobey God. They carry along the future manifestation of their choices as whichever tree they eat from; their seed will manifest according to the seed of the tree consumed.

Their image will take on the likeness of the tree that they join. God makes its clear what the outcomes will be if they eat of the Tree of the Knowledge of Good and Evil. We cannot miss the fact that they are both wise and the very crown of God's creation (manifestation). The Tree of Life presents a singular unity and the Tree of the Knowledge of Good and Evil presents a duality and mixture of experience. The first is based upon faith and trust in God and the second is based upon a lack of faith in God. The fruit that they manifest will be born in the lives of Adam and Eve and all of their descendants.

Let's not skip over the very clear fact that both of these trees are presented within the Garden of Eden before Adam and Eve fell into sin and were presented with all of creation on the Seventh Day Sabbath. Both trees are present within the Garden of Eden when God takes man and places him in the Garden. Within that Garden, within that Tree of the Knowledge of Good and Evil lies a beast.

> Genesis 3:1, Now the serpent was more subtil than any beast of the field which the Lord God had made. And he said unto the woman, Yea, hath God said, Ye shall not eat of every tree of the garden?

Of all the animals that Adam had named this is the only one that is mentioned as speaking to Eve. We will not pause to reflect upon whether this is the only creature that had the ability to speak aside from Adam and Eve, or whether all creatures had the ability to speak and communicate with the Image of God, Adam and Eve. As Adam was brought forth by God as His Own Image, God brought forth from Adam His Own Image, Eve.

Before glancing over that knowledge, think carefully about the rest of the Bible, Old and New Testament, and contemplate the deep significance of God's sole purpose to manifest His image and have it replicate in all creation. And how that very purpose was subverted by the most cunning of God's creation, the serpent. God's manifested image was beguiled and subverted by the Image of a Beast!

> Revelation 13:15, And he had power to give life unto the image of the beast, that the image of the beast should both speak, and cause that as many as would not worship the image of the beast should be killed.

This conflict between the Image of God and the Image of the Beast that is presented in the Book of Revelation (Manifestation) is the final act of the conflict that began in the Garden of Eden between the seed of the serpent and the seed of the woman.

Believe it or not this is the same conflict that the Apostle Paul repeatedly talked about in all of his letters to the Churches. It is central to his message of redemption for all creation and centers around the need for death and resurrection. But the Church has forgotten the reason why there is a need for a redeemer and a redeeming seed.

Romans 1:18, For the wrath of God is revealed from heaven against all ungodliness and unrighteousness of men, who hold the truth in unrighteousness; 19 Because that which may be known of God is manifest in them; for God hath shewed it unto them. 20 For the invisible things of him from the creation of the world are clearly seen, being understood by the things that are made, even his eternal power and Godhead; so that they are without excuse:21 Because that, when they knew God, they glorified him not as God, neither were thankful; but became vain in their imaginations, and their foolish heart was darkened. 22 Professing themselves to be wise, they became fools, 23 And changed the glory of the uncorruptible God into an image made like to corruptible man, and to birds, and fourfooted beasts, and creeping things.

For far too long the Christian church has allegorized away the redeeming work of Jesus the Christ (Yeshua the Messiah) as literally being the Seed of the Kingdom of God and that we need to become one with that seed in order to be restored to the state of the original Image of God. The first curse brought forth, by taking the seed of the Tree of the Knowledge of Good and Evil and taking on the Image of the Beast, death.

Genesis 3:19, In the sweat of thy face shalt thou eat bread, till thou return unto the ground; for out of it wast thou taken: for dust thou art, and unto dust shalt thou return.

Within that first curse lay the seed of a promise of redemption back to our original state, the Image of God. This is the first promise of the Messiah Yeshua and our redeeming seed.

Genesis 3:14, And the Lord God said unto the serpent, Because thou hast done this, thou art cursed above all cattle, and above every beast of the field; upon thy belly shalt thou go, and dust shalt thou eat all the days of thy life:15 And I will put enmity between thee and the woman, and between thy seed and her seed; it shall bruise thy head, and thou shalt bruise his heel.

Dedicated teachers for millennia have allegorized away the plain teaching of scripture by saying that Yeshua taught in parables about seed and fruit simply because they were living in an agrarian society and He was teaching within the context of their reality. Many think that because we live in the industrial and post-industrial world these teachings don't apply to us or only do so in an agrarian context. The error of this assumption is to refuse the real application of these truths.

The Messiah came teaching about seed and manifestation because all of creation is based upon and manifests itself as seed and image. Every plant, every creature, every man woman and child is a manifestation of a seed and presents itself by the love of God as an image. Every single thing in the Universe manifests itself according to the Tree of the Knowledge of Good and Evil and as such is subject to death and suffering. When Adam and Eve joined themselves to the Tree of the Knowledge of Good and Evil, they joined their seed with its seed. Their seed became corrupted by that tree and the outcome since then, and until redeemed, has been as the image of a beast. As such everything in the Universe manifests, but manifests in death and separation from God needing a redeeming seed to correct our corrupted state.

Romans 9:29, And as Esaias said before, Except the Lord of Sabaoth <u>had left us a seed</u>, we had been as Sodoma, and been made like unto Gomorrha.

The world has bought into the presumption that we are still in the Image of God, because Adam and Eve were created and manifested as such. But we are forgetting that fall and sin of the Image of God. When sin entered the world all of creation (manifestation) took on the broken image of the seed of the Tree of the Knowledge of Good and Evil. That perfect Image of God could no longer reproduce in His image. Adam and Eve now took on the characteristics and manifestation of the Tree of the Knowledge of Good and Evil and all its seed traits. Since Adam was responsible for all of creation and participated in the naming of all creatures, they also became subject to the traits of that tree; death and suffering.

Genesis 3:16, Unto the woman he said, <u>I will greatly multiply thy sorrow and thy conception; in sorrow thou shalt bring forth children</u>; and thy desire shall be to thy husband, and he shall rule over thee. 17 And unto Adam he said, Because thou hast hearkened unto the voice of thy wife, and hast eaten of the tree, of which I commanded thee, saying, Thou shalt not eat of it: cursed is the ground for thy sake; in sorrow shalt thou eat of it all the days of thy life; 18 Thorns also and thistles shall it bring forth to thee; and thou shalt eat the herb of the field; 19 In the sweat of thy face shalt thou eat bread, till thou return unto the ground; for out of it wast thou taken: for dust thou art, and unto dust shalt thou return. 20 And Adam called his wife's name Eve; because she was the mother of all living.

We need to remember that when Adam and Eve joined with the Tree of the Knowledge of Good and Evil, so did all of creation. They made a choice that all of their subjects would be a part of...and in this case the result was a multiplication of sorrow.

Romans 8:18, For I reckon that the sufferings of this present time are not worthy to be compared with the glory which shall be revealed in us. 19 For the earnest expectation of the creature waiteth for the manifestation of the sons of God. 20 For the creature was made subject to vanity, not willingly, but by reason of him who hath subjected the same in hope,

So, all of creation (manifestation) became subject to sin and all of its sorrows; sickness, death, and decay. This is not the naturally intended state of creation. It is the consequential state of being joined to the Tree of the Knowledge of Good and

Evil and having taken on the nature of its seed. The remedy is provided in God manifesting His true Image, the Messiah Yeshua, and participating in His seed, literally, so that our corruptible images may be restored back to the original Image of God.

For millennia, Christian and Jewish teachers have been saying that man is currently the Image of God. This is scripturally and factually inaccurate. Adam and Eve were the Image of God and then they broke the Image of God by taking of the seed of the Tree of the Knowledge of Good and Evil. Most skip over the truth of our current state…we are still fallen.

> Genesis 5:1, This is the book of the generations of Adam. In the day that God created man, <u>in the likeness of God made he him</u>; 2 Male and female created he them; and blessed them, and called their name Adam, in the day when they were created. 3 And Adam lived an hundred and thirty years, and <u>begat a son in his own likeness, and after his image</u>; and called his name Seth:

A careful reading of this verse shows that Adam was no longer producing the Image of God, but now was producing his own fallen image. This is the image that needs to be restored by the coming of the Messiah, who is the fulfillment of that first redemptive prophecy of Genesis 3 and is correctly called "the seed of the woman". For just as all creation was broken by joining with a disavowed seed, so we must consume a new seed to restore God's image in all creation.

- I John 3:9, Whosoever is born of God doth not commit sin; for his seed remaineth in him: and he cannot sin, because he is born of God.
- 1 Peter 1:23, Being born again, not of corruptible seed, but of incorruptible, by the word of God, which liveth and abideth for ever.

Paul touches on this very issue and then expounds on it over and over again. All of creation is the result of this wonderful pattern and fractal; Seed then Image…not just for plants, but for every image in creation, every animal, every creature, every man, woman, and child.

> 1 Corinthians 15:38, But God giveth it a body as it hath pleased him, and to every seed his own body.

To properly and accurately frame the truth of the current state of affairs, Adam and Eve were the Image of God and because they joined their seed with the seed of the Tree of the Knowledge of Good and Evil, consequently all of creation has a fallen, broken, and corruptible image that can only be restored through the promised seed. That seed joins with all those that partake in it and restores the original Image of God.

Creation's current broken image is associated with the image of the Beast, just as the Tree of the Knowledge of Good and Evil is associated with the subtlest beast of the Garden of Eden, the Original image of the Beast. Just as the serpent beguiled Eve, all of creation is going to be subject to an end-time test of the Beast.

The fractal presented in the Garden of Eden will be replicated in the end-times. The image of the Beast will persecute those with the true seed, The Image of God.

Revelation 12:17, And the dragon was wroth with the woman, and went to make war with the remnant of her seed, which keep the commandments of God, and have the testimony of Jesus Christ.

Time and again Yeshua, the Prophets, Moses, and the Apostles bear out these repeating patterns and fractals of seed then image, death then resurrection, duality then singularity, exile then restoration. What can we learn about our true state and how to escape the image of the Beast? Is death the curse and the natural consequence of the seed of the Tree of the Knowledge of Good and Evil? We have a choice to make. Which seed will you partake of? The Image of God or the Image of the Beast?

2 Corinthians 4:4, In whom the god of this world hath blinded the minds of them which believe not, lest the light of the glorious gospel of Christ, who is the Image of God, should shine unto them.

The promised Messiah is the pro-typical Image of God that Adam was originally created in. In fact, He is the creator of all things.

Colossians 1:15, Who is the image of the invisible God, the firstborn of every creature:

The Apostle John clarifies for us that it was by Yeshua that all things were made. With great clarity, we see the nature of the Messiah and His role in bringing forth all creation.

John 1:1, In the beginning was the Word, and the Word was with God, and the Word was God. 2 The same was in the beginning with God. 3 All things were made by him; and without him was not any thing made that was made. 4 In him was life; and the life was the light of men. 5 And the light shineth in darkness; and the darkness comprehended it not. 6 There was a man sent from God, whose name was John. 7 The same came for a witness, to bear witness of the Light, that all men through him might believe. 8 He was not that Light, but was sent to bear witness of that Light. 9 That was the true Light, which lighteth every man that cometh into the world. 10 He was in the world, and the world was made by him, and the world knew him not. 11 He came unto his own, and his own received him not. 12 But as many as received him, to them gave he power to become the sons of God, even to them that believe on his name:

John is clarifying the essential nature of all creation, every image, every creature and their creator, the Light and Image of God and how every creature is a temple that God's light and life dwells within. Every image is currently fallen and broken and are unable to perceive the coming of the redeeming seed, the Image of God,

Yeshua the Messiah. Those who reject that seed become associated with darkness and a broken image, the image of the Beast…the serpent.

The Fractal of the choice of which tree to eat from will be repeated again in the end time and all mankind will manifest the fruit of their seed.

Participants	Seed	Image	Choice	Outcome
Adam & Eve	Tree of the Knowledge of Good & Evil vs. The Tree of Life	Image of God vs. Image of the Beast	Which fruit to eat, faith & obedience or lack of faith and disobedience	Broken Image, Separation from God, Multiplied Sorrow, & Death
Israel & Egypt	Firstborn Seed vs. the Second born seed	Gods of Egypt or the Name of the Lord (YHWH)	Free the people or keep them in bondage	Death of the firstborn of Egypt and release of the Children of Israel
Esau & Jacob	Spirit of disobedience vs. Spirit of Christ	Flesh vs. Spirit	Faith vs. Unbelief	Walk in the flesh or Walk in the spirit
Yeshua & Barabbas	Seed of life vs. the Seed of Death	Yeshua the Son of God (Image of God/Life) vs. Bar-abba= literally, 'son of the father,' a murder (Mark 15:7)	Will you choose to save your life or loose it? Matthew 16:25, "For whosoever will save his life shall lose it:and whosoever will lose his life for my sake shall find it."	Barabbas is set free and Yeshua dies in his place. Philippians 2:8, "And being found in fashion as a man, he humbled himself, and became obedient unto death, even the death of the cross."
End Time Believers vs. the Image of the Beast	Save your flesh or trust in God? Revelation 12:11, "And they overcame him by the blood of the Lamb, and by the word of their testimony; and they loved not their lives unto the death."	Revelation 14:11, "And the smoke of their torment ascendeth up for ever and ever:and they have no rest day nor night, who worship the beast and his image, and whosoever receiveth the mark of his name."	Revelation 13:17, "And that no man might buy or sell, save he that had the mark, or the name of the beast, or the number of his name."	Revelation 19:20, "And the beast was taken, and with him the false prophet that wrought miracles before him, with which he deceived them that had received the mark of the beast, and them that worshipped his image. These both were cast alive into a lake of fire burning with brimstone."

God operates all creation through repeating patterns and fractals. The mark and image of the Beast cannot properly be understood without an accurate scriptural understanding of the Image of God, our fallen and broken Image of God, and the role of the Messiah to restore the Image of God. Just as this pattern was fulfilled by Adam and Eve, by all Creation, by Israel, by Yeshua the Messiah…it will also be fulfilled in the end-time called the Day of the Lord.

To properly understand the choices, you will be forced to make, you need to understand your true state as defined by the Bible. This end-time battle cannot be escaped, it will fall on all creation, and every man, woman, and child representing creation will be forced into a choice. It will demand every bit of your attention, and every emotion of your being and it will determine your fate. Don't be surprised…this battle has been raging for 6,000 years and will culminate in a choice…just like Eve had to make! What will you do? Switch on the football game or wake up to a reality that existed all around you that you chose to ignore because the deception was so entertaining?

2 Thessalonians 2:10, And with all deceivableness of unrighteousness in them that perish; because they received not the love of the truth, that they might be saved. 11 And for this cause God shall send them strong delusion, that they should believe a lie:12 That they all might be damned who believed not the truth, but had pleasure in unrighteousness.

It's just like in the beginning. God placed the Tree of the Knowledge of Good and Evil in the Garden with Adam and Eve…before the Fall! God created the serpent…subtler than any other creature…in the garden…with Adam and Eve. God made this circumstance for a choice to be made…and He's doing it again! What will you do? To better determine how to choose, we must first recalibrate our understanding about how God operates in patterns and fractals. What is a fractal?

Fractal:
A fractal is a natural phenomenon or a mathematical set that exhibits a repeating pattern that displays at every scale. It is also known as expanding symmetry or evolving symmetry. If the replication is exactly the same at every scale, it is called a self-similar pattern. (Wikipedia)

Notice a fractal is a natural God manifested phenomena and it repeats a pattern at every scale (above so below).

- Exodus 25:9, According to all that I shew thee, after the pattern of the tabernacle, and the pattern of all the instruments thereof, even so shall ye make it.
- Exodus 25:40, And look that thou make them after their pattern, which was shewed thee in the mount.

Here God is telling Moses that the earthly things need to be patterned after the heavenly things that God showed him on the mountain. The Apostle Paul reinforces this understanding.

1 Corinthians 15:49, And as we have borne the image of the earthy, we shall also bear the image of the heavenly.

Paul is clearly showing that our redemptive state will once again be patterned after the heavenly Image of God, the Messiah Yeshua. And consequently, we are currently not in that image, and as such we have a broken and earthly image, Adam.

1 Corinthians 15:44, It is sown a natural body; it is raised a spiritual body. There is a natural body, and there is a spiritual body. 45 And so it is written, The first man Adam was made a living soul; the last Adam was made a quickening spirit. 46 Howbeit that was not first which is spiritual, but that which is natural; and afterward that which is spiritual.

So, the God given pattern and fractal is "First Adam" (natural & earthly) and the "Last Adam" (Yeshua is a spiritual & heavenly image). We see first corruption then incorruption, first a broken image, then a restored image, first death, then resurrection, first seed then an ascended image (fruit)!

The pattern and fractal presented by the two trees in the Garden of Eden and hence for all of creation is seed then image, death then resurrection. We see that very clearly played out in Genesis 1 where the scriptural focus is on "herb bearing seeds". In Genesis 1 God focuses on creating seeds and then in Genesis 2 God is focusing on manifesting the images of those seeds on the Seventh Day Sabbath.

Genesis 3:4, These are the generations of the heavens and of the earth when they were created, in the day that the Lord God made the earth and the heavens, 5 And every plant of the field before it was in the earth, and every herb of the field before it grew: for the Lord God had not caused it to rain upon the earth, and there was not a man to till the ground. 6 But there went up a mist from the earth, and watered the whole face of the ground. 7 And the Lord God formed man of the dust of the ground, and breathed into his nostrils the breath of life; and man became a living soul.

All the seeds that were created in Genesis 1 had not grown until the Seventh Day Sabbath which focuses on the giving of water and the breath of life so that those seeds can manifest their images. Genesis 1 is about the creation of seed and Genesis 2 is about the manifestation of those seeds into fruit by watering and the giving of the breath of the Lord.

The fractal we are presented with, that all creation (manifestation) must be evaluated through, is "Seed then Image (fruit)". All perceived truth will come through that pattern of death and resurrection, death like a seed and resurrection like an ascended fruit.

John 12:24, Verily, verily, I say unto you, Except a corn of wheat fall into the ground and die, it abideth alone: but if it die, it bringeth forth much fruit.

This is not a reference to seeds because they lived in an agrarian society, it is because all creation is based off the fractal of "seed then image" and death then resurrection. And it all ends with a choice, The Image of God vs. the Image of the Beast. In the beginning came sin and the shadow of death. It was in the valley of that shadow that Aaron and Israel awaited the return of His brother Moses to cleanse their garments so that they could enter the Holy Place.

Psalm 23:4, Yea, though I walk through the valley of the shadow of death, I will fear no evil: for thou art with me; thy rod and thy staff they comfort me.

It is this joint work of the Levitical Priesthood (Aaron) and the Melchizedek (Moses) Priesthood that redemption of the fallen image of creation is restored and cleansed. But when Moses delayed to come down from the mountain from within the Shekinah Glory and the presence of God, Israel joined with a broken and fallen image and idol. The Image of the Beast!

Deuteronomy 9:12, And the Lord said unto me, Arise, get thee down quickly from hence; for thy people which thou hast brought forth out of Egypt have corrupted themselves; they are quickly turned aside out of the way which I commanded them; they have made them a molten image.

Moses, like Yeshua was sent down the mountain to deliver them from their corrupted state. Having seen the wonders and miracles of God in their deliverance from Egypt and having passed through the Red Sea, they came to a mountain to receive the Image of God, the Ten Commandments.

Exodus 19:14, And Moses went down from the mount unto the people, and sanctified the people; and they washed their clothes. 15 And he said unto the people, Be ready against the third day: come not at your wives. 16 And it came to pass on the third day in the morning, that there were thunders and lightnings, and a thick cloud upon the mount, and the voice of the trumpet exceeding loud; so that all the people that was in the camp trembled. 17 And Moses brought forth the people out of the camp to meet with God; and they stood at the nether part of the mount.

Man's fallen state had become so far removed from God that they could not bear to hear Him speak directly with them.

Exodus 20:18, And all the people saw the thunderings, and the lightnings, and the noise of the trumpet, and the mountain smoking: and when the people saw it, they removed, and stood afar off. 19 And they said unto Moses, Speak thou with us, and we will hear: but let not God speak with us, lest we die. 20 And Moses said unto the people, Fear not: for God is come to prove you, and that his fear may be before your faces, that ye sin not.

As the people were so afraid to hear the voice of God and see Him approach they begged that God would speak through Moses to them and not directly lest they die. At their request, Moses approached the dark cloud of the Shekinah Glory and God instructed him how to teach the people of Israel to walk. Due to his longer than expected absence they assumed that Moses had died and that they would need a new intercessor. They turned to the fallen image of a beast to fill in for the role of Moses.

Exodus 32:1, And when the people saw that Moses delayed to come down out of the mount, the people gathered themselves together unto Aaron, and said unto him, Up, make us gods, which shall go before us; for as for this Moses, the man that brought us up out of the land of Egypt, we wot not what is become of him.

Take note of the fact that the Shekinah Glory is still on the mountain. They can still see the visible presence of God. What was missing? God or an intercessor? Moses the intercessor was missing and presumed dead. The fallen image (the golden calf) was meant to replace Moses as intercessor between Israel and the presence of God. They were reverting back to their fallen and broken images instead of having faith and waiting on the intercessor that God had provided for them. This same fractal is repeated in the end-time. Just as Moses delays to come down from the mountain, so does Yeshua.

Matthew 24:44, Therefore be ye also ready: for in such an hour as ye think not the Son of man cometh. 45 Who then is a faithful and wise servant, whom his lord hath made ruler over his household, to give them meat in due season? 46 Blessed is that servant, whom his lord when he cometh shall find so doing. 47 Verily I say unto you, That he shall make him ruler over all his goods. 48 But and if that evil servant shall say in his heart, My lord delayeth his coming; 49 And shall begin to smite his fellowservants, and to eat and drink with the drunken; 50 The lord of that servant shall come in a day when he looketh not for him, and in an hour that he is not aware of, 51 And shall cut him asunder, and appoint him his portion with the hypocrites: there shall be weeping and gnashing of teeth.

Yeshua fulfills the same patterns as Moses. The purpose of this delay is to extend mercy.

2 Peter 3:9, The Lord is not slack concerning his promise, as some men count slackness; but is longsuffering to us-ward, not willing that any should perish, but that all should come to repentance.

But how can we be certain that Yeshua would fulfill the same patterns as Moses the Law-giver?

Deuteronomy 18:15, The Lord thy God <u>will raise up unto thee a Prophet from the midst of thee, of thy brethren, like unto me;</u> unto him ye shall hearken; 16 According to all that thou desiredst of the Lord thy God in Horeb in the day of the assembly, saying, <u>Let me not hear again the voice of the Lord my God, neither let me see this great fire any more, that I die not.</u> 17 And the Lord said unto me, They have well spoken that which they have spoken. 18 <u>I will raise them up a Prophet from among their brethren, like unto thee, and will put my words in his mouth; and he shall speak unto them all that I shall command him.</u> 19 And it shall come to pass, that whosoever will not hearken unto my words which he shall <u>speak in my name,</u> I will require it of him.

We should be looking for the Messiah to fulfill the same fractals as Moses. Just as He delayed to return, so will Yeshua. What will be the response of the people to this delay? It will be the same as the Children of Israel who turned to an image of a beast to serve as their intercessor with God. What is the outcome of this corrupted worship? Death.

Exodus 32:8, They have turned aside quickly out of the way which I commanded them: <u>they have made them a molten calf, and have worshipped it, and have sacrificed thereunto,</u> and said, These be thy gods, O Israel, which have brought thee up out of the land of Egypt. 9 And the Lord said unto Moses, I have seen this people, and, behold, it is a stiffnecked people:10 Now therefore let me alone, that my wrath may wax hot against them, and <u>that I may consume them</u>: and I will make of thee a great nation.

Israel had corrupted themselves with a fallen image on the very eve of their joining with the true Image of God. What has happened before, will happen again in the end. Just as Adam and Eve made a choice between the two trees or between the beast and their God given image, so also Israel fulfilled the same pattern. In the end-time the fractal will play itself out between the Image of God and the Image of the Beast!

Revelation 12:5, And she brought forth a man child, who was to rule all nations with a rod of iron: and her child was caught up unto God, and to his throne.

This Man-Child is none other than the Image of God. And what is the Beast's response to the birth of the Man-Child and the Image of God?

Revelation 12:13, And when the dragon saw that he was cast unto the earth, he persecuted the woman which brought forth the man child.

The result is the end-time battle, The Image of God vs the Image of the Beast!

1 Corinthians 15:25, For he must reign, till he hath put all enemies under his feet. 26 The last enemy that shall be destroyed is death. 27 For he hath put all

things under his feet. But when he saith all things are put under him, it is manifest that he is excepted, which did put all things under him.

What is your role in the end-time battle? Are you just sitting on the sidelines as an observer? Does your Pastor, Priest, or Rabbi do all the work for you? Is this something you can escape? Should you want to escape it? Or will you fulfill your God given fractal and participate in the seed and the role of redemption that has been engendered within you? Yeshua gave us His seed to give our testimony of resurrection life and the true Image of God. Can a pastor or priest or rabbi fulfill that God given calling for you? Or should you take a personal hand in carrying out the great commission?

How would you react, if God told you that He wanted to kill all of your family? Would you act like Moses and intercede or would you hope to escape the situation in a rapture?

Exodus 32:32, Yet now, if thou wilt forgive their sin--; and if not, blot me, I pray thee, out of thy book which thou hast written.

This is the same role that Yeshua fulfilled. Moses and Yeshua both fulfill the role of an intercessor between God and the people. Those of faith should also fulfill this role...just like Abraham, the "friend of God" (James 2:23) intervening for the inhabitants of Sodom.

Genesis 18:24, Peradventure there be fifty righteous within the city: wilt thou also destroy and not spare the place for the fifty righteous that are therein?

In both cases, we see God's chosen seed intervening on behalf of those trapped in a fallen state and a broken image. They were both willing to suffer the wrath of God in order to save others. The pattern of faith is intercession for the broken, unclean, and defiled...even if it means death for us. We will discuss the deep significance of the Baptism (Mikvah) and how it is related to taking on the fractal of death for the salvation of all creation. How do you restore a broken image? How do you turn all creation from a fractal and pattern of a death to a pattern of life?

Job 13:15, Though he slay me, yet will I trust in him: but I will maintain mine own ways before him.

2 THE MYSTERY OF INIQUITY VS THE LAW OF MOSES?

God was willing to kill all of Israel because of their refusal to hear the Law of Moses! Don't skip over that fact. It is critical and reinforced time and again in the scriptures. God mandates an existential choice between His way and the way of His enemy. Do you really think that God just caved on this issue? That He declared it was ok to ignore His law and that He would give everyone a pass that allowed them to do "whatever I think is best"? The modern teaching of "Grace vs. Law" has that belief as its foundational principle. It is completely unscriptural.

> Deuteronomy 30:19, I call heaven and earth to record this day against you, that I have set before you life and death, blessing and cursing: therefore choose life, that both thou and thy seed may live:

It is so important that the Prophet Jeremiah reminds the people of this choice and its implications on their seed.

> Jeremiah 21:8, And unto this people thou shalt say, Thus saith the Lord; Behold, I set before you the way of life, and the way of death.

It is such an important pattern that it is repeated over and over and over again, just like a fractal self-replicates. You can read the scriptures over and over again with the wrong paradigm and not get the message that God is telling you, but if you learn this one fractal, death (seed) and life (fruit), the mysteries of the Bible will open up to you. Why? Because you will begin to see the signature of God in what is written. You will read the Bible and begin to see the sub-text that is riding below the actual text.

Old Covenant	New Covenant
Torah of Sin and Death	Torah of Resurrection Life
Flesh	Spirit
Hagar	Sarah
Ishmael	Isaac
Sinai	Jerusalem
Moses	Yeshua
Torah	Resurrected Covenant
Letter	Spirit
Seed	Fruit
Death	Resurrection life
Ministration of condemnation	Ministration of grace & mercy
Law/Torah of works	Law/Torah of faith
Shadow	Image (manifestation)

If you take these symbols and events and apply the wrong assumptions you will end up with the wrong conclusions and their fruits. It doesn't matter what your intentions are saying. What matters is that you are accurately hearing what God is speaking.

Deuteronomy 29:4, Yet the Lord hath not given you an heart to perceive, and eyes to see, and ears to hear, unto this day.

Yeshua reiterates the call of the prophet as it relates to His work.

Matthew 11:14, And if ye will receive it, this is Elias, which was for to come. 15 He that hath ears to hear, let him hear. 16 But whereunto shall I liken this generation? It is like unto children sitting in the markets, and calling unto their fellows. . .

This hearkens back to the prophecy of Malachi that before the Day of the Lord, Elijah would be sent to cause those that "fear His Name" to remember the Law of Moses. Yeshua agreed that this would happen in the last days. Christians and Jews should be the quintessential embodiment of those who "fear the Lord" (Psalms 15:4, 22:23, 25:14, 34:7, Deuteronomy 6:13, Malachi 3:16).

Malachi 4:4, "Remember ye the law of Moses my servant, which I commanded unto him in Horeb for all Israel, with the statutes and judgments. 5 Behold, I will send you Elijah the prophet before the coming of the great and dreadful day of the Lord:6 And he shall turn the heart of the fathers to the children, and the heart of the children to their fathers, lest I come and smite the earth with a curse."

Yeshua reinforced the validity of this truth.

Matthew 17:11, And Jesus answered and said unto them, Elias truly shall first come, and restore all things.

That being the case let's briefly revisit what was covered in the first book in the "Restoring Truth" series "The Elijah Calling". We need to properly place the Law of Moses in alignment with the Word of God and with Yeshua the Messiah.

What is the most basic issue which the intercessor is faced? An angry God and a rebellious people.

Ezekiel 12:2, Son of man, thou dwellest in the midst of a rebellious house, which have eyes to see, and see not; they have ears to hear, and hear not: for they are a rebellious house.

Just as Abraham and Moses intervened for rebellious people so also Yeshua fulfilled this role...and still does. Yeshua clearly understood that in order to fulfill His fractal, he had to fulfill the same imagery of the seed, buried in death to await resurrection.

Yeshua the Messiah knew He had to fulfill the same imagery as the Torah: sin and death to await resurrection. This is why He also knew that the Father had no option, the fractal of death (sin) had to be fulfilled in Him, so that the fractal of resurrection life could also be fulfilled in him. This was the key to the kingdom in order for Yeshua to qualify to be the new administrator of the Resurrected Covenant (Torah of Resurrection Life).

2 Corinthians 3:6, Who also hath made us able ministers of the new testament; not of the letter, but of the spirit: for the letter killeth, but the spirit giveth life. 7 But if the ministration of death, written and engraven in stones, was glorious, so that the children of Israel could not stedfastly behold the face of Moses for the glory of his countenance; which glory was to be done away:8 How shall not the ministration of the spirit be rather glorious? 9 For if the

<u>ministration of condemnation be glory, much more doth the ministration of righteousness exceed in glory</u>.

If Yeshua was to be the administrator of this Resurrected Covenant (Torah), then He had to bear the marks of that same fractal of death and resurrection. He was taking our sin and death upon himself so that He could provide His resurrection life and place it upon us. He had to show that He was qualified through the power of resurrection life. If He could not prove it, then He could not qualify to be the new administrator.

Hebrews 7:15, And it is yet far more evident: for that after the similitude of Melchisedec there ariseth another priest, Who is made, not after the law of a carnal commandment, <u>but after the power of an endless life</u>.

Yeshua bears the same fractal hallmarks as the Torah of Sin and Death and then of the Torah of Resurrection Life! God has always desired to dwell within the temple of man. Our sin prevents that from happening. This can only occur through the work of the Messiah, circumcising the heart and preparing the mind and spirit of man.

1 Corinthians 6:17, But he that is joined unto the Lord is one spirit. 18 Flee fornication. Every sin that a man doeth is without the body; but he that committeth fornication sinneth against his own body. 19 What? know ye not that your body is the temple of the Holy Ghost which is in you, which ye have of God, and ye are not your own? 20 For ye are bought with a price: therefore glorify God in your body, and in your spirit, which are God's.

Accepting the teaching of death and resurrection affirmed by the resurrection of Yeshua would seal the Jew's judgment under the Law (Torah of Moses) and require that they seek entry into the resurrected Torah via the faith in the new resurrected administrator, Yeshua the Messiah. Scripturally there is no pass on the new administrator for the Jews or the Gentiles. The works of the Written Torah could not justify them. Why? It was a Torah of Sin and Death, designed to bring condemnation on the flesh.

Romans 3:26, To <u>declare, I say, at this time his righteousness</u>: that he might be just, <u>and the justifier of him which believeth in Yeshua. 27 Where is boasting then? It is excluded. By what law? of works? Nay</u>: but by the law of faith. 28 Therefore we conclude that <u>a man is justified by faith without the deeds of the law</u>.

Time and again Paul is testifying on behalf of the Written Torah about the fractal of death and resurrection. It was the proponents of the Oral Torah (Rabbinical Teachers) that were trying to make it seem that Paul, though saved, was not keeping the Written Torah Commandments.
This was an affront to the core of their Pharisaical beliefs, and rightfully so.

What could they not see?   That death and resurrection is the fractal of God and had to be fulfilled in the Commandments of God (the Written Torah), the administrations of the Written Torah, and their administrators, Moses and Yeshua.

TWO ADMINISTRATORS: DEATH (MOSES) & RESURRECTION (YESHUA):
This provides clear insight into why Moses could not be permitted to ascend to the Promised land and that another would have to prophetically fulfill his work. Moses had to fulfill the fractal of death and of the flesh.

> Exodus 31:1, And Moses went and spake these words unto all Israel. 2 And he said unto them, I am an hundred and twenty years old this day; I can no more go out and come in: also the Lord hath said unto me, Thou shalt not go over this Jordan.

Moses needed to remain descended, in exile, in the wilderness, and fulfill the imagery and fractal of death, the flesh, condemnation and judgment, while another fulfilled the imagery of resurrection life, the spirit. Moses is actually prophetic of the one to come; the Messiah.

> Deuteronomy 18:15, The Lord thy God will raise up unto thee a Prophet from the midst of thee, of thy brethren, like unto me; unto him ye shall hearken; 16 According to all that thou desiredst of the Lord thy God in Horeb in the day of the assembly, saying, Let me not hear again the voice of the Lord my God, neither let me see this great fire any more, that I die not. 17 And the Lord said unto me, They have well spoken that which they have spoken. 18 I will raise them up a Prophet from among their brethren, like unto thee, and will put my words in his mouth; and he shall speak unto them all that I shall command him.

This one who is like unto Moses would bear the fractal of resurrection life and of the spirit. This is the Messiah Yeshua, through whom we are sanctified. This is something Moses could not do, as he was a picture of sin and death, the flesh. God gives his judgment on Moses and says the reason he is not allowed to enter was because of his failure to sanctify God in the people.

> Deuteronomy 32:51, Because ye trespassed against me among the children of Israel at the waters of MeribahKadesh, in the wilderness of Zin; because ye sanctified me not in the midst of the children of Israel.

This was the essential failure of the Written Law (Torah) of Moses, not the Oral Torah. The Oral Torah is not even the focus here. The traditions of the rabbis (traditions of the elders, otherwise known as the Talmud, the Mishnah, or as the Takanot, Minhag, Halakha, or Ma'aseh) are not required to be in conformance with the covenant (meaning you would be without sin). Paul reaffirms Yeshua's declarations throughout the Gospels that the Oral Torah is not required for a believer. Both the Apostles and Yeshua describe the Rabbinical Oral Torah as a "burden" that is "borne" that causes "trouble". Yeshua and the Apostles clarified that the Rabbinical Oral Torah were extra burdens that were not required of believers in Yeshua. The Apostles in Acts 15 are talking about the Oral Torah not being required, not the Written Torah, as the Apostles address this issue in Acts 15:21, saying new believers should learn the Written Torah (the Law of Moses) every 7th day Sabbath in the Synagogue with other believers in Yeshua. We will delve into this more later. For added clarity, the Apostles go on to give some basic requirements for new believers while they learn the Written Torah of Moses in the Synagogue.

What was Moses' administration and that first generation's failure? The failure was Israel's willful disobedience to that Written Torah, which brought condemnation through their sin and death.

> Ephesians 2:2, Wherein in time past ye walked according to the course of this world, according to the prince of the power of the air, <u>the spirit that now worketh in the children of disobedience</u>:

It is this spirit that caused Israel to fail and the Covenant to be subjected to sin and death. This is also why they needed a new administrator, so they could receive a spirit of obedience to the Written Torah, turning it to a Torah of Resurrection Life. Why was this confusing to the rabbinic leaders of Paul's time?

> 1 Peter 1:1, Peter, an apostle of Yeshua, to the strangers scattered throughout Pontus, Galatia, Cappadocia, Asia, and Bithynia, 2 Elect according to the foreknowledge of God the Father, <u>through sanctification of the Spirit, unto obedience</u> and <u>sprinkling of the blood of Yeshua: grace</u> unto you, and peace, be multiplied. 3 Blessed be the God and Father of our Lord Yeshua, which <u>according to his abundant mercy hath begotten us again unto a lively hope by the resurrection</u> of Yeshua from the dead, 4 To an inheritance incorruptible, and undefiled, and that fadeth not away, reserved in heaven for you, 5 <u>Who are kept by the power of God through faith unto salvation ready to be revealed in the last time</u>.

It was confusing because they did not understand the death and resurrection fractal. Also, it was confusing because the fullness of the fractal was not revealed until the "last time". Peter is affirming the centrality of the death and resurrection fractal message and its new administrator, Yeshua the Messiah. How did Yeshua qualify to be the administrator of the Resurrected Covenant (the Written Torah)?

> Hebrews 7:15, And it is yet far more evident: for that after the similitude of Melchisedec there ariseth another priest, 16 <u>Who is made</u>, not after the law of a carnal commandment, <u>but after the power of an endless life</u>. 17 For he testifieth, Thou art a priest for ever after the order of Melchisedec.

Yeshua qualified to be the new administrator of the Law of Moses by the power of a resurrection (endless) life. Remember Moses is the picture of the death (seed) fractal, and Yeshua is the picture of the resurrection (fruit) fractal.

The Apostle Paul is examined time and again over this false accusation of the Pharisees that he was not keeping the Written Torah and time and again he is found in conformance with Yeshua's instruction in Matthew 5:17, "Think not that I am come to destroy the law (Written Torah), or the prophets: I am not come to destroy, but to fulfil."

Paul agrees with Yeshua, walks just as Yeshua walks, according to the Written Torah. He did not come to destroy the Torah, but to resurrect it to new life in the inward man. This is how Yeshua fulfills the Law. He does not do away with it, He resurrects it within the believer's heart. The same commandments are on the second set of tablets that were on the first set of tablets. Those who say Yeshua fulfilled the Law so that we do not have to keep the Law clearly do not understand the work of the Messiah.

Exodus 34:1, And the Lord said unto Moses, Hew thee two tablets of stone like unto the first: and I will write upon these tablets the words that were in the first tablets, which thou brakest.

While many Christians have done away with the written Law of Moses in the name of grace…on the other side there are many modern Christians who are saved by grace and keep the Written Law of Moses, who say the scriptures about being "under the law" or the "works of the law" or the "Law of Sin and Death" are referring to the Rabbinical Oral Torah (traditions of men).

Why would they misidentify the Written Law of Moses as the Rabbinical Oral Law (Traditions)? Because Paul associates the Written Law of Moses with sin and death. They say that cannot be for the Law is life and light. We will look more closely at why they mistakenly misinterpret these scriptures as the Oral Torah and not as the Written Torah of Moses.

Paul is so very clear that he is talking about the Written Torah by using the terms "under the law", "works of the law", and the "Law of Sin and Death". Both Yeshua and Paul, in many other scriptures, say the Oral Torah of the rabbis is not required. Unfortunately, some have misapplied the terms "under the law" or the "works of the law" or the "Law of Sin and Death" as referring to the Oral Torah.

The scriptural fractal clearly indicates that these terms point to the Written Law of Moses under the administration of condemnation and death prior to the resurrection of those same words under the administration of the Messiah Yeshua via resurrection life.

It is an injustice to the scriptures when we evaluate those references from Paul, the Apostles, and Yeshua within the context of the centrality of the fractal of death and resurrection, which applies to the Torah, to men, to the Messiah, and to all creation. This is why Paul brings it up every single time he is testifying to the truth of the revelation of resurrection.

Paul affirms:
- The Written Law of Moses is to be established by believers in Yeshua

- The Written Law of Moses has two administrations, one of sin and death and one of resurrection life.
- Both administrations have the same commandments.
- Each administration has its own administrator:
    o Sin and death (flesh)–Moses
    o Grace & abundant mercy and resurrection life (spirit)–Yeshua
- The Written Torah is required, the Oral Torah is not.
- The Law without the Messiah does what it should–it brings death to the flesh.
- The Law with the Messiah brings life to the spirit.

Here are some examples that confirm this understanding:
- Hagar and Sarah
- Torah of Sin and Death and the Torah of Resurrection Life
- Conflict between the flesh and the resurrection spirit

We need to restore the concepts of being "under the law" and "works of the law" as referencing the Written Torah just as the scriptures plainly indicate. Paul's central message is that we are unable to save ourselves, that we are "under a Torah of Sin and Death" and that the Law (Torah) referenced in the "works of the law" and "under the Law" is indeed the Written Torah.

Many Hebrew Roots teachers object to this statement because they say the Torah is life and light. That is true, the same commandments written twice are light and life, but the first set of tablets is "under sin and death" as we see the sin of the golden calf and the shedding of blood at the first giving of the Law of Moses (Exodus 20, 24:8, 32:4). This is the first administration of condemnation and judgment.

The second set of tablets is under resurrection life, grace and mercy as we see the manifestation of the Name of YHWH presented at the second giving of the Written Law of Moses (Exodus 34). The first administration must die and the new administration of resurrection life must be enacted. Those who deny faith in that new administrator, Yeshua, are indeed still under the law (Written Torah) of Sin and Death and cannot pass (baptized/Mikvah) to the Torah of Resurrection Life until they express faith in its administrator, Yeshua the Messiah. This is why there is only one way and one name by which we can all (Jew and Gentile) be saved.

Acts 4:12, Neither is there salvation in any other: for <u>there is none other name under heaven given among men, whereby we must be saved</u>.

Remember all Israel was baptized into Moses and Moses' name. This is the first administration of "sin and death". When Yeshua came, the administration changed to "resurrection life and abundant grace and mercy" and we must all be baptized into Him and His name.

- 1 Corinthians 10:2, And were all <u>baptized unto Moses</u> in the cloud and in the sea;
- Matthew 3:14, But John forbad him, saying, <u>I have need to be baptized of thee</u>, and comest thou to me?
- Matthew 3:11, I indeed baptize you with water unto repentance. but he that cometh after me is mightier than I, whose shoes I am not worthy to bear: he shall baptize you with the Holy Ghost, and with fire:
- Matthew 20:22, But Jesus answered and said, Ye know not what ye ask. Are ye able to drink of the cup that I shall drink of, <u>and to be baptized with the baptism that I am baptized with</u>? They say unto him, We are able.
- Mark 16:16, He that believeth and is baptized shall be saved; but he that believeth not shall be damned.
- Acts 2:38, Then Peter said unto them, Repent, and <u>be baptized every one of you in the name of Jesus Christ</u> for the remission of sins, and ye shall receive the gift of the Holy Ghost.

John the Baptist is puzzled by Yeshua's request to be baptized by John, but Yeshua knew He had to fulfill the fractal of death (old administration) before fulfilling the fractal of the Baptism of the Spirit that Yeshua would provide. But, as we have learned, that despite the glory of Moses' administration, it could not free the people from sin and death and was not qualified to save them due to their spirit of disobedience. This spirit kept them separated from God.

1 Corinthians 10:5, But with many of them God was not well pleased: for they were overthrown in the wilderness.

There is not one way for the Jews and another way for the Gentiles. All must confess faith in the new administrator the Messiah Yeshua, or they are still under the "Torah of Sin and Death" administration. All must confess faith in the Messiah Yeshua, for they are unable to bring about works of the Torah to justify themselves.

Romans 3:10, Seeing it is one God, which shall justify the circumcision by faith, and uncircumcision through faith.

How are we (Jew and Gentile) justified? By faith in Yeshua, the New administrator.

Galatians 3:7, <u>Know ye therefore that they which are of faith</u>, the same are the children of Abraham. 8 And the scripture, foreseeing that God would <u>justify the heathen through faith</u>, preached before the Gospel unto Abraham, saying, In thee shall all nations be blessed. 9 So <u>then they which be of faith are blessed with faithful Abraham</u>.

Are Jews saved a different way than Gentiles? No, all must come through faith in Yeshua.

Romans 3:1, What advantage then hath the Jew? or what profit is there of circumcision? 2 Much every way: chiefly, because that unto them were committed the oracles of God. 3 For what if some did not believe? shall their unbelief make the faith of God without effect? 4 God forbid: yea, let God be true, but every man a liar; as it is written, That thou mightest be justified in thy sayings, and mightest overcome when thou art judged.

The key issue is faith or lack thereof, from the start to end of the Bible. You cannot justify yourself or make yourself righteous. Avi Ben Mordechai suggests that Paul's letters were tampered with saying that the term "under the law" was added by Marcion. Why would Avi assume this? Apparently, he could not conceive of the Written Law of Moses being associated with "sin and death".

"Greek: For as many as are of the works of the law are under the Curse… (Galatians 3:10a)
Aramaic: For those who are servants (workers) of the law are still under a curse…
Marcion: For as many as are under the law are under the curse…
Gordon looked at this, then squarely looked at me, and said, here's a smoking gun. Works of, Greek ergon, was removed, permitting the text to imply that this thing called the Law of Moses is the real culprit; it was the curse!" (Galatians Commentary by Avi Ben Mordechai, page 252)

Avi spends much of the rest of the book trying to apply the "under the law" and "works of the law" to the Rabbinical Oral Torah (traditions of men) instead of the Written Law of Moses.

To clarify, we have a well–intended teacher, who, instead of adjusting his understanding of the scriptures, decides to edit out the scriptures (or translation) that do not agree with his paradigm. Some Hebrew Roots and Messianic teachers have chosen this path in order to avoid changing their paradigm to conform to the truth of the scriptures. Why did Avi do this? I assume it is because he did not see the death and resurrection fractal of the Messiah, the Torah, or their administrations.

We agree with Avi that in other locations of the scriptures, Yeshua, the Apostles, and Paul all affirm that we need not keep the Oral Torah. Unfortunately, this same brush is being applied to scriptures that are not discussing the Oral Torah. Why is this being done? We could not see what Paul saw, the fractal of death and resurrection. How can the Torah be a curse and still be light and life? It can, because it is fulfilling the same fractal as the Messiah, death and resurrection!

- Proverbs 6:23, For the commandment is a lamp; and the law is light; and reproofs of instruction are the way of life:
- Proverbs 13:4, The law of the wise is a fountain of life, to depart from the snares of death.

Both as statements are accurate, but we need to remember that God cannot be approached in the flesh no matter how good the light is.

Exodus 3:1, Now Moses kept the flock of Jethro his father in law, the priest of Midian: and he led the flock to the backside of the desert, and came to the mountain of God, even to Horeb. 2 And the <u>angel of the Lord appeared unto him in a flame of fire</u> out of the midst of a bush: and he looked, and, behold, the <u>bush burned with fire</u>, and the bush was not consumed. 3 And Moses said, I will now turn aside, and see this great sight, why the bush is not burnt. 4 And when the Lord saw that he turned aside to see, <u>God called unto him out of the midst of the bush</u>, and said, Moses, Moses. And he said, Here am I. 5 And he said, <u>Draw not nigh hither</u>: put off thy shoes from off thy feet, for the place whereon thou standest is holy ground.

God's warning to Moses is clear, do not come any closer lest you die. Just as many Hebrew Roots teachers say the Torah is a light, a fire, and a lamp, these same things can bring fallen flesh to destruction. (Genesis 3:3, Leviticus 10:6–9, Numbers 18:2–3). To oversimplify the allusions of the Torah as only being light and life do an injustice to the scriptures and keep us from seeing the fractal of death and resurrection.

It was because of the spirit of disobedience, that the Torah (Law of Moses) continually brought the people death. They needed to be freed from that administration in order to have the hope of resurrection life.

Romans 7:2, For the woman which hath an husband is bound by the law to her husband so long as he liveth; but if the husband be dead, <u>she is loosed from the law</u> of her husband.

Romans 7 illustrates the need of the woman to be loosed from the law of her current husband to be attached to the law of the new testator and administrator. Paul elaborates on the need for that new law because being under the law of the old testator brought only death.

Romans 7:3, So then if, while her husband liveth, she be married to another man, she shall be called an adulteress: but if her husband be dead, <u>she is free from that law</u>; so that she is no adulteress, though she be married to another man. 4 Wherefore, my brethren, <u>ye also are become dead to the law by the body of Christ; that ye should be married to another, even to him who is raised from the dead</u>, that we should bring forth fruit unto God. 5 For <u>when we were in the flesh, the motions of sins, which were by the law, did work in our members to bring forth fruit unto death</u>.

Again, Paul is contrasting the two administrations and showing how they brought out their respective fruit: death and resurrection. He is clearly saying that the fruit of the Law of Moses, the Written Torah, was death. There is no way around this scriptural fact. Remember Paul is always presenting a duality in contrast.

Flesh	Spirit
Seed	Fruit
Death	Resurrection
Works of the Law (Written Torah)	Faith
Torah of Sin & Death	Torah of Resurrection Life
Under the Law (Written Torah) (Old administration)	Under grace (Law of Spirit) (New administration)
Glorious	More Glorious
Cannot Justify Self	Justified by God's Son
Carnal Mind	Mind of Christ

Whose fault was it that the Law of Moses brought forth the fruit of death?

Hebrews 8:6, But now hath he obtained a more excellent ministry, by how much also he is the mediator of a better covenant, which was established upon better promises. 7 For if that first covenant had been faultless, then should no place have been sought for the second. 8 For finding fault with them, he saith, Behold, the days come, saith the Lord, when I will make a new covenant with the house of Israel and with the house of Judah:9 Not according to the covenant that I made with their fathers in the day when I took them by the hand to lead them out of the land of Egypt; because they continued not in my covenant, and I regarded them not, saith the Lord. 10 For this is the covenant that I will make with the house of Israel after those days, saith the Lord; I will put my laws into their mind, and write them in their hearts: and I will be to them a God, and they shall be to me a people:11 And they shall not teach every man his neighbour, and every man his brother, saying, Know the Lord: for all shall know me, from the least to the greatest. 12 For I will be merciful to their unrighteousness, and their sins and their iniquities will I remember no more.

The fault of the first covenant, the Written Torah of Moses, was their minds and their hearts. They have a spirit of disobedience that needs to be replaced with a new mediator. Knowing this we must re-evaluate what Yeshua said about the Law of Moses.

Matthew 5:17, Think not that I am come to destroy the law, or the prophets: I am not come to destroy, but to fulfil. 18 For verily I say unto you, Till heaven and earth pass, one jot or one tittle shall in no wise pass from the law, till all be fulfilled.

How long can Christians keep up this delusion that Yeshua fulfilled the Law so that we can violate the Law? Paul agreed with Yeshua.

Romans 3:31, Do we then make void the law through faith? God forbid, we establish the law.

There is no doubt that Yeshua fulfilled the Law, but He didn't do it so that we could ignore the Law. He fulfilled it to fulfill His fractal and pattern, and so should we.

Matthew 3:13, Then cometh Jesus from Galilee to Jordan unto John, to be baptized of him. 14 But John forbad him, saying, <u>I have need to be baptized of thee, and comest thou to me</u>? 15 And Jesus answering said unto him, Suffer it to be so now:<u> for thus it becometh **us** to fulfil all righteousness</u>. Then he suffered him.

How long can we ignore, deny, and obfuscate the truth of this statement? Notice He didn't say, "for thus it becometh <u>me</u> to fulfil all righteousness...", He said, "for thus it becometh <u>us</u> to fulfil all righteousness..." Yeshua and John both had a fractal to fulfill and so do we. John was a participant in the Mikva (Baptism) with Yeshua, and so are we. We have a role to fill, a fractal to live out. Nobody can fulfill that role for you or on your behalf. Sitting in a church and paying tithes just won't cut it. You need to live, speak it, and testify to it.

Just as John and Yeshua fulfill the work of Elijah, so also, we continue that work today with Yeshua. Knowing that Israel has returned to the Land of Promise, Israel, does that mean that God has forgiven them for the rejection of the new Administrator of Resurrection Life and the Resurrected Covenant. Many believers assume that God has indeed given two ways of salvation, one for the Jew and another for the Gentile. Is this true? Is this scripturally accurate?

Over and over again we hear Pastors and Ministers teach that the believer is grafted into Israel. Is this true? Is this scripturally accurate? Has God really forgiven Israel of their rejection of Yeshua the Messiah? You will be shocked by the clarity of the scriptures and the clear actions that God Himself is demanding from them and us.

Once again you will find that Yeshua, the Prophets, the Apostles, and Paul all agree on what needs to happen for all Israel to be saved. This doesn't deny God's love for Israel or ours. It does clarify the singular unity of the scriptures and the Body of Christ. We can't hide behind any delusions or false hopes. The prophecies for the end-times are grim for all peoples and especially the apple of God's eye, Israel.

Do you really think that God would move the goalposts of expectation from

2,000 years ago? Do you really think that once again God is just going to concede? If you have bought into those assumptions, you have a script running in your head that was placed there by someone who is not teaching the full council of the Bible. You need to start asking questions and reaffirming the truth of your beliefs. Why? You will be held accountable for your choices…just like Israel…just like Adam and Eve.

In the end time battle those who are in Yeshua and "keep His commandments" (Revelation 12:17) have a nemesis called the Antichrist. He is characterized by lawlessness.

> 2 Thessalonians 2:1, Now we beseech you, brethren, by the coming of our Lord Jesus Christ, and by our gathering together unto him, 2 That ye be not soon shaken in mind, or be troubled, neither by spirit, nor by word, nor by letter as from us, as that the day of Christ is at hand. 3 <u>Let no man deceive you by any means: for that day shall not come, except there come a falling away first, and that man of sin be revealed, the son of perdition;</u> 4 Who opposeth and exalteth himself above all that is called God, or that is worshipped; so that he as God sitteth in the temple of God, shewing himself that he is God. 5 Remember ye not, that, when I was yet with you, I told you these things? 6 And now ye know what withholdeth that he might be revealed in his time. 7 For the <u>mystery of iniquity doth already work</u>: only he who now letteth will let, until he be taken out of the way. 8 And <u>then shall that Wicked be revealed</u>, whom the Lord shall consume with the spirit of his mouth, and shall destroy with the brightness of his coming:9 Even him, whose coming is after the working of Satan with all power and signs and <u>lying wonders,</u> 10 And <u>with all deceivableness of unrighteousness</u> in them that perish; because <u>they received not the love of the truth, that they might be saved</u>. 11 And for this cause <u>God shall send them strong delusion, that they should believe a lie</u>:12 That <u>they all might be damned who believed not the truth, but had pleasure in unrighteousness</u>. 13 But we are bound to give thanks alway to God for you, brethren beloved of the Lord, because God hath from the beginning <u>chosen you to salvation through sanctification of the Spirit and belief of the truth</u>:14 Whereunto he called you by our gospel, to the obtaining of the glory of our Lord Jesus Christ. 15 Therefore, brethren, stand fast, and <u>hold the traditions which ye have been taught, whether by word, or our epistle</u>.

This is the most extensive explanation of the end time battle. We see two that are in opposition to one another.

- Truth is opposed to a lie (a delusion sent by God).
- A test is being performed to determine who love the truth and who love a lie.
- The "man of sin" is depicted as being contrary to the Law of Moses and performs the penultimate sin of the Golden Calf, making himself in God's place.
- The solution presented for those facing the quandary of darkness vs. light lies in their belief about "truth". Those truths will conform to the

traditions handed down by the Apostles. Not somebody else. Paul expresses great concern that deviation from those truths had already begun to occur in the first century after the death and resurrection of Yeshua. He calls that derivation from the truth, "the mystery of iniquity".

- Salvation is linked to the sanctification process that comes through our love of the truth and our conformance to it.

Revelation 2:1, Unto the angel of the church of Ephesus write; These things saith he that holdeth the seven stars in his right hand, who walketh in the midst of the seven golden candlesticks; 2 I know thy works, and thy labour, and thy patience, and how thou canst not bear them which are evil: and thou hast tried them which say they are apostles, and are not, and hast found them liars:3 And hast borne, and hast patience, and for my name's sake hast laboured, and hast not fainted. 4 Nevertheless I have somewhat against thee, because thou hast left thy first love. 5 Remember therefore from whence thou art fallen, and repent, and do the first works; or else I will come unto thee quickly, and will remove thy candlestick out of his place, except thou repent.

It is clear to see from this declaration about the Church of Ephesus that they had done the right thing in confronting false apostles over whether their teachings are truthful and scripturally accurate. However, over time they have left their first love. Many would like to say that our first love is God or Yeshua, but in actuality our first love is scripturally defined as the truth. So, after a while Ephesus had fallen away from their practice of testing apostles and their teachings and tolerated incorrect teaching. Yeshua gives them a stern warning to get back to their practice that they had fallen away from and get back into conformance with the teachings of the true apostles. 2 Thessalonians presents the culmination of this apostasy in the "man of sin" and a complete falling away from the traditions of the true apostles and the teachings of the Bible. God will allow signs and wonders to be performed by this Antichrist to really measure if His people will follow a lawless wonder or a persecuted truth.

What would you do if you discovered that what you were taught were Christian beliefs actually were contrary to the traditions of Christ's Apostles? Would you have the courage to continue listening or would you reject the warning because it was inconvenient, didn't feel right, or wasn't in line with what your priest, pastor, or rabbi teaches every weekend? Are you counting on the priest, pastor, and rabbi, to get you into heaven? Are you saved by your pastor?

The end-time conflict is centered around "Law". Christians around the world have bought into an unscriptural paradigm and they need to start having cold-sweats because the world is starting to manifest the fruit of that illegitimate seed and will bring forth a great falling away and resentment of the truth. Many justify their actions and their resentment. "Law, law, law…where is Christ? It has been 2,000 years and He isn't here…and doesn't appear to be coming…" What is the next step? Lawlessness and a false image, the Antichrist.

I John 4:3, And every spirit that confesseth not that Jesus Christ is come in the flesh is not of God: and this is that spirit of Antichrist, whereof ye have heard that it should come; and even now already is it in the world.

This Antichrist is characterized as having the image of a beast and not of God. It is this same beast the is battling the two true witnesses of God in the end time.

Revelation 11:7, And when they shall have finished their testimony, the beast that ascendeth out of the bottomless pit shall make war against them, and shall overcome them, and kill them.

It is this same beast that causes all who dwell on the earth to take the mark of the beast. He does this through a lie and a deception. Just as the markings of the beast and its image are contrary to truth, he will use lies as a tool to deceive people into worshiping the beast.

Revelation 13:9, If any man have an ear, let him hear. 10 He that leadeth into captivity shall go into captivity: he that killeth with the sword must be killed with the sword. Here is the patience and the faith of the saints. 11 And I beheld another beast coming up out of the earth; and he had two horns like a lamb, and he spake as a dragon. 12 And he exerciseth all the power of the first beast before him, and causeth the earth and them which dwell therein to worship the first beast, whose deadly wound was healed. 13 And he doeth great wonders, so that he maketh fire come down from heaven on the earth in the sight of men, 14 And deceiveth them that dwell on the earth by the means of those miracles which he had power to do in the sight of the beast; saying to them that dwell on the earth, that they should make an image to the beast, which had the wound by a sword, and did live. 15 And he had power to give life unto the image of the beast, that the image of the beast should both speak, and cause that as many as would not worship the image of the beast should be killed. 16 And he causeth all, both small and great, rich and poor, free and bond, to receive a mark in their right hand, or in their foreheads:17 And that no man might buy or sell, save he that had the mark, or the name of the beast, or the number of his name.

Notice that the prophecy is prefaced with "If any man has an ear, let him hear". This is code for those who love the truth. If you love the truth you need to hear what is coming next.

This man of lawlessness will cause the following:
- Causes the earth to worship the first beast.
- He makes fire to come down from heaven.
- He deceives those on the earth by those miracles.
- He tells all who dwell on the earth to make an image to the beast.
- He gives life to the image of the beast to speak and cause those who refuse to worship it to be killed.

- He causes a mark in their right hand or forehead which is required for buying or selling anything. Only those who have the mark, name, or number of the beast can buy and sell. Everyone else is outlawed and marked for death.

The enemy of the Image of God (Messiah Yeshua), will enact a mandatory law insisting worship that exalts the beast as God. This is a replay of the Golden Calf incident. Just as Israel was fulfilling the fractal of the choice of Eve and the Tree of the Knowledge of Good and Evil and the Image of God vs. The Image of the Beast, so will the whole world. The center of that battle is over the "tradition of the apostles", scriptural truth and accuracy, and our response to the violation of truth on a global scale.

So, is understanding the Law of Moses as the Apostles taught it important? Absolutely! Will all the world be confronted with that same choice? Yes. Can Christians and Jews sleepwalk their way through the end time. We won't be allowed to. Every single person will be forced to individually choose. So, if you had to choose your life vs your destiny...what would you do?

Remember, you can't make up your own moral law. You can't choose for yourself what is the law of God. You can't say, "I'm a good person and that should be enough..." What is your measure of "good"? What is your measure of truth? What is your measure of sin? The Apostles, Yeshua, and Paul all taught what the measure of sin was, is, and will be.

1 John 3:4, Whosoever committeth sin transgresseth also the law: for sin is the transgression of the law.

The Apostle John wasn't talking about your own self-defined moral law. He was talking about the Law of Moses. The Apostles told perspective believers to check their teaching against the truth of the scriptures. They gave no other measure for believers to use.

2 Timothy 3:15, And that from a child thou hast known the holy scriptures, which are able to make thee wise unto salvation through faith which is in Christ Jesus. All scripture is given by inspiration of God, and is profitable for doctrine, for reproof, for correction, for instruction in righteousness:

Paul went so far as to commend those that questioned the validity of his teaching. They went to the scriptures; the Torah, Writings, and the Prophets (Old Testament) to determine if his claims about Yeshua and His death and resurrection were true. At the time of Paul's writings there were no other scriptures to refer to than the Tanach-Torah, Writings, and Prophets. For the modern church to invalidate the very scriptures that Paul and the Apostles told potential believers to check their teaching against is astounding!

Acts 17:11, These were more noble than those in Thessalonica, in that they received the word with all readiness of mind, and searched the scriptures daily, whether those things were so.

So, if you think you as a Christian or a Jew can claim that you love the truth, yet refuse to correct your behavior in line with the truth of scripture...you have a serious problem. The church and Abrahams' physical descendants in the end time are characterized as being out of sync with the Messiah Yeshua and with the truth. The hallmarks of those days will be "strong delusion" and "idolatry".

Now that we have placed Law & Grace back in their scripturally accurate context, let's move onto redemption and how that occurs in the believer. Those who wish to read an extensive Bible Commentary on the issue of Law & Grace vs. the incorrect teaching of Law vs. Grace should read "The Elijah Calling".

The pursuit of truth is fraught with dangers on every side. Even when on the right path, the tendency is often to stray from the clarity of scriptures. You are moving from a pagan version of Christianity to a Biblical version of Christianity. In that journey, there will be many traps along the way that will seek to get you off course from the truth of the scriptures. The end goal is always truth and light vs. falsity and darkness. The days are growing dark and the darkness is popular and vengeful. Let your light grow in grace and knowledge, grounded in the truth of the scriptures. Make sure you are able to give accurate answers for what you believe.

I Peter 3:15, But sanctify the Lord God in your hearts: and be ready always to give an answer to every man that asketh you a reason of the hope that is in you with meekness and fear:

Knowing that God is at odds with mankind over His Law, not some arbitrary self-defined moral law, how do we proceed to fix the gap between God and man? The best way to identify the image and mark of the beast is to know the true Image of God, The Son of God.

2 John 1:7, For many deceivers are entered into the world, who confess not that Jesus Christ is come in the flesh. This is a deceiver and an Antichrist.

Mankind is going to be confronted with the choice between life and death. If you have the wrong paradigm. . . you might choose incorrectly. Sometimes what looks like life...may be death and vice versa.

Luke 17:33, Whosoever shall seek to save his life shall lose it; and whosoever shall lose his life shall preserve it.

Understanding the true nature of reality and our current fallen and broken image will help us identify if saving our flesh is really all it is made out to be. Or does it just seem important because we have a fallen and corrupted image that Adam and Eve joined themselves to in the beginning? Either way, by their disobedience all creation is paying a terrible price.

3 THE SPIRIT OF THE BEAST VS THE SPIRIT OF CHRIST

Many well intended Hebrew Roots groups are misidentifying the "Middle Wall of Partition" from Ephesians 2. Some are claiming that the "Middle Wall of Partition" is the Oral Torah (Traditions of Men) of the rabbis. Why are they misidentifying the Middle Wall as the Oral Torah? They envision the reunification of Judah (Southern Israel) and Ephraim (Northern Israel-10 tribes) and say it is the Oral Torah that keeps both groups from reconciling because of its offensive burdens. They state that the "one new man" of Ephesians 2 is Israel. So many Hebrew Roots teachers like to say that Ephesians 2 is talking about doing away with the Oral Torah so that Judah and Ephraim can be reunited as the "one new man". They run into a logical problem. If you assume Ephesians 2 is doing away with the Oral Torah of the Rabbis by Yeshua's work on the cross then that would presume that the Oral Torah was at one time recognized as valid by God...in order for Christ's work to "do it away". The scriptures are replete with testimony from Yeshua, the Apostles, and Paul that the Oral Torah was never valid or recognized by God!

We have already discussed that there are many scriptures in the Bible that show clearly that the Oral Torah is not required of believers in Yeshua. Ephesians 2 is not discussing the Oral Torah, nor is it identifying the Oral Torah as the "Middle Wall of Partition". So, what does Ephesians 2 say it is?

> Ephesians 2:2, Wherein in time past ye walked according to the course of this world, according to the prince of the power of the air, <u>the spirit that now worketh in the children of disobedience</u>:3 Among whom also we all had our conversation in times past in the lusts of our flesh, fulfilling the <u>desires of the flesh and of the mind;</u> and were by nature the children of wrath, even as others.

It is this "spirit of disobedience" that keeps us separated from God. This is why we must partake of the Spirit of Christ (the Holy Spirit). Paul is expounding on the Image of God, Yeshua vs. the Image of the Beast, and each spirit that manifests from each image. Can you understand the mystery of iniquity and not understand the Law? One requires the other. Can you understand the image of the beast and not understand the Image of God? One requires the other. Can you understand the administration of grace and not understand the administration of condemnation? One requires the other. Can you understand resurrection and not understand death? One requires the other. Can you understand the Antichrist and not understand the Christ? One requires the other. Let's go back and re-evaluate what the role, purpose, and need is for the Christ, the Image of God, and God manifest in the flesh, Immanuel.

- Romans 8:2, For the <u>law of the Spirit of life in Christ Yeshua hath made me free from the law of sin and death</u>.
- Romans 8:9, But ye are not in the flesh, but in the Spirit, if so be that the Spirit of God dwell in you. Now if <u>any man have not the Spirit of Christ, he is none of his</u>.
- Romans 8:10, And <u>if Christ be in you</u>, the body is dead because of sin; <u>but the Spirit is life because of righteousness</u>.
- Romans 8:11, But if the Spirit of him that raised up Yeshua from the dead dwell in you, he that raised up Christ from the dead shall also quicken your mortal bodies <u>by his Spirit that dwelleth in you</u>.
- 2 Corinthians 3:3, Forasmuch as ye are manifestly declared to be the epistle of Christ ministered by us, written not with ink, but with the Spirit of the living God; not in tablets of stone, but in fleshy tablets of the heart.

It is Christ's spirit that makes intercession between us (who had the spirit of disobedience, now replaced with Christ's Holy Spirit), and God…so that we would not be alienated from God any longer.

Romans 8:27, And he that searcheth the hearts knoweth <u>what is the mind of the Spirit, because he maketh intercession for the saints</u> according to the will of God.

God and man (the two) are made one in one body (Yeshua) by the cross. That Middle Wall of Partition is not the Oral Torah, it is the spirit of disobedience that is replaced with the Spirit of Christ (the Holy Spirit). We will elaborate further on this concept. Suffice to say, some teachers like to claim this new man is a picture of the joining of the House of Israel (Ephraim-Northern 10 tribes of Israel) and the House of Judah.

Ezekiel 37:19, Say unto them, Thus saith the Lord God; Behold, I will take the stick of Joseph, which is in the hand of Ephraim, and the tribes of Israel his fellows, and will put them with him, even with the stick of Judah, and make them one stick, and they shall be one in mine hand.

This concept does apply to Ezekiel 37, and indeed both houses will be joined together in the end time, but as verse 19 shows, they will be joined in "mine hand", which is a prophetic allusion to the Messiah, Yeshua.

However, the context of Ephesians 2 is not the separation between the House of Judah and Israel, it is the separation between God and man, and the cause of that separation, the Middle Wall of Partition, is the spirit of disobedience.

Paul goes into great detail in Ephesians 2 to indicate he is once again talking about death and resurrection and the insufficiency of the Law of Moses under the administration of sin and death.

Ephesians 2:1, And you hath he quickened, who were dead in trespasses and sins; 2 Wherein in time past ye walked according to the course of this world, according to the prince of the power of the air, the spirit that now worketh in the children of disobedience:

Does the Written Torah show this fractal? Yes. Moses is a picture of the heavenly mediator cleansing his brother and his garments so that he might enter within the Tabernacle and perform priestly service unto God. Until Moses provided that intercession for Aaron, he was incapable of entering into the presence of God. He was unclean and could not cleanse himself. Those who are unclean remain outside this Middle Wall of Partition. We see this same pattern of the "less" being blessed of the "better" in Abraham and Melchisedec.

Hebrews 7:1, For this Melchisedec, king of Salem, priest of the most high God, who met Abraham returning from the slaughter of the kings, and blessed him; 2 To whom also Abraham gave a tenth part of all; first being by interpretation King of righteousness, and after that also King of Salem, which is, King of peace; 3 Without father, without mother, without descent, having neither beginning of days, nor end of life; but made like unto the Son of God; abideth a priest continually. 4 Now consider how great this man was, unto whom even the patriarch Abraham gave the tenth of the spoils. 5 And verily they that are of the sons of Levi, who receive the office of the priesthood, have a commandment to take tithes of the people according to the law, that is, of their brethren, though they come out of the loins of Abraham:6 But he whose descent is not counted from them received tithes of Abraham, and blessed him that had the promises. 7 And without all contradiction the less is blessed of the better. 8 And here men that die receive tithes; but there he receiveth them, of whom it is witnessed that he liveth. 9 And as I may so say, Levi also, who receiveth tithes, payed tithes in Abraham. 10 For he was yet in the loins of his father, when Melchisedec met him. 11 If therefore perfection were by the Levitical priesthood, (for under it the people received the law,) what further need was there that another priest should rise after the order of Melchisedec, and not be called after the order of Aaron? 12 For the priesthood being changed, there is made of necessity a change also of the law.

Just as Abraham is blessed by Melchisedec, Aaron needs to have the assistance and blessing of Moses.

Priestly Imagery	
Intercessor	Redeemed
Melchisedec	Abraham
Moses	Aaron & Sons
Yeshua	Us

Numbers 8:5, And the <u>Lord spake unto Moses, saying, 6 Take the Levites from among the children of Israel, and cleanse them</u>. 7 And thus shalt thou do unto them, to cleanse them:<u> Sprinkle water of purifying upon them</u>, and let them shave all their flesh, and let them <u>wash their clothes, and so make themselves clean</u>.

Moses is prophetic of Yeshua after the order of Melchisedec. The Torah's focus was to keep the unclean out of the tabernacle precinct.

- Leviticus 15:30, And the priest shall offer the one for a sin offering, and the other for a burnt offering; and the priest shall <u>make an atonement for her before the Lord for the issue of her uncleanness</u>. 31 Thus shall <u>ye separate the children of Israel from their uncleanness</u>; that they die not in their uncleanness, <u>when they defile my tabernacle that is among them</u>.
- Leviticus 16:16, And he shall make an atonement for the holy place, <u>because of the uncleanness of the children of Israel, and because of their transgressions in all their sins</u>: and so shall he do for the tabernacle of the congregation, that remaineth among them in the midst of their uncleanness.

The Torah is replete with similar examples of when someone is not allowed beyond the Middle Wall of Partition. Later this was characterized as the separation wall between Jews and Gentiles, as the Gentiles were viewed as unclean. What do you do when those within the tabernacle are rendered unclean and under judgment, the same as the Gentiles?

Galatians 3:21, Is the law then against the promises of God? God forbid: for if there had been a law given which could have given life, verily righteousness should have been by the law. 22 But the <u>scripture hath concluded all under sin</u>, that the promise by faith of Yeshua might be given to them that believe. 23 But before faith came, <u>we were kept under the law, shut up unto the faith</u> which should afterwards be revealed.

They, both Jew and Gentile, were determined by God as "under sin" and are one and the same in exile. Both, without Christ, are outside the Middle Wall of Partition and separated from God because of an unclean spirit, the spirit of disobedience. They need someone like Moses, to cleanse them so that they may enter within, just as Moses did for Aaron and his sons. Notice how Paul uses the same terminology of "under sin" and "under the law". Every year the Levitical priests could tell that they had the favor of God and that the sins of Israel were forgiven.

Isaiah 1:18, Come now, and let us reason together, saith the Lord: though your sins be as scarlet, they shall be as white as snow; though they be red like crimson, they shall be as wool.

Then something changed.

Our rabbis taught: During the last forty years before the destruction of the Temple the lot ['For the Lord'] did not come up in the right hand; nor did the crimson–colored strap become white; nor did the western most light shine; and the doors of the Hekel [Temple] would open by themselves (Soncino version, Yoma 39b)

This terminology from Galatians 3:21 indicates that "all" are under condemnation and judgment, the law of sin and death, without the Messiah and His Holy Spirit. Why? We are separated from God and cannot be reconciled to Him without the intercessor that tears down the old Middle Wall of Partition (spirit of disobedience) and creates a new intercessor (mediator) between God and man via the Holy Spirit of Yeshua.

Judah and Israel are the same as all Gentiles, and were rendered unclean and unfit to serve within the tabernacle, hence they are all placed outside that Middle Wall of Partition, separated from God. This is the focus of Ephesians 2.

Seeing that Yeshua's work is purifying our spirit through the removal of the Middle Wall of Partition, we may understand more clearly why Yeshua is frequently healing people of unclean spirits and restoring their minds.

- Mark 5:15, And they come to Yeshua, and see him that was <u>possessed</u> with the devil, and had the legion, sitting, and clothed, <u>and in his right mind</u>: and they were afraid.
- Mark 5:8, For he said unto him, Come out of the man, <u>thou unclean spirit</u>.
- Mark 6:7, And he called unto him the twelve, and began to send them forth by two and two; and <u>gave them power over unclean spirits;</u>
- Luke 4:33, And in the synagogue there was a man, which had a spirit of an unclean devil, and cried out with a loud voice,
- Luke 4:36, And they were all amazed, and spake among themselves, saying, What a word is this! <u>for with authority and power he commandeth the unclean spirits, and they come out.</u>

The emphasis of our deliverance is having a new spirit, a new image, a new mind, a new baptism. Why new? Because the old administration of the Torah of Moses could not deliver us from the spirit of disobedience.

- Romans 3:14, But <u>put ye on the Lord Yeshua</u>, and make not provision for the flesh, to fulfil the lusts thereof.
- Galatians 3:27, For as many of you as <u>have been baptized into Christ have put on Christ</u>.

Putting on Yeshua and being baptized into His name results in His mind being placed within our temple, the heart.

- 1 Peter 3:18, For Christ also hath once suffered for sins, the just for the unjust, that he might bring us to God, being <u>put to death in the flesh, but quickened by the Spirit</u>:
- Romans 8:6, For <u>to be carnally minded is death</u>; but to be <u>spiritually minded</u> is life and peace. 7 Because the <u>carnal mind is enmity against God: for it is not subject to the law of God, neither indeed can be</u>. 8 So then <u>they that are in the flesh cannot please God</u>.
- Romans 8:27, And he that searcheth the hearts knoweth what is <u>the mind of the Spirit, because he maketh intercession for the saints</u> according to the will of God.
- Ephesians 4:23, And <u>be renewed in the spirit of your mind</u>;
- Philippians 2:5, <u>Let this mind be in you, which was also in Christ Yeshua</u>:
- Hebrews 8:10, For this is the covenant that I will make with the house of Israel after those days, saith the Lord; <u>I will put my laws into their mind, and write them in their hearts</u>: and I will be to them a God, and they shall be to me a people:

What intercedes between us and God?   The Spirit of God.

- Romans 8:26, Likewise the Spirit also helpeth our infirmities: for we know not what we should pray for as we ought: but the <u>Spirit itself maketh intercession for us</u> with groanings which cannot be uttered.
- Romans 8:34, Who is he that condemneth? It is <u>Christ that died, yea rather, that is risen again, who is even at the right hand of God, who also maketh intercession for us</u>.
- **He intercedes between what two?**   Israel and Judah?   No. Between us and God.
- Hebrews 7:24, But <u>this man, because he continueth ever, hath an unchangeable priesthood</u>. 25 Wherefore <u>he is able also to save them to the uttermost that come unto God by him</u>, seeing <u>he ever liveth to make intercession for them</u>. 26 For such an high priest became us, who is holy,

harmless, undefiled, <u>separate from sinners</u>, and made higher than the heavens;

Christ has broken down that Middle Wall of Partition between man and God. For what purpose?   To save our flesh?   No; to save our spirit.

1 Corinthians 5:5, To deliver such an one unto Satan <u>for the destruction of the flesh,</u> that <u>the spirit may be saved</u> in the day of the Lord Yeshua.

As Aaron was cleansed by Moses, we are cleansed by Yeshua.

1 Corinthians 6:10, Nor thieves, nor covetous, nor drunkards, nor revilers, nor extortioners, shall inherit the kingdom of God. 11 And such were some of you:<u> but ye are washed</u>, but <u>ye are sanctified</u>, but <u>ye are justified in the Name of the Lord Yeshua, and by the Spirit of our God</u>. 12 All things are lawful unto me, but all things are not expedient: all things are lawful for me, but I will not be brought under the power of any.

How are we are cleansed and justified?   By the Spirit of our God and by the Name of the Lord Yeshua.

Are you starting to see the pattern?
- Flesh then spirit
- Spirit of disobedience then the Spirit of Christ
- The fallen mind then the exalted mind
- Death then resurrection life
- Moses then Yeshua
- Torah of Sin and Death then the Torah of Resurrection Life

There are two administrations and two administrators. Both were intercessors and mediators between us and God. One was not able to save (death), the other is able to save (resurrection life).

GRAFTED INTO AND FOR WHAT PURPOSE?
Are we established by being in Israel? No. How then?

2 Corinthians 1:21, Now he which <u>stablisheth us with you in Christ,</u> and hath anointed us, is God; 22 Who hath also <u>sealed us, and given the earnest of the Spirit in our hearts.</u>

Ephesians 2 comes sharply into focus. You were dead, and now in Christ are made alive.

Ephesians 2:1, And you hath he quickened, <u>who were dead in trespasses and sins;</u>

What were we without? The Torah? No.

Ephesians 2:12, That at that time <u>ye were without Christ</u>, being aliens from the Commonwealth of Israel, and strangers from the covenants of promise, having no hope, <u>and without God in the world</u>:

Being without Christ, we had no covenant with God and were therefore separated from _____?

- Israel
- Judah
- The Torah
- God

The correct answer is given in Ephesians 2:12, "and without God in the world". It is so plain to see that the Middle Wall of Partition that is separating us from God is our spirit of disobedience.

Ephesians 2:2, Wherein in time past ye walked according to the course of this world, according to the prince of the power of the air, the <u>spirit that now worketh in the children of disobedience</u>:

What tears down this Middle Wall of Partition separating us and God?

Ephesians 2:13, <u>But now in Christ Yeshua ye who sometimes were far off are made nigh by the blood of Christ</u>.

We are made near by the blood of Christ, which grants to us His Holy Spirit. Christ is reconciling "both" unto God. Both need deliverance.

Who are the "both" of Ephesians 2:16, "And that he might <u>reconcile both unto God</u> in one body by the cross, having slain the enmity thereby"?

- Gentiles
- Jews
- Jews and Gentiles

The correct answer is "Jews and Gentiles".

Romans 3:9, What then? Are we better than they? No, in no wise: for we have before proved both Jews and Gentiles, that <u>they are all under sin</u>;

Being under sin, we are separated from God and under condemnation and death. We are both, Jews and Gentiles, made near unto God by Yeshua's blood.

The principal issue of Ephesians 2 is being separated from _____?

A. "Aliens of the Commonwealth of Israel"
B. "Strangers from the Covenants of Promise"
C. "Having no hope"

D. "Being without God in the World"
E. All of the Above
F. A, B, and C are systemic of D, "Being without God in the World"

The correct answer is F, A, B, and C are systemic of "D Being without God in the World".

Why not only A? Israel was under the Torah of Sin and Death and still is without the new administrator, the Messiah Yeshua.

Why not only B? The Covenants of Promise were broken.

Why not only C? They could not bring hope to themselves and effect their own salvation.

Why not only D? They could not approach God, God does the calling.

Why not all of the above? It does not answer what the root cause of the separation is and who you are separated from.

Jews and Gentiles are both under sin. Both are freed by Yeshua, by His body on the cross. Is Israel's body on the cross? No. Is Judah's body on the cross? No. Is the Commonwealth of Israel on the cross? No. Is the Covenant of Promise on the cross? No.

Is God manifest in the flesh on the cross? Yes.

Why is God manifest on the cross? Because being under sin and death we were separated from God and without God in the world.

If we have a spirit of disobedience separated from God, what then is the Middle Wall of Partition? Is it the Oral Torah separating the Gentiles from the Jews? No, both the Jews and the Gentiles are one under sin and death.

Ephesians 2:14, For he is our peace, who hath made both one, and hath broken down the middle wall of partition between us; 15 Having abolished in his flesh the enmity, even the law of commandments contained in ordinances; for to make in himself of twain one new man, so making peace; 16 And that he might reconcile both unto God in one body by the cross, having slain the enmity thereby:

We are all far off because we are all under sin. We need to draw near to God, since we are separated from Him. We are separated from God, because He hates sin, therefore He has enmity against us.

Ephesians 2:13, But now in Christ Yeshua ye who sometimes were far off are made nigh by the blood of Christ. 14 For he is our peace, who hath made both one, and hath broken down the middle wall of partition between us;

Christ has paid the penalty of sins, our violations of the Torah as described in Ephesians 2:15 allowing God's enmity to be removed and for us to draw near. We are separated from God by His hatred of our spirit of disobedience that has now been replaced by Christ's Holy spirit.

Who is the "ye" of Ephesians 2:13? Those separated from God by the spirit of disobedience and those under sin and death, both Jews and Gentiles, who are now "made nigh by the blood of Christ."

Is this one new man Yeshua or Israel? Paul has already identified that both Jews and Gentiles are in the same state of separation from God and under enmity. Paul has also confirmed that both Jews and Gentiles must come through the new administrator, Yeshua the Messiah. He is the one new man.

Ephesians 2:13, But now in Christ Yeshua ye who sometimes were far off are made nigh by the blood of Christ. 14 For he is our peace, who hath made both one, and hath broken down the middle wall of partition between us; 15 Having abolished in his flesh the enmity, even the law of commandments contained in ordinances; for to make in himself of twain one new man, so making peace; 16 And that he might reconcile both unto God in one body by the cross, having slain the enmity thereby:

Some teachers would like to tell you that the "us" and the "twain" are Judah and Israel. The House of Judah and Israel will be united as the prophets testify but Ephesians 2 is talking about God and man, not Israel and Judah. For those of you who are still doubters, Paul seals the deal.

Ephesians 2:17, And came and preached peace to you which were afar off, and to them that were nigh. 18 For through him we both have access by one Spirit unto the Father.

Both Jews and Gentiles need to have the Gospel preached to them so that they may enter into Yeshua and His Body. Notice Paul says "through Him" and "we both" to identify who we are redeemed through ("Him"-Yeshua) and who is redeemed ("we both"–Jews and Gentiles). Being near or far off does not change your status. We are all under sin and death and all need to express faith in the new administrator of resurrection life, Yeshua the Messiah. The far off are not grafted into the near. Both the far off and the near are grafted "into the Lord" (Isaiah 56:3)! **Why?** So, both can have access by Yeshua's spirit to the Father.

Ephesians 2:5, Even when we were dead in sins, hath quickened us together with Christ, (by grace ye are saved;) 6 And hath raised us up together, and made us sit together in heavenly places in Christ Yeshua:

Let's analyze Ephesians 2 to determine if this is describing the separation of Israel and Judah, Israel and the Gentiles, or God and man.

EPHESIANS 2 ANALYSIS VERSE BY VERSE:
v1 And you hath he quickened, who were dead in trespasses and sins;
* Death and resurrection are being contrasted.

- **Without Christ versus having Christ.**

v2 Wherein in time past ye walked according to the course of this world, according to the prince of the power of the air, the spirit that now worketh in the children of disobedience:
- Those now redeemed were as others under the spirit of disobedience.
- And now are **redeemed by Christ.**

v3 Among whom also we all had our conversation in times past in the lusts of our flesh, fulfilling the desires of the flesh and of the mind; and were by nature the children of wrath, even as others.
- Our fallen state was focused on the flesh and as such we were children of wrath, those who are exiled.
- Our present state is **focused on the flesh.**

v4 But God, who is rich in mercy, for his great love wherewith he loved us,
- Who are the "us"? These children of wrath who are exiled from God.
- Our redemption is initiated **by God through His mercy.**

v5 Even when we were dead in sins, hath quickened us together with Christ, (by grace ye are saved ;)
- The remedy from this exile from God is to be quickened alive in Christ.
- **Quickened with Christ.**

v6 And hath raised us up together, and made us sit together in heavenly places in Christ Yeshua:
- Who is the us? It is us (Redeemed Jews & Gentiles).
- Verse 5 detailed that this is how we leave sin and death and are resurrected to life.
- **Raised with Christ.**

v7 That in the ages to come he might shew the exceeding riches of his grace in his kindness toward us through Christ Yeshua.
- **Who is the "he"?** It is God.
- **Who is the "us"?** Those who were in exile from God.
- **Through "whom"?** Christ Yeshua
- **Through Christ.**

v8 For by grace are ye saved through faith; and that not of yourselves: it is the gift of God:
- We are saved by grace through faith by God.
- We cannot end the separation.
- **By grace and faith from God.**

v9 Not of works, lest any man should boast.
- Nothing we can do can cause that resurrection to occur.
- Not by our works.
- **All are under sin.**

v10 For we are his workmanship, created in Christ Yeshua unto good works, which God hath before ordained that we should walk in them.
- **Who is the "we"?** Those in Christ
- **Created in "who"?** Christ Yeshua
- **For what purpose?** Unto good works.
- **Created in Christ.**

v11 Wherefore remember, that ye being in time past Gentiles in the flesh, who are called Uncircumcision by that which is called the Circumcision in the flesh made by hands;
- Those with the spirit of disobedience are of the flesh.
- Without Christ, our status is flesh.
- **With Christ, our status is spirit.**

v12 That at that time ye were without Christ, being aliens from the Commonwealth of Israel, and strangers from the covenants of promise, having no hope, and without God in the world:
- **What caused the spirit of disobedience and being of the flesh?**
  - We were without Christ.
- Being without Christ, we are therefore without God in the world.
- Our problem is being without Christ.
- **Without Christ, we are without God in the world.**

v13 But now in Christ Yeshua ye who sometimes were far off are made nigh by the blood of Christ.
- **How can we avoid being without God?** Be in Christ Yeshua.
- **What are we afar off from?** God (see verse 12)
- **Our solution is presented…in Christ, by His blood.**

v14 For he is our peace, who hath made both one, and hath broken down the middle wall of partition between us;
- Christ has made both one.
- **Who is the both?**
  - Israel & Judah? No.
  - Jew & Gentile? No.
  - You and Yeshua? No, it is through Yeshua.
  - **You and God? Yes.**
- Notice Paul is talking to the Ephesians about our peace (shalom or

oneness) after stating they had been without God in the world. It is hard to conceive within the context of Ephesians 2 that he is referring to the "miracle" of Oral Torah "not being required" as the great work of Yeshua, so that Gentiles can draw near to Israel.

- Paul has already indicated Jew and Gentile are both under sin, so conceivably they are not separate in the eyes of God, and both are outside the Middle Wall of Partition separated from God.
- Paul starts and ends Ephesians 2 stating that we are separated from God due to the spirit of disobedience of man. (See verse 4, 12, 18, 21).

v15 Having abolished in his flesh the enmity, even the law of commandments contained in ordinances; for to make in himself of twain one new man, so making peace;
- **The enmity is between?**
    - Israel and Judah? No.
    - Jew and Gentile? No.
    - You and Yeshua? No, it is through Yeshua.
    - You and God? Yes.
- **Who is the twain?**
    - Israel and Judah? No.
    - Jew and Gentile? No.
    - You and Yeshua? No, it is through Yeshua.
    - **You and God? Yes.**
    - Paul starts and ends Ephesians 2 stating that we (mankind) are separated from God due to the spirit of disobedience. (See verse 4, 12, 18, 21). Paul's focus is the enmity caused by our sin and the subsequent removal of God's presence from the world.

v16 And that he might reconcile both unto God in one body by the cross, having slain the enmity thereby:
- **Who is the body?** Paul has already stated it is by Yeshua, "raised up together", "through Christ Yeshua", "created in Christ Yeshua", "with Christ Yeshua", "now in Christ Yeshua", and "make in himself one new man".
- Paul addresses who the enmity is between, "both unto God" (see verses 1–3). Those now redeemed along with the others under the spirit of disobedience that receive Christ Yeshua are restored to God.
- The enmity is God's hatred for those under the spirit of disobedience.

v17 And came and preached peace to you which were afar off, and to them that were nigh.
- **Who is the "afar" and the "nigh"?** Both Jews and Gentiles, as both are under sin and death.
- Both need the Gospel of the new administration of resurrection life.
    - Galatians 3:22, But the scripture hath concluded all

under sin, that the promise by faith of Yeshua might be given to them that believe.

- Notice verse 19, The former "strangers" are now "fellow citizens" with the saints who have accepted Yeshua. These are the "we both" in verse 18.

v18 For through him we both have access by one Spirit unto the Father.
- **Who is the "through him"?** Paul has already identified that it is Yeshua.
- Who is the "we both"? Those now redeemed and those others under the spirit of disobedience that have now received Christ Yeshua.

- **The end goal is access by one Spirit (Yeshua) to the Father.**

v19 Now therefore ye are no more strangers and foreigners, but fellowcitizens with the saints, and of the household of God;
- **What is the outcome of having Yeshua's spirit?** The redeemed are fellowcitizens of Israel? No, the context of Ephesians 2 is focused on deliverance in, though, and by Yeshua. The answer is given plainly that we are fellow citizens with others that have expressed faith in Yeshua.
- **We are fellow citizens in the household of God, Yeshua.**
- This ties to verse 10, "For we are his workmanship, <u>created in Christ Yeshua</u> unto good works, which God hath before ordained that we should walk in them."
- Hebrews 3:6, But <u>Christ as a son over his own house; whose house are we</u>, if we hold fast the confidence and the rejoicing of the hope firm unto the end.
- The former "strangers" are now "fellow citizens" with the saints who have accepted Yeshua. These are the "we both" in verse 18.
- The "household of God" is Christ.

v20 And are built upon the foundation of the Apostles and Prophets, Yeshua himself being the chief corner stone;
- We are built upon Christ, the Apostles, and the Prophets.

v21 In whom all the building fitly framed together groweth unto an holy temple in the Lord:
- **The outcome is a temple wherein God can reside**, as it is holy.
- Matthew 26:61, And said, This fellow said, I am able to destroy the temple of God, and to build it in three days.
- Romans 8:11, But if the Spirit of him that raised up Yeshua from the dead dwell in you, he that raised up Christ from the dead shall also <u>quicken your mortal bodies by his Spirit that dwelleth in you.</u>

v22 In whom <u>ye also are builded together for an habitation of God through the Spirit</u>.

- We become one with God's temple through the Spirit.
- Romans 8:9, But ye are not in the flesh, but in the Spirit, if so be that the Spirit of God dwell in you. Now if any man have not the Spirit of Christ, he is none of his.

Ephesians chapter two is an elaborate explanation of the events of Genesis 3 and the breaking of the original Image of God and how His image is restored by the promised seed of the Messiah.

Genesis 3:15, And <u>I will put enmity between thee and the woman, and between thy seed and her seed</u>; it shall bruise thy head, and thou shalt bruise his heel.

Paul elaborates on the promised seed of the Messiah and His role as the "Image of God".

2 Corinthians 4:4, In whom the god of this world hath blinded the minds of them which believe not, lest the light of the <u>glorious Gospel of Christ, who is the Image of God</u>, should shine unto them.

The image and Countenance of God is central to the Aaronic Benediction, which focuses upon the transcription of the Countenance of God onto the believer via the utterance of the High Priest.

Colossians 1:12, Giving thanks unto the Father, which hath made us meet to be <u>partakers of the inheritance of the saints in light</u>:13 Who hath delivered us from the power of darkness, and hath <u>translated us into the kingdom of his dear Son</u>:14 In whom <u>we have redemption through his blood</u>, even the forgiveness of sins:15 <u>Who is the image of the invisible God</u>, the firstborn of every creature:16 For by him were all things created, that are in heaven, and that are in earth, visible and invisible, whether they be thrones, or dominions, or principalities, or powers: all things were created by him, and for him:17 And he is before all things, and by him all things consist. 18 And he is the head of the body, the church: who is the beginning, the firstborn from the dead; that in all things he might have the preeminence. 19 For it pleased the Father that in him should all fulness dwell; 20 And, <u>having made peace through the blood of his cross, by him to reconcile all things unto himself; by him</u>, I say, whether they be things in earth, or things in heaven. 21 And <u>you, that were sometime alienated and enemies in your mind</u> by wicked works, <u>yet now hath he reconciled</u> 22 <u>In the body of his flesh through death, to present you</u> holy and unblameable and unreproveable in his sight:23 <u>If ye continue in the faith</u> grounded and settled, <u>and be not moved away from the hope of the Gospel</u>, which ye have heard, <u>and which was preached to every creature</u>

which is under heaven; whereof I Paul am made a minister; 24 Who now rejoice in my sufferings for you, and fill up that which is behind of the afflictions of Christ in my flesh for his body's sake, which is the church:25 Whereof I am made a minister, according to the dispensation of God which is given to me for you, to fulfil the word of God; 26 Even the mystery which hath been hid from ages and from generations, but now is made manifest to his saints:27 To whom God would make known what is the riches of the glory of this mystery among the Gentiles; which is Christ in you, the hope of glory:28 Whom we preach, warning every man, and teaching every man in all wisdom; that we may present every man perfect in Christ Yeshua:29 Whereunto I also labour, striving according to his working, which worketh in me mightily.

It is the restoration of God's image that is the central purpose and theme of the work of the Messiah. It is His seed that ensures our redemption. Notice this Gospel is not just preached to Judah, exiled Israel, or to the Gentiles. It is to be "preached to every creature which is under heaven" (Colossians 1:23). Every creature under the current administration of condemnation and death (the flesh) needs their image restored in Christ Yeshua (spirit). This is also the central issue during the Great Tribulation.

Revelation 15:2, And I saw as it were a sea of glass mingled with fire: and them that had gotten the victory over the beast, and over his image, and over his mark, and over the number of his name, stand on the sea of glass, having the harps of God.

Paul elaborates on how God is full of wrath over the breaking of His image in man.

Romans 1:18, For the wrath of God is revealed from heaven against all ungodliness and unrighteousness of men, who hold the truth in unrighteousness; 19 Because that which may be known of God is manifest in them; for God hath shewed it unto them. 20 For the invisible things of him from the creation of the world are clearly seen, being understood by the things that are made, even his eternal power and Godhead; so that they are without excuse:21 Because that, when they knew God, they glorified him not as God, neither were thankful; but became vain in their imaginations, and their foolish heart was darkened. 22 Professing themselves to be wise, they became fools, 23 And changed the glory of the uncorruptible God into an image made like to corruptible man, and to birds, and fourfooted beasts, and creeping things. 24 Wherefore God also gave them up to uncleanness through the lusts of their own hearts, to dishonour their own bodies between themselves:25 Who changed the truth of God into a lie, and worshipped and served the creature more than the Creator, who is blessed for ever. Amen.

This Godly wrath is centered upon the corruption of His image in man through the spirit of disobedience that man willfully embraced causing his own separation from God. These are not coincidental thematic connections related to: image, wrath, separation, corruption, and darkness. They repeat over and over again as biblical fractals and patterns.

From start to finish Paul is focusing on our fallen state that is subject to sin and death, being without Christ and therefore without God in the world. He states that because of the spirit of disobedience that causes our separation from God, we can only approach God through Yeshua's spirit. Without His spirit, we are separated from God because of His anger over our transgressions of the Law of Moses (Ephesians 2:15). Without Christ both Jew and Gentile are under sin and death and need to accept the administrator of Resurrection life.

Those that say that the goal of Ephesians 2 is to draw nigh to Judah or Israel or to be grafted into Judah or Israel clearly do not understand man's fundamental problem, that God will not dwell in a house of sin or with those who have a broken image.

Matthew 23:38, Behold, <u>your house is left unto you desolate</u>. 39 For I say unto you, Ye shall not see me henceforth, till ye shall say, <u>Blessed is he that cometh in the Name of the Lord</u>.

As a result of Yeshua's redemptive work between man and God, will Israel and Judah be united? Yes, but Ephesians 2 is not talking about that as the principal theme or problem that is remedied by Christ.

What is Israel/Judah's status with God? They are just like the Gentiles. They need to be in Christ and through Christ. Why? They must leave being under the administration of sin and death and transition to the new administration of resurrection life. The "we both" and the "us" focus upon sinful man and God being reconciled by Yeshua's spirit, casting down the enmity and the Middle Wall of Partition between man and God. This is what Ephesians 2 is focusing upon.

Paul is setting the ground work of the two administrations of the Torah, death and resurrection life. To suggest that the enmity is between Judah and Israel or Israel and the Gentiles due to the Middle Wall of Partition denies the clarity of Ephesians 2.

Ephesians 2:2, Wherein in time past ye walked according to the course of this world, according to the prince of the power of the air, <u>the spirit that now worketh in the children of disobedience</u>:3 Among whom also <u>we all had our conversation in times past</u> in the lusts of our <u>flesh,</u> fulfilling the desires of the <u>flesh and of the mind;</u> and were <u>by nature the children of wrath</u>, even <u>as others</u>.

The issue is that there is enmity between two parties, and this enmity is caused by wrath of one of the parties due to the conduct of the other. To suggest Ephesians 2:15 is saying this enmity is between the Jews and the Gentiles due to the Oral Torah and ignore the context of the earlier and later verses about man's separation from God is a significant flaw in their logic. Notice Paul is contrasting our corrupt flesh with Yeshua, and that the remedy is brought about by a change in our image.

Ephesians 5:15, Having abolished <u>in his flesh the enmity</u>, even the law of commandments contained in ordinances; for to make in himself of twain one new man, <u>so making peace</u>; 16 And that he might reconcile both <u>unto God in one body by the cross, having slain the enmity thereby</u>:

Clearly the enmity is between us (those in the flesh, Jews and Gentiles) and God. It is through a new image, Yeshua's blood and body, that the enmity between us (all mankind) and God is remedied.

Ephesians 2:18, For through him we both have access by one Spirit unto the Father.

Again, to suggest that Ephesians 2:14–16 is referring to the Oral Torah as the Middle Wall of Partition between Jews and Gentiles has several scriptural unintended consequences.

Ephesians 2:14, For <u>he is our peace</u>, who <u>hath made both one</u>, and hath <u>broken down the middle wall of partition between us</u>; 15 Having <u>abolished in his flesh the enmity, even the law of commandments contained in ordinances</u>; for to make in himself of twain one new man, so making peace;

Avi Ben Mordechai and many Hebrew Roots (Messianic) teachers will say this Middle Wall of Partition is the law of commandments contained in ordinances otherwise called the Oral Torah. You can find Avi's interpretation of Ephesians 2 on page 325 of his Galatians Commentary.

If you follow Avi's train of thought, it means that the great work of Yeshua was to tear down an Oral Torah that separated Jews and Gentiles and make them one. What are the unintended consequences of his interpretation? If you accept that this is Yeshua's work on the cross (Ephesians 2:15–16), you imply that God saw the rabbinic Oral Torah as valid and enforced by His command and that all the people indeed should have been keeping the Written and the Oral Torah to remain in covenant with Him. If it was validated by God, the people were under sin and death by the Oral Torah at God's will.

Of course, we have already established from the beginning that Yeshua taught that God did not endorse the Oral Torah, the traditions of the elders, the traditions of the rabbis, or the traditions of men. In fact, Paul establishes in many other scriptures that he is in full agreement with Yeshua that the Oral Torah has never been required to be in covenant with God.

- Matthew 15:3, But he answered and said unto them, Why do ye also transgress the commandment of God by your tradition?
- Matthew 15:6, And honour not his father or his mother, he shall be free. Thus have ye made the commandment of God of none effect by your tradition.
- Mark 7:8, For laying aside the commandment of God, ye hold the

tradition of men, as the washing of pots and cups: and many other such like things ye do.

- Mark 7:9, And he said unto them, Full well ye reject the commandment of God, that ye may keep your own tradition.
- Colossians 2:8, Beware lest any man spoil you through philosophy and vain deceit, after the tradition of men, after the rudiments of the world, and not after Christ.
- Galatians 1:14, And profited in the Jews' religion above many my equals in mine own nation, being more exceedingly zealous of the traditions of my fathers.

These scriptures are sufficient to clearly prove that Yeshua and Paul firmly reject the Oral Torah as a requirement to remain in covenant with God. Aside from that, we can see clearly from the Tanach that there is no validity to the idea of an Oral Torah that supersedes the Written Torah.

Joshua 8:34, And afterward he read all the words of the law (Towrah-Strongs 8451), the blessings and cursings, according to all that is written in the book of the law (Towrah-Strongs 8451). 35 There was not a word of all that Moses commanded, which Joshua read not before all the congregation of Israel, with the women, and the little ones, and the strangers that were conversant among them.

"There was not a word of all that Moses commanded, which Joshua read not before all the congregation of Israel..." What are the implications of this statement? Everything was written in the book of the Law, the Written Torah, and by consequence there is no Oral Torah. All that God commanded, Moses wrote in the Book of the Law. There is no Oral Torah acknowledged by God.

To say that the "law of commandments contained in ordinances" from Ephesians 2:15 is the Oral Torah that Yeshua came to do away with is to imply that this same Oral Torah was initially recognized, endorsed, approved, and required of God. Yeshua and Paul have already made it clear that this is not the case.

WHICH LAW?
Furthermore, this same term "law of commandments contained in ordinances" is used in Luke 1:1–7.

Luke 1:1, Forasmuch as many have taken in hand to set forth in order a declaration of those things which are most surely believed among us, 2 Even as they delivered them unto us, which from the beginning were eyewitnesses, and ministers of the word; 3 It seemed good to me also, having had perfect understanding of all things from the very first, to write unto thee in order, most excellent Theophilus, 4 That thou mightest know the certainty of those things, wherein thou hast been instructed. 5 There was in the days of Herod, the king of Judaea, a certain priest named Zacharias, of the course of Abia: and his wife was of the daughters of Aaron, and her name was Elisabeth. 6 And they were

<u>both righteous before God, walking in all the commandments (Entole–Strong's 1785) and ordinances (Dikaioma–Strong's 1345) of the Lord blameless</u>.

Entole:
The KJV New Testament Greek Lexicon
Strong's Number:1785
Original Word Origin:
ejntolhv from (1781)
Transliterated Word TDNT Entry
Entole 2:545, 234
Phonetic Spelling Parts of Speech
en–tol–ay'   Noun Feminine
Definition:
·an order, command, charge, precept, injunction that which is prescribed to one by reason of his office
·a commandment a prescribed rule in accordance with which a thing is done a precept relating to lineage, of the Mosaic precept concerning the priesthood
·ethically used of the commandments in the Mosaic law or Jewish tradition
King James Word Usage–Total:71
commandment 69, precept 2

Dikaioma:
The KJV New Testament Greek Lexicon
Strong's Number:1345
Original Word Origin:
dikaivwma from (1344)
Transliterated Word TDNT Entry
Dikaioma 2:219, 168
Phonetic Spelling Parts of Speech
dik–ah'–yo–mah   Noun Neuter
Definition:
·that which has been deemed right so as to have force of law what has been established, and ordained by law, an ordinance
·a judicial decision, sentence of God 1b

·either the favourable judgment by which he acquits man and declares them acceptable to Him 1b
·unfavourable:sentence of condemnation
·a righteous act or deed
King James Word Usage–Total:10
righteousness 4, ordinance 3, judgment 2, justification 1

Both Luke 1:6 and Ephesians 2:15 use the same terminology, the "law of commandments contained in ordinances".

Ephesians 2:15, Having abolished in his flesh the enmity, even <u>the law (Nomos–Strong's 3551) of commandments (Entole–Strong's 1785) contained in ordinances (Dogma–Strong's 1378)</u>; for to make in himself of twain one new man, so making peace;

Nomos:
The KJV New Testament Greek Lexicon
Strong's Number:3551
Original Word Origin:
novmoß from a primary nemo (to parcel out, especially food or grazing to animals)
Transliterated Word TDNT Entry
Nomos 4:1022, 646
Phonetic Spelling Parts of Speech
nom'–os   Noun Masculine
Definition:
·anything established, anything received by usage, a custom, a law, a command of any law whatsoever a law or rule producing a state approved of God.
·By the observance of which is approved of God a precept or injunction the rule of action prescribed by reason
·of the Mosaic law, and referring, acc. to the context. either to the volume of the law or to its contents
·the Christian religion:the law demanding faith, the moral instruction given by Christ, esp. the precept concerning love
·the name of the more important part (the Pentateuch), is put for the entire collection of the sacred books of the OT
King James Word Usage–Total:197
law 197

Dogma
The KJV New Testament Greek Lexicon
Strong's Number:1378
Original Word Origin:
dovgma from the base of (1380)
Transliterated Word TDNT Entry
Dogma 2:230, 178
Phonetic Spelling Parts of Speech
dog'–mah   Noun Neuter
Definition:
·doctrine, decree, ordinance of public decrees
·of the Roman Senate
·of rulers
·the rules and requirements of the law of Moses; carrying a suggestion of severity and of threatened judgment
·of certain decrees of the Apostles relative to right living
King James Word Usage–Total:5
decree 3, ordinance 2

The difference between the word used for "ordinances" (Dogma–Strong's 1378) in Ephesians 2:15 is that it has the definition of "severity of threatened judgment" or guilt of violating the Law, where in Luke 1:6, "Ordinances" (Dikaioma, Strong's 1345) has a definition of "favourable judgment by which he acquits". Both are referring to the same Law of Moses; Ephesians 2:15 is implying that the accused is guilty of violation of the Law of Moses, whereas in Luke 1:6, Zacharias and Elisabeth have been determined by "God" to be innocent of any violation of the Law of Moses.

Luke 1:6 says very clearly that the evaluation of Zacharias and his wife was "before God", not any earthly judge, and they were both determined to be blameless in regard to walking in all the commandments and ordinances of the Lord.

Simple logic should tell you if the term "the law of commandments contained in ordinances" means the Oral Torah, then Luke 1:6 is telling you that the Oral Torah is valid and is used as a measuring stick of judgment by God. So, then we have a problem. Why? Yeshua and Paul have already plainly stated that God does not use the Oral Torah for judgment.

What conclusion can we then draw? That "the law of commandments contained in ordinances" is the Written Torah, which leaves us under condemnation and becomes a Torah of Sin and Death that must be annulled and be replaced with the Torah of Resurrection Life with its new administrator, Yeshua the Messiah. He qualified for that role by the power of an eternal life.

This issue is rather simple when you look through the fractal of death and resurrection, which is the central message of Paul the Apostle. Now if Luke 1:6 had said that Zacharias and his wife were both righteous before the rabbis, you might have a leg to stand on when saying "the law of commandments contained in ordinances" is the Oral Torah. It does not. You should now be able to see that death and resurrection is the breaking and restoration of the Image of God.

Genesis 1:26, And God said, <u>Let us make man in our image, after our likeness</u>: and let them have dominion over the fish of the sea, and over the fowl of the air, and over the cattle, and over all the earth, and over every creeping thing that creepeth upon the earth.

This Image of God was broken by the spirit of disobedience displayed in Genesis 3.

Genesis 3:13, And the Lord God said unto the woman, What is this that thou hast done? And the woman said, The serpent beguiled me, and I did eat. 14 And the Lord God said unto the serpent, Because thou hast done this, thou art cursed above all cattle, and above every beast of the field; upon thy belly shalt thou go, and dust shalt thou eat all the days of thy life:15 And <u>I will put enmity between thee and the woman, and between thy seed and her seed; it shall bruise thy head, and thou shalt bruise his heel</u>.

This broken image was cursed by God, exiled from the Garden of Eden and subjected to sin and death. The hope of their redemption occurs with the promised "seed of the woman", the Messiah.

Genesis 3:19, In the sweat of thy face shalt thou eat bread, till thou return unto the ground; for out of it wast thou taken: for dust thou art, and <u>unto dust shalt thou return</u>.

The fractal of death and resurrection, seed then fruit, was set from the beginning. Adam no longer produced in God's image, but after the fall, they only produced seed after his own fallen image.

Genesis 5:1, This is the book of the generations of Adam. In the day that God created man, in the likeness of God made he him; 2 Male and female created he them; and blessed them, and called their name Adam, in the day when they were created. 3 And Adam lived an hundred and thirty years, and <u>begat a son in his own likeness, and after his image</u>; and called his name Seth:

This broken image needed to be restored to God, by restoring the true Image of God. This is the work of the Messiah. Paul is not merely talking about a separation between Jews and Gentiles or the House of Judah and the House of Israel. He is talking about the creation being separated from the Father. Ephesians is not talking about the removal of the Oral Torah as the great work of the Messiah. "Commandments" (Entole–Strong's number 1785) in Luke 1:6 is defined as "commandments in the Mosaic law". Ephesians 6:2 uses the same word, "Entole", and shows this is the Written Torah and not the Oral Torah.

Ephesians 6:2, Honour thy father and mother; (which is the first commandment (Entole–Strong's 1785) with promise ;)

The word "Law" (Nomos) is also used in Ephesians 2:15.

Ephesians 2:15, Having abolished in his flesh the enmity, even the law ("of the Mosaic Law"–Nomos–Strong's 3551) of commandments (Entole–Strong's 1785) contained in ordinances (Dogma–Strong's 1378); for to make in himself of twain one new man, so making peace;

Clearly, we have both scriptures referring to the Written Torah of Moses. The term "Ordinances" is basically the same in Ephesians 2:15 with the slight difference that in Luke 1:6 it is with a positive connotation of being in conformance with the Written Torah of Moses, which has the allusion of the righteousness of Zachariah and his wife. In Ephesians 2:15 it connotes our violation of the Written Law (Torah) which leaves us under the judgment of sin and death. The key emphasis is the issue of being under condemnation or not under condemnation of the Written Law of Moses.

Let's review the words used for "ordinances" one more time so there is no confusion later. "Ordinances" (Dikaioma, Strong's 1345) in Luke 1:6, is defined as being "ordained by the Law (Torah)". Dikaioma is used here because it connotes "adherence or righteousness and conformance to the Law (the Written Torah)". However, in Ephesians 2:15, "Ordinances" uses the term Dogma– (Dogma–Strong's 1378) meaning "rule and requirements of the law of Moses; carrying a suggestion of severity and of threatened judgment". This term is used for man's stated spirit of disobedience and consequential universal status of man as being in exile from God. Fallen man is under wrath and judgment for violation of the Written Torah.

Galatians 3:22, But the scripture hath concluded all under sin, that the promise by faith of Yeshua might be given to them that believe.

Colossians bears out this fact by using the same word "Dogma" indicating the judgment against us and our impending doom without Yeshua.

Colossians 2:14, Blotting out the handwriting of ordinances (Dogma–Strong's 1378) that was against us, which was contrary to us, and took it out of the way, nailing it to his cross;

Take notice that each of these scriptures is discussing the Written Torah. On the contrary, each and every time Yeshua or Paul criticize the Oral Torah, the Oral Law, the Traditions of men, the Tradition of the Elders, Commandments of Men, or the Tradition of the rabbis, they use a different word. They use the word "Paradosis" (Strong's 3862) meaning ritual that was orally transmitted.

Paradosis:
The KJV New Testament Greek Lexicon
Strong's Number:3862
Original Word Origin:
paravdosiß from (3860)
Transliterated Word TDNT Entry
Paradosis 2:172, 166
Phonetic Spelling Parts of Speech
par–ad'–os–is   Noun Feminine
Definition:
·giving up, giving over the act of giving up
the surrender of cities
·a giving over which is done by word of mouth or in writing, i. e. tradition by instruction, narrative, precept, etc. objectively, that which is delivered, the substance of a teaching
·of the body of precepts, esp. ritual, which in the opinion of the later Jews were orally delivered by Moses and orally transmitted in unbroken succession to subsequent generations, which precepts, both illustrating and expanding the Written Law, as they did were to be obeyed with equal reverence
King James Word Usage–Total:13
tradition 12, ordinance 1

Here are some examples of Yeshua referring to the rabbi's Oral Laws that violate His Written Law of Moses.

- Matthew 15:2, Why do thy disciples transgress the tradition (Paradosis–Strong's 3862) of the elders? for they wash not their hands when they eat bread.
- Mark 7:3, For the Pharisees, and all the Jews, except they wash their hands oft, eat not, holding the tradition (Paradosis–Strong's 3862) of the elders.
- Mark 7:8, For laying aside the commandment (Entole–Strong's 1785) of God, ye hold the tradition (Paradosis–Strong's 3862) of men, as the washing of pots and cups: and many other such like things ye do.

Notice how in the above scriptures we see "Entole" (Strong's 1785-Written Law of Moses) being contrasted with "Paradosis" (Strong's 3862)– (Oral Law or Tradition). Yeshua is clearly saying that their Paradosis (Oral Law) is violating His Entole (Written Law). Logically we can deduce that Entole is not "Rabbinical Oral Law or Tradition", it is the "Written Law of Moses". Sometimes the word Entalma (Strong's 1778) is used, meaning "precept" which is used to describe these same traditions or commandments of men and not of God.

- Matthew 15:9, But in vain they do worship me, teaching for doctrines the commandments (Entalma–Strong's 1778) of men.
- Mark 7:7, Howbeit in vain do they worship me, teaching for doctrines the commandments (Entalma–Strong's 1778) of men.
- Colossians 2:22, Which all are to perish with the using;) after the commandments (Entalma–Strong's 1778) and doctrines of men?

Entalma
The KJV New Testament Greek Lexicon
Strong's Number:1778
Original Word:
e[ntalma
Word Origin:
from (1781)
Transliterated Word:
Entalma
Phonetic Spelling:
en'–tal–mah
Parts of Speech:
Noun Neuter
Definition:
1. a precept
King James Word Usage–Total:3
commandment 3

In summary, to claim that Ephesians 2 is saying that Yeshua came to do away with an Oral Torah that God and Yeshua never recognized as valid in the first place simply does not hold water, logically or scripturally.

Avi Ben Mordechai has my thanks for his book, but there are sections that need to be corrected to align accurately with the paradigms of scripture. Some teachers are reluctant to make their teachings conform to the scriptures, whatever their motivations may be. You can decide for yourself if those are mature scriptural arguments or not. But you will be able to tell if they are in submission to Yeshua, if they recognize the scriptural inaccuracy of their teachings and change them to conform to the scriptures, instead of calling it an argument of semantics.

Can I ask a candid question? Or several?
- Does Easter have pagan or scriptural foundations?
- Does Christmas have pagan or scriptural foundation?
- Does Sunday observance have pagan or scriptural foundation?
- What other holidays and observances might the church adopt in the name of inclusiveness?

Believe it or not many Christians can't even answer these questions. Many refuse to answer these questions. They are comfortable with their level of truth or more candidly, lack of truth. They have bought into the idea that they are saved by grace and have no real responsibility to conform to the Image of His Son, Yeshua the Messiah. So, if they are not conforming to the Image of His son, whose image are they conforming to?

Many would rather not delve further into these pressing questions. Why? "Those are Jewish Holy Days" they say. But is that a scripturally accurate statement? If they understood the true meaning of the Lord's Holy Days and how those real days of worship repeat the patterns and fractals of God created nature, perhaps they would look twice at the Sabbath and the Holy Days and question whether the apostles that taught them were actually in the truth and of the truth. But like Ephesus many don't want to be bothered with actually being responsible for their beliefs. It is just too easy to let the Pastor, Priest, and Rabbi do the thinking and deciding. Does this rationale hold any weight with Yeshua? The book of Revelation (Manifestation) does not make it sound that way.

What camp will you be in when the Antichrist shows himself to the world? Will you be firmly on the side of scriptural truth and what the Apostles and Yeshua considered to be lawful behavior or will you be on the side of lawlessness and tolerance? What would Yeshua say? What will Elijah say? Two spirits are contrasted at the end of the age...a lawless spirit and a lawful spirit. One is depicted as being after the Image of the Beast and the Antichrist and the other is depicted as following the Spirit of Elijah and lawfulness. The end time scenario cannot be understood without having a scripturally accurate understanding of the Law of Moses and the Image of God.

4 PURGING THE TEMPLE OF THE ANTICHRIST

Why was it so important for Yeshua to purge the temple of those who bought and sold?

> Matthew 21:9, And the multitudes that went before, and that followed, cried, saying, Hosanna to the son of David: Blessed is he that cometh in the name of the Lord; Hosanna in the highest. 10 And when he was come into Jerusalem, all the city was moved, saying, Who is this? 11 And the multitude said, This is Jesus the prophet of Nazareth of Galilee. 12 And Jesus went into the temple of God, and cast out all them that sold and bought in the temple, and overthrew the tables of the moneychangers, and the seats of them that sold doves, 13 And said unto them, It is written, My house shall be called the house of prayer; but ye have made it a den of thieves.

There are very few times that the Son of God shows an act of anything but love and compassion. Everywhere He went the sick were healed, those tormented by demons were released from them, and truth was proclaimed. Every act was an act of clarity for the observer, every situation became a teaching moment.

Christians have been cowed by a new theology of Psychology that demands that Christians accept others as they are and without judgment on their thoughts and behaviors. Believers have abandoned the truths of scripture in light of this new measure of truth, tolerance. The new era has declared that you are not truly a Christian if you have a measure of good and bad conduct. You are not truly loving or following the example of Jesus Christ if you tell people to repent of their fleshly and unlawful behaviors.

The teachings of Yeshua and Paul have been turned into a politic of multiculturalism, where Christians accept people of other faiths and their religious observances as being just as valid and honored as those of the Bible. To say anything otherwise is viewed as sacrilegious. America, which was founded on the principles of Christian biblical beliefs, so that Christians could freely follow the teachings of the Bible without the interference of lords, governmental officials, and people of political authority dominating their ability to follow Sola Scriptura.

> Sola scriptura (Latin ablative, "by Scripture alone") is the Christian doctrine that the Bible is the supreme authority in all matters of doctrine and practice. Sola scriptura does not deny that other authorities govern Christian life and devotion, but sees them all as subordinate to and corrected by the written word of God...Luther said, "a simple layman armed with Scripture is greater than the mightiest pope without it". The intention of the Reformation was to correct what he asserted to be the errors of the Catholic Church by appeal to the uniqueness of the Bible's authority and to reject what Catholics considered to be Apostolic Tradition as a source of original authority alongside the Bible, wherever Tradition did not have Biblical support or where it supposedly contradicted Scripture. (Wikipedia)

America was not made to be a breeding ground for every religion of the world. The historical context of its founding was to provide a place of freedom for Christians to be free from the "New Pharisees" of religion that were now dominating the temple of God. This was an internal conflict between Christians and their self-appointed leaders. They sought freedom from their control and domination. This land was settled to establish Christian freedom from domineering Christian Pharisees. It was not settled with the intent of giving "religious freedom" to every religion of the world. Multiculturalism is a failure and every other religion knows this and in their own countries refuse and persecute other religions that are not their own. America, which was established upon Christian and Biblical truths has adopted an unbiblical philosophy while still garnering the historical benefits of its Christian heritage and law. This will remain only as long as the law is honored and unchanged from its historical context and history. The seeds have been planted over the past 50 years to ensure the Christianity is exiled to the wilderness of truth and purged from the temple of multiculturalism. Any Christians that think they can get by in this system will soon find out differently. They have been preached to by the multiculturalist spirit of co-existence and tolerance...only to find out decades later that these same lawless ones have no intention of co-existing with Christians or being tolerant of their beliefs.

The 2,000-year-old battle of truth is still raging in the Church and justifiably so. The temple is still dominated by the Pharisees of today, where scripture and truth is not held in the highest regard, but other goals are. Traditionally those goals are aligned with buying, selling, profit, taxation, and control. The temple of God, Man, that was designed for the highest unity between creation and God, in the state of prayer, has time and again been subverted for transactional trade. It was the case in Yeshua's time and still is today. The end-time battle will be over this very issue.

The Mark of the Beast and its image is centered around, worship, buying, selling, and control. They don't care about your hearts and your beliefs, but they do demand your worship.

Daniel 3:6, And whoso falleth not down and worshippeth shall the same hour be cast into the midst of a burning fiery furnace. 7 Therefore at that time, when all the people heard the sound of the cornet, flute, harp, sackbut, psaltery, and all kinds of musick, all the people, the nations, and the languages, fell down and worshipped the golden image that Nebuchadnezzar the king had set up.

Following in the pattern of the Golden Calf incident, we see the pattern repeated in the time of Israel's exile to Babylon. This time it is played out on a global scale. Everyone must worship or they will die. This is a template for what will occur in the end-time. Just as Yeshua had purged the temple of those that buy and sell and those who subvert the prayer and worship of man in his highest service to God, the Beast and his image will seek to purge his temple of those who would subvert his worship of buying and selling with any truth that is not approved by the Beast and the Antichrist.

Just as Daniel and His companions are forced to make a choice, so will everyone upon the earth. Understanding the nature of your fallen image and dual state of flesh and spirit will help you decide whom you will worship and if the Kings' command should make you afraid.

Daniel 3:17, If it be so, our God whom we serve is able to deliver us from the burning fiery furnace, and he will deliver us out of thine hand, O king. 18 But if not, be it known unto thee, O king, that we will not serve thy gods, nor worship the golden image which thou hast set up. 19 Then was Nebuchadnezzar full of fury, and the form of his visage was changed against Shadrach, Meshach, and Abednego: therefore he spake, and commanded that they should heat the furnace one seven times more than it was wont to be heated. 20 And he commanded the most mighty men that were in his army to bind Shadrach, Meshach, and Abednego, and to cast them into the burning fiery furnace. 21 Then these men were bound in their coats, their hosen, and their hats, and their other garments, and were cast into the midst of the burning fiery furnace...And the princes, governors, and captains, and the king's counsellors, being gathered together, saw these men, upon whose bodies the fire had no power, nor was an hair of their head singed, neither were their coats changed, nor the smell of fire had passed on them.

Yeshua was preparing His people for this end-time battle by destroying the incorrect ideas (idols) that they held and restoring the universal truths about the reality of our current fallen state, and our destiny.

Matthew 10:28, And fear not them which kill the body, but are not able to kill the soul: but rather fear him which is able to destroy both soul and body in hell.

We will all be confronted with this same choice. Will we worship this fallen body of death, this broken image, or will we have faith and trust in God and His deliverance from evil? Take note of the fact that the central issue of Daniel 3 is the change in Nebuchadnezzar's "visage" (countenance or image). This change in his countenance coincides with his demand of the people that they worship his image. Because of his arrogance his image is changed into an Image of the Beast, until he recognizes the true power and author of all that is, God Almighty.

That terrible fate of joining with (worshiping) an idol is warned against time and again in the 10 Commandments, the Torah, the Tanach, and the New Testament. It is the penultimate fall from what God intended for all creation and for the height of His creation, His very own image.

Just as Nebuchadnezzar was trying to force the whole world to accept a fallen and broken image and worship it, he is forced to accept that very fate that he was trying to force on others. His image (visage and countenance) is turned from a King to a beast. The significance of his and our countenance (image) being changed will be addressed in later chapters. Having been ignored for millennia it will become the central issue of the end-time battle.

> Daniel 4:14, <u>Let his heart be changed from man's, and let a beast's heart be given unto him; and let seven times pass over him</u>...This is the interpretation, O king, and this is the decree of the most High, which is come upon my lord the king:25 That <u>they shall drive thee from men, and thy dwelling shall be with the beasts of the field</u>, and they shall make thee to eat grass as oxen, and they shall wet thee with the dew of heaven, and <u>seven times shall pass over thee</u>, till thou know that the most High ruleth in the kingdom of men, and giveth it to whomsoever he will.

The decree of God's judgment was clear and plain, Nebuchadnezzar's image would be broken and fall just as God's image was broken and fallen. This image needs restoration and a new seed to redeem it. So also, would Nebuchadnezzar's image. It would be changed from being like a King to being like a beast. Just like creation would bear out this fallen image for 7,000 years following the template of the 7-day creation week, so also would Nebuchadnezzar fulfill 7 years as a beast.

> Daniel 3:30, "At the end of twelve months he walked in the palace of the kingdom of Babylon. 30 The king spake, and said, <u>Is not this great Babylon, that I have built</u> for the house of the kingdom by the might of my power, and for the honour of my majesty? 31 While the word was in the king's mouth, there fell a voice from heaven, saying, O king Nebuchadnezzar, to thee it is spoken; <u>The kingdom is departed from thee.</u> 32 And they shall drive thee from men, and <u>thy dwelling shall be with the beasts of the field</u>: they shall make thee to eat grass as oxen, and seven times shall pass over thee, <u>until thou know that the most High ruleth in the kingdom of men</u>, and giveth it to whomsoever he will. 33 The same hour was the thing fulfilled upon Nebuchadnezzar: and he was driven from men, and did eat grass as oxen, and his body was wet with the dew of heaven, till his hairs were grown like eagles' feathers, and his nails like birds' claws. 34 And at the <u>end of the days</u> I Nebuchadnezzar lifted up mine eyes unto heaven, and mine <u>understanding</u>

<u>returned unto me, and I blessed the most High, and I praised and honoured him that liveth for ever,</u> whose dominion is an everlasting dominion, and his kingdom is from generation to generation:

Nebuchadnezzar's judgment as an image of a beast was sealed by his arrogance of mind, exalting himself above the Most High God, declaring his greatness because he had built the Kingdom of Babylon. He lived as a beast and his mind was turned to that of beast for 7 years. His punishment is relieved only when He blesses and worships the Most High God. This same pattern will be lived out in the final 7 years of the end-time preceding the return of Yeshua, the true Image of God.

This battle between worship and the domination of worshippers happened between Yeshua and the Pharisees and between those who bought and sold in the temple. It will also play out again the end-time between those who have the "testimony of Yeshua and keep His commandments" (Revelation 12:17) and the Beast that controls who may buy and sell.

The Apostle Paul has made it clear that the goal of the believing Christian is to conform to the truth and separate holy from the unholy. This is the foundational issue of the choice and outcomes of the Garden of Eden. Will you bind yourself to singular truths or will you seek a mixture of the Tree of the Knowledge of Good and Evil? The tree is the essential nature of a duality and an ungodly mixture of truth and a lie. When Adam and Eve partook of this tree, they sealed the fate of all creation to be bound to the nature of this tree and its image. Just as Nebuchadnezzar was depicted as a tree that is cut down and became like a beast, this is also what happened to all creation.

Daniel 4:10, Thus were the visions of mine head in my bed; I saw, and behold a tree in the midst of the earth, and the height thereof was great. 11 The tree grew, and was strong, and the height thereof reached unto heaven, and the sight thereof to the end of all the earth:12 The leaves thereof were fair, and the fruit thereof much, and <u>in it was meat for all</u>: the beasts of the field had shadow under it, and the fowls of the heaven dwelt in the boughs thereof, and <u>all flesh was fed of it</u>. 13 I saw in the visions of my head upon my bed, and, behold, a watcher and an holy one came down from heaven; 14 He cried aloud, and said thus, <u>Hew down the tree</u>, and cut off his branches, shake off his leaves, and scatter his fruit: let the beasts get away from under it, and the fowls from his branches:15 Nevertheless <u>leave the stump of his roots in the earth, even with a band of iron and brass</u>, in the tender grass of the field; and let it be wet with the dew of heaven, and <u>let his portion be with the beasts</u> in the grass of the earth:

The Image of God was turned to the image of beasts. The temple of God where God and man meet and talk in unified oneness has been cut down and serves only beastly (fleshly) desires. Can this image ever be restored or will it reach its final depths in the slavery to the image of the beast? Can this temple ever be purged? Who can deliver us from this body of death…this fallen image of a beast?

Romans 7:24, O wretched man that I am! who shall deliver me from the body of this death?

Paul has shown that man is a duality, a mixture of spirit and flesh...needing to be delivered from that unholy mixture to a singularity of the spirt. The end time cry is, "who will deliver us"?

Revelation 5:2, And I saw a strong angel proclaiming with a loud voice, Who is worthy to open the book, and to loose the seals thereof? 3 And no man in heaven, nor in earth, neither under the earth, was able to open the book, neither to look thereon. 4 And I wept much, because no man was found worthy to open and to read the book, neither to look thereon. 5 And one of the elders saith unto me, Weep not: behold, the Lion of the tribe of Judah, the Root of David, hath prevailed to open the book, and to loose the seven seals thereof.

From start to finish, the role of the Messiah is to restore the Image of God and provide the Seed of the Kingdom to purge the temple, to cast out those who dominate a broken image, and to restore the unity between God and man that was intended from the beginning. We cannot begin to hope to understand this conflict without understanding the work of the Messiah between God and man. The conflict between the Image of God and the image of the beast is real and personal for every living creature. The choice of the Tree of the Knowledge of Good and Evil manifested itself through the consummation of a seed from a tree and manifested itself though the corruption of our seed and every creatures' seed. This Tree of the Knowledge of Good and Evil needs to be cut down and we need to partake of the seed and fruit of the Tree of Life. This is the tree that believers in Yeshua are grafted into. It requires faith in the redeeming work of the Messiah Yeshua, the Seed and Image of the Kingdom of God.

Romans 11:22, Behold therefore the goodness and severity of God: on them which fell, severity; but toward thee, goodness, if thou continue in his goodness: otherwise thou also shalt be cut off. 23 And they also, if they abide not still in unbelief, shall be grafted in: for God is able to graft them in again. 24 For if thou wert cut out of the olive tree which is wild by nature, and wert grafted contrary to nature into a good olive tree: how much more shall these, which be the natural branches, be grafted into their own olive tree? 25 For I would not, brethren, that ye should be ignorant of this mystery, lest ye should be wise in your own conceits; that blindness in part is happened to Israel, until the fulness of the Gentiles be come in. 26 And so all Israel shall be saved: as it is written, There shall come out of Sion the Deliverer, and shall turn away ungodliness from Jacob:27 For this is my covenant unto them, when I shall take away their sins.

This tree is the Tree of Life that is manifested through faith in the work of the

Messiah Yeshua. Paul is not presenting fallen and unfaithful Israel as this tree, but He is clearly showing that they will become part of this tree when they accept the work of the Messiah Yeshua as restoring the Image of God to all creation. For an in-depth teaching on this subject I suggest you read "The Elijah Calling" which clarifies the scriptural accuracy that this tree is faith in the true Image of God, Yeshua the Messiah as the administrator of resurrection life and the Resurrected Covenant.

As we have seen through evaluating Ephesians 2 we are delivered by, through, and for the true Image of God. Let's examine what that means and what it means to have a change of name from Jacob to Israel and how we are not grafted into Israel, but we are grafted into "the Lord" and as a consequence, just like Jacob, we have a change of nature and image from Jacob to Israel by receiving that name and that seed.

In order to understand the conflict of the Christ and the Antichrist, the Image of God with the Image of the Beast, we need to understand the fundamental nature of seed then manifestation, of name…and then manifestation of that name. This pattern and fractal is what the universe runs upon. What does the Bible mean when it says that the Name of the Lord is presented to Moses?

> Exodus 34:4, And he hewed two tables of stone like unto the first; and Moses rose up early in the morning, and went up unto mount Sinai, as the Lord had commanded him, and took in his hand the two tables of stone. 5 And the Lord descended in the cloud, and stood with him there, and proclaimed the name of the Lord. 6 And the Lord passed by before him, and proclaimed, The Lord, The Lord God, merciful and gracious, longsuffering, and abundant in goodness and truth, 7 Keeping mercy for thousands, forgiving iniquity and transgression and sin, and that will by no means clear the guilty; visiting the iniquity of the fathers upon the children, and upon the children's children, unto the third and to the fourth generation. 8 And Moses made haste, and bowed his head toward the earth, and worshipped. 9 And he said, If now I have found grace in thy sight, O Lord, let my Lord, I pray thee, go among us; for it is a stiffnecked people; and pardon our iniquity and our sin, and take us for thine inheritance.

Take notice of several facts, God had already been talking with Moses while giving him the new set of tablets of the Law…with the "same words that were in the first tablets" and along with those new tablets God was introducing Moses to the new administrator, the manifestation of the Name of the Lord (YHWH). His administration is of those "same words" (commandments) now under "grace, mercy, longsuffering…abundant in goodness and truth" (resurrection life) whereas the prior administration was under "judgment and condemnation" (death). This is the same fractal presented between the Tree of Life and the Tree of the Knowledge of Good and Evil, the same fractal as the Image of God vs. the Image of the Beast.

This presentation of the Name of YHWH is different than when God was talking with Moses as He was receiving a re-giving of the Law. Moses is being presented with the manifestation of the Name of YHWH, the pre-incarnate Yeshua the Messiah, the Image of God. Just as the Messiah is manifesting a name, so are we. It is the natural pattern and fractal of existence. The problem we are faced with is that we are manifesting a corrupted name and image and it needs to be restored to the true Image of God by receiving His name and Image.

In order to understand the end-time conflict we need to understand the underlying nature of what the conflict is…it is a conflict of names, images, and manifestation. The beast is going to compel the world to take on his image, his name, and the number (meaning) of his name. To avoid this, we need to re-educate ourselves on what, not just who is Yeshua the Messiah. Let's familiarize ourselves with the authentic Image of God so that we may avoid the image of the beast. Believe it or not you can't do this without the "Law"! The purpose of the Law of Moses was to manifest "heavenly patterns" for the world to see and understand. That is why Yeshua had to purge the temple as this heavenly pattern that was meant to enlighten the world was being corrupted into an image of a beast that served only commerce, money, control, and power. It was no longer manifesting the truth of God.

> Exodus 25:8, And let them make me a sanctuary; that I may dwell among them. 9 According to all that I shew thee, after the pattern of the tabernacle, and the pattern of all the instruments thereof, even so shall ye make it.

These patterns were for the sole purpose of rectifying the broken image of the Garden. When Adam and Eve took of the fruit and seed of the Tree of the Knowledge of Good and Evil they took on the nature of that tree and joined their seed with its seed. Man's image was now corrupted by that seed and could no longer replicate the Image of God. What was the result?

> Genesis 3:23, Therefore the Lord God sent him forth from the garden of Eden, to till the ground from whence he was taken. 24 So he drove out the man; and he placed at the east of the garden of Eden Cherubims, and a flaming sword which turned every way, to keep the way of the tree of life.

The result was separation from God. Man could no longer enter God's presence. The tabernacle of Moses was presenting imagery of the reunion of God and man, and how that reunion would take place. The end goal of the tabernacle and the temple, was so that God "may dwell among them" (Exodus 25:8). The separation and exile caused in the Garden of Eden was on the path of restoration (Romans 5:14). As we have already discussed, Ephesians 2 is clarifying how Yeshua is that new body and new temple where God and man can once again dwell in Edenic unity.

What happens when that pattern and symbol takes on the same broken image of Adam and Eve's sinful choice? Corruption. How do you remove the corruption? You purge the temple of false idols and images and restore the true image to its proper state. This is why Yeshua cleansed the temple.

> Mark 11:9, And they that went before, and they that followed, cried,

saying, Hosanna; <u>Blessed is he that cometh in the name of the Lord</u>:

Notice when we see the presence of the manifest name of the Lord, the outcome is to purge the image and pattern of God of all false images and idols and those who dominate the temple of God with ungodly goals.

> Mark 11:15, And they come to Jerusalem: and Jesus went into the temple, and began to <u>cast out them that sold and bought in the temple, and overthrew the tables of the moneychangers, and the seats of them that sold</u> doves; 16 And would not suffer that any man should carry any vessel through the temple. 17 And he taught, saying unto them, Is it not written, <u>My house shall be called of all nations the house of prayer</u>? but ye have made it a den of thieves. 18 And the <u>scribes and chief priests heard it, and sought how they might destroy him</u>: for they feared him, because all the people was astonished at his doctrine.

The Image of God that had fallen into corruption was being purged by the manifestation of the Name of the Lord (YHWH), the true Image of God. How did the religious and political leaders respond to the true Image of God? They sought to destroy Him. This is the same pattern that will play out between the Image of the Beast and those who hold the true Image of God and "keep the commandments of God, and have the testimony of Jesus Christ" (Revelation 12:17) in the end-time. The Beast and the Antichrist's response to the end time preaching of the Gospel and the truth will be violent and extreme. They will perform upon the true children of the King, believers in Yeshua, that which was fulfilled in Yeshua during the crucifixion week. The pattern that happened with Yeshua will also be fulfilled by us.

> Luke 9:23, And he said to them all, If any man will come after me, let him deny himself, and take up his cross daily, and follow me.

How will you respond? Will you seek to save your life and take the Image of the Beast, or will you fulfill your calling and be a living example of the Image of God? We have to wonder if everything that happened to the Apostles during that week was prophetic of what will happen to Christians during the final 7 years. A close examination of the events that occurred to the disciples preceding and during the crucifixion may be very telling of what will be fulfilled in us during the reign of the Beast.

5 ANTICHRIST?

If you want to understand the Image of the Beast we need a clear scriptural understanding of the Image of God, the Messiah. For two millennia Jews and Christians have been alienated over this very issue. Can God be "manifest in the flesh" (1 Timothy 3:16)? Jews will tell you that this is a violation of the 10 Commandments.

Exodus 20:3, <u>Thou shalt have no other gods before me</u>. 4 Thou shalt not make unto thee any graven image, or any likeness of any thing that is in heaven above, or that is in the earth beneath, or that is in the water under the earth. 5 <u>Thou shalt not bow down thyself to them, nor serve them</u>: for I the Lord thy God am a jealous God, visiting the iniquity of the fathers upon the children unto the third and fourth generation of them that hate me;

Given the placement of this command at the beginning of the 10 commandments it is very important and needs our attention. I would contend that due to 6,000 of man refusal of truth, we have lost the meaning of this command as it relates to the creation of Adam and Eve in God's image and then subsequent fall into a broken image. Hence mankind is no longer in God's image.

When Moses interceded for Israel so that God would pass over them and not destroy them for their sin of worshiping the Golden Calf, Moses pleaded with God to show him His face (countenance/image).

Exodus 33:12, And Moses said unto the Lord, See, thou sayest unto me, Bring up this people: and <u>thou hast not let me know whom thou wilt send with me</u>. Yet thou hast said, <u>I know thee by name</u>, and thou hast also <u>found grace</u> in my sight. 13 Now therefore, I pray thee, <u>if I have found grace in thy sight, shew me now thy way, that I may know thee</u>, that I may find grace in thy sight: and consider that this nation is thy people. 14 And he said, <u>My</u>

presence shall go with thee, and I will give thee rest. 15 And he said unto him, If thy presence go not with me, carry us not up hence. 16 For wherein shall it be known here that I and thy people have found grace in thy sight? is it not in that thou goest with us? so shall we be separated, I and thy people, from all the people that are upon the face of the earth. 17 And the Lord said unto Moses, I will do this thing also that thou hast spoken: for thou hast found grace in my sight, and I know thee by name. 18 And he said, I beseech thee, shew me thy glory. 19 And he said, I will make all my goodness pass before thee, and I will proclaim the name of the Lord before thee; and will be gracious to whom I will be gracious, and will shew mercy on whom I will shew mercy. 20 And he said, Thou canst not see my face: for there shall no man see me, and live.

This is perhaps one of the most important prophecies of the entire Bible. Moses is pleading with God to give him proof of His deliverance of Israel. God responds with proof of how He would deliver grace to Israel. What follows next is the presentation of the "Name of the Lord (YHWH)", the Image and Glory of God that would "pass by" and "go before" all of Israel. This is the manifestation of the Name of God. The same name that Jerusalem declared before Yeshua purged the temple in Jerusalem.

> Matthew 21:9, And the multitudes that went before, and that followed, cried, saying, Hosanna to the son of David: Blessed is he that cometh in the name of the Lord; Hosanna in the highest.

Israel understood Yeshua to be the manifestation of the name of YHWH, the same "glory" that passed before Moses in Exodus 33 and 34. This is the same "name of the Lord" that Israel's leaders rejected and consequentially their house has been vacated by the presence of God until…

> Luke 13:35, Behold, your house is left unto you desolate: and verily I say unto you, Ye shall not see me, until the time come when ye shall say, Blessed is he that cometh in the name of the Lord.

This Yeshua is the same child that the glory of the Lord was manifested for at Yeshua's birth.

> Luke 2:9, And, lo, the angel of the Lord came upon them, and the glory of the Lord shone round about them: and they were sore afraid.

This is the same glory that manifested to the Apostles when Moses and Elijah appeared with Yeshua on the mount of Transfiguration.

> Matthew 17:2, And was transfigured before them: and his face did shine as the sun, and his raiment was white as the light. 3 And, behold, there appeared unto them Moses and Elias talking with him. 4 Then answered

Peter, and said unto Jesus, Lord, it is good for us to be here: if thou wilt, let us make here three tabernacles; one for thee, and one for Moses, and one for Elias. 5 While he yet spake, behold, a bright cloud overshadowed them: and behold a voice out of the cloud, which said, This is my beloved Son, in whom I am well pleased; hear ye him.

Notice that this is the same "Glory of the Lord" and the "Name of the Lord" from Exodus 33 and 34, and is fulfilled time and again in the coming of Yeshua the Messiah. Each time the focus is upon a transfiguration from an earthly image to that of a heavenly image. Each time deliverance and grace is established though a change of image, visage, and countenance. Each time it happens through the manifestation of the Glory of God and the appearance and presentation of His manifested Name, YHWH. Yeshua is the name that Israel must still accept to come under the new administration of Grace and abundant mercy of resurrection life...the seal of His authority.

Just as Israel was afraid of Moses when he descended with the new set of tablets and a glorified countenance, so also Israel has been fulfilling a prophetic fractal and being afraid of Yeshua the Messiah... one "like unto" (Moses).

Exodus 34:29, And it came to pass, when Moses came down from mount Sinai with the two tables of testimony in Moses' hand, when he came down from the mount, that Moses wist not that the skin of his face shone while he talked with him. 30 And when Aaron and all the children of Israel saw Moses, behold, the skin of his face shone; and they were afraid to come nigh him. 31 And Moses called unto them; and Aaron and all the rulers of the congregation returned unto him: and Moses talked with them.

Just as they initially rejected Moses, being in fear of him, they also fulfilled this same pattern in the resurrected Yeshua. The time is coming and is near, that they will return to Yeshua, just as they returned to Moses. The same pattern is fulfilled in both Moses and Yeshua. Yeshua's statement to John becomes clearer and clearer.

Matthew 3:15, And Jesus answering said unto him, Suffer it to be so now: for thus it becometh us to fulfil all righteousness. Then he suffered him.

Yeshua had to fulfill certain prophetic patterns in order to manifest the truth and authenticity of His office as the manifest Name of the Lord (YHWH), the Countenance of God.

Deuteronomy 18:15, The Lord thy God will raise up unto thee a Prophet from the midst of thee, of thy brethren, like unto me; unto him ye shall hearken; 16 According to all that thou desiredst of the Lord thy God in Horeb in the day of the assembly, saying, Let me not hear again the voice of the Lord my God, neither let me see this great fire any more, that I die not. I will raise them up a Prophet from among their brethren, like unto thee, and will put my words in his mouth; and he shall speak unto them all that I shall command him. 19 And it shall come to pass, that whosoever will not hearken unto my words which he shall speak in my name, I will require it of him.

Just as Israel had rejected God's manifested name at Mt. Sinai, due to the fear of His glory, they also initially rejected Moses and withdrew from Him when they beheld his glorified countenance. They also rejected Yeshua in fear when He manifested His power in resurrection life. Notice this manifestation was at Israel's request because they thought they would die if they heard God's word directly from His presence. So, what does God do? He answers their prayer and sends the Messiah fulfilling the same pattern as Moses (one "...like unto me" --Moses) having God's very own Word in His mouth and God's very own Name in His being.

Exodus 23:21, Beware of him, and obey his voice, provoke him not; for he will not pardon your transgressions: for my name is in him.

This is what Yeshua declared about Himself.

John 8:28, Then said Jesus unto them, When ye have lifted up the Son of man, then shall ye know that I am he, and that I do nothing of myself; but as my Father hath taught me, I speak these things.

Yeshua makes it extremely clear He is the fulfillment of the promise of God. He is the "one like unto" Moses, the one with the "Word of God" in His mouth, the one manifesting the "Name" of the Lord (YHWH). Just as Moses was displaying the restored Image of God before the people as a consequence of his interaction with the presentation of the Name of the Lord on Mt. Sinai, so Yeshua was manifesting the Glory and Name of the Lord, which is the Image and Countenance of God before the people. People are still afraid of this truth and even believers with a foundation in Biblical truth try and shy away from the clarity of scripture on this point. In an effort to follow the Shema (the Oneness of God-Deuteronomy 6:4) they try to demote Yeshua from being the Manifest Name of the Lord (God manifest in the flesh) to something less controversial. In doing so we start to see the battle of the Image of God with the Image of the Beast. Truth vs. Tradition. Written Law of Moses vs. the Oral Law of Moses. Apostles of Christ vs. the religious establishment. A purified temple vs. a temple dominated by buying and selling. Coexistence vs. Holiness.

Is Yeshua the manifestation of the Torah? Believe it or not the Apostles and Paul actually address this question. There are some groups that say that He is. Why? They, like many Christians, are trying to reconcile the scriptures but their paradigm is inaccurate.

Rabbinic Judaism and many Messianic assemblies reject the idea of the manifestation of God. Those Rabbinic and Messianic Jews that have not recognized Yeshua the Messiah as being the manifest Name of the Lord (YHWH) are in conflict with the clear teachings of the Torah and the testimony of the

Apostles.

2 John 1:7, For many deceivers are entered into the world, who confess not that Jesus Christ is come in the flesh. This is a deceiver and an Antichrist.

Some groups try to affirm the Shema (the Oneness of God-Deuteronomy 6:4) by saying that Yeshua is the manifestation of the Torah instead of the scripturally accurate statements that Yeshua is the "fullness of the Godhead bodily", the "manifest Name of YHWH", and "the Image of God". They do so because they cannot reconcile the scriptures with their incorrect paradigm regarding the nature of God, nor recognize their own fallen image and countenance.

Romans 3:21, But now the righteousness of God without the law is manifested, being witnessed by the law and the prophets;

Literally God manifested His own righteousness for our redemption...but Paul says God could not save us by the Law of Moses. We have already covered the reasons why in the chapter discussing the fractal of death and resurrection and how the Law of Moses had to first appear under the broken image/fractal of death, just like Adam and Eve and all creation. Then that same Law of Moses would be re-written under a new administration of grace, mercy, and resurrection life. This was the fractal of the Messiah and had to be fulfilled without the fractal of death. The old administration of a fallen image is "done away" and a new fractal of "everlasting" life has begun. Being the Image of God, the Messiah had to first take on our sin and broken image, so that He could manifest the "righteousness of God" in resurrection life and restore His image to fallen creation. We who are without the "seed of life" have been give His new seed. Those who have no seed (death), have been given a new seed (resurrection life).

Numbers 20:5, And wherefore have ye made us to come up out of Egypt, to <u>bring us in unto this evil place? it is no place of seed</u>, or of figs, or of vines, or of pomegranates; neither is there any water to drink.

This is the same problem that God told Eve she would have after consuming the Tree of the Knowledge of Good & Evil

Genesis 3:16, Unto the woman he said, I will greatly multiply thy sorrow and thy conception; in sorrow thou shalt bring forth children; and thy desire shall be to thy husband, and he shall rule over thee.

Eve's seed and our image has been corrupted by the seed of the Tree of the Knowledge of Good and Evil. This seed causes separation from God and ultimately sickness and death. We are unable by any means to deliver ourselves without that promised seed that would redeem us back to our original state as the Image of God.

Genesis 3:15, And I will put enmity between thee and the woman, and between thy seed and her seed; it shall bruise thy head, and thou shalt bruise his heel.

We need an accurate scriptural paradigm of the nature of our original state as the Image of God and also of our current fallen state as the image of the beast. We cannot hope to understand the nature, purpose and role of the "promised seed of the Kingdom of God" without understanding our broken images. This broken image can only be restored by the true Image of God, the Messiah.

To understand this, we must look deeply at the nature of existence through the fractal of seed then manifestation. It will show itself in nature and in the scriptures. The fractal of seed (death) and image (life) repeats itself over and over again. We must come to greater clarity of what the Messiah is and not just who. We must also understand how the Messiah is related to the Law of Moses and clarify what is the Word of God and what is the Law of God. How is it that we move from death to life?

2 Timothy 1:10, But is now made manifest by the appearing of our Savior Jesus Christ, who hath abolished death, and hath brought life and immortality to light through the gospel:

Can the Law of Moses bring clarity to this issue? What is and was the Messiah? What is the Word of God? What is the Logos? What is Christ?

- Deuteronomy 6:4, Hear, O Israel: The Lord our God is one Lord:

- John 1:1, In the beginning was the Word (Logos–Strong's 3056), and the Word (Logos–Strong's 3056) was with God, and the Word (Logos–Strong's 3056) was God. 2 The same was in the beginning with God. 3 All things were made by him; and without him was not any thing made that was made. 4 In him was life; and the life was the light of men. 5 And the light shineth in darkness; and the darkness comprehended it not.

Logos
The KJV New Testament Greek Lexicon
Strong's Number:3056
Original Word
lovgoß
Transliterated Word:
Logos
Phonetic Spelling:

log'–os
Parts of Speech:
Noun Masculine
Word Origin:
from (3004)
Definition:
1. of speech
a word, uttered by a living voice, embodies a conception or idea
what someone has said
a word
the sayings of God
decree, mandate or order
of the moral precepts given by God
Old Testament prophecy given by the prophets
what is declared, a thought, declaration, aphorism, a weighty saying, a dictum, a maxim
discourse
the act of speaking, speech
the faculty of speech, skill and practice in speaking
a kind or style of speaking
a continuous speaking discourse–instruction
doctrine, teaching
anything reported in speech; a narration, narrative
matter under discussion, thing spoken of, affair, a matter in dispute, case, suit at law
the thing spoken of or talked about; event, deed
2. Its use as respect to the MIND alone
reason, the mental faculty of thinking, meditating, reasoning, calculating
account, i. e. regard, consideration
account, i. e. reckoning, score
account, i. e. answer or explanation in reference to judgment
relation, i. e. with whom as judge we stand in relation

reason would
reason, cause, ground
3. In John, denotes the essential Word of God, Jesus Christ, the personal wisdom and power in union with God, his minister in creation and government of the universe, the cause of all the world's life both physical and ethical, which for the procurement of man's salvation put on human nature in the person of Jesus the Messiah, the second person in the Godhead, and shone forth conspicuously from His words and deeds.
A Greek philosopher named Heraclitus first used the term Logos around 600 B. C. to designate the divine reason or plan which coordinates a changing universe. This word was well suited to John's purpose in John 1.
King James Word Usage—Total:330
word 218, saying 50, account 8, speech 8, Word (Christ) 7, thing 5, not translated 2, miscellaneous 32

Some in the Hebrew Roots and Messianic movements say that because Yeshua is the Word of God, He is in actuality the Torah. They make the mental and logical leap of saying that the "Word" in Hebrew is Dabar and means Torah. Let's examine if that statement is scripturally true.

The Hebrew word used for "Word" in the Old Testament is Dabar.

Dabar:
The KJV Old Testament Hebrew Lexicon
Strong's Number:01697
Original Word Origin:
rbd from (01696)
Transliterated Word TDNT Entry
Dabar TWOT–399a
Phonetic Spelling Parts of Speech
daw–baw'   Noun Masculine
Definition:
·speech, word, speaking, thing speech
·saying, Utterance
·word, words
·business, occupation, acts, matter, case, something, manner (by extension)

However, "Word" from the Greek "Logos (Strong's 3056), is used time and again in the New Testament Scriptures and not once in the Old Testament Scriptures. If indeed John is referring to Yeshua being the Word and therefore equating Him with the Torah or a divine Torah, you would expect to find that same word or an equivalent "Word" used when John refers to the "Law", "Commandments", or the "Law (Torah) of Moses".

John 1:45, Philip findeth Nathanael, and saith unto him, We have found him, of whom Moses in the law (Nomos–Strong's 3551), and the prophets, did write, Yeshua of Nazareth, the son of Joseph.

The word "law" in John 1:45 is "Nomos" (Strong's 3551) and is used repeatedly by John in reference to the Law (Torah) of Moses ("of the Mosaic Law").

- John 1:17, For the law (Nomos) was given by Moses, but grace and truth came by Yeshua.
- John 7:19, Did not Moses give you the law (Nomos), and yet none of you keepeth the law (Nomos)? Why go ye about to kill me?
- John 7:23, If a man on the sabbath day receive circumcision, that the law (Nomos) of Moses should not be broken; are ye angry at me, because I have made a man every whit whole on the sabbath day?
- John 7:49, But this people who knoweth not the law (Nomos) are cursed.
- John 7:51, Doth our law (Nomos) judge any man, before it hear him, and know what he doeth?
- John 8:5, Now Moses in the law (Nomos) commanded us, that such should be stoned: but what sayest thou?
- John 8:17, It is also written in your law (Nomos), that the testimony of two men is true.
- John 10:34, Yeshua answered them, Is it not written in your law (Nomos), I said, Ye are gods?
- John 12:34, The people answered him, We have heard out of the law (Nomos) that Christ abideth for ever: and how sayest thou, The Son of man must be lifted up? Who is this Son of man?
- John 15:25, But this cometh to pass, that the word might be fulfilled that is written in their law (Nomos), They hated me without a cause.
- John 18:31, Then said Pilate unto them, Take ye him, and judge him according to your law (Nomos). The Jews therefore said unto him, It is not lawful for us to put any man to death:
- John 19:7, The Jews answered him, We have a law (Nomos), and by our law (Nomos) he ought to die, because he made himself the Son of God.

Each and every time, John uses "Nomos" for the "law", which is the Written Law (Torah) of Moses. Not once does he refer to Yeshua being the "Word" using the term "Nomos". Instead John always uses the term "Logos" for Yeshua.

If John were trying to say that Yeshua being the "Word", was in actuality the divine "Torah", he would have used "Nomos" to refer to Yeshua. He never does. What does John do? He contrasts the Torah of Moses with Yeshua, showing they are not one and the same, nor the manifestation of the other.

John 1:17, For the law (Nomos-Strong's 3551) was given by Moses, but grace and truth came by Yeshua.

Paul affirms that Yeshua is not the Torah, the Torah in the flesh, the living Torah, or one with the Torah, and he does so in great detail. What does the Torah say?

Genesis 15:1, After these things the word (Debar-Strong's 1697) of the Lord came unto Abram in a vision, saying, Fear not, Abram: I am thy shield, and thy exceeding great reward.

The "Word" (Logos-Strong's 3056) of John 1:1 (Debar-Strong's 1697) is the same "Word" of Genesis 15:1, the pre-incarnate Christ ("word" is preeminently used of *Christ* (John 1:1), expressing the *thoughts* of the Father through the Spirit). However, you will not find that the "Word" is the same word as "Law or Torah" in the scriptures. The word "law" in the Old Testament (Towrah–Strong's 08451) is used 219 times and not once as the "Word" (Dabar–Strong's 01697).

Towrah:
The KJV Old Testament Hebrew Lexicon
Strong's Number:08451
Original Word Origin:
hrwt from (03384)
Transliterated Word TDNT Entry
Towrah TWOT–910d
Phonetic Spelling Parts of Speech
to–raw'   Noun Feminine
Definition:
·law, direction, instruction, direction (human or divine) body of prophetic teaching
· instruction in Messianic age
·body of priestly direction or instruction
·body of legal directives
·law of the burnt offering
·of special law, codes of law

·custom, manner
·the Deuteronomic or Mosaic Law
King James Word Usage—Total:219
law 219

In short, you have to make a huge mental leap…disregarding scriptural proof to make the "Word" of John 1:1 the divine Torah. John uses separate words for "Word" and "Law", as we have already discussed.

Since there is no logical or scriptural justification between John's choice of separate words for "law" and "Word", many Hebrew Roots teachers make the segue from "Logos" to "Dabar" since they both mean "Word". Unfortunately, you will not find "Dabar" meaning "Law" or "Torah" anywhere in the Old Testament scriptures.

Clearly the "Word" is the Utterance of God and gives the Law (Torah). There is no debate necessary on this topic. What becomes a problem is the fact that many Hebrew Roots teachers say that since Yeshua is the "Word" and gives the "Torah", He is therefore the divine Torah, the Torah in the flesh, or the living Torah. If that is true, it should be affirmed by Yeshua, the Apostles, and Paul. What do we find? Paul is extremely clear that the Torah could not save, could not be sent, and could not be manifested to save. We will dig into these scriptural proofs in detail.

This is one of the more critical issues in the Hebrew Roots and Messianic Movements. Why? Because they are essentially trying to maintain the oneness of God with the truth of God manifest in the flesh. Unfortunately, they violate the scriptures in their efforts to do so. This is the Shema. There is only one God.

Deuteronomy 6:4, Hear, O Israel: The Lord our God is one Lord:

But the Apostles affirm that Yeshua is the manifestation of God in the flesh. Rabbinic Judaism and many Messianic groups say that this statement from 1 Timothy is a violation of the Shema.

1 Timothy 3:16, And without controversy great is the mystery of godliness: God was manifest in the flesh, justified in the Spirit, seen of angels, preached unto the Gentiles, believed on in the world, received up into glory.

The outcome is that many groups ignore this scripture, many reject the writings of Paul, and many reject the entire New Testament. They go to great efforts to support a flawed paradigm instead of fixing their paradigm to fit all of the facts. All well intended…and all wrong.

Many of the Hebrew Roots and Messianic teachers have tried to hedge from the truth of the scriptures and shy away from 1 Timothy 3:16, thinking that this presents more than one God. The common outcome is an attempt to demote Yeshua from being God "manifest in the flesh" to being the living Torah or the manifestation of the Torah or One with the Torah.

Instead of sticking with the exactness of the scriptures, some teachers provide an explanation that contradicts Paul and even sometimes choose a rabbinical commentary that suggests that the Torah is divine. To say the least, a refusal to be open to self–reflection in regards to the scriptural accuracy of this teaching is concerning. Correctable, but still concerning.

When a teacher becomes un–learning and rigid, you need to evaluate the veracity of what he/she is teaching. If he/she is unwilling to keep searching for truth and to be open to correcting his/her beliefs then the believer has entered dangerous ground. This is the case when a Messianic or Hebrew Roots teacher goes off into an incorrect teaching, saying,

"You have the word of God written in the Old Testament and that word manifested itself…and that was Yeshua our Messiah, now you can see what was previously written doing those things".

He is saying the Messiah is the Torah manifested. At best he is confused, at worst he is couching what he believes in semantics. Why is this important? Hebrew Roots teaching is likely some of the best biblical teaching you will hear…but it can get caught up in error just like any other group.

Paul, is terribly clear on the nature of Yeshua:
- Yeshua is not the Torah
- The Torah is not what saves you
- The Messiah was not the Torah that was manifested in the flesh.

So where is the proof? Those teachers that affirm the validity of Paul the Apostle, and that Paul was pro–Written Torah and anti–Oral Torah are applauded. Yet this particular teacher, who claims Yeshua is the Torah manifested, fails to follow through on allowing Paul's confirmed authority to help us reconcile the scriptures.

What does Paul say was manifested to save us? What does Paul say was able to save us and was therefore sent by the Father? Paul contrasts one that is not able to save and could not be sent, with one who was able to save and was sent. By nature of Paul's presentation, they are not one and the same, or one manifesting the seed of the other.

Romans 8:1, There is therefore now no condemnation to them which are in Christ Yeshua, who walk not after the flesh, but after the Spirit. 2 For the law of the Spirit of life in Christ Yeshua hath made me free from the law of sin and death. 3 For <u>what the law could not do</u>, in that it was weak through the flesh, <u>God sending his own Son</u> in the likeness of sinful flesh, and for sin, condemned sin in the flesh:

The Torah could not free us from the Torah of Sin and Death. Hence the Torah could not free us and could not be sent to free us. What was sent? Someone who could free us, God's own son.

Romans 3:19, Now we know that what things soever the law saith, it saith to them who are under the law: that every mouth may be stopped, and all the world may become guilty before God. 20 Therefore by the deeds of the law there shall no flesh be justified in his sight: for by the law is the knowledge of sin. 21 But <u>now the righteousness of God without the law is manifested</u>...

Do you see that? The Written Torah is doing what it was designed to do. It is condemning the flesh, so that no flesh can be justified. The Written Torah is doing what it is designed to do, it is manifesting sin and death, which brings condemnation and judgment. Notice Paul says, "But now..." God's son, who is the righteousness of God, is sent to free us from the Torah of Sin and Death. So, the Torah was not manifested to free us, God's righteousness was manifested to free us. One is not a manifestation of the other. For those who would say "under the law" refers to the Oral Torah, please take note.

Hebrews 9:14, How much more shall the blood of Christ, who through the eternal Spirit offered himself without spot to God, purge your conscience from dead works to serve the living God? 15 And <u>for this cause he is the mediator of the new testament</u>, that <u>by means of death</u>, for the <u>redemption of the transgressions that were under the first testament</u>, they which are called <u>might receive the promise of eternal inheritance</u>. 16 For where a testament is, there must also <u>of necessity be the death of the testator</u>.

The book of Hebrews clarifies what we are under; the first testament (covenant/Torah). Not only this, he associates it with death, which caused the need for a new mediator of a new testament. So, do you send the mediator (Moses) of the first testament, or manifest the first testament? No. You send a new mediator with the "power of an eternal inheritance", resurrection life. You do not manifest the old, the dead, and the one that brought death. You manifest the new.

Romans 8:3, For <u>what the law (Nomos-Torah) could not do</u>, in that it was weak through the flesh, <u>God sending his own Son</u> in the likeness of sinful flesh, and for sin, condemned sin in the flesh:

Why was God's righteousness sent to free us from the Torah of Sin and Death?

Because God could not send the Torah to free us. What does this mean?

What was manifested to man to free us from the Torah of Sin and Death and was not the Torah?

The manifest Name of YHWH, God's Son, was sent. The Torah was NOT able to save; hence it was not sent to be manifested. The Torah was NOT manifested, the Righteousness of God was manifested.

Does this mean we are not to keep the Torah?

No. We are to keep the Written Torah.

Romans 3:31, Do we then make void the law (Nomos-Torah) through faith? God forbid, we establish the law (Nomos-Torah).

What many teachers are failing to see is the seed then fruit of the dual giving's of the Torah. First it is given in death (Torah of Sin and Death), like a seed, then it is given again like a risen fruit (Torah of Resurrection Life). One does not manifest the other, the administrations are distinct and cannot engender the other. The Utterances are the same on both sets of tablets though (Exodus 34:1).

Romans 8:2, For the <u>law of the Spirit of life in Christ Yeshua</u> hath made me <u>free from the law of sin and death</u>.

We see the contrasting of two laws (Torah), one that brings eternal life and one that cannot free us from sin and death. One is fleshly, carnal, subject to sin and subject to death like a seed. The other is spirit and subject to endless life. It is able to free us from sin and death, affirming life, like a fruit. One is not the manifestation of the other. If it were, Paul would not have said they were not the manifestation of the other. He clearly says the first could not be sent or manifested to save, so another had to be sent.

Galatians 3:21, Is the law then against the promises of God? God forbid: for <u>if there had been a law given which could have given life, verily righteousness should have been by the law</u>.

Paul is clearly saying the Torah could not bring forth life and could not free us from sin and death.

Hebrews 7:15, And it is yet far more evident: for that after the similitude of Melchisedec there ariseth another priest, <u>Who is made, not after the law of a carnal commandment</u>, but after the power of an endless life.

Paul is contrasting the Torah, which is subject to sin and death, with the High Priest, Yeshua, who is made or manifested not by the Torah, but by the power of endless life as we saw in Romans 8:2. Paul is continually contrasting the spirit with the flesh, and what many teachers are missing is that this fractal of seed (death) and fruit (resurrection) applies to the Torah, just like the Messiah. It is the Torah (the Law of Moses) that was indeed the Torah of Sin and Death. It was sent to condemn, not to bring life. You see the fractal of death and resurrection repeated over and over again in the scriptures.

Romans 5:18, Therefore as by the offence of one judgment came upon all men to condemnation; even so by the righteousness of one the free gift came upon all men unto justification of life.

Again, Paul is contrasting the roles of the Torah of Sin and Death (seed) with the Torah of Resurrection Life (fruit). They present a fractal of death and resurrection. You must have one to have the other. We cannot make the mistake of assuming that the second is the fruit of the first, in that it is manifesting the first. Paul is contrasting the essential nature of both Torah's: one in death (flesh) and one in resurrection life (spirit).

Romans 8:1, There is therefore now no condemnation to them which are in Christ Yeshua, who walk not after the flesh, but after the Spirit.

The scriptures show the contrast of the flesh (death and condemnation) and the spirit (resurrection life and no condemnation).

BAPTIZED INTO MOSES OR BAPTIZED INTO YESHUA?

2 Corinthians 3:9, For if the ministration of condemnation be glory, much more doth the ministration of righteousness exceed in glory.

Paul is again contrasting the two giving's of the Torah (Exodus 20/24 and Exodus 34), one under sin and death and the other under righteousness and resurrection life (grace). You cannot have the administrator of the first covenant, the Torah, be the administrator of the second giving of the Torah. Hence why the Torah is called the Law of Moses.

- Romans 7:25, I thank God through Yeshua our Lord. So then with the mind I myself serve the law of God; but with the flesh the law of sin.
- Romans 8:2, For the law of the Spirit of life in Christ Yeshua hath made me free from the law of sin and death.
- Galatians 2:21, I do not frustrate the grace of God: for if righteousness come by the law, then Christ is dead in vain.

Notice the Law of Moses is contrasted with the Law of Christ. One is designed to bring death, and the other is designed to bring resurrection life. This also clarifies why Moses cannot be the administrator of the Resurrected Torah (New Covenant). He is the administrator of the Torah of Sin and Death. This is the reason why Israel was baptized into Moses. This is also why the first generation which was saved from Egypt died in the Wilderness with Moses, and only two (Joshua and Caleb) were saved to ascend to the Promised land with the second generation. Once again, the firstborn is a picture of death (flesh), and the second born is a picture of resurrection life (spirit).

1 Corinthians 10:21, Moreover, brethren, I would not that ye should be ignorant, how that all our fathers were under the cloud, and all passed through the sea; 2 And were all baptized unto Moses in the cloud and in the sea;

This is why we are not baptized into Moses as Israel was, we are baptized into Yeshua. It provides added significance to why John told the people to now be baptized into Yeshua. It also confirms why you are not grafted into the Torah or Israel. The new body is Yeshua, not Israel.

- Romans 12:5, So we, being many, are <u>one body in Christ</u>, and every one members one of another.
- Matthew 3:11, I indeed baptize you with water unto repentance. but he that cometh after me is mightier than I, whose shoes I am not worthy to bear: <u>he shall baptize you with the Holy Ghost, and with fire</u>:
- Acts 2:38, Then Peter said unto them, Repent, and <u>be baptized every one of you in the name of Yeshua for the remission of sins</u>, and ye shall receive the gift of the Holy Ghost.

Israel was baptized into the name of Moses and we (Jews and Gentiles) are now baptized into the name of Yeshua. This is a picture of death and resurrection, just as there were two giving's of the Torah, one under death (Exodus 20/24) and one under resurrection life and grace (Exodus 34). Notice that both sets of tablets have the same commandments. This is why we keep the commandments even though we are saved by the work of Yeshua through His grace and mercy. The book of Hebrews contrasts two houses, one in death and one in resurrection life.

Hebrews 3:5, And <u>Moses verily was faithful in all his house</u>, as a servant, for a testimony of those things which were to be spoken after; 6 <u>But Christ as a son over his own house</u>; whose house are we, if we hold fast the confidence and the rejoicing of the hope firm unto the end. 7 Wherefore (as the Holy Ghost saith, To day if ye will hear his voice…

Moses' house is left desolate and those who wish to enter life need to seek that one name…it's not Moses. Why desolate? Because it is a picture of death which is the separation of spirit from the manifest body…an empty house.

Luke 13:34, O Jerusalem, Jerusalem, which killest the prophets, and stonest them that are sent unto thee; how often would I have gathered thy children together, as a hen doth gather her brood under her wings, and ye would not! 35 <u>Behold, your house is left unto you desolate</u>: and verily I say unto you, <u>Ye shall not see me, until the time come when ye shall say, Blessed is he that cometh in the Name of the Lord</u>.

There is only one way and one name, for Jew and Gentile.

Hebrews 3:2, Who was faithful to him that appointed him, <u>as also Moses was faithful in all his house</u>. 3 For <u>this man was counted worthy of more glory than Moses, inasmuch as he who hath builded the house hath more honour than the house</u>. 4 For every house is builded by some man; but he that built all things is God. 5 And Moses verily was faithful in all his house, as a servant, for a testimony of those things which were to be spoken after; 6 <u>But Christ as a son over his own house; whose house are we</u>, if we hold fast the confidence and the rejoicing of the hope firm unto the end. 7 Wherefore (as the Holy Ghost saith, To day if ye will hear his voice, 8 Harden not your hearts, as in the provocation, in the day of temptation in the wilderness:9 When your fathers tempted me, proved me, and saw my works forty years. 10 Wherefore I was grieved with that generation, and said, <u>They do alway err in their heart</u>; and they have not known my ways. 11 So I sware in my wrath, They shall not enter into my rest.)12 <u>Take heed, brethren, lest there be in any of you an evil heart of unbelief</u>, in departing from the living God.

It is clear this new house is not Judah or Israel, this house is Yeshua the Messiah. All those who join themselves to the Lord are Israel/Jews inwardly. If you think you can keep the Written Torah and take a pass on the new administrator of Resurrection Life, then you are still under the administration of condemnation, the Torah of Sin and Death.

Isaiah 56:3, Neither let the son of the stranger, <u>that hath joined himself to the Lord</u>, speak, saying, The Lord hath utterly separated me from his people: neither let the eunuch say, <u>Behold, I am a dry tree</u>.

YESHUA, MANIFESTATION OF...
We are to learn the Torah, but it is NOT able to save you, only Yeshua can do that. Beware the false teaching that says you are saved by the Torah or by keeping the Torah, or says that Yeshua is the Torah manifested, the living Torah, or the Torah in the flesh. Scripturally you do not see the manifestation of the Torah in the Messiah. It could not be sent because it could not save, it brought only sin and death.

So, if Yeshua is not the manifestation of the Torah, what is He the manifestation of?

Romans 3:21, <u>But now the righteousness of God without the law is manifested</u>, being witnessed by the law and the prophets;

Yeshua is not a manifestation of the Torah of Moses. Yeshua is the manifestation of the righteousness of God who saves us from the Torah of Sin and Death and brings us resurrection life, of which He is the administrator. Beware anyone who denies that Yeshua is God manifest in the flesh.

1 Timothy 3:16, And without controversy great is the mystery of godliness: <u>God was manifest in the flesh</u>, justified in the Spirit, seen of angels, preached unto the Gentiles, believed on in the world, received up into glory.

We now clearly see what has changed between the Torah of Sin and Death and the Torah of Resurrection Life. There is a new administrator.

2 Corinthians 3:3, Forasmuch as ye are manifestly declared to be the epistle of Christ ministered by us, written not with ink, but with the Spirit of the living God; not in tablets of stone, but in fleshy tablets of the heart. 4 And such trust have we through Christ to God–ward:5 Not that we are sufficient of ourselves to think any thing as of ourselves; but our sufficiency is of God; 6 Who also hath made us able ministers of the new testament; not of the letter, but of the spirit: for the letter killeth, but the spirit giveth life. 7 But if the ministration of death, written and engraven in stones, was glorious, so that the children of Israel could not stedfastly behold the face of Moses for the glory of his countenance; which glory was to be done away:8 How shall not the ministration of the spirit be rather glorious? 9 For if the ministration of condemnation be glory, much more doth the ministration of righteousness exceed in glory. 10 For even that which was made glorious had no glory in this respect, by reason of the glory that excelleth. 11 For if that which is done away was glorious, much more that which remaineth is glorious.

Can Paul be any clearer? He says the ministration of death is written and engraven in stones. This is the Written Torah of Moses, not the Oral Torah. He then clarifies what the new administration is, the spirit. Logically you can only come to one conclusion about the "ministration of death" then, it is the flesh.

Notice the old administration is not manifested in the new, it is done away. This does not mean the commandments are done away, only the administration of sin and death. At the second giving of the Torah, the same commandments are written the second time according to the ministration of the spirit and righteousness in Yeshua, the manifest Name of YHWH.

Exodus 34:1, And the Lord said unto Moses, Hew thee two tablets of stone like unto the first: and I will write upon these tablets the words that were in the first tablets, which thou brakest.

We are to keep the Written Torah, we are not saved by the Torah. Take careful notice of the comparing and contrasting of the two administrators.

Hebrews 3:1, Wherefore, holy brethren, partakers of the heavenly calling, consider the Apostle and High Priest of our profession, Christ Yeshua; 2 Who was faithful to him that appointed him, as also Moses was faithful in all his house. 3 For this man was counted worthy of more glory than Moses, inasmuch as he who hath builded the house hath more honour than the house. 4 For every house is builded by some man; but he that built all things is God. 5 And Moses verily was faithful in all his house, as a servant, for a testimony of those things which were to be spoken after; 6 But Christ as a son over his own house; whose house are we, if we hold fast the confidence and the rejoicing of the hope firm unto the end.

Are we called into Moses' house or Yeshua's house?   Are we called to be baptized into Moses or Yeshua?   Are we saved by our faith (confidence) in Moses or Yeshua?   This scripture says the house we are called to is Yeshua's and we are saved by his better name (Hebrews 1:4). The writer goes on to contrast the two administrations. The prior administration suffered from hard hearts full of error, always tempting God and therefore subject to sin and death. These were all symptoms of a lack of faith (unbelief). This is remedied in the second administration by holding our faith steadfast to the end. The first administration and generation brought out by Moses was plagued with a lack of faith which brought sin and death.

Hebrews 3:7, Wherefore (as the Holy Ghost saith, To day if ye will hear his voice, 8 Harden not your hearts, as in the provocation, in the day of temptation in the wilderness:9 When your fathers tempted me, proved me, and saw my works forty years. 10 Wherefore I was grieved with that generation, and said, They do alway err in their heart; and they have not known my ways. 11 So I sware in my wrath, They shall not enter into my rest.) 12 Take heed, brethren, lest there be in any of you an evil heart of unbelief, in departing from the living God. 13 But exhort one another daily, while it is called To day; lest any of you be hardened through the deceitfulness of sin. 14 For we are made partakers of Christ, if we hold the beginning of our confidence stedfast unto the end; 15 While it is said, To day if ye will hear his voice, harden not your hearts, as in the provocation. 16 For some, when they had heard, did provoke: howbeit not all that came out of Egypt by Moses. 17 But with whom was he grieved forty years?   was it not with them that had sinned, whose carcases fell in the wilderness? 18 And to whom sware he that they should not enter into his rest, but to them that believed not?   19 So we see that they could not enter in because of unbelief.

We are saved by faith (full belief) in Yeshua the Messiah, the new ministration of grace and mercy.

Is the Torah our savior?   No. It brought sin and death and separated us from God.

Hebrews 7:15, And it is yet far more evident: for that after the similitude of Melchisedec there ariseth another priest, 16 Who is made, not after the law of a carnal commandment, but after the power of an endless life. 17 For he testifieth, Thou art a priest for ever after the order of Melchisedec. 18 For there is verily a disannulling of the commandment going before for the weakness and unprofitableness thereof. 19 For the law made nothing perfect, but the bringing in of a better hope did; by the which we draw nigh unto God. 20 And inasmuch as not without an oath he was made priest:21 (For those priests were made without an oath; but this with an oath by him that said unto him, The Lord sware and will not repent, Thou art a priest for ever after the order of Melchisedec:) 22 By so much was Yeshua made a surety of a better testament.

Can the Torah be manifested to deliver us from sin and death?   No.

Hebrews 7:18, For there is verily a disannulling of the commandment going before for the weakness and unprofitableness thereof 19 For the law made nothing perfect, but the bringing in of a better hope did; by the which we draw nigh unto God.

It is clear that this Torah of Sin and Death and its administration is disannulled. It is replaced by a new administration and a new Torah of Resurrection Life. As the administrator fulfills the fractal of death and resurrection, so does the Torah. Why? The old proved to have a lack of faith, hardness of heart, and disobedience of commandments, causing separation from God.

Does this mean that the new Torah of Resurrection Life has different commandments?   If we follow the pattern of Exodus 34 and the second giving of the Torah, the new administration and the new Torah have the same commandments.

Exodus 34:1, And the Lord said unto Moses, Hew thee two tablets of stone like unto the first: and I will write upon these tablets the words that were in the first tablets, which thou brakest.

This may help clarify why we are instructed in the end times to remember the Law (Torah) of Moses, yet we are not saved by it. It has a new administrator and a new administration of grace and mercy, yielding faith and resurrection life. This is the better hope spoken of in Hebrew 7:19.

Malachi 4:4, Remember ye the law of Moses my servant, which I commanded unto him in Horeb for all Israel, with the statutes and judgments. 5 Behold, I will send you Elijah the prophet before the coming of the great and dreadful day of the Lord:

Considering the commandments are to be remembered, we can see clearly what is being done away. 2 Timothy 1:10 already touched on this and the Book of Hebrews reinforces the message of what is abolished. Is it the Law or is it the Broken Image of Death which is a corrupted state of a mixture of flesh and spirit?

Hebrews 8:6, But now hath he obtained a more excellent ministry, by how much also he is the mediator of a better covenant, which was established upon better promises. 7 For if that first covenant had been faultless, then should no place have been sought for the second. 8 For finding fault with them, he saith, Behold, the days come, saith the Lord, when I will make a new covenant with the house of Israel and with the house of Judah:9 Not according to the covenant that I made with their fathers in the day when I took them by the hand to lead them out of the land of Egypt; because they continued not in my covenant, and I regarded them not, saith the Lord. 10 For this is the covenant that I will make with the house of Israel after those days, saith the Lord; I will put my laws into their mind, and write them in their hearts: and I will be to them a God, and they shall be to me a people:11 And they shall not teach every man his neighbour, and every man his brother, saying, Know the Lord: for all shall know me, from the least to the greatest. 12 For I will be merciful to their unrighteousness, and their sins and their iniquities will I remember no more. 13 In that he saith, A new covenant, he hath made the first old. Now that which decayeth and waxeth old is ready to vanish away.

Consider the fact that you have two Torah's: one of Sin and Death (the flesh buried like a seed in death) and the other Torah of Resurrection Life (the spirit and like a manifested fruit). You also have two administrations, one that brought sin, condemnation and death (Moses), which needed to pass away, and the new one that brings grace, mercy and resurrection life with faith in Yeshua. In the old administration, you were baptized into Moses. In the new administration, you are baptized into Yeshua. In both you have the same commandments (Exodus 34:1), but now they are written on our hearts (Hebrews 8:10).

6 TWO WITNESSES? MOSES & ELIJAH?

Can Paul be any clearer?

Romans 7:23, But I see another law in my members, warring against the law of my mind, and bringing me into captivity to the law of sin which is in my members. 24 O wretched man that I am! who shall deliver me from the body of this death? 25 I thank God through Yeshua our Lord. So then with the mind I myself serve the law of God; but with the flesh the law of sin.

Paul is continually reflecting upon the duality of the flesh versus the spirit, the corruptible body versus the mind, the Law of Moses versus the Law of Christ, the Torah of Sin and Death versus the Torah of Resurrection Life. To deny the reality of this scriptural fact would be irresponsible.

Galatians 4:19, My little children, of whom I travail in birth again until Christ be formed in you, 20 I desire to be present with you now, and to change my voice; for I stand in doubt of you. 21 Tell me, ye that desire to be under the law, do ye not hear the law? 22 For it is written, that Abraham had two sons, the one by a bondmaid, the other by a freewoman. 23 But he who was of the bondwoman was born after the flesh; but he of the freewoman was by promise. 24 Which things are an allegory: for these are the two covenants; the one from the mount Sinai, which gendereth to bondage, which is Agar. 25 For this Agar is mount Sinai in Arabia, and answereth to Jerusalem which now is, and is in bondage with her children. 26 But Jerusalem which is above is free, which is the mother of us all. 27 For it is written, Rejoice, thou barren that bearest not; break forth and cry, thou that travailest not: for the desolate hath many more children than she which hath an husband. 28 Now we, brethren, as Isaac was, are the children of promise. 29 But as then he that was born after the flesh persecuted him that was born after the Spirit, even so it is now. 30 Nevertheless what saith the scripture? Cast out the bondwoman and her son: for the son of the bondwoman shall not be heir with the son of the freewoman. 31 So then, brethren, we are not children of the bondwoman, but of the free.

Do we throw out the Commandments?   No, we have already seen the commandments remain. It is the administration of the flesh and death with sin and condemnation that are passing away.

THE HOLY SPIRIT

Yeshua is always contrasting the flesh and the spirit. Which is typified by their administrations, Moses and Elijah. Just as both appear with Yeshua on the Mount of Transfiguration, Yeshua fulfills the pattern and fractal of both administrators, death (seed) and resurrection (manifested fruit).

- John 6:63, It is the spirit that quickeneth; the <u>flesh profiteth nothing</u>: the words that I speak unto you, they are spirit, and they are life.
- John 3:6, That which is born of the flesh is flesh; and that which is <u>born of the Spirit is spirit</u>.

This should give us new insight on the importance of eating and drinking Christ. We suffer from the spirit of disobedience (Ephesians 2:2) and need a new spirit (heart). This spirit of disobedience is the middle wall of partition between us and God, the two that need to be made one.

John 6:54, Whoso eateth my flesh, and drinketh my blood, hath eternal life; and I will raise him up at the last day.

We are indeed consuming Yeshua's spirit and becoming one with Him. Paul is continually contrasting the flesh and the spirit.

Romans 3:20, Therefore by the deeds of the law there shall <u>no flesh be justified in his sight</u>: for by the law is the knowledge of sin.

The ultimate fate of all flesh is destruction and death. Only the spirit will live.

Romans 7:25, I thank God through Yeshua our Lord. So then <u>with the mind I myself serve the law of God; but with the flesh the law of sin</u>.

This dictates how we should walk.

- Romans 8:1, There is therefore now no condemnation to them which <u>are in Christ Yeshua, who walk not after the flesh, but after the Spirit</u>.
- Romans 8:5, For they that are <u>after the flesh do mind the things of the flesh</u>; but they that are <u>after the Spirit the things of the Spirit</u>.

We see the same pattern. Yeshua gave His spirit to us to replace our spirit of disobedience.

John 1:33, And I knew him not: but he that sent me to baptize with water, the same said unto me, Upon whom thou shalt <u>see the Spirit descending, and remaining on him, the same is he which baptizeth with the Holy Ghost</u>.

This was the hallmark sign that would show that He was the Messiah and the one that was promised to come and prophesized by Moses.

Acts 2:3, And there appeared unto them <u>cloven tongues like as of fire, and it sat upon each of them</u>. 4 And <u>they were all filled with the Holy Ghost</u>, and began to speak with other tongues, as the Spirit gave them Utterance. 5 And there were dwelling at Jerusalem Jews, devout men, out of every nation under heaven.

In fact, this is how we are sealed in Christ. The spirit of disobedience is removed and a new spirit is placed within us: The Holy Spirit.

Ezekiel 11:19, And I will give them one heart, and <u>I will put a new spirit within you</u>; and I will take the stony heart out of their flesh, and will give them an heart of flesh:

Why do we need a new spirit? Because the old spirit is disobedient.

Ephesians 1:12, That we should be to the praise of his glory, who first trusted in Christ. 13 <u>In whom ye also trusted</u>, after that ye heard the word of truth, the Gospel of your salvation: in whom also <u>after that ye believed, ye were sealed with that holy Spirit of promise, 14 Which is the earnest of our inheritance until the redemption of the purchased possession</u>, unto the praise of his glory.

How do we know this is the hallmark sign of the promised Messiah? We need to look at the prophetic fractal that occurs with Moses. This same sealing occurs with Moses' spirit in the old administration. God takes Moses' spirit and gives it to the seventy elders.

Numbers 11:24, And Moses went out, and told the people the words of the Lord, and <u>gathered the seventy men of the elders of the people</u>, and set them round about the tabernacle. 25 And the <u>Lord came down in a cloud</u>, and spake unto him, <u>and took of the spirit that was upon him, and gave it unto the seventy elders: and it came to pass, that, when the spirit rested upon them</u>, they prophesied, and did not cease.

The pattern of death and resurrection occurs in the Messiah, all creation, mankind, Israel, and God's spirit. It was Yeshua's ability to cast out unclean spirits that caused Him to be known far and wide. This was something new.

Mark 1:22, And they were astonished at his doctrine: for he taught them as one that had authority, and not as the scribes. 23 And there was in their synagogue a man with an unclean spirit; and he cried out, 24 Saying, Let us alone; what have we to do with thee, thou Yeshua of Nazareth? art thou come to destroy us? I know thee who thou art, the Holy One of God. 25 And Yeshua rebuked him, saying, Hold thy peace, and come out of him. 26 And when the unclean spirit had torn him, and cried with a loud voice, he came out of him. 27 And they were all amazed, insomuch that they questioned among themselves, saying, What thing is this? what new doctrine is this? for with authority commandeth he even the unclean spirits, and they do obey him. 28 And immediately his fame spread abroad throughout all the region round about Galilee.

Have you underestimated the need for your unclean spirit to be removed and a new spirit to live within you? For too long Paul has been allegorized away. He is being very specific and completely literal. The flesh must pass away.

What does the wine of the Passover symbolize? It is Christ's spirit. You must consume it.

- Romans 8:8, So then they that are in the flesh cannot please God.
- 1 Corinthians 1:29, That no flesh should glory in his presence.
- 1 Corinthians 5:5, To deliver such an one unto Satan for the destruction of the flesh, that the spirit may be saved in the day of the Lord Yeshua.

Are you hearing the clarity of Paul? The flesh is passing away... the spirit needs to be saved by Yeshua.

1 Corinthians 10:16, The cup of blessing which we bless, is it not the communion of the blood of Christ? The bread which we break, is it not the communion of the body of Christ? 17 For we being many are one bread, and one body: for we are all partakers of that one bread. 18 Behold Israel after the flesh: are not they which eat of the sacrifices partakers of the altar?

Notice Paul clarifies our identity in the body of Yeshua, not in the body of Israel. In fact, he contrasts the members of the body of Yeshua with the members of the body of Israel by what sacrifice they each take part of. He even cites Israel in relation to the flesh, while he is contrasting them with those who are members of Yeshua after the spirit. To miss this point is to be willfully blind of the truth of the scriptures about the flesh and the spirit, what is passing away (the flesh) and what needs to be saved (the spirit).

1 Corinthians 15:49, And as we have borne the image of the earthy, we shall also bear the image of the heavenly. 50 Now this I say, brethren, that flesh and blood cannot inherit the kingdom of God; neither doth corruption inherit

incorruption. 51 Behold, I shew you a mystery; We shall not all sleep, but <u>we</u> <u>shall all be changed,</u>

Paul reminds us that just as there was a necessity in the change of the covenant, we also must be changed, from fallen corruptible flesh to incorruptible spirit.

- 1 Corinthians 15:38, But <u>God giveth it a body</u> as it hath pleased him, and <u>to every seed his own body. 39 All flesh is not the same flesh:</u> but there is one kind of flesh of men, another flesh of beasts, another of fishes, and another of birds. 40 There <u>are also celestial bodies, and bodies terrestrial: but the glory</u> <u>of the celestial is one, and the glory of the terrestrial is another.</u>
- 1 Corinthians 15:32, So also is the resurrection of the dead. It is sown in corruption; it is raised in incorruption:
- 1 Corinthians 15:50, Now this I say, brethren, that <u>flesh and blood</u> <u>cannot inherit the kingdom of God; neither doth corruption inherit</u> <u>incorruption</u>. 51 Behold, I shew you a mystery; We shall not all sleep, but <u>we</u> <u>shall all be changed,</u> 52 In a moment, in the twinkling of an eye, at the last trump: for the trumpet shall sound, and <u>the dead shall be raised incorruptible,</u> <u>and we shall be changed</u>. 53 For <u>this corruptible must put on incorruption,</u> and this mortal must put on immortality. 54 So <u>when this corruptible shall have put</u> <u>on incorruption,</u> and this mortal shall have put on immortality, then shall be brought to pass the saying that is written, Death is swallowed up in victory. 55 <u>O death, where is thy sting</u>? O grave, where is thy victory?

Once again Paul affirms the duality of seed then fruit, corruptible then incorruptible, death then resurrection life—the necessity of both, the glory of both, and the absolute necessity of the passing of the former things because of the exceeding glory of the latter things.

This present duality of the Tree of the Knowledge of Good (Spirit) and Evil (Flesh) must pass away and become the unity of the faith in the singularity of the Tree of Life (Spirit of Yeshua).

Topic	Law of Moses	Law of Christ
Baptized into	Moses	Yeshua
Nature	Flesh	Spirit
Outcome	Failure	Success
Focus	Hard hearts/failure to obey/lack of faith	Full faith/writing commandments on our hearts
Purpose	Torah of Sin & Death, to bring condemnation to the flesh	Torah of Resurrection Life, to bring eternal life to those of faith in Yeshua; life to the spirit

Topic	Law of Moses	Law of Christ
Imagery	Seed (buried in death)	Fruit (risen to eternal life)
Mediator	Moses	Yeshua
Administration	Condemnation	Righteousness
Commandments	The words written on the first set of tablets	The same words written on the first set of tablets are also written on the second set of tablets
Outcome	Covenant is disannulled; it could not free us from sin and death	Covenant is resurrected with a new administration and the same commandments are written in our minds and hearts
Glory of the Covenant	Glorious	More glorious
What is passing away?	The flesh	The spirit remains
High Priest(s)	Aaron (Levitical)	Yeshua (Melchisedec)
Covenant with	Israel	House of Israel & House of Judah & Gentiles (all whosoever's)
Saved by	Not saved	Yeshua
Grafted into	Moses	Yeshua
Who is a Jew/Israel?	Outwardly	Inwardly (Romans 2:28–29)
What profits?	Who you are related to… your flesh; am I a descendant of Abraham?	Do I have faith in Yeshua? Do I have the Son of God?
What is manifest?	Sin and death	Righteousness of God and resurrection life
Symbols	Agar (Hagar)/Mt. Sinai/Ishmael	Jerusalem/Sarah/Isaac
Symbolic meaning	Bondage to the flesh	Freedom above (Spirit)
Galatians 4:29, But as then he that was born after the flesh persecuted him that was born after the	Bondage to the flesh which brings condemnation, sin, and death	Free of the flesh, we live to the Spirit

Topic	Law of Moses	Law of Christ
Spirit, even so it is now.		
Image	Earthly	Heavenly

The central issue of the image of the beast is focused upon whether or not Yeshua came as the Image of God to deliver us "from" our current broken and fallen image of the beast.

> 1 John 2:21, I have not written unto you because ye know not the truth, but because ye know it, and that no lie is of the truth. 22 Who is a liar but he that denieth that Jesus is the Christ? He is Antichrist, that denieth the Father and the Son. 23 Whosoever denieth the Son, the same hath not the Father: he that acknowledgeth the Son hath the Father also.

Denial or acceptance of Yeshua the Messiah is mandatory upon all creation because He is the only one that has conquered the image of the beast. Our joining with Him in His body is indicative of our acceptance not of what we see with our senses, but what we know with our minds.

> Hebrews 11:1, Now faith is the substance of things hoped for, the evidence of things not seen. 2 For by it the elders obtained a good report. 3 Through faith we understand that the worlds were framed by the word of God, so that things which are seen were not made of things which do appear. 4 By faith Abel offered unto God a more excellent sacrifice than Cain, by which he obtained witness that he was righteous, God testifying of his gifts: and by it he being dead yet speaketh.

Currently we are under sin and death and a corrupted flesh and image and can only be delivered into a state of life by the author of resurrection life. Just as Cain's countenance was fallen because of His sin, he had the choice to repent.

> Genesis 4:6, And the Lord said unto Cain, Why art thou wroth? and why is thy countenance fallen? 7 If thou doest well, shalt thou not be accepted? and if thou doest not well, sin lieth at the door. And unto thee shall be his desire, and thou shalt rule over him.

Just as Nebuchadnezzar's visage (countenance) was changed so also was Cain's when he offered an inappropriate sacrifice. His countenance (image) could be restored. These archetypes (fractal/pattern) repeat over and over again in nature, in world events, and in the scriptures. It will also play out in our lives in the end-time battle between the Image of God vs. the Image of the Beast.

Just as Cain was focused on the flesh, just as Esau's only desire was to fill his belly, so also the Beast will focus the world on one thing. Worship me or you will not eat. When confronted with this choice will you do the same as Esau or will you do what Daniel's companions did and worship the Most High God? Will you try to save your flesh or will you trust in the deliverance of your spirit?

I Corinthians 5:5, o deliver such an one unto Satan for the destruction of the flesh, that the spirit may be saved in the day of the Lord Jesus.

The prosperity doctrine of modern Christian teachers has set the church up for destruction. It is no wonder that God ponders if He will find faith when He returns.

Luke 18:7, And shall not God avenge his own elect, which cry day and night unto him, though he bear long with them? 8 I tell you that he will avenge them speedily. Nevertheless when the Son of man cometh, shall he find faith on the earth? 9 And he spake this parable unto certain which trusted in themselves that they were righteous, and despised others:

This same question is posed to the Church of Laodicea only in different words. Yeshua is depicted as knocking at the door of the Church pleading with the inhabitants to unlock the door and let Him in. They are cast in the light of having no faith and no part in the Messiah. He declares them to be poor, blind, and naked...essentially without faith and without deliverance. He issues a warning "anoint your eyes", "open the door", and let the Messiah give you His image. Characteristic of that age, they will believe that they are covered, rich, healthy, and have perfect vision...all the while being deceived by the image of the beast with which they have covered themselves.

2 Timothy 3:13, But evil men and seducers shall wax worse and worse, deceiving, and being deceived.

It is this deception that is a hallmark of the mark of the beast and of its image.

Revelation 19:20, And the beast was taken, and with him the false prophet that wrought miracles before him, with which he deceived them that had received the mark of the beast, and them that worshipped his image. These both were cast alive into a lake of fire burning with brimstone.

The choice between Christ and Antichrist is the choice between the spirit and the flesh and which image you express faith in.

7 Correcting Christian Imagery…

Some teachers say the following, all of which are in violation of the truth of the Scriptures and the Testimony of the Apostles.

Popular Sayings That Are Scripturally Inaccurate:
Yeshua is the Torah in the flesh
Yeshua is the Torah
Yeshua is one with the Torah
The Torah was manifested
You must be grafted into Judah
You must be grafted into Israel
You must be grafted into the Torah
The tree of Romans 11 is Israel/Judah
"Under the Law" means being under the Oral Torah
"Works of the Law" means being under the Oral Torah
Sarah versus Hagar means being under the Oral Torah
That the Middle Wall of Partition of Ephesians 2:14 is the Oral Torah (Rabbinical Traditions)

We have already seen that Yeshua has his own house, just like Moses had a house (Hebrews 3:6). These houses are contrasted. Many teachers are saying you need to enter the House of Israel or the House of Judah. Why would you seek to enter any other house than that of Yeshua? God is still waiting on physical Israel to repent (Matthew 23:29) and enter Yeshua's house and become a Jew inwardly (Romans 2:29). The Torah could not provide redemption, hence God sent (manifested) His own fullness to redeem the sinful.

Hebrews 10:1, For the law having <u>a shadow of good things to come, and not the very image of the things</u>, can never with those sacrifices which they offered year by year continually make the comers thereunto perfect.

Can it be any clearer? The Torah is not the Image of God that was manifested to the world. The manifest Name of YHWH, Yeshua the Messiah, is the Image of God. He is literally God's righteousness! The Torah is not able to save you. The Messiah Yeshua is not the Torah in the flesh, one with the Torah, or the Torah manifested. He gave the Torah, but He is not the Torah.

Even the Written Torah makes it clear that it cannot save you and there was a need for a second giving of the Torah by the manifest Name of YHWH, Yeshua the Messiah. Remember, the second giving of the Torah is in Exodus 34.

Exodus 34:4, And he hewed two tablets of stone like unto the first; and Moses rose up early in the morning, and went up unto mount Sinai, as the Lord had commanded him, and took in his hand the two tablets of stone. 5 And the Lord descended in the cloud, and stood with him there, and proclaimed the Name of the Lord. 6 And <u>the Lord passed by before him, and proclaimed, The Lord, The Lord God, merciful and gracious, longsuffering, and abundant in goodness</u> and truth, 7 Keeping mercy for thousands, forgiving iniquity and transgression and sin, and that will by no means clear the guilty; visiting the iniquity of the fathers upon the children, and upon the children's children, unto the third and to the fourth generation. 8 And <u>Moses made haste, and bowed his head toward the earth, and worshipped</u>.

Moses did not bow down to worship the Torah, he was worshipping the manifest (declared) Name of YHWH, Yeshua the Messiah, presented in verse 6. Hopefully those few teachers will acknowledge their error and cease from teaching that Yeshua is the Torah manifested. At best, it is because of a lack of understanding, at worst it is because of an unwillingness to accept the reconciliation of the scriptures.

Let's be clear, Yeshua is the Word of God (John 1:1). All of those "unscriptural statements" (see table at the beginning of the chapter) are contrary to the scriptures and fundamentally lead new and scripturally inexperienced believers astray from the solid truths of the Bible.

What do the scriptures say?
- Yeshua and the Father are One and God manifest in the flesh (1

Timothy 3:16, 2 John 1:9).

- The Torah was NOT manifested to save us, God's righteousness was manifested (John 17:11, 1 John 5:7, John 10:30).
- What are you grafted into? You must be grafted into the Lord, Yeshua (Isaiah 56:3).
- What is the tree of Romans 11? Is it Judah/Israel? No. It is the tree of faith. The natural branches are those who once displayed faith and are cut off when they stop exhibiting faith. Why would you be grafted into a dead and cut off branch (Judah) that needs to be grafted back in? Was Judah baptized for you? Were you baptized into the name of Judah/Israel? (1 Corinthians 1:12–14, Galatians 3:27)
    - We are grafted into Yeshua.
        - o Colossians 2:7, Rooted and built up in him, and stablished in the faith, as ye have been taught, abounding therein with thanksgiving.
- Yeshua is the manifest Name of YHWH (John 17:6, 2 Corinthians 4:4, Colossians 1:15, Colossians 11:7)

Now is this just an issue of semantics? Paul did not seem to think so and neither did Yeshua. In fact, Yeshua refers to the Torah, not as Himself, but as "your law". Notice Yeshua does not identify Himself with the Torah in the Gospel of John (John 10:34).

John 8:16, And yet if I judge, my judgment is true: for I am not alone, but I and the Father that sent me. 17 It is also written in your law, that the testimony of two men is true.

He says "your law". He is not talking about the Oral Torah, He is talking about the Written Torah, the Law of Moses. You will find this in the description of Two Witnesses in the Written Torah, not the Oral Torah.

Deuteronomy 17:6, At the mouth of Two Witnesses, or three witnesses, shall he that is worthy of death be put to death; but at the mouth of one witness he shall not be put to death.

Be cautious of teachers who make these unscriptural statements, until they publicly confess that Yeshua is NOT the Torah manifested, the living Torah, or one with the Torah, but is indeed God manifest in the flesh (I Timothy 3:16), and that we are grafted into Him (not Israel/Judah). When we are grafted into Him, we are Israel. So, truly those who exhibit faith are Sons of Abraham, and a Jew inwardly (Romans 9:29).

Before you conclude that this is about an issue with Messianics or Hebrew Roots, understand this is about scriptural truth and accuracy. This is the result of over forty years of study as a believer in Yeshua and as a follower of the Written Torah of Moses.

2 John 1:8, Look to yourselves, that we lose not those things which we have wrought, but that we receive a full reward. 9 Whosoever transgresseth, and abideth not in the doctrine of Christ, hath not God. He that <u>abideth in the doctrine of Christ,</u> he hath both the Father and the Son. 10 If there come any unto you, and bring not this doctrine, receive him not into your house, neither bid him God speed:11 For he that biddeth him God speed is partaker of his evil deeds.

Hopefully all who hope to teach the Gospel will humble themselves and consider the need to perfect all teachings to conform to the truth of scripture. Unfortunately, these issues can be grossly confused by those who know only a little of the scriptures. Those who are new in the faith need help to learn accurately what the scriptures teach.

The scriptures affirm the following:

- Yeshua is the Word of God (John 1:1, 14)
- Yeshua is the manifest Name of YHWH (Exodus 34, Matthew 23:39, Hebrews 1:4)
- Yeshua is the fullness of the Godhead bodily (Colossians 2:9)
- Yeshua is God manifest in the flesh (1 Timothy 3:16)
- Yeshua is the Image of God (1 Corinthians 11:7, 2 Corinthians 4:4, Colossians 1:15)
- Yeshua and the Father are one (John 10:30, John 17:11, 22, 1 John 5:7)
- Yeshua is NOT the manifestation of the Torah (John 17:6, 2 Corinthians 4:4, Colossians 1:15, Colossians 11:7)
- The Torah is NOT able to save (Hebrews 10:1)
- The Torah was NOT sent to save (Romans 8:1)
- The Torah could NOT be sent to save (Romans 8:3)
- Yeshua is the manifestation of God's righteousness (John 17:11, 1 John 5:7, John 10:30)
- Yeshua is able to save, hence why He was sent (Romans 8:3, Hebrews 7:16)
- Yeshua is NOT the Torah manifested, in the flesh, or one with the Torah (Romans 8:1, Romans 3:19, Romans 8:3, Hebrews 10:1)
- Israel is not able to save (Matthew 23:39)
- Israel was not sent to save (John 3:17)
- We are not baptized into Judah/Israel (Romans 6:3)
- We are not saved by the name of Israel (Acts 2:21)
- We are not grafted into Judah/Israel (Romans 11:10–19)
- We are grafted into the Lord (Yeshua) (Isaiah 56:3)
- **Whose witnesses, are we?** Israel? No. Judah? No. Yeshua? Yes.

Acts 22:14–16, And he said, The God of our fathers hath chosen thee, that thou shouldest know his will, and <u>see that Just One,</u> and shouldest hear the voice of his mouth. 15 For <u>thou shalt be his witness</u> unto all men of what thou hast seen and heard. 16 And now why tarriest thou? arise, and be baptized, and wash away thy sins, <u>calling on the Name of the Lord</u>.

IS THE TORAH DIVINE?

One Hebrew Roots (Messianic) teacher quotes Avraham Heschel's "Heavenly Torah", which is quite alarming given that Heschel believed that the Torah was divine. This teacher says Avraham Herschel is his favorite rabbi. This does not appear in this teacher's presentation accidentally and gives great insight into what he may be saying.

- Is the Torah the Utterance (Word) of God? It is uttered by God, but it is not the Utterance (Word) of God. All of creation was created via the Utterance of God, so being an Utterance does not make you the Word of God.
- So, are you an Utterance of God? You were spoken into existence. Does that make you divine? No.
- Does that make the Torah divine? No.
- Does that make the Torah the Son of God? No.
- Being uttered by God, does that make you equal to the Son of God? No. Satan was also spoken into existence by God, so is he qualified to save or to be manifested to save? No.
- Yeshua is the Image of God and I am in Yeshua, conformed to His image. Am I therefore qualified to save? No.
- Therefore, to be spoken into existence by God does not make you the Word of God (John 1:1) or qualified to save.

John 1:1, In the <u>beginning was the Word, and the Word was with God, and the Word was God</u>. 2 The same was in the beginning with God. 3 All things were made by him; and without him was not any thing made that was made. 4 In him was life; and the life was the light of men.

Avraham Herschel is promoting that the Torah is divine primordial wisdom as the first created "word" who was with the Father in the beginning and was the agent of creation of the world. He is saying the Torah is the Word. So in reality, what is promoted by Herschel and some teachers is the worship of the Torah and that you are saved by the Torah. This conflicts with the statements of the Apostles that the Torah could not save, could not be sent, and was not manifested, because someone else had to be sent that could save, could be sent, and could be manifested.

Some teachers may claim, it was not actually the Torah that was sent, but the divine essence of the Torah that was sent. They are still attempting to say that the divine essence of the Torah is the Messiah who saves. As we have already addressed, Paul clarified the Torah's "essence" could not be sent. Why? Because it could not save.

Romans 8:3, For <u>what the law could not do</u>, in that it was weak through the flesh, <u>God sending his own Son</u> in the likeness of sinful flesh, and for sin, condemned sin in the flesh:4 That the righteousness of the law might be fulfilled in us, who walk not after the flesh, but after the Spirit.

What must we conclude? The Torah, essence or not, could not be sent because it could not save. In contrast one was judged by God as being able to save and was sent. Paul identifies that one or "essence" as the Son of God. He contrasts the Son of God with the Torah, hence to conclude that the "essence" of the Torah was sent, and is the Son of God, is not only contrary to the scriptures, it is illogical.

The common explanation of many Hebrew Roots teachers is that the Torah is the Word, but they spend most of their time avoiding 1 Timothy 3:16 that clearly says Yeshua was "God manifest in the flesh". This strays far too close to the spirit of Antichrist.

Hence, why we are spending so much time re-establishing the foundational elements of Christian faith. Being on the right path of Biblical truth does not mean that there are not pitfalls along the way where misinterpretation can lead to the path of Antichrist. Indeed, Yeshua came to His own temple, among His own people to which He had given His own Law. And the result, they rejected the Image and Presence of God for a false paradigm.

Can you be Torah observant and end up with the Mark and image of the Beast. Yes indeed. The Torah is not what saves you. It is the manifest name, image, and countenance of God that saves all things.

The arrogance of mind that we can save ourselves or establish our own righteousness is fundamentally flawed and expresses the same broken image of the beast that was fulfilled in Eve, Cain, Nebuchadnezzar, Judah, and a myriad of others.

Romans 10:3, For they being ignorant of God's righteousness, and going about to establish their own righteousness, have not submitted themselves unto the righteousness of God.

This is essentially the same declaration as Nebuchadnezzar.

Daniel 4:30, The king spake, and said, Is not this great Babylon, that I have built for the house of the kingdom by the might of my power, and for the honour of my majesty?

What was the outcome? Humility...brought on by a decree from God.

Daniel 4:31, While the word was in the king's mouth, there fell a voice from heaven, saying, O king Nebuchadnezzar, to thee it is spoken; <u>The kingdom is departed from thee</u>. 32 And <u>they shall drive thee from men</u>, and <u>thy dwelling shall be with the beasts of the field</u>: they shall make thee to eat grass as oxen, <u>and seven times shall pass over thee</u>, until thou know that the most High ruleth in the kingdom of men, and giveth it to whomsoever he will.

This same fractal was fulfilled by Judah when they rejected the coming of the Image of God, the Messiah Yeshua.

Luke 13:34, O Jerusalem, Jerusalem, which killest the prophets, and stonest them that are sent unto thee; how often would I have gathered thy children together, as a hen doth gather her brood under her wings, and ye would not! 35 Behold, your house is left unto you desolate: and verily I say unto you, Ye shall not see me, until the time come when ye shall say, Blessed is he that cometh in the name of the Lord.

Before you think that this fractal was not fulfilled by Israel as well as Nebuchadnezzar consider the following. Just as Nebuchadnezzar abandoned his house for 7 years to live with the beasts of the field, so also judgment was declared by Yeshua over the House of Israel that resulted in His departure from their midst until the days of restoration.

Acts 1:6, When they therefore were come together, they asked of him, saying, Lord, wilt thou at this time restore again the kingdom to Israel?

Just as Nebuchadnezzar had to fulfill his time as a beast, so did Israel. Why? Because of their rejection of the true Image of God, Yeshua. They were left with an abandoned house and forced into thousands of years of exile into the wilderness of the gentile nations. Before you reject the possibility that they had to fulfill this image of death and exile just like Nebuchadnezzar think about the following. Just as the administration of the flesh brings exile and death, so also Israel fulfilled this same prophetic fractal. Even the rabbi's Oral Torah says that the Gentiles are as beasts of the field. Israel, who had rejected the Messiah was cast out of their house and had to live among the gentiles (goyim). The Rabbi's depict the goyim as "beasts".

"The seed of the goyim is like an animal." Sanhedrin 74b

"All Gentile children are animals." Yebamoth 98a

God had given them the Kingdom and His Laws (the Written Torah of Moses). Because they rejected His ways and started following their own ways, God gave them over to their fallen image and let that seed manifest itself in their history. They moved from having the imagery of God to having the imagery of beasts. We will not at this point go into how long Israel's exile would last as detailed in Daniel's prophecies. But only remark that they were fulfilling a fractal that was destined to be fulfilled and concluded in their "resurrection" and acceptance of the new administrator of Resurrection life, the Image of God, Yeshua the Messiah.

Daniel 9:25, Know therefore and understand, that from the going forth of the commandment to restore and to build Jerusalem unto the Messiah the

Prince shall be seven weeks, and threescore and two weeks: the street shall be built again, and the wall, even in troublous times.

Just as a portion of this prophecy was fulfilled in seed form preceding the first coming of the Son of God, so also a greater manifestation of this same prophecy is fulfilled over a greater duration of time preceding Yeshua's second coming. We will delve more into the timing and nature of this prophecy later in the book.

Acts 1:6, When they therefore were come together, they asked of him, saying, Lord, wilt thou at this time restore again the kingdom to Israel? 7 And he said unto them, It is not for you to know the times or the seasons, which the Father hath put in his own power.

This horror of exile and banishment was presaged in the exile of Israel to Egypt and is again typified by the conflict between Moses and Pharaoh and the God of Israel vs. the false gods of Egypt.

Genesis 15:12, And when the sun was going down, a deep sleep fell upon Abram; and, lo, an horror of great darkness fell upon him. 13 And he said unto Abram, Know of a surety that thy seed shall be a stranger in a land that is not theirs, and shall serve them; and they shall afflict them four hundred years;

Each time God comes into covenant with someone, terrible and wonderful things happen. Imagine how Abraham must have felt, having the joy of coming into personal covenant with God, then to be told that his very own children would suffer exile and bondage for hundreds of years. That doesn't sound like a gift or a blessing, does it? But it does sound like Abraham and His seed were chosen to manifest ultimate realities and patterns, just like the tabernacle was to show mankind heavenly realties. What a choice and what destiny. Terrible and wonderful...just like the Tree of the Knowledge of Good and Evil! I dare say many of us would pass on such a "gift". But in reality, that is what we have chosen as Christians...that we would fulfill His pattern and fractal...like a seed in death and then as an ascended fruit in resurrection life.

Think about all the calamities that the "Chosen people" have suffered to manifest the Glory of God.
- Abraham was promised children beyond counting...yet he and Sarah couldn't even have one child.
- Ishmael was born first through the planning of Abraham and was rejected.
- Isaac was the promised seed, but in his old age, he couldn't see to determine who the next seed would be.
- Jacob through events of circumstance obtained the inheritance, yet is forced into exile by his brother Esau.
- Jacob, who finally returns to the land, loses his son Joseph to an

imaginary "beast" and believes for several decades that his promised seed is dead.

> o   Genesis 37:20, Come now therefore, and let us slay him, and cast him into some pit, and we will say, Some evil beast hath devoured him: and we shall see what will become of his dreams.

- Joseph is exiled to Egypt (as an allegory of death) by his very own brothers.
- Moses is raised to be a prince of Egypt and is exiled for 40 years.
- Moses is raised by God to deliver His people from Egypt then is told that he cannot enter the Promised Land.
- The first generation saved from Egypt, dies in the wilderness (except Joshua & Caleb) and do not get to enter the promised land.
- The judges were given the right to rule Israel and were rejected by the people.
- The people of Israel demanded a king like the gentiles and God rejected Him.
- Saul was promised the kingdom then it was given to David.
- David was promised a kingship that would last forever and the nation was exiled into the nations.
- Israel was returned to Israel only to reject the Messiah…
- The Image of God was given for the world and the world demanded and finally manifested the image of the Beast.
- Israel was promised the Land of Israel and has spent most of their existence in exile…until…
- The pattern of death and resurrection continues until the restoration of all things.

What a blessing… I think many of us would like to pass on these kinds of gifts. But this is what we have signed up for, that we would fulfill the patterns and images of God…according to His will and not ours. We must follow in Yeshua's footsteps and that means we must fulfill the same patterns that He fulfilled.

Romans 6:3, Know ye not, that so many of us as were baptized into Jesus Christ were baptized into his death?. . . 10 Let their eyes be darkened, that they may not see, and bow down their back alway. 11 I say then, Have they stumbled that they should fall? God forbid: but rather through their fall salvation is come unto the Gentiles, for to provoke them to jealousy. 12 Now if the fall of them be the riches of the world, and the diminishing of them the riches of the Gentiles; how much more their fulness? 13 For I speak to you Gentiles, inasmuch as I am the apostle of the Gentiles, I magnify mine office:14 If by any means I may provoke to emulation them which are my flesh, and might save some of them. 15 For if the casting away of them be the reconciling of the world, what shall the receiving of them be, but life from the dead?

Death and then resurrection. Shall we as those grafted into the Covenants of

Promise through Yeshua the Messiah look down upon Abraham's physical descendants that are in exile and fulfilling the prophecies of God? No.

> Romans 11:1, I say then, Hath God cast away his people? God forbid. For I also am an Israelite, of the seed of Abraham, of the tribe of Benjamin.

Israel is fulfilling the same pattern of death and resurrection as the covenant and the Law. The same pattern as the administrators. The same pattern as the shadow and the manifestation. . . seed and resurrection. Yeshua is not the manifestation of the Law, He is the manifestation of God's presence, name, and Image. What the old administration couldn't do, He was sent to do. What the Law couldn't do, God's righteousness was sent and manifested to do. Paul's comments hang in the air without rebuttal. Whether you are talking about the Torah or the "essence" of the Torah, the answer is the same from God's perspective. The Law could not be sent because it could not save.

- Romans 8:1, There is therefore now no condemnation to them which are in Christ Yeshua, who walk not after the flesh, but after the Spirit. 2 For the law of the Spirit of life in Christ Yeshua hath made me free from the law of sin and death. 3 For what the law could not do, in that it was weak through the flesh, God sending his own Son in the likeness of sinful flesh, and for sin, condemned sin in the flesh:
- Romans 3:19, Now we know that what things soever the law saith, it saith to them who are under the law: that every mouth may be stopped, and all the world may become guilty before God. 20 Therefore by the deeds of the law there shall no flesh be justified in his sight: for by the law is the knowledge of sin. 21 But now the righteousness of God without the law is manifested.
- Hebrews 10:1, For the law having a shadow of good things to come, and not the very image of the things, can never with those sacrifices which they offered year by year continually make the comers thereunto perfect.

The scriptures are clear, the Torah was only a shadow, and not the very image of the things; it could not save and was therefore not sent to save. We have already seen that the shadow is associated with death (Psalm 23:4, Job 10:22, Matthew 4:16). The first administration of the Law of Moses is also associated with that shadow of death and rightfully so. It was fulfilling the same pattern and fractal of a seed (death) then fruit (resurrection). It was indeed a shadow of good things to come, but because it brought death it could not be the very image of what was hoped for...only the Son of God with unending life could be the true Image of God. Why? He manifested unending life, God in the flesh.

Considering the Apostles are all very clear that the "image" that was sent is "God manifest in the flesh" (1 Timothy 3:16), "the fullness of the Godhead bodily" (Colossians 2:9), and "the image of the invisible God" (Colossians 1:15), we can only conclude that the Messiah is the Image of God, not the image of the Torah. The un–scriptural teaching that Yeshua is the image of the Torah, manifestation of the Torah, the living Torah, or one with the Torah, are in conflict with the truth of the scriptures.

- Zechariah 3:8, Hear now, O Joshua the high priest, thou, and thy fellows that sit before thee: for they are men wondered at: for, <u>behold, I will bring forth my servant the Branch</u>.
- Zechariah 6:12, And speak unto him, saying, Thus speaketh the Lord of hosts, saying, <u>Behold the man whose name is The Branch; and he shall grow up out of his place, and he shall build the temple of the Lord</u>:

All of these scriptures and Yeshua's own testimony confirm that we are to be grafted into the Lord, and as a consequence of that covenant of faith and belief in His name, we are saved and not by any work or worth of our own. Being joined to the Messiah Yeshua we are of "the Commonwealth of Israel". Being joined to the Torah does not save us.

Acts 4:11, This is the stone which was set at nought of you builders, which is become the head of the corner. 12 <u>Neither is there salvation in any other: for there is none other name under heaven given among men, whereby we must be saved</u>. 13 Now when they saw the boldness of Peter and John, and perceived that they were unlearned and ignorant men, they marvelled; and they took knowledge of them, that they had been with Yeshua.

You must be grafted into the Messiah Yeshua, the manifest Name of YHWH, in order to be saved. It does not matter if you are Jew or Gentile, bond or free, at home or abroad. Keeping the Torah will not save you, it will leave you under condemnation and death without the resurrected manifest Name of YHWH, the Messiah Yeshua, the administrator of the Resurrected Covenant (Torah). Once you have the Messiah and are grafted into Him, you are then of the Commonwealth of Israel and you should follow Yeshua's command to "keep my commandments", the Law of Moses (John 15:10).

It is easy to see why people would assume this tree is Israel or Judah. But the scriptures are clear that this tree is the Covenant of faith in the Messiah Yeshua, the manifest Name of YHWH. There is none other name under heaven whereby we must be saved.

The assumption that being "grafted into the Torah" will save the sinner is completely erroneous and unscriptural. Also, the term "works of the Law" (Torah) is not talking about the Oral Torah. It is talking about the natural consequence of the Torah of Moses (the Written Torah) under the administration of sin and death, the flesh.

Galatians 2:16, Knowing that a man is <u>not justified by the works of the law</u>, but by the faith of Yeshua, even we have believed in Yeshua, that we might be justified by the faith of Christ, and <u>not by the works of the law: for by the works of the law shall no flesh be justified</u>.

CONDEMNATION BY THE TORAH; THE FRUIT OF DEATH

Paul affirms that the Torah of Moses cannot bring about the fruit that God desires because of our flesh. Remember Paul is always contrasting the flesh and the spirit. Notice in Galatians 2 Paul moves from talking about the works of the law to describing what they produce.

Galatians 2:17, But if, while we seek to be justified by Christ, <u>we ourselves also are found sinners,</u> is therefore Christ the minister of sin? God forbid. 18 For if I build again the things which I destroyed, <u>I make myself a transgressor. 19 For I through the law am dead to the law,</u> that I might live unto God. 20 I am crucified with Christ: nevertheless I live; yet not I, but Christ liveth in me: and the life which I now live in the flesh I live by the faith of the Son of God, who loved me, and gave himself for me. 21 I do not frustrate the grace of God: for <u>if righteousness come by the law, then Christ is dead in vain.</u>

The Written Torah under the old administration does what it should, it identifies you as a sinner and a transgressor and brings about the death of our flesh. This is the "works of the law" under the old administration.

Galatians 5:16, This I say then, <u>Walk in the Spirit, and ye shall not fulfil the lust of the flesh.</u> 17 For the <u>flesh lusteth against the Spirit, and the Spirit against the flesh: and these are contrary the one to the other:</u> so that ye cannot do the things that ye would. 18 But <u>if ye be led of the Spirit, ye are not under the law</u> 19 Now the <u>works of the flesh are manifest,</u> which are these; Adultery, fornication, uncleanness, lasciviousness, 20 Idolatry, witchcraft, hatred, variance, emulations, wrath, strife, seditions, heresies, 21 Envyings, murders, drunkenness, revellings, and such like: of the which I tell you before, as I have also told you in time past, that they which do such things shall not inherit the kingdom of God. 22 But the <u>fruit of the Spirit is</u> love, joy, peace, longsuffering, gentleness, goodness, faith, 23 Meekness, temperance: against such there is no law. 24 And <u>they that are Christ's have crucified the flesh with the affections and lusts. 25 If we live in the Spirit,</u> let us also walk in the Spirit.

Paul is contrasting the old administration of the Written Torah, which brings about the manifestation of sin and death in our flesh, with the new administration of the Written Torah that brings about resurrection life. It does what it was intended to do, it condemns us and bring about the fractal of death to the flesh. This old administration afflicted with the spirit of disobedience needs to be replaced by the new administration of the Spirit of Christ and manifest His fruits and resurrection life.

Romans 7:24, O wretched man that I am! who shall deliver me from the body of this death?

Paul, even though saved, is in great desperation. Why? His body is still flesh and under judgment. He has a broken image. Under the old administration of the

Torah we are left under sin and death and need to be saved. How? Our fallen and broken image needs to be restored by taking on the Messiah's image.

> Colossians 1:13, Who hath delivered us from the power of darkness, and hath translated us into the kingdom of his dear Son:14 In whom we have redemption through his blood, even the forgiveness of sins:15 Who is the image of the invisible God, the firstborn of every creature:16 For by him were all things created, that are in heaven, and that are in earth, visible and invisible, whether they be thrones, or dominions, or principalities, or powers: all things were created by him, and for him:17 And he is before all things, and by him all things consist. 18 And he is the head of the body, the church: who is the beginning, the firstborn from the dead; that in all things he might have the preeminence. 19 For it pleased the Father that in him should all fulness dwell; 20 And, having made peace through the blood of his cross, by him to reconcile all things unto himself; by him, I say, whether they be things in earth, or things in heaven. 21 And you, that were sometime alienated and enemies in your mind by wicked works, yet now hath he reconciled 22 In the body of his flesh through death, to present you holy and unblameable and unreproveable in his sight:

God, through Yeshua, is reconciling the world back to the Father. Notice all things are being reconciled to the Father, not back to the Torah, and not back to Israel.

How long is the old administration of the Written Torah in effect? Until you die, hence you must die in Yeshua. We die into the baptism of His death.

> Romans 7:1, Know ye not, brethren, (for I speak to them that know the law,) how that the law hath dominion over a man as long as he liveth?

How do you become freed of the old administration of the Written Torah? By the body of Christ.

> Romans 7:4, Wherefore, my brethren, ye also are become dead to the law by the body of Christ; that ye should be married to another, even to him who is raised from the dead, that we should bring forth fruit unto God.

What did the old administration of the Written Torah produce? Death.

> Romans 7:5, For when we were in the flesh, the motions of sins, which were by the law, did work in our members to bring forth fruit unto death.

Paul even clarifies that the Torah was supposed to be light and life, as many teachers say, but it still brought forth death. He is not referring to the Oral Torah (Rabbinical Traditions), as some mistakenly teach to be the Middle Wall of Partition described in Ephesians 2:14 (which God never acknowledged as valid in the first place).

Romans 7:7, What shall we say then? <u>Is the law sin? God forbid</u>. Nay, <u>I had not known sin, but by the law</u>: for I had not known lust, except the law had said, Thou shalt not covet. 8 But <u>sin, taking occasion by the commandment, wrought in me all manner of concupiscence. For without the law sin was dead</u>. 9 For I was alive without the law once: but <u>when the commandment came, sin revived, and I died</u>. 10 And the <u>commandment, which was ordained to life, I found to be unto death</u>. For sin, taking occasion by the commandment, deceived me, and by it slew me.

Paul makes no equivocation in calling the Written Torah "good", but "death to me".

Romans 7:12 Wherefore <u>the law (nomos-Strong's 3551) is holy, and the commandment (entole-Strong's 1785) holy, and just, and good. 13 Was then that which is good made death unto me</u>? God forbid. But sin, that it might appear sin, <u>working death in me by that which is good</u>; that sin by the commandment might become exceeding sinful.

The Written Torah, which is good and should be light and life to us, brought us sin and death under the old administration. Hence it is the Law (Torah) of Sin and Death. Recognizing his absolute condemnation under the Torah of Sin and Death, the Written Torah, Paul begs for deliverance, realizing he cannot save himself. Notice again Paul starts by recognizing the Written Torah is good but it is still the Torah of Sin and Death to him.

Romans 7:14, For we know that the <u>law is spiritual: but I am carnal, sold under sin</u>. 15 For that which I do I allow not: for what I would, that do I not; but what I hate, that do I. 16 If then I do that which I would not, <u>I consent unto the law that it is good</u>. 17 Now then it is no more I that do it, but sin that dwelleth in me. 18 For I know that <u>in me (that is, in my flesh,) dwelleth no good thing</u>: for to will is present with me; but how to perform that which is good I find not.

SAVED BY THE NEW ADMINISTRATOR OF THE TORAH
Paul shows that his flesh is incapable of fulfilling the Written Torah and leaves him under sin and death, without the Messiah Yeshua, the new administrator.

Romans 7:19, For the good that I would I do not: but the evil which I would not, that I do. 20 Now if I do that I would not, it is no more I that do it, but sin that dwelleth in me. 21 I find <u>then a law, that, when I would do good, evil is present with me</u>.

Then Paul recognizes that though his flesh comes under the condemnation of the Written Torah, the Law of Sin and Death, his inward man still delights in the goodness of the Written Torah, even though it condemns him.

> Romans 7:22, For I delight in the law of God after the inward man:23 But I see another law in my members, warring against the law of my mind, and bringing me into captivity to the law of sin which is in my members. 24 O wretched man that I am! who shall deliver me from the body of this death?

Again, Paul contrasts the spirit with the flesh and recognizes he needs to be delivered from his flesh, which is condemned by the Written Torah. How does this come about if he cannot do it himself? He serves God with his mind, putting on the mind of Christ.

> Romans 7:25, I thank God through Yeshua our Lord. So then with <u>the mind I myself serve the law of God; but with the flesh the law of sin</u>.

Paul serves God with his mind while his flesh is under the law of sin and is condemned. He says he needs to be delivered from the body of death…his flesh.

> 1 Corinthians 2:16, For who hath known the mind of the Lord, that he may instruct him? but <u>we have the mind of Christ.</u>

- **Is the Torah good?** Yes.
- **Does the Torah condemn our flesh?** Yes.
- **Do we need to die to the old administration of the flesh**? Yes.
- **The new administration lives according to the** _____?
Spirit.
- **Does any of this happen through our own effort?** No.
- **How does it happen?** Through Christ, being buried with Him in baptism.

> Romans 6:1, What shall we say then? <u>Shall we continue in sin</u>, that grace may abound? 2 God forbid. How <u>shall we, that are dead to sin, live any longer therein</u>? 3 Know ye not, that so many of us as were <u>baptized into Yeshua were baptized into his death</u>? 4 Therefore <u>we are buried with him by baptism into death: that like as Christ was raised up from the dead by the glory of the Father, even so we also should walk in newness of life</u>.

Notice we are to share in the imagery with Christ. We die to the old administration, the Written Torah of Sin and Death under the flesh. We become buried with Christ and then rise with Him in the new administration of resurrection life, according to the Written Torah under grace and abundant mercy. We fulfill the death and resurrection fractal, just like the Messiah and just like the Law of Moses. It is the same pattern: seed then fruit, death then resurrection, flesh then spirit, Torah of Sin and Death then Torah of Resurrection Life.

Romans 6:5, For if we have been <u>planted together in the likeness of his death, we shall be also in the likeness of his resurrection</u>:6 Knowing this, that <u>our old man is crucified with him, that the body of sin might be destroyed</u>, that henceforth we should not serve sin. 7 For <u>he that is dead is freed from sin</u>. 8 Now <u>if we be dead with Christ, we believe that we shall also live with him</u>:9 Knowing that <u>Christ being raised from the dead dieth no more; death hath no more dominion over him</u>.

This is why the imagery of Yeshua's death and our joining with him in His death is so important.

Now that you are passed from death to life, to what are you restored? Is the end goal simply to rejoin the House of Judah with the House of Israel (Ephraim-Northern 10 tribes)? What does Paul say we are restored to?

Romans 6:10, For in that <u>he died, he died unto sin once: but in that he liveth, he liveth unto God</u>. 11 Likewise reckon ye also yourselves to be <u>dead indeed unto sin, but alive unto God</u> through Yeshua our Lord. 12 Let not sin therefore reign in your mortal body, that ye should obey it in the lusts thereof. 13 Neither yield ye your members as instruments of unrighteousness unto sin: but <u>yield yourselves unto God</u>, as those that are alive from the dead, and your members as instruments of righteousness unto God.

Paul once again reaffirms, just as he had in Ephesians 2:15–16, that the goal is to be restored to God and have His enmity towards us (all mankind) removed. Through that effectual work of the Messiah we are unified with God.

Are we still under the Torah of Sin and Death, the Written Torah, which condemns the flesh?

Romans 6:14, For sin shall not have dominion over you: for <u>ye are not under the law</u>, but under grace. 15 What then? <u>shall we sin, because we are not under the law, but under grace? God forbid</u>.

Paul says we are not. If we were, it would condemn us. We have left the old administration of sin, death, and condemnation, and now in Yeshua, we are under the new administration of grace.

Does the Witten Torah remain? Yes. Paul says we are not to sin and emphatically says, "God forbid".

Romans 3:31, Do we then make void the law through faith? God forbid, <u>we establish the law</u>.

Clearly this is the same Written Torah, the Law of Moses, under the new administration of grace and mercy as depicted in Exodus 34, with the new administrator, Yeshua the Messiah, under resurrection life. Being in the flesh, we cannot do the work, we cannot save ourselves. With circumcised hearts and unclean flesh, we serve the Messiah. This is the "offense of the cross" (Galatians 5:11) and the circumcision of the flesh is performed by the "minister of the circumcision" (Romans 15:8) the Messiah Yeshua.

Acts 4:11, This is the stone which was set at nought of you builders, which is become the head of the corner. 12 Neither is there salvation in any other: for there is none other name under heaven given among men, whereby we must be saved. 13 Now when they saw the boldness of Peter and John, and perceived that they were unlearned and ignorant men, they marvelled; and they took knowledge of them, that they had been with Yeshua.

You must be grafted into the Messiah Yeshua, the manifest Name of YHWH, in order to be saved. It does not matter if you are Jew or Gentile, bond or free, at home or abroad. Keeping the Torah will not save you, it will leave you under condemnation and death without the resurrected manifest Name of YHWH, the Messiah Yeshua, the administrator of the Resurrected Covenant (Torah). Once you are saved you should do as Yeshua says, "keep my commandments" (John 14:15). Once you have the Messiah and are grafted into Him, you are then of the Commonwealth of Israel and a Jew inwardly. What do we have in common? We have the Messiah and the new administration of resurrection life with grace and abundant mercy.

Notice the contrasting of the administrations. Remember that Exodus 20/24 shows the first giving of the law, presented with judgment and sacrifice (blood). The second giving of those same words are seen with grace and abundant mercy and a new administrator, the manifest name of the Lord, the one to whom Moses' bows to and worships.

Exodus 34:1, And the Lord said unto Moses, Hew thee two tablets of stone like unto the first: and I will write upon these tablets the words that were in the first tablets, which thou brakest. 2 And be ready in the morning, and come up in the morning unto mount Sinai, and present thyself there to me in the top of the mount. 3 And no man shall come up with thee, neither let any man be seen throughout all the mount; neither let the flocks nor herds feed before that mount. 4 And he hewed two tablets of stone like unto the first; and Moses rose up early in the morning, and went up unto mount Sinai, as the Lord had commanded him, and took in his hand the two tablets of stone. 5 And the Lord descended in the cloud, and stood with him there, and proclaimed the Name of the Lord. 6 And the Lord passed by before him, and proclaimed, The Lord, The Lord God, merciful and gracious, longsuffering, and abundant in goodness and truth, 7 Keeping mercy for thousands, forgiving iniquity and transgression and sin, and that will by no means clear the guilty; visiting the iniquity of the fathers upon the children, and upon the children's children, unto the third and to the fourth generation. 8 And Moses made haste, and bowed his head toward the earth, and worshipped. 9 And he said, If now I have found grace in thy sight, O Lord, let my Lord, I pray thee, go among us; for it is a stiffnecked people; and pardon our iniquity and our sin, and take us for thine inheritance. 10 And he said, Behold, I make a covenant: before all thy people I will do marvels, such as have not been done in all the earth, nor in any nation: and all the people among which thou art shall see the work of the Lord: for it is a terrible thing that I will do with thee.

The separation mentioned in Ephesians 2 is between God and man, not between the Jews and Gentiles or the House of Judah and the House of Israel. Both houses plus the Gentiles were concluded as "all under sin" and can only be saved by the manifest Name of YHWH, Yeshua the Messiah. The Torah could not be sent to save or manifested to save, but God's righteousness could. This is why Yeshua is the manifestation of God in the flesh, the Image of God, and the fullness of the Godhead bodily. This is also why Moses typifies the administration of death (seed) and the flesh and why he could not ascend to the Promised Land. This is also why Elijah typifies the administration of (fruit) resurrection life and ascending into the Shekinah Glory and receiving the manifest Name of the Lord, Yeshua the Messiah.

8 THE IMAGE OF GOD VS. THE SON OF PERDITION

Isaiah 7:14, Therefore the Lord himself shall give you a sign; Behold, a virgin shall conceive, and <u>bear a son, and shall call his name Immanuel</u>.

What does "Immanuel" (Emmanuel) mean? What is the significance of this prophecy? Is it just about the coming of the Son of God or is it something more? Why is the coming of the Son of God or "Son of Man" (Matthew 9:6, 10:23, 12:8, 40, 13:41) significant?

Matthew 1:22, Now all this was done, that it might be fulfilled which was spoken of the Lord by the prophet, saying, 23 Behold, a virgin shall be with child, and shall bring forth a son, and <u>they shall call his name Emmanuel, which being interpreted is, God with us</u>.

What is being made one? God in man.

Ephesians 4:3, <u>Endeavouring to keep the unity of the Spirit</u> in the bond of peace. 4 There is one body, and <u>one Spirit</u>, even as ye are called in one hope of your calling; 5 One Lord, one faith, one baptism, 6 <u>One God and Father of all, who is above all, and through all, and in you all</u>.

The work of the Messiah is to keep the unity of the Spirit, "God…in you all".

How is the unification between God and man going to occur? By God's manifest Name, the Messiah.

Exodus 34:5, And <u>the Lord descended</u> in the cloud, and stood with him there, and proclaimed the Name of the Lord. 6 And <u>the Lord passed by</u> before him, and <u>proclaimed, The Lord, The Lord God, merciful and gracious,</u> longsuffering, and abundant in goodness and truth…8 And <u>Moses made haste, and bowed his head toward the earth, and worshipped.</u>

Moses is given a personal preview of the new administration, the new administrator, and a declaration of the better promises.

What is the same between the old and the new administrations? They have the same commandments.

Exodus 34:1, And the Lord said unto Moses, <u>Hew thee two tablets of stone like unto the first: and I will write upon these tablets the words that were in the first tablets,</u> which thou brakest.

Why have a Law (Torah) of Sin and Death? To condemn the flesh and conclude "all under sin".

Galatians 3:19, <u>Wherefore then serveth the law</u>? It was added because of transgressions, till the seed should come to whom the promise was made; and it was ordained by angels in the hand of a mediator. 20 Now a mediator is not a mediator of one, <u>but God is one.</u>

Notice the emphasis of this scripture is to identify the purpose of the Law (Torah), since it will not justify you.

Galatians 3:10, For <u>as many as are of the works of the law are under the curse</u>: for it is written, <u>Cursed is every one that continueth not in all things which are written in the book of the law to do them.</u>

Paul even cites that this is referring to the Law of Moses (the Written Torah), not the Oral Torah, by clarifying "which are written in the book of the law…" Since we have transgressed the law, death is our penalty. The Messiah came to pay that penalty for us. In reality we should be hung upon the tree.

Deuteronomy 21:22, <u>And if a man have committed a sin worthy of death, and he be to be put to death, and thou hang him on a tree:</u>

Paul reiterates over and over again that it is the Written Torah, under the administration of sin and death (the flesh), that condemns us and leaves us "under the law" or "under sin" or "under judgment". Some Messianics say that it was the Oral Torah (Rabbinical Traditions/Traditions of Men) that was nailed to the cross. This is an error. We have already confirmed we are saved by grace and that we are to walk the Written Torah, and the Oral Torah is not required for salvation. You are saved by the Messiah, and then you are to walk the Written Torah. Colossians

2:14 is not talking about the Oral Torah.

Colossians 2:14, Blotting out the handwriting of ordinances that was against us, which was contrary to us, and took it out of the way, nailing it to his cross;

It is talking about the "writ of judgment" of our transgressions of our violations of the Written Torah, which is the penalty that is paid by Yeshua on the cross. It appears that some teachers want to make the Oral Torah the Middle Wall of Partition, when in reality the Middle Wall of Partition is our spirit of disobedience that refuses to follow God's Written Torah. Ephesians 2 makes it so clear what is causing the separation between us and God.

Ephesians 2:2, Wherein in time past ye walked according to the course of this world, according to the prince of the power of the air, the spirit that now worketh in the children of disobedience:

It is the spirit of disobedience that is the Middle Wall of Partition! This spirit has placed all "under sin" outside the Temple precinct as unclean people.

Who are the "two" that are separated in Ephesians 2? Us and God!

How are these two reconciled? By that one body, Yeshua, the Image of God, the temple restored, God in man, who is bearing the penalty of our sins on His cross! Yes, the Torah was meant for light and life for us, but it has become "a curse to us".

Galatians 3:11, But that no man is justified by the law in the sight of God, it is evident: for, The just shall live by faith. 12 And the law is not of faith: but, The man that doeth them shall live in them. 13 Christ hath redeemed us from the curse of the law, being made a curse for us: for it is written, Cursed is every one that hangeth on a tree:

Again, the goal is to remove the spirit of disobedience and have it replaced with the Holy Spirit, so that God may dwell in us without enmity and remove the wall of separation which is between us and God.

Galatians 3:14, That the blessing of Abraham might come on the Gentiles through Yeshua; that we might receive the promise of the Spirit through faith. 15 Brethren, I speak after the manner of men; Though it be but a man's covenant, yet if it be confirmed, no man disannulleth, or addeth thereto.

Since the law (the Written Torah) could not bring life, and only brought death, it had to be annulled.

Galatians 3:21, Is the law then against the promises of God? God forbid: for if there had been a law given which could have given life, verily righteousness should have been by the law.

Jews and Gentiles are concluded to be "all under sin" and outside the Middle Wall of Partition of the tabernacle. All have an unclean spirit and need to die to the flesh and to the old administration and take hold, by faith, of the new administration of the Torah of Resurrection Life with the resurrected administrator, Yeshua the Messiah. Why? This is the only way that God can end the separation and dwell with us by one spirit.

Galatians 3:22, But the scripture hath concluded all under sin, that the promise by faith of Yeshua might be given to them that believe. 23 But before faith came, we were kept under the law, shut up unto the faith which should afterwards be revealed. 24 Wherefore the law was our schoolmaster to bring us unto Christ, that we might be justified by faith. 25 But after that faith is come, we are no longer under a schoolmaster. 26 For ye are all the children of God by faith in Christ Yeshua. 27 For as many of you as have been baptized into Christ have put on Christ. 28 There is neither Jew nor Greek, there is neither bond nor free, there is neither male nor female: for ye are all one in Christ Yeshua.

REVIEW OF EPHESIANS 2 IN REGARD TO THE MIDDLE WALL OF PARTITION AND IMMANUEL (EMMANUEL)
Some Hebrew Roots (Messianic) teachers believe that Judah is still on the inside of the court and the Gentiles need to be grafted into them, and that Yeshua is doing away with the Middle Wall of Partition (typifying the Oral Torah/Traditions of Men) that causes conflict between Jew and Gentile. They believe this is the focus of Ephesians 2. It is not. Jew and Gentile are both "under sin" and need the wall of separation between them and God to be removed by the Spirit of Christ.

Ephesians 2:8, For by grace are ye saved through faith; and that not of yourselves: it is the gift of God:9 Not of works, lest any man should boast. 10 For we are his workmanship, created in Christ Yeshua unto good works, which God hath before ordained that we should walk in them. 11 Wherefore remember, that ye being in time past Gentiles in the flesh, who are called Uncircumcision by that which is called the Circumcision in the flesh made by hands; 12 That at that time ye were without Christ, being aliens from the Commonwealth of Israel, and strangers from the covenants of promise, having no hope, and without God in the world:13 But now in Christ Yeshua ye who sometimes were far off are made nigh by the blood of Christ. 14 For he is our peace, who hath made both one, and hath broken down the middle wall of partition between us; 15 Having abolished in his flesh the enmity, even the law of commandments contained in ordinances; for to make in himself of twain one new man, so making peace; 16 And that he might reconcile both unto God in one body by the cross, having slain the enmity thereby:

Notice this "peace" was referred to in Colossians.

Who is the peace between?

Colossians 1:19, For it pleased the Father that in him should all fulness dwell; 20 And, having made peace through the blood of his cross, <u>by him to reconcile all things unto himself</u>; by him, I say, whether they be things in earth, or things in heaven. 21 And you, that were sometime <u>alienated and enemies in your mind by wicked works, yet now hath he reconciled 22 In the body of his flesh through death, to present you holy and unblameable and unreproveable in his sight</u>:

Again, who is the "peace", or lack of enmity, between?
All creation is being reconciled. : "reconcile all things unto himself."

Who is all creation being reconciled to? Judah/Israel?
No. This is not Judah or Israel; "all things" are being "reconciled to himself".

Who is "himself"?
Galatians 1:19 identifies "himself" as the Father (God).

How was the Father and all creation separated?

Galatians 1:21, sometime <u>alienated and enemies in your mind</u> by wicked works

This is the very same enmity and Middle Wall of Partition that is referred to in Ephesians 2:15–16.

Once again, how is this remedied?

Galatians 1:22, <u>In the body of his flesh through death</u>, to present you holy and unblameable and unreproveable in his sight.

Whose flesh are we talking about? Israel/Judah?
No. This is Yeshua's flesh. In the body of His flesh… and created in Christ.

Is it through the Torah's flesh?
No.

Is it through the name of the Torah? No. It is through Yeshua's name. Some have incorrectly stated that this one new man is Israel or Judah or the joining of both. If you look more closely you will see that it is through the redemption of the Messiah that we (both Jews and Gentiles) become a part of His Body, Christ.

Without the Messiah, there is no Commonwealth of Israel and there is no peace between man and God. The enmity that is slain is not between Jew and Gentile, nor the two houses of Israel, though they will surely be joined together in the Messiah Yeshua. The enmity that is slain is between God and us, through our violations of the covenant and our lack of faith in His provision of the manifest Name of YHWH to become our righteousness through faith in His name.

Notice those who are strangers to the Commonwealth of Israel and the covenants of promise are "without Christ". This is what makes you either a part of the Commonwealth of Israel or apart from it. Being without the Messiah makes you a stranger from God.

> Ephesians 2:12, That <u>at that time ye were without Christ</u>, being aliens from the Commonwealth of Israel, and strangers from the covenants of promise, having no hope, and without God in the world:13 But now in Christ Yeshua ye who sometimes were far off are made nigh by the blood of Christ.

It is not the Torah that makes you of the Commonwealth of Israel, it is having the Messiah via faith in His manifest Name, YHWH. This tree of Romans 11 is all about faith in the manifest Name of YHWH, the Messiah Yeshua. He bears the branches; the branches do not bear Him…by their own works or worth. Paul addresses this very same issue with the Corinthians.

> 1 Corinthians 13:1, And I, brethren, could not speak unto you as unto spiritual, but as unto carnal, even as unto babes in Christ. 2 I have fed you with milk, and not with meat: for hitherto ye were not able to bear it, neither yet now are ye able. 3 For ye are yet carnal: for whereas there is among you envying, and strife, and divisions, are ye not carnal, and walk as men? 4 For while one saith, I am of Paul; and another, I am of Apollos; are ye not carnal? 5 Who then is Paul, and who is Apollos, but ministers by whom ye believed, even as the Lord gave to every man? 6 I have planted, Apollos watered; but God gave the increase. 7 So then neither is he that planteth any thing, neither he that watereth; but God that giveth the increase. 8 Now he that planteth and he that watereth are one: and every man shall receive his own reward according to his own labour. 9 For we are labourers together with God: ye are God's husbandry, ye are God's building. 10 According to the grace of God which is given unto me, as a wise masterbuilder, <u>I have laid the foundation,</u> and another buildeth thereon. But let every man take heed how he buildeth thereupon. 11 <u>For other foundation can no man lay than that is laid, which is Yeshua</u>.

Paul is clear, redemption comes only by the manifest Name of YHWH, the Messiah Yeshua. It does not matter who taught you or who baptized you. Paul did not save you; Yeshua did!

> 1 Corinthians 1:12, Now this I say, that every one of you saith, I am of Paul; and I of Apollos; and I of Cephas; and I of Christ. 13 <u>Is Christ divided? was Paul crucified for you? or were ye baptized in the name of Paul?</u>. . . 23 But <u>we preach Christ crucified</u>, unto the Jews a stumblingblock, and unto the Greeks foolishness; 24 But unto them which are called, both Jews and Greeks, Christ the power of God, and the wisdom of God.

It is this crucifixion tree that the manifest Name of YHWH, Yeshua the Messiah, was affixed to that pictures the engrafting of the believer into the covenant of faith. We should conform our image to His image.

Matthew 16:23, But he turned, and said unto Peter, Get thee behind me, Satan: thou art an offence unto me: for thou savourest not the things that be of God, but those that be of men. 24 Then said Yeshua unto his disciples, If any man will come after me, let him deny himself, and take up his cross, and follow me. 25 For whosoever will save his life shall lose it: and whosoever will lose his life for my sake shall find it.

Will keeping the Written Torah save you? No.

Romans 9:9, For I was alive without the law once: but when the commandment came, sin revived, and I died. 10 And the commandment, which was ordained to life, I found to be unto death. 11 For sin, taking occasion by the commandment, deceived me, and by it slew me.

This covenant, the Written Torah, under the administration of judgment brought condemnation and death to the flesh. We are all guilty under sin, which is the transgression of the law (Torah). We are not saved by keeping the Torah; we are saved by the new administration of grace and its resurrected administrator, the Countenance of YHWH, the Messiah Yeshua.

Romans 8:1, There is therefore now no condemnation to them which are in Christ Yeshua, who walk not after the flesh, but after the Spirit. 2 For the law of the Spirit of life in Christ Yeshua hath made me free from the law of sin and death. 3 For what the law could not do, in that it was weak through the flesh, God sending his own Son in the likeness of sinful flesh, and for sin, condemned sin in the flesh:

The Covenant (the Torah) brought death and judgment, but now the Resurrected Covenant and its resurrected administrator, the Name of YHWH, the Messiah, is administered with grace and mercy, which brings resurrected life via His righteousness.

Ephesians 2:8, For by grace are ye saved through faith; and that not of yourselves: it is the gift of God:9 Not of works, lest any man should boast. 10 For we are his workmanship, created in Christ Yeshua unto good works, which God hath before ordained that we should walk in them. 11 Wherefore remember, that ye being in time past Gentiles in the flesh, who are called Uncircumcision by that which is called the Circumcision in the flesh made by hands; 12 That at that time ye were without Christ, being aliens from the Commonwealth of Israel, and strangers from the covenants of promise, having no hope, and without God in the world:13 But now in Christ Yeshua ye who sometimes were far off are made nigh by the blood of Christ. 14 For he is our peace, who hath made both one, and hath broken down the middle wall of partition between us; 15 Having abolished in his flesh the enmity, even the law of commandments contained in ordinances; for to make in himself of twain one new man, so making peace; 16 And that he might reconcile both unto God in one body by the cross, having slain the enmity thereby:17 And came and preached peace to you which were afar off, and to them that were nigh. 18 For through him we both have access by one Spirit unto the Father. 19 Now therefore ye are no more strangers and foreigners, but fellowcitizens with the saints, and of the household of God; 20 And are built upon the foundation of the Apostles and prophets, Yeshua himself being the chief corner stone;

Notice what the exiles and uncircumcised were without that made them strangers to the Commonwealth of Israel: The Messiah Yeshua. It was the lack of the resurrected administrator of the Resurrected Covenant that made them strangers. Anyone is able to be identified with the Commonwealth of Israel if they have the resurrected administrator, the Messiah Yeshua. Notice Paul did not say it was the lack of the Torah that kept them from being identified as a part of the Commonwealth of Israel.

Romans 10:3, For they being ignorant of God's righteousness, and going about to establish their own righteousness, have not submitted themselves unto the righteousness of God.

Why is that? Even Judah, who has the Written Torah and is trying to "establish their own righteousness" thereby, is not a part of the Commonwealth of Israel because they are still under the tablets associated with death and judgment.

Romans 11:23, And they also, if they abide not still in unbelief, shall be grafted in: for God is able to graft them in again.

They rejected the new administrator, Yeshua the Messiah. Just like the Gentiles they also need the Gospel preached to them.

Romans 1:16, For I am not ashamed of the Gospel of Christ: for it is the power of God unto salvation to every one that believeth; to the Jew first, and also to the Greek.

The Jews along with those who keep the Torah also need to identify with and accept the administrator of the Resurrected Covenant, the resurrected Messiah Yeshua, in order to be in the Commonwealth of Israel. The goal is to be in Yeshua, and as a result of being in Yeshua, we become part of the Commonwealth of Israel.

We are not grafted into Judah or Israel. The Commonwealth of Israel is identified by the presence of the Messiah. It is His work that abolishes the Law (Torah) of Sin and Death, the first set of tablets, which identify sin and cause judgment and death via the flesh. Through the Messiah's flesh, He resurrects the tablets, the same commandments, the Torah, the covenant, this time with grace, mercy, and resurrected life, which is Spirit, and places it within our hearts. The conflict between the Torah and our hearts is now gone.

It is the state of the "spirit of disobedience" that causes God to separate Himself from His people. This is the middle wall of partition that is caused by the violation of the terms of the covenant. Notice Paul is talking about how we, without the Messiah Yeshua, are in exile from God and are separated from God. This Middle Wall of Partition is not referring to the separation between Jew and Gentile, nor Judah and the northern ten tribes of Israel that are in exile (Diaspora).

The Gospel of the Messiah is preached to both those that are far off and to those that are near. Both are separated from God and need the middle wall of partition, which separates us from God, to be brought down. This is the work of the manifest Name of YHWH. The wall went up between mankind and God because of our sin and violation of the covenant. When the wall of separation goes up we are without God in the world, Jews and Gentiles alike.

The two, God and man, are made one in Yeshua's resurrected flesh and image because he is administrating the Resurrected Covenant based upon grace and mercy, the covenants of promise. Remember God's goal is to be glorified in the eyes and the presence of His people (Numbers 27:14, Psalms 86:9, John 12:28, Revelation 15:4). We can only behold His image and countenance through the divine union of the glorified and resurrected countenance, the literal end and fulfillment, or embodiment of the manifest Name of YHWH. His image and countenance is transcribed on to ours.

Yeshua slays the enmity of the two (God and man) and makes them one with a resurrected heart. It is the enmity and separation between God and man that is abolished, which is caused by our transgression of the Covenant of God, the Torah.

> Ephesians 4:23, And be renewed in the spirit of your mind; 24 And that ye put on the new man, which after God is created in righteousness and true holiness. 25 Wherefore putting away lying, speak every man truth with his neighbour: for we are members one of another.

Yeshua the Messiah has made it possible for us to put on the image of the new man which is after the pattern and Image of God: Righteous, Holy, and without sin. Consequently, there is no transgression and therefore no enmity between us and God. We become temples that God can dwell within. There is no separation and we then have the embodiment of God in the world. Through Yeshua's work, God is made manifest in the world and His name is declared to all nations.

> Colossians 3:9, Lie not one to another, seeing that ye have put off the old man with his deeds; 10 And have put on the new man, which is renewed in knowledge after the image of him that created him:11 Where there is neither Greek nor Jew, circumcision nor uncircumcision, Barbarian, Scythian, bond nor free: but Christ is all, and in all.

Those who think that these scriptures are only talking about the re-unification of Israel are sadly mistaken. The goal is clear. They are not only to be reconciled with one another; the final goal is for all creation to be reconciled to God.

Ephesians 2:16, And that he might reconcile both unto God in one body by the cross, having slain the enmity thereby:

What is the goal? Reconcile all under sin to God.
...reconcile <u>BOTH</u> unto God. . . It is not the reconciliation of the near to the far. "Both" (Jew and Gentile) under sin need reconciliation to God.

How is the accomplished? Through Yeshua.
"...in one body by the cross. . ." This is not Israel or Judah's body. This is the body of the manifest Name of YHWH, the Messiah Yeshua.

Whose enmity is slain? The enmity between the Father and man.
"...God in one body..." Our spirit is in conflict with God's spirit. The conflict between our hearts and the Torah is done away via the Spirit of the Messiah. Notice Ephesians 2 is talking about the conflicting spirits that operate in the heart and mind of man separated from God.

Ephesians 2:1, And you hath he quickened, who were dead in trespasses and sins; 2 Wherein in time past ye walked according to the course of this world, according to the prince of the power of the air, the spirit that now worketh in the children of disobedience:

This spirit cannot keep the Torah and is therefore subject to condemnation, enmity, and death as a result. It must die and be replaced with the Spirit of the Messiah so that this separation and enmity from God can end and man can have God in the world. The enmity is brought about because we violate the Torah and are then subject to death. That being the case, we must die and be buried with Yeshua (the breaking of the original tablets) so that we might be resurrected with Him and the Resurrected Covenant (ascended new tablets), no longer subject to the flesh but to the Ruach Hakodesh (Holy Spirit), which we receive through the Messiah Yeshua. The Torah is no longer written on stone, but on fleshly tablets. The focus is no longer on uncircumcised flesh but on resurrected spirit, which is a picture of removing the flesh and being circumcised. We then have access to that Spirit of Messiah that gives us access to God. The image of the Messiah is passed on to His people and Immanuel (Emmanuel), which means God with us, becomes a manifest reality.

- Isaiah 7:14, Therefore the Lord himself shall give you a sign; Behold, a virgin shall conceive, and bear a son, and <u>shall call his name Immanuel</u>.
- Matthew 1:23, Behold, a virgin shall be with child, and shall bring forth a son, and <u>they shall call his name Emmanuel, which being interpreted is, God with us</u>.

What is the result of the coming of "Emmanuel" (Immanuel)? The restored Image of God in man.

Matthew 1:21, And she shall bring forth a son, and thou shalt call his name Jesus: for he shall save his people from their sins.

Why is it so critical to understand this? Because the end time will manifest the Image of the Beast instead of the Image of God, it will manifest the lawless vs the end-time mandate of Malachi 4 to remember of the Law of Moses. The end-time will manifest the Son of Perdition who will try to destroy and take the place of the Image of God, the Christ.

2 Thessalonians 2:3, Let no man deceive you by any means: for that day shall not come, except there come a falling away first, and that man of sin be revealed, the son of perdition;

This Son of Perdition is associated with a falling away from truth and conformance to the Image of God. You cannot understand and identify this Son of Perdition without a scripturally accurate view of the true Image of God and the restoration of God in man. Once you have an accurate scriptural understanding of the true Image of God, then you can easily identify the traits of the Son of Perdition. Where Elijah will come to restore the Law of Moses to believers, the Son of Perdition will be promoting lawlessness.

John 17:12, While I was with them in the world, I kept them in thy name: those that thou gavest me I have kept, and none of them is lost, but the son of perdition; that the scripture might be fulfilled.

Whereas the true Image of God is typified by the manifestation of the Name of the Lord in the Messiah and believers are sealed and kept by His name, the Son of Perdition will come in another name.

John 5:42, But I know you, that ye have not the love of God in you. 43 I am come in my Father's name, and ye receive me not: if another shall come in his own name, him ye will receive.

This "another" is an end time prophecy of Israel accepting the Antichrist, the Son of Perdition after having rejected the true Christ, the Son of God. A titanic battle is coming that will pit the Image of God, Immanuel, who comes in the Name of the Lord vs. the Image of the Beast, the Son of Perdition, who comes in his own name. Sadly, because so many Christians and Jews are so woefully ignorant of the scriptures they don't understand the players, the identifying characteristics, or the central issues that will be at play in the end time. They will still be chortling an unscriptural idea, "law vs. grace" all the way to Armageddon. If you don't like the message of what the scriptures are actually saying...you might be a candidate for the mark of the beast.

But there is hope, whenever terrible things are about to come to pass, God sends a messenger of repentance to His people to repent and how to repent. It will be the same in the end. While a popular Antichrist is promoting lawlessness, God will send a messenger of truth and lawfulness…enter Elijah knocking at your door. What will you do? Will you listen or will you do as a wayward people did 2,000 years ago?

Matthew 11:14, And if ye will receive it, this is Elias (Elijah), which was for to come. 15 He that hath ears to hear, let him hear.

Will you hear? Will you open the door? Or will you insist on lawlessness?

Zechariah 7:11, But they refused to hearken, and pulled away the shoulder, and stopped their ears, that they should not hear.

9 BEHOLD I WILL SEND ELIJAH

What does this mean in the end–times?   Embrace the administrator of the Resurrected Covenant, the Image of God, the Messiah Yeshua for your salvation thereby obtaining grace and mercy. Then what?

Malachi 4:1, For, behold, <u>the day cometh, that shall burn as an oven</u>; and all the proud, yea, and all that do wickedly, shall be stubble: and the day that cometh shall burn them up, saith the Lord of hosts, that it shall leave them neither root nor branch. 2 <u>But unto you that fear my name shall the Sun of righteousness</u> arise with healing in his wings; and ye shall go forth, and grow up as calves of the stall. 3 And ye shall tread down the wicked; for they shall be ashes under the soles of your feet <u>in the day that I shall do this</u>, saith the Lord of hosts. 4<u>Remember ye the law of Moses my servant</u>, which I commanded unto him in Horeb for all Israel, with the statutes and judgments. 5 Behold, <u>I will send you Elijah the prophet before the coming of the great and dreadful day of the Lord</u>:

Follow the leading of the Spirit of the Messiah and return to the Law of Moses as it was given at Mt. Horeb (Mt. Sinai) with the statutes and ordinances under the new administrator of resurrection life, Yeshua the Messiah. The prophet Ezekiel sums this up perfectly in an end–time prophecy.

Ezekiel 11:18, And they shall come thither, and they shall take away all the detestable things thereof and all the abominations thereof from thence. 19 And <u>I will give them one heart, and I will put a new spirit within you</u>; and I will take the stony heart out of their flesh, and will give them an heart of flesh:20 <u>That they may walk in my statutes, and keep mine ordinances, and do them: and they shall be my people, and I will be their God</u>.

Does this mean you can just do what your heart says to do because you are a good person? Can you define your own moral law? Does this mean the Torah, the Law of Moses, is done away?

Ezekiel is clear we are to follow God's statutes and His ordinances, not ours. The Torah, the Written Law of Moses, is resurrected! This is the way we are commanded to walk.

What is the purpose of the Written Torah?
To condemn the flesh and the spirit of disobedience.

Romans 3:19, Now we know that what things soever the law saith, it saith to them who are <u>under the law: that every mouth may be stopped, and all the world may become guilty before God</u>. 20 Therefore by the deeds of the law there shall <u>no flesh be justified in his sight: for by the law is the knowledge of sin</u>.

How are we "all under sin" justified?
By the righteousness of God manifested, Yeshua.

Romans 3:21, But now the righteousness of God without the law is manifested, being witnessed by the law and the prophets; 22 Even <u>the righteousness of God which is by faith of Yeshua unto all and upon all them that believe</u>: for there is no difference:

What is this new administration?
Grace and abundant mercy via faith in His Name, Yeshua (the new administrator).

Romans 3:23, For all have sinned, and come short of the glory of God; 24 Being justified freely by his grace through the redemption that is in Christ Yeshua:25 Whom God hath set forth to be a propitiation through faith in his blood, to declare his righteousness for the remission of sins that are past, through the forbearance of God;

Does this justification come by our obedience to the Written Torah?
No.

Romans 3:26, <u>To declare, I say, at this time his righteousness: that he might be just, and the justifier of him which believeth in Yeshua</u>. 27 Where is boasting then? It is excluded. By what law? of works? Nay: but by the law of faith. 28 Therefore <u>we conclude that a man is justified by faith without the deeds of the law</u>.

Do we then stop obeying the Written Torah?
No. We establish the Written Law of Moses under the new administration of Yeshua, the Messiah, via faith in His Name, His righteousness, and His abundant

grace and mercy.

Romans 3:29, Is he the God of the Jews only? is he not also of the Gentiles? Yes, of the Gentiles also:30 Seeing it is one God, which shall justify the circumcision by faith, and uncircumcision through faith. 31 <u>Do we then make void the law through faith? God forbid, we establish the law.</u>

What identifies sin?
The Law, the Written Torah, the Covenant.

What makes us righteous?
The righteousness of God by faith of Yeshua the Messiah, the administrator of the Resurrected Covenant.

Being in violation of the Torah/Covenant, how are we reconciled to God?
By His grace through the redemption that is in Yeshua the Messiah, through faith in His blood.

Does our righteousness or faithful observance of the Torah save us?
No; God's righteousness saves us through belief on the administrator of the Resurrected Covenant, the resurrected and manifest Name of YHWH, the Messiah Yeshua.

Are there two ways of reconciliation with God, one for those who keep the Torah and one for those who do not?
No; there is only one way, the Law of faith–the Resurrected Covenant.

Does this Law of faith nullify our keeping of the Written Torah?
No. We establish the Torah and the Covenant for both those that are "near" and "far". This law that is established is the Resurrected Covenant (Written Law of Moses), based on better promises, placed in a better location (our hearts), and administered by the Countenance of YHWH, the Resurrected Messiah. This is the same promise of faith that delivered Abraham.

Romans 4:20, He staggered not at the promise of God through unbelief; but was strong in faith, giving glory to God; 21 And being fully persuaded that, what he had promised, he was able also to perform. 22 And therefore it was imputed to him for righteousness. 23 Now it was not written for his sake alone, that it was imputed to him; 24 But for us also, to whom it shall be imputed, if we believe on him that raised up Yeshua our Lord from the dead; 25 Who was delivered for our offences, and was raised again for our justification.

So, let's be clear, are you saved by being grafted into Israel or Judah?
No.

Is Judah/Israel, who is without the Messiah Yeshua, worthy to be grafted into?

No.

If Judah/Israel had the Messiah Yeshua would they be worthy to be grafted into?

No. You are only grafted into the Messiah Yeshua via faith in His name. He saves you, not Judah or Israel. Once you have the Messiah Yeshua, you are circumcised without hands and made of the Commonwealth of Israel. You become a Jew inwardly (Romans 2:29)

Colossians 2:6, As ye have therefore received Christ Yeshua the Lord, so walk ye in him:7 Rooted and built up in him, and stablished in the faith, as ye have been taught, abounding therein with thanksgiving. 8 Beware lest any man spoil you through philosophy and vain deceit, after the tradition of men, after the rudiments of the world, and not after Christ. 9 For in him dwelleth all the fulness of the Godhead bodily. 10 And ye are complete in him, which is the head of all principality and power:11 In whom also ye are circumcised with the circumcision made without hands, in putting off the body of the sins of the flesh by the circumcision of Christ:12 Buried with him in baptism, wherein also ye are risen with him through the faith of the operation of God, who hath raised him from the dead. 13 And you, being dead in your sins and the uncircumcision of your flesh, hath he quickened together with him, having forgiven you all trespasses; 14 Blotting out the handwriting of ordinances that was against us, which was contrary to us, and took it out of the way, nailing it to his cross; 15 And having spoiled principalities and powers, he made a shew of them openly, triumphing over them in it.

Can the scriptures be any clearer? We are saved by the manifest Name of YHWH, Yeshua the Messiah, via faith in His name.

Acts 4:11, This is the stone which was set at nought of you builders, which is become the head of the corner. 12 Neither is there salvation in any other: for there is none other name under heaven given among men, whereby we must be saved. 13 Now when they saw the boldness of Peter and John, and perceived that they were unlearned and ignorant men, they marvelled; and they took knowledge of them, that they had been with Yeshua.

This is who you must be grafted into to be saved!

Philippians 2:9, Wherefore God also hath highly exalted him, and given him a name which is above every name:10 That at the name of Yeshua every knee should bow, of things in heaven, and things in earth, and things under the earth; 11 And that every tongue should confess that Yeshua is Lord, to the glory of God the Father.

Blessed be He who comes in the Name of the Lord. You cannot be grafted into a dead and cut off branch (Judah/Israel). You need to be grafted into the living branch (Yeshua). Just like the Gentiles, Judah also needs to be grafted into Yeshua.

- Matthew 23:37, O Jerusalem, Jerusalem, thou that killest the prophets, and stonest them which are sent unto thee, how often would I have gathered thy children together, even as a hen gathereth her chickens under her wings, and ye would not! 38 Behold, your house is left unto you desolate. 39 For I say unto you, Ye shall not see me henceforth, till ye shall say, Blessed is he that cometh in the Name of the Lord.
- Romans 11:23, And they also, if they abide not still in unbelief, shall be grafted in: for God is able to graft them in again.

If you were redeemed by being grafted into Israel/Judah then why would it suffer that only a remnant is saved (Romans 9:27) and not the whole nation of Israel?

Isaiah 4:1, And in that day seven women shall take hold of one man, saying, We will eat our own bread, and wear our own apparel: only let us be called by thy name, to take away our reproach. 2 In that day shall the branch of the Lord be beautiful and glorious, and the fruit of the earth shall be excellent and comely for them that are escaped of Israel. 3 And it shall come to pass, that he that is left in Sion, and he that remaineth in Jerusalem, shall be called holy, even every one that is written among the living in Jerusalem:

We must all take hold of the one man, the Messiah Yeshua, in order to be saved, to be forgiven, and to have our reproach taken away. It is by exhibiting faith in the Name of the Lord, the manifest Name of YHWH, the Messiah Yeshua, that we are grafted into His tree.

Acts 3:15, And killed the Prince of life, whom God hath raised from the dead; whereof we are witnesses. 16 And his name through faith in his name hath made this man strong, whom ye see and know: yea, the faith which is by him hath given him this perfect soundness in the presence of you all.

Once again, the tree of Romans 11 is not Israel or Judah. It is all about faith and how Israel and Judah should have a natural graft due to the faith of their father Abraham, not because the tree is Judah or Israel. They were cut out of the tree for a lack of faith in the administrator of the Resurrected Covenant, the Messiah Yeshua, the manifest Name of YHWH.

Ephesians 2:12, That at that time ye were without Christ, being aliens from the Commonwealth of Israel, and strangers from the covenants of promise, having no hope, and without God in the world:13 But now in Christ Yeshua ye who sometimes were far off are made nigh by the blood of Christ.

It is not the Torah that makes you of the Commonwealth of Israel, it is having the Messiah via faith in His manifest Name, YHWH. This tree is all about faith in the manifest Name of YHWH, the Messiah Yeshua. He bears the branches; the branches do not bear Him by their own works or worth. We are not grafted into Israel/Judah. We are grafted into Yeshua (the Lord).

Isaiah 56:3, Neither let the son of the stranger, that hath <u>joined himself to the Lord</u>, speak, saying, The Lord hath utterly separated me from his people: neither let the eunuch say, Behold, <u>I am a dry tree</u>.

Before concluding that this is a disagreement with Messianics or Hebrew Roots Movement, remember this is really about scriptural truth and accuracy. Question your teachers on what they are teaching. If they cannot affirm in writing, in person, and publicly that: Yeshua is God manifest in the flesh and that He is not the living Torah or the manifestation of the Torah, and that we are grafted into Yeshua (both Jews and Gentiles) and not Israel/Judah, send them quickly on their way.

Why is this so important?

1 John 2:21, I have not written unto you because ye know not the truth, but because ye know it, and that no lie is of the truth. 22 <u>Who is a liar but he that denieth that Jesus is the Christ? He is Antichrist, that denieth the Father and the Son. 23 Whosoever denieth the Son, the same hath not the Father: he that acknowledgeth the Son hath the Father also.</u> 24 Let that therefore abide in you, which ye have heard from the beginning. If that which ye have heard from the beginning shall remain in you, ye also shall continue in the Son, and in the Father. 25 And this is the promise that he hath promised us, even eternal life. 26 These things have I written unto you concerning them that seduce you. 27 But the anointing which ye have received of him abideth in you, and ye need not that any man teach you: but as the same anointing teacheth you of all things, and is truth, and is no lie, and even as it hath taught you, ye shall abide in him. 28 And now, little children, abide in him; that, when he shall appear, we may have confidence, and not be ashamed before him at his coming. 29 If ye know that he is righteous, ye know that every one that doeth righteousness is born of him.

John, the Apostle of love, leaves no room for untruthful and inaccurate statements about the nature of the Messiah and God. The Father is one with Yeshua.

John 10:29, My Father, which gave them me, is greater than all; and no man is able to pluck them out of my Father's hand. 30 <u>I and my Father are one</u>. 31 Then the Jews took up stones again to stone him.

Yeshua leaves no ambiguity on this issue and the Jews sought to stone Him for the clarity of His statements. Yeshua further clarifies that just as He and God are one, we will share the same destiny, "Immanuel".

John 17:11, And now I am no more in the world, but these are in the world, and I come to thee. Holy Father, keep through thine own name those whom thou hast given me, that they may be one, as we are.

If you ever come across someone who tries to say that Yeshua is not really "God manifest in the flesh", remember why Yeshua was condemned and crucified.

Matthew 26:63, But Jesus held his peace, And the high priest answered and said unto him, I adjure thee by the living God, that thou tell us whether thou be the Christ, the Son of God. 64 Jesus saith unto him, Thou hast said: nevertheless I say unto you, Hereafter shall ye see the Son of man sitting on the right hand of power, and coming in the clouds of heaven. 65 Then the high priest rent his clothes, saying, He hath spoken blasphemy; what further need have we of witnesses? behold, now ye have heard his blasphemy. 66 What think ye? They answered and said, He is guilty of death.

Beware of teachers that confess these things and then teach that Yeshua was the "Torah in the flesh" or the "Torah manifested" …pleading semantics as an excuse. The scriptures are clear.

2 Corinthian 5:19, To wit, that God was in Christ, reconciling the world unto himself, not imputing their trespasses unto them; and hath committed unto us the word of reconciliation.

10 REVELATION & THE FRACTAL OF SEED...THEN MANIFESTATION!

WHAT IS THE PURPOSE OF FLESHLY EXISTENCE (PRODUCING AN IMAGE)?

> Genesis 2:5, And every plant of the field <u>before it was in the earth</u>, and <u>every herb of the field before it grew</u>: for the Lord God had <u>not caused it to rain</u> upon the earth, and there was not a man to till the ground.

Notice how God mentions Adam's purpose for existence in connection with causing flesh (images) to grow from seeds—none had produced flesh yet. Adam is intimately tied to the earth bringing forth fruit. We have typically viewed this verse as Adam needing to go out and work in the garden to prune the shrubs when in reality God viewed the filling of the earth with Adam's seed and fleshly descendants as the tilling that God was hoping would be fruitful.

> - Genesis 1:28, And God blessed them, and God said unto them, <u>Be fruitful</u>, and multiply, and <u>replenish the earth</u>, and subdue it: and have dominion over the fish of the sea, and over the fowl of the air, and over every living thing that moveth upon the earth.
> - Genesis 9:1, And God blessed Noah and his sons, and said unto them, <u>Be fruitful</u>, and multiply, and <u>replenish the earth</u>.

Contrary to God's command for man's flesh to fill (replenish) the earth, man disobeys and starts to build a tower to avoid filling the earth.

> Genesis 11:4, And they said, Go to, let us build us a city and a tower, whose top may reach unto heaven; and let us make us a name, lest we be <u>scattered</u>

abroad upon the face of the whole earth.

The fruit that God is looking for is that which is born of man and woman who obey His Torah (Law of Moses) and cling to the Tree of Life from the beginning to the end.

- Matthew 7:15, Beware of false prophets, which come to you in sheep's clothing, but inwardly they are ravening wolves. 16 Ye shall know them by their fruits. Do men gather grapes of thorns, or figs of thistles? 17 Even so every good tree bringeth forth good fruit; but a corrupt tree bringeth forth evil fruit. 18 A good tree cannot bring forth evil fruit, neither can a corrupt tree bring forth good fruit. 19 Every tree that bringeth not forth good fruit is hewn down, and cast into the fire. 20 Wherefore by their fruits ye shall know them.
- Acts 14:17, Nevertheless he left not himself without witness, in that he did good, and gave us rain from heaven, and fruitful seasons, filling our hearts with food and gladness.
- Galatians 5:22, But the fruit of the Spirit is love, joy, peace, longsuffering, gentleness, goodness, faith, 23 Meekness, temperance: against such there is no law.
- Psalms 127:3, Lo, children are an heritage of the Lord: and the fruit of the womb is his reward. 4 As arrows are in the hand of a mighty man; so are children of the youth.

Just as God sowed seed in expectation of good fruit, Yeshua has commissioned us to also go into the whole world sowing His seed.

Mark 16:15, And he said unto them, Go ye into all the world, and preach the Gospel to every creature.

What is the Gospel?

Luke 23:46, And when Jesus had cried with a loud voice, he said, Father, into thy hands I commend my spirit: and having said thus, he gave up the ghost.

Yeshua's own testimony is that He viewed the cessation of His physical (fleshly) life with the departure of His spirit. His death occurs simultaneously with His last breath. That being the case for all creatures, what is the hope of the Gospel? All flesh has its life contained in the blood. The Messiah directly relates the promises of a covenant in Him by His body and by His blood. But what does that really mean and why is it significant?

Leviticus 17:11, For the life of the flesh is in the blood: and I have given it to you upon the altar to make an atonement for your souls: for it is the blood that maketh an atonement for the soul.

As Leviticus 17:11 shows, there is an intimate relationship between the blood and the breath that makes man a living soul. This is the message of the Gospel, blood making atonement for the soul to ensure the deathless joining of heaven (spirit) and earth (resurrected incorruptible image/flesh).

- Leviticus 17:11, For the life of the flesh is in the blood: and I have given it to you upon the altar to make an atonement for your souls: for it is the blood that maketh an atonement for the soul.
- Genesis 2:7, And the Lord God formed man of the dust of the ground, and breathed into his nostrils the breath of life; and man became a living soul.

It is by the blood that atonement is made for the breath (soul). As we have seen, life is the breath of God and it is in the blood. A living soul dies when it gives up the breath of God. The blood carries the breath. Medical science has confirmed the breath of life is in the blood.

The circulatory system includes: the pulmonary circulation, a loop through the lungs where blood is oxygenated; and the systemic circulation, a loop through the rest of the body to provide oxygenated blood. An average adult contains five to six quarts (roughly 4. 7 to 5. 7 liters) of blood, which consists of plasma, red blood cells, white blood cells, and platelets. Also, the digestive system works with the circulatory system to provide the nutrients the system needs to keep the heart pumping. (Wikipedia)

Science confirms that breath does indeed circulate via the blood and nourishes all of the body's systems. The life is in the blood. The focus of the Torah at Adam's formation of flesh and image on the seventh day is the giving of the breath of the Almighty, not the giving of blood. Take notice of the state of all of God's creation early on the seventh day. All had been "made", but nothing had grown flesh/image since YHWH had not yet caused the creation to be watered. The seeds are "made" and planted, but nothing has produced flesh as a fleshly living soul.

The Bible begins with a seed in Genesis and concludes with the manifestation of images in the Book of Revelation (Manifestation). Everything that occurs in the end-time as it relates to the events of the Book of Revelations must be viewed through the natural and biblical pattern of seed (male) and manifestation (female). Once we do this the confusing imagery of events in the Book of Revelation become clear and the characters become clearly defined by their attributes and roles. So, whenever you see the title "Book of Revelation" think of it within its natural and biblical pattern and fractal as the "Book of Manifestation".

Romans 8:19, For the earnest expectation of the creature waiteth for the manifestation of the sons of God.

Just as the Messiah fulfills the fractal of seed then manifestation, so also believers fulfill this same pattern.

11 WHY HAS CHRIST BEEN ABSENT FOR 2,000 YEARS? A REAL ANSWER FOR CHRISTIANS AND JEWS.

The natural pattern of God and His universe is always the same, "seed then flesh (image/manifestation)". This is why the end-times are focused on choice between the Image of God and the Image of the Beast. The time for seed has passed and now the time for the manifestation of those seeds into images is about to occur. Often there is confusion about why there are two creation chapters, one in Genesis 1 and another in Genesis 2. Few understand what they are seeing. Some think Genesis 2 is just a retelling of Genesis 1 with some unexplainable differences. Many claim this leaves the Bible open for criticism. Let's clear up the confusion. It all starts with a fractal (pattern) of seed then manifested image.

> Genesis 2:5, And every plant of the field before it was in the earth, and every herb of the field before it grew: for the Lord God had not caused it to rain upon the earth, and there was not a man to till the ground.

It is only after the watering on the 7th day Sabbath that all seeds begin to grow and man receives the breath of life and becomes a living soul with flesh.

> Genesis 2:6, But there went up a mist from the earth, and watered the whole face of the ground. 7 And the Lord God <u>formed</u> man of the dust of the ground, and breathed into his nostrils the breath of life; and man became a living soul. 8 And the Lord God planted a garden eastward in Eden; and there he put the man whom he had formed. 9 And out of the ground <u>made the Lord God to grow</u> every tree that is pleasant to the sight, and good for food; the Tree of Life also in the midst of the garden, and the tree of knowledge of good

and evil.

How can this be? All things were made in Genesis 1, right? Notice the key words! Genesis 2 shows YHWH "forming" all flesh/manifest images. Genesis 1 shows Elohim making all "seed".

> Genesis 1:11, And God said, Let the earth bring forth grass, the herb yielding seed, and the fruit tree yielding fruit after his kind, whose seed is in itself, upon the earth: and it was so. 12 And the earth brought forth grass, and herb yielding seed after his kind, and the tree yielding fruit, whose seed was in itself, after his kind: and God saw that it was good.

Notice the focus is on Elohim creating seed bearing plants. We must reconcile this with Genesis 2. The seeds are created in Genesis 1, but as Genesis 2 states, none of those seeds have grown until YHWH causes a mist to come up from the face of the ground on the 7th day Sabbath in Genesis 2.

> Genesis 2:5, And every plant of the field before it was in the earth, and every herb of the field before it grew: for the Lord God had not caused it to rain upon the earth, and there was not a man to till the ground.

What about the rest of Genesis 1? Throughout Genesis 1, we see the name of "El" being used. God always uses the name "El" when He is dealing with the promised seed and the multiplicity of seed in secret or in hiding (for example: exile, Egypt, or wilderness).

Notice the seeds are hidden in the earth and do not form flesh until Genesis 2 when YHWH (Lord God) causes the watering of the earth. Water is also synonymous with breath of the Almighty. In Genesis 2 we see the seeds in the earth watered and grow and we see Adam given the breath of the Almighty (water of life). The name YHWH also appears later when the LORD (YHWH) promises to deliver the land of Israel to Abraham's descendants. We see the name YHWH again when He delivers Israel's descendants (flesh) from the wilderness (exile) and into the Promised land.

> Exodus 1:5, And all the souls that came out of the loins of Jacob were seventy souls: for Joseph was in Egypt already.

These living souls (seed producing flesh) need YHWH to deliver them from bondage (death) to the land of promise (incorruptible life).

> Exodus 6:3, And I appeared unto Abraham, unto Isaac, and unto Jacob, by the name of God Almighty, but by my name JEHOVAH (YHWH) was I not known to them.

The name "EL" is used for the causation of the hidden multiplication of "seed", and the name YHWH is used for the causation of the deliverance/formation of manifestation (image/flesh/fruit). Abram had El's promise of multiplicity of seed and Abram experienced God through the promise of multiplicity.

God reveals Himself to man through various names and each name has meaning and significance. He is always communicating with us, but we are not always able to understand what He is saying. It is up to us to be an active participant in our redemption and come out of sin so that we can come to the point of hearing the voice of YHWH.

In Exodus, the God of Abraham, Isaac, and Jacob begins to reveal Himself to the children of Israel in a way that He had not done with their forefathers. He has brought about His promise of multiplicity of seed and now He is working to deliver their flesh to the Promised land. Hence God (Adonai) switches from using the name El which is associated with the promise of multiplicity of hidden seed (in Egypt), and starts using the name YHWH fulfilling the promise to deliver the seed's flesh (images) to the promised land.

> Exodus 6:2, And God spake unto Moses, and said unto him, I am the Lord:3 And I appeared unto Abraham, unto Isaac, and unto Jacob, by the name of God Almighty, but by my name JEHOVAH (YHWH) was I not known to them. 4 And I have also established my covenant with them, to give them the land of Canaan, the land of their pilgrimage, wherein they were strangers.

YHWH is telling the children of Israel that He is going to reveal or manifest Himself to them by the Name of YHWH and by all that the name means. Now it is clear that the promises that were made to Abram and Jacob were given in two names of God: El Shaddai (El, Elohim) and YHWH (Lord). It is the same pattern of seed (El) then manifestation of flesh (YHWH)! This provides added significance to the deliverance presented in Exodus 34 of the manifestation of the Name of YHWH as the new administrator of the Resurrected Covenant. It also clarifies why Yeshua is the manifestation of His name when He came to the earth to save our fallen and corruptible minds and bodies. Our fallen and broken images are restored by His new seed as the Image of God and that image is placed upon our image (countenance).

> Matthew 23:39, For I say unto you, Ye shall not see me henceforth, till ye shall say, Blessed is he that cometh in the Name of the Lord (YHWH).

Every time you see the word "Lord" it is actually using the name YHWH.

> Genesis 15:4, And, behold, the word of the Lord (YHWH-Strong's 3068) came unto him, saying, This shall not be thine heir; but he that shall come forth out of thine own bowels shall be thine heir. 5 And he brought him forth abroad, and said, Look now toward heaven, and tell the stars, if thou be able to number them: and he said unto him, So shall thy seed be. 6 And he believed in the Lord (YHWH); and he counted it to him for righteousness. 7 And he said unto him, I am the Lord (YHWH) that brought thee out of Ur of the Chaldees,

to give thee this land to inherit it. 8 And he said, Lord God, whereby shall I know that I shall inherit it?

Notice the focus of this passage is the promise of inheritance of the promised land. God promises the land to Abraham's descendants in the Name of YHWH (Lord). So, Abraham knew the name YHWH. When God promises to Abram the multiplicity of seed, He makes His promises via the name El Shaddai.

Genesis 17:1, And when Abram was ninety years old and nine, the Lord appeared to Abram, and said unto him, I am the Almighty God (El Shaddai-Strong's 7706); walk before me, and be thou perfect. 2 And I will make my covenant between me and thee, and will multiply thee exceedingly.

Let's recap seed then flesh in regard to God's promises to Abraham.

Notice:
- The covenant with Abram and his descendants included great multiplicity of seed/descendants and the promise of the inheritance of the Promised land. When God promises multiplicity of seed, He uses a derivation of the name El, as in El Shaddai or Elohim (Genesis 1).
- When God promises the deliverance of the land He uses YHWH-Lord-(Genesis 2).
- The creation and promise of seed is hidden and the deliverance of the land is out in the open for all to see (revealed and manifested).
- Conception (hidden) then birth (revealed/manifested).
- Seed then manifestation (image/flesh).
- Exile then return to the land.
- Womb then birth.
- Descend (Egypt) then ascend (Promised Land).

You see the same patterns of God working His mighty hand in the events of the world. The Book of Esther is a great example of God operating in hiding but moving His will in the events of the world. Not once is God's name mentioned in the Book of Esther, but His will is manifest throughout.

The Book of Esther is about the preservation of the seed of Israel while hidden in exile under bondage to Persia. The seed is in Diaspora or hiding. The miracles seem to occur as a part of natural events. Other nations cannot tell that these are God's people. Dispersed Israel is very similar to Joseph in Egypt. Even his brothers could not tell he was not Egyptian but really was of their own seed. He was hidden so that their eyes could not see him.

Genesis 42:8, And Joseph knew his brethren, but they knew not him.

Abraham did have YHWH's promise of deliverance of his seed's flesh, but that name was to be known or directly experienced by his seed's flesh and not by his own flesh.

Genesis 22:8, And Abraham said, My son, God (Elohim-Strong's 430) will provide himself a lamb for a burnt offering: so they went both of them together. 9 And they came to the place which God had told him of; and Abraham built an altar there, and laid the wood in order, and bound Isaac his son, and laid him on the altar upon the wood. 10 And Abraham stretched forth his hand, and took the knife to slay his son. 11 And the angel of the Lord called unto him out of heaven, and said, Abraham, Abraham: and he said, Here am I. 12 And he said, Lay not thine hand upon the lad, neither do thou any thing unto him: for now I know that thou fearest God, seeing thou hast not withheld thy son, thine only son from me. 13 And Abraham lifted up his eyes, and looked, and behold behind him a ram caught in a thicket by his horns: and Abraham went and took the ram, and offered him up for a burnt offering in the stead of his son. 14 And Abraham called the name of that place Jehovahjireh: as it is said to this day, In the mount of the Lord it shall be seen. 15 And the angel of the Lord called unto Abraham out of heaven the second time, 16 And said, By myself have I sworn, saith the Lord, for because thou hast done this thing, and hast not withheld thy son, thine only son:17 That in blessing I will bless thee, and in multiplying I will multiply thy seed as the stars of the heaven, and as the sand which is upon the sea shore; and thy seed shall possess the gate of his enemies; 18 And in thy seed shall all the nations of the earth be blessed; because thou hast obeyed my voice.

Just as Isaac is a prophetic type of the Messiah, he had to bear the same imagery of the death of a seed so that the second part of the fractal of death and resurrection could be fulfilled. We see that Isaac is directly associated by Paul with "the seed of promise".

Romans 9:7, Neither, because they are the seed of Abraham, are they all children: but, In Isaac shall thy seed be called.

And as a prophetic type of the "seed of the woman" that would be the Messiah, he must also fulfill the imagery of a seed death, only to be replaced by the true image of the seed, the Messiah (a lamb).

Hebrew 11:17, By faith Abraham, when he was tried, offered up Isaac: and he that had received the promises offered up his only begotten son, 18 Of whom it was said, That in Isaac shall thy seed be called:19 Accounting that God was able to raise him up, even from the dead; from whence also he received him in a figure.

We see God (Elohim) providing the lamb (image or seed of YHWH) and we then see the fleshly appearance of the seed as the lamb in the mount of the Lord (YHWH). Again, the pattern is seed then manifestation (flesh). Take note of the name Jehovahjireh in Genesis 22:14.

- Jehovah–jireh = Jehovah sees, proper locative noun
- It is through Yeshua's flesh that YHWH sees us. Remember it was after Adam and Eve fell, lost their proper covering and became naked that YHWH was not able to locate them and had to call out, "Where are you". YHWH subsequently had to cover them with a temporary covering, a (tabernacle or sukkot) which is made from that which grows from the earth.
   o Genesis 3:8 And they heard the voice of the Lord God walking in the garden in the cool of the day: and Adam and his wife hid themselves from the presence of the Lord God amongst the trees of the garden. 9 And the Lord God called unto Adam, and said unto him, Where art thou?
- Israel makes 42 journeys in the wilderness (exile/hiding) in temporary dwellings until they enter the Promised land (incorruptible flesh–a redeemed covering). The Feast of Tabernacles (Sukkot) commemorates this journey in temporary dwellings.
   o Leviticus 23:42, Ye shall dwell in booths seven days; all that are Israelites born shall dwell in booths:43 That your generations may know that I made the children of Israel to dwell in booths, when I brought them out of the land of Egypt: I am the Lord your God.

Let's do a quick review on the name of El and the name of YHWH. There is a connection between the Name of "El" and seed, which is a picture of a temporary shelter, being in exile and a state of hiding and multiplication. The Name of YHWH is a picture of manifestation or flesh/fruit (image) as something permanent and incorruptible, which is a picture of receiving the Promised land and being revealed (ascending in resurrection life).

Name of Elohim:
- Genesis 1, Genesis 17, and Exodus 1
- It bears the hallmarks of blessing and multiplicity of the promised seed in hiding.
   o Exodus 1:18, And the king of Egypt called for the midwives, and said unto them, Why have ye done this thing, and have saved the men children alive? 19 And the midwives said unto Pharaoh, Because the Hebrew women are not as the Egyptian women; for they are lively, and are delivered ere the midwives come in unto them. 20 Therefore God (Elohim-Strong's 430) dealt well with the midwives: and the people multiplied, and waxed very mighty.
- The Name of "El" and seed is a picture of a temporary shelter, being in exile and a state of hiding and multiplication.

Name of YHWH:
- Genesis 2, Genesis 15, Genesis 22, and Exodus 6
- Deliverance of the flesh (image) of the promised seed.

- The Name of YHWH is a picture of manifestation or flesh/fruit/image as something permanent and incorruptible, which is a picture of receiving the Promised land and being revealed.

If we know that Genesis 2 shows YHWH forming Adam's flesh (image) we can then see that El is making Adam and the plant and animal seeds (DNA) in Genesis 1.

Genesis 1:20, And <u>God</u> (Elohim-Strong's 430) said, Let the waters bring forth abundantly the moving creature that hath life, and fowl that may fly above the earth in the open firmament of heaven. 21 And God created great whales, and every living creature that moveth, which the waters brought forth abundantly, after their kind, and every winged fowl after his kind: and God saw that it was good. 22 And God blessed them, saying, <u>Be fruitful, and multiply,</u> and fill the waters in the seas, and let fowl <u>multiply in the earth</u>.

MESSIAH BEN JOSEPH & MESSIAH BEN DAVID:
Many Jews reject Yeshua as Messiah because of their claim that He did not regather the lost ten tribes of Israel and reunite the Kingdom of Israel and Judah (all the sons of Jacob). As such they feel He disqualified Himself as being the Messiah. Rabbinical literature proposes two separate Messiahs, one a picture of suffering and death and one a picture of victory and resurrection power.

Finally, there must be mentioned a Messianic figure peculiar to the rabbinical apocalyptic literature—<u>that of Messiah ben Joseph</u>. The earliest mention of him is in Suk. 52a, b, where three statements occur in regard to him, for the first of which R. Dosa (c. 250) is given as authority. In the last of these statements only his name is mentioned, but the first two speak of the fate which he is to meet, namely, to fall in battle (as if alluding to a well–known tradition). Details about him are not found until much later, but he has an established place in the apocalypses of later centuries and in the midrash literature—in Saadia's description of the future ("Emunot we–De'ot, " ch. viii.) and in that of Hai Gaon ("Ṭa'am Zeḳenim, " p. 59). According to these, Messiah b. Joseph will appear prior to the coming of Messiah b. David; he will gather the children of Israel around him, march to Jerusalem, and there, after overcoming the hostile powers, reestablish the Temple–worship and set up his own dominion. Thereupon Armilus, according to one group of sources, or Gog and Magog, according to the other, will appear with their hosts before Jerusalem, wage war against <u>Messiah b. Joseph, and slay him. His corpse, according to one group, will lie unburied in the streets of Jerusalem; according to the other, it will be hidden by the angels with the bodies of the Patriarchs, until Messiah b. David comes and resurrects him.</u> (comp. Jew. Encyc. i. 682, 684 [§§ 8 and 13]; comp. also Midr. Wayosha' and Agadat ha–Mashiaḥ in Jellinek, "B. H." i. 55 et seq. , iii. 141 et seq.)

It is clear that this rabbinic tradition arises since they see the pattern of death and resurrection presented in the Torah: death as a seed and resurrection as a manifested fruit. Instead of seeing the fulfillment of both in the singular Messiah Yeshua, they apply each part of the fractal to a separate individual Messiah. We can see that Yeshua made it incredibly clear that He would fulfill both parts of the fractal and uses specific terminology that relates to the seed and the harvest of the manifestation of the fruit of that seed. Within the dealayed time gap of this growth period He remains hidden as the seed of the Kingdom of God, until the point of manifestation and harvest of its fruit. When it appears, so does He.

Matthew 13:3, And he spake many things unto them in parables, saying, Behold, a sower went forth to sow; ... 9 Who hath ears to hear, let him hear. 10 And the disciples came, and said unto him, Why speakest thou unto them in parables? 11 He answered and said unto them, Because it is given unto you to know the mysteries of the kingdom of heaven, but to them it is not given. ...14 And in them is fulfilled the prophecy of Esaias, which saith, By hearing ye shall hear, and shall not understand; and seeing ye shall see, and shall not perceive:15 For this people's heart is waxed gross, and their ears are dull of hearing, and their eyes they have closed; lest at any time they should see with their eyes and hear with their ears, and should understand with their heart, and should be converted, and I should heal them. 16 But blessed are your eyes, for they see: and your ears, for they hear. ... 18 Hear ye therefore the parable of the sower. 19 When any one heareth the word of the kingdom, and understandeth it not, then cometh the wicked one, and catcheth away that which was sown in his heart. ... 23 But he that received seed into the good ground is he that heareth the word, and understandeth it; which also beareth fruit, and bringeth forth, some an hundredfold, some sixty, some thirty. 24 Another parable put he forth unto them, saying, The kingdom of heaven is likened unto a man which sowed good seed in his field:25 But while men slept, his enemy came and sowed tares among the wheat, and went his way. 26 But when the blade was sprung up, and brought forth fruit, then appeared the tares also.... The servants said unto him, Wilt thou then that we go and gather them up? 29 But he said, Nay; lest while ye gather up the tares, ye root up also the wheat with them. 30 Let both grow together until the harvest: and in the time of harvest I will say to the reapers, Gather ye together first the tares, and bind them in bundles to burn them: but gather the wheat into my barn.

Yeshua is clearly presenting the work of the Messiah as sowing seed that must wait and grow in hiding (exile) and be given the time to manifest (reveal) its fruit. Then He sends forth the reapers. The Jews reject Yeshua as the Messiah because they expected an immediate fulfillment of the seed and the fruit, but as the fractal presents itself in nature there is a built-in time lapse that requires a hiding of the seed, time to pass, growth to occur and then a reaping at the harvest time. Harvest does not occur at the time of sowing but according to the images, patterns, and fractals of God. We must look to the seasons for our prophetic pattern. The fractal of seed (death and sorrow) and manifested fruit (resurrection life) and joy is built into the design of the universe.

Psalm 126:5, They that sow in tears shall reap in joy.

As those who have expressed faith in the Messiah Yeshua, we should be fulfilling the same fractal and image that He fulfilled. He gives us the express command to do what He did during His ministry. We are to fulfill the role of the Sower.

- Matthew 24:13, But he that shall endure unto the end, the same shall be saved. 14 And this Gospel of the kingdom shall be preached in all the world for a witness unto all nations; and then shall the end come.
- Mark 16:15, And he said unto them, Go ye into all the world, and preach the Gospel to every creature.
- Matthew 28:18, And Yeshua came and spake unto them, saying, All power is given unto me in heaven and in earth. 19 Go ye therefore, and teach all nations, baptizing them in the name of the Father, and of the Son, and of the Holy Ghost:20 Teaching them to observe all things whatsoever I have commanded you: and, lo, I am with you always, even unto the end of the world. Amen.

Once this work and fractal has been completed and the manifestation of that sowing has occurred, then the second part of the fractal of seed and fruit will commence, the reaping.

Revelation 14:5, And another angel came out of the temple, crying with a loud voice to him that sat on the cloud, Thrust in thy sickle, and reap: for the time is come for thee to reap; for the harvest of the earth is ripe.

By all accounts the delayed time gap between Yeshua's first coming and His second coming will bear the imagery of hiddenness, suffering, and death like a seed, only to break forth in the end like a manifested and resurrected fruit. Yeshua makes it clear that the timing of that "season" is completely up to God the Father and only He knows when it will be.

Matthew 24:30, And then shall appear the sign of the Son of man in heaven: and then shall all the tribes of the earth mourn, and they shall see the Son of man coming in the clouds of heaven with power and great glory. 31 And he shall send his angels with a great sound of a trumpet, and they shall gather together his elect from the four winds, from one end of heaven to the other. 32 Now learn a parable of the fig tree; When his branch is yet tender, and putteth forth leaves, ye know that summer is nigh:33 So likewise ye, when ye shall see all these things, know that it is near, even at the doors. 34 Verily I say unto you, This generation shall not pass, till all these things be fulfilled. 35 Heaven and earth shall pass away, but my words shall not pass away. 36 But of that day and hour knoweth no man, no, not the angels of heaven, but my Father only.

Notice Yeshua presents His second coming with the imagery of a seed manifesting its image as the "branch is yet tender, and putteth forth leaves". This is not a coincidence. He further clarifies that the "day and the hour" of these events are known only to the Father. This question is so important to the disciples that they ask Him again after His resurrection if now was the time.

Acts 1:6, When they therefore were come together, they asked of him, saying, Lord, wilt thou at this time restore again the kingdom to Israel? 7 And he said unto them, It is not for you to know the times or the seasons, which the Father hath put in his own power. 8 But ye shall receive power, after that the Holy Ghost is come upon you: and ye shall be witnesses unto me both in Jerusalem, and in all Judaea, and in Samaria, and unto the uttermost part of the earth.

Notice the disciples connect the "coming of the son of man in power" with the restoration of the Kingdom to Israel. They are wondering if His comments from Matthew 24 are being fulfilled and if the new season has arrived. Yeshua gives the same answer as before and indicates the fulfillment of that day will occur in its "season" and that only the Father knows when that season is. We should ask why is it that only the Father knows when this season is?

1 Corinthians 3:7, So then neither is he that planteth any thing, neither he that watereth; but God that giveth the increase.

The end will come when the fruit is fully manifested from the seed and God has increased it to the point of being harvested.

James 5:7, Be patient therefore, brethren, unto the coming of the Lord. Behold, the husbandman waiteth for the precious fruit of the earth, and hath long patience for it, until he receive the early and latter rain. 8 Be ye also patient; stablish your hearts: for the coming of the Lord draweth nigh.

Let's not assume that these are random references to the "seasons", but that they are very meaningful and should give us insight into what season we are in. It should also give us the pattern and fractal of our hope in Christ!

1 Corinthians 15:36, Thou fool, that which thou sowest is not quickened, except it die:37 And that which thou sowest, thou sowest not that body that shall be, but bare grain, it may chance of wheat, or of some other grain:38 But God giveth it a body as it hath pleased him, and to every seed his own body. 39 All flesh is not the same flesh: but there is one kind of flesh of men, another flesh of beasts, another of fishes, and another of birds...42 So also is the resurrection of the dead. It is sown in corruption; it is raised in incorruption:43 It is sown in dishonour; it is raised in glory: it is sown in weakness; it is raised in power:44 It is sown a natural body; it is raised a spiritual body. There is a natural body, and there is a spiritual body. 45 And so it is written, The first man

Adam was made a living soul; the last Adam was made a quickening spirit. 46 Howbeit that was not first which is spiritual, but that which is natural; and afterward that which is spiritual. 47 The first man is of the earth, earthy; the second man is the Lord from heaven. 48 As is the earthy, such are they also that are earthy: and as is the heavenly, such are they also that are heavenly. 49 And as we have borne the image of the earthy, we shall also bear the image of the heavenly. 50 Now this I say, brethren, that flesh and blood cannot inherit the kingdom of God; neither doth corruption inherit incorruption. 51 Behold, I shew you a mystery; We shall not all sleep, but we shall all be changed, 52 In a moment, in the twinkling of an eye, at the last trump: for the trumpet shall sound, and the dead shall be raised incorruptible, and we shall be changed. 53 For this corruptible must put on incorruption, and this mortal must put on immortality.

Just as the Messiah bears the imagery of death and resurrection, so will those who express faith in His work. The angels affirm that both the death and resurrection fractal occur within a singular Messiah, not in two.

- Acts 1:11, Which also said, Ye men of Galilee, why stand ye gazing up into heaven? this same Jesus, which is taken up from you into heaven, shall so come in like manner as ye have seen him go into heaven. 12 Then returned they unto Jerusalem from the mount called Olivet, which is from Jerusalem a sabbath day's journey.
- Matthew 24:30, And then shall appear the sign of the Son of man in heaven: and then shall all the tribes of the earth mourn, and they shall see the Son of man coming in the clouds of heaven with power and great glory.

The critical question on the lips of the Apostles at the time of Yeshua's resurrection was the timing of the Kingdom of God, is it now or is it later? Notice how Yeshua answers the question in relation to the imagery of the seasons of nature and what they should be doing in the appropriate season.

Acts 1:6, When they therefore were come together, they asked of him, saying, Lord, wilt thou at this time restore again the kingdom to Israel? 7 And he said unto them, It is not for you to know the times or the seasons, which the Father hath put in his own power. 8 But ye shall receive power, after that the Holy Ghost is come upon you: and ye shall be witnesses unto me both in Jerusalem, and in all Judaea, and in Samaria, and unto the uttermost part of the earth. 9 And when he had spoken these things, while they beheld, he was taken up; and a cloud received him out of their sight. 10 And while they looked stedfastly toward heaven as he went up, behold, two men stood by them in white apparel; 11 Which also said, Ye men of Galilee, why stand ye gazing up into heaven? this same Yeshua, which is taken up from you into heaven, shall so come in like manner as ye have seen him go into heaven.

The Apostles are told very plainly that they need to focus on their appropriate season of sowing the word (seed) of God, fulfilling the same fractal and image that Yeshua initiated in His first coming. After the season of sowing, hiding, and death, when fullness and maturation has come to the fruit of the seed, then the same Messiah will return and fulfill the season and imagery of reaping and resurrection of the fruit. Just as the Messiah ascended in resurrection, so will those that conform to His image and fractal. The delay is designed by God according to the appropriate work and imagery of its season. Judah's inability to see this fractal is one of the major obstacles to accept the Messiah Yeshua. This blindness is directed by God and will be lifted in its season.

- Romans 11:1, I say then, Hath God cast away his people? God forbid. For I also am an Israelite, of the seed of Abraham, of the tribe of Benjamin.
- Romans 11:7, What then? Israel hath not obtained that which he seeketh for; but the election hath obtained it, and the rest were blinded. 8 (According as it is written, God hath given them the spirit of slumber, eyes that they should not see, and ears that they should not hear;) unto this day. ...10 Let their eyes be darkened, that they may not see, and bow down their back alway. 11 I say then, Have they stumbled that they should fall? God forbid: but rather through their fall salvation is come unto the Gentiles, for to provoke them to jealousy. 12 Now if the fall of them be the riches of the world, and the diminishing of them the riches of the Gentiles; how much more their fulness?...15 For if the casting away of them be the reconciling of the world, what shall the receiving of them be, but life from the dead?
- Romans 11:25, For I would not, brethren, that ye should be ignorant of this mystery, lest ye should be wise in your own conceits; that blindness in part is happened to Israel, until the fulness of the Gentiles be come in. 26 And so all Israel shall be saved:... 31 Even so have these also now not believed, that through your mercy they also may obtain mercy. 32 For God hath concluded them all in unbelief, that he might have mercy upon all.

Notice all of the thematic connections:
- The casting away of Israel is temporary (casting a seed in death/exile).
- God intentionally blinded part of Israel so that the Gentiles might be brought in.
- The receiving of Israel once again will coincide with the resurrection of the dead (ascension like a manifested fruit).
- God has kept in mystery the blindness of Israel until the fullness of the Gentiles be come in, then all Israel will be saved.
- Both Jews and Gentiles are concluded as "one" under sin and as "one" under condemnation and death, fulfilling the fractal of death like a seed and then later the fractal of grace and abundant mercy, fulfilling the fullness of a fruit in resurrection life.

Just as Moses fulfilled the imagery of death and Elijah fulfilled the imagery of resurrection, the Messiah and those who bear His image will fulfill the imagery of death and resurrection. Just as the tablets of stone had to descend and ascend, we must also fulfill the same pattern. The sowing is the descending, and the reaping and fullness is the ascending. This is why the resurrection shows followers of Yeshua fulfilling the same imagery of ascension into the clouds at the resurrection of the dead.

> 1 Thessalonians 4:13, But I would not have you to be ignorant, brethren, concerning them which are asleep, that ye sorrow not, even as others which have no hope. 14 For if we believe that Yeshua died and rose again, even so them also which sleep in Yeshua will God bring with him. 15 For this we say unto you by the word of the Lord, that we which are alive and remain unto the coming of the Lord shall not prevent them which are asleep. 16 For the Lord himself shall descend from heaven with a shout, with the voice of the archangel, and with the trump of God: and the dead in Christ shall rise first:17 Then we which are alive and remain shall be caught up together with them in the clouds, to meet the Lord in the air: and so shall we ever be with the Lord. 18 Wherefore comfort one another with these words.

Now we can see why Elijah is a pattern of the end–time call to repentance and the necessity of his coming before the day of the Lord as Malachi 4 describes. We can also see why Moses as an image of death like a seed and exile from the land of Promise appears in conjunction with Elijah, who is a picture of resurrection and repentance and the call to return to the Law of Moses before Yeshua's return. Elijah bears the hallmarks of resurrection!

> 1 Kings 17:17, And it came to pass after these things, that the son of the woman, the mistress of the house, fell sick; and his sickness was so sore, that there was no breath left in him. 18 And she said unto Elijah, What have I to do with thee, O thou man of God? art thou come unto me to call my sin to remembrance, and to slay my son? 19 And he said unto her, Give me thy son. And he took him out of her bosom, and carried him up into a loft, where he abode, and laid him upon his own bed. 20 And he cried unto the Lord, and said, O Lord my God, hast thou also brought evil upon the widow with whom I sojourn, by slaying her son? 21 And he stretched himself upon the child three times, and cried unto the Lord, and said, O Lord my God, I pray thee, let this child's soul come into him again. 22 And the Lord heard the voice of Elijah; and the soul of the child came into him again, and he revived. 23 And Elijah took the child, and brought him down out of the chamber into the house, and delivered him unto his mother: and Elijah said, See, thy son liveth. 24 And the woman said to Elijah, Now by this I know that thou art a man of God, and that the word of the Lord in thy mouth is truth.

Elijah is thematically connected to resurrection and how it occurs, applying his own image upon the child and pleading with God to restore his soul to him. Elijah is cast in the end-time battle against the Antichrist. A messenger of the truth battling with the ultimate lie. The restorer of the Law of Moses battling with the

Man of Lawlessness leading a great falling away from the truth of God. This battle has always been cast as lawlessness and iniquity vs obedience to the Law of God, death vs. life, denial of the flesh vs life of the spirit. This battle has moved from its seed form to its full-blown manifestation in the lives of fallen creation. Yeshua's words are as true as ever, "Elias (Elijah) truly shall first come, and restore all things" (Matthew 17:11).

The Spirit of Elijah is coming to restore the true Image of God and ensure the destruction of the Image of the Beast. It is time for him to raise up the dead child and restore his life as God intended. You cannot attempt to understand the end-time battle that is about to ensue without understanding the necessity of the Law of Moses and its proper relationship to the administration of Grace. Those that would like a full briefing on this topic should read the book, "The Elijah Calling". Before we move onto this end-time battle we need to make sure that we have a deep understanding of the Biblical fractals of seed then image. It will help us understand the prophetic patterns revealed in the end-time and what the Apostles meant by "the fullness of time" and the "fullness of the gentiles".

12 THE END-TIME TRAVAIL OF THE WOMAN

Yes, the seed is multiplying. Yes, the seed is alive. Yes, the originally created seed of Adam has YHWH's image. Yes, the seed of Adam is given dominion over all other seed and their kinds before receiving the formation of manifestation and flesh. The pattern is always the same: seed then manifestation (fruit or flesh/image). This applies to Adam, to Abraham, to Yeshua, and to us.

> Genesis 1:24, And God said, Let the earth bring forth the living creature after his kind, cattle, and creeping thing, and beast of the earth after his kind: and it was so. 25 And God made the beast of the earth after his kind, and cattle after their kind, and every thing that creepeth upon the earth after his kind: and God saw that it was good. 26 And God said, Let us make man in our image, after our likeness: and let them have dominion over the fish of the sea, and over the fowl of the air, and over the cattle, and over all the earth, and over every creeping thing that creepeth upon the earth. 27 So God created man in his own image, in the Image of God created he him; male and female created he them…29 And God said, Behold, I have given you every herb bearing seed, which is upon the face of all the earth, and every tree, in the which is the fruit of a tree yielding seed; to you it shall be for meat.

The seed (DNA) for all things is made in Genesis 1 and the formation of all manifestation and flesh (image) for that created living seed is formed in Genesis 2.

> Genesis 2:7, And the Lord God formed man of the dust of the ground, and breathed into his nostrils the breath of life; and man became a living soul. 8 And the Lord God planted a garden eastward in Eden; and there he put the man whom he had formed.

In Genesis 1, Adam is not formed of the dust of the ground, nor does he have the breath of life, but he is made in God's image and he is multiplying. We need to remember what a seed is. It's a word, a code, a program, an image, a transfer of life. We call it DNA.

Deoxyribonucleic acid (DNA) is a nucleic acid that <u>contains the genetic instructions</u> used in the development and functioning of all known living organisms and some viruses. The main role of DNA molecules is the long–term storage of information. DNA is often compared to a set of blueprints or a recipe, or a code, since it contains the instructions needed to construct other components of cells, such as proteins and RNA molecules. The <u>DNA segments that carry this genetic information</u> are called genes, but other DNA sequences have structural purposes, or are involved in regulating the use of this genetic information…It is the sequence of these four bases along the backbone that encodes information. This information is read using the genetic code, which specifies the sequence of the amino acids within proteins. The code is read by copying stretches of DNA into the related nucleic acid RNA, in <u>a process called transcription</u>. (Wikipedia)

We can see that DNA fits Genesis 1 quite well. Remember the pattern of seed then manifestation of flesh and image. Before sin entered the world, this manifestation was not corrupt or broken. Then the Image of God was broken by Adam and Eve. They became one with a corrupt seed that corrupted their seed and resulted in death. It is restored by the "promised seed", the Messiah. He transcribes His seed and image upon us, thereby restoring the image and Countenance of God. We are currently fulfilling the fractal of a seed, not yet manifested in incorruptible flesh (image).

I John 3:2, Beloved, now are we the sons of God, and it doth not yet appear what we shall be: but we know that, when he shall appear, we shall be like him; for we shall see him as he is.

We are not yet born again, but we are a seed that is growing.

John 3:5, Jesus answered, Verily, verily, I say unto thee, Except a man be born of water and of the Spirit, he cannot enter into the kingdom of God. 6 That which is born of the flesh is flesh; and that which is born of the Spirit is spirit. 7 Marvel not that I said unto thee, Ye must be born again.

How do we receive this new life? We have to take the "promised seed".

1 Peter 1:21, Who by him do believe in God, that raised him up from the dead, and gave him glory; that your faith and hope might be in God. 22 Seeing ye have purified your souls in obeying the truth through the Spirit unto unfeigned love of the brethren, see that ye love one another with a pure heart fervently:23 <u>Being born again, not of corruptible seed, but of incorruptible, by the word of God</u>, which liveth and abideth for ever.

As we have already learned this new seed and new life begins in death and is pictured as the hiding of the seed, the Word of God, in our hearts. When that seed begins to grow, it will eventually manifest itself outwardly.

Mark 4:14, The <u>sower soweth the word</u>. 15 And these are they by the way side, where the word is sown; but when they have heard, Satan cometh immediately, and taketh away the <u>word that was sown in their hearts</u>...19 And the cares of this world, and the deceitfulness of riches, and the lusts of other things entering in, choke the word, and it becometh unfruitful. 20 And these are they which are <u>sown on good ground; such as hear the word, and receive it, and bring forth fruit</u>, some thirtyfold, some sixty, and some an hundred. 21 And he said unto them, Is a candle brought to be put under a bushel, or under a bed? and not to be set on a candlestick? 22 For <u>there is nothing hid, which shall not be manifested</u>; neither was any thing kept secret, but that it should come abroad. 23 If any man have ears to hear, let him hear. ...26 And he said, <u>So is the kingdom of God, as if a man should cast seed into the ground</u>; 27 And should sleep, and rise night and day, and the seed <u>should spring and grow up</u>, he knoweth not how. 28 For the earth <u>bringeth forth fruit of herself; first the blade</u>, then the ear, after that the full corn in the ear. 29 But when the fruit is brought forth, <u>immediately he putteth in the sickle, because the harvest is </u>come.

Indeed, we have the seed conceived within us, but the new birth happens when we are resurrected. How can we tell? Are we not once saved, always saved? Yeshua makes it quite clear that the seed that is planted within us can wither and die (Matthew 13:6). If we are already "born again", the seed would not have the capacity to die.

IF WE ARE NOT BORN AS YET, ARE WE ALIVE?
Is the baby in the womb alive? Perhaps Yeshua can enlighten us. Let's return to the breath of life. If we are expecting that a child is not alive until the blood is coursing through the body or the breath of life is in him/her what does that tell us about a baby that does not breathe on his/her own until being born after 9 months?

"Is the child alive in the womb? Or does this mean the child is not alive in the womb?"
I am wondering how the baby breathes while in the amniotic fluid? How can the baby breathe in water? Many people ponder this, as I get this question from time to time. The answer is: he/she does not. A baby's first breath usually happens at birth when he begins to cry. <u>While in the womb, his lungs are filled with fluid and are not involved in supplying oxygen</u> to his body. The <u>Baby gets his oxygen from the mother, via the umbilical cord</u>. He also gets his nutrients from the mother the same way. This is why it is important that a pregnant mother eats healthy food, and breathes healthy air (i. e. do not smoke). (Ask Dr. Sears. com)

This provides an interesting insight on when life begins for the child. He/she cannot breathe on his/her own during the whole 9 months in the womb. What about blood supply?

Your baby at week five: At week five, your baby is 1/17 of an inch long — about the size of the tip of a pen. This week, your baby's heart and circulatory system are taking shape. Your baby's blood vessels will complete a circuit, and his or her heart will begin to beat. Although you will not be able to hear it yet, the motion of your baby's beating heart may be detected with an ultrasound exam. With these changes, blood circulation begins — making the circulatory system the first functioning organ system. (MayoClinic. com)

Prior to week 5 the unborn baby does not even have his/her own blood and is not breathing, but is growing and multiplying in hiding (the womb). The baby in the womb is fully reliant upon his/her mother for breath of life (oxygen), blood (life is in the blood–oxygen), and food. The child is growing and is living upon his/her mother's blood and breath. Without the mother, the child cannot grow or multiply or come to maturity and be born. What is the child to do until he/she can breathe on his/her own? He/she must let the mother provide the breath and the blood.

WHAT IS OUR STATUS?
Are we born? Are we conceived? Are we alive? Are we multiplying? Are we a living soul? Do we have the breath of the Almighty? Do we have the blood?

John 3:2, The same came to Yeshua by night, and said unto him, Rabbi, we know that thou art a teacher come from God: for no man can do these miracles that thou doest, except God be with him. 3 Yeshua answered and said unto him, Verily, verily, I say unto thee, Except a man be born again, he cannot see the kingdom of God. 4 Nicodemus saith unto him, How can a man be born when he is old? can he enter the second time into his mother's womb, and be born? 5 Yeshua answered, Verily, verily, I say unto thee, Except a man be born of water and of the Spirit, he cannot enter into the kingdom of God. 6 That which is born of the flesh is flesh; and *that which is born of the Spirit is spirit.* 7 Marvel not that I said unto thee, Ye must be born again. 8 The wind bloweth where it listeth, and thou hearest the sound thereof, but canst not tell whence it cometh, and whither it goeth: so is every one that is born of the Spirit. 9 Nicodemus answered and said unto him, How can these things be? ...15 That whosoever believeth in him should not perish, but have eternal life. ...18 He that believeth on him is not condemned: but he that believeth not is condemned already, because he hath not believed in the name of the only begotten Son of God.

Our status of being born again as a living soul is completely dependent on believing upon the name of the only begotten Son of YHWH, the Image of

YHWH. Being born of water and the Holy Spirit is the only way that we can see the Kingdom of YHWH. How is our belief upon the name of the only begotten Son of God expressed? By living through Yeshua.

> John 6:47, Verily, verily, I say unto you, He that believeth on me hath everlasting life. 48 I am that bread of life…52 The Jews therefore strove among themselves, saying, How can this man give us his flesh to eat? 53 Then Yeshua said unto them, Verily, verily, I say unto you, Except ye eat the flesh of the Son of man, and drink his blood, ye have no life in you. 54 Whoso eateth my flesh, and drinketh my blood, hath eternal life; and I will raise him up at the last day. 55 For my flesh is meat indeed, and my blood is drink indeed. 56 He that eateth my flesh, and drinketh my blood, dwelleth in me, and I in him…63 It is the spirit that quickeneth; the flesh profiteth nothing: the words that I speak unto you, they are spirit, and they are life.

Yeshua is making it possible for us to born again. It is through abiding in Yeshua that we receive the nourishment of life; the breath, the blood, the water, and the bread of life comes only through Yeshua. He has made the womb (mikvah/baptism) for us to exist in until our second birth (resurrection).

Yeshua presently (now) gives us eternal life, yet we will be raised up (born) on the last day. Notice we are in the womb, we are alive, we have eternal life or the life of the second birth even though we are currently within the womb drinking the blood of Yeshua and eating His flesh. We are living in Him! We are one with Him, as He is one with the Father. So, we know that we are not yet born, yet we are viewed by God as currently having eternal life so long as we abide in Yeshua. We see that Yeshua has provided the flesh, the water, and the blood, but what about the breath?

HOW DO WE LIVE IN AND THROUGH YESHUA?
We must have the breath of the Almighty in order to be considered a living soul. The blood carries the breath of the Almighty, the life. Yeshua gives us the breath of life, the Holy Spirit (Ruach Hakodesh).

> John 7:37, In the last day, that great day of the feast, Yeshua stood and cried, saying, If any man thirst, let him come unto me, and drink. 38 He that believeth on me, as the scripture hath said, out of his belly shall flow rivers of living water. 39 (But this spake he of the Spirit, which they that believe on him should receive: for the Holy Ghost was not yet given; because that Yeshua was not yet glorified.)

Notice the fulfillment of this promise after Yeshua's resurrection. We are given the breath of life, the breath of the Almighty, the Ruach Hakodesh (Holy Spirit).

> John 20:19, Then the same day at evening, being the first day of the week, when the doors were shut where the disciples were assembled for fear of the Jews, came Yeshua and stood in the midst, and saith unto them, Peace be unto

you. 20 And when he had so said, he shewed unto them his hands and his side. Then were the disciples glad, when they saw the Lord. 21 Then said Yeshua to them again, Peace be unto you: as my Father hath sent me, even so send I you. 22 And when he had said this, he breathed on them, and saith unto them, Receive ye the Holy Ghost:

After Yeshua's resurrection the Apostles still could not breathe on their own. Yeshua had to do it for them. He made them breathe the Holy Spirit by giving them His breath. This preliminary breath occurred shortly after Yeshua's resurrection. Not all of the Apostles are there, as Thomas is absent. It is not until the day of Pentecost (Shavuot) that the Apostles are given a full portion of the Ruach Hakodesh (Holy Spirit) when they all come together as one. This is also the same day that commemorated the first giving of the Law of Moses to Israel. Just as we see the fire of God (Shekinah Glory), the Utterance of God, and the giving of the "commandments of God", we see all of these same manifestations of God's glory within the Apostles with the Holy Spirit. The Ten Commandments that are expressions of the Image of God are being put within the hearts of those redeemed by Yeshua. Along with that restored image come the manifestations of God's presence.

Acts 1:6, When they therefore were come together, they asked of him, saying, Lord, wilt thou at this time restore again the kingdom to Israel? 7 And he said unto them, It is not for you to know the times or the seasons, which the Father hath put in his own power. 8 But ye shall receive power, after that the Holy Ghost is come upon you: and ye shall be witnesses unto me both in Jerusalem, and in all Judaea, and in Samaria, and unto the uttermost part of the earth. 9 And when he had spoken these things, while they beheld, he was taken up; and a cloud received him out of their sight.

It is after receiving this power and the Holy Spirit that all 12 Apostles are fully able to give testimony that they are alive in Yeshua. They are fully breathing as Yeshua breathed by the power of the Holy Spirit, the breath of the Almighty. It is by Yeshua that the Holy Spirit is given for a full testimony that they are alive in Yeshua.

Acts 2:1, And when the day of Pentecost was fully come, they were all with one accord in one place. 2 And suddenly there came a sound from heaven as of a rushing mighty wind, and it filled all the house where they were sitting. 3 And there appeared unto them cloven tongues like as of fire, and it sat upon each of them. 4 And they were all filled with the Holy Ghost, and began to speak with other tongues, as the Spirit gave them Utterance. 5 And there were dwelling at Jerusalem Jews, devout men, out of every nation under heaven. 6 Now when this was noised abroad, the multitude came together, and were confounded, because that every man heard them speak in his own language....And they were all amazed, and were in doubt, saying one to another, What meaneth this?

The breath of the Almighty has given them Utterance and a complete testimony of Yeshua's redemptive work for mankind: the deliverance of their image and flesh. Yeshua came to manifest the Name of the Father, YHWH, for the redemption of the flesh of all fallen creation. Their testimony is that they received the Holy Spirit because of Yeshua's blood. The blood has made atonement for the soul (spirit).

Acts 2:31, He seeing this before spake of the resurrection of Christ, that his soul was not left in hell, neither his flesh did see corruption. 32 This Yeshua hath God raised up, whereof we all are witnesses. 33 Therefore being by the right hand of God exalted, and having received of the Father the promise of the Holy Ghost, he hath shed forth this, which ye now see and hear.

The promise of deliverance is through Yeshua's blood atonement so that we might receive the breath of the almighty (Holy Spirit).

HOW DOES THE BLOOD MAKE ATONEMENT FOR THE SOUL?

Leviticus 17:11, For the life of the flesh is in the blood: and I have given it to you upon the altar to make an atonement for your souls: for it is the blood that maketh an atonement for the soul.

We can see how Yeshua made this blood atonement that we might become living souls.

- Romans 3:25, Whom God hath set forth to be a propitiation through faith in his blood, to declare his righteousness for the remission of sins that are past, through the forbearance of God;
- Romans 5:9, Much more then, being now justified by his blood, we shall be saved from wrath through him.
- Ephesians 1:7, In whom we have redemption through his blood, the forgiveness of sins, according to the riches of his grace;
- Colossians 1:14, In whom we have redemption through his blood, even the forgiveness of sins:
- Colossians 1:20, And, having made peace through the blood of his cross, by him to reconcile all things unto himself; by him, I say, whether they be things in earth, or things in heaven.
- Hebrews 13:11, For the bodies of those beasts, whose blood is brought into the sanctuary by the high priest for sin, are burned without the camp. 12 Wherefore Yeshua also, that he might sanctify the people with his own blood, suffered without the gate. 13 Let us go forth therefore unto him without the camp, bearing his reproach.
- 1 Peter 1:1, Peter, an apostle of Yeshua, to the strangers scattered throughout Pontus, Galatia, Cappadocia, Asia, and Bithynia, 2 Elect according to the foreknowledge of God the Father, through sanctification of the Spirit, unto obedience and sprinkling of the blood of Yeshua: grace unto you, and

peace, be multiplied. 3 Blessed be the God and Father of our Lord Yeshua, which according to his abundant mercy hath begotten us again unto a lively hope by the resurrection of Yeshua from the dead,

It is always for the same goal! Yeshua's blood has made it possible that we might breathe the Holy Spirit!

- John 20:22, And when he had said this, he breathed on them, and saith unto them, Receive ye the Holy Ghost:
- Acts 1:8, But ye shall receive power, after that the Holy Ghost is come upon you: and ye shall be witnesses unto me both in Jerusalem, and in all Judaea, and in Samaria, and unto the uttermost part of the earth.
- Acts 2:33, Therefore being by the right hand of God exalted, and having received of the Father the promise of the Holy Ghost, he hath shed forth this, which ye now see and hear.
- Acts 2:38, Then Peter said unto them, Repent, and be baptized every one of you in the name of Yeshua for the remission of sins, and ye shall receive the gift of the Holy Ghost.
- Acts 8:15, Who, when they were come down, prayed for them, that they might receive the Holy Ghost:
- Acts 8:17, Then laid they their hands on them, and they received the Holy Ghost.
- Acts 8:19, Saying, Give me also this power, that on whomsoever I lay hands, he may receive the Holy Ghost.
- Acts 10:47, Can any man forbid water, that these should not be baptized, which have received the Holy Ghost as well as we?
- Acts 19:2, He said unto them, Have ye received the Holy Ghost since ye believed? And they said unto him, We have not so much as heard whether there be any Holy Ghost.
- 1 Corinthians 6:19, What? know ye not that your body is the temple of the Holy Ghost which is in you, which ye have of God, and ye are not your own?

Yes, the life is in the blood. Without Yeshua's blood we cannot breathe the Holy Spirit (the life)! We know we are alive, we are in the womb (baptism/mikvah) with Yeshua providing us the blood, the water, the flesh, and the breath. If we remain in Him we stay alive. If we remain in Him we will be born again. In essence we are in seed form. We are in hiding. We are multiplying and being blessed in the womb (mikvah). Yeshua has given us His DNA (image) so that we might be born again with His image (flesh) to stand in the presence of God. What does Paul say about being born again with new flesh? It starts with the sowing of a seed and it ends with being grafted into Yeshua's image (flesh).

I Corinthians 15:35, But some man will say, How are the dead raised up? and with what body do they come? 36 Thou fool, that which thou sowest is not quickened, except it die:37 And that which thou sowest, thou sowest not that body that shall be, but bare grain, it may chance of wheat, or of some other grain:38 But God giveth it a body as it hath pleased him, and to every seed his own body. 39 All flesh is not the same flesh: but there is one kind of flesh of men, another flesh of beasts, another of fishes, and another of birds...It is sown in corruption; it is raised in incorruption:43 It is sown in dishonour; it is raised in glory: it is sown in weakness; it is raised in power:44 It is sown a natural body; it is raised a spiritual body. There is a natural body, and there is a spiritual body. 45 And so it is written, The first man Adam was made a living soul; the last Adam was made a quickening spirit. 46 Howbeit that was not first which is spiritual, but that which is natural; and afterward that which is spiritual. 47 The first man is of the earth, earthy; the second man is the Lord from heaven. 48 As is the earthy, such are they also that are earthy: and as is the heavenly, such are they also that are heavenly. 49 And as we have borne the image of the earthy, we shall also bear the image of the heavenly. 50 Now this I say, brethren, that flesh and blood cannot inherit the kingdom of God; neither doth corruption inherit incorruption. 51 Behold, I shew you a mystery; We shall not all sleep, but we shall all be changed, 52 In a moment, in the twinkling of an eye, at the last trump: for the trumpet shall sound, and the dead shall be raised incorruptible, and we shall be changed. 53 For this corruptible must put on incorruption, and this mortal must put on immortality. 54 So when this corruptible shall have put on incorruption, and this mortal shall have put on immortality, then shall be brought to pass the saying that is written, Death is swallowed up in victory. 55 O death, where is thy sting? O grave, where is thy victory?

Is the seed alive? Yes. Yeshua is the seed (image/DNA) of YHWH.

John 12:23, And Yeshua answered them, saying, The hour is come, that the Son of man should be glorified. 24 Verily, verily, I say unto you, Except a corn of wheat fall into the ground and die, it abideth alone: but if it die, it bringeth forth much fruit. 25 He that loveth his life shall lose it; and he that hateth his life in this world shall keep it unto life eternal. 26 If any man serve me, let him follow me; and where I am, there shall also my servant be: if any man serve me, him will my Father honour.

The seed must be alive in order for it to die. The seed must be alive in order for it to "keep it unto life eternal". Yeshua is the image (DNA) of the Father (YHWH). Yeshua is sowing the seed, His seed, and YHWH's image in us. We are made alive by His death.

This is why we do not see the Kingdom of Heaven manifest as yet. It is in hiding while it multiplies and grows in the womb. It is yet to be born of manifestation (flesh/image). We are literally grafted into Yeshua's incorruptible flesh and blood. Through Him we receive eternal and spiritual life. We are able to breathe the Holy Spirit by Yeshua's blood. We partake of His image, the image of the Father (YHWH). We become one in Him.

I John 3:1, Behold, what manner of love the Father hath bestowed upon us, that we should be called the sons of God: therefore the world knoweth us not, because it knew him not. 2 Beloved, now are we the sons of God, and it doth not yet appear what we shall be: but we know that, when he shall appear, we shall be like him; for we shall see him as he is. 3 And every man that hath this hope in him purifieth himself, even as he is pure. 4 Whosoever committeth sin transgresseth also the law: for sin is the transgression of the law. 5 And ye know that he was manifested to take away our sins; and in him is no sin.

We can see that Yeshua's work in the New Testament is just like Genesis 1 and Genesis 2: seed then manifestation (flesh/image)! There is multiplication of seed, then formation of image and flesh, hidden then revealed, sown then raised. The Apostles and disciples are instructed to continue Yeshua's work of sowing seed. If we are in His image, we should be doing His work and fulfilling His fractal.

Matthew 28:18, And Yeshua came and spake unto them, saying, All power is given unto me in heaven and in earth. 19 Go ye therefore, and teach all nations, baptizing them in the name of the Father, and of the Son, and of the Holy Ghost:20 Teaching them to observe all things whatsoever I have commanded you: and, lo, I am with you always, even unto the end of the world. Amen.

What have we seen? The patterns and fractals of conception, growth in the womb, and birth are the same patterns of joining with the Messiah in the baptism (mikvah) as a type of the womb and the subsequent growth that happens to the believer that remains "in Christ". The fractals of God's design in nature also apply to the redemption process and our future destiny. What can we conclude about the child in the womb? It is alive and has the presence of God dwelling within him/her. It is holy and must be treated as such! We, like the child in the womb, await our birth in the Messiah.

Conception and growth in the womb is associated with a state of exile, hiddenness, and great multiplicity. It is the very act of the replication of images, moving from one cell to many cells, from one child (promised seed) to many children. This aspect of hiding the seed is associated with burying (hiding) the seed in the Earth and fulfilling the imagery of death. The same associations apply to the Baptism (Mikvah) and our being buried with the Messiah (Colossians 2:12). We are fulfilling the same imagery as the Messiah Yeshua. Elijah's ministry fulfills this same fractal of exile, death, and hiddenness.

1 Kings 19:1, And Ahab told Jezebel all that Elijah had done, and withal how he had slain all the prophets with the sword. 2 Then Jezebel sent a messenger unto Elijah, saying, So let the gods do to me, and more also, if I make not thy life as the life of one of them by to morrow about this time. And when he saw that, he arose, and went for his life, and came to Beersheba, which belongeth to Judah, and left his servant there. 4 But he himself went a day's

journey into the wilderness, and came and sat down under a juniper tree: and he requested for himself that he might die; and said, It is enough; now, O Lord, take away my life; for I am not better than my fathers. 5 And as he lay and slept under a juniper tree, behold, then an angel touched him, and said unto him, Arise and eat.

Take note of how after God's display of power in response to Elijah's prayer in testing the priests of Baal, Elijah is now pursued by the Queen and flees for his life into the wilderness. Elijah, just like Joseph is banished into exile from the Promised Land, just like Israel leaving Egypt and going into the wilderness, just like Moses fleeing into the wilderness for forty years before returning at God's command to work for their redemption from their taskmasters...he also flees to a place of death (wilderness, exile, and hiddenness). A careful analysis will show that Elijah flees to the same mountain that God spoke from when He gave the Law to Israel. It is in the wilderness that that an angel touches him and restores his will to live.

I Kings 19:6, And he looked, and, behold, there was a cake baken on the coals, and a cruse of water at his head. And he did eat and drink, and laid him down again. 7 And the angel of the Lord came again the second time, and touched him, and said, Arise and eat; because the journey is too great for thee.

The angel actually prepares a cake for Elijah to consume and places a container of water by Elijah's head. Elijah eats and drinks and then lays back down apparently still in despair for his own life...even after seeing an angel of God. Imagine how great his distress was that even after God's display of the Shekinah Glory over Elijah's sacrifice at the confrontation with the priests of Baal and after seeing and being fed by an angel, he still has to lay back down and recover himself. The angel actually appears to Elijah twice and has Elijah eat twice, stating that the journey will be too difficult for Elijah.

Let's not casually dismiss the significance of the imagery that Elijah is manifesting or the fact that God personally sends an angel to restore him and to literally "touch" him twice, feed him twice, and give him water to drink twice...before having him continue his journey. This should give us some insight into Yeshua's own declaration about Elijah, the role he would fulfill and that he would indeed serve twice!

Matthew 11:12, And from the days of John the Baptist until now the kingdom of heaven suffereth violence, and the violent take it by force. 13 For all the prophets and the law prophesied until John. 14 And if ye will receive it, this is Elias, which was for to come. 15 He that hath ears to hear, let him hear.

Yeshua's plain declaration was that John the Baptist fulfilled the role of Elijah. But is that the whole story? Is this all just historical fulfillment?

Matthew 17:10, And his disciples asked him, saying, Why then say the scribes that Elias must first come? 11 And Jesus answered and said unto them,

Elias truly shall first come, and restore all things. 12 But I say unto you, That Elias is come already, and they knew him not, but have done unto him whatsoever they listed. Likewise shall also the Son of man suffer of them. 13 Then the disciples understood that he spake unto them of John the Baptist.

At the Mount of Transfiguration, the subject of Elijah comes up again after Elijah and Moses appear with Yeshua in a transfigured state. The Apostles ask why it was such a common teaching that Elijah would come again. Yeshua clearly explains that Elijah's role is to "restore all things". Notice that Yeshua responds not in a past tense, but in a future tense, "Elias truly <u>shall</u> first come" while establishing also that John the Baptist also fulfilled this role. Given the Angel's interaction with Elijah, touching and feeding him twice before continuing his journey to the very place that God gave the Law to Israel, it would seem very plausible that Elijah, whether personally or one appointed with the "Spirit of Elijah" would indeed serve twice in the restoration process.

2 Kings 2:9, And it came to pass, when they were gone over, that Elijah said unto Elisha, Ask what I shall do for thee, before I be taken away from thee. And Elisha said, I pray thee, let a double portion of thy spirit be upon me.

Just as Elijah passed on his image to the dead boy who was brought back to life, now his spirit rests as a double portion upon his protégé, Elisha.

2 Kings 2:15, And when the sons of the prophets which were to view at Jericho saw him, they said, The spirit of Elijah doth rest on Elisha. And they came to meet him, and bowed themselves to the ground before him.

It is quite possible that someone or someone's could fulfill the role of Elijah and not be Elijah, having Elijah's spirit, commission, and divine decree placed upon them. What is especially amazing about this is that he then continues his journey to the place where the Law was given to Israel and just as Moses saw the Name of the Lord presented to him in Exodus 34, so also Elijah has an encounter with the Word of YHWH.

I Kings 19:8, And he arose, and did eat and drink, and went in the strength of that meat forty days and forty nights unto Horeb the mount of God. 9 And he came thither unto a cave, and lodged there; and, behold, the word of the Lord came to him, and he said unto him, What doest thou here, Elijah? 10 And he said, I have been very jealous for the Lord God of hosts: for the children of Israel have forsaken thy covenant, thrown down thine altars, and slain thy prophets with the sword; and I, even I only, am left; and they seek my life, to take it away. 11 And he said, Go forth, and stand upon the mount before the Lord. And, behold, the Lord passed by, and a great and strong wind rent the mountains, and brake in pieces the rocks before the Lord; but the Lord was not in the wind: and after the wind an earthquake; but the Lord was not in the earthquake:12 And after the earthquake a fire; but the Lord was not in the fire:

and after the fire a still small voice. 13 And it was so, when Elijah heard it, that he wrapped his face in his mantle, and went out, and stood in the entering in of the cave. And, behold, there came a voice unto him, and said, What doest thou here, Elijah?

For those who thought the references to the Name of YHWH with the glorified countenance of Moses at the second giving of the Law, was happenstance, might want to look again. God's presents to Elijah what God is in…not the wind, nor the earthquake, and not the fire…but only in the still small voice. The Word! Literally the manifest Name of the Lord (YHWH). As John 1:1 indicates this is none other than Yeshua the Messiah.

Exodus 34:5, And the Lord descended in the cloud, and stood with him there, and proclaimed the name of the Lord. 6 And the Lord passed by before him, and proclaimed, The Lord, The Lord God, merciful and gracious, longsuffering, and abundant in goodness and truth…

Are you seeing how this same imagery that Moses lived though at the second giving of the Torah is now being fulfilled by Elijah? How does Elijah respond? He wraps his face (countenance) in a mantle. This is exactly what Moses did at the second giving of the Torah.

Exodus 34:28, And he was there with the Lord forty days and forty nights; he did neither eat bread, nor drink water. And he wrote upon the tables the words of the covenant, the ten commandments. 29 And it came to pass, when Moses came down from mount Sinai with the two tables of testimony in Moses' hand, when he came down from the mount, that Moses wist not that the skin of his face shone while he talked with him. 30 And when Aaron and all the children of Israel saw Moses, behold, the skin of his face shone; and they were afraid to come nigh him. 31 And Moses called unto them; and Aaron and all the rulers of the congregation returned unto him: and Moses talked with them. 32 And afterward all the children of Israel came nigh: and he gave them in commandment all that the Lord had spoken with him in mount Sinai. 33 And till Moses had done speaking with them, he put a vail on his face. 34 But when Moses went in before the Lord to speak with him, he took the vail off, until he came out. And he came out, and spake unto the children of Israel that which he was commanded. 35 And the children of Israel saw the face of Moses, that the skin of Moses' face shone: and Moses put the vail upon his face again, until he went in to speak with him.

Elijah had the same glorification experience that Moses had. His countenance was changed by his encounter with the Name of YHWH. If we follow the pattern of what occurred to Moses and to Elijah we can see what happens next in the role of Elijah, the restoration of the written Law of Moses.

Malachi 4:4, Remember ye the law of Moses my servant, which I commanded unto him in Horeb for all Israel, with the statutes and judgments. 5 Behold, I will send you Elijah the prophet before the coming of the great and dreadful day of the Lord:

Elijah's role is very clear, restore those who worship God and fear His name (the Messiah) to the Law of Moses. This prophecy has a very clear time element of being "before the coming of the great and dreadful day of the Lord". This was not fulfilled in its entirety at the first coming of Yeshua. We must look to the angel touching and feeding Elijah twice and having a very long journey to fulfill this prophecy. Just as Moses and Elijah have an encounter with the Countenance (Image) of God, so can we. Just as that image has been hidden and exiled due to the sin of Adam and Eve, it will be revealed again by the work of the "promised seed", the Messiah Yeshua. After Elijah encounters the Word of God, his countenance is also changed just as Moses countenance was and he wraps his face in his mantle. Think of the symbolism here of the glorified countenance being wrapped in a garment. What happens to that image wrapped in a garment?

1 Kings 19:18, And Jehu the son of Nimshi shalt thou anoint to be king over Israel: and Elisha the son of Shaphat of Abelmeholah shalt thou anoint to be prophet in thy room…Yet I have left me seven thousand in Israel, all the knees which have not bowed unto Baal, and every mouth which hath not kissed him. 19 So he departed thence, and found Elisha the son of Shaphat, who was plowing with twelve yoke of oxen before him, and he with the twelfth: and Elijah passed by him, and cast his mantle upon him. 20 And he left the oxen, and ran after Elijah, and said, Let me, I pray thee, kiss my father and my mother, and then I will follow thee. And he said unto him, Go back again: for what have I done to thee? 21 And he returned back from him, and took a yoke of oxen, and slew them, and boiled their flesh with the instruments of the oxen, and gave unto the people, and they did eat. Then he arose, and went after Elijah, and ministered unto him.

Just as Elijah buries his countenance in his mantle and he is comforted that there are seven thousand in Israel that have not bowed to Baal, Elijah departs and finds Elisha and throws that same countenance covered mantle upon Elisha. Once again, we see the transference of the Image and Countenance of God moving from seed to manifestation and revelation. Along with that revelation comes a "double" portion of the Spirit of God.

2 Kings 2:9, And it came to pass, when they were gone over, that Elijah said unto Elisha, Ask what I shall do for thee, before I be taken away from thee. And Elisha said, I pray thee, let a double portion of thy spirit be upon me.

The pattern of Elijah is to pass on the Image of God. We cannot miss the inescapable similarities of Elijah fulfilling the same pattern as Moses. We can see why it was such a prevalent teaching that Elijah must come again and restore all things. A church blinded by an unscriptural presupposition of "grace vs. law" is blindly disregarding a host of Old and New Testament scriptures showing end time believers restoring and establishing the Law of Moses.

We cannot deny the imagery of a dual coming of "Elijah" or "Elijah's office (room)" or "Elijah's Spirit" being fulfilled by someone or several people. Just as the seed portion of the fractal has a limited presentation of imagery, the manifestation portion of the imagery has a double portion of the Spirit of God.

The purpose of Moses and Elijah's role was and is associated with transference of the Image of God. Those without the Word…cannot fulfill this. Those with the Word and without the Law of Moses cannot hope to fulfill this. Those with the Word and the Law of Moses will have the seed of the Kingdom of God in their mouths and will be sharing it with the world (Revelation 12:17). This is why we see the Book of Revelation focused on manifesting the Image of God, the Image of the Beast, and the birth of the Man-Child. Just as there is a time for sowing, there is a time for reaping…seed then manifestation.

Ecclesiastes 3:1, To every thing there is a season, and a time to every purpose under the heaven:2 A time to be born, and a time to die; a time to plant, and a time to pluck up that which is planted;

This isn't just a philosophical concept. This is the fractal of creation and manifestation. This is the pattern of Genesis 1-Seed, and Genesis 2-Manifestation of the Image. This is the pattern of the Image of God, the Messiah. The first coming was associated with Him planting the seed of the Word of God. His seconding coming will be to harvest the fruit of that seed. Make no mistake He won't be harvesting bad fruit into his barn.

Matthew 7:18, A good tree cannot bring forth evil fruit, neither can a corrupt tree bring forth good fruit.

So those who think "once saved always saved" might want to re-evaluate if this idea is actually a scriptural teaching or a man-made tradition.

2 Corinthians 13:5, Examine yourselves, whether ye be in the faith; prove your own selves. Know ye not your own selves, how that Jesus Christ is in you, except ye be reprobates?

Here Paul is addressing the church and warning them of the possibility that though they may be professing Christ, He may not be in them. Yeshua made it quite plain that there would be many "believers" thinking that they were in union with Yeshua and are not.

Matthew 25:10, And while they went to buy, the bridegroom came; and they that were ready went in with him to the marriage: and the door was shut. 11 Afterward came also the other virgins, saying, Lord, Lord, open to us. 12 But he answered and said, Verily I say unto you, I know you not.

This is a warning from the Messiah Himself that "once saved always saved" is not a scriptural truth.

> Philippians 2:12, Wherefore, my beloved, as ye have always obeyed, not as in my presence only, but now much more in my absence, work out your own salvation with fear and trembling.

Paul's warning to believers is to "work" and be cautious and diligent. This is hardly the advice of today's "let Jesus do it" philosophy. There are many that hold to this philosophy and fail to weigh lies vs truth, and tradition vs scripture. Every believer is responsible for who they learn from and associate. The pastor, the preacher, nor the rabbi, will be held solely accountable for your actions on that day...you will be the one held responsible if you have conformed to the Image of Christ or not (Romans 8:29).

13 THE IMAGE OF GOD-THE MESSIAH

The Messiah came to sow His seed, the Image of God. If you go back and look at the ministry of Yeshua, you will see that He was telling the people this message continually.

Yeshua is sowing the image, the word, His seed, some on good ground and some on cursed ground. Remember the first Adam's purpose is to till the ground. This is also the purpose of the last Adam. The first Adam brought death (like a seed), the last Adam brings life (like a manifested fruit). Also keep in mind that before Adam's fall, the ground was good and would produce good fruit. After Adam fell, the ground was cursed and would bring forth thorns and thistles.

> Genesis 2:5, And every plant of the field before it was in the earth, and every herb of the field before it grew: for the Lord God had not caused it to rain upon the earth, and there was not a man to till the ground.

We must acknowledge that in this account Yeshua is associated with water (God/Holy Spirit) and the people he is teaching are associated with the "land". Remember Yeshua is "tilling the ground" just like the first Adam.

> Mark 4:1, And he began again to teach by the sea side: and there was gathered unto him a great multitude, so that <u>he entered into a ship, and sat in the sea</u>; and the <u>whole multitude was by the sea on the land</u>. 2 And he taught them many things by parables, and said unto them in his doctrine, 3 Hearken; Behold, there went out a sower to sow:...22 For <u>there is nothing hid, which shall not be manifested</u>; neither was any thing kept secret, but that it should come abroad. 23 If <u>any man have ears to hear, let him hear</u>...26 And he said, <u>So is the kingdom of God, as if a man should cast seed into the ground; 27 And should sleep, and rise night and day, and the seed should spring and grow up</u>, he knoweth not how. 28 For the earth bringeth forth fruit of herself; first the

blade, then the ear, after that the full corn in the ear. 29 But <u>when the fruit is brought forth, immediately he putteth in the sickle, because the harvest is come</u>. 30 And he said, Whereunto shall we liken the kingdom of God? or with what comparison shall we compare it? 31 It is like a grain of mustard seed, which, when it is sown in the earth, is less than all the seeds that be in the earth:32 But when it is sown, it groweth up, and becometh greater than all herbs, and shooteth out great branches; so that the fowls of the air may lodge under the shadow of it. 33 And with many such parables spake he the word unto them, as they were able to hear it. 34 But without a parable spake he not unto them: and when they were alone, he expounded all things to his disciples.

Yeshua is sowing the seed of the Kingdom of God (Image of YHWH) throughout the New Testament. This is not an ethereal kingdom. Do not spiritualize it away. Yeshua is sowing His seed (DNA, image). The seed, the DNA, is the Word. Just like DNA, it is an encoded program that takes root in the soil and changes it and makes it a new image (manifestation/flesh/image).

Chemically, DNA consists of two long polymers of simple units called nucleotides, with backbones made of sugars and phosphate groups joined by ester bonds...It is the sequence of these four bases along the backbone that encodes information. This information is read using the genetic code, which specifies the sequence of the amino acids within proteins. The code is read by copying stretches of DNA into the related nucleic acid RNA, in a process called transcription. (Wikipedia)

We see Yeshua sowing His word, His seed, His image, the seed of the Kingdom of God for the deliverance of incorruptible flesh. The word is read by the hearing of the word (code) and it grows in some and not in others. God's word must be written upon the tablets of our hearts in order for us to obtain eternal life.

Exodus 34:1, And the Lord said unto Moses, Hew thee two tablets of stone like unto the first: and I will write upon these tablets the words that were in the first tablets, which thou brakest. 2 And be ready in the morning, and come up in the morning unto mount Sinai, and present thyself there to me in the top of the mount.

This is the sowing of the Word of God, the Image of God upon our circumcised hearts. This is the transcription of God's image (DNA) upon our lives.

Matthew 13:24, Another parable put he forth unto them, saying, The kingdom of heaven is likened unto a man which sowed good seed in his field:...37, He answered and said unto them, He that soweth the good seed is the Son of man;

The seed is sown in the hearts of people. Those who receive the seed cultivate it and allow it to grow by remaining in Yeshua. These are covered by His blood and are able to breathe the Holy Spirit. These are alive. These are unborn. These are in the mikvah (womb) and live thorough Yeshua.

What does this tell us about the unborn? Between Yeshua's testimony and the proof found in Genesis 1, we can clearly see that these seeds are alive, they multiply, they have movement, they have dominion, and they are created "kind after kind" in the "image of their kind".

The first phase is the planting of the seed (Genesis 1 and Yeshua's first coming). The second phase is the formation of an image (manifested fruit/flesh) and birth as a living soul (Genesis 2 and Yeshua's second coming/the resurrection).

LIFE BEGINS WITH THE WRITING OF A CODE ON A SEED:

Romans 8:22, For we know that the whole creation groaneth and travaileth in pain together until now...29 For whom he did foreknow, he also did predestinate to be conformed to the image of his Son, that he might be the firstborn among many brethren. 30 Moreover whom he did predestinate, them he also called: and whom he called, them he also justified: and whom he justified, them he also glorified. 31 What shall we then say to these things? If God be for us, who can be against us?

Using the Torah and Yeshua's testimony as our guide we should be able to clearly know when life begins.

When does life begin?
- The image, code, Word, (DNA) multiplies.
- El's involvement in the creation of life begins with the seed (DNA).
- God always works the same way, seed then flesh (image).
- The seed grows in hiding (womb/mikvah/exile).
- The seed's life is dependent upon the blood and the breath.
- The blood and the breath are provided to the seed by the work of Yeshua.
- The seed remains alive so long as it abides in Yeshua.
- The blood carries the life (breath of the Almighty).
- Yeshua's blood atonement makes us able to breathe the Holy Spirit.
- Yeshua says we (seed in the womb) currently have eternal life but we are awaiting our birth (incorruptible flesh/image).
- The name El brings seed multiplicity and the name YHWH brings deliverance of manifested image/flesh.
- The name Elohim begins the Torah, "the book of the generations of heaven and earth" and "the book of the generations of Adam", with the creation of seed. God only concerns Himself with life. He is life. The creative work by the name EL and then the name YHWH causes life from the beginning. In the beginning of life was the Word (seed).
- Genesis clarifies that the Torah is "the Book of the Generations of

Adam", so we are being shown Adam's beginning which is inseparable from "the Generations of the Heavens and the earth".

- Life begins at conception!

Genesis 5:1, This is the book of the generations of Adam. In the day that God created man, in the likeness of God made he him; 2 Male and female created he them; and blessed them, and called their name Adam, in the day when they were created. 3 And Adam lived an hundred and thirty years, and begat a son in his own likeness, and after his image; and called his name Seth:

The Torah is explaining the making of the Image of God and how Adam, originally made in God's image (DNA/seed), fell and no longer made seed in God's image. The book starts with seed and ends with the deliverance of flesh to the Promised land. The generations of Adam begin with the making of a seed in God's image, just as life begins with the making of the seed. As we have learned, the seed may die if it is not cared for properly or does not abide where the blood can give it the breath of the almighty. The seed is alive. Genesis 1 is showing a seed that is alive and multiplying, but has not yet received the formation of flesh which happens at the appearance of YHWH and the watering of the ground on the 7th day Sabbath. Take notice that we need the blood, the water, and the breath (ruach/spirit). These three-bear witness in the earth (ground).

I John 5:2, By this we know that we love the children of God, when we love God, and keep his commandments. 3 For this is the love of God, that we keep his commandments: and his commandments are not grievous. 4 For whatsoever is born (Gennao, Strong's 1080, "to be Begotten") of God overcometh the world: and this is the victory that overcometh the world, even our faith. 5 Who is he that overcometh the world, but he that believeth that Yeshua is the Son of God? 6 This is he that came by water and blood, even Yeshua; not by water only, but by water and blood. And it is the Spirit that beareth witness, because the Spirit is truth. 7 For there are three that bear record in heaven, the Father, the Word, and the Holy Ghost: and these three are one. 8 And there are three that bear witness in earth, the Spirit, and the water, and the blood: and these three agree in one. 9 If we receive the witness of men, the witness of God is greater: for this is the witness of God which he hath testified of his Son. 10 He that believeth on the Son of God hath the witness in himself: he that believeth not God hath made him a liar; because he believeth not the record that God gave of his Son

Yeshua and the Torah give testimony that life begins at the making of the seed, not at birth, not when the blood starts flowing, not when the breath starts. The breath and the blood are necessary for continued life. Birth is also necessary when the baby is ready to be born. The baby cannot remain in the womb forever. Life begins when God makes the seed. The planting of the seed is the hearing of the Word (the seed of the Kingdom of Heaven). It is alive but it can die. Life begins with the writing of the seed.

Proofs of Life from Conception:

- "God hath from the beginning chosen you." (2 Thessalonians 2:13)
- "Known unto God are all his works from the beginning of the world." (Acts 15:18)
- "Whither shall I flee from thy presence? . . . thou hast possessed my reins: thou hast covered me in my mother's womb." (Psalm 139:7, 13)
- "Thine eyes did see my substance, yet being unperfect; and in thy book all my members were written, which in continuance were fashioned, when as yet there was none of them." (Psalm 139:16)
- "They shall enter into my rest: although the works were finished from the foundation of the world." (Hebrews 4:3)
- "Declaring the end from the beginning, and from ancient times the things that are not yet done." (Isaiah 46:10)
- "In whom also we have obtained an inheritance, being predestinated according to the purpose of him." (Ephesians 1:11)
- "According as he hath chosen us in him before the foundation of the world." (Ephesians 1:4)
- "Whose names were not written in the book of life from the foundation of the world." (Revelation 17:8)

The inscription in the book of life happened at the foundation of the world (Genesis 1). Those who say that which is growing in the womb is just a clump of cells need to learn the patterns and fractals of God's divine plan. That plan of life starts with a seed and it is holy to God. God is life.

John 1:2, The same was in the beginning with God. 3 All things were made by him; and without him was not any thing made that was made. 4 In him was life; and the life was the light of men.

Anyone choosing to kill and destroy where God has placed His own life, has placed themselves in great jeopardy. Life begins with a seed!

Exodus 32:31, And Moses returned unto the Lord, and said, Oh, this people have sinned a great sin, and have made them gods of gold. 32 Yet now, if thou wilt forgive their sin—; and if not, blot me, I pray thee, out of thy book which thou hast written. 33 And the Lord said unto Moses, Whosoever hath sinned against me, him will I blot out of my book.

What is this book?   It is the book of life!

Philippians 4:3, And I intreat thee also, true yokefellow, help those women which laboured with me in the Gospel, with Clement also, and with other my fellowlabourers, whose names are in the book of life.

YESHUA, THE WORD, THE SEED, THE IMAGE, THE CODE, THE LIGHT OF LIFE:

Life begins when God writes a name in the book and ends if or when the name is blotted out from the book. The seed is created with the writing, it is planted, it grows and dies. It is born again if the name remains in the book: seed then manifestation. Any other definition of life that does not encompass the start of creation with the seed and the fulfillment of the creation with delivered manifestation (fruit and flesh) has not taken into consideration the whole testimony of Yeshua or the Torah.

Life begins with the coding of the seed. All seeds are planted. Life is to be protected. Remember the Torah and Genesis is the "book of the generations of Adam" (Genesis 5:1).

Genesis 1:1, In the beginning God created the heaven and the earth. 2 And the earth was without form, and void; and darkness was upon the face of the deep. And the Spirit of God moved upon the face of the waters.

Keep in mind that Adam is made of water and earth which becomes a living soul by the breath of the Almighty. Adam in his unfallen state is a part of the world. His generations are connected to "the generations of the heaven and earth" (Genesis 2:4) and always will be. His original unfallen state is of the world and in his redeemed state remains that way. Just as Adam and his generations receive new flesh and image, so also the heavens and earth are made new.

Revelation 21:1, And I saw a new heaven and a new earth: for the first heaven and the first earth were passed away; and there was no more sea.

Adam and Eve and all humanity are sharing the same patterns and fractals as the natural world.

Genesis 2:4, These are the generations of the heavens and of the earth when they were created, in the day that the Lord God made the earth and the heavens, 5 And every plant of the field before it was in the earth, and every herb of the field before it grew: for the Lord God had not caused it to rain upon the earth, and there was not a man to till the ground. 6 But there went up a mist from the earth, and watered the whole face of the ground. 7 And the Lord God formed man of the dust of the ground, and breathed into his nostrils the breath of life; and man became a living soul. 8 And the Lord God planted a garden eastward in Eden; and there he put the man whom he had formed.

Adam's unfallen state is of "the generations of the heavens and earth" and he is intimately connected with them via the seed, which was created in Genesis 1. Remember manifested flesh did not appear until Genesis 2. In Genesis 1:1, we see a part of Adam's beginning. Adam cannot exist in chapter 2 of Genesis without the events of Genesis 1:1.

> Genesis 1:1, In the beginning God created the heaven and the earth. 2 And the earth was without form, and void; and darkness was upon the face of the deep. And the Spirit of God moved upon the face of the waters.

Adam's beginning starts with unformed earth and the creative action of the Spirit of God hovering over the face of the waters. We see this same event in the New Testament. We need to look for unformed earth and the hovering Holy Spirit planting seed.

> Luke 1:30, And the angel said unto her, Fear not, Mary: for thou hast found favour with God. 31 And, behold, thou shalt conceive in thy womb, and bring forth a son, and shalt call his name YESHUA. 32 He shall be great, and shall be called the Son of the Highest: and the Lord God shall give unto him the throne of his father David:33 And he shall reign over the house of Jacob for ever; and of his kingdom there shall be no end. 34 Then said Mary unto the angel, How shall this be, seeing I know not a man? 35 And the angel answered and said unto her, The Holy Ghost shall come upon thee, and the power of the Highest shall overshadow thee: therefore also that holy thing which shall be born of thee shall be called the Son of God.

This matches the events of Genesis 1. The same pattern is being fulfilled first in the natural world, then in the woman who brings forth the promised seed (Messiah). First, we see the hovering or overshadowing of the Holy Spirit over that which is about to receive seed (just as the Shekinah Glory "covered" Mount Sinai-Exodus 24:15-16). First the spirit moved over the earth and later it covered the woman, Mary. This is the planting of the seed. This is where the seed begins to grow in the world. Both are conceived with the seed and then later manifest the fruit of the seed, just as we see in Genesis 2. The purpose and plan for both is designed before the planting of the seed. It is holy to God and is going to fulfill His purposes as He predestinates. What man would attempt to violate the sanctity of that conception and call it nothing more than a lump of cells that has no meaning? Just like Adam, Yeshua is intimately tied to the heavens and earth.

> I Corinthians 15:44, It is sown a natural body; it is raised a spiritual body. There is a natural body, and there is a spiritual body. 45 And so it is written, The first man Adam was made a living soul; the last Adam was made a quickening spirit. 46 Howbeit that was not first which is spiritual, but that which is natural; and afterward that which is spiritual.

We see Yeshua after His resurrection is still of heaven and earth.

> John 20:24, But Thomas, one of the twelve, called Didymus, was not with them when Yeshua came. 25 The other disciples therefore said unto him, We have seen the Lord. But he said unto them, Except I shall see in his hands the

print of the nails, and put my finger into the print of the nails, and thrust my hand into his side, I will not believe. 26 And after eight days again his disciples were within, and Thomas with them: then came Yeshua, the doors being shut, and stood in the midst, and said, Peace be unto you. 27 Then saith he to Thomas, Reach hither thy finger, and behold my hands; and reach hither thy hand, and thrust it into my side: and be not faithless, but believing.

We also have Yeshua's promise to eat and drink (have an image, yet without corruption) in the Kingdom of God.

Luke 22:15, And he said unto them, With desire I have desired to eat this passover with you before I suffer:16 For I say unto you, I will not any more eat thereof, until it be fulfilled in the kingdom of God. 17 And he took the cup, and gave thanks, and said, Take this, and divide it among yourselves:

Knowing that Yeshua will have an intimate relationship with the manifested world, we need to ask ourselves, did Yeshua's life begin with His conceived seed being planted within Mary's fallen flesh? We already know that Yeshua is the Image and Word of YHWH. We know that Adam was made in the image of YHWH. The first Adam who fell is earthly (cursed ground–earthy) and the second Adam who causes our fallen flesh to ascend is heavenly (blessed ground–spiritual). But they were both in the image of YHWH and they both are intimately tied to the manifested world. Adam's seed was created in the beginning of Genesis 1. What about Yeshua? Was Yeshua alive before being planted in Mary's womb? Let's look back at the beginning and see if Yeshua is alive.

John 1:1, In the beginning was the Word, and the Word was with God, and the Word was God. 2 The same was in the beginning with God. 3 All things were made by him; and without him was not any thing made that was made. 4 In him was life; and the life was the light of men. 5 And the light shineth in darkness; and the darkness comprehended it not. 6 There was a man sent from God, whose name was John. 7 The same came for a witness, to bear witness of the light, that all men through him might believe. 8 He was not that light, but was sent to bear witness of that light. 9 That was the true light, which lighteth every man that cometh into the world. 10 He was in the world, and the world was made by him, and the world knew him not. 11 He came unto his own, and his own received him not. 12 But as many as received him, to them gave he power to become the sons of God, even to them that believe on his name:13 Which were born, not of blood, nor of the will of the flesh, nor of the will of man, but of God. 14 And the Word was made flesh, and dwelt among us, (and we beheld his glory, the glory as of the only begotten of the Father,) full of grace and truth. 15 John bare witness of him, and cried, saying, This was he of whom I spake, He that cometh after me is preferred before me: for he was before me. 16 And of his fulness have all we received, and grace for grace.

We have confirmation of several facts:

- Yeshua (the Word) was with God in the beginning.
- Yeshua (the Word) was God.
- All things were made by Yeshua (the Word).
- Yeshua (the Word) had life in the beginning.
- Yeshua (the Word) is the light of the world (Genesis 1).
- Yeshua (the Word) gives us power to become the sons of God, having His image.
- Yeshua (the Word) gives us the power to be born (born again) of God, having His image.
- Yeshua (the Word) was made flesh and dwelt among fallen man.
- Yeshua (the Word) was before and is the fullness of the Godhead bodily.
  - o Colossians 2:8, Beware lest any man spoil you through philosophy and vain deceit, after the tradition of men, after the rudiments of the world, and not after Christ. 9 For <u>in him dwelleth all the fulness of the Godhead bodily</u>. 10 And <u>ye are complete in him</u>, which is the head of all principality and power:11 In whom also ye are circumcised with the circumcision made without hands, in putting off the body of the sins of the flesh by the circumcision of Christ:12 Buried with him in baptism, wherein also ye are risen with him through the faith of the operation of God, who hath raised him from the dead.
- We live through Yeshua. He makes it possible for us to breathe in the womb as we await our birth. It is through His blood that we receive the breath (Holy Spirit) of the Almighty.
  - o Job 33:3, My words shall be of the uprightness of my heart: and my lips shall utter knowledge clearly. 4 The spirit of God hath made me, and the breath of the Almighty hath given me life. 5 If thou canst answer me, set thy words in order before me, stand up.

SOWING THE SEED (IMAGE) OF THE KINGDOM OF GOD:
In the beginning Yeshua is not here in the flesh, but is He alive? Yes. He is moving, making, multiplying, and creating. We should clearly be able to apply this to the life of the unborn child to determine if he/she is alive and if it is murder to kill that which is alive in the womb. The answer is self–evident. Our commission from the beginning is to be fruitful and multiply. The blessings of obeying the Torah results in having "fruitful seed" and having life. God is life!

The Promise was to Adam & Eve.
- Genesis 1:22, And God blessed them, saying, Be fruitful, and multiply, and fill the waters in the seas, and let fowl multiply in the earth.
- Genesis 1:28, And God blessed them, and God said unto them, Be fruitful, and multiply, and replenish the earth, and subdue it: and have

dominion over the fish of the sea, and over the fowl of the air, and over every living thing that moveth upon the earth.

The Promise was to Noah and his Sons.
- Genesis 9:1, And God blessed Noah and his sons, and said unto them, Be fruitful, and multiply, and replenish the earth.

The Promise was to Abraham.
- Genesis 17:6, And I will make thee exceeding fruitful, and I will make nations of thee, and kings shall come out of thee.

The Promise was to Ishmael.
- Genesis 17:20, And as for Ishmael, I have heard thee: Behold, I have blessed him, and will make him fruitful, and will multiply him exceedingly; twelve princes shall he beget, and I will make him a great nation.

The Promise was to Isaac.
- Genesis 26:22, And he removed from thence, and digged another well; and for that they strove not: and he called the name of it Rehoboth; and he said, For now the Lord hath made room for us, and we shall be fruitful in the land.

The Promise was to Jacob.
- Genesis 28:3, And God Almighty bless thee, and make thee fruitful, and multiply thee, that thou mayest be a multitude of people;
- Genesis 35:11, And God said unto him, I am God Almighty: be fruitful and multiply; a nation and a company of nations shall be of thee, and kings shall come out of thy loins;

The Promise was to Joseph.
- Genesis 41:52, And the name of the second called he Ephraim: For God hath caused me to be fruitful in the land of my affliction.
- Genesis 48:4, And said unto me, Behold, I will make thee fruitful, and multiply thee, and I will make of thee a multitude of people; and will give this land to thy seed after thee for an everlasting possession.
- Genesis 49:22, Joseph is a fruitful bough, even a fruitful bough by a well; whose branches run over the wall:

The Promise was to the Children of Israel.
- Exodus 1:7, And the children of Israel were fruitful, and increased abundantly, and multiplied, and waxed exceeding mighty; and the land was filled with them.
- Leviticus 26:9, For I will have respect unto you, and make you fruitful, and multiply you, and establish my covenant with you.

- Deuteronomy 30:6, And the Lord thy God will circumcise thine heart, and the heart of thy seed, to love the Lord thy God with all thine heart, and with all thy soul, that thou mayest live.
- Deuteronomy 30:19, I call heaven and earth to record this day against you, that I have set before you life and death, blessing and cursing: therefore choose life, that both thou and thy seed may live:

The blessings of God result in the living and multiplying of seed. The curse for disobedience to God's Torah is having your "seed cut off", which is death.

- Leviticus 20:3, And I will set my face against that man, and will cut him off from among his people; because he hath given of his seed unto Molech, to defile my sanctuary, and to profane my holy name.
- Leviticus 22:3, Say unto them, Whosoever he be of all your seed among your generations, that goeth unto the holy things, which the children of Israel hallow unto the Lord, having his uncleanness upon him, that soul shall be cut off from my presence: I am the Lord.
- 1 Samuel 24:21, Swear now therefore unto me by the Lord, that thou wilt not cut off my seed after me, and that thou wilt not destroy my name out of my father's house.
- Psalm 37:28, For the Lord loveth judgment, and forsaketh not his saints; they are preserved for ever: but the seed of the wicked shall be cut off.
- Isaiah 48:19, Thy seed also had been as the sand, and the offspring of thy bowels like the gravel thereof; his name should not have been cut off nor destroyed from before me.

"Cutting off" seed is the same as:
- Having your name cut off.
- Destroying my name out of my father's house.
- Having your soul cut off.
- Being cut off from among his people.
- Death.

This is contrasted with, "therefore choose life, that both thou and thy seed may live". This shows us the significance of the Tree of Life being a tree that produces "living seed". Adam is instructed to only eat of those herbs and trees that produce living seed.

Genesis 1:27, So God created man in his own image, in the Image of God created he him; male and female created he them. 28 And God blessed them, and God said unto them, Be fruitful, and multiply, and replenish the earth, and subdue it: and have dominion over the fish of the sea, and over the fowl of the air, and over every living thing that moveth upon the earth. 29 And God said, Behold, I have given you every herb bearing seed, which is upon the face of all the earth, and every tree, in the which is the fruit of a tree yielding seed; to you

<u>it shall be for meat</u>.

The Tree of Life was good for food. Why? It produced seed. The tree of the Knowledge of Good and Evil was not good for food. It did not produce living seed. In fact, when mixed with the seed of Adam and Eve, it brought death and corrupted their seed so it would always die. Life is carried on by the seed. Yeshua gives us His seed so we could be redeemed and re–enter God's living presence. It is imperative that we are circumcised so that we might receive Yeshua's seed of the Kingdom of God that we may continue to live.

Deuteronomy 30:5, And the Lord thy God will bring thee into the land which thy fathers possessed, and thou shalt possess it; and he will do thee good, <u>and multiply thee</u> above thy fathers. 6 And the Lord thy God <u>will circumcise thine heart</u>, and <u>the heart of thy seed</u>, to love the Lord thy God with all thine heart, and with all thy soul, that thou mayest live. 7 And the Lord thy God will put all these curses upon thine enemies, and on them that hate thee, which persecuted thee.

This requires the implantation and growth of Yeshua's seed so that we might live. We must be grafted into Yeshua, the Tree of Life, the seed of life, the image of life, the Image of God. This is how we return to God's presence. It is not through our own righteousness but through Yeshua's redemptive work.

The seed is the life. The seed is the light. The seed is the beginning. The seed is Yeshua. Yeshua is the Image of YHWH. Yeshua is YHWH. We live in, by, and through Yeshua. We cannot live by our own effort. The seed is alive and death occurs when you give up the breath of the Almighty.

Our life is connected with having the breath of the Almighty, the Holy Spirit. Without it we cannot give testimony and Utterance of the voice of God. Speaking contrary to the inspiration of the testimony of the Holy Spirit is blasphemy.

Luke 12:11, And when they bring you unto the synagogues, and unto magistrates, and powers, take ye no thought how or what thing ye shall answer, or what ye shall say:12 For the <u>Holy Ghost shall teach you in the same hour what ye ought to say</u>.

This is how we know we are alive and reside in Yeshua. His blood brings us the breath of life. We live and reside by and through Yeshua. There is no way around it. He is the only way to life.

- Romans 6:7, For <u>he that is dead is freed from sin</u>. 8 Now if we be dead with Christ, we believe that we shall also live with him:9 Knowing that Christ being raised from the dead dieth no more; death hath no more dominion over him.
- 2 Timothy 2:10, Therefore I endure all things for the elect's sakes, that they may also obtain the salvation which is in Christ Yeshua with eternal glory. 11 It is a faithful saying: For <u>if we be dead with him, we shall also live with</u>

him:12 If we suffer, we shall also reign with him: if we deny him, he also will deny us:

- I John 4:8, He that loveth not knoweth not God; for God is love. 9 In this was manifested the love of God toward us, because that God sent his only begotten Son into the world, that we might live through him. 10 Herein is love, not that we loved God, but that he loved us, and sent his Son to be the propitiation for our sins.
- Revelation 12:10, And I heard a loud voice saying in heaven, Now is come salvation, and strength, and the kingdom of our God, and the power of his Christ: for the accuser of our brethren is cast down, which accused them before our God day and night. 11 And they overcame him by the blood of the Lamb, and by the word of their testimony; and they loved not their lives unto the death.

Our victory is by and through Yeshua, His blood, and the subsequent giving of the Holy Spirit that bestows the breath of the Almighty, the word of testimony. This is life!

John 20:30, And many other signs truly did Yeshua in the presence of his disciples, which are not written in this book:31 But these are written, that ye might believe that Yeshua is the Christ, the Son of God; and that believing ye might have life through his name.

That life comes via having His name. This name is associated with grace and abundant mercy in Exodus 34 at the second giving of the Law of Moses. That abundant grace is associated with the "abundant" life that Yeshua came to give to believers in His name (John 10:10) ...Just as the Name of the Lord was presented to Moses and Elijah on the mountain where God gave his Law. His name is Yeshua YHWH.

2 Timothy 1:8, Be not thou therefore ashamed of the testimony of our Lord, nor of me his prisoner: but be thou partaker of the afflictions of the Gospel according to the power of God; 9 Who hath saved us, and called us with an holy calling, not according to our works, but according to his own purpose and grace, which was given us in Christ Yeshua before the world began, 10 But is now made manifest by the appearing of our Savior Yeshua, who hath abolished death, and hath brought life and immortality to light through the Gospel:...13 Hold fast the form of sound words, which thou hast heard of me, in faith and love which is in Christ Yeshua. 14 That good thing which was committed unto thee keep by the Holy Ghost which dwelleth in us.

Paul is once again declaring the pattern and fractal of seed and then manifestation. "But is now made manifest by the appearing of our Savior Yeshua..." Just as the universe and nature follows this pattern, so does Yeshua, and so do we. Breathe deep of the breath of the Almighty by the grace of Yeshua YHWH and His blood! The life is in the seed. The unborn child is alive and needs to remain in Yeshua to stay alive. The book of Revelation (Manifestation) tells about our birth. This long-awaited event is called the birth of the man–child and the preparing of the Bride.

- Revelation 12:1, And there appeared a great wonder in heaven; a woman clothed with the sun, and the moon under her feet, and upon her head a crown of twelve stars:2 And she being with child cried, travailing in birth, and pained to be delivered. 3 And there appeared another wonder in heaven; and behold a great red dragon, having seven heads and ten horns, and seven crowns upon his heads. 4 And his tail drew the third part of the stars of heaven, and did cast them to the earth: and the dragon stood before the woman which was ready to be delivered, for to devour her child as soon as it was born. 5 And she brought forth a man child, who was to rule all nations with a rod of iron: and her child was caught up unto God, and to his throne.

- Revelation 19:7, Let us be glad and rejoice, and give honor to him: for the marriage of the Lamb is come, and his wife hath made herself ready.

The Holy Spirit will have finally birthed those who are currently hidden in the womb and are being kept alive via the blood of Yeshua.

THE BOOK OF REVELATION IS ABOUT THE BIRTH OF THE MAN–CHILD AND THE OPENING OF THE DOOR OF HEAVEN; FORTY-TWO

Revelation 4:1, After this I looked, and, behold, a door was opened in heaven: and the first voice which I heard was as it were of a trumpet talking with me; which said, Come up hither, and I will shew thee things which must be hereafter. 2 And immediately I was in the spirit: and, behold, a throne was set in heaven, and one sat on the throne.

You should be very interested in this door. Revelation focuses upon it. It is central to our future. Most do not know why. The size and dimensions of the door will give you the answer.

Ezekiel 41:1, Afterward he brought me to the temple, and measured the posts, six cubits broad on the one side, and six cubits broad on the other side, which was the breadth of the tabernacle. 2 And the breadth of the door was ten cubits; and the sides of the door were five cubits on the one side, and five cubits on the other side: and he measured the length thereof, forty cubits: and the breadth, twenty cubits. 3 Then went he inward, and measured the post of the door, two cubits; and the door, six cubits; and the breadth of the door, seven cubits.

We see time and again that the Messiah is the door that we must pass through.

- John 10:1, Verily, verily, I say unto you, <u>He that entereth not by the door</u> into the sheepfold, but climbeth up some other way, the same is a thief and a robber. 2 But <u>he that entereth in by the door is the shepherd of the sheep</u>. 3 To him the porter openeth; and the sheep hear his voice: and he calleth his own sheep by name, and leadeth them out.
- John 10:7, Then <u>said Jesus unto them</u> again, Verily, verily, I say unto you, <u>I am the door of the sheep</u>. 8 All that ever came before me are thieves and robbers: but the sheep did not hear them. 9 <u>I am the door: by me if any man enter in, he shall be saved</u>, and shall go in and out, and find pasture.

Yeshua is associated with the rending of the veil to the temple.

Matthew 27:50, The rest said, Let be, let us see whether Elias will come to save him. 50 Jesus, when he had cried again with a loud voice, yielded up the ghost. 51 And, behold, the veil of the temple was rent in twain from the top to the bottom; and the earth did quake, and the rocks rent; 52 And the graves were opened; and many bodies of the saints which slept arose, 53 And came out of the graves after his resurrection, and went into the holy city, and appeared unto many. 54 Now when the centurion, and they that were with him, watching Jesus, saw the earthquake, and those things that were done, they feared greatly, saying, Truly this was the Son of God.

Yeshua is the "door" or the entryway to God. It is provided by His gift of the Holy Spirit and is coincident with the rending of the veil of the temple, the Messiah's death and the resurrection of the saints. Even the gentile Centurion standing nearby at His crucifixion gives His personal testimony that Yeshua is the Image and Son of God. All of these are signets of the purpose and role of the Son of God as the Promised Seed and what that seed was intended to do for fallen creation.

John 14:6, Jesus saith unto him, I am the way, the truth, and the life: no man cometh unto the Father, but by me.

This entryway to God could only occur by the death and burial of His seed (rending of His flesh), so that we might enter the Holy of Holies.

- Luke 23:44, And it was about the sixth hour, and there was a darkness over all the earth until the ninth hour. 45 And the <u>sun was darkened, and the veil of the temple was rent in the midst</u>. 46 And when Jesus had cried with a loud voice, he said, Father, into thy hands I commend my spirit: and having said thus, he gave up the ghost.
- Hebrews 10:14, For by one offering he hath perfected for ever them that are sanctified. 15 Whereof the Holy Ghost also is a witness to us: for after that he had said before, 16 This is the covenant that I will make with them after those days, saith the Lord, <u>I will put my laws into their hearts, and in their</u>

minds will I write them; 17 And their sins and iniquities will I remember no more. 18 Now where remission of these is, there is no more offering for sin. 19 Having therefore, brethren, boldness to enter into the holiest by the blood of Jesus, 20 By a new and living way, which he hath consecrated for us, through the veil, that is to say, his flesh; 21 And having an high priest over the house of God; 22 Let us draw near with a true heart in full assurance of faith, having our hearts sprinkled from an evil conscience, and our bodies washed with pure water.

The door to the Holy Place is Yeshua's image. The flesh and blood that we must become one with is 6x7=42 (Ezekiel 41:3). The book of Revelation begins with the opening of this door and allowing the redeemed to enter the Holy Place. His flesh is not profane, it is Holy. His flesh (image) and His Spirit are in the mikvah (baptism). This is the bread of God, Yeshua's flesh. What does 42 have to do with seed then flesh? If we are in the womb and our life is through Yeshua and His blood allows us to breathe the Holy Spirit, we must pass through that door with the dimensions of 42 in order to be born again. When is a pregnancy considered overdue?

A pregnancy is usually completed in 38 to 42 weeks. Post–term pregnancy, prolonged pregnancy and post–date pregnancy are all words used to describe a pregnancy that lasts beyond 42 weeks. (familydoctor. org)

Approximately 5 to 10 percent of all pregnancies continue to at least 42 weeks' gestation. 1, 2 Advances in obstetric and neonatal care have lowered the absolute mortality risk; however, retrospective studies of these so–called post–term pregnancies have found an increased risk to the mother and fetus. (aafp.org)

Remember the woman from Revelation 12 is having a difficult birth which is typically associated with an overdue birth.

Revelation 12:1, And there appeared a great wonder in heaven; a woman clothed with the sun, and the moon under her feet, and upon her head a crown of twelve stars:2 And she being with child cried, travailing in birth, and pained to be delivered. 3 And there appeared another wonder in heaven; and behold a great red dragon, having seven heads and ten horns, and seven crowns upon his heads. 4 And his tail drew the third part of the stars of heaven, and did cast them to the earth: and the dragon stood before the woman which was ready to be delivered, for to devour her child as soon as it was born.

This birth is difficult because it has been delayed and is going to a maximum term. Many conclude that this "man–child" is Yeshua. This begs the question, why would Yeshua being born in heaven be a "great wonder"? After all, the Son of God came from heaven, did He not? If this is not the Messiah, then who is it? We will explore this in-depth in coming chapters.

Luke 12:45, But and if that servant say in his heart, <u>My Lord delayeth his coming</u>; and shall begin to beat the menservants and maidens, and to eat and drink, and to be drunken; 46 The Lord of that servant will come in a day when he looketh not for him, and at an hour when he is not aware, and will cut him in sunder, and will appoint him his portion with the unbelievers.

We also see the circumstances that occur over the period of time lasting 42 months causing her tribulation.

Revelation 11:1, And there was given me a reed like unto a rod: and the angel stood, saying, Rise, and measure the temple of God, and the altar, and them that worship therein. 2 But the court which is without the temple leave out, and measure it not; for it is given unto the Gentiles: and the holy city <u>shall they tread under foot forty and two months</u>. 3 And I will give power unto my Two Witnesses, and they shall prophesy a thousand two hundred and threescore days, clothed in sackcloth. 4 These are the two olive trees, and the two candlesticks standing before the God of the earth.

The man–child is born through the door in heaven having the dimensions of 6 by 7 equaling 42. In Hebrew, the number 6 is Vav:ו Vav–6, the picture of a man standing upright, a pillar, or a vertical line. The number 7 is Zayin, 7–ז.

ו Vav–6

ו Vav–6, In the beginning of creation, when Infinite light filled all reality, G d contracted His light to create hollow empty space, as it were, the place necessary for the existence of finite worlds. Into this vacuum <u>God drew down, figuratively speaking, a single line of light, from the Infinite Source. This ray of light is the secret of the letter vav</u>. Though the line is singular in appearance, it nonetheless possesses two dimensions, an external as well as an internal force, both of which take part in the process of creation and the continuous interaction between the creative power and created reality.

Zayin, 7–ז,

The Maggid of Mezeritch, the successor of the Ba'al Shem Tov, teaches that the verse <u>A woman of valor is the crown of her husband alludes to the form of the letter zayin</u>. The previous letter, vav, portrays the or yashar (straight light) descending from God into the worlds. The zayin, whose form is similar to a vav, though with a crown on top, reflects the or yashar of the vav as or chozer (returning light). Or chozer ascends with such great force that it reaches a higher state of consciousness than that of the revealed origin–point of the or yashar. When reaching the initially superconscious realm of keter (the crown), it broadens its awareness to both the right and the left. In truth there is no left in that Ancient One [the level of keter], for all is right. This means that the awe of God (left) at this initially superconscious level is indistinguishable, in its nature to cling directly to God, from the highest manifestation of the love of

God (right). (www. inner. org)

Can you see the interplay of the male and the female and the planting of the seed and then the birth of the new image (manifestation or flesh)? Can you see the imagery of the conception and the birth? (6 x 7=birth 42)? This may be why the book of Revelation focuses on the holy city being "under foot forty and two months" (Revelation 11:2) and the beast being allowed to continue for "forty and two months" (Revelation 13:4-6). The Two Witnesses are also given power to witness for "a thousand two hundred and three score days" or 42 months (1260 days divided by 30 equals 42 months) (Revelation 11:3). We will not delve into the significance of the treading down of the holy city being associated with the counting in months (having the female aspect-moon). Also, the preaching of the gospel by the Two Witnesses (having the male aspect-sun) being counted by days (sun) and the tribulation of the holy city (the female) being counted in months (moon).

Those who live in Yeshua are given an incorruptible image and incorruptible flesh when they ascend (opposite of fallen). We are then born again. This matches up with the pattern within the Torah of Israel's journeys through the wilderness for 40 years. They were saved by grace and delivered from Egypt. They did nothing of worth to be delivered. They are baptized (mikvah) in the Red Sea, and given the seed of the Kingdom at Mount Sinai during their first Pentecost (Shavuot). They received the seed, the Ten Commandments which are expressions of the Image of God. Then they traveled through the wilderness making 42 journeys until they were ready to be born (ascend) into the Promised land by the Hand of YHWH.

COUNT THE NUMBERS OF JOURNEYS OF ISRAEL IN THE WILDERNESS:
Numbers 33:2, And Moses wrote their goings out according to their journeys by the commandment of the Lord: and these are their journeys according to their goings out.

1. 3 And they departed from Rameses in the first month, on the fifteenth day of the first month; on the morrow after the passover the children of Israel went out with an high hand in the sight of all the Egyptians. 4 For the Egyptians buried all their firstborn, which the Lord had smitten among them: upon their gods also the Lord executed judgments.

2. 5 And the children of Israel removed from Rameses, and pitched in Succoth.

3. 6 And they departed from Succoth, and pitched in Etham, which is in the edge of the wilderness.

4. 7 And they removed from Etham, and turned again unto Pihahiroth, which is before Baalzephon: and they pitched before Migdol.

5. 8 And they departed from before Pihahiroth, and passed through the midst of the sea into the wilderness, and went three days'journey in the wilderness of Etham, and pitched in Marah.

6. 9 And they removed from Marah, and came unto Elim:and in

Elim were twelve fountains of water, and threescore and ten palm trees; and they pitched there.

7. 10 And they removed from Elim, and encamped by the Red sea.

8. 11 And they removed from the Red sea, and encamped in the wilderness of Sin.

9. 12 And they took their journey out of the wilderness of Sin, and encamped in Dophkah.

10. 13 And they departed from Dophkah, and encamped in Alush.

11. 14 And they removed from Alush, and encamped at Rephidim, where was no water for the people to drink.

12. 15 And they departed from Rephidim, and pitched in the wilderness of Sinai.

13. 16 And they removed from the desert of Sinai, and pitched at Kibrothhattaavah.

14. 17 And they departed from Kibrothhattaavah, and encamped at Hazeroth.

15. 18 And they departed from Hazeroth, and pitched in Rithmah.

16. 19 And they departed from Rithmah, and pitched at Rimmonparez.

17. 20 And they departed from Rimmonparez, and pitched in Libnah.

18. 21 And they removed from Libnah, and pitched at Rissah.

19. 22 And they journeyed from Rissah, and pitched in Kehelathah.

20. 23 And they went from Kehelathah, and pitched in mount Shapher.

21. 24 And they removed from mount Shapher, and encamped in Haradah.

22. 25 And they removed from Haradah, and pitched in Makheloth.

23. 26 And they removed from Makheloth, and encamped at Tahath.

24. 27 And they departed from Tahath, and pitched at Tarah.

25. 28 And they removed from Tarah, and pitched in Mithcah.

26. 29 And they went from Mithcah, and pitched in Hashmonah.

27. 30 And they departed from Hashmonah, and encamped at Moseroth.

28. 31 And they departed from Moseroth, and pitched in Benejaakan.

29. 32 And they removed from Benejaakan, and encamped at Horhagidgad.

30. 33 And they went from Horhagidgad, and pitched in Jotbathah.

31. 34 And they removed from Jotbathah, and encamped at Ebronah.

32. 35 And they departed from Ebronah, and encamped at Eziongaber.

33. 36 And they removed from Eziongaber, and pitched in the wilderness of Zin, which is Kadesh.

34. 37 And they removed from Kadesh, and pitched in mount Hor, in the edge of the land of Edom. 38 And Aaron the priest went up into mount Hor at the commandment of the Lord, and died there, in the fortieth year after the children of Israel were come out of the land of

Egypt, in the first day of the fifth month. 39 And Aaron was an hundred and twenty and three years old when he died in mount Hor. 40 And king Arad the Canaanite, which dwelt in the south in the land of Canaan, heard of the coming of the children of Israel.

35. 41 And they departed from mount Hor, and pitched in Zalmonah.

36. 42 And they departed from Zalmonah, and pitched in Punon.

37. 43 And they departed from Punon, and pitched in Oboth.

38. 44 And they departed from Oboth, and pitched in Ijeabarim, in the border of Moab.

39. 45 And they departed from Iim, and pitched in Dibongad.

40. 46 And they removed from Dibongad, and encamped in Almondiblathaim.

41. 47 And they removed from Almondiblathaim, and pitched in the mountains of Abarim, before Nebo.

42. 48 And they departed from the mountains of Abarim, and pitched in the plains of Moab by Jordan near Jericho. 49 And they pitched by Jordan, from Bethjesimoth even unto Abelshittim in the plains of Moab. 50 And the Lord spake unto Moses in the plains of Moab by Jordan near Jericho, saying, 51 Speak unto the children of Israel, and say unto them, When ye are passed over Jordan into the land of Canaan; 52 Then ye shall drive out all the inhabitants of the land from before you, and destroy all their pictures, and destroy all their molten images, and quite pluck down all their high places:53 And ye shall dispossess the inhabitants of the land, and dwell therein: for I have given you the land to possess it.

At the conclusion of their 42 journeys, they enter the land and dispossess the current inhabitants, destroying their false images! The false images are replaced with the true and ascended images, made like unto the manifest Name of YHWH, the Messiah Yeshua.

The name YHWH is used for the deliverance of images and manifestation (flesh/fruit) after the seed has grown and is ready to be born. The seed is alive awaiting its birth.

The dragon of Revelation 12 has no desire to be dispossessed and smashed and is therefore waiting to kill the man–child at his birth! This should give us insight into why the first generation that came out of Egypt died before entering the land. This is a type of the deliverance provided by Yeshua, taking on the imagery of a seed in death buried in the exile of the wilderness (manifest universe). He died so that His seed could be manifested, inherit the land, and receive the image of YHWH and incorruptible flesh. It may be that this "man–child" of Revelation 12 has the Image of God and is therefore easily confused by many as being Yeshua the Messiah. The goal and purpose of the "promised seed" is to transcribe His likeness and image upon the redeemed. Now that is a great wonder. As God told Moses…

Exodus 34:10, And he said, Behold, I make a covenant: before all thy people I will do marvels, such as have not been done in all the earth, nor in any nation: and all the people among which thou art shall see the work of the Lord:

for it is a terrible thing that I will do with thee. 11 Observe thou that which I command thee this day: behold, I drive out before thee the Amorite, and the Canaanite, and the Hittite, and the Perizzite, and the Hivite, and the Jebusite. 12 Take heed to thyself, lest thou make a covenant with the inhabitants of the land whither thou goest, lest it be for a snare in the midst of thee:13 But ye shall destroy their altars, break their images, and cut down their groves:14 For thou shalt worship no other god: for the Lord, whose name is Jealous, is a jealous God:...17 Thou shalt make thee no molten gods.

God has promised to do "marvels" such has not been done. He goes so far as to say it is a "terrible thing that I will do with thee." The word "terrible" means "awesome" or "wonderful". Notice the conclusion of this Resurrected Covenant. It results in the "break(ing) of the images" of those who currently dwell in the Promised land. Once the redeemed ascend with the Image of God, the "molten images" of those currently residing in the land will be shattered. This is the same phraseology that we saw after the 42 journeys of Israel right before they ascend to the Promised land. For what goal?

Numbers 33:58, Then ye shall drive out all the inhabitants of the land from before you, and destroy all their pictures, and destroy all their molten images, and quite pluck down all their high places:

We see the same thing happens in the end–time.

Revelation 12:7, And there was war in heaven: Michael and his angels fought against the dragon; and the dragon fought and his angels, 8 And prevailed not; neither was their place found any more in heaven. 9 And the great dragon was cast out, that old serpent, called the Devil, and Satan, which deceiveth the whole world: he was cast out into the earth, and his angels were cast out with him.

The Image of God is restored and those in the Messiah ascend into the Heavens. Just as Elijah restored the life of the boy who dies in 1 Kings 17:20-24 by stretching out His own image upon the boy three times (the pattern of resurrection) and prayed that God would restore his soul to him, so also Yeshua has stretched His image upon our fallen images and restored us to life via His breath. It was through this act that the boy's mother confessed, "Now by this I know that thou art a man of God, and that the word of the Lord in thy mouth is truth." (1 Kings 17:24)

There is an inextricable link between the role of the Elijah, resurrection, and the restoration of breath to the dead child that results in confession that this "Elijah" is a man of God and that the Word of the Lord spoken by him is truth. This is the same purpose of the coming of "Elijah" before the Day of the Lord. He comes to pit truth vs. the Great Delusion (2 Thessalonians 2:11). Just as Elijah is pitted against the priests of Baal, in the end time Elijah is pitted against the Antichrist.

1 Kings 18:21, And Elijah came unto all the people, and said, How long halt ye between two opinions? if the Lord be God, follow him: but if Baal, then follow him. And the people answered him not a word.

This is quite simply a replay of the fractal that God presented to Israel before they entered the Land of Promise.

Deuteronomy 30:19, I call heaven and earth to record this day against you, that I have set before you life and death, blessing and cursing: therefore choose life, that both thou and thy seed may live:

Nobody will be exempt from this test of truth. Everyone must choose light vs. dark.

John 3:19, And this is the condemnation, that light is come into the world, and men loved darkness rather than light, because their deeds were evil.

Just as Elijah forces idolatrous Israel to choose who is God, so will the whole world. The choice of the Garden of Eden will be replayed in the last days. Elijah is the template for what will happen and what the central issue will be in the end times…Lawlessness vs. Lawfulness, False Worship vs. True Worship.

1 Kings 18:30, And Elijah said unto all the people, Come near unto me. And all the people came near unto him. And he repaired the altar of the Lord that was broken down. 31 And Elijah took twelve stones, according to the number of the tribes of the sons of Jacob, unto whom the word of the Lord came, saying, Israel shall be thy name:32 And with the stones he built an altar in the name of the Lord: and he made a trench about the altar, as great as would contain two measures of seed. 33 And he put the wood in order, and cut the bullock in pieces, and laid him on the wood, and said, Fill four barrels with water, and pour it on the burnt sacrifice, and on the wood. 34 And he said, Do it the second time. And they did it the second time. And he said, Do it the third time. And they did it the third time. 35 And the water ran round about the altar; and he filled the trench also with water. 36 And it came to pass at the time of the offering of the evening sacrifice, that Elijah the prophet came near, and said, Lord God of Abraham, Isaac, and of Israel, let it be known this day that thou art God in Israel, and that I am thy servant, and that I have done all these things at thy word. 37 Hear me, O Lord, hear me, that this people may know that thou art the Lord God, and that thou hast turned their heart back again. 38 Then the fire of the Lord fell, and consumed the burnt sacrifice, and the wood, and the stones, and the dust, and licked up the water that was in the trench. 39 And when all the people saw it, they fell on their faces: and they said, The Lord, he is the God; the Lord, he is the God.

The end goal of this confrontation is the same goal that was achieved by Elijah

RESTORING TRUTH SERIES

resurrecting the dead boy to life. His mother and in this case "all Israel" would know that Elijah is God's servant. That they would know that YHWH is the God in Israel and that all that Elijah does, is by the Word of the Lord (YHWH).

By doing all these things all the people would clearly know that God has turned the hearts of the Children of Israel back from false worship of idols and pagan gods to the True and Only God. This happens through the manifestation of God's presence in the appearance of the Shekinah Glory consuming the sacrifice and the immediate response of the people. They fall on their faces and worship the presentation of "The Lord". This is none other than an exact replay of the presentation of the "Name of the Lord" to Moses in Exodus 34 when he was given the new administration of grace and abundant mercy when God re-wrote the "same words" that were on the first set of tablets. God confirmed His mercy by answering Moses prayer that God would show him His glory. He did so by presenting the "Name of the Lord" and Moses responded the same way as the people...he bowed and worshipped.

> Exodus 34:1, And the Lord said unto Moses, Hew thee two tables of stone like unto the first: and I will write upon these tables the words that were in the first tables, which thou brakest...4 And he hewed two tables of stone like unto the first; and Moses rose up early in the morning, and went up unto mount Sinai, as the Lord had commanded him, and took in his hand the two tables of stone. 5 And the Lord descended in the cloud, and stood with him there, and proclaimed the name of the Lord. 6 And the Lord passed by before him, and proclaimed, The Lord, The Lord God, merciful and gracious, longsuffering, and abundant in goodness and truth, 7 Keeping mercy for thousands, forgiving iniquity and transgression and sin, and that will by no means clear the guilty; visiting the iniquity of the fathers upon the children, and upon the children's children, unto the third and to the fourth generation. 8 And Moses made haste, and bowed his head toward the earth, and worshipped.

There is an undeniable connection between the role of Elijah restoring the Law of Moses to Israel by combating the priests of Baal and God introducing the administration of grace to Moses at the second giving of the Law (Written Torah). So many Christians are deluded by a false teaching of "grace vs. law" and they have willfully ignored the plain teaching of the scriptures. It is the role of "Elijah" to present that choice to the world once again and restore what was intended. Since the fall of Adam and Eve, God had chosen to not reveal Himself with such wonders and miracles as were seen at the Exodus of Egypt and thereafter. Would modern Christianity have us believe, contrary to the scriptures, that God came down to give us something unimportant and insignificant? The Church has lost its measuring stick for truth and light if it denies the plain teaching of Yeshua and the Apostles.

> Matthew 5:17, Think not that I am come to destroy the law, or the prophets: I am not come to destroy, but to fulfil. 18 For verily I say unto you, Till heaven and earth pass, one jot or one tittle shall in no wise pass from the

463 | P a g e

law, till all be fulfilled.

How long can we deny the literalness of the teaching of the Son of God?

In the end time the man of lawlessness will be juxtaposed with the man of lawfulness. One is of Satan and the other is commissioned by God.

2 Thessalonians 2:3, Let no man deceive you by any means: for that day shall not come, except there come a falling away first, and that man of sin be revealed, the son of perdition; 7 For the mystery of iniquity doth already work: only he who now letteth will let, until he be taken out of the way. 8 And then shall that Wicked be revealed, whom the Lord shall consume with the spirit of his mouth, and shall destroy with the brightness of his coming:

The Antichrist comes with lies, lawlessness, and lying wonders. The Elijah comes with the Word of God and the declaration to repent and return to the Law of God under the administration of "grace and abundant mercy".

Malachi 4:4, "Remember ye the law of Moses my servant, which I commanded unto him in Horeb for all Israel, with the statutes and judgments. 5 Behold, I will send you Elijah the prophet before the coming of the great and dreadful day of the Lord:6 And he shall turn the heart of the fathers to the children, and the heart of the children to their fathers, lest I come and smite the earth with a curse.

This scripture was so well known and the atmosphere of expectancy so strong that when Moses and Elijah appeared with Yeshua on the Mount of Transfiguration the apostles asked why people said that the coming of Elijah needed to occur again.

Matthew 17:10, And his disciples asked him, saying, Why then say the scribes that Elias must first come? 11 And Jesus answered and said unto them, Elias truly shall first come, and restore all things. But I say unto you, That Elias is come already, and they knew him not, but have done unto him whatsoever they listed. Likewise shall also the Son of man suffer of them. 13 Then the disciples understood that he spake unto them of John the Baptist.

Take note that Yeshua declares that Elijah comes in the same fractal that we have already presented in both seed and manifestation, fulfilling the pattern of a death like a seed in John the Baptist who also fulfills the role of having the spirit of Elijah and then coming again at the Day of the Lord when you have the fulfillment of the manifestation of images, when the Image of the Beast battles the Image of God. Yeshua makes it absolutely clear that Elijah (Spirit of Elijah) had come in John the Baptist and as Yeshua declared after John had died that Elijah would come again, "Jesus answered and said unto them, Elias (Elijah) truly shall first come, and restore all things..." (Matthew 17:11)

	Elijah	Antichrist
Law of Moses	Restores it	Lawlessness
God vs. Idols	Image of God	Image of the Beast
Worship	YHWH	Baal
Word	Truth	Lies & Lying Wonders
Principal Act	Return believers to the Law of Moses and restore the altar of God	Set himself in the temple as god and demand to be worshipped. Those who do not worship are killed by the Image of the Beast
State of the World	Preaching the Gospel of Truth	Great deception
Response of Every person	Repent & Return; Accept Christ	Take the mark of the beast and worship the beast

As you are confronted with these end time choices, be sure to remember that everyone receives a mark, either from the Antichrist or from God. One will look like life and will deliver you to ultimate death. The other will look like death and ultimately deliver you to eternal life.

> Revelation 15:2, And I saw as it were a sea of glass mingled with fire: and them that had gotten the victory over the beast, and over his image, and over his mark, and over the number of his name, stand on the sea of glass, having the harps of God.

This is our battle. Our goal is to be marked with the Name of the Lord, just as Moses was presented the Name of the Lord in Exodus 34 and came down from the mountain with a glorified countenance. And also, just as Elijah manifested the Glory of the Lord for all of Israel to see the Name of the Lord restoring the heart of the people to himself.

> Revelation 3:12, Him that overcometh will I make a pillar in the temple of my God, and he shall go no more out: and I will write upon him the name of my God, and the name of the city of my God, which is new Jerusalem, which cometh down out of heaven from my God: and I <u>will write upon him my new name.</u>

God is judging the world just as He did at Mount Sinai after the Golden Calf incident.

> Exodus 32:26, Then Moses stood in the gate of the camp, and said, Who is on the Lord's side? let him come unto me. And all the sons of Levi gathered themselves together unto him. 27 And he said unto them, Thus saith the Lord God of Israel, Put every man his sword by his side, and go in and out from gate to gate throughout the camp, and slay every man his brother, and every man his companion, and every man his neighbour. 28 And the children of Levi did

according to the word of Moses: and there fell of the people that day about three thousand men.

Just as 3,000 were killed on this day of idolatry, so also when Pentecost arrived after Yeshua's resurrection 3,000 were saved on that day (Acts 2:41). Just as Idolatry is being contrasted with the true worship of God then, so also it will be in the Day of the Lord. Just as following the Law of God was contrasted with Lawlessness then, so will it be in the Day of the Lord. Just as 3,000 died of that first Golden Calf worship (false image-seed in death), so also 3,000 were saved on the first Pentecost after Yeshua's (the true Image of God-manifested life) resurrection. Just as the false image is contrasted with the true Image of God, so also will the Image of the Beast be contrasted with the true Image of God. Just as Israel was saved by a true mark of God on that first Passover, all the world will be judged by whether they accept a false mark of the beast in the End of Days.

> Ezekiel 9:3, And the glory of the God of Israel was gone up from the cherub, whereupon he was, to the threshold of the house. And he called to the man clothed with linen, which had the writer's inkhorn by his side; 4 And the Lord said unto him, Go through the midst of the city, through the midst of Jerusalem, and set a mark upon the foreheads of the men that sigh and that cry for all the abominations that be done in the midst thereof. 5 And to the others he said in mine hearing, Go ye after him through the city, and smite: let not your eye spare, neither have ye pity:6 Slay utterly old and young, both maids, and little children, and women: but come not near any man upon whom is the mark; and begin at my sanctuary. Then they began at the ancient men which were before the house.

Whether the world likes it or not, the Law of Moses is going to be the central issue before the Day of the Lord. Remaining scripturally uneducated about this fact will not be excusable. Everyone will be forced to pick one image or the other.

14 SEED THEN MANIFESTATION; TORAH PROOFS

Let's take a quick look at the twins inside of Tamar's womb.

> Genesis 38:24, And it came to pass about three months after, that it was told Judah, saying, Tamar thy daughter in law hath played the harlot; and also, behold, she is with child by whoredom. And Judah said, Bring her forth, and let her be burnt...27 And it came to pass in the time of her travail, that, behold, twins were in her womb. 28 And it came to pass, when she travailed, that the one put out his hand: and the midwife took and bound upon his hand a scarlet thread, saying, This came out first. 29 And it came to pass, as he drew back his hand, that, behold, his brother came out: and she said, How hast thou broken forth? this breach be upon thee: therefore his name was called Pharez (breach). 30 And afterward came out his brother, that had the scarlet thread upon his hand: and his name was called Zarah (rising).

It is as if Yeshua, the Arm of God, came first and offered for His twin to be born first. The second is made first and the first is made last. We have seen the pattern of the firstborn (the broken Image of God), the flesh, trying to kill the second born, the spirit, in this fallen world. However, in order to put things right to the true Image of God, the true firstborn sacrifices His position so that His twin may take on His image and live.

Yeshua (the Arm of God) returns to the womb (mikvah) and we receive the right and opportunity to be the firstborn. The scarlet thread on the arm goes back into the mikvah (womb) and is dipped into the waters and we (Pharez) are treated like the one who came out first, Yeshua (Zarah). We receive the image of the firstborn, we receive His image, and are given the birthright and inheritance. We inherit with Him. He died so that His seed might inherit the land of Promise of an incorruptible image. Yeshua came to sow His seed so that we might inherit the Kingdom of God, the land of promise, eternal life. Just like Pharez and Zarah, the first and second generation saved from Egypt share prophetic imagery with the Messiah and those He redeems.

Israel delivered from bondage of Egypt by the saving of the firstborn	Yeshua is called out of Egypt	Fallen man is called out of death and fallen flesh
Israel is baptized in the Red Sea on the 8th day of Unleavened Bread	Yeshua enters the mikvah of the Jordan with John (prophetic of the Holy Spirit)	We enter the womb (mikvah) with Yeshua and the Holy Spirit
Israel receives the foreshadow Ten expressions of the seed/image of YHWH, the Torah, on Pentecost	Yeshua is the image of YHWH sowing His seed of the Kingdom of YHWH	We receive the image of YHWH
Israel makes 42 journeys in the wilderness (hidden from the world in exile)	Those who receive Yeshua enter the mikvah (womb) to multiply (hidden in the womb with Yeshua) and are born again through the door of heaven with the dimensions of 42, Yeshua's image	We, the multiplying seed, live through Yeshua's blood, which gives us the ability to breathe the Holy Spirit while we are hidden in the womb (mikvah) and are born again at the end of the 42 weeks
All of the first generation of Israel delivered from Egypt die in the Wilderness, except 2 witnesses of that generation. They become a picture of the Word of God taking death upon Himself so their/His seed might live	Yeshua dies so that we might inherit with Him and He provides Two Witnesses that teach the Testimony of Yeshua and the keeping of His Torah for 42 months before the birth of the man–child	We inherit through Yeshua who has made atonement through His blood for our soul (spirit–breath of the almighty); Our seed and fallen flesh are caused to ascend to its intended state; life with an incorruptible image
The second generation inherit the land that the first generation (who died) was promised to receive–seed then fruit, death then ascension	The born again are resurrected and inherit through Yeshua (who died)	We will appear like Yeshua when we are born with His image
The seed cross over the water of the Jordan and are	The born again enter through the door of	We are resurrected (born again) when we receive

Israel delivered from bondage of Egypt by the saving of the firstborn	Yeshua is called out of Egypt	Fallen man is called out of death and fallen flesh
born again and receive the promised land through driving out the inhabitants	heaven, Yeshua's flesh and blood	Yeshua's flesh while the dragon is waiting to devour us as soon as we are born

Now we can finally understand why there are two events with Moses before the rock, when the people are dying of thirst. The first event of Moses bringing water from the rock happens with the first generation of Israel that came out of Egypt (Exodus 17:6).

The second event of Moses bringing water from the rock happens with the second generation that came out of Egypt (Numbers 20:8). The second event happens right before they are about to enter the Promised land. Remember entering the Promised land is a type of receiving the incorruptible image of the Messiah Yeshua and the gift of eternal life. Remember the prophetic significance of the following:

First generation of Israel called out of Egypt dies in the wilderness (Exodus 17:6)	Second generation of Israel called out of Egypt is delivered from the wilderness ((Numbers 20:8)
Prophetic of Yeshua	Prophetic of the seed planted by Yeshua that manifests itself in ascended fruit
Yeshua is killed	Because Yeshua is killed we may live through Him
Yeshua is the seed of the Kingdom of God, the image of YHWH	The seed of the Image of God is written upon our circumcised hearts
First tablets of the Torah are broken	Second set of tablets are made by Moses and transcribed with the same words that were on the first set of tablets
First Adam (dies)	Last Adam (Yeshua lives and we live through Him)
Seed/hidden	New Flesh (Incorruptible Image) revealed

Remember what we learned earlier about the transcription of DNA/RNA and transcribing the code (Word) of the seed. Now we can understand the two events of Moses and the rock.

TRANSCRIBING THE SEED (IMAGE) OF GOD:

Exodus 17:1, And all the congregation of the children of Israel journeyed from the wilderness of Sin, after their journeys, according to the commandment of the Lord, and pitched in Rephidim: and there was no water for the people to drink. 2 Wherefore the people did chide with Moses, and said, Give us water that we may drink. And Moses said unto them, Why chide ye with me? wherefore do ye tempt the Lord? 3 And the people thirsted there for water; and the people murmured against Moses, and said, Wherefore is this that thou hast brought us up out of Egypt, to kill us and our children and our cattle with thirst? 4 And Moses cried unto the Lord, saying, What shall I do unto this people? they be almost ready to stone me. 5 And the Lord said unto Moses, Go on before the people, and take with thee of the elders of Israel; and thy rod, wherewith thou smotest the river, take in thine hand, and go. 6 Behold, I will stand before thee there upon the rock in Horeb; and thou shalt smite the rock, and there shall come water out of it, that the people may drink. And Moses did so in the sight of the elders of Israel. 7 And he called the name of the place Massah, and Meribah, because of the chiding of the children of Israel, and because they tempted the Lord, saying, Is the Lord among us, or not?

The people that came out of Egypt are about to die of thirst and Moses keeps pointing them to God for deliverance. To save the lives of the children of Israel, the Angel of YHWH (Yeshua) stands before the rock and tells Moses to strike it so that water will spring forth so that the people may drink.

This vicarious striking of the Angel of YHWH before the rock is clearly a picture of the killing of the Messiah, the seed, the Image of YHWH so that waters would be brought forth to water the people. Remember the picture of Genesis 2 of water being brought forth so that the seeds planted in the earth could grow flesh (an image).

The seed must die and be planted in the earth so that it may bring forth much life (John 12:24). This is why the first generation had to die in the wilderness—they were prophetic of the work of the seed, the Image of God, Yeshua, who had to die and be planted in the ground so that His/their seed might inherit the land (prophetic of an incorruptible image). Let's not miss the fact that this happens to the rock, just like it did to the first set of tablets of stone that the covenant was written upon in Exodus 20/24. Like the first generation it symbolizes death like a seed.

Now what about the second striking of the rock? This event happened to the second generation that came out of Egypt right before they entered the Promised land. Most of the first generation has died in the wilderness. God was very displeased with Moses and Aaron and how this played out and punishes Moses and Aaron for not following His instructions. Keep in mind in both events Moses is supposed to use the staff of God, but in the first occurrence he is told to strike the rock with the staff of God.

In the second occurrence with the second generation, Moses is told to speak to the rock while holding the staff of God in his hand. By striking the rock instead of speaking to it as God told him to, Moses is fulfilling the pattern of the "old administration" of condemnation and judgment which results in death. Since Moses is the administrator of that administration he brings forth death and exile from the land of Promise. He is not allowed by God to enter the Promised Land. Moses has fulfilled the will of God and the pattern and fractal he was destined and purposed to fulfill. It would not have been possible for Moses to be the administrator of "condemnation and judgment" and also be allowed to enter the promised land, a picture of resurrection life and "grace and abundant mercy".

Numbers 20:1, Then came the children of Israel, even the whole congregation, into the desert of Zin in the first month: and the people abode in Kadesh; and Miriam died there, and was buried there. 2 And there was no water for the congregation: and they gathered themselves together against Moses and against Aaron. 3 And the people chode with Moses, and spake, saying, Would God that we had died when our brethren died before the Lord! 4 And why have ye brought up the congregation of the Lord into this wilderness, that we and our cattle should die there? 5 And wherefore have ye made us to come up out of Egypt, to bring us in unto this evil place? it is no place of seed, or of figs, or of vines, or of pomegranates; neither is there any water to drink. 6 And Moses and Aaron went from the presence of the assembly unto the door of the tabernacle of the congregation, and they fell upon their faces: and the glory of the Lord appeared unto them. 7 And the Lord spake unto Moses, saying, 8 Take the rod, and gather thou the assembly together, thou, and Aaron thy brother, and speak ye unto the rock before their eyes; and it shall give forth his water, and thou shalt bring forth to them water out of the rock: so thou shalt give the congregation and their beasts drink. 9 And Moses took the rod from before the Lord, as he commanded him. 10 And Moses and Aaron gathered the congregation together before the rock, and he said unto them, Hear now, ye rebels; must we fetch you water out of this rock? 11 And Moses lifted up his hand, and with his rod he smote the rock twice: and the water came out abundantly, and the congregation drank, and their beasts also. 12 And the Lord spake unto Moses and Aaron, Because ye believed me not, to sanctify me in the eyes of the children of Israel, therefore ye shall not bring this congregation into the land which I have given them. 13 This is the water of Meribah; because the children of Israel strove with the Lord, and he was sanctified in them.

Notice these key points between the first event of striking the rock and the second event of bringing forth water for the people.

First Event of Moses Bringing Water From the Rock–Exodus 17	Second Event of Moses Bringing Water From the Rock– Numbers 20
Happened to the first generation	Happened to the second generation
Angel of YHWH stands before the rock; The rock is a picture of Yeshua, the Image of God	The Angel of YHWH does not stand before the rock; The rock is a picture of us, the second set of tablets that are to receive the transcribing of the Image of God
Moses is commanded to strike the rock with the staff of God	Moses is commanded to speak to the rock with the staff of God
Moses has the staff of God in his hand	Moses has the staff of God in his hand
Picture of the Messiah Yeshua being killed to bring forth water so they might live	God is angry that Moses did not obey and speak to the rock as He instructed, and the picture is not what He wanted painted for the people to see
The key question that the people ask, "is YHWH among us or not?" (Exodus 17:7)	The key issue of the people is that they have been brought to a place that "is no place of seed" (Numbers 20:5)
This is a picture of the first tablets of the Torah which are broken	This is a picture of the words of the first tablets (image of YHWH, Yeshua) being written upon the second set of tablets (our hearts)
God's image (Angel of YHWH) is struck as He stands before the rock and He is broken	God's image is restored in Adam and Eve's redeemed seed
Principal action is the striking of the image	Principal action is supposed to be the speaking of the Word (Image of God) transcribed to the rock so that the people would live
Yeshua is killed so that we might receive living waters	We receive Yeshua's image so that we might produce living waters
"Is YHWH among us or not?" (Exodus 17:7)	"Because ye believed me not, to sanctify me in the eyes of the children of Israel. . . Israel strove with the Lord, and he was sanctified in them" (Numbers 20:12)

Remember the manifestation of God is in the voice.

Exodus 20:18, When the people saw the thunder and lightning and heard the trumpet and saw the mountain in smoke, they trembled with fear. They stayed at a distance 19 and said to Moses, Speak to us yourself and we will listen. But <u>do not have God speak to us or we will die</u>. 20 Moses said to the people, Do not be afraid. God has come to test you, so that the fear of God will be with you to keep you from sinning. 21 The people remained at a distance, while Moses approached the thick darkness where God was.

With the completion of the tabernacle, the consummating event was the appearance of the voice of God.

Numbers 7:89, And when Moses was gone into the tabernacle of the congregation to speak with him, <u>then he heard the voice of one speaking unto him from off the mercy seat that was upon the ark of testimony</u>, from between the two cherubims: and he spake unto him.

When we have the Image of God, our eyes and ears are opened to see the Glory of God, Yeshua, that God may be glorified in the people and in the eyes of the children of Israel. God's image is transcribed upon us and His countenance is glorified in our eyes, not just by what we see and hear, but when others look upon our eyes and see God's countenance. Now we can fully understand the need for the two events of Moses and the rock. We can see the full implications of the Aaronic blessing.

THE AARONIC BLESSING; SEED TO FRUIT, TRANSCRIBING THE COUNTENANCE (IMAGE) OF GOD:

Numbers 6:22, And the Lord spake unto Moses, saying, 23 Speak unto Aaron and unto his sons, saying, On this wise ye shall bless the children of Israel, saying unto them, 24 The Lord bless thee, and keep thee:25 The <u>Lord make his face shine upon thee</u>, and be gracious unto thee:26 The Lord lift up his countenance upon thee, and give thee peace. 27 And <u>they shall put my name upon the children of Israel,</u> and I will bless them.

May the Lord bless you and guard you– יְבָרֶכְךָ יְהֹוָה, וְיִשְׁמְרֶךָ

May the Lord shine His countenance toward you and be gracious to you– יָאֵר
יְהֹוָה פָּנָיו אֵלֶיךָ, וִיחֻנֶּךָּ

May the Lord lift up His countenance toward you and give you peace– יִשָּׂא יְהֹוָה
פָּנָיו אֵלֶיךָ, וְיָשֵׂם לְךָ שָׁלוֹם

"Hashem spoke to Moses, saying, Speak to Aaron and his sons, saying: So shall you bless the children of Israel, saying to them: May Hashem bless you and safeguard you. May Hashem illuminate His countenance for you and be gracious to you. May <u>Hashem lift His countenance to you</u> and establish peace for you. Let them <u>place My Name upon the children of Israel</u> and I shall bless them." (Chumash–Numbers 6:22–27)

God is transcribing His image, His countenance, His face, and His name upon us. He is not just shinning upon us, He is shining from us because we have received His image, Yeshua the Messiah, and we live through him. Yeshua is the manifestation of the Glory of God before the people. God's great desire was to be manifest before the people.

Numbers 20:12, And the Lord spake unto Moses and Aaron, Because ye believed me not, <u>to sanctify me in the eyes</u> of the children of Israel, therefore ye shall not bring this congregation into the land which I have given them. 13 This is the water of Meribah; because the children of Israel strove with the Lord, and <u>he was sanctified in them</u>.

The people need to see and hear the Glory of God in order to have the waters of life.

John 12:27, Now is my soul troubled; and what shall I say? Father, save me from this hour: but for this cause came I unto this hour. 28 Father, <u>glorify thy name</u>. Then came there a voice from heaven, saying, I have both glorified it, and will glorify it again. 29 The people therefore, that stood by, and heard it, said that it thundered: others said, An angel spake to him.

It is through seeing the glory of the manifest Name of God, Yeshua, that we receive His image. Just as waters flowed from Yeshua to bring life to the people, so also the transcribing of His image produces the same effect in us, waters of life.

John 7:37, In the last day, that great day of the feast, Yeshua stood and cried, saying, <u>If any man thirst, let him come unto me, and drink. 38 He that believeth on me, as the scripture hath said, out of his belly shall flow rivers of living water</u>. 39 (But this spake he of the Spirit, which they that believe on him should receive: for the Holy Ghost was not yet given; because that Yeshua was not yet glorified.)

The living water is the Breath of the Almighty, the Holy Spirit and with it comes life.

John 4:7, There cometh a woman of Samaria <u>to draw water</u>: Yeshua saith unto her, Give me to drink. 8 (For his disciples were gone away unto the city to buy meat.) 9 Then saith the woman of Samaria unto him, How is it that thou, being a Jew, askest drink of me, which am a woman of Samaria? for the Jews have no dealings with the Samaritans. 10 Yeshua answered and said unto her, If thou knewest the gift of God, and who it is that saith to thee, Give me to drink; thou wouldest have asked of him, and <u>he would have given thee living water</u>. 11 The woman saith unto him, Sir, thou hast nothing to draw with, and the well is deep: from whence then hast thou that living water? 12 Art thou greater than our father Jacob, which gave us the well, and drank thereof himself, and his children, and his cattle? 13 Yeshua answered and said unto her, Whosoever drinketh of this water shall thirst again:14 But <u>whosoever drinketh of the water that I shall give him shall never thirst; but the water that I shall give him shall be in him a well of water springing up into everlasting life</u>. 15 The woman saith unto him, Sir, give me this water, that I thirst not, neither come hither to draw.

We see the fulfillment of these promises in the book of Revelation (Manifestation).

Revelation 7:13, And one of the elders answered, saying unto me, <u>What are these which are arrayed in white robes</u>? and whence came they? 14 And I said unto him, Sir, thou knowest. And he said to me, These are they which came out of great tribulation, and have washed their robes, and made them white in the blood of the Lamb. 15 Therefore are they before the throne of God, and serve him day and night in his temple: and he that sitteth on the throne shall dwell among them. 16 They shall hunger no more, <u>neither thirst any more</u>; neither shall the sun light on them, nor any heat. 17 For the Lamb which is in the midst of the throne shall feed them, and <u>shall lead them unto living fountains of waters</u>: and God shall wipe away all tears from their eyes.

The blood of the Lamb makes atonement for the soul (breath of the Almighty) and gives us water that we might live. We now know why the first generation from Egypt had to die and why Moses approached the rock in need of water twice!

So, what then ought we to be doing?

Romans 8:28, And we know that all things work together for good to them that love God, to them who are the called according to his purpose. 29 For whom he did foreknow, he also did <u>predestinate to be conformed to the image of his Son</u>, that he might be the firstborn among many brethren. 30 Moreover whom he did predestinate, them he also called: and whom he called, them he also justified: and whom he justified, them he also glorified.

May the countenance of Yeshua YHWH be upon your lives and His name written in your flesh.

Revelation 3:11, Behold, I come quickly: hold that fast which thou hast, that no man take thy crown. 12 Him that overcometh will I make a pillar in the temple of my God, and he shall go no more out: and <u>I will write upon him the name of my God</u>, and the name of the city of my God, which is new Jerusalem, which cometh down out of heaven from my God: and I will write upon him my new name. 13 He that hath an ear, let him hear what the Spirit saith unto the churches.

HEARING THE VOICE OF GOD

The Almighty reveals Himself to man through various names and each name has meaning and significance. In the book of Exodus, the God of Abraham, Isaac, and Jacob begins to reveal Himself to the children of Israel in a way that He had not done with their forefathers.

Exodus 6:2, And God spake unto Moses, and said unto him, I am the Lord:3 And I appeared unto Abraham, unto Isaac, and unto Jacob, by the name of God Almighty, but by my name JEHOVAH (YHWH) was I not known to them. 4 And I have also established my covenant with them, to give them the land of Canaan, the land of their pilgrimage, wherein they were strangers.

God is telling the children of Israel that He is going to reveal himself to them by the Name of YHWH and all that the name means. Now it is clear that the promises that were made to Abram and Jacob were given in two names of God, El Shaddai (El, Elohim) and YHWH (Lord).

Genesis 15:4, And, behold, the word of the Lord came unto him, saying, This shall not be thine heir; but he that shall come forth out of thine own bowels shall be thine heir. 5 And he brought him forth abroad, and said, Look now toward heaven, and tell the stars, if thou be able to number them: and he said unto him, So shall thy seed be. 6 And he believed in the Lord; and he counted it to him for righteousness. 7 And he said unto him, I am the Lord that brought thee out of Ur of the Chaldees, to give thee this land to inherit it...13 And he said unto Abram, Know of a surety that thy seed shall be a stranger in a land that is not theirs, and shall serve them; and they shall afflict them four hundred years; 14 And also that nation, whom they shall serve, will I judge: and afterward shall they come out with great substance.

Notice the focus of this passage is the promise of inheritance of the Promised land. God promises the land to Abraham's descendants in the Name of YHWH (Lord). So, Abraham knew the name YHWH. When God promises to Abraham the multiplicity of seed He makes His promises via the name El Shaddai.

Genesis 17:1, And when Abram was ninety years old and nine, the Lord appeared to Abram, and said unto him, I am the Almighty God (El Shaddai-Strong's 7706); walk before me, and be thou perfect. 2 And I will make my covenant between me and thee, and will multiply thee exceedingly. 3 And Abram fell on his face: and God talked with him, saying, As for me, behold, my covenant is with thee, and thou shalt be a father of many nations.

The covenant with Abram and his descendants included great multiplicity of seed (descendants) and the promise of the inheritance of the Promised land. When God promises multiplicity of seed He uses the name El Shaddai.

When God promises the deliverance of the land (Aliyah-ascended inheritance) He uses the name YHWH (Lord). The creation and promise of seed is hidden and the deliverance of the land is out in the open for all to see (revealed/manifested).

Aliyah (US /ˌæ. lı. ˈɑː/, UK /ˌɑː. lı. ˈɑː/; Hebrew:עֲלִיָּה aliyah, "ascent") is the immigration of Jews from the diaspora to the Land of Israel (Eretz Israel in Hebrew). Also defined as "the act of going up"—that is, towards Jerusalem— "making Aliyah" by moving to the Land of Israel is one of the most basic tenets of Zionism. The opposite action, emigration from the Land of Israel, is referred to in Hebrew as yerida ("descent"). [1] The State of Israel's Law of Return gives Jews and their descendants automatic rights regarding residency and Israeli citizenship. (Wikipedia)

THE HIDDEN SEED OF JOSEPH

These patterns are very similar to the events we see in the life of Joseph when he was exiled (caused to descend) to Egypt by his brothers. Joseph's role was for the saving of "much people alive" (seed).

Genesis 50:19, And Joseph said unto them, Fear not: for am I in the place of God? 20 But as for you, ye thought evil against me; but God meant it unto good, to bring to pass, as it is this day, to save much people alive. 21 Now therefore fear ye not: I will nourish you, and your little ones. And he comforted them, and spake kindly unto them.

God is operating in the life of Joseph through seemingly natural everyday events, not through great visible miracles. Even Joseph's brothers have difficulty seeing the divine hand of God in the events of their lives. That is because God is operating through natural events and hiding the miraculous in common everyday circumstances.

Notice the same pattern is observed in Genesis 1 and 2. In Genesis 1, God is revealing himself (making himself known) via the name El, Elohim (a derivation of El Shaddai). So, we know that God is operating in hidden everyday natural events. In Genesis 1, we learned that God is creating seed for all his creation and their ability to multiply in hiding. This passing on of seed and multiplicity is divine and miraculous and seems to be common and a part of nature.

Genesis 1:27, So God (Elohim-Strong's 430) created man in his own image, in the Image of God created he him; male and female created he them. And God blessed them, and God said unto them, Be fruitful, and multiply, and replenish the earth, and subdue it: and have dominion over the fish of the sea, and over the fowl of the air, and over every living thing that moveth upon the earth.

Genesis shows us that the creative fractal happens "image after image" and "kind after kind". They all proceed in the same pattern of seed then manifested flesh. Before the fall, that manifested image (flesh) was unfallen and unbroken. After the fall, the manifested image (flesh) is corruptible and broken. We keep seeing the imagery of a hidden duality that needs to be restored to an ascended state.

Just as Joseph was hidden in exile while God prospered him, the fractal and pattern repeats itself in his sons, Ephraim and Manasseh. This "seed" of Joseph has been hidden from Israel (Jacob) and is now revealed to him right before his death. This hidden seed ascends by the blessing of Israel as his image is passed on to his grandsons. They ascend from being grandsons to being full sons of inheritance with the other twelve sons of Jacob. They literally take Joseph's place. This is the same imagery that is presented to believers in Yeshua.

Romans 8:17, And if children, then heirs; heirs of God, and joint–heirs with Christ; if so be that we suffer with him, that we may be also glorified together.

Now let's review that the promises to Ephraim and Manasseh.

Genesis 48:4, And said unto me, Behold, I will make thee fruitful, and multiply thee, and I will make of thee a multitude of people; and will give this land to thy seed after thee for an everlasting possession. 5 And now thy two sons, Ephraim and Manasseh, which were born unto thee in the land of Egypt before I came unto thee into Egypt, are mine; as Reuben and Simeon, they shall be mine. 6 And thy issue, which thou begettest after them, shall be thine, and shall be called after the name of their brethren in their inheritance...8 And Israel beheld Joseph's sons, and said, Who are these? 9 And Joseph said unto his father, They are my sons, whom God hath given me in this place. And he said, Bring them, I pray thee, unto me, and I will bless them. 10 Now the eyes of Israel were dim for age, so that he could not see. And he brought them near unto him; and he kissed them, and embraced them...16 The Angel which redeemed me from all evil, bless the lads; and let my name be named on them, and the name of my fathers Abraham and Isaac; and let them grow into a multitude in the midst of the earth. 17 And when Joseph saw that his father laid his right hand upon the head of Ephraim, it displeased him: and he held up his father's hand, to remove it from Ephraim's head unto Manasseh's head. 18 And Joseph said unto his father, Not so, my father: for this is the firstborn; put thy right hand upon his head. 19 And his father refused, and said, I know it, my son, I know it: he also shall become a people, and he also shall be great: but truly his younger brother shall be greater than he, and his seed shall become a multitude of nations. 20 And he blessed them that day, saying, In thee shall Israel bless, saying, God make thee as Ephraim and as Manasseh: and he set Ephraim before Manasseh. 21 And Israel said unto Joseph, Behold, I die: but God shall be with you, and bring you again unto the land of your fathers.

Notice these promises. They are about the recognition or lack thereof of Israel's seed. They key question is stated by Jacob, "Whose are these?" He answers his own question, "let my name be named on them." Jacob's eyes were dim so he could not discern his own seed. He had to touch the lads to tell who the greater blessing would go to. Even Joseph protests because Jacob cannot tell who the firstborn is and as such would get the greater blessing.

Jacob instructs Joseph that these two would be "great in the earth" and one of the sons would become a multitude "in the midst of the earth". This term most likely is an allusion to their future Diaspora (exile) and their being hidden in the earth like a seed with the promise to ascend and return to the land of their fathers. This great multiplicity happens in hiding (exile) during seemingly natural events.

> Exodus 1:7, And the <u>children of Israel were fruitful, and increased abundantly, and multiplied</u>, and waxed exceeding mighty; and the land was filled with them. 8 Now there arose up a new king over Egypt, which knew not Joseph. 9 And he said unto his people, Behold, the people of the children of Israel are more and mightier than we: Come on, let us deal wisely with them; <u>lest they multiply</u>, and it come to pass, that, when there falleth out any war, they join also unto our enemies, and fight against us, and so get them up out of the land.

ELOHIM (SEED) & YHWH (MANIFESTED IMAGE)

Keep in mind that while Israel was in Egypt (exile) God (Elohim) caused their seed to multiply exceedingly and later YHWH delivered their flesh from Egypt. Just as we see Ephraim and Manasseh multiplying in the "midst of the earth", we see in Genesis 2 the multiplicity of the created seed of the image of YHWH occurring "in the midst of the Garden" of Eden.

> Genesis 2:9, And out of the ground made the Lord God to grow every tree that is pleasant to the sight, and good for food; the Tree of Life also <u>in the midst of the garden</u>, and the tree of knowledge of good and evil.

Both multiplicity of seeds and deliverance of a manifested image, our flesh, occur "in the midst of" the garden and the earth. The hidden seed is revealed by YHWH as living flesh (image).

The pattern is always the same:
- Hidden seed–Elohim–Genesis 1
- Ascended and manifested image (flesh)–YHWH–Genesis 2

As with Adam, so it is with Israel. As in the beginning, so it is in the end. Seed is sown and flesh (image) is reaped. The Egyptians could not tell that Israel was the betrothed of YHWH, just as Joseph's brothers could not tell that Joseph was of Jacob's seed, and just as Pharaoh could not tell that Sarai was Abram's wife. They are hidden from sight so that God can cause them to grow and prosper.

> Genesis 12:18, So Pharaoh summoned Abram. "What have you done to me? " he said. "Why did not you tell me she was your wife? 19 Why did you say, 'She is my sister, ' so that I took her to be my wife? Now then, here is your

wife. Take her and go!" 20 Then Pharaoh gave orders about Abram to his men, and they sent him on his way, with his wife and everything he had.

God is going to reveal Himself as the groom of Israel in the end–time. That requires the revealing of the groom and the bride. That is why God begins to show Himself (make Himself known) as YHWH. He is about to provide deliverance of the seed, as manifested fruit, to the land. He no longer operates in the hidden events of man, but in the revealed miraculous events of the Exodus and the events of the second coming of Christ as described in the book of Revelation (Manifestation). He delivers the seed that multiplied in hiding (exile). The same will be the case at the end of the age.

Now notice Genesis 2 again. You see the appearance of YHWH (Lord God). Why? Because He is delivering their images and causing them to ascend out of the earth after their seed has multiplied.

> Genesis 2:5, And <u>every plant of the field before it was in the earth, and every herb of the field before it grew</u>: for <u>the Lord God had not caused it to rain upon the earth</u>, and there was not a man to till the ground. 6 But there went up a mist from the earth, and watered the whole face of the ground. 7 And the Lord God formed man of the dust of the ground, and breathed into his nostrils the breath of life; and man became a living soul. 8 And the Lord God planted a garden eastward in Eden; and there he put the man whom he had formed.

The Lord God (YHWH Elohim) brings forth the images through the bringing of water, just like we have seen Yeshua the Messiah offering the living waters to the redeemed. We saw Yeshua making this offer at the Water Libation Ceremony on the Last Day of the Feast of Tabernacles in Jerusalem (John 7:37–38). He also made the same offer to the Samaritan woman at the well (John 4:6–27). This is just another confirmation that we are in the season of seeds and are awaiting the watering that occurs on the 7th day Sabbath that causes the manifestation of the restored image of those redeemed seeds (hearts-Luke 2:35).

> Luke 2:35, (Yea, a sword shall pierce through thy own soul also,) that the thoughts of many hearts may be revealed.

Yeshua is fulfilling the same pattern as Genesis 1 and 2. Our hearts are the seeds that need to be circumcised and watered so that they can manifest the Image of God.

Let's read this carefully. Genesis is clarifying that nothing grew until the seventh day. That means all the seed of Genesis 1 multiplied but did not deliver an image or flesh as yet. That could only happen with the watering on the 7th day Sabbath and the revealing of the Lord God (YHWH).

After the formation of the image and flesh of man, YHWH gives him the breath of life and places him in the garden that He created. God is revealing Himself to man with a new name, YHWH.

Now why is it that He says He did not make Himself known to the Patriarchs by the Name of YHWH? We've already established that they knew the name YHWH and that the promise of the land was given to them in the Name of YHWH. But He says He did not "make Himself known" nor reveal Himself by the Name of YHWH. The answer is in the "land". Did Abraham, Isaac, and Jacob possess the land?

Exodus 35:27, And Jacob came unto Isaac his father unto Mamre, unto the city of Arbah, which is Hebron, where Abraham and Isaac <u>sojourned</u>.

Notice they sojourned, they did not possess the Promised Land.

Genesis 17:7, And I will establish my covenant <u>between me and thee and thy seed after thee</u> in their generations for an everlasting covenant, to be a God unto thee, <u>and to thy seed after thee</u>. 8 And I will give unto thee, and <u>to thy seed after thee, the land wherein thou art a stranger</u>, all the land of Canaan, for an everlasting possession; and I will be their God. 9 And God said unto Abraham, Thou shalt <u>keep my covenant therefore, thou, and thy seed</u> after thee in their generations.

The Patriarchs did not possess the land, they were aliens (strangers) in the land. God made the promise but did not deliver the promise until a future generation of Abraham's seed. So, YHWH was not known (revealed) as YHWH to the fathers. That was to come later when God would deliver their seed from Egypt. That is why you see the repeated phrase that they were "to go up to possess the land".

Deuteronomy 1:20, And I said unto you, Ye are come unto the mountain of the Amorites, which the Lord our God doth give unto us. 21 Behold, the Lord thy God hath set the land before thee: <u>go up and possess it,</u> as the Lord God of thy fathers hath said unto thee; fear not, neither be discouraged. 22 And ye came near unto me every one of you, and said, We will send men before us, and they shall search us out the land, and bring us word again by what way we must go up, and into what cities we shall come.

YHWH is revealing Himself to Israel's multiplied delivered seed and bringing them to the land to "possess" it. They will not be aliens or sojourners. They will possess the land unlike their fathers. Hence the name of YHWH is used, the name the promise was originally given in. God was no longer going to operate in the background but now manifested where everyone could see Him and know His name! It will be the same in the end.

THE END OF ISRAEL'S EXILE

Ezekiel 37:1, The hand of the Lord was upon me, and he brought me out by the Spirit of the Lord and set me in the middle of a valley; it was full of bones. 2 He led me back and forth among them, and I saw a great many bones on the floor of the valley, bones that were very dry. 3 He asked me, "Son of man, can these bones live?" I said, "O Sovereign Lord, you alone know."

This is YHWH returning all of Israel from Diaspora (exile). It happens on the 7th day Sabbath and involves the creation of new manifested images (flesh) and the giving of the breath of life just as in Genesis 2.

Ezekiel 37:7, So I prophesied as I was commanded. And as I was prophesying, there was a noise, a rattling sound, and the bones came together, bone to bone. 8 I looked, and tendons and flesh appeared on them and skin covered them, but there was no breath in them. 9 Then he said to me, "Prophesy to the breath; prophesy, son of man, and say to it, 'This is what the Sovereign Lord says: Come from the four winds, O breath, and breathe into these slain, that they may live. ' " 10 So I prophesied as he commanded me, and breath entered them; they came to life and stood up on their feet—a vast army. Then he said to me: "Son of man, these bones are the whole house of Israel.

This shows Israel about to be delivered by YHWH for all to see in a miraculous fashion.

Ezekiel 37:21, And say unto them, Thus saith the Lord God; Behold, I will take the children of Israel from among the heathen, whither they be gone, and will gather them on every side, and bring them into their own land:22 And I will make them one nation in the land upon the mountains of Israel; and one king shall be king to them all: and they shall be no more two nations, neither shall they be divided into two kingdoms any more at all. 23 Neither shall they defile themselves any more with their idols, nor with their detestable things, nor with any of their transgressions: but I will save them out of all their dwellingplaces, wherein they have sinned, and will cleanse them: so shall they be my people, and I will be their God.

This will happen on the last day in the end-time! Who will do it? YHWH! It will be visible and miraculous! Yeshua is YHWH manifested for all people to see the glory of God's manifested name.

YESHUA THE MANIFESTED IMAGE OF GOD (HIS FLESH)
Mark 14:24, And he said unto them, This is my blood of the new testament, which is shed for many. 25 Verily I say unto you, I will drink no more of the fruit of the vine, until that day that I drink it new in the kingdom of God.

It is Yeshua's flesh and blood that provides deliverance and the restoration of the Kingdom of God, the reunification of Israel, and the gathering of Israel back to the land.

John 11:50, Nor consider that it is expedient for us, that one man should die for the people, and that the whole nation perish not. 51 And this spake he not of himself: but being high priest that year, he prophesied that Yeshua should die for that nation; 52 And not for that nation only, but that also <u>he should gather together in one the children of God that were scattered abroad</u>.

It is through Yeshua's flesh that believers (Israel) receive life and are re–gathered to the Promised land!

Exodus 14:12, Is not this the word that we did tell thee in Egypt, saying, Let us alone, that we may serve the Egyptians? For it had been better for us to serve the Egyptians, than that we should die in the wilderness. 13 And Moses said unto the people, Fear ye not, <u>stand still, and see the salvation of the Lord</u>, which he will shew to you to day: for the Egyptians whom ye have seen to day, ye shall see them again no more for ever. 14 The Lord shall fight for you, and ye shall hold your peace.

- "Stand still and see the Yeshua of YHWH."
- "Stand still and see the Salvation of YHWH."

Yeshua (ישוע, with vowel pointing יֵשׁוּעַ–yēšūă' in Hebrew) Yeshua in Hebrew is verbal derivative from "to rescue", "to deliver". [9] Its usage among the Jews of the Second Temple Period, the Biblical Aramaic/Hebrew name יֵשׁוּעַ Yeshua's was common: the Hebrew Bible mentions several individuals with this name–while also using their full name Joshua. (Wikipedia)

Israel is fulfilling the same pattern and fractal as we saw in creation, seed (hidden) then manifestation (revealed). This is why Paul referred to Israel and their "casting away" (Romans 11:15) as fulfilling the imagery of a seed being cast was for the purpose of reaping the whole world. So, as a seed they fulfil the imagery of hiddenness and death until the day of fruitfulness and resurrection life. This is the same pattern of Genesis 1 and 2.

Unlocking the simple pattern and fractal of Genesis 1 and 2 also unlocks the meaning of the two giving's of the Torah of Moses, the deliverance from Egypt and death in the wilderness of the first generation of Israel, and the first and second coming of the Messiah Yeshua. It finally unlocks the two administrations, one of judgment and condemnation-death (Moses) and the final administration of grace and abundant mercy-resurrection life (Yeshua).

Having an incorrect paradigm of the beginning will ensure you have an incorrect paradigm of the end. If we fix our ideas about the creation and cause our paradigm to conform to the scriptural model, our end-time conclusions will have a greater chance of being biblically accurate.

GENESIS 1 & 2 REVISITED

Notice the often-supposed repeated accounts of the creation in Genesis. It begins in Genesis 1 and then appears to repeat in Genesis 2. What is the reason for this? And why do both chapters have subtle differences? Did Moses mistakenly write down what YHWH told Him to write? Did the scribes erroneously copy this section of scripture so we can now assume the account of Genesis is just some allegory that we can spiritualize away? No. We need to pay close attention to the details and follow the path of clues laid before us back to the garden.

Genesis 1:
The creation of all seeds and their programs/rules of existence.

Genesis 1:26, And <u>God said,</u> Let us make man in our image, after our likeness: and let them have dominion over the fish of the sea, and over the fowl of the air, and over the cattle, and over all the earth, and over every creeping thing that creepeth upon the earth. 27 So <u>God created</u> man in his own image, in the Image of God created he him; male and female created he them. 28 And God blessed them, and <u>God said unto them,</u> Be fruitful, and multiply, and replenish the earth, and subdue it: and have dominion over the fish of the sea, and over the fowl of the air, and over every living thing that moveth upon the earth. 29 And <u>God said,</u> Behold, I have given you <u>every herb bearing seed, which is upon the face of all the earth, and every tree, in the which is the fruit of a tree yielding seed</u>; to you it shall be for meat. 30 And to every beast of the earth, and to every fowl of the air, and to every thing that creepeth upon the earth, wherein there is life, I have given every green herb for meat: and it was so. 31 And <u>God saw every thing that he had made,</u> and, behold, it was very good. And the evening and the morning were the sixth day.

Genesis 2:
Forming of the flesh (images) of the seeds of the ground after watering on the Seventh day.

Genesis 2:3, And God blessed the seventh day, and sanctified it: because that in it he had rested from all his work which God created and made. 4 These are the generations of the heavens and of the earth when they were created, in the day that the <u>Lord God</u> made the earth and the heavens, 5 <u>And every plant of the field before it was in the earth, and every herb of the field before it grew: for the Lord God had not caused it to rain upon the earth, and there was not a man to till the ground</u>. 6 But there went up a mist from the earth, and watered the whole face of the ground. 7 And the <u>Lord God formed</u> man of the dust of the ground, and breathed into his nostrils the breath of life; and man became a living soul. 8 And the <u>Lord God planted</u> a garden eastward in Eden; and there he put the man whom he had formed. 9 And out of the ground made the <u>Lord God to grow</u> every tree that is pleasant to the sight, and good for food; the Tree of Life also in the midst of the garden, and the tree of knowledge of good and evil. . . . . 15 And the <u>Lord God took the man,</u> and put him into the garden of Eden to dress it and to keep it. 16 And the Lord God commanded the man, saying, Of every tree of the garden thou mayest freely eat:17 But of the Tree of the Knowledge of Good and Evil, thou shalt not eat of it: for in the day that thou eatest thereof thou shalt surely die. 18 And the <u>Lord God said,</u> It is not good that the man should be alone; I will make him an help meet for him. 19 And out of the ground the <u>Lord God formed</u> every beast of the field, and every fowl of the air; and brought them unto Adam to see what he would call them: and whatsoever Adam called every living creature, that was the name thereof. 20 <u>And Adam gave names</u> to all cattle, and to the fowl of the air, and to every beast of the field; but for Adam there was not found an help meet for him. 21 And the <u>Lord God caused</u> a deep sleep to fall upon Adam, and he slept: and he took one of his ribs, and closed up the flesh instead thereof; 22 And the rib, which the <u>Lord God had taken</u> from man, made he a woman, and brought her unto the man. 23 And Adam said, This is now bone of my bones, and flesh of my flesh: she shall be called woman, because she was taken out of man.

Let's review the differences in the two passages.

Genesis 1: SEED
The creation of all seeds and their programs/rules of existence:
- Not of dust
- "MADE" In God's image
- Male/female
- Dominion over all things in the earth
- Blessed by God
- Fruitful, multiply, and replenish the earth
- Every herb, tree yielding seed for meat, flesh of trees and herbs
- All very good
- God is known as El, Elohim, and El Shaddi; the miraculous divine hand of God is hidden in the natural
- Rules of existence are put in place and the multiplication of seed occurs.

Genesis 2: MANIFESTED IMAGE
Forming of the images of the seeds of the ground after watering on the 7th day Sabbath:
- First watering is on the 7th day Sabbath
- Every plant and herb grows
- "FORMED" man
- Of the dust of the ground
- Breathed into his nostrils the breath of life
- Man becomes a living soul
- Every tree grows that is pleasant to sight and good for food (bearing seeds); The Tree of the Knowledge of Good and Evil and the Tree of Life are placed in the garden
- Man put in the garden to dress and keep it
- Every tree he may eat of, but the Tree of the Knowledge of Good and Evil will cause him to die

- Man is alone and it is not good
- Formation of all beasts and fowls from the ground
- Adam names the animals
- No help meet for Adam
- Deep sleep on Adam
- Woman is "made" from Adam's rib (womb) and brought to him.
- "This is now bone of my bones and flesh of my flesh"
- Both Adam and Eve are naked and not ashamed
- God is known as the Lord God (YHWH); the miraculous is done openly for deliverance of redeemed flesh (image)

Now let's look at Genesis 3.

Genesis 3: CORRUPTING SEED THROUGH MIXING
Mixing two kinds of seed, corruption enters, then death
- Serpent lies about what they can eat, seed producing or not
- They eat of the Tree of Knowledge of Good and Evil and their eyes are opened and they know they are naked
- They seek to cover the areas of their bodies that produce seed
- YHWH is not able to locate them as He normally would
- They realize they need a covering, which is related to the need for circumcision to return to the garden; the covering applied to them needs to be removed because it is corruptible
- God is known as YHWH; the miraculous is done openly for deliverance of redeemed flesh

Let's first address the practice of mixing two types of seed. We have specific instruction in the Torah to never mix seed. YHWH intended for kind to produce their own kind. To mix seeds is to cause corruption and death (to descend or fall).

DO NOT MIX; THE REAL REASON FOR THE FALL
Leviticus 19:19, Ye shall keep my statutes. Thou shalt not let thy cattle gender with a diverse kind: thou shalt not sow thy field with mingled seed: neither shall a garment mingled of linen and woollen come upon thee.

- Keep my statutes.
- 'Do not mate different kinds of animals.
- Do not plant your field with two kinds of seed.
- Do not wear clothing woven of two kinds of material.

These statutes must be important, but some of them seem unnecessary to the casual observer. What is the underlying theme between all of these decrees? Paul understood these basics concepts, that everybody comes from a seed and every seed produces a body. This is not about living in an agrarian society, this is about the pattern and fractals of the universe. These natural patterns should teach us about heavenly realities. They should also clearly illustrate our current state and why we have need for a new "seed", the Messiah.

1 Corinthians 15:36, Thou fool, <u>that which thou sowest is not quickened, except it die</u>:37 And <u>that which thou sowest, thou sowest not that body that shall be</u>, but bare grain, it may chance of wheat, or of some other grain:38 But God giveth it a body as it hath pleased him, and <u>to every seed his own body</u>. 39 All flesh is not the same flesh: but there is one kind of flesh of men, another flesh of beasts, another of fishes, and another of birds.

In order for Abraham to have his seed redeemed, he needed to come into covenant with YHWH. This required the symbolic fixing of the act of Adam covering the parts of himself that produce seed. Abraham was told to circumcise the male part that produces "seed". The foreskin must be removed and replaced by a new image or flesh that is incorruptible.

Genesis 17:9, And God said unto Abraham, Thou shalt keep my covenant therefore, thou, and thy seed after thee in their generations. 10 This is my covenant, which ye shall keep, between me and you and thy seed after thee; <u>Every man child among you shall be circumcised</u>. 11 And ye shall circumcise the flesh of your foreskin; and it shall be a token of the covenant betwixt me and you.

In Revelation 12, the "man–child" is also the focus of God's attention.

Revelation 12:5, And she <u>brought forth a man child</u>, who was to rule all nations with a rod of iron: and her child was caught up unto God, and to his throne.

Perhaps we should not assume this is a coincidental use of the term "man–child" and that indeed this man–child could be the First-Fruits of the promised Image of God that ascends in deliverance from this fallen world. This man–child could be the First-Fruits of the redeemed "Sons of God".

Romans 8:19, For the earnest expectation of the creature waiteth for the manifestation of the sons of God.

Now this event truly would be a "great wonder". The Messiah, who came down from heaven, has fulfilled His promises to Abraham and delivered His seed! Notice the first mention of circumcision is to seal the covenant between Abraham and YHWH so that he and his seed would remain in covenant with YHWH. This covenant is tied to the promise of fruitfulness and the promise of land for an everlasting inheritance. Prior to this event Sarah's womb was barren or dead and Abraham lamented that he did not have an heir. He could not produce seed, just as

Adam could not produce seed until Eve was made from His flesh.

Genesis 17:12, And he that is eight days old shall be circumcised among you, every man child in your generations, he that is born in the house, or bought with money of any stranger, which is not of thy seed. 13 He that is born in thy house, and he that is bought with thy money, must needs be circumcised: and my covenant shall be in your flesh for an everlasting covenant. 14 And the uncircumcised man child whose flesh of his foreskin is not circumcised, that soul shall be cut off from his people; he hath broken my covenant. 15 And God said unto Abraham, As for Sarai thy wife, thou shalt not call her name Sarai, but Sarah shall her name be. 16 And I will bless her, and give thee a son also of her: yea, I will bless her, and she shall be a mother of nations; kings of people shall be of her. 17 Then Abraham fell upon his face, and laughed, and said in his heart, Shall a child be born unto him that is an hundred years old? and shall Sarah, that is ninety years old, bear?

Sarah, symbolic of a dead branch that cannot produce life, is restored to fruitfulness through Abraham's covenant with YHWH and the circumcision of his entire male household.

Deuteronomy 30:5, And the Lord thy God will bring thee into the land which thy fathers possessed, and thou shalt possess it; and he will do thee good, and multiply thee above thy fathers. 6 And the Lord thy God will circumcise thine heart, and the heart of thy seed, to love the Lord thy God with all thine heart, and with all thy soul, that thou mayest live. 7 And the Lord thy God will put all these curses upon thine enemies, and on them that hate thee, which persecuted thee.

YHWH talks about the importance of circumcision throughout the Torah, Tanach, and the New Testament. He appeals to Israel not only to circumcise their flesh, but to circumcise their hearts that "they may live". Yeshua was frequently criticized by the Pharisees for healing on the Sabbath. Is there a connection between healing and circumcision?

John 7:21, Yeshua answered and said unto them, I have done one work, and ye all marvel. 22 Moses therefore gave unto you circumcision; (not because it is of Moses, but of the fathers;) and ye on the sabbath day circumcise a man. 23 If a man on the sabbath day receive circumcision, that the law of Moses should not be broken; are ye angry at me, because I have made a man every whit whole on the sabbath day?

The rabbis knew it was needful to circumcise even on the Sabbath because it symbolized coming into covenant with YHWH and being redeemed or "made whole". Yeshua instructed them that he was literally and physically making someone whole on the Sabbath and releasing them from the fruits of death by healing them. In addition, Yeshua was telling them that healing on the Sabbath is also lawful because it fulfills the same purpose of restoring corruptible flesh to full life, which is a picture of restoring a broken image to the Image of God.

Circumcision symbolizes healing, restoration, redemption of seed, and coming into covenant with YHWH. Those who were circumcised would not associate with those who were uncircumcised. The uncircumcised were viewed by the rabbis as dead flesh and not redeemed. Peter was faced with trying to reconcile his traditional beliefs about not associating with those out of covenant with YHWH to accepting those uncircumcised believers in Yeshua back into fellowship with Judah.

God is clarifying that those who produce the fruit of the Tree of Life are in covenant with Him, and it is Yeshua who will judge who is really alive and producing fruit and upon those people will dwell the Holy Spirit. At this point it is clear no one should be saying they are not in covenant with God and forbidding water so that they might be baptized (mikvah), which symbolizes becoming one flesh with Yeshua and receiving His uncorrupted image. This is how we, as dead branches from the Tree of the Knowledge of Good and Evil that produce no life, can be grafted into a Tree of Life that produces fruit.

Yeshua is the tree we are grafted into. When the northern ten tribes (Ephraim) left the covenant, their branches were cut off because they no longer believed. Yeshua came to graft our dead branches back into the tree of faith. This is the "fulness of the Gentiles" (Romans 11:12,25), the return from exile (hiddenness, death) of the northern ten tribes of Israel along with their companions (the gentiles) to the covenants of promise. This "fullness" is the allusion of "fruitfulness" and the bringing forth of an image from a seed.

> Numbers 18:27, And this your heave offering shall be reckoned unto you, as though it were the corn of the threshingfloor, and as the fulness of the winepress.

It denotes a time of harvest where the plant has finally sprung forth branches and is ready to have its fruit harvested.

> Isaiah 61:11, For as the earth bringeth forth her bud, and as the garden causeth the things that are sown in it to spring forth; so the Lord God will cause righteousness and praise to spring forth before all the nations.

Yeshua depicted the Day of the Lord and His imminent return as being associated with the season of "fruit" (resurrection) as opposed to the season of "seed" (death).

> Matthew 13:27, And then shall he send his angels, and shall gather together his elect from the four winds, from the uttermost part of the earth to the uttermost part of heaven. 28 Now learn a parable of the fig tree; When her branch is yet tender, and putteth forth leaves, ye know that summer is near:29 So ye in like manner, when ye shall see these things come to pass, know that it is nigh, even at the doors.

Yeshua is using very clear references to times and seasons of seed and fruit and just as God reaches forth to collect the fruit in harvest, He will do the same to His people. When this event occurs all the world will know it and see it and know that the time is nearly at the door. After Yeshua's resurrection the Apostles asked if this was the time that God would restore the Kingdom to Israel. How does the Messiah respond? What symbols does He use?

Acts 1:5, For John truly baptized with water; but ye shall be baptized with the Holy Ghost not many days hence. 6 When they therefore were come together, they asked of him, saying, Lord, <u>wilt thou at this time restore again the kingdom to Israel?</u> 7 And he said unto them, It is not for you <u>to know the times or the seasons</u>, which the Father hath put in his own power.

Yeshua is giving the Apostles very clear indications that the regathering and the restoration of the Kingdom of all of Israel will be in its appropriate season related to fruit and harvest and only the Father can dictate when He will grant the appropriate factors for that season to occur. So just as the Northern 10 tribes of Israel went into exile due to their lawlessness, they will return according to God's blessing and lawfulness.

2 Chronicles 13:8, And now ye think to withstand the kingdom of the Lord in the hand of the sons of David; and ye be a great multitude, and there are with your golden calves, which Jeroboam made you for gods. 9 Have ye not cast out the priests of the Lord, the sons of Aaron, and the Levites, and have made you priests after the manner of the nations of other lands? so that whosoever cometh to consecrate himself with a young bullock and seven rams, the same may be a priest of them that are no gods. 10 But as for us, the Lord is our God, and we have not forsaken him; and the priests, which minister unto the Lord, are the sons of Aaron, and the Levites wait upon their business:11 And they burn unto the Lord every morning and every evening burnt sacrifices and sweet incense: the shewbread also set they in order upon the pure table; and the candlestick of gold with the lamps thereof, to burn every evening: for we keep the charge of the Lord our God; but ye have forsaken him.

Just as Israel was split by the Golden Calf incident at Mt. Sinai, so also the twelve tribes of Israel were split when Ephraim and the Northern 10 tribes set up golden calves for worship in the north. This resulted in the division of the Kingdom of Israel, the banishment of the Northern 10 tribes and the eventual fall of the Southern Kingdom of Judah. To this day only Judah and his companions have returned and the Northern 10 tribes are still yet to return from their diaspora amongst the Gentiles (Goyim-synonymous with "cattle", Mas. K'rithoth 6b, Mas. Yevamoth 61b). Once these tribes have fulfilled the same fractal as a seed (in death) amongst the Gentiles, God will harvest them out and reunite them with their brothers in the Land of Israel.

Isaiah 49:22, 22 Thus saith the Lord God, Behold, I will lift up mine hand to the Gentiles, and set up my standard to the people: and they shall bring thy sons in their arms, and thy daughters shall be carried upon their shoulders.

This is the work of the Messiah and is typified by the work of Elijah and returning God's people to the Law of Moses. God's full intention for His people is to gather their children (fruit) from the nations that they have been exiled into. This is that end time gathering that the prophets allude to. The context of this return is inextricable from God's expectation that His people will repent and return to the Law of Moses that He personally gave to the people.

Ezekiel 37:19, The word of the Lord came again unto me, saying, 16 Moreover, thou son of man, take thee one stick, and write upon it, For Judah, and for the children of Israel his companions: then take another stick, and write upon it, For Joseph, the stick of Ephraim and for all the house of Israel his companions:17 And join them one to another into one stick; and they shall become one in thine hand. 18 And when the children of thy people shall speak unto thee, saying, Wilt thou not shew us what thou meanest by these? 19 Say unto them, Thus saith the Lord God; Behold, I will take the stick of Joseph, which is in the hand of Ephraim, and the tribes of Israel his fellows, and will put them with him, even with the stick of Judah, and make them one stick, and they shall be one in mine hand. 20 And the sticks whereon thou writest shall be in thine hand before their eyes. 21 And say unto them, Thus saith the Lord God; Behold, I will take the children of Israel from among the heathen, whither they be gone, and will gather them on every side, and bring them into their own land:22 And I will make them one nation in the land upon the mountains of Israel; and one king shall be king to them all: and they shall be no more two nations, neither shall they be divided into two kingdoms any more at all. 23 Neither shall they defile themselves any more with their idols, nor with their detestable things, nor with any of their transgressions: but I will save them out of all their dwellingplaces, wherein they have sinned, and will cleanse them: so shall they be my people, and I will be their God.

Take note of the facts that both of these houses are depicted as "trees" or "sticks" and they are currently exiled due to their transgressions of the Law of Moses and their disregard for accurate scriptural worship. These two houses (sticks) are made one in the Hand of the Lord, the Messiah Yeshua, under an administration of grace, mercy, and forgiveness. This does not mean that there is an abolishment of the Law, but that they are forgiven so that they may return to the Law of Moses.

Modern Christianity has committed the same errors as Israel and have forsaken the Law of Moses and joined themselves to detestable pagan practices. We need to repent and return to the God of Israel...who we claim to be joined to...through His Messiah, the Seed of the Kingdom of God, and the Restorer of the Kingdom. We cannot hope to approach the truth of God without the Law of God or a natural understanding of the patterns and fractals of God via seed then flesh (manifestation, image).

The pretext and basis of this return at the Day of the Lord is now upon the people, the fruit gathered out of the earth, returning to God's law. When Adam and Eve disobeyed God's command about eating of the Tree of the Knowledge of Good and Evil, their flesh and their seed was changed, as was the serpent's.

Serpent Flesh/Seed Result:

- "Cursed above all cattle and every beast of the field, upon your belly shalt thou go."
- "Dust shall you eat all the days of your life, Enmity between thee and the woman."
- "Between thy seed and her seed, It (her seed) shall bruise thy head, and you shalt bruise his heel."

Female Seed Result:

- Multiply thy sorrow (because her seed dies), multiply thy conception (she has many seeds but they all die).
- Enmity between the female seed and serpent's seed, in sorrow bring forth children (because they will die/pain)
- Desire towards husband and he will rule over you

Male Seed Result:

- Cursed is the ground for his sake
- In sorrow, you will eat of it all the days of your life
- Thorns and thistles, it will produce
- "Eat the herb of the field, in the sweat of your face will you eat bread, till you return to the ground, for out of it wast thou taken."
- Lord God makes coats of skins to cover their nakedness, flesh (It does not say animal skins as many assume.)
- Adam and Eve know good and evil like God, if they eat of the Tree of Life they will live forever
- Driven from the Tree of Life and also the garden, because that is where the Tree of Life is located

Let's compare the two trees and their symbolism, and maybe we will learn something new

Tree of Knowledge of Good and Evil:

- Not good for food
- Causes death
- Adam is alone, not good
- Male alone at first and cannot produce fruit
- Eve is grafted from Adam's flesh
- Symbolic of natural Adam

- First Adam
- Natural man
- Corruptible

REMEMBER: Man is allowed to eat ONLY "tree and herb yielding seeds", and animals are allowed to eat "every herb".

Tree of Life:
- Bears seed
- Good for food
- Causes eternal life
- Male and female
- Yeshua and His bride
- The Bride of Messiah is grafted from Yeshua's flesh
- Produces fruit
- Symbolic of the Messiah and the Holy Spirit joined in us
- Last Adam
- Spiritual man
- Incorruptible

WHAT IS THE HIDDEN THEMATIC CONNECTION BETWEEN THE TREE OF THE KNOWLEDGE OF GOOD AND EVIL AND THE TREE OF LIFE?

Adam and Eve ate of a tree that "does not produce seed". This is the violation of God's command. It was not good for food and brought death to Adam and Eve and their seed. The fruit of the Tree of the Knowledge of Good and Evil does not bear seed. This is the same complaint that the second generation of Israel that left Egypt made about the wilderness.

> Numbers 20:5, And wherefore have ye made us to come up out of Egypt, to bring us in unto this evil place? it is no place of seed, or of figs, or of vines, or of pomegranates; neither is there any water to drink.

What can we conclude from this? Eating of the fruit of the Tree of the Knowledge of Good and Evil changed and corrupted the seed of the manifest universe to be like the Tree of the Knowledge of Good and Evil. Creation fell and became dual and divided. It produces "no seed" of life and must be restored by the "promised seed" (Genesis 3:15).

This fruit corrupted Adam and Eve's seed by becoming one flesh with it. To consume something, to eat of something, is to become one flesh with it. That is why eating is symbolic of coming into covenant with someone. You are becoming one flesh with them. That is why the Passover meal is our becoming one flesh with Yeshua. We become one with the tree of the fruit that we consume.

It is either going to produce good fruit or bad fruit. There is no middle ground.

It does not matter what our intentions are. You are one with those you affiliate with. That is why we are to work out our own salvation in fear and trembling. The consequences are eternal. We need to consume the tree that produces seed, the Tree of Life. This is why Yeshua came sowing the seed of the Kingdom of God for our redemption. This is also why you cannot save yourself by your own righteousness. Without the Messiah, you do not have the "seed of the Kingdom" in your current state. Our current state without the Messiah is "no seed" of the Tree of the Knowledge of Good and Evil

How do you heal a branch that has been growing from a tree that does not bear seed or fruit?   Cut the branch off and graft it into a Tree of Life that produces seed. When we are circumcised in our hearts we are to repent and be baptized into the name of Yeshua (His image and flesh) and receive the Holy Spirit. Once we have done this, we need to follow Yeshua's commandments (John 15:10).

The difference between the two trees is that one has broken and divided our seed and manifestation and created a duality (flesh and spirit). This duality needs to put off the flesh and cling to the unity of the faith (spirit) in Christ. He is the only one that can turn our duality into a singularity. Notice how the Apostle Paul wraps all these concepts into one.

Colossians 2:10, And ye are complete in him, which is the head of all principality and power:11 In whom also ye are circumcised with the circumcision made without hands, in putting off the body of the sins of the flesh by the circumcision of Christ:12 Buried with him in baptism, wherein also ye are risen with him through the faith of the operation of God, who hath raised him from the dead.

What have we learned?
We are complete (whole) in the Messiah. We are made whole just like the person Yeshua healed on the 7th day Sabbath. The healing is associated with circumcision and putting off the flesh. This circumcision happens without hands, by Yeshua. When does it happen?   At the resurrection, when we, flesh and spirit, become spirit only. The body of flesh is associated with sin.

How does this transition occur?
We join Yeshua in the imagery of a seed buried in death of the baptism (mikvah). The baptism is our womb in which we are conceived and awaiting our new birth (resurrection–circumcision of the flesh).

How does this new birth occur?
Our spirit is raised with Yeshua in ascended and resurrected life.

1 Corinthians 15:44, It is sown a natural body; it is raised a spiritual body. There is a natural body, and there is a spiritual body.

Our dead branch from the Tree of the Knowledge of Good and Evil is grafted into the Messiah Yeshua, the Tree of Life. We are saved by faith in His name and we take His seed upon us. By doing so we are conformed to His image.

Romans 8:29, For whom he did foreknow, he also did predestinate to be conformed to the image of his Son, that he might be the firstborn among many brethren.

Our dead branches are turned to lively branches in Yeshua.

How do we know that the end is near?
Look to the season of growth and the harvest of those in Yeshua.

Mark 13:27, And then <u>shall he send his angels, and shall gather together his elect from the four winds,</u> from the uttermost part of the earth to the uttermost part of heaven. 28 Now learn a parable of the fig tree<u>; When her branch is yet tender, and putteth forth leaves, ye know that summer is near:</u>29 So ye in like manner, when ye shall see these things come to pass, know that it is nigh, even at the doors.

The Apostles kept asking Yeshua when all things would be fulfilled. His answer is always the same, in its proper "season". This is when the seed is no longer hidden (El) and is going to be revealed and manifested in ascended fruit (YHWH). El works His divine intervention through the seemingly natural events of creation. YHWH works an open revelation (manifestation) so that all might know the salvation of His name.

- Exodus 5:2, And Pharaoh said, Who is the Lord, that I should obey his voice to let Israel go? <u>I know not the Lord</u>, neither will I let Israel go.
- Exodus 6:7, And I will take you to me for a people, and I will be to you a God: and <u>ye shall know that I am the Lord your God</u>, which bringeth you out from under the burdens of the Egyptians.
- Exodus 31:13, Speak thou also unto the children of Israel, saying, Verily <u>my sabbaths ye shall keep</u>: for it is a sign between me and you throughout your generations; <u>that ye may know that I am the Lord</u> that doth sanctify you.
- Isaiah 49:26, And I will feed them that oppress thee with their own flesh; and they shall be drunken with their own blood, as with sweet wine: and <u>all flesh shall know that I the Lord am thy Savior and thy Redeemer</u>, the mighty One of Jacob.
- Ezekiel 21:5, That <u>all flesh may know that I the Lord</u> have drawn forth my sword out of his sheath: it shall not return any more.
- Hebrews 8:11, And they shall not teach every man his neighbour, and every man his brother, saying, Know the Lord: for <u>all shall know me</u>, from the least to the greatest.

The scriptures are showing us very clear patterns of seed then flesh, death then resurrection, divided then united, hidden then revealed, exiled then returned, and descended then ascended. Let's delve into the Lord's Holy Days and see if we can learn about the necessary union of male and female and what those patterns tell us about God's mysteries.

Just as we see that "seed" is associated with death and burial, notice that it is within the "promised seed" that we see the hope of restoration and resurrection to the restored Image of God.

We see the worst in sinful behavior and corruption of the Image of God when we see the King of Israel disregarding the Prophet of God. We won't take the time now to extensively cover the prophetic role and typology of the King and the Prophet besides to note that this is one of the greatest secrets of the bible and it all relates to the Countenance of God as the Prophet serving as the Conscience (Consciousness) of the King.

When the Kings of Israel become corrupt God sends His countenance to deliver Israel from their sins and to restore the King to a right relationship with God. Often the King and the Prophet are found in deep disagreement and outright conflict over the will of God and how to righteously rule His Kingdom. Many of the books of the Old Testament seemingly ignore the Kings or treat them as a sidelight to the activities of the Prophets. The deep meaning behind this is centered upon the Image of God, its fall and restoration through the manifestation of the Countenance of God. Just as the Messiah came to transcribe His image upon us, the Aaronic Benediction focuses on God placing His countenance upon those who have His name and His mark placed upon their lives. Elijah does not appear by coincidence. He is sent by the Most High God to oppose the most evil king that Israel had up to that point in time.

> 1 Kings 16:30, And <u>Ahab the son of Omri did evil in the sight of the Lord above all that were before him</u>. 31 And it came to pass, as if it had been a light thing for him to walk in the sins of Jeroboam the son of Nebat, that he took to wife Jezebel the daughter of Ethbaal king of the Zidonians, and <u>went and served Baal, and worshipped him</u>. 32 And <u>he reared up an altar for Baal</u> in the house of Baal, which he had built in Samaria. 33 And <u>Ahab made a grove; and Ahab did more to provoke the Lord God of Israel to anger than all the kings of Israel that were before him</u>.

What was God's response to this provocation of iniquity and lawlessness?

> 1 Kings 17:1, <u>And Elijah the Tishbite</u>, who was of the inhabitants of Gilead, said unto Ahab, <u>As the Lord God of Israel liveth, before whom I stand, there shall not be dew nor rain these years, but according to my word</u>.

Just as Ahab's idolatry and disregard for the Law of Moses resulted in Ahab setting up places of worship to the pagan god Baal, God declares through His true prophet that there will be no rain for 3 years. With this one act and declaration Elijah has judged the King of Israel and all its inhabitants placing a curse of the removal of water that sustains life. As Ahab joined himself to those symbols (seeds) that depict death, Elijah brought forth the Word of God and allowed the results of those seeds to manifest into reality. The worship of lies leads to the removal of the source of life…water.

With this one act, Elijah condemned the actions of the king and his wife and all those who followed the edicts of the king. With this one act Elijah declared that he was standing with God and with the Law of Moses. Elijah was standing in opposition to this lawless one and his ways. Elijah became a hunted man, an outlaw because of his lawfulness. The same will happen in the end time to those who remain faithful the Yeshua the Messiah and His commandments (Revelation 12:17). It is not by chance that the end times will be associated with famine and a lack of food.

Matthew 24:7, For nation shall rise against nation, and kingdom against kingdom: and there shall be famines, and pestilences, and earthquakes, in divers places.

Just as the worship of Baal was being endorsed, God sent His Word through a prophet to bring the people back to God and His law. Will that be the case in these days?

Christians should watch out for two events that would take place simultaneously on April 19 (2016) in New York City and London, Christian author Michael Synder says. On that day, reproductions of the arch that stood in front of the Temple of Baal in Palmyra, Syria are going to be erected in Times Square and in Trafalgar Square. That would coincide with an occult festival related to the worship of a demon named Baal. (Christiantoday. com)

Elijah vs. Ahab and Jezebel is the pattern for the conflict that will happen in the Day of the Lord. The Lawful one will confront the Lawless one. It will become popular to worship pagan gods and idols. Those who follow the Bible and the teachings of Yeshua will become out of sync with the world…and rightfully so. We will be persecuted for it and all the world will be forced to make a choice…the Mark of the Beast or the Mark of God, the Image of the Beast or the Image of God, the favor of men or the favor of God.

Isaiah 5:20, Woe unto them that call evil good, and good evil; that put darkness for light, and light for darkness; that put bitter for sweet, and sweet for bitter!

This is the quandary of the End Times, be popular with men or fear the True God of Israel. Everyone will be forced to make a choice. Be certain to make it wisely and according to knowledge. Popularity is not a measure of truth. Every seed will eventually manifest the fullness of its image for good or evil.

Matthew 7:17, Even so every good tree bringeth forth good fruit; but a corrupt tree bringeth forth evil fruit.

Which tree are you grafted into? The Tree of Life or the Tree of the Knowledge of Good and Evil? Which seed are you manifesting in your choices? Whose image are you conforming to? Is every path truly equal in the eyes of God? We need to pay careful attention to the patterns and fractals that God has revealed in nature and see if those same patterns and fractals appear in the Bible and the Law of Moses. This is how we can validate the truthfulness of our beliefs and determine if they conform to God's expectations or if they will leave you under His judgement.

15 POLITICALLY CORRECT BELIEVERS? ANTICHRIST APPROVED!

We have discussed the ultimate importance of being grafted into the Messiah and how there is no substitute for His redemptive work. In prior chapters, we clarified how we are grafted into the tree of the Messiah via faith in His name and that there is no other Tree of Life that we can be grafted into and be redeemed. We will continue to clarify the necessity of becoming one with the Messiah and what that means. This union of redemption is depicted as the grafting of branches into the Tree of faith through the work of the Messiah (the seed of the Kingdom of God). We see the scriptural pattern of seed and branches revealing the means of ascension.

As we have previously learned, seed is associated with the firstborn and death (judgment and condemnation, seed planting–male) and branches are associated with the second born and resurrected or ascended life (grace and abundant mercy, manifested fruit harvest–female). We need to ask ourselves if there is any natural God given truths in pagan holy days like Easter, Christmas, and myriad of other pagan holy days that the world observes.

Why does the Catholic Encyclopedia declare so many of the Easter observances as having pagan origins? Why is Christmas also focused on pagan observances? Why do both of these holidays pre-date Christ? Why didn't Christ observe either of these days? The answer lies in the measure of truth. Why are some Christian Churches now turning to observing other religions' festivals in the name of "joint faith initiatives"? Are these initiatives based on any measure of truth from the Bible or are they based in a psychological con that has turned Christians into "self-hating" believers, where love and compassion are used as tools to wedge Christians away from adhering to the truth. What would Elijah say if the Priests of Baal told him he was being mean for not being more accepting of their pagan sacrifices or religious observances? Is it really the measure of a Christian to see how "tolerant" he/she can be of religious deceit and lawless behavior? Or is it the role of a Christian to set the Image of God as a role model in his/her community?

Have we really gotten to the point that we assume the measure of truth is only by determining how accepting you are of deviant behavior? What is divinely inspiring about that? To use this as your model of righteousness would have resulted in a different result at Mt. Sinai as the people made a golden idol.

Those who made the idol would say you must accept the Golden Calf as your "god". Furthermore, they would declare that you must accept those who worship the idol because you need to be inclusive of your neighbors. They would then declare a "safe space" if their favorite idol was nearby to exempt them from anybody who disagreed. This psychological con is becoming mainstream in how people, communities, and governments make decisions and it will lead to the overturning of truth (proven right and wrong) for the mainstreaming of the most vile behavior and private agendas. It is all done in the name of "inclusiveness" and "coexistence".

Many Christians have bought into this psychological con job and their children will pay the price of their deception. They will not figure it out till it is much too late. Those who plead for coexistence will seek to literally eradicate anyone who believes or practices anything different from their profane behavior. It is the strategy of a fifth column. Gullible and unscriptural Christians have bought it hook line and sinker. What is the fix? How do we cure Christians of this pathological gullibility? We need to get back to scriptural teaching and evaluate how it reinforces the natural God given patterns of the universe, of life, and reproduction of the Image of God!

Christians are leaving the Church in the name of Evolution and for other reasons because the Church has ceased to give factual, real, and self-verifying truths straight from nature and the Bible that sync up and establish themselves as truth over and over again. People can smell the con of psychobabble coming from the pulpits. College professors steeped in atheism can easily point out the contradictions of Christian erroneous teachings, which are unscriptural. It is easy for these college "educators" to overturn the faith of so many young people. How do we fix this? Start giving the real scriptural explanations that are undisputable. Stop using the terminology of the priesthood and start using scriptural language that gives its own definitions in the scriptures.

We need to abandon oral traditions that do not conform to the written scriptures. We need to forsake observances that were not observed by the author and finisher of our faith. Anyone that can convince themselves that they are Christian, yet ignore all those Holy Days that Yeshua observed is simply deluding themselves. Anyone that can ignore the very Law that Yeshua said would never pass away is utterly confused. Anyone who can openly say Christ kept the Law so I wouldn't have to…has not read the Bible. Will we be held unaccountable for our passivity in the name of grace? What is the Christian expected by Christ to do?

2 Peter 3:18, But grow in grace, and in the knowledge of our Lord and Savior Jesus Christ. To him be glory both now and for ever. Amen.

Let's begin by examining the Holy Days that Yeshua observed and observes still today! Let's examine the very Holy Days in which Elijah pays a critical part for our restoration.

Why are there two sets of Holy Days in the Bible (Passover, Unleavened Bread,

First Fruits, then Trumpets, Atonement, and the Feast of Tabernacles) split by Pentecost (Shavuot) in the middle? Why did Yeshua observe these days and not observe other pagan days?

We must also ask why there is so much confusion about the end–times, the second coming of Yeshua, and how modern Christianity tries to fit the Holy Days into a flawed paradigm of what they signify prophetically and the sequence of their fulfillment.

> 1 Kings 18:21, And Elijah came unto all the people, and said, How long halt ye between two opinions? if the Lord be God, follow him: but if Baal, then follow him. And the people answered him not a word.

The role of the end-time Elijah is to present the world with a choice to love the truth or to love a lie. The establishment of the world will be encouraging all to apostatize from the truth in the name of love, peace and safety.

> 1 Thessalonians 5:3, For when they shall say, Peace and safety; then sudden destruction cometh upon them, as travail upon a woman with child; and they shall not escape.

The Antichrist will be demanding that people be tolerant of everything except the truth, while Elijah will be presenting the judgement of God for those who reject the light and truth of the Gospel. The seeds of the Antichrist's gospel will bear a terrible fruit and finally manifest itself in a worldwide oppression of anything that opposes the darkness of his lawlessness. In all respects, he will be against God, the Law of Moses, and natural God given laws that all things exist by. Where only God's image can be replicated by man and woman giving birth to a child, he will mandate against the sanctity of that singular way of reproducing. Where men are to fulfill a masculine role and women a feminine role, he will encourage a mixing of roles and an obscuring of God given natural roles of their appropriate sex. Where truth is clearly defined, he will obscure and deny the speaking of truth in the name of inclusiveness. All of these and more are an apostasy.

> 2 Thessalonians 2:3, Let no man deceive you by any means: for that day shall not come, except there come a falling away (Strong's #646) first, and that man of sin be revealed, the son of perdition; 4 Who opposeth and exalteth himself above all that is called God, or that is worshipped; so that he as God sitteth in the temple of God, shewing himself that he is God.

Tree of Knowledge of Good and Evil:	Tree of Life:
Dual in nature	Singular in nature
Unclean and mixture	Purity and no mixture
Mixture of flesh and spirit	Spirit only
Comes about by a lack of faith in the Word of YHWH	Comes about by faith in the Word of YHWH
Produces death, uncleanness, exile, corruption	Produces resurrection life, cleanness, return from exile, incorruption
Picture of separation and division	Picture of unity and singular faith
Fear	Love
Mixture of darkness and light	Pure light, no darkness
Darkened mirror that Paul refers to	Lighted mirror
Divided male and female	Unified male and female

What is amazing is that much of the church is already steeped in these deceptions in the name of love and inclusiveness. The church has been fed a spiritual and psychological con that tells them they are not good Christians if they don't accept lawlessness in the name of diversity.

Daniel 7:25, And he shall speak great words against the most High, and shall wear out the saints of the most High, and think to change times and laws: and they shall be given into his hand until a time and times and the dividing of time.

Much of those "diversities" are becoming law and are becoming a formalized rebellion against God and nature. Christians and Torah abiding Jews are being marginalized in the name of inclusiveness. Soon those formalized seeds of lawlessness will result in the outlawing of truth, the scriptures, and anything branded as intolerant. Yeshua, the Apostles, Paul, nor Elijah would be a welcome visitor in any of these chambers of government and in fact they would not be welcomed in the synagogues, nor the churches. This is, in fact, the state of the Christian Church today as well as the Jewish synagogue. Oral traditions are elevated against the written Word of God. Acceptance is valued more than truth. Silence is demanded in the place of the Gospel. Most Christians have been cowed into silence by small groups of radical lawless ones that use the law to sue and silence anyone who disagrees with them. They appear to actually be winning, but in reality, they are sowing the seeds of judgement against themselves. They think because they have not seen an immediate response from the Creator that they have His approval. God is only doing what He has always done. He is allowing us to sow the seeds of sin or righteousness and then He grants a space of time for those seeds to grow and manifest into their own fruits. Then judgment comes.

Ecclesiastes 8:11, Because sentence against an evil work is not executed speedily, therefore the heart of the sons of men is fully set in them to do evil.

As the day grows darker and believers in Christ are persecuted for standing for Christ, the judgment grows more likely and more severe.

Luke 18:7, And shall not God avenge his own elect, which cry day and night unto him, though he bear long with them? 8 I tell you that he will avenge them speedily. Nevertheless when the Son of man cometh, shall he find faith on the earth? 9 And he spake this parable unto certain which trusted in themselves that they were righteous, and despised others:

Yeshua knew this would happen to the His elect. We are to bear the same image as Yeshua. Just as Yeshua was persecuted and tortured in His final days of His earthly ministry, so will those that bear His image.

Luke 9:23, And he said to them all, If any man will come after me, let him deny himself, and take up his cross daily, and follow me.

Surprisingly this is God's plan for some of those who hold faith in His manifested name, Yeshua the Messiah. This certainly isn't something that an earthly minded, sensually and fleshly driven person would aspire to.

Revelation 6:11, And white robes were given unto every one of them; and it was said unto them, that they should rest yet for a little season, until their fellowservants also and their brethren, that should be killed as they were, should be fulfilled.

Sadly, the enlightenment of Christ will have left most of the world and they will be wholly following and worshiping the beast. Having conformed themselves to his image, they will act like beasts and seek to kill and destroy anyone who says anything different. Just as Yeshua was persecuted, the Apostles driven away, and Peter forced to deny Christ, this is likely the pattern and fractal that will play out in world events at the time of the Antichrist.

Matthew 26:39, And he went a little farther, and fell on his face, and prayed, saying, O my Father, if it be possible, let this cup pass from me: nevertheless not as I will, but as thou wilt. 40 And he cometh unto the disciples, and findeth them asleep, and saith unto Peter, <u>What, could ye not watch with me one hour?</u> 41 Watch and pray, that ye enter not into temptation: the spirit indeed is willing, but the flesh is weak.

Shockingly…this is God's plan. There is no way around it. Those looking for an escape may be surprised if and when we are expected to fulfill the same pattern and fractal as the Messiah and the Apostles. Just as Yeshua was expected to take on the imagery of the Seed in death, so also believers in His name are expected to do the same. Why? God needs and expects an accurate testimony of His will in the earth. God literally is waiting while faithful believers are being killed for their testimony of Yeshua and for keeping the Law of Moses. So much for the wealth and prosperity teaching of today's modern false teachers. Who wouldn't want the escape of a rapture from such a scenario? But is it a scripturally accurate outcome? While the church is proclaiming its righteousness, while being out of step with the scriptures in every regard, they declare they will escape because of grace. Meanwhile the accurate scriptural scenario is that Yeshua is about to spit the end-time church out of His mouth for their terrible state of mind and body. He doesn't sound like a groom waiting to welcome His favored bride. He sounds like a groom who is in distress over the state of His bride.

Revelation 3:14, And unto the angel of the church of the Laodiceans write; These things saith the Amen, the faithful and true witness, the beginning of the creation of God; 15 I know thy works, that thou art neither cold nor hot: I would thou wert cold or hot. 16 So then because thou art lukewarm, and neither cold nor hot, I will spue thee out of my mouth. 17 Because thou sayest, I am rich, and increased with goods, and have need of nothing; and knowest not that thou art wretched, and miserable, and poor, and blind, and naked:18 I counsel thee to buy of me gold tried in the fire, that thou mayest be rich; and white raiment, that thou mayest be clothed, and that the shame of thy nakedness do not appear; and anoint thine eyes with eyesalve, that thou mayest see. 19 As many as I love, I rebuke and chasten: be zealous therefore, and repent . 20 Behold, I stand at the door, and knock: if any man hear my voice, and open the door, I will come in to him, and will sup with him, and he with me. 21 To him that overcometh will I grant to sit with me in my throne, even as I also overcame, and am set down with my Father in his throne. 22 He that hath an ear, let him hear what the Spirit saith unto the churches.

What is the cure? Repent! Change your ways. Return to the truth of the scriptures. Stop apostatizing yourself from the truth of the scriptures. Just as the rabbinic scholars of Yeshua's time were so caught up in their own teachings and self-righteousness, so also is the church of today. We have spent so much time justifying our own superiority to the plain truth of the scriptures that we have set ourselves in opposition to the truths that God gave us. The church itself looks more like a corporation that has elevated its own beliefs and rules over and above the Law of God and has corrupted itself. Simply stated it has bought its own press. The result of this state of mind keeps the believer from accurately seeing him/herself as they actually are. It makes them deluded and self-satisfied. In the end, it keeps them from being able to perceive truth and respond to it. This is apostasy. How does God respond to this? He sends the Spirit of Elijah.

2 Kings 2:15, And when the sons of the prophets which were to view at Jericho saw him, they said, The spirit of Elijah doth rest on Elisha. And they came to meet him, and bowed themselves to the ground before him.

This answers why Yeshua said, "Elijah must first come" (Matthew 17:10, Mark 9:19, Malachi 4:1-6). He was not only speaking of how John the Baptist fulfilled this role, but how we must fulfill this role in partnership with Yeshua in the end-time. The Antichrist will think he has won. He will be given power to dominate for a short time, just as Pharaoh was given that leeway to do evil. Why? To glorify the Name of the Lord (YHWH), Yeshua the Messiah.

Exodus 5:2, And Pharaoh said, Who is the Lord, that I should obey his voice to let Israel go? I know not the Lord, neither will I let Israel go.

This is the same purpose that is accomplished through the Spirit of Elijah.

1 Kings 17:24, And the woman said to Elijah, Now by this I know that thou art a man of God, and that the word of the Lord in thy mouth is truth.

Elijah's confrontation with the false teachers of his day focuses on this very issue.

1 Kings 18:21, And Elijah came unto all the people, and said, <u>How long halt ye between two opinions? if the Lord be God, follow him: but if Baal, then follow him.</u> And the people answered him not a word...24 And call ye on the name of your gods, and <u>I will call on the name of the Lord</u>: and the God that answereth by fire, let him be God. And all the people answered and said, It is well spoken...27 And it came to pass at noon, that Elijah mocked them, and said, Cry aloud: for he is a god; either he is talking, or he is pursuing, or he is in a journey, or peradventure he sleepeth, and must be awaked...30 And Elijah said unto all the people, <u>Come near unto me.</u> And all the people came near unto him. And <u>he repaired the altar of the Lord that was broken down.</u> 31 And <u>Elijah took twelve stones, according to the number of the tribes of the sons of Jacob,</u> unto whom the word of the Lord came, saying, Israel shall be thy name:32 And <u>with the stones he built an altar in the name of the Lord</u>: and he made a trench about the altar, as great as would contain <u>two measures of seed</u>...36 And it came to pass at the time of the offering of the evening sacrifice, that Elijah the prophet came near, and said, Lord God of Abraham, Isaac, and of Israel, <u>let it be known this day that thou art God in Israel, and that I am thy servant, and that I have done all these things at thy word.</u> 37 Hear me, O Lord, hear me, <u>that this people may know that thou art the Lord God, and that thou hast turned their heart back again.</u> 38 Then the fire of the Lord fell,

and consumed the burnt sacrifice, and the wood, and the stones, and the dust, and licked up the water that was in the trench. 39 And <u>when all the people saw it, they fell on their faces: and they said, The Lord, he is the God; the Lord, he is the God</u>. 40 And Elijah said unto them, Take the prophets of Baal; let not one of them escape. And they took them: and Elijah brought them down to the brook Kishon, and slew them there.

What have we learned?

- The central problem is that the people are double minded.
- The central question is, "Who is God?".
- Elijah's response to this question is to "call upon the name of the Lord (YHWH)".
- Elijah calls the people near to him. He rebuilds the altar with the imagery (stones) of the 12 tribes of Israel and he does so in the "Name of the Lord (YHWH)".
- The altar and the sacrifice is doused with water and the trench filled with water is associated with "seed".
- Elijah asks God to manifest to all Israel that He only is God in Israel and that Elijah is His servant and that he has done these things by God's word.
- When God responds, and sends His fire to consume the sacrifice, the people respond just like Moses in Exodus 34! They bow and worship.

This whole chapter shows Elijah replaying the second giving of the Torah to Moses in Exodus 34 where God presents to Moses "the Name of the Lord" (the Messiah) with grace and mercy with the second set of tablets (stones) with the "same words" that were written in the first tablets.

> Exodus 34:5, And the <u>Lord descended in the cloud, and stood with him there, and proclaimed the name of the Lord</u>. 6 And the <u>Lord passed by before him, and proclaimed, The Lord, The Lord God, merciful and gracious, longsuffering, and abundant in goodness and truth,</u> 7 Keeping mercy for thousands, forgiving iniquity and transgression and sin, and that will by no means clear the guilty; visiting the iniquity of the fathers upon the children, and upon the children's children, unto the third and to the fourth generation. 8 And <u>Moses made haste, and bowed his head toward the earth, and worshipped</u>.

Just as Moses fulfilled the pattern of death and resurrection and served as the administrator of condemnation and death, so also Elijah fulfills his fractal. He fulfills the imagery of the administration of grace and mercy by calling the people back in repentance and "drawing them near" to the true God of Israel. Like it or not Moses had to fulfill his pattern, just as Elijah fulfills his pattern, so also Yeshua fulfilled both patterns to "fulfill all righteousness".

Matthew 3:14, But John forbad him, saying, I have need to be baptized of thee, and comest thou to me? 15 And Jesus answering said unto him, <u>Suffer it to be so now: for thus it becometh us to fulfil all righteousness</u>. Then he suffered him. 16 And Jesus, when he was baptized, went up straightway out of the water: and, lo, the heavens were opened unto him, and he saw the Spirit of God descending like a dove, and lighting upon him:

Just as they had to fulfill their pattern and fractal, so must we. Take notice what happens to Elijah and to Moses in regard to the people.

- I Kings 18:30, 30 And Elijah said unto all the people, <u>Come near unto me</u>. And all the people came near unto him.
- Exodus 34:30, And when Aaron and all the children of Israel saw Moses, behold, the skin of his face shone; and they were afraid to come nigh him. 31 And Moses called unto them; and <u>Aaron and all the rulers of the congregation returned unto him</u>: and Moses talked with them. 32 And <u>afterward all the children of Israel came nigh</u>: and he gave them in commandment all that the Lord had spoken with him in mount Sinai.

The Spirit of Elijah calls to all who are willing to recognize the manifest Name of the Lord (Yeshua YHWH), the administrator of the Law of Moses under the administration of Grace and abundant mercy (resurrection life).

Just as Elijah fulfilled this pattern with ancient Israel, it will be fulfilled again in the end-time. The goal is for the people to be restored to the truth of the Law of Moses, for all the tribes of Israel to be gathered by and to Elijah for the restoration of true scriptural worship of the Name of the Lord (YHWH), Yeshua the Messiah. Just as God is presenting truth to the world, the Antichrist will produce a counterfeit that will deceive the nations.

Revelation 13:12, And he exerciseth all the power of the first beast before him, and causeth the earth and them which dwell therein to worship the first beast, whose deadly wound was healed. 13 And <u>he doeth great wonders, so that he maketh fire come down from heaven on the earth in the sight of men</u>, 14 And <u>deceiveth them that dwell on the earth by the means of those miracles which he had power to do in the sight of the beast; saying to them that dwell on the earth, that they should make an image to the beast</u>, which had the wound by a sword, and did live.

The choice is simple, truth or a lie, YHWH or Baal. The Antichrist or the Spirit of Elijah. Conformity or scriptural truth and accuracy. The Image of Christ or the Image of the Beast. The mark of God or the mark of the beast. The world has made itself ripe to manifest the pinnacle of lawlessness. It will be popular to do all the wrong things. Doing the right things will be made a great burden. So, if you think prosperity doctrines and escaping the end-times is scripturally accurate, you might be ripe for the doctrines of Antichrist. Every seed will manifest its appropriate fruit, to think we can escape this basic rule of nature may leave you devastated and disillusioned.

Luke 18:8, I tell you that he will avenge them speedily. Nevertheless, when the Son of man cometh, shall he find faith on the earth?

Those so steeped in an unscriptural teaching of "law vs grace" will be ripe for the Antichrist. Lawlessness is always confronted by Lawfulness. This pattern repeats itself over and over again in Israel and in the scriptures.

16 THEY SHALL BE ONE FLESH (IMAGE)

Some have stated that the spring Holy Days are a prophecy of the First Coming of the Messiah and that the fall Holy Days are about the Second Coming of the Messiah. At the conclusion of this study you may find that this premise is not completely focused though it may be accurate. We will attempt to bring some additional clarity to this idea. Unfortunately, just as the modern church attempts to make all the Levitical sacrifices about the Messiah, they also attempt to make all the Holy Days about the Messiah. The modern church is inherently blind to the one that the Messiah redeems and how she appears in the prophetic patterns and fractals of God.

Let's briefly detail what the modern church believes about the Holy Days:
- Passover–Death of the Messiah
- Unleavened Bread–Removal of Sin
- Pentecost/Shavuot–Birth of the church
- Trumpets–Day of Blowing Trumpets–Stand in judgment before God–Call to repentance
- Atonement–Yeshua enters into the Holy of Holies with His blood covering our sins
- Feast of Tabernacles–picture of the Millennium after the return of the Messiah and God tabernacling with man
- Last Great Day- White Throne Judgement

It is possible that these meanings have been derived less from a scriptural viewpoint and more from a traditional church paradigm. In other words, the church is reading our current understanding into the scriptures, instead of deriving a scripturally accurate paradigm from what the scriptures actually do say.

To be unwilling to consider that our current understanding may be partial or even flawed will certainly keep us from growing in accurate understanding of the scriptures. We must ask ourselves at what point we are willing to consider that we need to correct our paradigm to ensure it conforms to actual scriptural patterns and symbols, instead of applying the symbols we would like these days to refer to.

So, let us begin by reaffirming that those things that appear below are patterns and images of heavenly realities and will instruct us in truths that are currently beyond our understanding. This is the fundamental truth of our existence, that though all things are set before us to observe, our ability to understand what they mean is hampered by our ability to see the accurate meaning and connection of the symbols. God is always talking with us, but the question is if we are listening to Him.

> Mark 4:20, And these are they which are sown on good ground; such as hear the word, and receive it, and bring forth fruit, some thirtyfold, some sixty, and some an hundred. 21 And he said unto them, Is a candle brought to be put under a bushel, or under a bed? and not to be set on a candlestick? 22 For there is nothing hid, which shall not be manifested; neither was any thing kept secret, but that it should come abroad.

This parable about "hearing" is presented to us again in the fractal of seed and then fruit (harvest). What you are willing and able to hear is indicative of the quality of ground the seed of the Kingdom of God is planted in and will determine the quality of your harvest.

Let us also reaffirm that the objective of the Messiah is to restore the Image of God that was given to Adam which was then broken in Genesis 3. This is the fundamental goal of the Messiah communicated by the scriptures from start to finish.

> Genesis 1:27, So God created man in his own image, in the Image of God created he him; male and female created he them.

God's purpose in Genesis 1 was to manifest His image in all things. It began with the manifestation of His light on day 1 and culminated in the manifestation of His image on the 7th day Sabbath. This image was broken by Adam and Eve's sin and they no longer produced God's image, but only their own flawed and fallen image.

> Genesis 5:1, This is the book of the generations of Adam. In the day that God created man, in the likeness of God made he him; 2 Male and female created he them; and blessed them, and called their name Adam, in the day when they were created. 3 And Adam lived an hundred and thirty years, and begat a son in his own likeness, and after his image; and called his name Seth:

The true likeness and Image of God was lost in Genesis 3 and could only be restored via the promised seed (the Messiah).

Genesis 3:15, And I will put <u>enmity between thee and the woman, and between thy seed and her seed; it shall bruise thy head, and thou shalt bruise his heel</u>. 16 Unto the woman he said, I will greatly multiply thy sorrow and thy conception; in sorrow thou shalt bring forth children; and thy desire shall be to thy husband, and he shall rule over thee.

In the first chapters of Genesis, we see the breaking of the Image of God, its condemnation, judgment, decree of death, exile, and uncleanness. The rest of the scriptures detail the redemption, ascension, mercy, decree of resurrected life, restoration, and cleansing of the Image of God through the work of the promised seed, the Messiah, the Second Adam, the heavenly male, the Image of God, and the manifest Name of YHWH. This interplay of male and female and duality continues in all the images and fractals of this Tree of the Knowledge of Good and Evil (the manifest universe).

Genesis 3:17, Because thou hast hearkened unto the voice of thy wife, and hast eaten of the tree, of which I commanded thee, saying, Thou shalt not eat of it: cursed is the ground for thy sake; in sorrow shalt thou eat of it all the days of thy life;

The critical difference between this tree and the Tree of Life is their essential nature. The Tree of the Knowledge of Good and Evil is dual (male and female) in nature.

Genesis 2:8, And the Lord God planted a garden eastward in Eden; and there he put the man whom he had formed. 9 And out of the ground made the Lord God to grow every tree that is pleasant to the sight, and good for food; the Tree of Life also in the midst of the garden, and the tree of knowledge of good and evil.

It is divided in nature and those who consume its seed will also manifest a divided nature (male and female separately). The Tree of Life (the Messiah) is singular in nature and depicts a unity of male and female (in consummation of marriage). Hence the Tree of the Knowledge of Good and Evil depicts separation, exile, and death, while the Tree of Life depicts unity, inclusion, and resurrection life.

Tree of Knowledge of Good and Evil:	Tree of Life:
Dual in nature	Singular in nature
Unclean and mixture	Purity and no mixture
Mixture of flesh and spirit	Spirit only
Comes about by a lack of faith in the Word of YHWH	Comes about by faith in the Word of YHWH
Produces death, uncleanness, exile, corruption	Produces resurrection life, cleanness, return from exile, incorruption
Picture of separation and division	Picture of unity and singular faith
Fear	Love
Mixture of darkness and light	Pure light, no darkness
Darkened mirror that Paul refers to	Lighted mirror
Divided male and female	Unified male and female

The purpose of the Messiah, the seed of the woman, is to rectify this duality (divided nature) and cause it to ascend into a unity with the Messiah in the bridal chamber. Then the exiled and unclean woman (Leviticus 15) becomes clean by receiving her new covering in the Messiah. This is not a discussion of cultural custom but of scriptural symbolism. Those that are unwilling to follow the prophetic patterns and fractals of scripture in the name of political correctness ensure that they will progress no further.

2 Timothy 3:7, Ever learning, and never able to come to the knowledge of the truth. 8 Now as Jannes and Jambres withstood Moses, so do these also resist the truth: men of corrupt minds, reprobate concerning the faith. 9 But they shall proceed no further: for their folly shall be manifest unto all men, as their's also was.

All of the scriptures and prophetic patterns we find therein will teach us about the healing and restoration of this divided and broken image into one of unity and ascension. Let us use this as our paradigm for reviewing the Holy Days and see where the scriptural patterns lead us.

We must ask ourselves the critical question, what good is the second coming of the Messiah (as He judges the world) if He has not changed and restored our image? If He does not come in each of us, but only near, we will find ourselves in judgment and under condemnation. Our torment would only continue. What benefit is there in having the spring Holy Days be only about the Messiah's first coming and the fall Holy Days be only about His second coming? What about the unclean woman (fallen manifested universe)?

Let us not forget that generation, of His beloved Israel, that rejected Him as the Messiah and ended up being condemned and destroyed by the Romans in 70 AD. What is to say that the same fate does not await us at the second coming? Are we more righteous than they? No. We are as flawed and broken as they were and in as much need of a redeemer as they were. Are we more righteous because we have accepted Him? No. We are still sinners, broken and disobedient. Our redemption lies not only in the Messiah coming to the earth once again, but in His coming in us! Only then are we healed, restored, and alive! Redemption begins in the heart and then manifests itself outwardly.

It is most likely that the Biblically ordained fulfillment of the Biblical Holy Days that all believers should observe occur prophetically as follows.

THE LIKELY PROPHETIC FULFILLMENT OF THE HOLY DAYS:
- Passover–Death of the Messiah
- Feast of First-Fruits-Resurrection of the Messiah
- Feast of Unleavened Bread–Removal of sin & baptism of believers on the Last Day of Unleavened Bread (just as initially fulfilled by Israel crossing the Red Sea on Unleavened the Last Day of Unleavened Bread).
- Day of Pentecost/Shavuot–Presentation of the True Image of God (Shekinah Glory upon the Apostles' heads/the Divine Utterance of tongues, and the preaching of the message of repentance). 3,000 come to repentance in contrast to the 3,000 who died during the day of worship of the Golden Calf. This may have a dual fulfillment in the Final Week of Daniel's 70 weeks prophecy, where Yeshua pours out His spirit on Believers giving them irrefutable testimony of His saving work.
- Feast of Trumpets– "The day and hour that no one knows." An idiom of the time period of the first century church refering to the Feast of Yom Teruah. This is very possibly the Pre-Wrath Rapture (Occurs at the Sixth Seal) that occurs after 6 years during the final week of Daniel's 70-week prophecy. Half of "Believers" will be worthy and half will not be worthy and have to endure a year of God's wrath. Those that are worthy are raptured and spend the next year in heaven while God's wrath is poured out.
- Day of Atonement–At the conclusion of the year of wrath at the end of the 7th year of Daniels final week, Yeshua and the Saints return to the Earth for Armageddon.
- Feast of Tabernacles–The Wedding Feast of the Lamb.

17 ELIJAH VS JEZEBEL (LIGHT VS DARKNESS)

The current explanation of the spring and fall Holy Days being about the first and second coming of the Messiah is incomplete to the purpose of the seed of the woman (the Messiah). Our understanding of the Holy Days needs to incorporate a fuller comprehension of the redemptive work of the Messiah on the broken Image of God and our restoration and ascension back to the Garden of Eden. Our explanation of the spring and fall Holy Days needs to elaborate on the division of the male and female (the breaking of the Image of God) and their restoration by the work of the Messiah (the seed of the woman).

To this end, a complete reading of the following is recommended:
- Leviticus 23
- Deuteronomy 16
- Numbers 28 and 29
- Numbers 9

These chapters will give you an intensive look at the Feasts of the Lord. These are the same feasts and Holy Days that Yeshua observes. As a follower of Yeshua, you should be observing these very same days to absorb the meaning encompassed in them. Notice they are not Jewish feasts, they are called, "the feasts of the Lord".

Leviticus 23:2, Speak unto the children of Israel, and say unto them, Concerning the feasts of the Lord, which ye shall proclaim to be holy convocations, even these are my feasts.

Those that wish to look for prophetic and divinely inspired meaning in any holidays or observances that are not detailed in the Torah of the scriptures will likely find themselves looking at meaningless man made traditions and will proceed no further.

It is highly recommended that you begin to keep the same days that Yeshua the Messiah observed so that you may be found in His image. They are detailed in the above listed chapters and are the divinely communicated images and patterns that will lead us to greater truth. By design prophetic fractals and patterns are repeated in all aspects of nature and the events of life. This is how we can affirm their truthfulness.

Now we must ask the following question: "Why does the advent of the promised "seed of the woman" (the Messiah) appear neither at the beginning of the fall of man nor at the conclusion of the 7,000 years of man…to work the redemptive imagery?"

2 Peter 3:8, But, beloved, be not ignorant of this one thing, that one day is with the Lord as a thousand years, and a thousand years as one day.

Why does the Messiah (the Image of God) appear on the millennial fourth day of the week? Perhaps the creation week will give us some insight on the meaning of the fourth day.

Genesis 1:16, And God made two great lights; the greater light to rule the day, and the lesser light to rule the night: he made the stars also. 17 And God set them in the firmament of the heaven to give light upon the earth, 18 And to rule over the day and over the night, and to divide the light from the darkness: and God saw that it was good. 19 And the evening and the morning were the fourth day.

In the creation week, God caused His light to be manifest on day 1. This light is not the same light that is discussed in Genesis 1:14. On day 4 we see the two great lights are brought forth, one for the day and one for the night to give light upon the earth.

God's goal in Genesis 1 is to manifest His image; it begins with the manifestation of His light on day 1 and concludes on the 7th day Sabbath with the manifestation of that light in His manifested image of Adam and Eve. It is mid–week (day 4) that pictures the interaction of the sun and the moon to bring light upon the earth. We see throughout the creation week the presentation of singularities that are split into dualities.

Creation Week:
- Day 1– Light divided from Darkness, day from night.
- Day 2–Firmament (Heaven) divides the waters above and below the firmament.
- Day 3–Waters divided from the land and seeds are brought forth
- Day 4–Two great lights appointed, one for the day (sun) and one for the night (moon) to divide light from darkness.
- Day 5–Creatures brought forth in the waters and creatures brought forth in the firmament of heaven (seeds created, not formation).

- Day 6–Man brought forth in His image, male and female (seed created, not image formation).
- Day 7– Manifestation of seeds (formation–seeds are watered, grow and manifest images, flesh).
  - Genesis 2:3, And God blessed the seventh day, and sanctified it: because that in it he had rested from all his work which God created and made…5 And <u>every plant of the field before it was in the earth, and every herb of the field before it grew: for the Lord God had not caused it to rain upon the earth, and there was not a man to till the ground</u>. 6 But there went up a mist from the earth, and watered the whole face of the ground. 7 And the <u>Lord God formed man of the dust of the ground,</u> and breathed into his nostrils the breath of life; and <u>man became a living soul</u>.

Day	Imagery
1	Light–day/Night
2	Water/Water
3	Water/land–seed
4	Light–sun/moon
5	Water creatures/Air creatures
6	God's image and earth creatures–Male & Female
7	Manifestation of seeds via formation of images/flesh

Each day is presented as a duality starting from a singularity, light. The mixture of these dualities brings forth the manifestation of the images of God with their watering and breath upon the 7th day Sabbath of Rest. The plants created upon day 3 do not grow until day 7. The creatures created on day 5 are in seed form (DNA) and receive their formation and names on day 7 (Genesis 2:19).

Man is created on day 6 in the Image of God in seed form (DNA) and does not have the breath of life until the 7th day Sabbath, when he is then formed and receives breath from the Lord God (YHWH). We cannot miss the interplay of the dualities presented in the creation week, nor can we miss the significance that they will play through the manifest creation of His universe and His images throughout time. We should be able to see the connections between the symbols and images presented in this week.

Light (Day)	Darkness (Night)
Water above	Water below
Water	Earth
Sun	Moon
Water creatures	Air creatures
Male	Female
Seed (creation)	Manifestation (Formation)
Singular and united	Divided and dual
Unity	Division
Breath in	Breath out
Day	Night
Right	Left
Rest	Motion
Faith	Unbelief
Clean	Unclean
Ascended	Descended
Spirit	Flesh
Tree of Life	Tree of the Knowledge of Good and Evil

Just as each day of the creation week has a singularity that is separated into a duality, so also Adam, who is first created a singularity, both male and female, is then separated on the seventh day into male and female.

Genesis 2:21, And the Lord God caused a deep sleep to fall upon Adam, and he slept: and he took one of his ribs, and closed up the flesh instead thereof; 22 And the rib, which the Lord God had taken from man, made he a woman, and brought her unto the man. 23 And Adam said, This is now bone of my bones, and flesh of my flesh: she shall be called woman, because she was taken out of man. 24 Therefore shall a man leave his father and his mother, and shall cleave unto his wife: and they shall be one flesh. 25 And they were both naked, the man and his wife, and were not ashamed.

We can assume that the division we see in Adam from unified male and female to divided male and female is a prototypical separation that can also be applied to all of the events that occurred in the first 6 days of creation. The concept of seed then manifestation is borne out by the patterns of the Bible and nature. Just as all things were separated in Days 1-6, Adam is separated from all animals that are given names and they are all deemed as being incapable as being a "help-meet" for Adam (Genesis 2:18-25). Once God had determined it was not good from man to be alone, God first brings forth the animals and every living creature. Once they are found to be unsuitable for Adam, God brings Eve forth from Adam (1 Corinthians 11:7-9)

Days 1–6	Day 7
Creation and seed (Adam)	Formation and manifestation of images (Eve)

We see that the Apostle Paul affirms this understanding!

1 Corinthians 15:38, But God giveth it a body as it hath pleased him, and to every seed his own body.

The fractal of male and female separation that occurred in days 1–6 also occurs in Adam on day 7. This separation is presented in tandem with the presentation of the Tree of the Knowledge of Good and Evil (duality) and the Tree of Life (singularity).

Genesis 2:8, And the Lord God planted a garden eastward in Eden; and there he put the man whom he had formed. 9 And out of the ground made the Lord God to grow every tree that is pleasant to the sight, and good for food; the Tree of Life also in the midst of the garden, and the tree of knowledge of good and evil. . . 15 And the Lord God took the man, and put him into the garden of Eden to dress it and to keep it. 16 And the Lord God commanded the man, saying, Of every tree of the garden thou mayest freely eat:17 But of the Tree of the Knowledge of Good and Evil, thou shalt not eat of it: for in the day that thou eatest thereof thou shalt surely die. 18 And the Lord God said, It is not good that the man should be alone; I will make him an help meet for him.

Notice this presentation of the two trees and the instruction not to eat of the

Tree of the Knowledge of Good and Evil occurs while Eve is still one with Adam. In conjunction with the instruction regarding the two trees and the curse, the first "not good" is stated by God in relation to man being alone and the subsequent need for Eve to be separated from Adam!

We see that both of the trees, one representing life and the other representing death, exist in the perfect Garden of Eden before the entering of sin into the world! Do not hurry past this significant fact.

Remember that all things manifested below are images of heavenly things and should be teaching us truth. Both trees are presented and then divided by whether you can eat them (make them one flesh with the eater) and what the outcome will be if eaten; life or death. They are separated just as everything else was during the creation week. On the 7th day Sabbath we see the separation of the two trees and the separation of Adam and Eve. These two separations are no less significant than those other separations or divisions that occurred on days 1 through 6!

The pattern of the original oneness and then separation (duality) of all things during the creation week into a male (above) and a female (below) needs to be applied to the Holy Days. This will help us understand why Yeshua came on the fourth day, midway through the 7,000-year period. We need to remember what occurred on the fourth day and how the end goal was to bring light upon the earth.

> Genesis 1:14, And God said, <u>Let there be lights in the firmament of the heaven to divide the day from the night</u>; and let them be for signs, and for seasons, and for days, and years:15 And let them be for lights in the firmament of the heaven <u>to give light upon the earth</u>: and it was so. 16 And God made two great lights; the greater light to rule the day, and the lesser light to rule the night: he made the stars also. 17 And God set them in the firmament of the heaven to give light upon the earth, 18 And to rule over the day and over the night, and to divide the light from the darkness: and God saw that it was good. 19 And the evening and the morning <u>were the fourth day</u>.

On the fourth day, God is manifesting light upon and for the earth. The two lights are meant to divide day and night and divide light from darkness. As we have already seen, this duality of light is male (sun/day) and female (moon/night). The goal of the creation week was to manifest God's light and cause it to manifest in His images.

It is brought forth in a unity on day 1 of creation and then split into a duality on day 4 so that seeds and then their manifest images can be brought forth on the 7th day Sabbath. The light is not in the manifest universe at first, then it is brought forth. It is brought forth in the firmament (heaven) and then is divided into lights (sun/moon) so that it may be brought forth in living images on the earth.

We cannot over emphasize the importance of the previous chapter and that the creation week is really the manifestation week of God's presence through His images!

This happens through a singularity (light/life) that is made into dualities that manifest themselves in images on the 7th day Sabbath. God is manifesting His images in all things. It is through this interplay between the sun and the moon, that light is brought to the earth and causes God to manifest His images. It begins with light and through division ends with manifest images.

The internalization of light cannot happen without day 4 of the creation week. Light moves progressively from above to below. We asked the question of what benefit the coming of the Messiah will have for the sinner if He only comes near you and does not come within you. If the Messiah, the seed, only comes next to you and does not come within you and fix your broken image, you will find yourself under His judgment and not under His mercy. The seed without dying cannot multiply His image in you.

John 12:23, And Yeshua answered them, saying, The hour is come, that the Son of man should be glorified. 24 Verily, verily, I say unto you, Except a corn of wheat fall into the ground and die, it abideth alone: but if it die, it bringeth forth much fruit.

Progression of light in Genesis:
- Above to below, outward to inward
- Manifestation of the singular light of God–universal–day 1
- Waters divided from waters by the firmament (heaven)–day 2
- Earth divided from waters, seeds (seed/DNA) are created–day 3
- Light divided from darkness–division of light into sun (male, day) and moon (female, night)–firmament of heaven over the earth–day 4
- Water and air creatures (but not earth creatures–above (air) and below (sea), but not middle–earth (seed/DNA) (there is no mention of the sex of the creatures)–day 5
- Earth creatures and Image of God (seed/DNA) (only herb and trees bearing seeds are to be eaten, and the sex is specified for the creatures/images)–day 6
- All seeds receive a body–mixture of earth (female) and water (male) (formation)–day 7 (1 Corinthians 15:38, But God giveth it a body as it hath pleased him, and to every seed his own body)

Genesis 2:5, And every plant of the field before it was in the earth, and every herb of the field before it grew: for the Lord God had not caused it to rain upon the earth, and there was not a man to till the ground. 6 But there went up a mist from the earth, and watered the whole face of the ground. 7 And the Lord God formed man of the dust of the ground, and breathed into his nostrils the breath of life; and man became a living soul. 8 And the Lord God planted a garden eastward in Eden; and there he put the man whom he had formed.

Items of note about the 7ᵗʰ day Sabbath:
- Mist (water) comes out from the earth on the 7ᵗʰ day Sabbath.
- Man becomes a singularity with formation.

- God goes into man via His breath (man is the Image of God, man is not his own image, man projects God).
- Woman comes out from the man on the 7th day and their new fleshly union begins.
- All seeds receive formation (image/flesh).

On days 1 through 6, we see division into male and female, and then on day 7, the Sabbath, we see the formation of all images/flesh for all seeds through the union of earth (female) and water (male). Adam is created a singularity, both male and female, but is then divided like all of the rest of manifestation/creation.

Genesis 1:26, And God said, Let us make man in our image, after our likeness: and let them have dominion over the fish of the sea, and over the fowl of the air, and over the cattle, and over all the earth, and over every creeping thing that creepeth upon the earth. 27 So God created man in his own image, in the Image of God created he him; male and female created he them.

We must ask, is Adam in Genesis 1:26 male and female? Or does the pattern of the creation week hold true and Adam is created a singularity (male as a unified male and female) like the rest of creation? "In the Image of God created he him; male and female created he them" may be indicating that Adam was created as a male and that the rest of the earth creatures were created male and female. It could also be clarifying that Adam was created a male but was in fact an ascended male, a unity of male and female, as you would see a man and a woman unified in the bridal chamber.

This verse in Genesis 1:26 is either clarifying how the Image of God, man, is different from the rest of the earth creatures created on day 6 by being an ascended male (unified male and female) while the other creatures are separated male and female, or it is stating that the Image of God is a male and this ascended male is both male and female in a singularity. The other creatures need no separation of the male and the female after formation of their bodies on the 7th day Sabbath, but man does require this separation as we see in Genesis 2. In Genesis 2 Adam is formed and is truly still a singularity. Even though he is in the Garden of Eden it is clear that there are no other living creatures with him. He is totally alone.

Genesis 2:18, And the Lord God said, It is not good that the man should be alone; I will make him an help meet for him. 19 And out of the ground the Lord God formed every beast of the field, and every fowl of the air; and brought them unto Adam to see what he would call them: and whatsoever Adam called every living creature, that was the name thereof. 20 And Adam gave names to all cattle, and to the fowl of the air, and to every beast of the field; but for Adam there was not found an help meet for him. 21 And the Lord God caused a deep sleep to fall upon Adam, and he slept: and he took one of his ribs, and closed up the flesh instead thereof; 22 And the rib, which the Lord

God had taken from man, made he a woman, and brought her unto the man. 23 And Adam said, This is now bone of my bones, and flesh of my flesh: she shall be called woman, because she was taken out of man. 24 Therefore shall a man leave his father and his mother, and shall cleave unto his wife: and they shall be one flesh. 25 And they were both naked, the man and his wife, and were not ashamed.

Items of note on the first 7th day Sabbath:
- Man is truly alone in the Garden.
- There are not even creatures formed yet.
- When creatures are formed, and named they cannot serve as Adam's help meet.
- Man receives a name at the same time as the creatures.
- The Lord God separates Adam from a singularity (unified male and female) into a duality (separated male and female).
- The goal of separated male and female is to become unified and one flesh (ascended unified male and female).
- Water is drawn out of the earth, just as the Messiah comes from the bosom of the Father. This process brings about formation and manifestation.
   - John 1:18, No man hath seen God at any time, the only begotten Son, which is in the bosom of the Father, he hath declared him.
- Just as the light is alone on day 1, so also is Adam at the beginning of the 7th day Sabbath.

This goal of union through the redemptive seed is depicted in Genesis 1–3 and reiterated in our joining to the Messiah.

1 Corinthians 6:13, Meats for the belly, and the belly for meats: but God shall destroy both it and them. Now the body is not for fornication, but for the Lord; and the Lord for the body. 14 And God hath both raised up the Lord, and will also raise up us by his own power. 15 Know ye not that your bodies are the members of Christ? shall I then take the members of Christ, and make them the members of an harlot? God forbid. 16 What? know ye not that he which is joined to an harlot is one body? for two, saith he, shall be one flesh. 17 But he that is joined unto the Lord is one spirit.

Our redemption by the Messiah from a broken image to a restored Image of God is depicted as the union of male and female into one flesh and one body. This same fractal is applied to our union with the promised seed, the Messiah, as becoming one spirit, just as a man and a woman become one flesh.

Messianic seed and manifestation symbols:
- Spirit–heavenly and ascended male (unified male and female in the bridal chamber)

o Ephesians 4:7, But unto every one of us is given grace according to the measure of the gift of Christ. 8 Wherefore he saith, When he ascended up on high, he led captivity captive, and gave gifts unto men. 9 (Now that he ascended, what is it but that he also descended first into the lower parts of the earth? 10 He that descended is the same also that ascended up far above all heavens, that he might fill all things.)

• Flesh–fallen and exiled, earthly and as the unclean woman of Leviticus 15 (man in his dual and broken state with a corrupted image). The flesh is said to be destined for destruction and the spirit is destined to be with the Lord (the promised seed), raised up and ascended. This is why things that are of this fallen and broken image are depicted as female and our ultimate resurrected state is as Sons of God (male).

o Romans 8:13, For if ye live after the flesh, ye shall die: but if ye through the Spirit do mortify the deeds of the body, ye shall live. 14 For as many as are led by the Spirit of God, they are the sons of God. 15 For ye have not received the spirit of bondage again to fear; but ye have received the Spirit of adoption, whereby we cry, Abba, Father.

o Romans 8:18, For I reckon that the sufferings of this present time are not worthy to be compared with the glory which shall be revealed in us. 19 For the earnest expectation of the creature waiteth for the manifestation of the sons of God. 20 For the creature was made subject to vanity, not willingly, but by reason of him who hath subjected the same in hope,

o 1 John 3:1, Behold, what manner of love the Father hath bestowed upon us, that we should be called the sons of God: therefore the world knoweth us not, because it knew him not. 2 Beloved, now are we the sons of God, and it doth not yet appear what we shall be: but we know that, when he shall appear, we shall be like him; for we shall see him as he is. 3 And every man that hath this hope in him purifieth himself, even as he is pure.

The state of glory and resurrection is depicted as:
• Male
• Sons
• Pure
• Spirit–unified and singular (unity of the faith)
• Freedom

Our current state is depicted as:
• Female
• Daughters
• Unclean/corruption
• Flesh and spirit–dual (division of unbelief)

- Bondage

Matthew 25:1, Then shall <u>the kingdom of heaven be likened unto ten virgins,</u> which took their lamps, and <u>went forth to meet the bridegroom.</u> 2 And <u>five of them were wise, and five were foolish.</u> 3 They that were foolish took their lamps, and took no oil with them:4 But the wise took oil in their vessels with their lamps. 5 While the bridegroom tarried, they all slumbered and slept. 6 And at midnight there was a cry made, Behold, the bridegroom cometh; go ye out to meet him. 7 Then all those virgins arose, and trimmed their lamps. 8 And the foolish said unto the wise, Give us of your oil; for our lamps are gone out. 9 But the wise answered, saying, Not so; lest there be not enough for us and you: but go ye rather to them that sell, and buy for yourselves. 10 And <u>while they went to buy, the bridegroom came; and they that were ready went in with him to the marriage: and the door was shut. 11 Afterward came also the other virgins, saying, Lord, Lord, open to us. 12 But he answered and said, Verily I say unto you, I know you not.</u> 13 Watch therefore, for ye know neither the day nor the hour wherein the Son of man cometh.

Items of note about the "ten virgins":
- They are virgins.
- They are unwed.
- They are female.
- They are dual (wise and foolish).
- They need the light of the promised seed within their vessels.
- They need redemption.
- They are depicted as being separated from their heavenly male and needing to join with Him in order to enter within and ascend with Him.
- All are depicted with a state of consciousness of sleeping and then being awakened by the announcement of the coming of the seed of the woman, the Messiah.
- All are required to respond to the announcement of the Messiah by going out to meet Him and only the wise do so, while the foolish go to buy oil to restart their lamps and do not go out to meet Him.
- The wise have lamps that are burning continuously, even while sleeping, and they go out to meet the Messiah.
- All of them have lamps, but the distinction between the wise and the foolish is whether they took oil with their lamps.
- We are seeing the presentation of the flesh (vessel) and the spirit (oil) again.

John 6:57, As the living Father hath sent me, and I live by the Father: <u>so he that eateth me, even he shall live by me</u>. 58 This is that bread which came down from heaven: not as your fathers did eat manna, and are dead: he that eateth of this bread shall live for ever. 59 These things said he in the synagogue, as he taught in Capernaum. 60 Many therefore of his disciples, when they had heard this, said, This is an hard saying; who can hear it? 61 When Yeshua knew in himself that his disciples murmured at it, he said unto them, Doth this offend you? 62 What and if ye shall see the Son of man ascend up where he was before? <u>63 It is the spirit that quickeneth; the flesh profiteth nothing: the words that I speak unto you, they are spirit, and they are life</u>.

Those with broken images are depicted as separated females (vessels) who need to join with their ascended male (oil) and enter within and share the light of God. Notice the lamps are distinguished by being full or empty, complete or lacking. The joining with the Messiah brings the light of God within them, above to below, outside to inside. The issue is whether their lamps are full or empty of oil and manifesting the light of God, the indwelling of the Messiah.

Luke 17:20, And when he was demanded of the Pharisees, when the kingdom of God should come, he answered them and said, <u>The kingdom of God cometh not with observation:21 Neither shall they say, Lo here! or, lo there! for, behold, the kingdom of God is within you</u>. 22 And he said unto the disciples, The days will come, when ye shall desire to see one of the days of the Son of man, and ye shall not see it.

The life and proof of life is hidden within the vessel (female).

John 7:37, In the last day, that great day of the feast, Yeshua stood and cried, saying, If any man thirst, let him come unto me, and drink. 38 <u>He that believeth on me, as the scripture hath said, out of his belly shall flow rivers of living water</u>. 39 (But this spake he of the Spirit, which they that believe on him should receive: for the Holy Ghost was not yet given; because that Yeshua was not yet glorified.) 40 Many of the people therefore, when they heard this saying, said, Of a truth this is the Prophet.

Like the first 7th day Sabbath, water (male) comes up out of the female (the ground), just like Yeshua offering the living waters to the Samaritan woman (John 4:7–16) and to all those who thirst. We cannot escape the fact that when Yeshua offered these waters to the Samaritan woman and she agreed that she would like to have those "living waters", He told her, "Go, call thy husband".

John 4:15, The woman saith unto him, Sir, give me this water, that I thirst not, neither come hither to draw. 16 Jesus saith unto her, Go, call thy husband, and come hither. 17 The woman answered and said, I have no husband. Jesus said unto her, Thou hast well said, I have no husband:

Yeshua is associating those living waters and redemption with the unity of the male and the female in a faithful covenant. These "living waters" are typified as "fire" and the Holy Spirit.

Luke 3:16, John answered, saying unto them all, I indeed baptize you with water; but one mightier than I cometh, the latchet of whose shoes I am not worthy to unloose: he shall baptize you with the Holy Ghost and with fire:

This association between living waters and fire (the Holy Spirit) and the female needing her husband (male) manifests itself in the concept of the broken Image of God being restored by the reunification of male (spirit) and female (manifested image–flesh) in the marriage chamber, making them one flesh (an ascended male or son of God). After Yeshua's resurrection, He promised that He would send His disciples that living water (fire) in a heavenly baptism that restores their image to a unified male (Shekinah Glory–cloven tongues of fire) and female (manifested Image of God).

Acts 2:3, And <u>there appeared unto them cloven tongues like as of fire, and it sat upon each of them</u>. 4 And they were all filled with the Holy Ghost, and began to speak with other tongues, as the <u>Spirit gave them Utterance</u>. 5 And there were dwelling at Jerusalem Jews, devout men, out of every nation under heaven.

Proof of life manifests itself in the divine Utterance (breath of God) and the manifestation of His fire, the Shekinah Glory, upon the vessel.

John 1:32, And John bare record, saying, I saw the Spirit descending from heaven like a dove, and it abode upon him. 33 And I knew him not: but he that sent me to baptize with water, the same said unto me, Upon whom thou shalt see the Spirit descending, and remaining on him, <u>the same is he which baptizeth with the Holy Ghost</u>. 34 And I saw, and bare record that this is the Son of God.

The oil (Spirit of the Messiah) is akin to the immersion of the believer in the womb and the waters of conception sent by the Messiah, just like the waters coming up from the earth to water the seeds on the first 7th day Sabbath.

John 7:38, He that believeth on me, as the scripture hath said, out of his belly shall flow rivers of living water.

The concept of being born again is tied to the woman bringing forth the waters of conception, first in sorrow and then in joy, seed then manifestation!

John 16:3, And these things will they do unto you, because they have not known the Father, nor me. 4 But these things have I told you, that when the time shall come, ye may remember that I told you of them. And these things I said not unto you at the beginning, because I was with you. 5 But now I go my way to him that sent me; and none of you asketh me, Whither goest thou? 6 But because I have said these things unto you, sorrow hath filled your heart. 7 Nevertheless I tell you the truth; <u>It is expedient for you that I go away: for if I</u>

go not away, the Comforter will not come unto you; but if I depart, I will send him unto you. 8 And when he is come, he will reprove the world of sin, and of righteousness, and of judgment:9 Of sin, because they believe not on me; 10 Of righteousness, because I go to my Father, and ye see me no more; 11 Of judgment, because the prince of this world is judged. 12 I have yet many things to say unto you, but ye cannot bear them now. 13 Howbeit when he, the Spirit of truth, is come, he will guide you into all truth: for he shall not speak of himself; but whatsoever he shall hear, that shall he speak: and he will shew you things to come. 14 He shall glorify me: for he shall receive of mine, and shall shew it unto you. 15 All things that the Father hath are mine: therefore said I, that he shall take of mine, and shall shew it unto you. 16 A little while, and ye shall not see me: and again, a little while, and ye shall see me, because I go to the Father. 17 Then said some of his disciples among themselves, What is this that he saith unto us, A little while, and ye shall not see me: and again, a little while, and ye shall see me: and, Because I go to the Father? 18 They said therefore, What is this that he saith, A little while? we cannot tell what he saith. 19 Now Yeshua knew that they were desirous to ask him, and said unto them, Do ye enquire among yourselves of that I said, A little while, and ye shall not see me: and again, a little while, and ye shall see me? 20 Verily, verily, I say unto you, That ye shall weep and lament, but the world shall rejoice: and ye shall be sorrowful, but your sorrow shall be turned into joy. 21 A woman when she is in travail hath sorrow, because her hour is come: but as soon as she is delivered of the child, she remembereth no more the anguish, for joy that a man is born into the world. 22 And ye now therefore have sorrow: but I will see you again, and your heart shall rejoice, and your joy no man taketh from you. 23 And in that day ye shall ask me nothing. Verily, verily, I say unto you, Whatsoever ye shall ask the Father in my name, he will give it you. 24 Hitherto have ye asked nothing in my name: ask, and ye shall receive, that your joy may be full. 25 These things have I spoken unto you in proverbs: but the time cometh, when I shall no more speak unto you in proverbs, but I shall shew you plainly of the Father. 26 At that day ye shall ask in my name: and I say not unto you, that I will pray the Father for you:27 For the Father himself loveth you, because ye have loved me, and have believed that I came out from God. 28 I came forth from the Father, and am come into the world: again, I leave the world, and go to the Father. 29 His disciples said unto him, Lo, now speakest thou plainly, and speakest no proverb. 30 Now are we sure that thou knowest all things, and needest not that any man should ask thee: by this we believe that thou camest forth from God. 31 Yeshua answered them, Do ye now believe? 32 Behold, the hour cometh, yea, is now come, that ye shall be scattered, every man to his own, and shall leave me alone: and yet I am not alone, because the Father is with me. 33 These things I have spoken unto you, that in me ye might have peace. In the world ye shall have tribulation: but be of good cheer; I have overcome the world.

Notice:
- The Kingdom of God is within you and is not observable outwardly.

- Belief on the "seed of the woman" causes waters to flow from the believer, just as water flowed up from the earth (mist) on the 7th day Sabbath and caused the manifestation of forms for all created seeds during days 1 through 6.

- The seed of the Kingdom (the Messiah Yeshua) causes God's Spirit (breath) to dwell within you (likened to the Shekinah Glory on the Tabernacle). This runs parallel to God giving Adam the breath of life in Genesis 2.

- The breath of God (the Spirit) gives you Utterance (the Word, the indwelling of the Messiah via His Spirit and consciousness).

- The seed of the Kingdom (the Messiah) baptizes the believer with the heavenly waters (the Holy Spirit) and causes growth from above to below and from outward to inward.

- The death and ascension of the seed (the Messiah) is likened to a birth of a male child into the world (bringing down the Spirit of God within the world and the believer). The seed must die in order for the work of multiplication and fruit (resurrection) to occur. The fractal of a seed death and manifestation of its fruit in resurrection occurs repeatedly in the scriptures.

- Our redemption is depicted as a union of male and female in conception of a child, just as we saw during the creation week.

- Our redemption is depicted as the growth of a hidden seed buried in death which emerges in fruit and resurrection life (spirit).

- Our redemption is depicted as water (spirit) rising up in ascension from the earth (our bodies).

- Our redemption is depicted as the sexual union of male and female in which fallen creation is the female needing redemption and receives it through the work of her divine (heavenly–spirit) male.

- Our redemption is depicted as the manifestation of an internal light and breath (Utterance via the Holy Spirit), the Shekinah Glory (cloven tongues of fire), as it was manifested over the Apostles at Shavuot (Pentecost).

Redemption is depicted as the ultimate unity of male and female in marriage. This is the same role of the Messiah Yeshua and the Church. Yeshua is the divine and ascended male (mind) and the redeemed Church is his female mate (body).

Ephesians 5:23, For the husband is the head of the wife, even as Christ is the head of the church: and he is the savior of the body.

Just as the husband fills the wife with his seed so that she can manifest his image, so also Yeshua does the same with His body (wife, believers).

Ephesians 4:7, But unto every one of us is given grace according to the measure of the gift of Christ. 8 Wherefore he saith, When he ascended up on high, he led captivity captive, and gave gifts unto men. 9 (Now that he ascended, what is it but that he also descended first into the lower parts of the earth? 10 He that descended is the same also that ascended up far above all heavens, that he might fill all things.)… 22 That ye <u>put off concerning the former conversation the old man</u>, which is corrupt according to the deceitful lusts; 23 And be renewed in the spirit of your mind; 24 And that <u>ye put on the new man</u>, which after God is created in righteousness and true holiness.

Clearly the redemption process is a divine union of Christ and the redeemed. That perfect unity is manifested as the perfect union of the mind of Christ (male) and His body (female).

Colossians 1:18, And he is the head of the body, the church: who is the beginning, the firstborn from the dead; that in all things he might have the preeminence.

The God ordained relationship shows the body properly in submission to the mind and the church properly in submission to Christ, and the female properly in submission to the male in unity and oneness. This is the true image of Christ and of God. When Adam and Eve sinned, this God given image was broken and thrown into disarray.

Genesis 3:6, Unto the woman he said, I will greatly multiply thy sorrow and thy conception; in sorrow thou shalt bring forth children; <u>and thy desire shall be to thy husband, and he shall rule over thee</u>.

This is showing a relationship where now the female (body) is in rebellion to the male (mind). The result is a duality and not a unity. We see the same disunity between Cain and Abel.

Genesis 4:7, If thou doest well, shalt thou not be accepted? and if thou doest not well, sin lieth at the door. And <u>unto thee shall be his desire, and thou shalt rule over him</u>.

This pattern is showing the upending of the natural order that God had intended between male and female and mind and body. As we have already stated being fallen and broken images, all of creation is manifesting itself as a fallen female. It doesn't matter if you are physically a male or female, all creation is the manifest female that needs to be restored by the Ascended Male (the Messiah Yeshua). Why is this important? This duality in the beginning is depicted as a conflict between Adam and Eve and male and female.

Genesis 3:12, And the man said, The woman whom thou gavest to be with me, she gave me of the tree, and I did eat.

In the time of Elijah, it is depicted as a confrontation between the one who comes as the Prophet of God (male) and Jezebel (Queen of Israel/female).

1 Kings 19:1, And Ahab told Jezebel all that Elijah had done, and withal

how he had slain all the prophets with the sword. 2 Then Jezebel sent a messenger unto Elijah, saying, So let the gods do to me, and more also, if I make not thy life as the life of one of them by to morrow about this time.

This same confrontation of truth vs. deception, lawfulness, vs. lawlessness, Elijah vs. Jezebel, true worship vs. pagan worship is the manifestation of the initial male/female conflict that was engendered by the sin of Adam and Eve. The seed that was sown by the Tree of the Knowledge of Good and Evil will finally manifest itself in the end-times.

Revelation 17:1, And there came one of the seven angels which had the seven vials, and talked with me, saying unto me, Come hither; I will shew unto thee the judgment of the great whore that sitteth upon many waters:2 With whom the kings of the earth have committed fornication, and the inhabitants of the earth have been made drunk with the wine of her fornication. 3 So he carried me away in the spirit into the wilderness: and I saw a woman sit upon a scarlet coloured beast, full of names of blasphemy, having seven heads and ten horns. 4 And the woman was arrayed in purple and scarlet colour, and decked with gold and precious stones and pearls, having a golden cup in her hand full of abominations and filthiness of her fornication:5 And upon her forehead was a name written, Mystery, Babylon The Great, The Mother Of Harlots And Abominations Of The Earth.

This end-time abomination is depicted as the ultimate rebellion against God that has been playing out throughout human history. She is portrayed as a Queen that rules via fornication. This fornication is simply an inappropriate God condemned sexual bodily union or an inappropriate mixing. It is the antithesis of what the purpose of the Messiah is typified as.

1 Corinthians 6:15, Know ye not that your bodies are the members of Christ? shall I then take the members of Christ, and make them the members of an harlot? God forbid. 16 What? know ye not that he which is joined to an harlot is one body? for two, saith he, shall be one flesh. 17 But he that is joined unto the Lord is one spirit.

Just as Jezebel was the sponsor of the Priests of Baal, the Great Whore of the end-times will once again be espousing the worship of pagan gods over the true God of Israel.

2 Kings 9:22, And it came to pass, when Joram saw Jehu, that he said, Is it peace, Jehu? And he answered, What peace, so long as the whoredoms of thy mother Jezebel and her witchcrafts are so many?

This end-time whore will fulfill the same imagery of the original Jezebel. She will set the righteous to be condemned. Just as the two-witnesses of God are presented in the book of Revelation, she will present two false witnesses to kill the servants of God.

1 Kings 21:7, And Jezebel his wife said unto him, Dost thou now govern the kingdom of Israel? arise, and eat bread, and let thine heart be merry: I will give thee the vineyard of Naboth the Jezreelite. 8 So she wrote letters in Ahab's name, and sealed them with his seal, and sent the letters unto the elders and to the nobles that were in his city, dwelling with Naboth. 9 And she wrote in the letters, saying, Proclaim a fast, and set Naboth on high among the people:10 And set two men, sons of Belial, before him, to bear witness against him, saying, Thou didst blaspheme God and the king. And then carry him out, and stone him, that he may die.

Every time the whore presents an upended counterfeit, God will produce a true image and a true witness.

Revelation 11:2, But the court which is without the temple leave out, and measure it not; for it is given unto the Gentiles: and the holy city shall they tread under foot forty and two months. 3 And I will give power unto my Two Witnesses, and they shall prophesy a thousand two hundred and threescore days, clothed in sackcloth. 4 These are the two olive trees, and the two candlesticks standing before the God of the earth.

There is no doubt that one of these two witness is someone(s) with the Spirit of Elijah. Just as Elijah confronted the wickedness of Jezebel, God will provide a witness against the manifestation of the Whore of Mystery Babylon. Scripturally we cannot get past the clearly associated link between a wicked ruler sponsoring lawless pagan worship being confronted by Elijah as he works to restore Israel to true worship and the Law of Moses.

For the church to ignore these correlations and the centrality of the Elijah's role then and now in regard to restoring the Law of Moses to all believers in the Messiah Yeshua is astounding. Meanwhile they declare "law vs. grace", highlighting how far gone the Church of God is from the truth of the scriptures.

The spirit of Laodicea is alive and well today. Elijah is foretold to come right before the Day of the Lord, standing at the door on Passover Eve, just like the Messiah depicts Himself outside Laodicea's door (Revelation 3:20). We have an inescapable conclusion. The church of Laodicea is the final generation of the church at the time of the end...when Elijah is promised to come and restore the Law of Moses...to all believers.

Opening the Door for Elijah
1) The Torah describes the night of Passover as leil shimurim, a "guarded night." It is the night when long ago G-d protected the Jews from the plague which slew all the Egyptian firstborn, and the night when G-d's protection over His chosen nation is most apparent. Opening the door expresses our trust in G-d's protection.
2) When opening the door, we take the opportunity to invite in the prophet

Elijah. Elijah is the one who visits the circumcision ceremony of every Jewish child, and testifies that the Jewish people are scrupulous regarding the mitzvah of circumcision. 2 Males were permitted to partake of the paschal offering only if they were circumcised. Thus, Elijah comes to the Seder to "testify" that all present are indeed circumcised.

Additionally, according to the Midrash, on the night prior to the Exodus, the Seder night, the entire Jewish male population circumcised themselves—in order to be eligible to eat from the paschal lamb. Thus the clear connection between circumcision, and Elijah, and Passover eve.

Cup of Elijah

1) There is an open question in the Talmud whether we are obligated to have four or five cups on the night of Passover. Since the issue was never resolved, we pour a fifth cup, but do not drink it.

After heralding the coming of the Messiah, one of Elijah's tasks will be to resolve all hitherto unanswered halachic questions. Thus, this fifth cup whose status is in doubt is dubbed "Elijah's Cup," in anticipation of the insight he will shed on the matter.

2) The four cups correspond to the four "expressions of redemption" promised by G-d:"I will take you out from the suffering of Egypt, and I will deliver you from their bondage; I will redeem you with an outstretched arm and with great judgments. I will take you to Myself as a nation . . ."3 The fifth cup corresponds to the fifth expression of redemption, which comes in the following verse: "I will bring you to the Land . . ." This expression, however, is an allusion to the future messianic redemption, which will be announced by Elijah. This is also why we do not drink, "enjoy," the fifth cup—as we have not yet experienced this redemption.

The timing of the pouring of the "Cup of Elijah" is also apropos, right before we start reading the Hallel, whose focus is on the future redemption (see Why do we divide the Hallel into two at the Passover Seder?). After commemorating the very first redemption of the Jewish people from Egypt we express our hope and firm belief in the coming of Moshiach, who will usher in the new and final redemption very soon. (Chabad. org)

It is inescapable that there is a very meaningful connection between Yeshua standing at Laodicea's door, their call to repentance and Elijah's role in checking that all within the house are a part of the covenant. Instead of endorsing lawlessness He is instructing believers in lawfulness! The message that believers should be "Jews inwardly" (Romans 2:29) should not be spiritualized away.

18 PENTECOST AND THE IMAGE OF GOD - (RAPTURE OR RESURRECTION?)

What is of great interest is that this manifestation of divine union did not happen at the beginning of the Holy Days or at the Holy Days in the fall. It occurred on Pentecost seven weeks/fifty days (generally) from the week of Passover and five months before the Feast of Trumpets. We will not go into detail of the counting of the Omer and from what Holy Day the count should begin.

This should lead you to ask some very important questions.
- Why did the manifestation of God's glory occur on Pentecost?
- Why did Yeshua come on the fourth day of the 7,000-year week?
- Why do we see the repetition of the number 7 as it relates to males?
- Why do we see the repetition of the number 5 as it relates to females?
- Why do we see 7 and 5 interact in the events related to the Holy Days, Sabbaths, and new moons?
- Why do we see 7 related to the Image of God and the promised seed?
- Why do we see 5 related to manifestation and habitation?

Now we need to examine these concepts in light of the Lord's Holy Days to gain a deeper understanding of what they mean and why they occur on the dates and times they are scheduled.

Genesis 1:14, And God said, <u>Let there be lights in the firmament of the heaven to divide the day from the night; and let them be for signs, and for seasons, and for days, and years</u>:15 And let them be for lights in the firmament of the heaven to give light upon the earth: and it was so. 16 And God made two great lights; the greater light to rule the day, and the lesser light to rule the night:

he made the stars also. 17 And God set them in the firmament of the heaven to give light upon the earth, 18 And to rule over the day and over the night, and to divide the light from the darkness: and God saw that it was good. 19 And the evening and the morning were the fourth day.

These two great lights are the duality that rule the earth, the seeds in the earth, and their eventual manifestation when they interact with the two great lights by internalizing their light into themselves. The sun (male) and the moon (female) not only divide the day from the night, they determine signs, seasons, days, and years. We have already commented on those signs, seasons, days, and years. Remember what you have read in the following chapters.

- Leviticus 23
- Deuteronomy 16
- Numbers 28 and 29
- Numbers 9

Let's briefly review what the modern church believes about the Holy Days:
- Passover–Death of the Messiah.
- Unleavened Bread–Removal of sin.
- **Pentecost/Shavuot–Birth of the church.**
- Trumpets–Day of blowing trumpets–Stand in judgment before God–the call to repentance.
- Atonement–Yeshua enters into the Holy of Holies with His blood covering our sins.
- Feast of Tabernacles–Picture of the millennium after the return of the Messiah, God tabernacling with man.
- Last Great Day- Entrance to eternity.

Having re–evaluated the events of the creation week and determined the patterns and images of how God creates seed and then manifests images, we should be able to more accurately define the meaning of these days but now with the emphasis of healing a broken Image of God that was divided and needs unity once again. The purpose of the coming of the Messiah is to restore the broken and divided Image of God!

Ephesians 4:3, Endeavouring to keep the unity of the Spirit in the bond of peace. 4 There is one body, and one Spirit, even as ye are called in one hope of your calling; 5 One Lord, one faith, one baptism, 6 One God and Father of all, who is above all, and through all, and in you all. 7 But unto every one of us is given grace according to the measure of the gift of Christ. 8 Wherefore he saith, When he ascended up on high, he led captivity captive, and gave gifts unto men. 9 (Now that he ascended, what is it but that he also descended first into the lower parts of the earth?   10 <u>He that descended is the same also that ascended up far above all heavens, that he might fill all things.</u>) 11 And he gave some, Apostles; and some, prophets; and some, evangelists; and some, pastors and teachers; 12 For the perfecting of the saints, for the work of the ministry, for the edifying of the body of Christ:13 <u>Till we all come in the unity of the faith, and of the knowledge of the Son of God, unto a perfect man, unto the measure of the stature of the fulness of Christ</u>:14 That we henceforth be no more children, tossed to and fro, and carried about with every wind of doctrine, by the sleight of men, and cunning craftiness, whereby they lie in wait to deceive; 15 But speaking the truth in love, <u>may grow up into him in all things, which is the head, even Christ</u>:16 <u>From whom the whole body fitly joined together and compacted by that which every joint supplieth, according to the effectual working in the measure of every part, maketh increase of the body</u> unto the edifying of itself in love.

We should take notice of the following. The redemption of the believers is to attain the unity–oneness of the Spirit (the Messiah Yeshua). When we are redeemed there is no more duality or division. In the redeemed there is a singular body, a singular spirit, God (breathed) in that one body, the Messiah Yeshua. Yeshua the Messiah (the seed of the woman) came down (descended and then ascended) in order that He would fill the redeemed body (us) with light and breath. The Father is in the Son and the Son is in us. Yeshua manifested the Father's name and gave that name to us, so that we may be one as He is one with the Father.

John 17:4, <u>I have glorified thee</u> on the earth: I have finished the work which thou gavest me to do. 5 And now, O <u>Father, glorify thou me with thine own self</u> with the glory which I had with thee before the world was. 6 <u>I have manifested thy name</u> unto the men which thou gavest me out of the world: thine they were, and thou gavest them me; and they have kept thy word. 7 Now they have known that all things whatsoever thou hast given me are of thee. 8 For I have given unto them the words which thou gavest me; and they have received them, and have known surely that <u>I came out from thee</u>, and they have believed that <u>thou didst send me</u>. 9 I pray for them: I pray not for the world, but for them which thou hast given me; for they are thine. 10 And all mine are thine, and thine are mine; and <u>I am glorified in them</u>. 11 And now I am no more in the world, but these are in the world, and I come to thee. Holy Father, <u>keep through thine own name those whom thou hast given me, that they may be one, as we are</u>. 12 While I was with them in the world, <u>I kept them in thy name</u>: those that thou gavest me I have kept, and none of them is lost, but the son of perdition; that the scripture might be fulfilled.

This redemption comes through singular faith and non–broken/non–divided (non–dual) Image of God, oneness with the Messiah (seed). We are joined to the Messiah (1 Corinthians 6:13–17). Through unity with the Messiah's Spirit (the ascended male), we (the descended female) become one flesh with Him and become of one spirit with Him, making us one ascended male (male & female united in marriage). This is called the unity of the faith or the unity of the spirit in the bond of peace (shalom).

- Shalom (שָׁלוֹם) (Sephardic Hebrew/Israeli Hebrew: Shalom; Ashkenazi Hebrew/Yiddish: sholom, sholem, shoilem, shulem) is a Hebrew word meaning peace, <u>completeness</u>, Prosperity, and welfare and can be used idiomatically to mean both hello and goodbye. [1][2][3] As it does in English, it can refer to either peace between two entities (especially between man and God or between two countries), or to the well–being, welfare or safety of an individual or a group of individuals. (Wikipedia)

    o Ephesians 2:14, For he is our peace, who hath made both one, and hath broken down the middle wall of partition between us;

This concept of shalom is best expressed as peace, wholeness, and completeness, of something that was divided. We call it oneness or singularity. It is best expressed in the creation week as the Sabbath (the 7th day of creation) where the singular Image of God is made manifest in all things.

Shalom: Shabbat shalom (שַׁבָּת שָׁלוֹם) is a common greeting used on Shabbat. This is most prominent in areas with Mizrahi, Sephardi, or modern Israeli influence. Many Ashkenazi communities in the Jewish Diaspora use Yiddish Gut shabbes in preference or interchangeably. Ma sh'lom'cha (מַה שְׁלוֹמְךָ; what is your well–being/peace?) is a Hebrew equivalent of the <u>English how are you? This is the form addressed to a single male. The form for addressing a single female is Ma sh'lomech? For addressing several females, Ma sh'lomchen? For a group of males or a mixed–gender group, Ma sh'lomchem?</u> (Wikipedia)

Notice that the greeting is typically male in gender and pictures an ultimate fulfillment of becoming an ascended male (Sons of God). When we use the terms of salvation and redemption, the essential issue is whether you have joined yourself to the Messiah Yeshua, the promised seed of the woman who would restore the Image of God, turning a duality (division, brokenness, female) into a singularity (unity, oneness, ascended male). Let's look at the patterns of the number 7 and the number 5.

7	5
Sabbath	Days 1–6
Ascended male	Descended female
Belief/faith	Unbelief
Manifestation of image	Seed image
No Sin	Sin
Incorruption	Corruption
Unity	Divided
Oneness	Duality
Tree of Life	Tree of the Knowledge of Good and Evil
Sun	Moon
Light	Darkness and Partial light
Spirit	Flesh & Spirit
Life	Death

Knowing that the principal theme of the Holy Days is the restoration of the Image of God through the promised seed, we should see a male/female interaction in the spring and fall Holy Days in order to manifest the restored and ascended Image of God. If we use this premise, we can look for a male/female (Messiah-redeemed or seed/manifestation) interaction in the Holy Days. Remember we learned that 3 is the number of resurrection.

Mark 9:31, For he taught his disciples, and said unto them, The Son of man is delivered into the hands of men, and they shall kill him; and after that he is killed, he shall rise the third day. 32 But they understood not that saying, and were afraid to ask him.

We have seen that this third day (3) is associated with male and female sexual union and oneness, which is a picture of ascension and resurrection.

John 2:1, And the third day there was a marriage in Cana of Galilee; and the mother of Yeshua was there:2 And both Yeshua was called, and his disciples, to the marriage. 3 And when they wanted wine, the mother of Yeshua saith unto him, They have no wine.

This is the first miracle of Yeshua's (the seed) ministry, commanded by Mary (the woman) and typifies the purpose of the coming of the Messiah! The fundamental problem at the marriage in Cana was that they had no wine when they wanted it. This issue is miraculously resolved by the coming of the Messiah (seed) at the behest of Mary (woman). We have already learned that wine is symbolic of the Spirit. At this joining of the duality there is a lack of the spirit (the true Image of God) and it can only be remedied by the miraculous work of the Messiah (the promised seed of the woman) and the release of the water of the grapes (spirit) from their vessels (flesh). We see a similar pattern at Pentecost (Shavuot) after Yeshua's resurrection.

Acts 2:3, And there appeared unto them cloven tongues like as of fire, and it sat upon each of them. 4 And they were all filled with the Holy Ghost, and began to speak with other tongues, as the Spirit gave them Utterance...12 And they were all amazed, and were in doubt, saying one to another, What meaneth this? 13 Others mocking said, These men are full of new wine. 14 But Peter, standing up with the eleven, lifted up his voice, and said unto them, Ye men of Judaea, and all ye that dwell at Jerusalem, be this known unto you, and hearken to my words:15 For these are not drunken, as ye suppose, seeing it is but the third hour of the day. 16 But this is that which was spoken by the prophet Joel; 17 And it shall come to pass in the last days, saith God, I will pour out of my Spirit upon all flesh: and your sons and your daughters shall prophesy, and your young men shall see visions, and your old men shall dream dreams:18 And on my servants and on my handmaidens I will pour out in those days of my Spirit; and they shall prophesy:19 And I will shew wonders in heaven above, and signs in the earth beneath; blood, and fire, and vapour of smoke:20 The sun shall be turned into darkness, and the moon into blood, before the great and notable day of the Lord come:21 And it shall come to pass, that whosoever shall call on the Name of the Lord shall be saved. 22 Ye men of Israel, hear these words; Yeshua of Nazareth, a man approved of God among you by miracles and wonders and signs, which God did by him in the midst of you, as ye yourselves also know:23 Him, being delivered by the determinate counsel and foreknowledge of God, ye have taken, and by wicked hands have crucified and slain:24 Whom God hath raised up, having loosed the pains of death: because it was not possible that he should be holden of it.

Do you see the connections?
- The Shekinah glory is on their heads.
- They are given Utterance of the Holy Spirit.
- It is the third (3) hour of the day. (3 is the number of resurrection)
- Those filled with unbelief claim they are drunken with new wine.

- God has poured out His spirit on to men.
- Those who call on the promised "seed of the woman", the Messiah Yeshua, shall be saved and raised up with Him.

Colossians 2:6, As ye <u>have therefore received Christ Yeshua the Lord, so walk ye in him</u>:7 Rooted and built up in him, and <u>stablished in the faith</u>, as ye have been taught, abounding therein with thanksgiving. 8 Beware lest any man spoil you through philosophy and vain deceit, after the tradition of men, after the rudiments of the world, and not after Christ. 9 <u>For in him dwelleth all the fulness of the Godhead bodily</u>. 10 And <u>ye are complete in him</u>, which is the head of all principality and power:11 In whom also ye are circumcised with the circumcision made without hands, in <u>putting off the body of the sins of the flesh by the circumcision of Christ</u>:12 Buried with him in baptism, wherein also <u>ye are risen with him through the faith of the operation of God, who hath raised him from the dead</u>.

We see the scriptures reaffirming the purpose of the Messiah (the promised "seed of the woman") is to restore the image and fullness of God, to make us one from a fractured duality. He causes the redeemed to ascend with Him in singular faith. When this union is manifested, it occurs with the Glory of God, the Shekinah Glory upon the believer and the manifestation of the Utterance of the Holy Spirit (the breath of God).

Why did this event and manifestation of the union of God with the believer occur on Pentecost/Shavuot and not on any of the other Holy Days? To find the answer to this question we need to abandon many of the unscriptural doctrines and traditions of men that we have been taught over the past two millennia and stick to the scriptural prophetic patterns to find the answer. Redemption is not just about the Messiah, it is also about the one needing to be redeemed, both the male (7) and the female (5), the seed and the manifestation/habitation of the seed.

Matthew 13:18, Hear ye therefore the parable of the sower. 19 When <u>any one heareth the word of the kingdom</u>, and understandeth it not, then cometh the wicked one, and catcheth away that which was sown in his heart. This is he which received seed by the way side…23 <u>But he that received seed into the good ground is he that heareth the word, and understandeth it; which also beareth fruit, and bringeth forth, some an hundredfold, some sixty, some thirty.</u>

The interaction of the seed (male) and the working of the operation of God requires earth (female) to sow it in. We should expect to see the Holy Days not only showing imagery about the seed but also about what the seed is sown into.

We should be looking for duality then singularity, for separation then unity, for descending then ascension, for male and female, and then unified male and female. Instead of viewing the Holy Days as a linear progression, we should view them as a male/female union needing to take place. Notice this pattern is the same as the division of the waters above and below the firmament (heaven) that are divided by the firmament.

Genesis 1:6, And God said, <u>Let there be a firmament in the midst of the waters, and let it divide the waters from the waters</u>. 7 And God made the firmament, and divided the waters which were under the firmament from the waters which were above the firmament: and it was so. 8 And <u>God called the firmament Heaven</u>. And the evening and the morning were the second day.

The dividing element is heaven.

Matthew 10:28, And<u> fear not them which kill the body, but are not able to kill the soul</u>: but rather fear him which is able to destroy both soul and body in hell. 29 Are not two sparrows sold for a farthing? and one of them shall not fall on the ground without your Father. 30 But the very hairs of your head are all numbered. 31 Fear ye not therefore, ye are of more value than many sparrows. 32 Whosoever <u>therefore shall confess me before men, him will I confess also before my Father which is in heaven</u>. 33 But whosoever shall deny me before men, him will I also deny before my Father which is in heaven. 34 <u>Think not that I am come to send peace on earth: I came not to send peace, but a sword</u>. 35 For I am come to set a man at variance against his father, and the daughter against her mother, and the daughter in law against her mother in law. 36 And a man's foes shall be they of his own household. 37 He that loveth father or mother more than me is not worthy of me: and he that loveth son or daughter more than me is not worthy of me. 38 And <u>he that taketh not his cross, and followeth after me, is not worthy of me. 39 He that findeth his life shall lose it: and he that loseth his life for my sake shall find it</u>.

The seed of the Kingdom, who is sent from heaven, is here to divide spirit and flesh, to divide those unified with Him from those who are not. This should provide added insight to Yeshua's warning. Integration and coexistence is not God's goal. Separation and holiness is the desired outcome.

Luke 17:33, Whosoever shall seek to save his life shall lose it; and whosoever shall lose his life shall preserve it.

Any attempts to preserve your fleshly life will ensure your demise, wherefore those who are circumcised from the flesh by the work of the Messiah and are unified with His spirit will find life. Our current fallen state and broken image is depicted as being uncircumcised and in a state of death. Exalting that state or seeking to create an environment of coexistence in that state only serves the enemy and not God.

Colossians 2:9, For in him dwelleth all the fulness of the Godhead bodily. 10 And <u>ye are complete in him</u>, which is the head of all principality and power:11 In whom also ye are circumcised with the circumcision made without hands, in <u>putting off the body of the sins of the flesh by the circumcision of Christ</u>:12 Buried with him in baptism, wherein also ye are risen with him through the faith of the operation of God, who hath raised him from the dead. 13 And you, being dead in your sins and the uncircumcision of your flesh, hath he quickened together with him, having forgiven you all trespasses; 14 Blotting out the handwriting of ordinances that was against us, which was contrary to us, and took it out of the way, nailing it to his cross; 15 And having spoiled principalities and powers, he made a shew of them openly, triumphing over them in it. 16 Let no man therefore judge you in meat, or in drink, <u>or in respect of an holyday, or of the new moon, or of the sabbath days:17 Which are a shadow of things to come; but the body is of Christ.</u>

Notice:
- The Father dwells in Heaven (Matthew 10:32).
- The fullness of the Godhead bodily dwells in the promised "seed of the woman", the Messiah Yeshua (Colossians 2:9).
- We are complete and one with Yeshua.
- We are circumcised by the work of the Messiah by putting off the flesh and being baptized into the Messiah's (seed) death and ascend through faith in His work.
- The Holy Days, New Moons, and Sabbath days are a shadow of things to come as they relate to the body of the Messiah and our redemption!

The Holy Days are not just about the seed of the woman, the Messiah Yeshua, they are also about His body, of which you are one. Yeshua and the Father are one and the Father resides in Yeshua, and the place where the Father resides is heaven. Heaven is the firmament that divides the waters above from the waters below. This is a prophetic pattern of the work of the Messiah, in whom we are destined to dwell. He is separating light from dark, upper from lower, earth from water, female from male, flesh from spirit.

Now let's clarify that the separation of flesh from spirit is due to the corruption of the flesh and the sin that occurs thereby. The original Image of God involved both seed and manifestation but without sin, without corruption, without death and duality of the Tree of the Knowledge of Good and Evil (mixture of fallen flesh and Spirit).

The circumcision made without hands is the work of the Messiah and is the operation of God to free us from the Tree of the Knowledge of Good and Evil (death–fallen flesh) and to graft/join us to the singularity of the Tree of Life (the Spirit). Within the Holy Days we should see the imagery of a duality being redeemed into a singularity. The prophetic pattern of the first 7th day Sabbath shows us the method of redemption.

Genesis 2:4, These are the generations of the heavens and of the earth when they were created, in the day that the Lord God made the earth and the heavens, 5 And <u>every plant of the field before it was in the earth, and every herb of the field before it grew</u>: for the Lord God had not caused it to rain upon the earth, and there was not a man to till the ground. 6 But <u>there went up</u>

a mist from the earth, and watered the whole face of the ground. 7 And the Lord God formed man of the dust of the ground, and breathed into his nostrils the breath of life; and man became a living soul.

All seeds were in the earth on the 7th day Sabbath, until the Lord God (YHWH) intervened and caused water to ascend up from the earth to water the seed. This imagery is connected to the formation of man as a living soul, through the operation of the Lord God (YHWH–Lord of the Sabbath, Mark 2:28) and imparting His breath (Spirit) to become one with man so that he could become a living soul, the Image of God.

How is Elijah associated with this restored image and the administration of resurrection life? Elijah is pivotal to the repentance of believers and a return to remembering the Law of Moses. The Law of Moses was a codified Image of God. Israel could not bear to hear God's own voice and pleaded that He would not talk with them anymore, except through Moses. Since they had descended to a state where they did not have "ears to hear" (Deuteronomy 9:24, Mark 4:9, Mark 8:18, Romans 11:8) God could only give them imagery that they could bear to behold. This resulted in the writing of the Law of Moses on tablets of stone. Elijah is depicted as the restoration and manifestation of that second administration of repentance and "grace and abundant mercy". As such his life is a depiction of imagery that is associated with the circumcision of Christ and the resurrection of the dead. At the conclusion of his ministry Elijah anointed Elisha to continue in his prophetic office, Elijah fulfills the imagery of ascension into the clouds of Glory (Shekinah Glory).

2 Kings 2:1, And it came to pass, when the Lord would take up Elijah into heaven by a whirlwind, that Elijah went with Elisha from Gilgal. 2 And Elijah said unto Elisha, Tarry here, I pray thee; for the Lord hath sent me to Bethel. And Elisha said unto him, As the Lord liveth, and as thy soul liveth, I will not leave thee. So they went down to Bethel. 3 And the sons of the prophets that were at Bethel came forth to Elisha, and said unto him, Knowest thou that the Lord will take away thy master from thy head to day? And he said, Yea, I know it; hold ye your peace.

This imagery of ascension and resurrection at the conclusion of Elijah's ministry is contrasted with the conclusion of Moses' ministry where he must fulfill the imagery of death and exile (condemnation and judgement) outside of the Promised Land.

Numbers 20:12, 12 And the Lord spake unto Moses and Aaron, Because ye believed me not, to sanctify me in the eyes of the children of Israel, therefore ye shall not bring this congregation into the land which I have given them.

Just as the pattern of death (Moses) and resurrection (Elijah) occurs in the lives of both prophets, so also Yeshua fulfills "all righteousness" (Matthew 3:15) of both administrations. His first coming resulted in His death (seed and administration of condemnation). His second coming results in resurrection life for His body (believers-manifestation and administration of grace and abundant mercy).

As Yeshua's final days also portrayed both judgement and death (first half of the Days of Unleavened Bread), three days later they portrayed grace and abundant mercy resulting in resurrection life (second half of the Days of Unleavened Bread). Forty days after His resurrection He manifested Himself in resurrection life by ascending into the Clouds of Glory. Fifty days after His resurrection He displayed His saving Spirit within His believers.

Acts 1:2, Until the day in which he was taken up, after that he through the Holy Ghost had given commandments unto the apostles whom he had chosen: To whom also he shewed himself alive after his passion by many infallible proofs, being seen of them forty days, and speaking of the things pertaining to the kingdom of God:

Just as Elijah was taken up, so also was Yeshua. Yeshua is fulfilling "all righteousness" or his prophetic pattern of death (descending) and resurrection (ascending), seed then manifested fruit. This is the pattern and fractal of the universe. Just as Moses entered the clouds (Shekinah Glory) on the mountain at the giving of the Torah of Moses (Exodus 16:10, Exodus 19:9, 16 Exodus 24:15-18, Exodus 33:9) so also Elijah enters the Shekinah Glory.

2 Kings 2:11, 11 And it came to pass, as they still went on, and talked, that, behold, there appeared a chariot of fire, and horses of fire, and parted them both asunder; and Elijah went up by a whirlwind into heaven.

Yeshua fulfills the same pattern as Elijah. We also see this presentation of the "cloud" and the "wind" of God after the resurrection of Yeshua.

Acts 1:9, And when he had spoken these things, while they beheld, he was taken up; and a cloud received him out of their sight. 10 And while they looked stedfastly toward heaven as he went up, behold, two men stood by them in white apparel; 11 Which also said, Ye men of Galilee, why stand ye gazing up into heaven? this same Jesus, which is taken up from you into heaven, shall so come in like manner as ye have seen him go into heaven.

We see the "wind" of God again at the first Pentecost after Yeshua's resurrection.

Acts 2:1, And when the day of Pentecost was fully come, they were all with one accord in one place. 2 And suddenly there came a sound from heaven as of a rushing mighty wind, and it filled all the house where they were sitting. 3 And there appeared unto them cloven tongues like as of fire, and it sat upon each of them.

Here the angel of God actually clarifies that Yeshua having fulfilled death and resurrection (the patterns of "all righteousness") has now ascended and will come again in the clouds of glory which is the Shekinah Glory of the tabernacle of God.

Exodus 33:9, And it came to pass, as Moses entered into the tabernacle, the cloudy pillar descended, and stood at the door of the tabernacle, and the Lord talked with Moses.

It is the same Shekinah Glory that was on the mountain with Moses when God declared the manifestation of the Name of the Lord (YHWH).

Exodus 34:5, And the Lord descended in the cloud, and stood with him there, and proclaimed the name of the Lord.

This is the same cloud that the voice of God declared Yeshua to be His Son on the mount of transfiguration.

Matthew 17:5, While he yet spake, behold, a bright cloud overshadowed them: and behold a voice out of the cloud, which said, This is my beloved Son, in whom I am well pleased; hear ye him.

These clouds of Glory are none other than the manifestation of the Shekinah Glory. Just as they appeared at the manifestation of the Name of the Lord (Yeshua the Messiah) they will manifest again at His return.

Matthew 24:30, And <u>then shall appear the sign of the Son of man in heaven</u>: and then shall all the tribes of the earth mourn, and <u>they shall see the Son of man coming in the clouds of heaven</u> with power and great glory.

These are not typical clouds that you would see in the sky.

Shekinah:

Shekinah, Shechinah, or Schechinah (Hebrew:שְׁכִינָה), is the English transliteration of a Hebrew noun meaning dwelling or settling, and denotes the dwelling or settling of the divine presence of God and his cosmic glory. This exact term does not occur in the Hebrew Bible, and is first encountered in rabbinic literature. [1]:148, [2] The Shekinah is held by some to represent the feminine attributes of the presence of God (Shekinah being a feminine word in Hebrew), based especially on readings of the Talmud. [5]

Manifestation:

The Shekinah is referred to as manifest in the Tabernacle and the Temple in Jerusalem throughout Rabbinic literature. It is also reported as being present in the acts of public prayer. In the Mishna the noun is used twice: once by Rabbi Hananiah ben Teradion (ca,135 CE):'If two sit together and the words between them are of the Torah, then the Shekinah is in their midst'; and Rabbi Halafta ben Dosa:'If ten men sit together and occupy themselves with the Law, the Shekinah rests among them. '[1]:148–149 So too in the Talmud Sanhedrin 39a, we read: "Whenever ten are gathered for prayer, there the Shekinah rests"; it also connotes righteous judgment ("when three sit as judges, the Shekinah is with them." Talmud tractate Berachot 6a), and personal need ("The Shekinah dwells over the headside of the sick man's bed." Talmud tractate Shabbat 12b; "Wheresoever they were exiled, the Shekinah went with them." Talmud tractate Megillah 29a). (Wikipedia)

We see this same "Clouds of Glory" in the book of Revelation.

Revelation 1:7, Behold, he cometh with clouds; and every eye shall see him, and they also which pierced him: and all kindreds of the earth shall wail because of him. Even so, Amen.

Here these clouds of Glory are directly associated with Yeshua the Messiah and His second coming. Notice earlier that the angel talking to the apostles at His ascension indicated that "this same" Jesus will come as He left descending in the Shekinah Glory. What is interesting is that the Two Witnesses that have been killed by the Beast and the Antichrist are fulfilling the same pattern of death and resurrection as Yeshua. After three and a half days of death laying openly in the streets, they are called up into the Shekinah Glory.

Revelation 11:3, And I will give power unto my Two Witnesses, and they shall prophesy a thousand two hundred and threescore days, clothed in sackcloth. 4 These are the two olive trees, and the two candlesticks standing before the God of the earth. 5 And if any man will hurt them, fire proceedeth out of their mouth, and devoureth their enemies: and if any man will hurt them, he must in this manner be killed. 6 These have power to shut heaven, that it rain not in the days of their prophecy: and have power over waters to turn them to blood, and to smite the earth with all plagues, as often as they will. 7 And when they shall have finished their testimony, the beast that ascendeth out of the bottomless pit shall make war against them, and shall overcome them, and kill them.

We cannot help but notice that these two are associated with the miracles that both Elijah and Moses did before all the people. Elijah declared that there would be no rain (1 Kings 17:1) and Moses turned the waters to blood (Exodus 7:17). Yeshua declared that Elijah must truly come again to restore all things (Matthew 17:11). Whether Yeshua meant literally Elijah or the Spirit of Elijah resting upon a modern-day Elisha we have yet to see. But we do see Moses and Elijah at the Mount of Transfiguration in the Clouds of Glory with Yeshua.

Matthew 17:2, And was transfigured before them: and his face did shine as the sun, and his raiment was white as the light. 3 And, behold, there appeared unto them Moses and Elias talking with him. 4 Then answered Peter, and said unto Jesus, Lord, it is good for us to be here: if thou wilt, let us make here three tabernacles; one for thee, and one for Moses, and one for Elias. 5 While he yet spake, behold, <u>a bright cloud overshadowed them: and behold a voice out of the cloud</u>, which said, This is my beloved Son, in whom I am well pleased; hear ye him.

We cannot dismiss the possibility that the Two Witnesses are either Moses and Elijah or someone who is anointed with their spirit and office. The Two Witnesses are depicted as the two olive trees and the two candlesticks that can be associated with the two administrations of the Law of Moses, one in death (Moses) and one in resurrection life (Elijah). Once these Two Witnesses are killed and fulfill the same imagery of death for three days, they are called to ascend into the Shekinah Glory.

Revelation 11:7, And when they shall have finished their testimony, the beast that ascendeth out of the bottomless pit shall make war against them, and shall <u>overcome them, and kill them.</u> 8 And their dead bodies shall lie in the street of the great city, which spiritually is called Sodom and Egypt, where also our Lord was crucified. 9 And they of the people and kindreds and tongues and <u>nations shall see their dead bodies three days and an half, and shall not suffer their dead bodies to be put in graves</u> . 10 And they that dwell upon the earth shall rejoice over them, and make merry, and shall send gifts one to another; <u>because these two prophets tormented them that dwelt on the earth</u>. 11 And <u>after three days and an half the spirit of life from God entered into them, and they stood upon their feet</u>; and great fear fell upon them which saw them. 12 And <u>they heard a great voice from heaven saying unto them, Come up hither. And they ascended up to heaven in a cloud</u>; and their enemies beheld them.

Just as Yeshua was killed they will follow His pattern and image and be left dead for 3 ½ days only to be resurrected to life and ascend into the Shekinah Glory. The very next time we see this cloud it is time for the harvest.

Revelation 14:4, And I looked, and behold a white cloud, and upon the <u>cloud one sat like unto the Son of man</u>, having on his head a golden crown, and in his hand a sharp sickle. And <u>he that sat on the cloud thrust in his sickle on the earth; and the earth was reaped</u>.

Paul talks about this event and how believers will follow the same pattern as Yeshua and will ascend into the Shekinah Glory.

2 Thessalonians 2:1, Now we beseech you, brethren, <u>by the coming of our Lord Jesus Christ, and by our gathering together unto him</u>, 2 That ye be not soon shaken in mind, or be troubled, neither by spirit, nor by word, nor by letter as from us, as that the day of Christ is at hand.

Paul goes into some depth on this event and what it will be like for believers in Yeshua.

1 Thessalonians 4:13, But I would not have you to be ignorant, brethren, <u>concerning them which are asleep</u>, that ye sorrow not, even as others which have no hope. 14 For if we believe <u>that Jesus died and rose again, even so them also which sleep in Jesus will God bring with him</u>. 15 For this we say unto you by the word of the Lord, that <u>we which are alive and remain unto the coming of the Lord shall not prevent them which are asleep</u>. 16 For the <u>Lord himself shall descend from heaven with a shout, with the voice of the archangel, and with the trump of God: and the dead in Christ shall rise first</u>:17 Then <u>we which are alive and remain shall be caught up together with them in the clouds, to meet the Lord in the air</u>: and so shall we ever be with the Lord. 18 Wherefore comfort one another with these words.

Notice the core question is "what about the dead"? What happens to them? Those who sleep in Yeshua, Paul says, "them also which sleep in Jesus will God bring with him". Then Paul says, "the dead in Christ shall rise first".

He answers the question if our being alive and remaining unto the coming of the Lord will prevent the dead in Christ from being resurrected. Paul is unequivocal that our being alive and waiting on the Lord does not prevent those who died in Christ from being resurrected first (rise first).

We should ask if that means if we will see them rise first from the earth or if they are literally just risen from death and given a resurrection body...and as Paul says, "even so them also which sleep in Jesus will God bring with him" (1 Thessalonians 4:14).

If we are to rise and be caught up together with them...this could mean that they rise from death. . . not necessarily from the earth to the sky, then it is likely that they are risen from the dead and Christ brings them with Him from where He is.

We can say that the dead in Christ rise when Yeshua appears, as Paul says that our resurrection occurs when Yeshua descends from heaven with the trump of God "and" the dead shall rise first. This could mean that they also rise at this same time or that they indeed are not prevented from rising as the question was initially asked and they are risen before this event and are brought with Yeshua as he had earlier stated.

1 Thessalonians 4:13, But <u>I would not have you to be ignorant, brethren, concerning them which are asleep</u>, that ye sorrow not, even as others which have no hope. 14 For if we believe that Jesus died and rose again, <u>even so them also which sleep in Jesus will God bring with him</u>...15 For this we say unto you by the word of the Lord, that <u>we which are alive and remain unto the coming of the Lord shall not prevent them which are asleep</u>...

Just as Yeshua and Elijah fulfill this pattern of ascension into the Shekinah Glory, so also will those who are alive at Yeshua's second coming. The Two Witnesses, whether they literally be Moses and Elijah, or those anointed with the Holy Spirit and the calling of God to fulfill those offices will also fulfill the fractal of death and resurrection, just like Yeshua. They give testimony for 3 ½ years and are killed by the Beast that ascends out of the bottomless pit. They lay in the streets dead for 3 ½ days for all to see that they are dead and then they are resurrected at the coming of the Lord in the clouds of glory (Shekinah). Immediately afterward the Man-Child is caught up to God and His throne.

Some additional thoughts on the timing of this "ascension". I don't use the term rapture as it is merely an expression of the resurrection of the dead. As the "rapture" is taught by many pastors and ministers it becomes a misleading term due to their personal beliefs of when they need it to occur to escape tribulation. Paul deals with this logical question of timing and clarifies for confused believers that the resurrection of the living in Christ and our gathering to the Lord in the air will occur only after this critical event.

> 2 Thessalonians 2:1, Now we beseech you, brethren, by <u>the coming of our Lord Jesus Christ, and by our gathering together unto him</u>, 2 That ye be not soon shaken in mind, or be troubled, neither by spirit, nor by word, nor by letter as from us, as that <u>the day of Christ is at hand</u>. 3 <u>Let no man deceive you by any means: for that day shall not come, except there come a falling away first, and that man of sin be revealed, the son of perdition</u>; 4 Who opposeth and exalteth himself above all that is called God, or that is worshipped; so that he as God sitteth in the temple of God, shewing himself that he is God.

Paul is unequivocal. The coming of Christ, our gathering (those alive at Christ's coming) to Him, and our resurrection and ascension into the Shekinah Glory will not happen until the Man of Sin declares himself to be God sitting in the temple of God. We know that the Two Witnesses testify for a period of 3 ½ years.

> Revelation 11:3, And I will give power unto my Two Witnesses, and they shall prophesy a thousand two hundred and threescore days, clothed in sackcloth.

After this 3 ½ year testimony they are killed and resurrected and ascend into the Shekinah Glory. The pivotal question we need to be asking is…can this death and resurrection of the Two Witnesses be a separate event from the resurrection of believers that Paul detailed to the Thessalonians or is it happening at the same time as the gathering together of all those "in Christ"? It would appear that this happens either immediately before or coincident with ascension of the Man-Child.

> Revelation 11:18, And the nations were angry, and thy wrath is come, and <u>the time of the dead, that they should be judged, and that thou shouldest give reward unto thy servants the prophets, and to the saints, and them that fear thy name</u>, small and great; and shouldest destroy them which destroy the earth.

Immediately following this statement, we see the presentation of the Image of God, the Man-Child. I would propose this Man-Child are resurrected believers in Christ…but which ones?

Revelation 12:5, And <u>she brought forth a man child</u>, who was to rule all nations with a rod of iron: and <u>her child was caught up unto God</u>, and to his throne... <u>Therefore rejoice, ye heavens, and ye that dwell in them</u>. Woe to the inhabiters of the earth and of the sea! for the devil is come down unto you, having great wrath, because <u>he knoweth that he hath but a short time</u>. 13 And when the dragon saw that he was cast unto the earth, he persecuted the woman which brought forth the man child.

And after this event we see the beast being depicted as continuing for 42 months.

Revelation 13:5, And there was given unto him a mouth speaking great things and blasphemies; and power was given unto him to continue forty and two months.

It would appear that the Two Witnesses are testifying for 1260 days (42 months) before the 42 months that beast "continues" for 42 months. The Son of Perdition can hardly be in the temple "showing himself that he is God" (2 Thessalonians 2:4) if there are two men outside in Jerusalem proving he is not God. The resurrection of the Two Witnesses happens at the conclusion of the second woe!

Revelation 11:12, And they heard a great voice from heaven saying unto them, <u>Come up hither</u>. And <u>they ascended up to heaven in a cloud</u>; and their enemies beheld them. 13 And <u>the same hour was there a great earthquake</u>, and the tenth part of the city fell, and in the earthquake were slain of men seven thousand: and <u>the remnant were affrighted, and gave glory to the God of heaven</u>. 14 The <u>second woe is past</u>; and, behold, the third woe cometh quickly.

Really the pivotal question is if the Two Witnesses and possibly all those in Christ happen at the same time, at the sixth seal...how logically can you have a Pre-Tribulation rapture (resurrection)? All we have to do is read just a little further to see the announcement that the dead are about to be judged...right after the Sixth Seal.

Revelation 11:18, And the nations were angry, and thy wrath is come, and <u>the time of the dead, that they should be judged, and that thou shouldest give reward unto thy servants the prophets, and to the saints, and them that fear thy name</u>, small and great; and shouldest destroy them which destroy the earth.

This certainly will give Pre-Tribulation Rapture proponents a simple logical and scriptural quandary to chew on. If you cannot reconcile all the scriptures into a unified whole, then likely you have a faulty and unscriptural paradigm. We cannot help but wonder if it is literally Elijah and Moses that are the Two Witnesses or if it is two individuals that have the spirit of their office upon them by the ordination of God. Just as the Antichrist and the Beast are proponents of Lawlessness, the Two

Witnesses of God will be proponents of Lawfulness and will be focusing believers on the Law of Moses and the Administration of Grace and abundant mercy. As we examine the third woe which follows immediately upon the heels of the scriptures above we see the ascension of the Man-Child and the descension of Satan and his angels.

Revelation 12:10, And I heard a loud voice saying in heaven, <u>Now is come salvation</u>, and strength, and the kingdom of our God, and the power of his Christ: for the <u>accuser of our brethren is cast down</u>, which accused them before our God day and night. 11 And <u>they overcame him by the blood of the Lamb</u>, and by the word of their testimony; and they loved not their lives unto the death. 12 Therefore <u>rejoice, ye heavens, and ye that dwell in them</u>. <u>Woe to the inhabiters of the earth</u> and of the sea! for <u>the devil is come down unto you, having great wrath, because he knoweth that he hath but a short time</u>. 13 And when the <u>dragon saw that he was cast unto the earth, he persecuted the woman which brought forth the man child</u>. 14 And <u>to the woman</u> were given two wings of a great eagle, that she might fly into the wilderness, into her place, <u>where she is nourished for a time, and times, and half a time, from the face of the serpent</u>.

Notice:
- This follows upon the murder of the two-witnesses.
- This follows the resurrection and ascension of the two-witnesses.
- This follows the second woe and is called a "woe" (third woe). We cannot pass over the fact that this is manifestation of the number 3 which is associated with males ascending on the 3 required holy days (3 number of the male).
- "Now" salvation has come…arrived.
- The Man-Child has ascended to heaven.
- The devil and his angels are forced to descend to the earth.
  - Deuteronomy 7:5, But thus shall ye deal with them; ye shall destroy their altars, and break down their images, and cut down their groves, and burn their graven images with fire.
- The devil has a short time…but how long?
  - Revelation 12:14, And to the woman were given two wings of a great eagle, that she might fly into the wilderness, into her place, where <u>she is nourished for a time, and times, and half a time, from the face of the serpent</u>.

Now why do we assume the Man-Child is not Christ? I would, as many have done, assume Christ is the Man-Child, but, as his appearance is connected to the 1260 days that the woman is sheltered by God in the wilderness, it looks very much like a literal end-time count of days. I find it rather difficult to make the Man-Child Christ as He ascended 2,000 years ago. Also, as we have already examined in the story of Tamar:

Genesis 38:24, And <u>it came to pass about three months</u> after, that it was told Judah, saying, Tamar thy daughter in law hath played the harlot; and also, behold, she is with child by whoredom. And Judah said, Bring her forth, and <u>let her be burnt.</u> 25 When she was brought forth, she sent to her father in law, saying, By the man, whose these are, am I with child: and she said, Discern, I pray thee, <u>whose are these, the signet, and bracelets, and staff.</u> 26 And Judah acknowledged them, and said, She hath been more righteous than I; <u>because that I gave her not to Shelah my son.</u> And he knew her again no more.

We see here again the count of three (resurrection) and she is pursued to be burnt. She proves her worthiness via the signet, bracelets, and staff of the one who gave her conception. So just as Joseph is hidden in Egypt, these events with Tamar are playing out in the midst of Joseph's brothers.

Genesis 38:27, And <u>it came to pass in the time of her travail</u>, that, behold, <u>twins were in her womb</u>. 28 And it came to pass, when she travailed, that the <u>one put out his hand: and the midwife took and bound upon his hand a scarlet thread, saying, This came out first</u>. 29 And it came to pass, as <u>he drew back his hand</u>, that, behold, <u>his brother came out:</u> and she said, How hast thou broken forth? this breach be upon thee: therefore his name was called Pharez. 30 And afterward came out his brother, that had the scarlet thread upon his hand: and his name was called Zarah.

It is very clear that this woman is with twins and one of them is a picture of the Messiah who allows his brother to break forth first before his appearing. I would contend that this twin of the Messiah is the one who is redeemed first by the Messiah and is typified as His twin, the Man-Child. Those typified by Joseph in Egypt are a symbol of the great multitude that comes out of Great Tribulation. Remember John is asked about the great multitude, "What are these which are arrayed in white robes? and whence came they?" (Revelation 7:9-13) We see Jacob say the same thing about Joseph's seed.

Genesis 48:8, And <u>Israel beheld Joseph's sons, and said, Who are these?</u> 9 And Joseph said unto his father, <u>They are my sons</u>, whom God hath given me in this place. And he said, Bring them, I pray thee, unto me, and I will bless them. 10 Now the eyes of Israel were dim for age, so that he could not see. And he <u>brought them near unto him;</u> and he kissed them, and embraced them. 11 And Israel said unto Joseph, <u>I had not thought to see thy face: and, lo, God hath shewed me also thy seed.</u>

Israel (Jacob) says, "Who are these?" We find that same question asked in the book of Revelation about the Great Multitude (Revelation 7:13). Joseph's seed in Egypt (a land associated with images/idols) are depicted as becoming a great multitude.

Genesis 48:16, The Angel which redeemed me from all evil, bless the lads; and let my name be named on them, and the name of my fathers Abraham and Isaac; and let them grow into a multitude in the midst of the earth. 17 And when Joseph saw that his father laid his right hand upon the head of Ephraim, it displeased him: and he held up his father's hand, to remove it from Ephraim's head unto Manasseh's head. 18 And Joseph said unto his father, Not so, my father: for this is the firstborn; put thy right hand upon his head. 19 And his father refused, and said, I know it, my son, I know it: he also shall become a people, and he also shall be great: but truly his younger brother shall be greater than he, and his seed shall become a multitude of nations.

Ephraim is also clearly associated with images/idols in Talmud sources.

When Isreael was about to bless Joseph's sons, he saw by the Holy Spirit that Jeroboam the son of Nebat would issue from Ephraim, and he exclaimed, "Who are these?", the word "these" (eleh) being an allusion to idols. (Soncino Zohar Volume I, p. 228b)

The northern ten tribes of Israel are known as Ephraim. They were the first to be dispersed from the Promised Land because they set up idols when the Kingdom was split from Judah.

I Kings 12:25, Then Jeroboam built Shechem in mount Ephraim, and dwelt therein; and went out from thence, and built Penuel. 26 And Jeroboam said in his heart, Now shall the kingdom return to the house of David:27 If this people go up to do sacrifice in the house of the Lord at Jerusalem, then shall the heart of this people turn again unto their lord, even unto Rehoboam king of Judah, and they shall kill me, and go again to Rehoboam king of Judah. 28 Whereupon the king took counsel, and made two calves of gold, and said unto them, It is too much for you to go up to Jerusalem: behold thy gods, O Israel, which brought thee up out of the land of Egypt. 29 And he set the one in Bethel, and the other put he in Dan. 30 And this thing became a sin: for the people went to worship before the one, even unto Dan. 31 And he made an house of high places, and made priests of the lowest of the people, which were not of the sons of Levi.

Israel is shown what is prophetically to occur to his grandsons in the end-time and how they will come out of idolatry as a "multitude of nations" or as Revelation puts it as a "great multitude" composed of "whosoever's" from every nation who have forsaken the image/idol of the beast and have joined themselves to the true Image of God, Yeshua the Messiah. Just as Israel had removed themselves far off from Moses' glorified countenance and were once again brought near to Moses, so also Israel 's grandchildren (and their companions-Gentiles) will be brought near for a final blessing.

Ezekiel 37:15, The word of the Lord came again unto me, saying,16

Moreover, thou son of man, take thee one stick, and write upon it, For Judah, and for the children of Israel his companions: then take another stick, and write upon it, <u>For Joseph, the stick of Ephraim and for all the house of Israel his companions</u>:17 And join them one to another into one stick; and they shall become one in thine hand.

Keep in mind that just as the Church has taken on the name and identity of Christ. The wife takes on the name of her husband and receives a new name and becomes and initiates a new creation (replication of life). Which is very good in God's eyes because God is life and replicating His image is the replication of the pattern of life. We like Jacob must believe and transform just a Jacob did by receiving his new name, Israel, and replicate the Image of God. Going from separation to unity to singularity to replication of the Image of God, Life. Now the pattern presents itself anew in Ephraim and Manasseh. Hidden and revealed. Seed then Image. Even Joseph who dreamed God's dreams was surprised by the replication of the pattern in his own sons.

Do not be surprised if this death and resurrection fractal is replicated in your life in the very end-time. Just when it appears darkest, have faith and do not worry. Death must appear the victor before ultimately being defeated by resurrection life. The honor is that God has selected us to replicate His divine pattern and fractal. It will take courage to deny what the Antichrist and the Beast will try and force you to believe. They will cajole, con, and kill to make you comply. Trust in the new name you've been given and don't worry about saving your life or the life of your loved ones. The Beast and the Antichrist will only be given a couple of years longer to live than those they are going to kill for rejecting them. So, taking the Mark of the Beast will at best give you a year or two more of misery before they and their companions are judged, convicted, and destroyed. Do not sell your souls for porridge like Esau did.

When their judgement occurs then the resurrection of the martyrs will occur sealing God's judgment and verdict against the wicked. Each aspect of the fractal must occur in its pattern. Death and Resurrection.

19 FRIEND OF THE BRIDEGROOM

Just as Tamar's twins are born together, Ephraim and Manasseh inherit the blessing together as full children of Abraham, not as grandsons. So, is it possible that we should be looking for a twin (someone in His image) of the Messiah just as we see Tamar's twins? Or someone who participates in His ministry? We should look to see if someone appears in conjunction with the Messiah.

> Matthew 3:3, In those days came John the Baptist, preaching in the wilderness of Judaea, 2 And saying, Repent ye: for the kingdom of heaven is at hand. 3 For this is he that was spoken of by the prophet Esaias, saying, The voice of one crying in the wilderness, Prepare ye the way of the Lord, make his paths straight. <u>11 I indeed baptize you with water unto repentance, but he that cometh after me is mightier than I, whose shoes I am not worthy to bear: he shall baptize you with the Holy Ghost, and with fire</u>:12 Whose fan is in his hand, and he will throughly purge his floor, and gather his wheat into the garner; but he will burn up the chaff with unquenchable fire. 13 Then cometh Jesus from Galilee to Jordan unto John, to be baptized of him. 14 But John forbad him, saying, <u>I have need to be baptized of thee</u>, and comest thou to me? 15 And Jesus answering said unto him, <u>Suffer it to be so now: for thus it becometh us to fulfil all righteousness</u>. Then he suffered him.

Not only was John born first and was related to Mary's family, but he participates in the baptism of Yeshua. Later Yeshua refers to John as the greatest born of women.

> Matthew 11:11, Verily I say unto you, Among them that are born of women there hath not risen a greater than John the Baptist: notwithstanding he that is least in the kingdom of heaven is greater than he.

The parallels here between John the Baptist and the Man-Child, and the 144,000 are striking. Not only that but John is not described as being of the bride, but he is associated with the male friend of the Bridegroom. John's words here are prophetic and bear all the imagery of the sealing of those who wish to escape the wrath of God. The 144,000 cited in Revelation need to be sealed before the earth and sea are hurt in the end-time events. Let's look at the similarities between John the Baptist and the Friend of the Bridegroom.

> John 3:26, And <u>they came unto John</u>, and said unto him, Rabbi, he that was with thee beyond Jordan, to whom thou barest witness, behold, the same baptizeth, and all men come to him. 27 John answered and said, A man can receive nothing, except it be given him from heaven. 28 Ye yourselves bear me witness, that I said<u>, I am not the Christ, but that I am sent before him</u>. 29 <u>He that hath the bride is the bridegroom: but the friend of the bridegroom, which standeth and heareth him, rejoiceth greatly</u> because of the bridegroom's voice: this my joy therefore is fulfilled. 30 He must increase, but I must decrease. 31 He that cometh from above is above all: he that is of the earth is earthly, and speaketh of the earth: he that cometh from heaven is above all. 32 And what he hath seen and heard, that he testifieth; and no man receiveth his testimony. 33 <u>He that hath received his testimony hath set to his seal that God is true</u>. 34 For he whom God hath sent speaketh the words of God: for God giveth not the Spirit by measure unto him. 35 The Father loveth the Son, and hath given all things into his hand. 36 He that believeth on the Son hath everlasting life: and he that believeth not the Son shall not see life; <u>but the wrath of God abideth on him</u>.

John is clearly noted as being sent and fulfilling the role of the friend of the bridegroom. The Man-Child and the 144,000 both have hallmarks associated with the male, the First-Fruits, and being on Mt. Sion with the Lamb (Bridegroom). They are also marked by God having the name of the Father written in their foreheads. Tamar's children bear the hallmarks of these same twins (Messiah & the Man-Child) and Joseph's children bear the hallmarks of the Great Multitude. These two groups are continually presented together and having separate roles, locations, garments, and markings. It would appear from Revelation 7 that these who are sealed (144,000) are upon the earth while the earth and sea are being hurt.

> • Revelation 7:1, And after these things I saw four angels standing on the four corners of the earth, holding the four winds of the earth, that the wind should not blow on the earth, nor on the sea, nor on any tree. 2 And I saw another angel ascending from the east, <u>having the seal of the living God:</u> and he cried with a loud voice to the four angels, to whom it was given to hurt the earth and the sea, 3 Saying, <u>Hurt not the earth, neither the sea, nor the trees, till we have sealed the servants of our God in their foreheads</u>.

- Revelation 9:4, And it was commanded them that <u>they should not hurt the grass of the earth, neither any green thing, neither any tree; but only those men which have not the seal of God in their foreheads</u>.

Since these who are sealed are 144,000 and appear to be on earth, as the angel was cautioned to hurt only those who have not the seal of God, it could be surmised that these are also on the earth and could have been hurt. Perhaps they are on the earth, sealed, and then ascend as the First-Fruits of God appearing as the Man-Child and the 144,000 on Mt. Sion with the Messiah. Many confuse this Man-Child with the Messiah. It would appear that these two are very much like when Yeshua and John the Baptist had appeared together. People thought Yeshua was actually John the Baptist.

Matthew 16:13, When Jesus came into the coasts of Caesarea Philippi, he asked his disciples, saying, <u>Whom do men say that I the Son of man am</u>? 14 And they said, <u>Some say that thou art John the Baptist:</u> some, Elias; and others, Jeremias, or one of the prophets. 15 He saith unto them, But whom say ye that I am? 16 And Simon Peter answered and said, Thou art the Christ, the Son of the living God.

Some thought the Messiah was John the Baptist resurrected. Peter, however, had a clear testimony that they were not one and the same, but that Yeshua, unlike John, was the Son of God. Even Herod thought Yeshua was John the Baptist raised from the dead (Matthew 14:1-3). John the Baptist appears to be a prophetic picture of the friend of the bridegroom, the Man-Child, the 144,000, and First-Fruits of resurrection. They look so much like the Messiah, because they have His image, His countenance, and His name that they are often confused with the Messiah in the book of Revelation. Just as we participate in the Baptism (Mikva) with Yeshua, so also Tamar's twins are prophetic pattern for the Messiah and the Friend of the Bridegroom.

The Bride's Reception
The bride's reception is usually the livelier one. It is an old tradition, referred to in the Talmud, for the bride to sit on an attractive throne. Surrounded by her attendants, close family members, and friends, she receives guests and well-wishers. As the musicians play, her friends dance in front of her.

The Groom's Tisch
The groom's reception (Yiddish: hoson's tisch) for men is held at a table laden with food and drink. Seated adjacent to the groom are his father and the bride's father, surrounded by the rabbis. Around the table are male guests, relatives, and friends of the groom, who toast the groom and sing. [Today, many grooms opt to have female friends and relatives at their tish as well.] Often, the room in which the groom's reception is held is where the late-afternoon Minchah prayer service takes place.

It is customary for a groom to deliver (or attempt to deliver) a learned discourse at the tisch ("table"). But traditionally he is interrupted by his friends shortly after beginning, with lively singing and rhythmic clapping in which all present join to prevent him from continuing. This custom is not intended as an affront or as an act of disrespect to the groom, but is designed to protect the groom who may be less than scholarly, lest he be shamed on what should be his most joyous day.

In many Hasidic circles, a badhan, or professional wedding jester, would be employed at the tish to entertain the assembled guests, by toasting the groom in rhymed couplets sung in traditional tunes.

The most crucial procedure at the groom's reception is the completion and validation of the ketubah, the marriage contract. The ketubah is carefully reviewed by the rabbi to determine that all details are correct.

The groom then formally accepts all the unilateral obligations to which he commits himself in the ketubah by executing a kinyan sudar, a traditional legal consent and agreement process. The officiating rabbi hands him a small article of clothing such as a handkerchief, and the groom, before Two Witnesses (who may not be close relatives of bride or groom), takes it and lifts it up symbolically to affirm consent, before returning it to the rabbi.

At the conclusion of this procedure, called kinyan, a scribe or the rabbi then adds to the end of the ketubah text the Aramaic word v'kanina (and we have properly concluded the legal act of transference), and the witnesses sign to affirm the groom's acceptance, through the act of kinyan, of all the conditions of the ketubah document, thereby validating the ketubah. In some communities, it is customary for the groom also to sign it.

The Veiling Ceremony

The groom is then escorted by his father and the bride's father, the rabbis, the dignitaries, and the others in his retinue to the bridal reception area for the veiling ceremony, known in Yiddish as the bedeken (Hebrew, hinuma). Accompanied by his friends, who dance and sing in front of him, the groom leads the procession to the bride. He approaches the bridal throne and covers the bride's face with a veil (Yiddish, dektich). He is then escorted back to the groom's reception room by the men, to prepare for the huppah ceremony [the public marriage ceremony that takes place under the marriage canopy, or huppah]. (myjewishlearning.com)

Notice how the Man-Child and the 144,000 have roles very similar to the Friend of the Bridegroom. They have a separate role from the Bride and are distinct from that great multitude. As such they have different hallmarks (singing a song only they can learn, name, and location on Mt. Sion with the Lamb).

Just as those who have taken the mark and image of the beast come under the wrath of God, so also those who take the mark and Image of God-The Resurrected First-Fruits (Yeshua the Messiah) are on Mount Sion with the Lamb of God, Yeshua.

Revelation 14:1, And I looked, and, lo, a Lamb stood on the mount Sion, and with him an hundred forty and four thousand, having his Father's name written in their foreheads…These are they which were not defiled with women; for they are virgins. These are they which follow the Lamb whithersoever he goeth. These were redeemed from among men, being the First-Fruits unto God and to the Lamb.

The book of Revelation (Manifestation) makes it clear that these 144,000 are the First-Fruits of resurrection. They have the mark and name of God's name sealed in their foreheads, they follow the Messiah wherever He leads and they have been redeemed out of mankind.

Exodus 13:1, And the Lord spake unto Moses, saying, Sanctify unto me all the firstborn, whatsoever openeth the womb among the children of Israel, both of man and of beast: it is mine…

Just as the First-Fruits in Christ are sealed, redeemed, and ascend into heaven because they are marked with the Image of God, Yeshua the Messiah, those who are marked with the image of the beast come under the judgment and wrath of God.

Revelation 14:8, And there followed another angel, saying, Babylon is fallen, is fallen, that great city, because she made all nations drink of the wine of the wrath of her fornication. 9 And the third angel followed them, saying with a loud voice, If any man worship the beast and his image, and receive his mark in his forehead, or in his hand, 10 The same shall drink of the wine of the wrath of God, which is poured out without mixture into the cup of his indignation; and he shall be tormented with fire and brimstone in the presence of the holy angels, and in the presence of the Lamb:11 And the smoke of their torment ascendeth up for ever and ever: and they have no rest day nor night, who worship the beast and his image, and whosoever receiveth the mark of his name. 12 Here is the patience of the saints: here are they that keep the commandments of God, and the faith of Jesus.

Notice the clear difference between those marked by the beast and those who are marked by the Father's name. Those marked with the Father's name keep the Law of Moses (commandments of God) and keep the faith of its new administrator, Yeshua the Messiah. Whether this group of 144,000 are solely of those who are dead in Christ we cannot at this point say.

Revelation 7:3, Saying, Hurt not the earth, neither the sea, nor the trees, till we have sealed the servants of our God in their foreheads. 4 And I heard the number of them which were sealed: and there were sealed an hundred and forty and four thousand of all the tribes of the children of Israel.

Obviously these 144,000 are sealed, but it does not indicate if they are alive on the earth and are sealed in protection from the wrath that is to come or if they are dead and are sealed by being raised in resurrection life having the name of the

Father written on their foreheads. It would be presumptuous to conclude adamantly one way or the other. It could be the case that this reaping of First-Fruits are only the resurrection of some of those who are dead in Christ as they fulfill a special role and are literally marked by the Father's name written in their foreheads. Either way it is apparent that these 144,000 are strictly from the tribes of Israel and are depicted as First-Fruits. It could very well be that at the ascension of the Two Witnesses and the Man-Child marks this event of the resurrection of the first fruits. This event happens in the middle of the tribulation after 1260 days of the Two Witnesses giving their testimony to the world.

144,000:
- Sealed before the earth and sea are hurt (Revelation 7:3-4)
- They are literally all from tribes of Israel (Revelation 7:4-8)
- They are marked with the Father's name (Revelation 14:1)
- They are on Mount Sion with the Lamb (Revelation 14:1)
- They sing a new song only they can learn before the throne of God (Revelation 14:3)
- They are not defiled with women and are virgins (Revelation 14:4)
- They are without guile or fault (Revelation 14:5)

These first fruits appear to serve as the Friend of the Bridegroom and are depicted as the birth of the Man-Child. If this scenario is accurate then it could explain why after the Two Witnesses go up and the devil is cast down to earth, there are still all the living in Christ that are on the earth to be persecuted and pursued by the beast.

Revelation 13:4, And they worshipped the dragon which gave power unto the beast: and they worshipped the beast, saying, Who is like unto the beast? who is able to make war with him? 5 And there was given unto him a mouth speaking great things and blasphemies; and power was given unto him to continue forty and two months. 6 And he opened his mouth in blasphemy against God, to blaspheme his name, and his tabernacle, and them that dwell in heaven. 7 And it was given unto him to make war with the saints, and to overcome them: and power was given him over all kindreds, and tongues, and nations. 8 And all that dwell upon the earth shall worship him, whose names are not written in the book of life of the Lamb slain from the foundation of the world.

It could very well be that the woman brings forth the first fruits, the Man-Child who ascends into heaven, and those who are left alive on the earth in Christ flee into the wilderness from the dragon.

Revelation 12:5, And she brought forth a man child, who was to rule all nations with a rod of iron: and her child was caught up unto God, and to his throne. 6 And the woman fled into the wilderness, where she hath a place

<u>prepared of God, that they should feed her there a thousand two hundred and threescore days</u>.

This event happens after the Two Witnesses have testified for 1260 days (3 ½ years) and are killed and called up to heaven. This woman (the body of Christ) is protected by God on earth for 1260 more days. So, what would make us think that this group of 144,000 are those that are dead in Christ and are the First-Fruits of the resurrection?

- Revelation 12:5, And <u>she brought forth a man child</u>, who was to rule all nations with a rod of iron: and <u>her child was caught up unto God, and to his throne</u>. . . And <u>they overcame him by the blood of the Lamb, and by the word of their testimony; and they loved not their lives unto the death</u>. 12 Therefore rejoice, ye heavens, and ye that dwell in them. Woe to the inhabiters of the earth and of the sea! for the devil is come down unto you, having great wrath, because he knoweth that he hath but a short time. 13 And when the dragon saw that he was cast unto the earth, he persecuted the woman which brought forth the man child. And to the woman were given two wings of a great eagle, that she might fly into the wilderness, into her place, where she is nourished for a time, and times, and half a time, from the face of the serpent.
- Revelation 14:1, And I looked, and, lo, <u>a Lamb stood on the mount Sion, and with him an hundred forty and four thousand, having his Father's name written in their foreheads</u>. 2 And I heard a voice from heaven, as the voice of many waters, and as the voice of a great thunder: and I heard the voice of harpers harping with their harps:3 And they sung as it were a new song before the throne, and before the four beasts, and the elders: and no man could learn that song but the hundred and forty and four thousand, which were redeemed from the earth. 4 These are they which were not defiled with women; for they are virgins. These are they which follow the Lamb whithersoever he goeth. <u>These were redeemed from among men, being the first fruits</u> unto God and to the Lamb.

The focus of this group of people is that they "loved not their lives unto the death". And after the presentation of the 144,000 with Yeshua in heaven as being the First-Fruits of the resurrection a declaration is made to those who "die" from that moment on.

Revelation 14:12, Here is the patience of the saints:<u> here are they that keep the commandments of God, and the faith of Jesus</u>. 13 And I heard a voice from heaven saying unto me, <u>Write, Blessed are the dead which die in the Lord from henceforth</u>: Yea, saith the Spirit, that they may rest from their labours; and their works do follow them.

We are shown a clear declaration that the resurrection of the First-Fruits has occurred and that there are still those who are faithful to Yeshua and to His law (Law of Moses) on earth. Consequently, it would seem that the resurrection of those who are alive in Christ has not yet occurred. We may be seeing that calling out of the living in Christ later at the judgement of Babylon the Whore.

Revelation 18:4, And I heard another voice from heaven, saying, <u>Come out of her, my people</u>, that ye be not partakers of her sins, and that ye receive not of her plagues.

It is immediately after this declaration of God's people to come out of Babylon and the description of what God is going to do to Babylon that we see the presentation of "much people in heaven".

Revelation 19:1, And after these <u>things I heard a great voice of much people in heaven</u>, saying, Alleluia; Salvation, and glory, and honour, and power, unto the Lord our God:2 For true and righteous are his judgments:<u> for he hath judged the great whore</u>, which did corrupt the earth with her fornication, and hath avenged the blood of his servants at her hand.

This great number of people in heaven is not happenstance. The time had come for the resurrection of those alive in Christ.

Revelation 19:6, And <u>I heard as it were the voice of a great multitude, and as the voice of many waters</u>, and as the voice of mighty thunderings, saying, Alleluia: for the Lord God omnipotent reigneth. 7 <u>Let us be glad and rejoice</u>, and give honour to him:<u> for the marriage of the Lamb is come, and his wife hath made herself ready</u>. 8 And to her was granted that she should be arrayed in fine linen, clean and white: for the fine linen is the righteousness of saints. 9 And he saith unto me, Write, <u>Blessed are they which are called unto the marriage supper of the Lamb</u>. And he saith unto me, These are the true sayings of God.

Regardless of what many teachers say about the rapture and resurrection if we simplify our terminology and only use scriptural terms, meaning, images, and patterns...a very clear picture emerges of the final tribulation week of 7 years. An understanding how the seed (male) and image (female) pattern reoccurs in nature in the scriptures and in the Holy Days is critical to having a scripturally accurate understanding of what is about to come to pass. Yeshua the seed of the Kingdom came in the middle of 7,000 years, Yeshua died on Passover and then His resurrected image appeared in the middle of the Days of Unleavened Bread. Yeshua ascended to the Father and sent His Holy Spirit in the middle of the annual Holy Days on the Feast of Shavuot (Pentecost) to give His image to believers in His name.

We see the apostles then fulfill the same fractal as the messiah spreading the seed in the imagery of death and testimony of His name. So, we see seed (death) then manifestation of image (resurrection life). In the middle of the Crucifixion Passover we see the manifestation of the seed of the Kingdom of God on the Holy Day of First-Fruits by the presentation of the resurrected Image of God, the

Messiah.

In the middle of the annual Holy Days we see the manifestation of the seed of the Kingdom of God in those who have been called by Christ who have received His seed in the giving of the Holy Spirit. All of this occurred in the middle of the 7,000-year period depicted by the 4th day of creation and the making of the sun (male) and moon (female). If we simplify and follow this pattern, we see the resurrection of the First-Fruits (144,000) in the middle of the Tribulation 7-year period fulfilling the imagery of the seed (those dead in Christ) who are depicted as the Man-Child (male 144,000). This is followed by the gathering together of those alive in Christ who are conformed to His image and have His seed within them at the conclusion of the 7-year tribulation period when Babylon the Whore is judged by God. Now many will rightfully say, "This great multitude (female-Bride of Christ) is there from the beginning of the Tribulation since we see them in Revelation 7". First John is shown the presentation of the 144,000.

> Revelation 7:2, And I saw another angel ascending from the east, having the seal of the living God: and he cried with a loud voice to the four angels, to whom it was given to hurt the earth and the sea, 3 Saying, <u>Hurt not the earth, neither the sea, nor the trees, till we have sealed the servants of our God in their foreheads</u>. 4 And I heard the number of them which were sealed: and <u>there were sealed an hundred and forty and four thousand of all the tribes of the children of Israel</u>.

We must acknowledge the possibility that the Man-Child ascends in resurrection life at the same time as all believers in Christ at the Pre-Wrath Rapture at the very latest if all Believers are resurrected at the same event, Yeshua's Appearing. We also must acknowledge that it would appear that they do not ascend in a Pre-Tribulation Rapture. It is the Author's belief that the timing of the Two Witnesses testimony...and their subsequent death and resurrection may or may not coincide with the General Resurrection of those in Christ at His appearing. Some would conclude that the resurrection of these groups all must occur on the same day...and that may be possible. If you place their testimony at the second half of the tribulation...they evidently stay beyond any Pre-Wrath Rapture. If you place their testimony in the first half of Daniel's Final Week...then they are called up well before a 6th year Pre-Wrath Rapture. There may be an as yet unidentified trigger for the start of their testimony somewhere during the final 7 years.

Then he is shown a separate group of resurrected people.

20 THE GREAT MULTITUDE

We see the presentation of the "great multitude" in Revelation seven.

> Revelation 7:9, After this <u>I beheld, and, lo, a great multitude</u>, which no man could number, <u>of all nations, and kindreds, and people, and tongues, stood before the throne, and before the Lamb, clothed with white robes</u>, and palms in their hands; 10 And cried with a loud voice, saying, Salvation to our God which sitteth upon the throne, and unto the Lamb. 11 And all the angels stood round about the throne, and about the elders and the four beasts, and fell before the throne on their faces, and worshipped God, 12 Saying, Amen: Blessing, and glory, and wisdom, and thanksgiving, and honour, and power, and might, be unto our God for ever and ever. Amen. 13 And one of the elders answered, saying unto me, <u>What are these which are arrayed in white robes? and whence came they</u>? 14 And I said unto him, Sir, thou knows. And he said to me, <u>These are they which came out of great tribulation, and have washed their robes, and made them white in the blood of the Lamb</u>. 15 Therefore are they before the throne of God, and serve him day and night in his temple: and he that sitteth on the throne shall dwell among them. 16 <u>They shall hunger no more, neither thirst any more; neither shall the sun light on them, nor any heat</u>. 17 For the Lamb which is in the midst of the throne shall feed them, and shall lead them unto living fountains of waters: and God shall wipe away all tears from their eyes.

Given the fact that John is being transported to a future time it is not impossible to think that he is given this image of the 144,000 and the great multitude and the rest of the Book of Revelation that follows this chapter is an answer to the question of "What are these which are arrayed in white robes? and whence came they?" (Revelation 7:13)

In fact, the answer given to him in this very chapter is that these are those "which came out of great tribulation…" So, it appears likely that he is presented with these groups and the chapters that follow answer the question as to who they are. Notice John isn't asking the question, one of the Elders is quizzing John to see if he knows who these people are. By John's response we see that he does not know. It would appear that John, late in life, persecuted and imprisoned could have been asking if he had fulfilled his purpose in life for Christ. This Revelation could have been an answer to those questions. The early presentation of this great multitude in the book of Revelation does not necessitate that they are resurrected (raptured) pre-tribulation or even mid-tribulation. You cannot both come "out of great tribulation" and be "saved from great tribulation". Notice they are described as no longer suffering heat or thirst as is characterized by the Great Tribulation. Since now they no longer suffer from it suggests that they had suffered from it and no longer have to.

Since the 144,000 are described as being a specific count of 12,000 from each tribe of Israel and the Great Multitude is from every nation and tongue, we see the presentation of the First-Fruits being from the Tribes of Israel and the great harvest is from the whole world. Those that are dead in Christ are viewed at the fifth seal.

Revelation 6:9, And when he had opened the fifth seal, I saw under the altar the souls of them that were slain for the word of God, and for the testimony which they held:10 And they cried with a loud voice, saying, How long, O Lord, holy and true, dost thou not judge and avenge our blood on them that dwell on the earth? 11 And white robes were given unto every one of them; and it was said unto them, that they should rest yet for a little season, until their fellowservants also and their brethren, that should be killed as they were, should be fulfilled.

The clothing of the dead in a white garment is indicative of resurrection, yet they are told to continue resting for a little while till the count of their brethren are killed just as they were, for their testimony of Yeshua and His commandments. This leads to the possibility that there is resurrection occurring, yet not in sight of those who are dwelling upon the earth. As we mentioned earlier that it could be that the "dead in Christ" are brought with Yeshua at His return and their resurrection may not happen in sight of those dwelling upon the earth. But those alive in Christ at His coming will ascend and meet them in the air.

1 Thessalonians 4:14, For if we believe that Jesus died and rose again, even so them also which sleep in Jesus will God bring with him.

Immediately after this event in Revelation 6:11 of the dead receiving white robes, the sixth seal is announced and there is a declaration that "day of wrath" has come.

Revelation 6:17, For the great day of his wrath is come; and who shall be able to stand?

Could the following chapters of Revelation be a response to those in Revelation 6:9-11 who are dead in Christ and killed for Christ that ask "how long" until you avenge our blood. Yeshua's response is that others, like them, must be killed, and we need to wait until that happens. Revelation 7 could be explaining to that group of souls and John what has yet to occur to these others. What follows Revelation 7 is their Great Tribulation story.

Revelation clearly defines the 144,000 being of each tribe of Israel and are described as the First Fruits of resurrection, which appears to happen at the time of the ascension of the Two Witnesses into heaven after 1260 days of testimony. Are these 144,000 the resurrection of those who (of the 12 tribes of Israel that are in Christ) are already dead as they are killed by the beast? Or are they alive and receive the testimony of the Two Witnesses in the first half of the tribulation? We need to come to some conclusion on this issue. It may very well be that the resurrection of the 144,000 (Israel) is appropriately the First-Fruits of God...as Israel should be. Paul described the resurrection as occurring as appropriate to their order or rank.

> I Corinthians 15:22, For as in Adam all die, even so in Christ shall all be made alive. 23 But every man in his own order: Christ the First-Fruits; afterward they that are Christ's at his coming. 24 Then cometh the end, when he shall have delivered up the kingdom to God, even the Father; when he shall have put down all rule and all authority and power.

All that are resurrected exhibit faith in Yeshua the Messiah, but clearly the First-Fruits have been described as being of each tribe of Israel (12,000 per tribe). Paul is clearly stating that each resurrection occurs at a different time. So easily we can assume that the resurrection of the First-Fruits occurs at a different time than those who are alive at His coming. So, the resurrection of the First-Fruits naturally occurs before His coming. This could easily explain the mid-tribulation resurrection of the Two Witnesses and the 144,000. Should we be offended that the Book of Revelation details these 144,000 as being from each tribe of Israel and not composed of Gentile believers?

> • Romans 1:16, For I am not ashamed of the gospel of Christ: for it is the power of God unto salvation to every one that believeth; to the Jew first, and also to the Greek.
> • Exodus 22:29, Thou shalt not delay to offer the first of thy ripe fruits, and of thy liquors: the firstborn of thy sons shalt thou give unto me.

The only question that seems to be unconfirmed is if those 144,000 are already dead in Christ during the Great Tribulation or are they alive and resurrected first?

> 1 Thessalonians 4:13, But I would not have you to be ignorant, brethren, concerning them which are asleep, that ye sorrow not, even as others which

have no hope. 14 For if we believe that Jesus died and rose again, even so them also which sleep in Jesus will God bring with him. 15 For this we say unto you by the word of the Lord, that we which are alive and remain unto the coming of the Lord shall not prevent them which are asleep. 16 For the Lord himself shall descend from heaven with a shout, with the voice of the archangel, and with the trump of God: and the dead in Christ shall rise first:17 Then we which are alive and remain shall be caught up together with them in the clouds, to meet the Lord in the air: and so shall we ever be with the Lord. 18 Wherefore comfort one another with these words.

Many teachers like to say that the 144,000 are of Israel because the Church has been raptured and is no longer upon the earth. The plain scriptures of Revelation would appear to negate this theory. The 144,000 are of Israel, but it appears to be obvious that the Church is still on earth. If the living at Christ's return shall not precede those who are dead in Christ, we can only assume that those resurrected mid-tribulation are dead in Christ and not alive, nor has Christ come yet when this resurrection occurs as those who are alive in Christ are resurrected at His coming and are gathered to Him in the air. This sealing of the 144,000 seems to occur after the Sixth Seal.

Revelation 6:17, For the great day of his wrath is come; and who shall be able to stand?

And it occurs before the Seventh Seal.

Revelation 8:1, And when he had opened the seventh seal, there was silence in heaven about the space of half an hour. 2 And I saw the seven angels which stood before God; and to them were given seven trumpets.

We see confirmation of this as it relates to the Mystery of God.

Revelation 10:7, But in the days of the voice of the seventh angel, when he shall begin to sound, the mystery of God should be finished, as he hath declared to his servants the prophets.

When Revelation 10 opens, it shows this seventh "angel" being depicted very much like the Son of Man having a countenance like the sun, feet as pillars of fire, roaring like a lion and having a book in his hand. We are never told what is said during this angels' uttering for it is sealed up and he declares that there should "be time no longer" (Revelation 10:6). Immediately after this the Two-Witnesses are introduced to the world and they give testimony for 1260 days. 1 Thessalonians 4:14-18 indicates very clearly that at the "coming of the Lord" and when He "descends" with the "voice of the archangel" and the "trump of God", then the dead rise first …then we "which are alive shall be caught up together with them in the clouds, to meet the Lord in the air". The dead in Christ rise first. Whether that means that Christ brings them with Him and they are observable in the air by those on the Earth or that it means literally that the graves are opened and the dead literally "rise" as it says and they ascend first, then we which are alive are changed and ascend also. It could be a literal rising from the dead graves on earth and they ascend first (rise), then those who are alive in Christ (rise) afterward. Or it could be that the dead in Christ rise from the dead and are given resurrection garments in heaven and Yeshua brings them with him and we join them both in the air. Both appear to occur when the Lord (Yeshua) descends with the voice of an archangel and the trump of God.

Revelation 14:13, And I heard a voice from heaven saying unto me, Write, Blessed are the dead which die in the Lord from henceforth: Yea, saith the Spirit, that they may rest from their labours; and their works do follow them. 14 And I looked, and behold a white cloud, and upon the cloud one sat like unto the Son of man, having on his head a golden crown, and in his hand a sharp sickle. 15 And another angel came out of the temple, crying with a loud voice to him that sat on the cloud, Thrust in thy sickle, and reap: for the time is come for thee to reap; for the harvest of the earth is ripe. 16 And he that sat on the cloud thrust in his sickle on the earth; and the earth was reaped.

As we have already studied, Yeshua is coming in the "clouds of Glory" otherwise known as the Shekinah Glory. What is interesting is that immediately preceding this it is indicating that believers who die from henceforth are "blessed". It seems to be indicating that after this event you still have believers in Christ dying, so we can assume that the resurrection has not taken place as yet for those who are in Christ alive on the earth.

What are the Critical Questions?
- If the Two Witnesses are resurrected after 1260 days and the beast continues another 1260 days after their resurrection, is this a resurrection only of the Two Witnesses?
- Is there another 1260 days until the resurrection of the dead in Christ and those alive in Christ?
- If the Two Witnesses are resurrected mid-tribulation and those who are dead in Christ rise first with them, is there a gap between the resurrection of the dead in Christ and those alive in Christ of about 1260 days?

Traditionally, the Letters to the Thessalonians seem to indicate that both the dead and those alive in Christ are seen to rise in Christ with the dead rising up first, then those alive in Christ rising shortly thereafter and meeting those who were dead in Christ in the air at the "appearing of the Lord".

Could it be that these Two Witnesses fulfill the image, pattern, and fractal of death and resurrection, just like Yeshua? They are called to ascend into heaven after their 1260 days after they are killed by the Beast for their testimony of Yeshua and His commandments.

The Book of Revelation may be showing these Two Witnesses serving among these angels and messengers that carry out the judgment of the Beast, the Antichrist, and Babylon. Take note of the fact that two of these heavenly messengers so conform to the Image of Christ that John mistakes them for Christ and attempts to bow and worship them. Both times these two "angels" declare "I am thy fellowservant, and of thy brethren..." and "for I am thy fellowservant, and of thy brethren the prophets..."

1.Revelation 17:1, And <u>there came one of the seven angels which had the seven vials</u>, and talked with me, saying unto me, Come hither; <u>I will shew unto thee the judgment of the great whore</u> that sitteth upon many waters:2 With whom the kings of the earth have committed fornication, and the inhabitants of the earth have been made drunk with the wine of her fornication. 3 So <u>he carried me away in the spirit into the wilderness</u>: and I saw a woman sit upon a scarlet coloured beast, full of names of blasphemy, having seven heads and ten horns.

- Revelation 19:10, And <u>I fell at his feet to worship him</u>. And he said unto me, See thou do it not<u>: I am thy fellowservant, and of thy brethren that have the testimony of Jesus</u>: worship God: for the testimony of Jesus is the spirit of prophecy.

2.Revelation 21:9, And there came unto me <u>one of the seven angels which had the seven vials full of the seven last plagues</u>, and talked with me, saying, Come hither, <u>I will shew thee the bride, the Lamb's wife</u>. 10 And <u>he carried me away in the spirit to a great and high mountain</u>, and shewed me that great city, the holy Jerusalem, descending out of heaven from God, 11 Having the glory of God: and her light was like unto a stone most precious, even like a jasper stone, clear as crystal; 12 And had a wall great and high, and had twelve gates, and at the gates twelve angels, and names written thereon, which are the names of the twelve tribes of the children of Israel:

- Revelation 22:8, And I John saw these things, and heard them. And when I had heard and seen, <u>I fell down to worship before the feet of the angel which shewed me these things</u>. 9 Then saith he unto me, <u>See thou do it not: for I am thy fellowservant, and of thy brethren the prophets, and of them which keep the sayings of this book: worship God</u>.

Notice that the first "angel" John attempts to worship associates himself with being a fellowservant and having the testimony of Yeshua. The second angel that John tries to worship associates himself as also being a fellowservant and being one of the prophets who keep the sayings of "this book". We assume they are two different "angels" as John would have surely remembered the countenance of the first angel that had spoken to him and warned him previously. Could these two "angels" be the ascended Two Witnesses that were killed and resurrected during the middle of the tribulation? Notice how one angel is showing him the great whore that comes under condemnation and judgement (death) and the second angel is showing him the Bride of the Lamb who is resurrected to life and is associated with grace, mercy, and blessing.

We see the juxtaposition of death and life, cursing and blessing, seed then flesh, one dwelling on the mountain of God and the other dwelling in a dead wilderness.

It may be likely that the resurrection of the Two Witnesses mid-tribulation is for those two alone having fulfilled the fractal of death and resurrection and are called up to serve God.

Zechariah 4:1, And the angel that talked with me came again, and waked me, as a man that is wakened out of his sleep. 2 And said unto me, What seest thou? And I said, I have looked, and behold a candlestick all of gold, with a bowl upon the top of it, and his seven lamps thereon, and seven pipes to the seven lamps, which are upon the top thereof:3 <u>And two olive trees by it, one upon the right side of the bowl, and the other upon the left side thereof</u>. 4 So I answered and spake to the angel that talked with me, saying, What are these, my lord? 5 Then the angel that talked with me answered and said unto me, <u>Knowest thou not what these be? And I said, No, my lord</u>... 11 Then answered I, and said unto him, <u>What are these two olive trees upon the right side of the candlestick and upon the left side thereof</u>? 12 And I answered again, and said unto him, <u>What be these two olive branches which through the two golden pipes empty the golden oil out of themselves</u>? 13 And he answered me and said, Knowest thou not what these be? And I said, No, my lord. 14 Then said he, <u>These are the two anointed ones, that stand by the Lord of the whole earth.</u>

At this point we have a hard time thinking that these are anyone but Moses and Elijah.

Matthew 17:1, And after six days Jesus taketh Peter, James, <u>and John</u> his brother, and bringeth them up into an high mountain apart, 2 And was <u>transfigured before them: and his face did shine as the sun, and his raiment was white as the light</u>. 3 And, behold, <u>there appeared unto them Moses and Elias talking with him</u>. 4 Then answered Peter, and said unto Jesus, Lord, it is good for us to be here: if thou wilt, <u>let us make here three tabernacles; one for thee, and one for Moses, and one for Elias</u>. 5 While he yet spake, behold, a <u>bright cloud overshadowed them: and behold a voice out of the cloud, which said, This is my beloved Son</u>, in whom I am well pleased; hear ye him. 6 And when the disciples heard it, <u>they fell on their face, and were sore afraid</u>. 7 And <u>Jesus came and touched them, and said, Arise</u>, and be not afraid.

The similarity between John's interaction with the two angels in the Book of Revelation and this event are striking. All three appear in a glorified form and all three are overshadowed by the clouds of Glory, the Shekinah, so much so that the disciples suggest building three tabernacles and not one. The voice of God clarifies that Yeshua is the Son of God. In fear they fall to the ground and Yeshua tells them to rise up. With all that we have learned about the two administrations and how Moses typifies the administration of the Law under condemnation and death and Elijah typifies the restoration to the Law of Moses under grace and abundant mercy, and that Yeshua fulfills "all righteousness" in walking out the patterns and fractals of both administrations so that He could become the administrator or the Law of Moses under the administration of grace and abundant mercy via resurrection life, it would seem possible that the Two Witnesses are either Moses and Elijah or those anointed with that office and the Spirit of that office.

As such the one angel shows condemnation of the Whore of Babylon and the other angel shows the mercy extended to the Bride of the Lamb, those who have faith in Yeshua and keep His commandments (Law of Moses).

One possibility is that we have the resurrection of the Two Witnesses mid-tribulation and the ascension of the Man-Child into heaven. Possibly we have the resurrection of the Two Witnesses mid-tribulation and the ascension of the Man-Child and the resurrection of the dead in Christ, while those alive in Christ are persecuted by the devil who has been cast down to earth. Maximally we have the resurrection of the Two Witnesses mid-tribulation and the ascension of the Man-Child and the resurrection of the dead in Christ and those alive in Christ. This would seem to contradict the fact that after this event there are those who are yet to die and are declared to be blessed (Revelation 14:3).

Revelation 14:3, And I heard a voice from heaven saying unto me, Write, Blessed are the dead which die in the Lord from henceforth: Yea, saith the Spirit, that they may rest from their labours; and their works do follow them.

This would seem to indicate that the resurrection of those alive in Christ cannot happen mid-tribulation...as believers are still dying. So, if we eliminate the un-factual we are left with the possibility that the resurrection of the Two Witnesses happens prior to the appearing of Christ at the middle of the Tribulation and there are yet 1260 days that the remnant need to take shelter from the continuance of the Beast and the Antichrist until the appearing of the Lord and the rising of the dead and our gathering unto Him in the air. What is confusing is that we see the ascension of the Man-Child right after the ascension of the Two Witnesses (Revelation 11:11-12, 12:5). Many try to say that this Man-Child is Yeshua that was brought forth by Israel. This would seem unlikely as this appears to be an end-time event with a literal count of 1260 days that the woman is sheltered by God while the devil who has been cast down tries to kill her.

Isaiah 66:5, Hear the word of the Lord, ye that tremble at his word; Your brethren that hated you, that cast you out for my name's sake, said, Let the Lord be glorified: but he shall appear to your joy, and they shall be ashamed. 6 A voice of noise from the city, a voice from the temple, a voice of the Lord that rendereth recompence to his enemies. 7 Before she travailed, she brought forth; before her pain came, she was delivered of a man child. 8 Who hath heard such a thing? who hath seen such things? Shall the earth be made to bring forth in one day? or shall a nation be born at once? for as soon as Sion travailed, she brought forth her children. 9 Shall I bring to the birth, and not cause to bring forth? saith the Lord: shall I cause to bring forth, and shut the womb? saith thy God.

This ascending of the Man-Child seems to be associated with the bringing forth of Sion and her children. It would seem that this Man-Child is the resurrection of the First-Fruits mid-tribulation immediately after the ascension of the Two Witnesses. This group of 144,000 are associated with being all male and on Mt. Sion with the Lamb.

As we already have learned, seed is associated with the male and fruit is associated with the female. Is there a possibility that the resurrection of the first fruits happens mid-tribulation and as such follow the seed then manifestation pattern? Seeing that Yeshua is the ascended male and these 144,000 appear with Him on Mount Sion? This viewing of the 144,000 happens shortly after the ascension of the Man-Child who was delivered of the woman who then flees into the wilderness for 1260 days.

Progression of Events:
- Two Witnesses give testimony for 1260 days.
- Beast kills the Two Witnesses.
- Two Witnesses lay dead for 3 ½ days then are resurrected to life and called up to heaven.
- The Man-Child is born and caught up to God and His throne
- The woman who gives birth to the Man-Child flees to the wilderness and is protected for 1260 days.
- The dragon makes war with the remnant of her seed who keep the testimony of Yeshua and keep the Commandments of God (Law of Moses).
- The image of the beast is worshiped by those not written in the book of life.
- Another beast gives life to the image of the beast causing it to speak and all who refuse to worship it to be killed. The Beast causes all to receive his mark permitting them to buy and sell.
- Seven angels (messengers) with the seven last plagues are released on the judgement of the beast and those with his mark. These are all clothed in white linen (Could they be resurrected saints?).
- One angel shows John the judgement of the Whore Babylon. John tries to worship this angel.
- Another angel declares that Babylon is fallen and God's people are called out from among Babylon before the plagues are poured out. Why before? This is the wrath of God poured out and is not for believers.
- The announcement of the Marriage of the Lamb goes out and his wife is arrayed in fine linen. John tries to worship this angel.
- Heaven is opened and the Word of God appears on a white horse with the armies of heaven arrayed in white linen.
- The beast and the false prophet are cast into a lake of fire and their

remnant are slain by the Word of God.

- The devil is bound in the bottomless pit.
- The souls of those that were beheaded for the witness of Yeshua, and for the Word of God, and had not worshipped the beast, neither his image, nor receive his mark live and reign with Christ for 1,000 years. This is the first resurrection.
- The rest of the dead and the next resurrection does not happen until the end of the 1,000 years.
- After the 1,000 years Satan is loosed and the nations are deceived again. The devil is cast into the same lake of fire as the beast and the false prophet.
- The great white throne judgment occurs and the dead are judged; death and hell are cast into the lake of fire and anyone not found written in the book of life is cast into the lake of fire.
- There is a new heaven and new earth.
- The new Jerusalem descends out of heaven.
- God dwells with man.
- The seven angels (messengers) show John the Bride of Christ.

It would appear that either way the first resurrection happens 1,000 years before the next resurrection. The question is, can we have the resurrection of the Two Witnesses and then a time gap of 1260 days until the coming of Christ and the resurrection of the dead in Christ and the ascension of those alive in Christ?

Or do we have the resurrection of the Two Witnesses and the dead in Christ and then a time gap of 1260 days until the coming of Yeshua and the gathering of those who are alive in Christ to meet Him in the air with those who were dead in Christ? 1 Thessalonians 4:14 seems to indicate that Christ brings the dead in Christ with Him and we do not see the graves break open and rise into the air.

1 Thessalonians 4:14, For if we believe that Jesus died and rose again, even so them also which sleep in Jesus will God bring with him.

It would appear that we who are alive in Christ will meet them in the air when we ascend at Christ's coming. Is it scriptural that those who are dead in Christ truly are resurrected to life at the same time as the ascension of the Two Witnesses? It would appear that we have "fellowservants of the prophets" in heaven, doing heavenly things in a resurrected state. Surely this glorified state was wondrous enough to confuse even the Apostle John. We need to look for any scriptural fact that clarifies that the dead in Christ must immediately precede those who are alive in Christ, or perhaps we have an illogical presumption that has not been factually verified. Can you have the resurrection of the dead 3 ½ years before the resurrection of those alive in Christ at His appearing and still call it the first resurrection? Paul seems to state that the order of resurrection is "Christ the First-Fruits…"

1 Corinthians 15:23, But every man in his own order: Christ the First-Fruits;

afterward they that are Christ's at his coming.

As the book of Revelation portrays the 144,000 as the First-Fruits (Revelation 14:3-5) and being conformed to the image of Christ having the name of the Father written in their foreheads, we have to question if the traditional order is correct.

Traditional Order:
- Christ the First Fruits
- They that are Christ's at His coming

Proposed Order:
- Christ (2,000 years ago)
- The First Fruits (mid-Tribulation after 3 ½ years)
- They that are Christ's at His coming

No doubt all of these are the first resurrection as they all precede the 1,000-year gap between the stated first resurrection and the resurrection of all the dead. The principal question of the Thessalonians is whether the scenario of events declared by Paul would consequently "prevent" the resurrection of those who are dead in Christ whose bodies sleep in the earth.

1 Thessalonians 4:15, For this we say unto you by the word of the Lord, that <u>we which are alive and remain unto the coming of the Lord shall not prevent them which are asleep.</u> 16 For the Lord himself shall descend from heaven with a shout, with the voice of the archangel, and with the trump of God: and the dead in Christ shall rise first:

Paul is clearly stating that the resurrection of the dead in Christ will happen before the resurrection of the living in Christ and our living and gathering to Christ will not "prevent" them from being resurrected. We have to question if the resurrection of the dead in Christ receive their resurrection bodies in heaven at the time of the fifth seal.

Revelation 6:9, And <u>when he had opened the fifth seal</u>, I saw <u>under the altar the souls of them that were slain for the word of God</u>, and for the testimony which they held:10 And they cried with a loud voice, saying, <u>How long, O Lord, holy and true, dost thou not judge and avenge our blood</u> on them that dwell on the earth? 11 And <u>white robes were given unto every one of them; and it was said unto them, that they should rest yet for a little season, until their fellowservants also and their brethren, that should be killed as they were</u>, should be fulfilled.

We see here that those who are slain for their testimony of Yeshua are given white robes and told to rest for a little while until their company is completed by the deaths of others who are killed for their testimony of Yeshua. This is the same apparel that the Lamb's wife and the seven angels (messengers) in heaven wear.

- Revelation 15:6, And the seven angels came out of the temple, having the seven plagues, <u>clothed in pure and white linen</u>, and having their breasts girded with golden girdles.

- Revelation 19:7, Let us be glad and rejoice, and give honour to him: for the marriage of the Lamb is come, and his wife hath made herself ready. 8 And to her was granted <u>that she should be arrayed in fine linen, clean and white: for the fine linen is the righteousness of saints</u>.

Both of these groups are clearly clothed in what appear to be resurrection garments (bodies) as early as the fifth seal. It would not seem impossible that if those who are the First-Fruits precede the resurrection of the living in Christ that it could be more than just moments between these ranks of the first resurrection, but indeed could be years based upon the scenarios presented by the book of Revelation. It would seem entirely possible that those that are killed for their testimony of Yeshua step directly into their ranks and receive their resurrection garments immediately upon death of their fallen and corruptible bodies. These saints become a part of Yeshua's heavenly army.

Revelation 19:14, And the armies which were in heaven followed him upon white horses, clothed in fine linen, white and clean.

We cannot skip over the fact that at Yeshua's resurrection two thousand years ago, that saints were resurrected and rose out of their graves in testimony of Yeshua's authority as the new administrator of grace and abundant mercy (resurrection life).

Matthew 27:52, And the graves were opened; and <u>many bodies of the saints which slept arose</u>, 53 And <u>came out of the graves after his resurrection, and went into the holy city, and appeared unto many</u>. 54 Now when the centurion, and they that were with him, watching Jesus, saw the earthquake, and those things that were done, they feared greatly, saying, Truly this was the Son of God.

It is entirely possible that this rank of First-Fruits is filled continuously as saints in Christ die and are conscious upon their death, instead of participating in some sort of soul sleep. Indeed, their carnal bodies are asleep in the ground, but Paul portrays the consciousness of the believer who has died in Christ having gained immediately upon death.

- Philippians 1:21, For to me to live is Christ, and to die is gain. 22 But if I live in the flesh, this is the fruit of my labour: yet what I shall choose I wot not. 23 For I am in a strait betwixt two, having a desire to depart, and to be with Christ; which is far better:

- Matthew 10:28, And fear not them which kill the body, but are not able to kill the soul: but rather fear him which is able to destroy both soul and body in hell.

To take these scriptures at face value, it would certainly indicate that those who kill the body cannot kill something else and as such it is still alive once the body is dead. They cannot kill the soul and it exists before the only one who can kill it…God, even after the body has been killed. The question lies in the clothing of the soul (consciousness-seed) with a garment (body-manifestation). Paul confirms this as being the natural pattern of how the world manifests images.

1 Corinthians 15:38, But God giveth it a body as it hath pleased him, and to every seed his own body.

This also clarifies the issue of predestination and what it is.

Ephesians 1:4, According as he hath chosen us in him before the foundation of the world, that we should be holy and without blame before him in love:5 Having predestinated us unto the adoption of children by Jesus Christ to himself, according to the good pleasure of his will, 6 To the praise of the glory of his grace, wherein he hath made us accepted in the beloved.

Just as those souls appear to be conscious and communicating with God under the altar of God it displays their awareness of their own state and the state of the world.

1 Corinthians 15:52, In a moment, in the twinkling of an eye, at the last trump: for the trumpet shall sound, and the dead shall be raised incorruptible, and we shall be changed.

We will not pass over the fact that Paul describes the rising of the dead and changing of the living in Christ as happening at the trump of God.

1 Thessalonians 4:15, For this we say unto you by the word of the Lord, that we which are alive and remain unto the coming of the Lord shall not prevent them which are asleep. 16 For the <u>Lord himself shall descend from heaven with a shout, with the voice of the archangel, and with the trump of God: and the dead in Christ shall rise first</u>:17 Then <u>we which are alive and remain shall be caught up together with them in the clouds</u>, to meet the Lord in the air: and so shall we ever be with the Lord.

It would appear that this event occurs at the sounding of the 7th angel as the "mystery of God" is finished.

Revelation 10:7, But in the days of the voice of the seventh angel, when he shall begin to sound, the mystery of God should be finished, as he hath declared to his servants the prophets. 8 And the voice which I heard from heaven spake unto me again, and said, Go and take the little book which is open in the hand of the angel which standeth upon the sea and upon the earth.

If we take the book of Revelation to be announcing a timeline of events, it is interesting to note that this seventh angel looks remarkably like the Son of Man in Revelation 1:12-16. It is after this 7th angel starts to sound that the work of the Two Witnesses is declared to be given power by this 7th angel to prophesy for 1260 days. This seventh angel sounds immediately after the death and resurrection of the Two Witnesses.

Revelation 11:15, And after three days and an half the spirit of life from God entered into them, and they stood upon their feet; and great fear fell upon them which saw them. 12 And they heard a great voice from heaven saying unto them, Come up hither. And they ascended up to heaven in a cloud; and their enemies beheld them. 13 And the same hour was there a great earthquake, and the tenth part of the city fell, and in the earthquake were slain of men seven thousand: and the remnant were affrighted, and gave glory to the God of heaven. 14 The second woe is past; and, behold, the third woe cometh quickly. 15 And the seventh angel sounded; and there were great voices in heaven, saying, The kingdoms of this world are become the kingdoms of our Lord, and of his Christ; and he shall reign for ever and ever.

What is interesting is that those who are alive in Christ see this event happen to the Two Witnesses and "give glory to God". This event is astounding and actually causes them to "fear". Why? The Two Witnesses have been resurrected and ascend into heaven...and the remnant have witnessed the reality of resurrection. Immediately after the resurrection and ascension of the Two Witnesses the following is declared.

Revelation 11:18, And the nations were angry, and thy wrath is come, and the time of the dead, that they should be judged, and that thou shouldest give reward unto thy servants the prophets, and to the saints, and them that fear thy name, small and great; and shouldest destroy them which destroy the earth.

It is immediately after this that we see the ascension of the Man-Child, the fleeing of the woman into the wilderness to be nourished for 1260 days, the devil is cast down and persecutes the remnant of her seed who have the testimony of Yeshua and keep the Commandments of God. Next, we are shown the beast, his mark, and his image. We can only assume that those alive in Christ have not been resurrected with the Two Witnesses after their testimony of 1260 days. If we view Revelation 13 to be after the death of the Two Witnesses, that would mean the mark of the beast does not happen until after the beast has killed the Two Witnesses' mid-tribulation.

Revelation 13:7, And it was given unto him to make war with the saints, and to overcome them: and power was given him over all kindreds, and tongues, and nations.

Does the beast rise at the end of the testimony of the Two Witnesses and commence his 1260-day persecution of the saints with the killing of the Two Witnesses?

Revelation 11:7, And when they shall have finished their testimony, the beast that ascendeth out of the bottomless pit shall make war against them, and shall overcome them, and kill them.

This would place the beast's ascension out of the bottomless pit coincident with the casting down of the devil and his "short time" of 1260 days to persecute those who are alive in Christ who have not been resurrected in the middle of the tribulation.

Revelation 14:12, Here is the patience of the saints: here are they that keep the commandments of God, and the faith of Jesus. 13 And I heard a voice from heaven saying unto me, Write, Blessed are the dead which die in the Lord from henceforth: Yea, saith the Spirit, that they may rest from their labours; and their works do follow them. 14 And I looked, and behold a white cloud, and upon the cloud one sat like unto the Son of man, having on his head a golden crown, and in his hand a sharp sickle.

Those who hold faith in Yeshua and keep His commandments (Law of Moses) are being killed for their faith and testimony during the reign of the beast during the 1260 days after the death and resurrection of the Two Witnesses. The seven angels pour out their plagues for one very clear reason, retribution.

Revelation 16:6, For they have shed the blood of saints and prophets, and thou hast given them blood to drink; for they are worthy.

To attempt to present believers escaping this time period in a pre-tribulation rapture appears to be a fantasy. The deliverance of God's people is from God's wrath upon Babylon at the end. Why then? Why so much wrath?

Revelation 18:4, And I heard another voice from heaven, saying, Come out of her, my people, that ye be not partakers of her sins, and that ye receive not of her plagues…20 Rejoice over her, thou heaven, and ye holy apostles and prophets; for God hath avenged you on her. 24 And in her was found the blood of prophets, and of saints, and of all that were slain upon the earth.

With this announcement to "come out of her my people" we see Babylon's destruction and then the presentation of their great deliverance…in heaven.

Revelation 19:1, And <u>after these things I heard a great voice of much people in heaven</u>, saying, Alleluia; Salvation, and glory, and honour, and power, unto the Lord our God:2 For true and righteous are his judgments: for <u>he hath judged the great whore,</u> which did corrupt the earth with her fornication, and hath avenged the blood of his servants at her hand…6 And I <u>heard as it were the voice of a great multitude,</u> and as the voice of many waters, and as the voice of mighty thunderings, saying, Alleluia: for the Lord God omnipotent reigneth. 7 Let us be glad and rejoice, and give honour to him:<u> for the marriage of the Lamb is come,</u> and his wife hath made herself ready. 8 And to her was granted that she should be arrayed in fine linen, clean and white: for the fine linen is the righteousness of saints.

This calling out of persecuted Christians and the marriage of the Lamb is announced having "come" "after these things". What things? The announcement of the judgement of Babylon. This marriage does not occur at the beginning of the tribulation, nor in the middle. It occurs when the seventh angel has sounded. It would appear that those who are alive in Christ at His coming are not the First-Fruits, they are the First Resurrection. The First-Fruits are declared to be the 144,000 (of Israel). As Paul indicated the timing of the resurrection of the First-Fruits is not at the same time as those who are alive at His coming.

1 Corinthians 15:23, But every man in his own order: Christ the First-Fruits; afterward they that are Christ's at his coming.

Notice Paul refers to the First-Fruits resurrection then indicates… "afterward" … "they that are Christ's at his coming". Whether those First-Fruits are those who were resurrected at the time of Yeshua's resurrection, or those who have died in Christ from Israel over the past 2,000 years, or if they be a select group of believers in Christ from Israel before the Great Tribulation…either way they are resurrected before those who are alive in Christ at His coming.

- Revelation 7:1, And after these things I saw four angels standing on the four corners of the earth, holding the four winds of the earth, that the wind should not blow on the earth, nor on the sea, nor on any tree. 2 And I saw another angel ascending from the east, having the seal of the living God: and he cried with a loud voice to the four angels, to whom it was given to hurt the earth and the sea, 3 Saying, Hurt not the earth, neither the sea, nor the trees, till we have sealed the servants of our God in their foreheads. 4 And I heard the number of them which were sealed: and there were sealed an hundred and forty and four thousand of all the tribes of the children of Israel.
- Revelation 14:1, And I looked, and, lo, a Lamb stood on the mount Sion, and with him an hundred forty and four thousand, having his Father's name written in their foreheads. 2 And I heard a voice from heaven, as the voice of many waters, and as the voice of a great thunder: and I heard the voice of harpers harping with their harps:3 And they sung as it were a new song before the throne, and before the four beasts, and the elders: and no man could

learn that song but the hundred and forty and four thousand, which were
redeemed from the earth. 4 These are they which were not defiled with women;
for they are virgins. These are they which follow the Lamb whithersoever he
goeth. These were redeemed from among men, being the First-Fruits unto God
and to the Lamb.

As such if this resurrection happens before those who are alive in Christ at His
coming, it would seem to be portrayed as happening before the earth and the sea
are hurt. In fact, after being shown the 144,000, and then a great multitude in white
robes, John is asked who is this great multitude. He is not asked who the 144,000
are. Why? They have already been identified as being 12,000 from each tribe of
Israel and the First-Fruits of God.

Revelation 7:9 After this I beheld, and, lo, a great multitude, which no man
could number, of all nations, and kindreds, and people, and tongues, stood
before the throne, and before the Lamb, clothed with white robes, and palms in
their hands;... 13 And one of the elders answered, saying unto me, What are
these which are arrayed in white robes? and whence came they?

The 144,000 are described as being sealed by God "in their foreheads" and then
"after this" the great multitude is described as being arrayed in "white robes". So,
the 144,000 are distinct in how they are sealed having the name of God in their
foreheads and they are viewed before the great multitude, who are described having
white robes. These two groups are distinct in their characteristics, grouping, and
timing of presentation. John is not asked who the 144,000 are since he is told they
come from each tribe of Israel. When asked about the great multitude and who
they are, he seems puzzled.

Revelation 7:14, And I said unto him, Sir, thou knows. And he said to me,
These are they which came out of great tribulation, and have washed their
robes, and made them white in the blood of the Lamb.

The 144,000 are not defined as coming out of "Great Tribulation" and are in
fact sealed before the earth and the sea are hurt. This would seem to indicate that
their sealing occurs before the earth and sea are hurt and before the Great
Tribulation. Whether this sealing is resurrection or just the mark of God's name
placed upon these 144,000 of Israel, either way it occurs right before the seventh
seal is broken and their protection is mentioned at the time of the fifth angel
sounding.

Revelation 9:4, And it was commanded them that they should not hurt the
grass of the earth, neither any green thing, neither any tree; but only those men
which have not the seal of God in their foreheads.

The question may remain in some people's minds if these 144,000 are the Man-
Child of Revelation 12:5 that ascend to God and his throne and if the great

579 | P a g e

multitude are the "remnant of the seed of the woman of Revelation 12:6, 13-17. As the beast persecutes the woman, who brings forth the Man-Child, we are then shown the Lamb on Mount Sion with the 144,000 who have the Father's name in their foreheads (Mark of God). Clearly this is the seal mentioned earlier in Revelation 7. So, we see these 144,000 with Christ on Mount Sion. They are stated as having been "redeemed from the earth" (Revelation 12:3), so we are assuming this is in heaven, as Christ is not shown as having come to the earth as yet. And an angel declares at this point that if anyone receives the mark of the beast then they will receive the wrath of God.

Revelation 14:9, And the third angel followed them, saying with a loud voice, If any man worship the beast and his image, and receive his mark in his forehead, or in his hand, 10 The same shall drink of the wine of the wrath of God, which is poured out without mixture into the cup of his indignation; and he shall be tormented with fire and brimstone in the presence of the holy angels, and in the presence of the Lamb:

These two marks are juxtaposed and the fate of each group is declared. The question remains if this sealing with the mark of God results in the resurrection of the 144,000 before people are forced to choose the mark of the beast. We see this group of 144,000 in heaven before the seven last plagues are poured out.

Revelation 15:2, And I saw as it were a sea of glass mingled with fire: and them that had gotten the victory over the beast, and over his image, and over his mark, and over the number of his name, stand on the sea of glass, having the harps of God. 3 And they sing the song of Moses the servant of God, and the song of the Lamb, saying, Great and marvellous are thy works, Lord God Almighty; just and true are thy ways, thou King of saints. 4 Who shall not fear thee, O Lord, and glorify thy name? for thou only art holy: for all nations shall come and worship before thee; for thy judgments are made manifest.

How do we know these are the 144,000?

Revelation 14:1, And I looked, and, lo, a Lamb stood on the mount Sion, and with him an hundred forty and four thousand, having his Father's name written in their foreheads. 2 And I heard a voice from heaven, as the voice of many waters, and as the voice of a great thunder: and I heard the voice of harpers harping with their harps:3 And they sung as it were a new song before the throne, and before the four beasts, and the elders: and no man could learn that song but the hundred and forty and four thousand, which were redeemed from the earth.

It is only after the 144,000 sing this song that the seven angels come out with the seven plagues.

Revelation 15:5, And after that I looked, and, behold, the temple of the tabernacle of the testimony in heaven was opened:6 And the seven angels came out of the temple, having the seven plagues, clothed in pure and white linen, and having their breasts girded with golden girdles.

Either way we have confirmed that the 144,000 are on a "sea of glass" and on "Mount Sion". Is this in heaven?

Revelation 4:5, And <u>out of the throne</u> proceeded lightnings and thunderings and voices: and there <u>were seven lamps of fire burning before the throne</u>, which are the seven Spirits of God. 6 <u>And before the throne there was a sea of glass like unto crystal: and in the midst of the throne, and round about the throne</u>, were four beasts full of eyes before and behind.

It would indeed appear that these 144,000 are in heaven and before the Throne of God on Mount Sion. This does not appear to be an earthly situation. This does not dismiss the possibility that this could be on earth.

Exodus 24:9, Then went up Moses, and Aaron, Nadab, and Abihu, and seventy of the elders of Israel:10 And they saw the God of Israel: and there was under his feet as it were a paved work of a sapphire stone, and as it were the body of heaven in his clearness. 11 And <u>upon the nobles of the children of Israel he laid not his hand: also they saw God, and did eat and drink</u>.

But given the fact that the Man-Child is caught "up" to God and His throne it would seem that this occurs in heaven.

Revelation 12:5, And she brought forth a man child, who was to rule all nations with a rod of iron: and her child was caught up unto God, and to his throne.

Also, the fact that these 144,000 are all male would seem to indicate that these 144,000 are the Man-Child of Revelation 12.

Revelation 14:1, And I looked, and, lo, a Lamb stood on the mount Sion, and with him an <u>hundred forty and four thousand, having his Father's name written in their foreheads</u>... 4 These are <u>they which were not defiled with women; for they are virgins</u>. These are they which follow the Lamb whithersoever he goeth. These were <u>redeemed from among men, being the First-Fruits unto God and to the Lamb</u>.

We are proposing the following order of events:
- Yeshua is resurrected and ascends.
- The Man-Child (144,000) are resurrected and ascend.
- Those who are in Christ are changed and ascend at His coming.

- 1 Corinthians 15:23, But every man in his own order: Christ the First-Fruits; afterward they that are Christ's at his coming.
- Exodus 23:14, <u>Three times thou shalt keep a feast unto me in the year</u>. 15 Thou shalt keep <u>the feast of unleavened bread</u>:(thou shalt eat unleavened bread seven days, as I commanded thee, in the time appointed of the month Abib; for in it thou camest out from Egypt: and none shall appear before me empty:)16 And <u>the feast of harvest, the First-Fruits of thy labours</u>, which thou hast sown in the field:<u> and the feast of ingathering</u>, which is in the end of the year, when thou hast gathered in thy labours out of the field. 17 Three times in the year all thy males shall appear before the Lord God.

The Scriptural Order of Resurrection:
- Yeshua's resurrection- The Feast of Unleavened Bread
- The Man-Child (144,000)- The Feast of Harvest, First-Fruits (Shavuot-Pentecost-12 tribes of Israel)
  - o Revelation 7:4, And I heard the number of them which were sealed: and there were sealed an hundred and forty and four thousand of all the tribes of the children of Israel. 5 Of the tribe of <u>Juda</u> were sealed twelve thousand. Of the tribe of <u>Reuben</u> were sealed twelve thousand. Of the tribe of <u>Gad</u> were sealed twelve thousand. 6 Of the tribe of <u>Aser</u> were sealed twelve thousand. Of the tribe of <u>Nephthalim</u> were sealed twelve thousand. Of the tribe of <u>Manasses</u> were sealed twelve thousand. 7 Of the tribe of <u>Simeon</u> were sealed twelve thousand. Of the tribe of <u>Levi</u> were sealed twelve thousand. Of the tribe of <u>Issachar </u>were sealed twelve thousand. 8 Of the tribe of <u>Zabulon</u> were sealed twelve thousand. Of the tribe of <u>Joseph</u> were sealed twelve thousand. Of the tribe of <u>Benjamin</u> were sealed twelve thousand.
  - o Where is Ephraim and where is Dan in the list of the 144,000? The leading tribes of the 10 tribes of Israel that were exiled for setting up golden calves for worship in the Northern Kingdom of Israel and were associated with images/idols. They need to repent and remember the Law of Moses. They will be tried and purified. They need to forsake the mark and image of the Beast.
- Those who are in Christ at His coming- The Feast of Ingathering (Sukkot-Tabernacles). We won't take the time to expound on the relationship between Sukkot and its sacrifices related to the 70 nations (Gentiles-Great Multitude-Ephraim & his companions).
  - o Joshua 17:17, And Joshua spake unto the house of Joseph, even to Ephraim and to Manasseh, saying, Thou art <u>a great people</u>, and hast great power: thou shalt not have one lot only:
  - o **FEAST OF TABERNACLES (SUKKOT): Trumpet and Shofar Blasts:** As an expression of the feeling of great joy which reverberated through the congregation on account of the

opportunity to fulfill the will of G-d through this precept, the bringing of these branches each day and their arrangement along the altar was accompanied by trumpet-blasts and the sounding of the shofar by the priests and Levites. **Surrounding the Altar:** Each day of the festival, after the willow branches were thus arranged firmly along the altar's foundation, the priests would march one time around the altar, making a circle with their lulavim in hand, appealing to the Almighty "We beseech You, O L-rd, please save us! We beseech You, O L-rd, please grant us success!" (Ibid.) On the last day of the festival, the seventh day, they would "surround" the altar seven times-as a remembrance of the conquest of Jericho (JT Sukkah 4, 3). It was customary on the last day of Sukkot, after the final circling of the altar, for the children to playfully snatch the four species from the adults, and eat their etrogs! The adults would graciously indulge the children. **The Sacrifice of Seventy Bulls:** During Sukkot in the time of the Holy Temple, a unique sacrifice was offered on the altar - with a unique intention. In chapter 29 of the book of Numbers, the Bible outlines the sacrifices that are to be offered over the span of the holiday. Counting the number of bulls that are offered over the seven day period, we find that the total number was seventy. And in chapter 10 of the book of Genesis, there are seventy nations mentioned. These are the primordial nations, sometimes referred to as the "seventy languages," which represent all humanity. The Talmud (BT Sukkah 55:B) teaches that the seventy bulls that were offered in the Holy Temple served as atonement for the seventy nations of the world. Truly, as the rabbis observed, "if the nations of the world had only known how much they needed the Temple, they would have surrounded it with armed fortresses to protect it" (Bamidbar Rabbah 1, 3). Here we can already sense that inherent within the very nature of the holiday, an inexorable bond - as expressed through its sacrificial requirements - links it to the earth's peoples. Sukkot was mandated by the Creator Himself to be a holiday for all the world. (templeinstitute.org)

Is there any merit to this idea that we are waiting on the harvesting of Israel as the First-Fruits before the Gentiles in Christ can be resurrected? The patterns and fractals of scriptures seem to indicate that this is a strong possibility.

21 THE RESTRAINER

2 Thessalonians 2:1, Now we beseech you, brethren, <u>by the coming of our</u> <u>Lord Jesus Christ, and by our gathering together unto him,</u> 2 That ye <u>be not</u> <u>soon shaken in mind,</u> or be troubled, neither by spirit, nor by word, nor by letter as from us, as that the day of Christ is at hand. 3 <u>Let no man deceive you</u> <u>by any means:</u> for <u>that day shall not come, except there come a falling away</u> <u>first, and that man of sin be revealed,</u> the son of perdition; 4 Who opposeth and exalteth himself above all that is called God, or that is worshipped; so that he as God sitteth in the temple of God, shewing himself that he is God. 5 Remember ye not, that, when I was yet with you, I told you these things? 6 <u>And now ye know what</u> **withholdeth (Strong's #2722)** <u>that he might be</u> <u>revealed in his time.</u> 7 For the mystery of iniquity doth already work: <u>only he</u> <u>who now</u> **letteth (Strong's #2722)** <u>will let, until he be taken out of the way.</u>

"LETTETH" Strong's Number 2722
katechó:to hold fast, hold back
Original Word:κατέχω
Part of Speech:Verb
Transliteration:katechó
Phonetic Spelling:(kat-ekh'-o)
Short Definition:I hold fast, bind, restrain
Definition:(a) I hold fast, bind, arrest, (b) I take possession of, lay hold of, (c) I hold back, detain, restrain, (d) I hold a ship, keep its head.
katechó:to hold fast, hold back

Paul is trying to clear up some misconceptions about the order of events that will occur as they relate to those in Christ at His coming and their gathering together unto Yeshua. He makes it clear that some people will be deceived and think that it occurs before the revealing of the man of sin, the Antichrist, and before the falling away occurs. He corrects them knowing this would be a common error. He then indicates that someone or something "what withholdeth that he might be revealed in his time" (2 Thessalonians 2:6).

It seems quite apparent that Paul had an expectation that something "withholds" the Antichrist to ensure he is revealed in his time. And "he" who withholds the Antichrist from being revealed until "he who now letteth will let, until he be taken out of the way." Could this "he" who lets and "what" that withholds the Antichrist be the Man-Child (144,000), the First-Fruits of the resurrection? Clearly the Man-Child is revealed by being a "wonder in heaven" via his ascension to the throne of God in heaven.

Revelation 12:1, And there appeared a great wonder in heaven; a woman clothed with the sun, and the moon under her feet, and upon her head a crown of twelve stars:2 And she being with child cried, travailing in birth, and pained to be delivered... 5 And she brought forth a man child, who was to rule all nations with a rod of iron: and her child was caught up unto God, and to his throne.

Notice Paul is writing to the Thessalonians who are a Gentile church and are not of the twelve tribes of Israel. They are wondering where they fit into the resurrection and the coming of Yeshua. Paul cautions them that their gathering together to be with the Lord is withheld by a "he" that will be revealed in "his" time. This "he" appears to "let" or withhold until "he" is taken out of the way. Could this be the ascension of the Man-Child, the First-Fruits of God, the 144,000? Paul appears to say that Israel's redemption is of key importance.

Romans 11:7, What then? Israel hath not obtained that which he seeketh for; but the election hath obtained it, and the rest were blinded. 8 (According as it is written, God hath given them the spirit of slumber, eyes that they should not see, and ears that they should not hear;) unto this day. 9 And David saith, Let their table be made a snare, and a trap, and a stumblingblock, and a recompence unto them:10 Let their eyes be darkened, that they may not see, and bow down their back alway. 11 I say then, Have they stumbled that they should fall? God forbid: but rather through their fall salvation is come unto the Gentiles, for to provoke them to jealousy. 12 Now if the fall of them be the riches of the world, and the diminishing of them the riches of the Gentiles; how much more their fulness? 13 For I speak to you Gentiles, inasmuch as I am the apostle of the Gentiles, I magnify mine office:14 If by any means I may provoke to emulation them which are my flesh, and might save some of them. 15 For if the casting away of them be the reconciling of the world, what shall the receiving of them be, but life from the dead? 16 For if the firstfruit be holy,

<u>the lump is also holy</u>: and if the root be holy, so are the branches.

It would appear that Paul is saying that the resurrection of the dead will occur when Israel's fullness has occurred. Perhaps it is the fulfilling of this full count from Israel that prevents, withholds, and lets (keeps) the resurrection of the Gentiles from occurring. Notice he says that the lump cannot be made holy without the First-Fruits as they are what makes the rest of the lump holy, just as Yeshua makes the redeemed holy.

Romans 11:25, For I would not, brethren, that ye should be ignorant of this mystery, lest ye should be wise in your own conceits; that <u>blindness in part is happened to Israel, until the fulness of the Gentiles be come in</u>. 26 And <u>so all Israel shall be saved</u>: as it is written, There shall come out of Sion the Deliverer, and shall turn away ungodliness from Jacob:

Just as the Gentiles cannot be gathered until "he" who withholds is "taken out of the way", Israel cannot be saved until the "fullness of the Gentiles" occurs.

The Talmud refers to Shavuot as Atzeret [6] (Hebrew:עצרת, literally, "refraining" or "holding back"[7] (Wikipedia)

Before Sukkot (Feast of Tabernacles) can be fulfilled, first Shavuot (Pentecost) must be fulfilled. Here we see a clear connection between the "First-Fruits" (144,000) and the "holding back" (withholding) and the "letteth" (restrainer or refrainer). Could it be that the sign indicating the time is near is associated with Pentecost?

Matthew 24:31, And <u>he shall send his angels with a great sound of a trumpet, and they shall gather together his elect from the four winds</u>, from one end of heaven to the other. 32 Now learn a parable of the fig tree; <u>When his branch is yet tender, and putteth forth leaves, ye know that summer is nigh</u>:33 So <u>likewise ye, when ye shall see all these things, know that it is near, even at the doors</u>.

It appears that Yeshua is saying the gathering together will be known to be near when the branch puts forth leaves and then we know summer is nigh. Could there be an underlying understanding that we have missed?

According to the Midrash, Mount Sinai suddenly blossomed with flowers in anticipation of the giving of the Torah on its summit. Greenery also figures in the story of the baby Moses being found among the bulrushes in a watertight cradle (Ex. 2:3) when he was three months old (Moses was born on 7 Adar and placed in the Nile River on 6 Sivan, the same day he later brought the Jewish nation to Mount Sinai to receive the Torah). [17]
For these reasons, many Jewish families traditionally decorate their homes and synagogues with plants, flowers and leafy branches in honor of Shavuot.

Some synagogues decorate the bimah with a canopy of flowers and plants so that it resembles a chuppah, as Shavuot is mystically referred to as the day the matchmaker (Moses) brought the bride (the nation of Israel) to the chuppah (Mount Sinai) to marry the bridegroom (God); the ketubah (marriage contract) was the Torah. Some Eastern Sephardi communities actually read out a ketubah between God and Israel as part of the service.

The Vilna Gaon cancelled the tradition of decorating with trees because it too closely resembles the Christian decorations for their holidays. (Wikipedia)

Could this "putteth forth leaves" be alluding to the actual fulfillment of Pentecost where the removal of the "withholder" that occurs is actually the ascension of the Man-Child (144,000) and the First-Fruits of Israel?

"Atzeret," means "refraining" or "holding back." On all festivals, in addition to refraining from work unconnected to food preparation, there is also a special mitzvah to perform: on Pesach one eats matzah, on Sukkot one sits in a sukkah and takes the four species, on Rosh Hashanah one blows the shofar, and on Yom Kippur one fasts. Shavuot, however, has no special mitzvah connected to it, except for refraining from work. Thus, we emphasize that the obvious mitzvah of the festival is "Atzeret" — refraining and holding back from doing any forbidden work. (Chabad.org)

Just as resurrection is a restoration of the original Image of God, resting in the Garden of Eden, unfallen and sinless, Shavuot depicts this same imagery of rest in a resurrected state. We cannot miss the fact that those who were to be first become last and the last become first.

Matthew 20:11, And when they had received it, they murmured against the goodman of the house, 12 Saying, These last have wrought but one hour, and thou hast made them equal unto us, which have borne the burden and heat of the day. 13 But he answered one of them, and said, Friend, I do thee no wrong: didst not thou agree with me for a penny? 14 Take that thine is, and go thy way: I will give unto this last, even as unto thee. 15 Is it not lawful for me to do what I will with mine own? Is thine eye evil, because I am good? 16 So the last shall be first, and the first last: for many be called, but few chosen.

This seems to be a recurring theme with the Jewish leaders having great opposition to their Messiah extending salvation to the Gentiles. They are typified as being unjust and having an evil eye. Yeshua (the Goodman) declares that He can do what He wants with what is His and they should go their way while He does so. Those called first (Jews) are made last for 2,000 years and those called last (Gentiles) are made first for 2,000 years. This disgruntled attitude leads the Chief Priests of the Jews to crucify Him (Matthew 20:17-17) and brings about His sacrifice for the redemption of the whole world.

The failure of the Jews is brought about by God...for the salvation of the Gentiles. The Jews are provoked to jealousy (Romans 10:19) for the Messiah by those same Gentiles. When their number (those of Israel) is come in and full, then it would appear that the First-Fruits are gathered and the 144,000 (Man-Child) ascends to the throne of God as the Friend of the Bridegroom. Then the Antichrist is revealed, the devil is cast down, and the woman and her remnant (those alive in Christ) flee to the wilderness for 1260 days until the judgment of Babylon is announced and all those who are alive in Christ are called out of her and meet the Lord and the dead in Christ that He brings with Him in the air.

These days Shavuot is known as the holiday that commemorates the giving of the Torah. In Temple times, however, Shavuot was significant for several other reasons. In fact, the Torah uses three names for the festival, none of them directly related to the event at Mount Sinai: Shavuot, Chag HaKatzir, and Yom HaBikurim.

"Shavuot" means "weeks," and refers to the seven weeks between Passover and Shavuot, during which each day is counted as part of Sefirat HaOmer. "Chag HaKatzir" means "the festival of the harvest"—in ancient Israel the holiday coincided with the wheat harvest, and "Yom HaBikurim" means "the day of the first produce," since on Shavuot the first offering from the new wheat crop, known as the "Shtei HaLechem" (the two loaves), was brought in the Temple.

In the agricultural society of ancient Israel, the wheat harvest was a very important event, and though it is not currently observed, the Shtei HaLechem bread offering was originally an essential part of the festival. Let's take a closer look at the offering and its significance, both practical and mystical.

How It Was Done

The Torah commands the Jewish people to bring an offering from the new wheat crop to the Temple on Shavuot. It was to be brought from the choicest wheat,7 which would be husked, ground into flour and sifted twelve times to ensure that only the finest flour was used.

The flour was brought to the Temple courtyard, where it was baked into two loaves of chometz, leavened bread, unlike almost all other offerings in the Temple, which were either flour or matzah (unleavened bread). (The korban toda, thanksgiving offering, was the only other sacrifice to have loaves of chometz brought with it.)

Along with the two loaves, two lambs were included in the offering. The priests would wave the lambs and the loaves in all four directions and up and down, and then place the lambs on the mizbeiach (altar). The loaves were eaten by the kohanim (priests).

The Talmud tells us that no offerings from the new crop of wheat were allowed in the Temple before the two loaves were brought. This is similar to the Omer offering brought on Passover, until which no one was allowed to eat from the new crop of barley... Many point to the contrast between the matzah we eat on Passover and the leavened bread used for the Shtei Halechem. Leavened bread was usually prohibited in sacrifices because dough that has risen is compared to pride and arrogance, traits associated with the yetzer hara (evil inclination). Studying Torah, however, subdues inappropriate pride, allowing us to use the energy of the evil inclination for good...

The famous chassidic master Rabbi Yehudah Aryeh Leib Alter of Ger (known by the name of his magnum opus, Sfas Emes) writes that the divine wisdom contained in the Torah is the power from which the world was created. Normally this wisdom is hidden, and physical beings feel that their own efforts are what count. At the giving of the Torah, however, G-d Himself spoke to man, meaning that the essential reality of all existence became visible and tangible. 29

He explains that the two loaves offered on Shavuot symbolize the duality that we perceive in creation: one signified divine blessings, the other the product of man's toil. On the anniversary of the giving of the Torah, they were both waived towards heaven as an acknowledgment that both come from G-d. (Chabad. org)

It is interesting to note that the first mention of the Feast of Weeks (Shavuot-Pentecost) occurs at the second giving of the Torah, the presentation of Name of the Lord (Yeshua), and the glorification of Moses' countenance.

Exodus 34:22, And thou shalt observe the feast of weeks, of the First-Fruits of wheat harvest, and the feast of ingathering at the year's end. 23 Thrice in the year shall all your menchildren appear before the Lord God, the God of Israel.

After so many "coincidental" references between the Feast of Weeks (Shavuot-Pentecost) and the ascension of the 144,000 (First-Fruits/Man-Child) to the throne of God we should no longer be surprised that Moses is instructed about how to observe Pentecost and that all males are to appear on this feast, on Unleavened Bread and The Feast of Ingathering (Tabernacles). Exodus 34 is showing the second giving of the Torah, the manifestation of the Name of the Lord, and the glorification of Moses' countenance. There are too many connections to resurrection to ignore.

Finally, can the one who "letteth" and "withholdeth" (refrains, restrains) be the 144,000 (Man-Child) and the completion of the full count from Israel that results in their ascension in resurrection to the throne of God? The Holy Spirit has historically been stated to be the restrainer. It would seem apparent that God will not remove His Holy Spirit from believers that are persecuted by the beast after the Man-Child has been called up to the throne of God. The remnant of the Seed of the Woman that birthed the Man-Child are killed and persecuted on the earth by the Beast, the Antichrist, the False Prophet, and the Devil who has been cast down.

It would also appear that there is a yet future fulfillment of Pentecost beyond the giving of the Holy Spirit to believers in Yeshua on that first Pentecost after His death and resurrection. Just as the apostles were a picture of the restored Image of God having the Shekinah Glory upon their heads and the testimony of Yeshua in their mouths, so also the 144,000 appear to have this same imagery having the name of the Father written on their foreheads and having a special song that only they could sing.

If we follow a process of elimination, Paul is stating that the coming of

Yeshua and the gathering to Him of those alive in Christ at His coming cannot occur until the falling away occurs and the man of sin be revealed. The man of sin cannot be revealed until "what" withholds him from being revealed and manifested is removed.

The man of sin will be revealed when this "what withholdeth": "only he who now letteth (Strong's #2722) will let, until he be taken out of the way..." So "what withholds" the man of sin from being revealed is a "he" that needs to be taken out of the way. This could either be the devil who is cast down to the earth or it could be the Man-Child and the First-Fruits that ascend up to the throne of God that results in the devil being cast down from heaven...who then has a short time and goes about persecuting the remnant of the seed of the woman who brought forth the Man-Child.

Scripturally we know that the resurrection of the First-Fruits happens before the resurrection of those who are alive in Christ at His coming as Paul describes the ranks of resurrection. Whether we on earth are aware that this resurrection has occurred is unknown unless the First-Fruits are the Man-Child and the great sign that appears in heaven at his accession to the throne of God (Revelation 12:5, 14:5). What is the distinction of the First-Fruits and the 144,000? The First-Fruits are on Mount Sion with the Lamb and before the throne of God having the name of the Father in their foreheads. They sing a song only they can learn. The great multitude is described as having white garments. Clearly these are two different classes of resurrected believers having two different roles. One group is of Israel and the other is of the Gentiles.

The devil and his angels are only cast down upon the ascension of the Man-Child. The man of sin who is possessed with the devil cannot be made manifest until the devil is cast down and that event is withheld until "he who now letteth (restrain or hold back from happening) ...until he be taken out of the way."

Could that be the devil "letting" until he is taken out of the way by the ascension of the Man-Child? Or is this the Man-Child letting until he is taken out of the way thereby causing the devil to be cast down and the man of lawlessness to be possessed by him?

The Thessalonians were worried because someone wrote a letter pretending to be Paul saying that Christ had already come and that they had missed the resurrection.

2 Thessalonians 2:1, Now we beseech you, brethren, by the coming of our Lord Jesus Christ, and by our gathering together unto him, 2 That ye be not soon shaken in mind, or be troubled, neither by spirit, nor by word, nor by letter as from us, as that the day of Christ is at hand.

Could it be that in the tribulation that this would be a common worry for those who are alive in Christ? Could it be that having witnessed this great sign in heaven and the Man-Child and the Two Witnesses ascending into heaven that they would be worried that they had missed the resurrection?

Revelation 11:12, And they heard a great voice from heaven saying unto them, Come up hither. And they ascended up to heaven in a cloud; and their enemies beheld them. 13 And the same hour was there a great earthquake, and the tenth part of the city fell, and in the earthquake were slain of men seven thousand: and the remnant were affrighted, and gave glory to the God of heaven.

Notice it is the beast that kills the Two Witnesses. The man of sin sitting in the temple showing himself that he is God occurs…when?

- 2 Thessalonians 2:3, Let no man deceive you by any means: for that day shall not come, except there come a falling away first, and that man of sin be revealed, the son of perdition; 4 Who opposeth and exalteth himself above all that is called God, or that is worshipped; so that he as God sitteth in the temple of God, shewing himself that he is God.
- Daniel 9:26, And after threescore and two weeks shall Messiah be cut off, but not for himself: and the people of the prince that shall come shall destroy the city and the sanctuary; and the end thereof shall be with a flood, and unto the end of the war desolations are determined. 27 And he shall confirm the covenant with many for one week: and in the midst of the week he shall cause the sacrifice and the oblation to cease, and for the overspreading of abominations he shall make it desolate, even until the consummation, and that determined shall be poured upon the desolate.

Here we see the "overspreading of abominations" and the sacrifices and oblations to cease. Both of these occur mid tribulation week. It would appear that these abominations occur because "he as God sitteth in the temple of God, shewing himself that he is God."

Daniel 11:31, And arms shall stand on his part, and they shall pollute the sanctuary of strength, and shall take away the daily sacrifice, and they shall place the abomination that maketh desolate… And they that understand among the people shall instruct many: yet they shall fall by the sword, and by flame, by captivity, and by spoil, many days. 34 Now when they shall fall, they shall be holpen with a little help: but many shall cleave to them with flatteries. 35 And some of them of understanding shall fall, to try them, and to purge, and to make them white, even to the time of the end: because it is yet for a time appointed. 36 And the king shall do according to his will; and he shall exalt himself, and magnify himself above every god, and shall speak marvellous things against the God of gods, and shall prosper till the indignation be accomplished: for that that is determined shall be done. 37 Neither shall he regard the God of his fathers, nor the desire of women, nor regard any god: for he shall magnify himself above all. 38 But in his estate shall he honour the God of forces: and a god whom his fathers knew not shall he honour with gold, and silver, and with precious stones, and pleasant things.

It would appear that this Son of Perdition causes his abomination mid-week, apparently in conjunction with the killing of the Two Witnesses, the ascension of the Man-Child and the descension of the devil down to the earth. Could it be that those alive in Christ witness these events of resurrection of the Two Witnesses and the ascension of the Man-Child and fear that Yeshua has already come and they are afraid that they failed to be gathered? Hence Paul's reminder that Yeshua will not come until the Man of Sin (2 Thessalonians 2:3) comes and the great falling away has occurred. We have been taught for so long that the resurrection of the dead in Christ and the First-Fruits would happen at the return of Yeshua, what if the First-Fruits resurrection happens mid-tribulation before Yeshua comes? After all the resurrection of the first fruits is a picture of Pentecost and the ascension of counting the omer to fifty.

Counting the Omer

The omer ("sheaf") is an old Biblical measure of volume of grain. On the day following the shabbat during Passover in Biblical times, observed today as the second day of Passover (The Feast of Unleavened Bread) on Day 16 of Hebrew Month 1 in Rabbinic Judaism, which is also known as "First Fruits", an omer of barley was offered in the Temple in Jerusalem, signalling the allowance of the consumption of chadash (grains from the new harvest). On the 50th day after the beginning of the count, corresponding to the holiday of Shavuot, two loaves made of wheat were offered in the Temple to signal the start of the wheat harvest.

The origins of the omer count (i. e. the Sefirat HaOmer), as enumerated in the Midrash Rabba Parashas Emor, explains that when the Children of Israel left ancient Egypt they were told by Moses that 49 days after the Exodus, they would be given the Torah. The populace was so excited at the prospect of a spiritual liberation, following the physical emancipation from Egypt, they kept a count of the passing days that ended with the giving of the Torah at the foot of Mount Sinai. The Torah itself, in Leviticus 23:15–16, and Deuteronomy 16:9, states that it is a commandment to count seven complete weeks from the day after Passover night ending with the festival of Shavuot on the fiftieth day. Shavuot is the festival marking the giving of the Torah to the Hebrew nation on the 6th of the Hebrew month of Sivan.

In keeping with the themes of spiritual growth and character development during this period, the Rabbinic literature [2] compares the process of growth to the two types of grain offered at either pole of the counting period. In ancient times, barley was simpler food while wheat was a more luxurious food. At Passover, the children of Israel were raised out of the Egyptian exile although they had sunken almost to the point of no return. The Exodus was an unearned gift from God, like the food of simple creatures that are not expected to develop their spiritual potential. The receiving of the Torah created spiritual elevation and active cooperation. Thus the Shavuot offering is "people food". [3] (Wikipedia)

The whole focus of Pentecost is the ascension of Israel to accept the Law of Moses on the fiftieth day. Could this be the very picture of the ascension of the Man-Child (144,000 all from the Tribes of Israel) and are the First Fruits in resurrection <u>before</u> the coming of the Lord and resurrection those alive in Christ at His coming? Just as Shavuot (Pentecost) requires a count linked to the Passover and is linked to the harvest of the first grain during the Days of Unleavened Bread, the timing occurs at the count of seven sevens (49 days plus 1) and the culmination of 50 in a Jubilee of freedom. This day occurs in the midst (middle) of the other holy days. Could it be that it will culminate during the middle of the tribulation in the ascension of the Man-Child (First Fruits) causing the descension of the devil?

Leviticus 25:8, And thou shalt number seven sabbaths of years unto thee, seven times seven years; and the <u>space of the seven sabbaths of years shall be unto thee forty and nine years</u>. 9 Then shalt thou <u>cause the trumpet of the jubile to sound on the tenth day of the seventh month, in the day of atonement</u> shall ye make the trumpet sound throughout all your land. 10 And <u>ye shall hallow the fiftieth year, and proclaim liberty throughout all the land unto all the inhabitants thereof</u>: it shall be a jubile unto you; and <u>ye shall return every man unto his possession, and ye shall return every man unto his family</u>. 11 A jubile shall that fiftieth year be unto you: ye shall not sow, neither reap that which groweth of itself in it, nor gather the grapes in it of thy vine undressed. 12 For it is the jubile; it shall be holy unto you: ye shall eat the increase thereof out of the field. 13 In the year of this jubile ye shall return every man unto his possession.

At the very least, even if we are forced to not draw an adamant conclusion on the timing of the resurrection of the First-Fruits and the gathering of those who are alive in Christ at His coming, we have certainly raised enough scriptural points to be open to a more scripturally accurate explanation of the nature and timing of the resurrection. Many will claim that Matthew 24 shows that believers are not going to go through the tribulation.

Matthew 24:24, For there shall arise false Christs, and false prophets, and shall shew great signs and wonders; insomuch that, if it were possible, they shall deceive the very elect. 25 Behold, I have told you before. 26 Wherefore if they shall say unto you, <u>Behold, he is in the desert</u>; go not forth: behold, he is in the secret chambers; believe it not. 27 For as the lightning cometh out of the east, and shineth even unto the west; so shall also the coming of the Son of man be. 28 For wheresoever the carcase is, there will the eagles be gathered together. 29 <u>Immediately after the tribulation of those days</u> shall the sun be darkened, and the moon shall not give her light, and the stars shall fall from heaven, and the powers of the heavens shall be shaken:30 And <u>then shall appear the sign of the Son of man in heaven</u>: and then shall all the tribes of the earth mourn, and <u>they shall see the Son of man coming in the clouds of heaven</u> with power and great glory. 31 And <u>he shall send his angels with a great sound of a trumpet, and they shall gather together his elect</u> from the four winds, from one end of heaven to the other.

The central issue of this section of scripture relates to the Thessalonians question, has Christ already come and did we miss the resurrection? Yeshua answers those who will be told that "He has already come" that they should not be deceived and that He will arrive "immediately after the tribulation of those days" for the purpose to "gather together his elect". This very gathering is necessary to avoid the certain death of those in Christ.

Matthew 24:22, And except those days should be shortened, there should no flesh be saved: but for the elect's sake those days shall be shortened.

If the elect had been raptured or resurrected pre-tribulation or mid-tribulation, then why would they be in jeopardy? Some would like to make this "elect" Israel or someone other than the church in order to show that the Church will not be on the Earth suffering tribulation. Why are those who are in jeopardy on the earth gathered "lest they die"? Because they are not destined for the wrath of the Lamb and of God upon Babylon (Revelation 18:4). This would appear to be what we as believers should aspire to "escape" from.

Luke 21:32, Verily I say unto you, <u>This generation shall not pass away, till all be fulfilled</u>. 33 Heaven and earth shall pass away: but my words shall not pass away. 34 And <u>take heed to yourselves, lest at any time your hearts be overcharged</u> with surfeiting, and drunkenness, and cares of this life, and so that day come upon you unawares. 35 For <u>as a snare shall it come on all them that dwell on the face of the whole earth</u>. 36 <u>Watch ye therefore, and pray always, that ye may be accounted worthy to escape all these things that shall come to pass</u>, and to stand before the Son of man.

It would appear that believers should aspire to escape from the "snare" that is coming to test all those who dwell on the earth. Does this mean that we are to aspire to escape from the earth or to aspire to escape from the snare that will be hidden by an overcharged heart? Only by watching and praying do we avoid the overcharged heart that is consumed by the cares of this life and will test everyone who dwells on the earth.

This is how we are delivered from the snare...not necessarily by being delivered literally from the earth, until Christ arrives to deliver us from the wrath of God on Babylon. Certainly, we can be counted "worthy to escape", while being on the earth, from the devil who has been cast down and pursues the woman and the remnant of her seed into the wilderness where she is nourished for 3 ½ years. Obviously, Christ details when the gathering of the living in Christ occurs... "after the tribulation of those days".

Matthew 24:29, <u>Immediately after the tribulation of those days</u> shall the sun be darkened, and the moon shall not give her light, and the stars shall fall from heaven, and the powers of the heavens shall be shaken:30 And <u>then shall</u>

appear the sign of the Son of man in heaven: and then shall all the tribes of the earth mourn, and they shall see the Son of man coming in the clouds of heaven with power and great glory. 31 And he shall send his angels with a great sound of a trumpet, and they shall gather together his elect from the four winds, from one end of heaven to the other.

The Man of Sin (Son of Perdition) cannot be in the temple of God showing himself to be God, if he has not first killed the Two Witnesses. You cannot convince anyone that you are God if you have two men outside the temple doing miracles showing that you are not God. So obviously the Two Witnesses must give testimony during the first 3 ½ years of the tribulation and the Man of Sin is revealed at the end of their ministry. Notice that the beast who ascends out of the bottomless pit kills them at the end of their ministry. That would put the beast who ascends out of the bottomless pit at the end of the 1260 days that they give testimony, after the opening of the seventh seal, during the sounding of the fifth angel and during the first woe.

Revelation 11:7, And when they shall have finished their testimony, the beast that ascendeth out of the bottomless pit shall make war against them, and shall overcome them, and kill them.

Whether we can draw conclusively what the series of events will be, we cannot say adamantly. What we can say is that there are enough legitimate scriptural passages to call into question the idea of a Pre-Tribulation rapture and whether the First-Fruits resurrection happens immediately before the resurrection and gathering together those who are alive at Christ's coming.

To try and say that the Holy Spirit is the restrainer and is removed from the earth (via the Church being raptured) so the Man of Sin can be revealed appears to be unscriptural, or to say that Michael the Archangel is the restrainer and is removed that Satan may go unhindered also appears to be unscriptural. To say that the elect are to hope to "escape" the things to come, but are shown going through the things to come would also appear to be unscriptural. We do see the elect being saved from, gathered, and escaping from the wrath of God on Babylon.

What we can say with certainty is that the Two Witnesses are killed and resurrected mid-tribulation after 1260 days of testimony. White robes are given to those who have been killed for the Word of God and for their testimony at the fifth seal. At the opening of the seventh seal and the sounding of the seventh angel the wonder of the Man-Child is seen in heaven and he is caught up to God. The woman who bore him is pursued into the wilderness by the devil who is cast down to Earth. He persecutes the remnant of her seed and she is protected and nourished for 1260 days, the same amount of time that the beast continues (42 months) after killing the Two Witnesses.

All the world is forced to accept the mark and image of the beast - they cannot buy or sell without that mark. On Mount Sion, the Lamb of God stands with the 144,000 who are described as the First-Fruits of the resurrection.

People are warned if they take the mark of the beast they will suffer the wrath of God. Those who die in the Lord from that point on are declared, "blessed". An angel in the cloud is told to reap the earth. Seven angels (messengers) begin to pour out the wrath of God on those who have the mark of the beast. Those who have gotten victory over the beast, his mark, and image are shown on sea of glass singing a new song.

Three angels pour out their plagues on those who have the mark of the beast and his image because they shed the blood of the saints and prophets. The other angels pour out their plagues. Babylon then comes into remembrance before God and He decides to then give her "the cup of the wine of the fierceness of His wrath" (Revelation 16:19). God calls His people out of Babylon that they might escape His wrath.

Revelation 18:4, And I heard another voice from heaven, saying, Come out of her, my people, that ye be not partakers of her sins, and that ye receive not of her plagues...20 Rejoice over her, thou heaven, and ye holy apostles and prophets; for God hath avenged you on her...24 And in her was found the blood of prophets, and of saints, and of all that were slain upon the earth.

Now after these things finally we see a conclusion to the matter.

Revelation 19:1, <u>And after these things I heard a great voice of much people in heaven,</u> saying, Alleluia; Salvation, and glory, and honour, and power, unto the Lord our God: . . . 5 And a voice came out of the throne, saying, Praise our God, all ye his servants, and ye that fear him, both small and great. 6 And <u>I heard as it were the voice of a great multitude,</u> and as the voice of many waters, and as the voice of mighty thunderings, saying, Alleluia: for the Lord God omnipotent reigneth. 7 <u>Let us be glad and rejoice, and give honour to him: for the marriage of the Lamb is come, and his wife hath made herself ready</u>. 8 And to her was granted <u>that she should be arrayed in fine linen, clean and white: for the fine linen is the righteousness of saints</u>. 9 And he saith unto me, Write, <u>Blessed are they which are called unto the marriage supper of the Lamb</u>. And he saith unto me, These are the true sayings of God.

Just as the souls under the altar were given white garments early on in the tribulation, so also those who are called out of Babylon and escape the wrath of God "after all these things" are clothed in her white garments as well. So perhaps we are seeing the resurrection of the First-Fruits early on (of Israel) and then the gathering of the great multitude (from the nations) at Christ's coming to judge Babylon. How can it be that going through the tribulation is still an "escape" from wrath?

- Matthew 10:28, Do not be afraid of those who kill the body but cannot kill the soul. Rather, be afraid of the One who can destroy both soul and body in hell.
- Luke 12:4, And I say unto you my friends, Be not afraid of them that kill the body, and after that have no more that they can do. 5 But I will

forewarn you whom ye shall fear: Fear him, which after he hath killed hath power to cast into hell; yea, I say unto you, Fear him.

This appears to be the fate of those who follow after the beast.

- Revelation 20:10, And the devil that deceived them was cast into the lake of fire and brimstone, where the beast and the false prophet are, and shall be tormented day and night for ever and ever. 11 And I saw a great white throne, and him that sat on it, from whose face the earth and the heaven fled away; and there was found no place for them. 12 And I saw the dead, small and great, stand before God; and the books were opened: and another book was opened, which is the book of life: and the dead were judged out of those things which were written in the books, according to their works. 13 And the sea gave up the dead which were in it; and death and hell delivered up the dead which were in them: and they were judged every man according to their works. 14 And death and hell were cast into the lake of fire. This is the second death. 15 And whosoever was not found written in the book of life was cast into the lake of fire.
- Revelation 14:9, And the third angel followed them, saying with a loud voice, If any man worship the beast and his image, and receive his mark in his forehead, or in his hand, 10 The same shall drink of the wine of the wrath of God, which is poured out without mixture into the cup of his indignation; and he shall be tormented with fire and brimstone in the presence of the holy angels, and in the presence of the Lamb:11 And the smoke of their torment ascendeth up for ever and ever: and they have no rest day nor night, who worship the beast and his image, and whosoever receiveth the mark of his name.

Given the fact that God's wrath carries with it an eternal punishment and not just a death of the body, but also the soul (consciousness), it would seem going through tribulation and having the body killed is still a good escape from the wrath of God. Ultimately it would appear that the demons and Satan know their ultimate fate will come and that it will be at the hands of the Messiah Yeshua.

Matthew 8:28, And when he was come to the other side into the country of the Gergesenes, there met him two possessed with devils, coming out of the tombs, exceeding fierce, so that no man might pass by that way. 29 And, behold, they cried out, saying, What have we to do with thee, Jesus, thou Son of God? art thou come hither to torment us before the time? 30 And there was a good way off from them an herd of many swine feeding. 31 So the devils besought him, saying, If thou cast us out, suffer us to go away into the herd of swine. 32 And he said unto them, Go. And when they were come out, they went into the herd of swine: and, behold, the whole herd of swine ran violently down a steep place into the sea, and perished in the waters.

Given the weight of all these scriptures the possibility looks very good that the scenario of a pre-tribulation rapture is unlikely and that the specificity of the scriptures shows a pattern of death and resurrection unlike what the Church has taught for thousands of years. Those that take the mark and image of the beast appear to seal their fate by making a covenant with death and hell (Revelation 20:12-15).

Isaiah 28:15, Because ye have said, We have made a covenant with death, and with hell are we at agreement; when the overflowing scourge shall pass through, it shall not come unto us: for we have made lies our refuge, and under falsehood have we hid ourselves:

We must also consider the following.

2 Timothy 2:1, I charge thee therefore before God, and the Lord Jesus Christ, who shall judge the quick and the dead at his appearing and his kingdom;

This could be a reference to the gathering together of those in Christ at His appearing and as it says "and the dead" this could refer to "at His appearing" or it could refer to "and his kingdom" where the rest of the dead are raised at the end of the 1,000 years.

Revelation 20:5, But the rest of the dead lived not again until the thousand years were finished. This is the first resurrection.

We must also take into account this scripture.

1 Corinthians 15:51, Behold, I shew you a mystery; <u>We shall not all sleep, but we shall all be changed</u>, 52 In a moment, <u>in the twinkling of an eye, at the last trump: for the trumpet shall sound, and the dead shall be raised incorruptible, and we shall be changed</u>. 53 For this corruptible must put on incorruption, and this mortal must put on immortality.

The implications of this scripture are staggering. How many different ways can we state what we think the author might have meant?

- Who are the "we" and the "all"? We would assume believers in Christ. Paul is saying the "we" are those dead in Christ and the living in Christ.
- The dead in Christ sleep and those alive in Christ at His appearing will not sleep.
- Both groups however will be changed.
- When is this to occur? At the Last Trump. What is the Last Trump? Is it the sounding of the seventh angel when the mystery of God is finished (Revelation 10:7, 11:5)? Is it the same angel that declares the Two Witnesses will prophesy for 1260 days? And then the beast continues another 42 months

after they have finished their testimony?

- The dead are raised incorruptible at the "last trump" …whenever it is.
- When the dead are raised and "we", those who are alive, will be changed. So, it could be that both the dead and the living in Christ are the "all" that are all changed, and the "but" is showing that the dead sleep, but the rest who are alive in Christ at His coming will not sleep, but go directly to their change. Whether this sleep means that their bodies sleep in the dust and their consciousness also sleeps can be debated continually. The book of Revelation clearly depicts the consciousness of those killed for their testimony and for keeping the commandments of God as being conscious enough to ask God, "How long?" (Revelation 6:9-10)

How does the modern teaching of the Pre-Tribulation Rapture and the Gathering together of those alive in Christ fail?

- It does not account for the souls under the altar receiving garments at the fifth seal and being told to wait for their brethren to be killed as they were.
- It does not account for the resurrection and ascension of the Two-Witnesses after 1260 days of witnessing.
- It does not account for the ascension of the Man-Child mid-tribulation and the remnant of her seed being persecuted for another 1260 days.
- It does not account for the gathering of those alive in Christ at His coming on the Last Trump, but indicates that He comes twice, once at the beginning and once at the end.
- Nor does it account for God calling His people out of Babylon before His wrath falls.

How does the modern teaching of the Mid-Tribulation Rapture and the Gathering together of those alive in Christ fail?

- It does not account for the gathering of those alive in Christ at His coming on the Last Trump, but indicates that He comes twice, once at the beginning and once at the end.
- It does not account for the ascension of the Man-Child mid-tribulation and the remnant of her seed being persecuted for another 1260 days.
- Nor does it account for God calling His people out of Babylon before His wrath falls.

How does the modern teaching of the Post-Tribulation Rapture and the Gathering together of those alive in Christ fail?

- It does not account for the souls under the altar receiving garments at the fifth seal and being told to wait for their brethren to be killed as they were.
- It does not account for the resurrection and ascension of the Two-Witnesses after 1260 days of witnessing.
- It does not account for the ascension of the Man-Child (144,000) mid-tribulation and the remnant of her seed being persecuted for another 1260 days.

What are the problems with modern teaching on the rapture and the resurrection?

- Characters are often un-identified with specificity.
  - o Example the Man-Child is stated to be Christ...who was killed 2,000 years ago, but is shown clearly being born and pursued to be killed during this end-time scenario and is connected to a 1260-day count of protection for the woman and that remnant of her seed that are pursued.
  - o Two Angels clearly identify themselves as being like John, of the prophets and a fellow servant, and are clearly resurrected beings before the gathering of those alive in Christ and the dead in Christ before He comes to gather together the living in Christ.
- Timelines are ignored or confused.
  - o Clearly the Two-Witnesses testify for 1260 days and then the beast continues for another 42 months. The Son of Perdition cannot likely show himself to be God if there are two men outside his temple doing miracles and showing that he is not God.
- Groups of resurrected saints are all lumped together as one group.
  - o The Man-Child and the 144,000 are clearly not the Great Multitude. They have different identifying characteristics and roles.
  - o The First-Fruits do not appear to be the gathering of those who are alive in Christ at His coming. Paul states that the order of resurrection is: Yeshua, the First-Fruits, those alive at His coming.
- Whether those who dead in Christ are conscious or not seems to be a settled issue, as they are still crying out to God from under the altar. Perhaps the real issue is, when are these "dead in Christ" given resurrection garments and when are they manifested to those alive on the earth. Could it be that they are resurrected/raised (given resurrection garments) before those who are alive in Christ see them manifested to the world? The key issue may not be when they receive resurrection garments, but when are they in resurrected garments manifested (revealed) to the creation and those on the Earth.
  - o Romans 8:18, For I reckon that the sufferings of this present time are not worthy to be compared with the glory which shall be revealed in us. 19 For the earnest expectation of the creature waiteth for the manifestation of the sons of God.

Given all these issues with the modern teaching of the rapture and the resurrection surely, we can see the legitimacy of raising these questions without being adamant about what must happen. Adamancy only breeds self-insured ignorance, just as the Jews could not perceive the coming of the Messiah due to their adamancy of what they thought must occur, we should be more open than they were to allow the truth of the scriptures to speak for themselves.

It would appear to be clear that the First-Fruits (1 Corinthians 15:23, Revelation 14:4) are not resurrected at the same time as those who are alive in Christ (Great

Multitude-Revelation 7:9-13) and gathered at His coming. It would also appear that these First-Fruits are associated with being male (seed, Friend of the Bridegroom) and the Great Multitude is associated with being female (manifested fruit, Lamb's bride).

One last note on this issue. Regardless of the timing of these events the reality is that many will be called to fulfill the same imagery as Yeshua the Messiah and be killed for their testimony of Him and for keeping His commandments. Should the church rightfully be happy in heaven rejoicing in a marriage supper while their own brothers and sisters in Christ are suffering and dying on the earth for their testimony of the Messiah? I think not. The souls under the altar have it right, they are mourning and yearning for vengeance upon those who kill those in Christ. Once the cup is full, the wrath will fall.

> Revelation 17:4, And the woman was arrayed in purple and scarlet colour, and decked with gold and precious stones and pearls, <u>having a golden cup in her hand full of abominations</u> and filthiness of her fornication:5 And upon her forehead was a name written, Mystery, Babylon The Great, The Mother Of Harlots And Abominations Of The Earth. 6 And <u>I saw the woman drunken with the blood of the saints, and with the blood of the martyrs of Jesus</u>: and when I saw her, I wondered with great admiration.

We may want to consider the possibility that the Tribulation will follow the pattern of seed (male-death) and manifestation (female-resurrection life) and that each half of the tribulation focuses on male and then female, just as the Spring Holy Days focus on the male (seed) and the Fall Holy Days focus on the female (fruit/manifestation).

Moses receives the Law of Moses (Written Torah) on Pentecost, while He is in the cloud being instructed for forty days. Meanwhile Israel is worshiping the golden calf in the valley (death-like a seed) and then the Law is broken and buried under the mountain. Moses intercedes for Israel for forty days and ascends a second time on Elul 1 where he receives that same law with the same words a second time. He returns with a glorified countenance on Tishri 10, Yom Kippur (Day of Atonement). This is traditionally the only day of the year that Aaron (the High Priest) can enter into the Holy of Holies. Just as Moses came down with a glorified countenance (manifestation of a resurrected fruit) some commentators say that the High Priest on this day would also come out with a glorified countenance.

Moses was the High Priest on the mountain and after he cleansed Aaron and his sons, Aaron served as the High Priest in the valley. They are presented as Two Witnesses before God, one cleansing the garments of the other, one needing to be cleansed and the other not needing to be cleansed. Moses was passing on his image, countenance, and cleansed garments to His brother so they could intercede on behalf of the "bride" of God, Israel. We see this presentation of Two Witnesses over and over again.

Patterns of Two Witnesses:

- Adam & Eve
- Melchizedek & Abraham
- Moses & Aaron
- Elijah & Elisha
- Moses & Elijah
- John the Baptist & Yeshua
- Peter (Apostle to the Jews) & Paul (Apostle to the Gentiles)
- Actual end-time Two Witnesses
- Man-Child (144,000) and the Great Multitude (Bride of the Lamb)

Could it be that the first half of the tribulation is focused on the male (seed) and the second half of the tribulation is focused on the female (manifested fruit)? After all the book is called "Revelation". Moses' goal was to cleanse His brother so that he might enter into the Holy of Holies, just like Moses was able to enter the Shekinah Glory on the mountain and then in turn intercede on behalf of the People of Israel, the Bride of God.

Romans 8:19, For the earnest expectation of the creature waiteth for the manifestation of the sons of God.

God is still in the business of creating and making His image and likeness, from the beginning of creation until the very end of this fallen world.

1 John 3:2, Beloved, now are we the sons of God, and it doth not yet appear what we shall be: but we know that, when he shall appear, we shall be like him; for we shall see him as he is.

Just as the Spring Holy Days begin with the harvest of the First of the First-Fruits, Christ, shortly after Passover...the harvest continues of those seeds until Shavuot (Pentecost) when the Wheat seed is harvested. All of those spring harvests are of seed (male) and concludes with the wave offering of the two-leavened loaves and the two lambs. Christ is indeed the first of the First-Fruits which takes place during the Days of Unleavened Bread and as such He is without leaven (sin). Those offerings on Shavuot (Pentecost-Feast of Weeks) are appropriately filled with leaven and appear as a duality (two loaves and two lambs).

Leviticus 23:15, And ye shall count unto you from the morrow after the sabbath, from the day that ye brought the sheaf of the wave offering; seven sabbaths shall be complete:16 Even unto the morrow after the seventh sabbath shall ye number fifty days; and ye shall offer a new meat offering unto the Lord. 17 Ye shall bring out of your habitations two wave loaves of two tenth deals; they shall be of fine flour; they shall be baken with leaven; they are the First-Fruits unto the Lord. 18 And ye shall offer with the bread seven lambs without blemish of the first year, and one young bullock, and two rams: they shall be for a burnt offering unto the Lord, with their meat offering, and their drink offerings, even an offering made by fire, of sweet savour unto the Lord. 19 Then ye shall sacrifice one kid of the goats for a sin offering, and two lambs of the first year for a sacrifice of peace offerings. 20 And the priest shall wave them with the bread of the First-Fruits for a wave offering before the Lord, with the two lambs: they shall be holy to the Lord for the priest.

We can see that Yeshua the Messiah, the sinless lamb, is depicted by the "sheaf of the wave offering from the "morrow after the Sabbath" during the Days of Unleavened Bread.

Leviticus 23:6, In the fourteenth day of the first month at even is the Lord's passover. 6 And on the fifteenth day of the same month is the feast of unleavened bread unto the Lord: seven days ye must eat unleavened bread. 7 In the first day ye shall have an holy convocation: ye shall do no servile work therein. 8 But ye shall offer an offering made by fire unto the Lord seven days: in the seventh day is an holy convocation: ye shall do no servile work therein. 9 And the Lord spake unto Moses, saying, 10 Speak unto the children of Israel, and say unto them, When ye be come into the land which I give unto you, and shall reap the harvest thereof, then ye shall bring a sheaf of the First-Fruits of your harvest unto the priest:11 And he shall wave the sheaf before the Lord, to be accepted for you: on the morrow after the sabbath the priest shall wave it.

This wave sheaf of the First-Fruits that is offered during the Days of Unleavened Bread depict the sinless Messiah Yeshua and is the hallmark of Paul's comment on the order of timing in the resurrection. Christ is first and without sin (leaven).

The first-fruit harvest concludes seven weeks later with the ascension and waving of the two loaves with sin and the two lambs. Pentecost (Shavuot) concludes the harvest of the First-Fruits and is focused on seeds and the male. There are three feasts that the males are commanded to appear.

Exodus 34:22, And thou shalt observe the feast of weeks, of the First-Fruits of wheat harvest, and the feast of ingathering at the year's end. 23 Thrice in the year shall all your menchildren appear before the Lord God, the God of Israel.

As such we can only conclude this is the scriptural rationale that Paul used for describing the ranking and ordering of the resurrection of the dead.

1 Corinthians 15:20, But now is Christ risen from the dead, and become the First-Fruits of them that slept. 21 For since by man came death, by man came also the resurrection of the dead. 22 For as in Adam all die, even so in Christ shall all be made alive. 23 But every man in his own order: Christ the First-Fruits; afterward they that are Christ's at his coming.

Some attempt to say that Yeshua is only the First-Fruits and there are no others, but the book of Revelation has made it plain that the 144,000 are also the First-Fruits.

> Revelation 14:1, And I looked, and, lo, a Lamb stood on the mount Sion, and <u>with him an hundred forty and four thousand,</u> having his Father's name written in their foreheads...4 These are they which were not defiled with women; for they are virgins. These are they which follow the Lamb whithersoever he goeth. <u>These were redeemed from among men, being the First-Fruits unto God and to the Lamb.</u>

This being the case we have to seriously wonder if the Man-Child is the 144,000 that serves as being the "Friend of the Bridegroom" much like Moses was the intercessor between Israel and God and Abraham served as the intercessor between God and Sodom.

- James 2:23, And the scripture was fulfilled which saith, Abraham believed God, and it was imputed unto him for righteousness: and he was called the Friend of God.
- Genesis 18:24, Peradventure there be fifty righteous within the city: wilt thou also destroy and not spare the place for the fifty righteous that are therein?

> We actually see Moses fulfilling this same role when Israel sinned against God and He wanted to destroy them.

Deuteronomy 9:13, Furthermore the Lord spake unto me, saying, I have seen this people, and, behold, it is a stiffnecked people:14 Let me alone, that I may destroy them, and blot out their name from under heaven: and I will make of thee a nation mightier and greater than they. 15 So I turned and came down from the mount, and the mount burned with fire: and the two tables of the covenant were in my two hands. 16 And I looked, and, behold, ye had sinned against the Lord your God, and had made you a molten calf: ye had turned aside quickly out of the way which the Lord had commanded you. 17 And I took the two tables, and cast them out of my two hands, and brake them before your eyes. 18 And I fell down before the Lord, as at the first, forty days and forty nights: I did neither eat bread, nor drink water, because of all your sins which ye sinned, in doing wickedly in the sight of the Lord, to provoke him to anger. 19 For I was afraid of the anger and hot displeasure, wherewith the Lord was wroth against you to destroy you. But the Lord hearkened unto me at that time also. 20 And the Lord was very angry with Aaron to have destroyed him: and I prayed for Aaron also the same time. 21 And I took your sin, the calf which ye had made, and burnt it with fire, and stamped it, and ground it very small, even until it was as small as dust: and I cast the dust thereof into the brook that descended out of the mount.

God was actually offering to Moses to take Israel's place and He would make of him a great people. How did Moses respond? Just like the Messiah.

Exodus 32:31, And Moses returned unto the Lord, and said, Oh, this people have sinned a great sin, and have made them gods of gold. 32 Yet now, if thou wilt forgive their sin--; and if not, blot me, I pray thee, out of thy book which thou hast written. 33 And the Lord said unto Moses, Whosoever hath sinned against me, him will I blot out of my book.

Can you see how Yeshua was fulfilling the same role as Moses, interceding for the People of God while they were steeped in their worst sin?

Luke 23:33, And when they were come to the place, which is called Calvary, there they crucified him, and the malefactors, one on the right hand, and the other on the left. 34 Then said Jesus, Father, forgive them; for they know not what they do. And they parted his raiment, and cast lots. 35 And the people stood beholding. And the rulers also with them derided him, saying, He saved others; let him save himself, if he be Christ, the chosen of God.

Given the fact that this pattern of intercession and how Moses is a type of the Messiah that was to come and how they are both associated with the ascended male, having the name of God written upon them, we may need to reconsider our assumptions about how the Tribulation will play out.

Consider: if the name of our great leader Moses is not really a name, might it mean something else? Interestingly, if we spell Moses' name in Hebrew backwards, Moshe becomes HaShem, which literally means "The Name," one of the ways some Jews refer to God.

Then consider: if Moses' name spelled backwards becomes HaShem, reflecting the Godly nature of the human being, might not God's name spelled backward similarly reflect something essential about humankind? Indeed it does.

Look at Yud–Hay–Vov–Hay, the ineffable Name of God. Known as the Tetragrammaton, the Name was permitted for everyday greetings until at least 586 B. C. E. , when the First Temple was destroyed (Mishnah Berakhot 9:5). In time its pronunciation was permitted only to the priests (Mishnah Sotah 7:6), who would pronounce it in their public blessing of the people. After the death of the High Priest Shimon HaTzaddik around 300 B. C. E. (Babylonian Talmud, Tractate Yoma 39b) the name was pronounced only by the High Priest in the Holy of Holies on Yom Kippur (Mishnah Sotah 7:6; Mishnah Tamid 7:2). The sages then passed on the pronunciation of the Name to their disciples only once (some say twice) every seven years (Babylonian Talmud, Tractate Kiddushin 71a). Finally, upon the destruction of the Second Temple in 70 C. E., the Name was no longer pronounced at all.

Later, some speculated that the Name had been pronounced "Jehovah," or possibly "Yahweh," but scholars did not agree. No one knew for a certainty how to pronounce the ineffable Name of God.

But what if Yud–Hay–Vov–Hay has long been unpronounceable for the simple reason that it is written in reverse?

Reversed, the Name of God becomes Hay Vov Hay Yud. And these two syllables, Hay Vov and Hay Yud, can be vocalized as the sound equivalents of the Hebrew pronouns hu and hi, which are rendered in English as he and she respectively. Combining them together, Hay Vov and Hay Yud become He-She.

He-She, I believe, is the long-unpronounceable Name of God! This secret has been hiding in plain sight for all these years, for it explicitly states in the Torah: God created the earth-creature in God's own image, male and female. (Mark Sameth, Hebrew Union College-Jewish Institute of Religion class of 1998, is rabbi of Pleasantville Community Synagogue, Pleasantville, New York.)

We cannot pass over the repeating nature of this mystery from the beginning of the Bible to the end and how God's focus is replicating His image by manifesting and glorifying His name. It starts with the separation of the original Image of God, Adam into male and female, their fall and cessation of reproducing the Image of God and then the book of Revelation (Manifestation) focuses on the end-time restoration of the Image of God through the joining of the Lamb (male) and His bride (female).

22 SPRING (SEED) VS. FALL (MANIFESTATION) HOLY DAYS

If we let the Bible interpret its own symbols and images, the number 7 is associated with the complete Image of God–a singular and unified manifestation of God in man (shalom, rest, and wholeness). The 7th day Sabbath is the quintessential height of days.

All other days aspire to ascend to be like the 7th day Sabbath, including all of the Holy Days and new moons. The number 7 is the symbol of the ascended male– The Son of God, a unified male and female, the manifest presence of the Godhead bodily. This should tell us something about those Holy Days that require the attendance of all males.

> Exodus 23:10, And six years <u>thou shalt sow thy land, and shalt gather in the fruits thereof:11 But the seventh year thou shalt let it rest and lie still</u>; that the poor of thy people may eat: and what they leave the beasts of the field shall eat. In like manner thou shalt deal with thy vineyard, and with thy oliveyard. 12 Six days thou shalt do thy work, <u>and on the seventh day thou shalt rest: that thine ox and thine ass may rest, and the son of thy handmaid, and the stranger, may be refreshed</u>. 13 And in all things that I have said unto you be circumspect: and make no mention of the name of other gods, neither let it be heard out of thy mouth. 14 <u>Three times thou shalt keep a feast unto me in the year</u>. 15 Thou shalt keep <u>the feast of unleavened bread</u>:(thou shalt <u>eat unleavened bread seven days</u>, as I commanded thee, in the time appointed of the month Abib; for in it thou camest out from Egypt: and none shall appear before me empty:) 16 <u>And the feast of harvest</u>, the First-Fruits of thy labours, which thou hast sown in the field:<u> and the feast of ingathering, which is in the end of the year</u>, when thou hast gathered in thy labours out of the field. 17 <u>Three times in the year all thy males shall appear before the Lord God</u>.

Three (number of resurrection) times a year males are commanded to appear before YHWH:
1. Feast of Unleavened Bread (Chag HaMatzot)
    a.   7 days eat unleavened bread (none are to appear before YHWH empty)
    b.   7 days from memorial date of freedom from Egypt
    c.   Pictures 7 days of affliction and sorrow
    d.   No leavened bread or flesh is to remain during the 7 days

2. Feast of Harvest (Shavuot-Pentecost)
    a.   First fruits of what you have sown is harvested
    b.   7 weeks from when you start to harvest (put the sickle to the Corn) (standing grain)
    c.   Bring a tribute of Free Will
    d.   We are commanded to rejoice without sorrow
    e.   You are to remember you were in bondage in Egypt

3. Feast of Ingathering (Sukkot-Feast of Tabernacles)
    a.   Gather in your labors out of the field
    b.   Keep it for 7 days after you have gathered in the "corn" (standing grain) and the wine (fruit harvest)
    c.   7 months from the new year
    d.   Commanded to rejoice in the blessing of God in your increase and the works of your hands

We see a connection between the number 3, resurrection, and the ascended male (unified male and female). We also see a connection between the number 7 with a rest from work, labor, and sowing seed.

The land rests every 7 years, man rests every 7 days. Seven (7) is the number of the ascended male, who does not labor, just as we saw in Genesis 2. We see that the males are required to appear at three of the feasts. Remember three is the number of resurrection of the Image of God. We will see an interplay between the number seven and the number three in the Holy Days.

Deuteronomy 16:1, Observe the month of Abib, and keep the passover unto the Lord thy God: for in the month of Abib the Lord thy God brought thee forth out of Egypt by night. 2 Thou shalt therefore sacrifice the passover unto the Lord thy God, of the flock and the herd, in the place which the Lord shall choose to place his name there. 3 Thou shalt eat no leavened bread with it; seven days shalt thou eat unleavened bread therewith, even the bread of affliction; for thou camest forth out of the land of Egypt in haste: that thou mayest remember the day when thou camest forth out of the land of Egypt all the days of thy life. 4 And there shall be no leavened bread seen with thee in all thy coast seven days; neither shall there any thing of the flesh, which thou sacrificedst the first day at even, remain all night until the morning. 5 <u>Thou mayest not sacrifice the passover within any of thy gates, which the Lord thy God giveth thee:6 But at the place which the Lord thy God shall choose to place his name</u> in, there thou shalt sacrifice the passover at even, at the going down of the sun, at the season that thou camest forth out of Egypt. 7 And thou shalt roast and eat it in the place which the Lord thy God shall choose: and thou shalt turn in the morning, and go unto thy tents. 8 Six days thou shalt eat unleavened bread: and on the seventh day shall be a solemn assembly to the Lord thy God: thou shalt do no work therein. 9 <u>Seven weeks shalt thou number unto thee: begin to number the seven weeks from such time as thou beginnest to put the sickle to the corn. 10 And thou shalt keep the feast of weeks unto the Lord thy God</u> with a tribute of a freewill offering of thine hand, which thou shalt give unto the Lord thy God, according as the Lord thy God hath blessed thee:11 And thou shalt rejoice before the Lord thy God, thou, and thy son, and thy daughter, and thy manservant, and thy maidservant, and the Levite that is within thy gates, and the stranger, and the fatherless, and the widow, that are among you, <u>in the place which the Lord thy God hath chosen to place his name there</u>. 12 And thou shalt remember that thou wast a bondman in Egypt: and thou shalt observe and do these statutes. 13 <u>Thou shalt observe the feast of tabernacles seven days</u>, after that thou hast gathered in thy corn and thy wine:14 And thou shalt rejoice in thy feast, thou, and thy son, and thy daughter, and thy manservant, and thy maidservant, and the Levite, the stranger, and the fatherless, and the widow, that are within thy gates. 15 Seven days shalt thou keep a solemn feast unto the Lord thy God in the place which the Lord shall choose: because the Lord thy God shall bless thee in all thine increase, and in all the works of thine hands, therefore thou shalt surely rejoice. 16 <u>Three times in a year shall all thy males appear before the Lord thy God in the place which he shall choose; in the feast of unleavened bread, and in the feast of weeks, and in the feast of tabernacles: and they shall not appear before the Lord empty</u>:17 Every man shall give as he is able, according to the blessing of the Lord thy God which he hath given thee. 18 Judges and officers shalt thou make thee in all thy gates, which the Lord thy God giveth thee, throughout thy tribes: and they shall judge the people with just judgment. 19 Thou shalt not wrest judgment; thou shalt not respect persons, neither take a gift: for a gift doth blind the eyes of the wise, and pervert the words of the righteous. 20 That which is altogether just shalt thou follow, that thou mayest live, and inherit the land which the Lord thy God giveth thee. 21 Thou <u>shalt not plant thee a grove of any trees near unto the altar of the Lord thy God</u>, which thou shalt make thee. 22 <u>Neither shalt thou set thee up any image; which the Lord thy God hateth</u>.

Make sure to observe that in relation to these Holy Days there is particular reference made to "images" and the absolute necessity of not setting any up. Why? These days are directly connected to the true and complete (unbroken) Image of God, the Messiah. Take notice of the following. The days of Unleavened Bread occur in the first month of the year (spring) and are to be kept for 7 days and all males must attend (7-day count). The Passover sacrifice can only be done where God places His name. The Feast of Weeks (Shavuot/Pentecost) occurs after 7 weeks and all males must attend (7-week count/50-day count). Remember what we have already learned about the 50-day ascension count (counting the omer) and how it is connected to the Jubilee and freedom from bondage.

- Leviticus 27:16, And if a man shall sanctify unto the Lord some part of a field of his possession, then thy estimation shall be according to the seed thereof: an homer of barley seed shall be valued at fifty shekels of silver
- Leviticus 27:2, Speak unto the children of Israel, and say unto them, When a man shall make a singular vow, the persons shall be for the Lord by thy estimation. 3 And thy estimation shall be of the male from twenty years old even unto sixty years old, even thy estimation shall be fifty shekels of silver, after the shekel of the sanctuary.

The Feast of Tabernacles are to be kept for 7 days and all males must attend (7 month/moon count) – also 5 moons (months) from Pentecost (Shavuot). The Holy Days that have a count of 7 require the appearance of the male and all that signifies as previously discussed. These males must appear 3 times. Three (3) is the number of the resurrection of the Image of God. This resurrection and redemption of the Image of God is the restoration of wholeness and oneness (rest/shalom) and pertains to restoring the original 7th day Sabbath of creation (Genesis 2). This is why you see the interplay between the males required attendance 3 times and the number 7, which shows the unity of the ascended male (male and female) in the Image of God. Restoring the original Image of God requires the destruction of all false images (verse 22), which God hates because they show death and duality. We have identified the male number (7) and the resurrection number (3), but where is the female number?

Symbols of the Male:	Symbols of the Female:
Light	Mixture of darkness and light
Sun	Moon
Oneness	Duality
Unity	Division
Intimate male and female	Female
Tree of Life	Tree of the Knowledge of Good and Evil
Ascended Life	Fallen manifestation (death)
Seed	Fruit

If we go back and look at the count of the Holy Days, we should see the interplay of the male number and the female number.

- Passover–14 days from New Year and new month (2 counts of 7)–spring.
- Feast of Unleavened Bread–15 days from New Year and new month (3 counts of 5)–spring.
- Pentecost/Shavuot–7 counts of 7 from the day after the Sabbath of the spring harvest (Feast of First Fruits)–spring.

Leviticus 23:7, In the first day ye shall have an holy convocation: ye shall do no servile work therein. 8 But ye shall offer an offering made by fire unto the Lord seven days: in the seventh day is an holy convocation: ye shall do no servile work therein. 9 And the Lord spake unto Moses, saying, 10 Speak unto the children of Israel, and say unto them, When ye be come into the land which I give unto you, and shall reap the harvest thereof, then ye shall bring a sheaf of the First-Fruits of your harvest unto the priest:11 And he shall wave the sheaf before the Lord, to be accepted for you: on the morrow after the sabbath the priest shall wave it. 12 And ye shall offer that day when ye wave the sheaf an he lamb without blemish of the first year for a burnt offering unto the Lord. 13 And the meat offering thereof shall be two tenth deals of fine flour mingled with oil, an offering made by fire unto the Lord for a sweet savour: and the drink offering thereof shall be of wine, the fourth part of an hin. 14 And ye shall eat neither bread, nor parched corn, nor green ears, until the selfsame day that ye have brought an offering unto your God: it shall be a statute for ever throughout your generations in all your dwellings. 15 And ye shall count unto you from the morrow after the sabbath, from the day that ye brought the sheaf of the wave offering; seven sabbaths shall be complete:16 Even unto the morrow after the seventh sabbath shall ye number fifty days; and ye shall offer a new meat offering unto the Lord.

- Feast of Trumpets–7 months/moons from the new year and 5 months/moons from Pentecost/Shavuot (1 count of 7 interplayed with a count of 5) – Fall
- Day of Atonement–10 days from new moon of 7th month (2 counts of 5 interplayed with a count of 7) – Fall
- Feast of Tabernacles–15 days from the new moon of the 7th month (3 counts of 5 interplayed with a count of 7) – Fall

Leviticus 23:23, And the Lord spake unto Moses, saying, 24 Speak unto the children of Israel, saying, In the seventh month, in the first day of the month, shall ye have a sabbath, a memorial of blowing of trumpets, an holy convocation. 25 Ye shall do no servile work therein: but ye shall offer an offering made by fire unto the Lord. 26 And the Lord spake unto Moses, saying, 27 Also <u>on the tenth day of this seventh month there shall be a day of atonement: it shall be an holy convocation unto you; and ye shall afflict your souls</u>, and offer an offering made by fire unto the Lord. 28 And ye shall do no work in that same day: for it is a day of atonement, to make an atonement for you before the Lord your God. 29 For whatsoever soul it be that shall not be afflicted in that same day, he shall be cut off from among his people. 30 And whatsoever soul it be that doeth any work in that same day, the same soul will I destroy from among his people. 31 Ye shall do no manner of work: it shall be a statute for ever throughout your generations in all your dwellings. 32 It shall be unto you a sabbath of rest, and ye shall afflict your souls:<u> in the ninth day of the month at even, from even unto even, shall ye celebrate your sabbath</u>. 33 And the Lord spake unto Moses, saying, 34 Speak unto the children of Israel, saying, The <u>fifteenth day of this seventh month shall be the feast of tabernacles for seven days unto the Lord. 35 On the first day shall be an holy convocation: ye shall do no servile work therein. 36 Seven days ye shall offer</u> an offering made by fire unto the Lord:<u> on the eighth day shall be an holy convocation unto you; and ye shall offer</u> an offering made by fire unto the Lord: it is a solemn assembly; and ye shall do no servile work therein. 37 These are the feasts of the Lord, which ye shall proclaim to be holy convocations, to offer an offering made by fire unto the Lord, a burnt offering, and a meat offering, a sacrifice, and drink offerings, every thing upon his day:38 Beside the sabbaths of the Lord, and beside your gifts, and beside all your vows, and beside all your freewill offerings, which ye give unto the Lord. 39 <u>Also in the fifteenth day of the seventh month, when ye have gathered in the fruit of the land, ye shall keep a feast unto the Lord seven days: on the first day shall be a sabbath, and on the eighth day shall be a sabbath</u>. 40 And <u>ye shall take you on the first day the boughs of goodly trees, branches of palm trees, and the boughs of thick trees, and willows of the brook</u>; and ye shall rejoice before the Lord your God seven days. 41 And ye shall keep it a feast unto the Lord seven days in the year. It shall be a statute for ever in your generations: ye shall celebrate it in the seventh month. 42 Ye shall dwell in booths seven days; all that are Israelites born shall dwell in booths:43 That your generations may know that I made the children of Israel to dwell in booths, when I brought them out of the land of Egypt: I am the Lord your God. 44 And Moses declared unto the children of Israel the feasts of the Lord.

Through this analysis, we should be able to determine that the number associated with the moon (female) is the number five (5). Five has frequently been associated with grace, but more accurately may be identified with the one needing grace and redemption, the fallen and corrupted Image of God, which is restored through union with the promised seed of the woman (the ascended male, Yeshua the Messiah). Before we further explain the female (moon) number of 5, we should confirm why the males appear at the count of 7.

Leviticus 23:2, Speak unto the children of Israel, and say unto them, <u>Concerning the feasts of the Lord</u>, which ye shall proclaim to be holy convocations, even these are my feasts. 3 <u>Six days shall work be done: but the seventh day is the sabbath of rest</u>, an holy convocation; <u>ye shall do no work therein</u>: it is the sabbath of the Lord in all your dwellings. 4 These are the feasts of the Lord, even holy convocations, <u>which ye shall proclaim in their seasons</u>. 5 In the <u>fourteenth day of the first month at even is the Lord's passover. 6 And on the fifteenth day of the same month is the feast of unleavened bread unto the Lord: seven days ye must eat unleavened bread. 7 In the first day ye shall have an holy convocation: ye shall do no servile work therein</u>. 8 But ye shall offer an <u>offering made by fire unto the Lord seven days: in the seventh day is an holy convocation: ye shall do no servile work therein</u>.

Take notice of the following. The Feasts of the Lord are a picture of the original creation week and Sabbath rest before the curse, without labor, sweat, and toil. These days aspire to ascend and become the image of the original 7th day Sabbath. These feasts are proclaimed in their season. The year begins and then there is a count of 14 days (2 sevens), when Passover occurs on the 14th after the new moon and New Year. Unleavened Bread commences on the 15th (3 fives), and requires the consumption of unleavened bread when no leavening is to be found in their habitations. This is the bread of affliction. You have Passover (male) joined to 7 days that aspire to ascend and become without sin. For Unleavened Bread, the first and seventh days are Holy and are a picture of rest without labor (before the curse).

Passover commences after the dual count of 7 days, and Unleavened Bread commences after a 3 count of 5 and proceeds for a count of 7. Again, the count of 7 is male and the count of 5 is female; 7 is seed (male), 5 is manifestation (female), 7 is wine, 5 is bread (leavened/unleavened), 7 is spirit, and 5 is flesh/body. The interplay between Passover and Unleavened bread is the picture of union between male and female. The spring Holy Days are all a picture of the harvest of seed.

Leviticus 23:7, In the first day ye shall have an holy convocation: ye shall do no servile work therein. 8 But ye shall offer an offering made by fire unto the Lord seven days: in the seventh day is an holy convocation: ye shall do no servile work therein. 9 And the Lord spake unto Moses, saying, 10 Speak unto the children of Israel, and say unto them, When ye be come into the land which I give unto you, <u>and shall reap the harvest thereof, then ye shall bring a sheaf of the First-Fruits of your harvest unto the priest</u>:

The Feast of First-Fruits, which occurs during the days of Unleavened Bread, results in the harvest of barley seed (grain/seed harvest begins). It is marked by the offering of the first barley sheaf. The seed harvest continues for 50 days until the wheat harvest concludes with Shavuot/Pentecost. The Feast of Pentecost (Shavuot) concludes the harvest of the wheat seed (grain/seed harvest ends), marked by the wave offering of the two wheat loaves.

The Feast of Tabernacles marks the end of the harvest of the fruit of the land ("corn"–standing grain) & wine (Deuteronomy 16:13). The fruit harvest continues through until the 8th day of the Feast of Tabernacles which is marked by the taking of branches from goodly trees.

Leviticus 23:34, Speak unto the children of Israel, saying, The fifteenth day of this seventh month <u>shall be the feast of tabernacles for seven days unto the Lord</u>. 35 On the first day shall be an holy convocation: ye shall do no servile work therein. 36 Seven days ye shall offer an offering made by fire unto the Lord: on the eighth day shall be an holy convocation unto you; and ye shall offer an offering made by fire unto the Lord: it is a solemn assembly; and ye shall do no servile work therein. 37 <u>These are the feasts of the Lord, which ye shall proclaim to be holy convocations,</u> to offer an offering made by fire unto the Lord, a burnt offering, and a meat offering, a sacrifice, and drink offerings, every thing upon his day:38 Beside the sabbaths of the Lord, and beside your gifts, and beside all your vows, and beside all your freewill offerings, which ye give unto the Lord. 39 <u>Also in the fifteenth day of the seventh month, when ye have gathered in the fruit of the land, ye shall keep a feast unto the Lord seven days: on the first day shall be a sabbath, and on the eighth day shall be a sabbath. 40 And ye shall take you on the first day the boughs of goodly trees, branches of palm trees, and the boughs of thick trees, and willows of the brook; and ye shall rejoice before the Lord your God seven days</u>. 41 And ye shall keep it a feast unto the Lord seven days in the year. It shall be a statute for ever in your generations: ye shall celebrate it in the seventh month.

Bough:	
Strong's Number:06529	
Original Word	Word Origin:
yrp	from 06509
Transliterated Word	
P@riy	TWOT–1809a
Phonetic Spelling	Parts of Speech
per–ee'	Noun Masculine
Definition:	
fruit	

Branches:	
Strong's Number:03709	
Original Word	Word Origin
@k	from 03721

Transliterated Word	
Kaph	TWOT–1022a
Phonetic Spelling	Parts of Speech
kaf	Noun Feminine
Definition:	
palm, hand, sole, palm of the hand, hollow or flat of the hand	

The fall Feast of Tabernacles focuses on fruit and branches (female) as opposed to the seed (male).

Genesis 1:29, And God said, Behold, I have given you every herb bearing seed, which is upon the face of all the earth, and every tree, in the which is the fruit of a tree yielding seed; to you it shall be for meat.

Plants that produce fruit (female) with seed (male) within, are good for food and permitted to be eaten as they follow the fractal of a unified male and female.

Those plants with fruit without a seed within, are not good for food as they depict a separated female (fruit) and male (seed), they are unripe and immature. Those with seeds within have reached maturity.

In the culinary sense of these words, a fruit is usually any sweet–tasting plant product, especially those associated with seeds; a vegetable is any savoury or less sweet plant product; and a nut is any hard, oily, and shelled plant product. . . Botanically, a cereal grain, such as corn, wheat or rice, is also a kind of fruit, termed a caryopsis. However, the fruit wall is very thin, and is fused to the seed coat, so almost all of the edible grain is actually a seed… In botany, seeds are ripened ovules; fruits are the ripened ovaries or carpels that contain the seeds and a nut is a type of fruit and not a seed. . .. In botany, a caryopsis (plural caryopses) is a type of simple dry fruit — one that is monocarpellate (formed from a single carpel) and indehiscent (not opening at maturity) and resembles an achene, except that in a caryopsis the pericarp is fused with the thin seed coat. The caryopsis is popularly called a grain and is the fruit typical of the family Poaceae (or Gramineae), such as wheat, rice, and corn. The term grain is also used in a more general sense as synonymous with cereal (as in cereal grains, which include some non–Poaceae). Considering that the fruit wall and the seed are intimately fused into a single unit, and the caryopsis or grain is a dry fruit, little concern is given to technically separating the terms fruit and seed in these plant structures. In many grains, the hulls to be separated before processing are actually flower bracts. . . A fruit results from maturation of one or more flowers, and the gynoecium of the flower(s) forms all or part of the fruit. . . Gynoecium (from Ancient Greek γυνή, gyne, meaning woman, and οἶκος, oikos, meaning house) is most commonly used as a collective term for all carpels in a flower. A carpel is the ovule and seed producing reproductive organ in flowering plants. Carpels are derived from ovule–bearing leaves which evolved to form a closed structure containing the ovules. They did this by folding and fusing at their edges to form a chamber in which the ovules develop. The gynoecium is often referred to as female because it gives rise to female (egg–producing) gametophytes, however, strictly speaking sporophytes do not have sex, only gametophytes do. [1] Successful germination of pollen and growth of pollen tubes results in fertilization of ova. Barley is a member of the grass family. It is a self–pollinating, diploid species with 14 chromosomes. Hulless or naked barley (Hordeum vulgare L. var. nudum Hook. f.) is a form of domesticated barley with an easier–to–remove hull. Naked barley is an ancient food crop, but a new industry has developed around uses of selected hulless barley to increase the digestible energy of the grain, especially for swine and poultry. . . . Wheat is one of the first cereals known to have been domesticated, and wheat's ability to self–pollinate greatly facilitated the selection of many distinct domesticated varieties. The four wild species of wheat, along with the domesticated varieties einkorn, [36] emmer[37] and spelt, [38] have hulls. This more primitive morphology (in evolutionary terms) consists of toughened glumes that tightly enclose the grains, and (in domesticated wheats) a semi–brittle rachis that breaks easily on threshing. The result is that when threshed, the wheat ear breaks up into spikelets. To obtain the grain, further processing, such as milling or pounding, is needed to remove the hulls or husks. In contrast, in free–threshing (or naked) forms such as durum wheat and common wheat, the glumes are fragile and the rachis tough. On threshing, the chaff breaks up, releasing the grains. Hulled wheats are often stored as spikelets because the toughened glumes give good protection against pests of stored grain. Wheat provides more nourishment for humans than any other food source. Wheat normally needs between 110 and 130 days between sowing and harvest, depending upon climate, seed type, and soil conditions (winter wheat lies dormant during a winter freeze). (Wikipedia)

The patterns and fractals of the universe have once again proven the concept of seed (male) then manifestation of fruit (female). Barley and wheat self–pollinating is a pattern for the promise of the "seed of the woman" and what happens within the heart of the believer in Yeshua.

We see the fall Feast of Tabernacles (Fruit Harvest) occurring on the 3 count of 5 days, the 15th day from the new moon of the 7th moon (month). Again, this shows the interplay of male and female.

Then the Feast proceeds for a count of 7 with a Holy Day of rest on the 1st and 8th day. We will examine how this last Holy day commences on the conclusion of the 7th day of the Feast and brings in the eighth day (female), just as it is a mirror image of the Passover and the count of 7 days of Unleavened Bread (male). Notice again the interplay between spring (seed, unleavened bread, spirit, male) and fall (fruit, branches, manifestation, and female).

Shemini Atzeret
    The Jewish Encyclopedia states that during the time of the Second Temple, the festival of Shavuot received the specific name of "'Atzarta" as cited by Josephus in Antiquities of the Jews (iii. 10, § 6) and in the Talmud's tractate Pesahim (42b, 68b), signifying "the closing feast" of Passover. [7] and commenting on this fact, the Rabbis in tractate Pesahim say that:
    The closing feast of Sukkot (i. e. , Shemini Atzeret) ought rightly to have been, like that of Passover (i. e. , Shavuot) on the fiftieth day; but, in order not to force the people to make another journey to Jerusalem in the rainy season, God fixed it as early as the eighth day. [7] (Wikipedia)

Event	Count	Pattern	Date	Sex
New Year (Rosh Chodashim)	New moon after 12th moon	5 moons after Trumpets/7th moon	Nisan 1	Male
Passover (Pesach)	2 counts of 7 days from new moon of new year	2 x 7 days	Nisan 14	Male (based on days of count only)
Feast of Unleavened Bread (7 days) (Chag HaMatzot)	15 days (3 counts of 5) from new moon of new year, 1 count of 7 days from Passover in length (8 days total:7 days UB + 1 Passover)	3 x 7 days	Nisan 15–Nisan 22	Male and female (unified)
Pentecost (Shavuot)	7 counts of 7 weeks from spring Harvest Offering/10 counts of 5	7 x 7 weeks	Based on Count of 7 and 5	Male and female (unified)
Feast of Trumpets (Yom Teruah)	7 counts of new moon from new year and 5 counts of new moon from Shavuot or Pentecost	7 x 1 moons from new year (5 x 1 moons from Pentecost)	Tishri 1	Male
Day of Atonement (Yom Kippur)	2 counts of 5 days from new moon of 7th moon/month	7 x 1 moon/ 2 x 5 days	Tishri 10	Female

Event	Count	Pattern	Date	Sex
Feast of Tabernacles (7 days) (Sukkot)	3 counts of 5 days from new moon of 7th month and 1 count of 5 days from the day of Atonement, 1 count of 7 days in length	7 x 1 moon/ 3 x 5 days	Tishri 15-Tishri 21	Male and female (unified)
Eighth day of the Feast of Tabernacles (Shemini Atzeret)	Mirror image of Passover, 1 day added onto the Feast of Tabernacles (7 days + 1)	3 x 7 days + 1	Tishri 22	Male (based on days of count only)

Keep in mind that there are two Jewish calendars in a given year. One calendar begins on Nisan 1 and the other calendar begins on Tishri 1 (Feast of Trumpets) which is the 7th month of the year. The calendar starting on Nisan 1 is for the male and the calendar beginning on Tishri 1 is for the female and as such they interplay with one another. This may also add some insight as to why Tishri 1, the Feast of Trumpets, is known as the day "when no man knows the day or the hour". It may also show us why the manifestation of the fruit of the Image of God happens in the 7th month, just as it did on the first 7th day Sabbath.

Mark 13:32, But of that day and that hour knoweth no man, no, not the angels which are in heaven, neither the Son, but the Father.

No man knows the day or the hour because the Holy Day begins on a new moon and is the first day of the month. All new moons must be sighted by Two Witnesses and declared to the nation that the Holy day has begun.

During the time of the Holy Temple, the drama of Rosh Hashanah (Head of the Year/Feast of Trumpets- Yom Teruah) began even before the onset of the holy day. This drama involved the sanctification of the new moon. Rosh Hashanah occurs on the first day of the month of Tishrei, and therefore, it cannot begin until the appearance of the new moon has been established. The commandment to declare the new moon and establish its appearance for all the children of Israel was the first commandment received by the Israelites, even before they emerged from their bondage in Egypt, (Exodus 12:2) It may seem ironic that G–d–the King of the universe–would call upon His people to determine, as it were, on what day He Himself created the universe! But this is, in fact, what G–d, in His love for His people did: he entrusted the children of Israel as "partners" in maintaining and perfecting His creation.

Two Witnesses who had seen the appearance of the new moon were required to testify before the Great Sanhedrin, which convened in the Chamber of Hewn Stone, which was located on the northern wall of the Inner Courtyard of the Holy Temple. There they would be questioned and cross examined to verify their fitness as witnesses, and the truth of their words. Only when this had been done to the satisfaction of the sages of the Great Sanhedrin, would the Rosh Hashanah service in the Holy Temple begin. (Templeinstitute.org)

This certainly adds significance to the role of the Two Witnesses in the book of Revelation and why they are mentioned concurrently with the measuring of the temple of God.

Revelation 11:1, And there was given me a reed like unto a rod: and the angel stood, saying, Rise, and measure the temple of God, and the altar, and them that worship therein. 2 But the court which is without the temple leave out, and measure it not; for it is given unto the Gentiles: and the holy city shall they tread under foot forty and two months. 3 And I will give power unto my Two Witnesses, and they shall prophesy a thousand two hundred and threescore days, clothed in sackcloth.

Remember that males are commanded to appear on only 3 of the Holy Days.
- Exodus 23:14, Three times thou shalt keep a feast unto me in the year. 15 Thou shalt keep the feast of unleavened bread:(thou shalt eat unleavened bread seven days, as I commanded thee, in the time appointed of the month Abib; for in it thou camest out from Egypt: and none shall appear before me empty:) 16 And the feast of harvest, the First-Fruits of thy labours, which thou hast sown in the field: and the feast of ingathering, which is in the end of the year, when thou hast gathered in thy labours out of the field. 17 Three times in the year all thy males shall appear before the Lord God.
- Deuteronomy 16:13, Thou shalt observe the feast of tabernacles seven days, after that thou hast gathered in thy corn and thy wine:14 And thou shalt rejoice in thy feast, thou, and thy son, and thy daughter, and thy manservant, and thy maidservant, and the Levite, the stranger, and the fatherless, and the widow, that are within thy gates. 15 Seven days shalt thou keep a solemn feast unto the Lord thy God in the place which the Lord shall choose: because the Lord thy God shall bless thee in all thine increase, and in all the works of thine hands, therefore thou shalt surely rejoice. 16 Three times in a year shall all thy males appear before the Lord thy God in the place which he shall choose; in the feast of unleavened bread, and in the feast of weeks, and in the feast of tabernacles: and they shall not appear before the Lord empty:17 Every man shall give as he is able, according to the blessing of the Lord thy God which he hath given thee.
- 2 Chronicles 8:12, Then Solomon offered burnt offerings unto the Lord on the altar of the Lord, which he had built before the porch, 13 Even after a certain rate every day, offering according to the commandment of Moses, on

the sabbaths, and on the new moons, and on the solemn feasts, <u>three times in the year, even in the feast of unleavened bread, and in the feast of weeks, and in the feast of tabernacles.</u>

The male (seed) is to appear at three of the Holy Days:
1. Feast of Unleavened Bread (7 days (1) count)
2. Feast of Harvest, also called the Feast of Weeks (7 weeks (7) count)
3. Feast of Ingathering, also called the Feast of Tabernacles (7 moons/months (1) count)

- All three of these feasts are harvest festivals.
- All three of these feasts begin after a multiple count of 5 (female) from the new moon.
  - o   Unleavened Bread starts on day 15 (counted from the new moon and the New Year)
  - o   Shavuot/Pentecost is counted both as the day after 7 counts of 7 days (weeks), but also as day 50 (multiple of 5 x 10)
  - o   Feast of Tabernacles is on the 15th day (3 x 5 days) from the new moon of the 7th month.
- All three of these feasts depict the union of male redeemer (7) and female needing to ascend and be redeemed (5).

Once again, the count of 7 begins with the manifestation of God's light until God's image (unified male and female) is manifested on the 7th day, which is also the 7th day Sabbath. The counts of 5 are for the fallen manifestation (universe), the exiled woman (female), and are associated (in multiples of 5) with the new moon (female).

Moon Associations:
- Moon
- Female
- Darkness
- Reflection
- Unclean
- Division
- Mixture of light and darkness
- Duality
- Tree of the Knowledge of Good and Evil
- Number 5
- Darkened mirror

From a scriptural standpoint, the defiled woman is not a sociological debasement of the female but a universal phenomenon. All of the manifest universe is fallen and separated from her divine male (the Messiah) and needs to be reunited with His spirit.

Leviticus 12:1, And the Lord spake unto Moses, saying, 2 Speak unto the children of Israel, saying, <u>If a woman have conceived seed, and born a man child: then she shall be unclean seven days</u>; according to the days of the separation for her infirmity shall she be unclean. 3 And in <u>the eighth day the flesh of his foreskin shall be circumcised</u>. 4 And she shall then continue in the blood of her purifying three and thirty days; she shall touch no hallowed thing, nor come into the sanctuary, until the days of her purifying be fulfilled. 5 But if she bear a maid child, then she shall be unclean two weeks, as in her separation: and she shall continue in the blood of her purifying threescore and six days.

Notice giving birth results in the female's uncleanness and needing purification. This purification comes though her separation for 33 days (notice the repeat of the number 3 in resurrection and redemption) if she bears a male child and doubles to 66 days if she bears a female. She cannot re–enter the sanctuary until the fulfillment of her separation.

The High Priest entering the Holy of Holies with the blood of the Messiah is not only a picture of the Messiah bearing His own blood. It is a picture of Aaron, who is symbolic of the Holy Spirit in the valley (us), being allowed to enter the Holy of Holies once the sacrifice of the Messiah has occurred. We are carrying His blood into the Holy of Holies to end our separation. This is the fulfillment of AT–One–Ment, the reunification of the fallen female with the ascended male (the Messiah). The Jewish wedding ceremony bears out the idea that the wedding day is a couple's own personal Yom Kippur (Day of Atonement). This is why we see Yom Kippur, the Day of Atonement reflecting the count of 3x5.

This fractal of the unity of the male (Messiah) and the female (us) is also patterned in every marriage between husbands and wives. The importance of the unity of the male and the female cannot be underestimated. Peter touches on this fact in regards to prayer.

1 Peter 3:7, Likewise, ye husbands, dwell with them according to knowledge, giving honour unto the wife, as unto the weaker vessel, and as being heirs together of the grace of life; that your prayers be not hindered.

The divided husband and wife that is in conflict does not go unnoticed by God. Peter makes it clear that a lack of harmony and shalom (oneness) in the marriage relationship will be reflected in the effectiveness of your prayers and God's willingness to answer them.

23 MELCHISEDEC AND LEVITICAL PRIESTHOODS

Remember that there are always two High Priests like Moses and Aaron. Moses is on the mountain (Melchisedec Priesthood) interceding for his brother with unclean flesh and unclean garments (Aaronic Priesthood). Moses did not need to be purified as he is a prophetic type of the sinless Messiah. He was interceding in the Shekinah Glory on the mountain so that his brother could be baptized (mikvah) and receive new garments and then enter into the Holy of Holies. Moses is a picture of the ascended male and Aaron is a picture of the fallen female who needs to be cleansed and enter within the Holy of Holies. There will always be two priesthoods before God, forever! The Aaronic is not done away.

Exodus 40:12, And thou shalt bring Aaron and his sons unto the door of the tabernacle of the congregation, and wash them with water. 13 And thou shalt put upon Aaron the holy garments, and anoint him, and sanctify him; that he may minister unto me in the priest's office. 14 And thou shalt bring his sons, and clothe them with coats:15 And thou shalt anoint them, as thou didst anoint their father, that they may minister unto me in the priest's office: for their anointing shall surely be an everlasting priesthood throughout their generations.

Everlasting means everlasting. Many will try to say that Yeshua took over the Aaronic priesthood. But a careful reading of the book of Hebrews will clarify that the Aaronic Priesthood was not taken over by the Messiah, but that He was given a better priesthood that would work in tandem with the Aaronic priesthood.

Hebrews 7:1, For this Melchisedec, king of Salem, priest of the most high God, who met Abraham returning from the slaughter of the kings, and blessed him; 2 To whom also Abraham gave a tenth part of all; first being by interpretation King of righteousness, and after that also King of Salem, which is, King of peace; 3 Without father, without mother, without descent, having neither beginning of days, nor end of life; but made like unto the Son of God; abideth a priest continually. 4 Now consider how great this man was, unto whom even the patriarch Abraham gave the tenth of the spoils. 5 And verily they that are of the sons of Levi, who receive the office of the priesthood, have a commandment to take tithes of the people according to the law, that is, of their brethren, though they come out of the loins of Abraham:6 But he whose descent is not counted from them received tithes of Abraham, and blessed him that had the promises. 7 And without all contradiction the less is blessed of the better. 8 And here men that die receive tithes; but there he receiveth them, of whom it is witnessed that he liveth. 9 And as I may so say, Levi also, who receiveth tithes, payed tithes in Abraham. 10 For he was yet in the loins of his father, when Melchisedec met him. 11 If therefore perfection were by the Levitical priesthood, (for under it the people received the law,) what further need was there that another priest should rise after the order of Melchisedec, and not be called after the order of Aaron? 12 For the priesthood being changed, there is made of necessity a change also of the law. 13 For he of whom these things are spoken pertaineth to another tribe, of which no man gave attendance at the altar. 14 For it is evident that our Lord sprang out of Juda; of which tribe Moses spake nothing concerning priesthood. 15 And it is yet far more evident: for that after the similitude of Melchisedec there ariseth another priest, 16 Who is made, not after the law of a carnal commandment, but after the power of an endless life. 17 For he testifieth, Thou art a priest for ever after the order of Melchisedec. 18 For there is verily a disannulling of the commandment going before for the weakness and unprofitableness thereof. 19 For the law made nothing perfect, but the bringing in of a better hope did; by the which we draw nigh unto God. 20 And inasmuch as not without an oath he was made priest:21 (For those priests were made without an oath; but this with an oath by him that said unto him, The Lord sware and will not repent, Thou art a priest for ever after the order of Melchisedec:) 22 By so much was Yeshua made a surety of a better testament. 23 And they truly were many priests, because they were not suffered to continue by reason of death:24 But this man, because he continueth ever, hath an unchangeable priesthood. 25 Wherefore he is able also to save them to the uttermost that come unto God by him, seeing he ever liveth to make intercession for them. 26 For such an high priest became us, who is holy, harmless, undefiled, separate from sinners, and made higher than the heavens; 27 Who needeth not daily, as those high priests, to offer up sacrifice, first for his own sins, and then for the people's: for this he did once, when he offered up himself. 28 For the law maketh men high priests which have infirmity; but the word of the oath, which was since the law, maketh the Son, who is consecrated for evermore.

Take notice of the following. The less (Levi/Aaronic Priesthood) is blessed by the better (Melchisedec Priesthood). The priesthood is changed, not removed. How is it changed? "Another priest" is added that brings perfection. Both priesthoods continue forever together. The Levitical/Aaronic Priesthood is not done away.

Malachi 3:2, But who may abide the day of his coming? and who shall stand when he appeareth? for he is like a refiner's fire, and like fullers' soap:3 <u>And he shall sit as a refiner and purifier of silver: and he shall purify the sons of Levi, and purge them as gold and silver, that they may offer unto the Lord an offering in righteousness.</u> 4 Then shall the offering of Judah and Jerusalem be pleasant unto the Lord, as in the days of old, and as in former years. 5 And I will come near to you to judgment; and I will be a swift witness against the sorcerers, and against the adulterers, and against false swearers, and against those that oppress the hireling in his wages, the widow, and the fatherless, and that turn aside the stranger from his right, and fear not me, saith the Lord of hosts. 6 For I am the Lord, I change not; therefore ye sons of Jacob are not consumed. 7 Even from the days of your fathers ye are gone away from mine ordinances, and have not kept them. Return unto me, and I will return unto you, saith the Lord of hosts. But ye said, Wherein shall we return?

There was a need for an additional (another) priest to arise to bring perfection. The Messiah's priesthood (Melchisedec–pictured by Moses on the mountain) is affirmed by the power of resurrection life. The role of the Melchisedec Priesthood is to bring us (typified by the Aaronic/Levitical Priesthood) near unto God. The Torah shows how fallen mankind can ascend and become high priests, by the intercession of the Melchisedec Priesthood (the Messiah) and by the power of His endless resurrection life. This is the picture of Yom Kippur and the day of Atonement. Moses is sanctifying and cleansing Aaron's garments so that he may enter into the Holy of Holies and draw near to God by the blood of the Melchisedec High Priest!

These are the same roles as the Messiah being the Bridegroom and the Man-Child (144,000/First-Fruits) serving as the Friend of the Bridegroom. The Groom is associated with the male and the Friend of the Bridegroom is in His image (male) working with the female in the valley of the shadow of death.

The division of being "halt between two opinions" is unbelief (divided male and female needing redemption) and manifests as duality. On the contrary, the unity of the faith (redeemed) manifests as a singularity (marriage – ascended male - joined male and female).

1 Kings 18:21, And Elijah came unto all the people, and said, How long halt ye between two opinions? if the Lord be God, follow him: but if Baal, then follow him. And the people answered him not a word.

The female (unbeliever who is lacking faith) is sanctified by the ascended male (believer–full of faith).

1 Corinthians 7:10, And unto the married I command, yet not I, but the Lord, <u>Let not the wife depart from her husband</u>:11 But and if she depart, let her remain unmarried or be reconciled to her husband: and let not the husband put away his wife. 12 But to the rest speak I, not the Lord: If any brother hath a wife that believeth not, and she be pleased to dwell with him, let him not put

her away. 13 And the woman which hath an husband that believeth not, and if he be pleased to dwell with her, let her not leave him. 14 <u>For the unbelieving husband is sanctified by the wife, and the unbelieving wife is sanctified by the husband: else were your children unclean; but now are they holy</u>. 15 But if the unbelieving depart, let him depart. A brother or a sister is not under bondage in such cases: but God hath called us to peace. 16 For what knowest thou, O wife, whether thou shalt save thy husband? or how knowest thou, <u>O man, whether thou shalt save thy wife</u>?

We also see the pattern of the coming of the male seed associated with a seven-day period and then a day of circumcision.

Passover	Unleavened Bread	Pentecost or Shavuot	Feast of Tabernacles	Last Great Day of the Feast of Tabernacles
1 day	7 days	7 weeks then 1 day	7 days	1 day
Seed-Conception-Birth	Day 8– Circumcision - Baptism in the Red Sea	Seed, Conception-Birth, day 8 (day 50) Baptized with the Holy Spirit	Seed, Conception-Birth	Day 8– Circumcision - Baptism

The woman who has conceived seed and born a male child has to wait for a 7-day period and then the male son has his flesh removed (circumcision) on the 8th day. Could this be a picture of the death and resurrection of the Messiah, and the ascension of the spirit? Is it the turning of the female (flesh) to the male (spirit)?

Leviticus 12:1, And the Lord spake unto Moses, saying, 2 Speak unto the children of Israel, saying, If a woman have conceived seed, and born a man child: then she shall be unclean seven days; according to the days of the separation for her infirmity shall she be unclean. 3 And <u>in the eighth day the flesh of his foreskin shall be circumcised</u>. 4 And she shall then continue in the blood of her purifying three and thirty days; she shall touch no hallowed thing, nor come into the sanctuary, until the days of her purifying be fulfilled. 5 But if she bear a maid child, then she shall be unclean two weeks, as in her separation: and she shall continue in the blood of her purifying threescore and six days.

Without getting too deep into the issue of the uncleanness of the female due to her conception and what that means, the intent is simply to show that there is an association between the female needing to be cleansed and that her purification is linked with the count of 7. In addition, there is a thematic tie between circumcision and baptism (mikvah). Universally all of manifest creation is the unclean female (Holy Spirit in the valley of the shadow of death) needing to be reunited with her husband (the Messiah).

Leviticus 15:24, And <u>if any man lie with her at all, and her flowers be upon him, he shall be unclean seven days</u>; and all the bed whereon he lieth shall be unclean. 25 And if a woman have an issue of her blood many days out of the time of her separation, or if it run beyond the time of her separation; all the days of the issue of her uncleanness shall be as the days of her separation: she shall be unclean. 26 Every bed whereon she lieth all the days of her issue shall be unto her as the bed of her separation: and whatsoever she sitteth upon shall be unclean, as the uncleanness of her separation. 27 And <u>whosoever toucheth those things shall be unclean, and shall wash his clothes, and bathe himself in water, and be unclean until the even. 28 But if she be cleansed of her issue, then she shall number to herself seven days, and after that she shall be clean.</u>

We have established that the number seven is associated with cleansing the unclean woman who has conceived seed. Seven is associated with faith, light, sun, rest, the 7th day Sabbath, the unfallen manifest Image of God, and the promised seed of the woman that would redeem fallen creation (the unclean female).

The unclean female is associated with unbelief, darkness, division, the moon, the count of 5, and the fallen Image of God needing to be restored. In the Holy Days, we see distinct patterns of the interplay of the numbers 7 and 5, and we also see the patterns of day, week, and month counts of 7 (male) and then day counts in multiples of 5 (female).

- Passover is counted from death of the cycle of the sun (male)–2 cycles of 7 days.
- Shavuot/Pentecost is counted from the death of the harvest– 7 cycles of 7 weeks.
- Trumpets is counted from the death of the cycle of the sun (male)–7 cycles of the moon.
- Atonement is counted from the death of the moon/Trumpets–2 cycles of 5 days.
- Tabernacles is counted from the death of the moon/Trumpets–3 cycles of 5 days.

Event	Union	Count	Moon	Creation	Creation Event
New Year (Rosh Chodashim)	Union of the year to the seed (7 moons from Trumpets)	7 count	Waxing moon		
Passover (Pesach)	Seed of the woman/the Messiah (seed death)	7 count	Full moon	Creation day 1	Light manifested and separated from darkness
Feast of Unleavened Bread (7 days) (Chag HaMatzot)	Union of days to the seed (7 day count)	7 count	Waning moon	Creation day 2	Upper waters separated from lower waters
Pentecost (Shavuot)	Union of Weeks to the seed (7 week count/50 day)	7 count & 5 count	Not tied to the moon	Creation day 3	Water & earth separated and seeds appear
Feast of Trumpets (Yom Teruah)	Union of moons/Month to the seed (7 moon count)	7 count	New moon	Creation day 4	Sun & moon created to divide day and night, to be for signs and seasons
Day of Atonement (Yom Kippur)	Principal count is now by 5's	7 count & 5 count	Waxing moon	Creation day 5	Water & air creatures seed/DNA created
Feast of Tabernacles (Sukkot) 1st day is Holy	Principal count is now by 5's	7 count & 5 count	Full moon	Creation day 6	Earth creatures DNA and Image of God seed/DNA created
Feast of Tabernacles (Sukkot) (7 days)	Union of days to the seed (7 day count)	7 count	Waning moon	Creation day 7	Manifestation of form and image for all created seeds
8th day of the Feast of Tabernacles (Shemini Atzeret)		7 count then 5 count, then 7 count	Waning moon		

UNITY IN THE MIDDLE OF THE PATTERN

Now we must determine if we should be viewing the Holy Days as a linear timeline for prophecy or view it as a scroll that is rolled up to meet in the middle at Shavuot. What can make us think that this holds any credibility?

If we view Pentecost/Shavuot (Male) and Trumpets (Female) as the fulfillment of the restoration of the Image of God with the utterance of God and the Shekinah Glory dwelling upon the heads of the redeemed Image of God (the Apostles serving as the Friend of the Bridegroom), then we could see this as the middle pattern of death and resurrection, just like the Messiah, the forerunner of our redemption in the end time. The incomplete male and incomplete female are joined in one and the restored Image of God once again produces the Shekinah Glory and the Utterance of God in the believer, who is one with the Messiah Yeshua, in the middle of the time frame. It could be that Pentecost is a prophetic picture of the "First-Fruits" of the seed harvest, foreshadowing what is going to occur in the final harvest pictured by the fall Holy Days (fruit harvest).

Patterns of the Middle			
Event Pattern	Beginning	Middle	End
Number	1	4	7
Creation week	First light manifested	Sun/moon manifested	Images of God manifested on the 7th day Sabbath
Exodus	Egypt and slavery–Israel begins their Exodus on the 1st day of Unleavened Bread	Original request to Pharaoh to go 3 days into the wilderness to serve God. This timing would prophetically line up with the Resurrection day of the Messiah. The first 3 days of Unleavened Bread are full of sorrow and the last 4 are full of joy because of resurrection life.	Cross the Red Sea on the last day of Unleavened Bread
Jericho	Begin marching around the city on the 1st day.	Continue Marching around the city for 6 days.	March, shout, and blow trumpets around the city. Walls fall down on the 7th day.
Yeshua's Death & Resurrection	Passover– Yeshua's death (3 days of Sorrow)	First of the First-Fruits– Yeshua's resurrection (joy). After 3 days and 3 nights in the grave of the earth . . . like a seed. Resurrection on the close of the 3rd day and commencement of the 4th day.	Last day of Unleavened Bread–conclusion of 3 days of Joy

Patterns of the Middle			
Event Pattern	Beginning	Middle	End
7,000 Years of creation	Genesis (Seed)	The Messiah's manifestation, death and resurrection	Second coming of the Messiah and our resurrection. Revelation (Manifestation)
Feast of Tabernacles	Yeshua is urged by His brethren to go to Jerusalem at the Feast of Tabernacles and He says His time is not yet; He goes secretly (John 7:8–10)	Yeshua goes to the temple in the middle of the Feast and reveals Himself openly teaching (John 7:14).	Yeshua goes to the temple in the last day of the Feast and offers the water of salvation (John 7:37–38).
Judgment of Jerusalem	Messiah's birth	Messiah's death and resurrection	Destruction of Jerusalem (35 years after the death and resurrection of the Messiah) 70 AD
Final Week of Prophecy	1260 days the Two Witnesses prophesy	Death & Resurrection of the 2 witnesses (Revelation 11:15–18); Image of God brought forth in Revelation 12. Mid–Tribulation	1, 260 days woman flees to the wilderness (remnant of her seed) in Revelation 12, and the beast continues 42 months (Revelation 13:5).

This is just a start of the review of the duality of the Holy Days and their meaning within the context of the unity of the male and the female and the restoration of the Image of God. We can now see the clear patterns and images of the spring Holy Days relating to the male seed and the fall Holy Days relating to the female fruit as they pertain to the redemptive work of God.

We should also be able to see a clearer picture of Pentecost (Shavuot) and how it pictures the manifestation of the restoration of the Image of God. This happens through the redeemed Image of God (Apostles) manifesting the indwelling of the Holy Spirit, the Utterance of the voice of God and the appearance of the Shekinah Glory upon their heads.

The count of 7 and 50 shows the restoration of our original inheritance, the 7th day Sabbath of Eden, and our unity with God through His countenance (the Messiah Yeshua). We should also have a clearer picture of why this manifested Image of God, the Messiah, appears in the middle of time. We can also see how this may be a redemptive pattern for those who are one with the Messiah.

24 THE ASCENDED MALE (THE MESSIAH)

This should clarify why you are not grafted into Israel (female), you must be grafted into your ascended male (Yeshua). Once again, we see a direct reference of who and what you are in. It's not Israel or Judah. It's not the Torah. It is Yeshua the Messiah, the manifest Name of YHWH! Peter condemns those who deny Yeshua is the Son of God and our redemption.

> 1 Peter 2:2, But there were false prophets also among the people, even as there shall be <u>false teachers among you</u>, who privily shall bring in damnable heresies, <u>even denying the Lord that bought them</u>, and bring upon themselves swift destruction.

It is so clear, we are a female needing to be joined and grafted into our ascended male (the manifest Name of YHWH).

> John 6:69, And we believe and are sure that thou art that Christ, the Son of the living God.

When Christ asked the disciples who people thought He was, Peter's bold claim was not the living Torah. Peter's answer is that Yeshua is the manifest Name of YHWH, the Son of God. More importantly, Yeshua does not refute this fact. He clarifies that for Peter to know this was a revelation from God.

> Matthew 16:13, When Jesus came into the coasts of Caesarea Philippi, he asked his disciples, saying, Whom do men say that I the Son of man am? 14 And they said, Some say that thou art John the Baptist: some, Elias; and others, Jeremias, or one of the prophets. 15 He saith unto them, But whom say ye that I am? 16 And Simon Peter answered and said, Thou art the Christ, the Son of the living God. 17 And Jesus answered and said unto him, Blessed art thou,

Simon Barjona: for flesh and blood hath not revealed it unto thee, but my Father which is in heaven.

It is only through this revelation that we are saved.

John 3:18, He that believeth on him is not condemned: but he that believeth not is condemned already, because he hath not <u>believed in the name of the only begotten Son of God</u>.

Yeshua is the manifest Name of YHWH, the Image of God, the fullness of the Godhead bodily, the Countenance of God, the one name under heaven whereby we must be saved. Yeshua the Messiah is God manifest in the flesh!

The Torah could not deliver man from sin and death. It was weak through the flesh. It could not do what needed to be done for our redemption. It could not serve as a propitiation. So, God did not send the Torah in the flesh for our deliverance. He sent His own Son

The first giving of the Torah is associated with the law in your flesh (sin) and it needed to be done away. It was then resurrected to life (spirit) which is done by the Son of God, the manifest Name of YHWH, so that it can now bring life to each of us, who by nature is a sinner (fleshly).

Romans 8:3, For <u>what the law could not do, in that it was weak through the flesh, God sending his own Son</u> in the likeness of sinful flesh, and for sin, condemned sin in the flesh:

Paul is contrasting the Torah and the Son of God. He is making it clear that Yeshua is not the Torah made flesh. He is none other than the manifest Name of YHWH. You need to join with your ascended male, the Messiah Yeshua. You do not join a female to a female (Israel or Judah), you join a female to a male (the Messiah).

Isaiah 56:6, Also the sons of the stranger, <u>that join themselves to the Lord</u>, to serve him, and <u>to love the Name of the Lord</u>, to be his servants, every one that keepeth the sabbath from polluting it, and taketh hold of my covenant; 7 Even them will I bring to my holy mountain, and make them joyful in my house of prayer: their burnt offerings and their sacrifices shall be accepted upon mine altar; for mine house shall be called an house of prayer for all people. 8 The Lord God, which gathereth the outcasts of Israel saith, Yet will I gather others to him, beside those <u>that are gathered unto him</u>.

You are joined and grafted into the Messiah. All those who have been grafted into the Messiah are of the Commonwealth of Israel. So, what is the change in the Law (Torah) that is spoken of in the book of Hebrews? Did it pass away? No.

Hebrews 7:12, For the priesthood being changed, there is made of necessity a change also of the law.

Just as the priesthood has been changed (not done away) from imperfection to the addition of that which makes perfect (the Melchisedec Priesthood), the Torah has now gone from the administration of death (seed), to a Torah with the administration of resurrection life with grace and abundant mercy (better promises or fruit). As Paul says it is no longer a Torah of Sin and Death.

> Romans 8:1, There is therefore now no condemnation to them which are in Christ Yeshua, who walk not after the flesh, but after the Spirit. 2 For the law of the Spirit of life in Christ Yeshua hath made me free from the law of sin and death. 3 For what the law could not do, in that it was weak through the flesh, God sending his own Son in the likeness of sinful flesh, and for sin, condemned sin in the flesh:

Being free from the Torah of Sin and Death (seed), we are now under the Torah with the same commandments with grace and abundant mercy (resurrection life–fruit).

> Exodus 34:1, And the Lord said unto Moses, Hew thee two tablets of stone like unto the first: and I will write upon these tablets the words that were in the first tablets, which thou brakest. . 5 And the Lord descended in the cloud, and stood with him there, and proclaimed the Name of the Lord. 6 And the Lord passed by before him, and proclaimed, The Lord, The Lord God, merciful and gracious, longsuffering, and abundant in goodness and truth, 7 Keeping mercy for thousands, forgiving iniquity and transgression and sin, and that will by no means clear the guilty; visiting the iniquity of the fathers upon the children, and upon the children's children, unto the third and to the fourth generation. 8 And Moses made haste, and bowed his head toward the earth, and worshipped.

We see the dual giving of the Torah. The first time the tablets are broken (like the flesh), and then the tablets are remade and caused to ascend the mountain with Moses for the re–Utterance of the same commandments. This time it is with grace and mercy assured. This is a picture of resurrection life (the spirit). The Utterances are the same for both sets of tablets. The first set were crushed and died like a seed, the second set ascend like a resurrected fruit.

When Moses descends the mountain with the new set of tablets that were written with grace and mercy and the manifest Name of YHWH is presented, we see a new wonder. Moses' countenance has been glorified by the work of the manifest Name of YHWH, the Messiah, Yeshua.

> Exodus 34:29, And it came to pass, when Moses came down from mount Sinai with the two tablets of testimony in Moses' hand, when he came down from the mount, that Moses wist not that the skin of his face shone while he talked with him. 30 And when Aaron and all the children of Israel saw Moses, behold, the skin of his face shone; and they were afraid to come nigh him. 31 And Moses called unto them; and Aaron and all the rulers of the congregation

returned unto him: and Moses talked with them. 32 And afterward all the children of Israel came nigh: and he gave them in commandment all that the Lord had spoken with him in mount Sinai. 33 And till Moses had done speaking with them, he put a vail on his face. 34 But when Moses went in before the Lord to speak with him, he took the vail off, until he came out. And he came out, and spake unto the children of Israel that which he was commanded. 35 And the children of Israel saw the face of Moses, that the skin of Moses' face shone: and Moses put the vail upon his face again, until he went in to speak with him.

Once again, we see the correction of the duality (two giving's of the Torah), one according to death and judgment (flesh) and the second according to the spirit (resurrection grace and mercy).

The first giving of the Torah occurs with a sprinkling of blood (flesh). The second giving of the Torah results in the glorification of the countenance of Moses. These events are all a prophetic type and image of our current fallen state and the promise of the resurrection.

This is how the Torah is easily understood to be a Law (Torah) of Sin and Death–flesh, which is then resurrected into a Torah of Life–the Spirit. Both have the same Utterances. Only the second is uttered with the manifest presence of the Name of YHWH, the Messiah Yeshua. His presence causes our countenances to be glorified.

Some Torah observant followers of Yeshua have mistakenly missed the dual imagery of the giving of the Torah and its significance as it relates to our fallen and dual existence of flesh and spirit. They do not understand the Apostle Paul because they still do not understand the imagery of the Torah.

Some mistakenly think Paul is saying we are free from the Torah. Some others mistakenly cannot understand how the Torah could have been both according to "sin and death" and then unto "resurrected life". Notice Paul prefaces his comments about the Torah with the clarification of the conflict between the flesh and the spirit. All of his comments must relate back to this basic conflict of duality.

Romans 8:1, There is therefore now no condemnation to them which are in Christ Yeshua, who walk not after the flesh, but after the Spirit. 2 For the law of the Spirit of life in Christ Yeshua hath made me free from the law of sin and death. 3 For what the law could not do, in that it was weak through the flesh, God sending his own Son in the likeness of sinful flesh, and for sin, condemned sin in the flesh:4 That the righteousness of the law might be fulfilled in us, who walk not after the flesh, but after the Spirit. 5 For they that are after the flesh do mind the things of the flesh; but they that are after the Spirit the things of the Spirit. 6 For to be carnally minded is death; but to be spiritually minded is life and peace. 7 Because the carnal mind is enmity against God: for it is not subject to the law of God, neither indeed can be. 8 So then they that are in the flesh cannot please God. 9 But ye are not in the flesh, but in the Spirit, if so be that the Spirit of God dwell in you. Now if any man have not the Spirit of Christ, he is none of his. 10 And if Christ be in you, the body is dead because of sin; but the Spirit is life because of righteousness. 11 But if the Spirit of him that raised up Yeshua from the dead dwell in you, he that raised up Christ from the dead shall also quicken your mortal bodies by his Spirit that dwelleth in you. 12 Therefore, brethren, we are debtors, not to the flesh, to live after the flesh. 13 For if ye live after the flesh, ye shall die: but if ye through the Spirit do mortify the deeds of the body, ye shall live. 14 For as many as are led by the Spirit of God, they are the sons of God.

Take notice of the following. The Torah was given the first time according to the duality of the Tree of the Knowledge of Good and Evil (duality of spirit and flesh), sin and death (the flesh/blood, Exodus 20/24). When the Torah was given the second time it was according to the Tree of Life (singular and spirit, Exodus 34). We are to put off the flesh and mind the things of the spirit. We must leave the flesh (literally at death) in order to please God and leave the duality of sin and death behind. If you are in Christ your spirit is living and your flesh is dying. It is the flesh that is passing away, not the Torah. God will quicken your body and make it spirit after death. It is the flesh that we need to be delivered from.

Romans 7:7, What shall we say then? <u>Is the law sin</u>? God forbid. Nay, I had not known sin, but by the law (Torah): for I had not known lust, except the law had said, Thou shalt not covet. 8 But sin, taking occasion by the commandment, wrought in me all manner of concupiscence. For without the law (Torah) sin was dead. 9 For I was alive without the law (Torah) once: but when the commandment came, sin revived, and I died. 10 And the commandment, which was ordained to life, I found to be unto death. 11 For sin, taking occasion by the commandment, deceived me, and by it slew me. 12 Wherefore the law (Torah) is holy, and the commandment holy, and just, and good. 13 Was then that which is good made death unto me? God forbid. But sin, that it might appear sin, working death in me by that which is good; that sin by the commandment might become exceeding sinful. 14 For <u>we know that the law (Torah) is spiritual: but I am carnal, sold under sin</u>. 15 For that which I do I allow not: for what I would, that do I not; but what I hate, that do I. 16 If then I do that which I would not, I consent unto the law that it is good. 17 Now then it is no more I that do it, but sin that dwelleth in me. 18 For I know that in me (that is, in my flesh,) dwelleth no good thing: for to will is present with me; but how to perform that which is good I find not. 19 For the good that I would I do not: but the evil which I would not, that I do. 20 Now if I do that I would not, it is no more I that do it, but sin that dwelleth in me. 21 I find then a law, that, when I would do good, evil is present with me. 22 <u>For I delight in the law of God after the inward man</u>:23 But I see another law in my members, warring against the law of my mind, and bringing me into captivity to the law of sin which is in my members. 24 O wretched man that I am! who shall deliver me from the body of this death? 25 I thank God through Yeshua our Lord. So then with the mind I myself serve the law of God; but with the flesh the law of sin.

What have we learned? The Torah of Moses defines what sin is and the Torah is holy and good. The Torah does what it should, it condemns the flesh because it is by nature like the Tree of the Knowledge of Good and Evil (dual and corrupt). The Torah identifies sin and condemns the flesh as it should. The flesh is not meant to survive. The Torah is rightfully the Law of Sin and Death. The Torah is spiritual and condemns the carnal (flesh) as it should. Those who are subject to the dual nature (flesh and sprit) are powerless to deliver themselves. We sin because we are subject to the flesh. That will not change until we are delivered from the flesh and are made singular (spirit). Paul rightfully concludes his outward man (flesh) cannot keep the Torah, so he does what he can and delights in the Torah after the inward man (the spirit). Paul asks, who can deliver us from the body of this death (flesh)? Only Yeshua the Messiah, the manifest Name of YHWH.

Knowing that we are in the battle of the duality of the Tree of the Knowledge of Good and Evil, the flesh versus the spirit, how do we proceed? Do we forsake the Torah? No, we delight in it. Do we cling to the flesh? No, we cling to the spirit.

25 WHAT IS "READY TO VANISH AWAY"?

Was there a fault with the covenant? Yes, the people were under a curse, the Tree of the Knowledge of Good and Evil. We all are dual in nature, flesh and spirit. By nature, it is not possible for us to keep the Torah (Law) of God successfully. Our tabernacle is flawed. We need a new tabernacle made by the Messiah Yeshua. We need a new body, singular in nature (spirit) and made in accordance with grace and mercy (resurrection life).

Hebrews 8:2, A <u>minister of the sanctuary, and of the true tabernacle, which the Lord pitched</u>, and not man. 3 For every high priest is ordained to offer gifts and sacrifices: wherefore it is of necessity that this man have somewhat also to offer. 4 For if he were on earth, he should not be a priest, seeing that there are priests that offer gifts according to the law:5 Who serve unto the example and <u>shadow of heavenly things</u>, as Moses was admonished of God when he was about to make the tabernacle: for, See, saith he, that thou make all things according to the pattern shewed to thee in the mount. 6 But now hath he obtained a more excellent ministry, by how much also he is the <u>mediator of a better covenant, which was established upon better promises</u>. 7 For if that first covenant had been faultless, then should no place have been sought for the second. 8 For <u>finding fault with them,</u> he saith, Behold, the days come, saith the Lord, when I will make a new covenant with the house of Israel and with the house of Judah:9 Not according to the covenant that I made with their fathers in the day when I took them by the hand to lead them out of the land of Egypt; because they continued not in my covenant, and I regarded them not, saith the Lord. 10 For <u>this is the covenant that I will make with the house of Israel after those days, saith the Lord; I will put my laws into their mind, and write them in their hearts</u>: and I will be to them a God, and they shall be to me a people:11 And they shall not teach every man his neighbour, and every man his brother, saying, Know the Lord: for all shall know me, from the least to the greatest. 12

For I will be merciful to their unrighteousness, and their sins and their iniquities will I remember no more. 13 In that he saith, A new covenant, he hath made the first old. <u>Now that which decayeth and waxeth old is ready to vanish away</u>.

What is old and decaying and ready to vanish away? The Torah? No, our fleshly bodies that are dual in nature (flesh and spirit) and subject to the Tree of the Knowledge of Good and Evil. We are corruption needing to put on incorruption (singularity–spirit). Yeshua is the minister of that new sanctuary. We are grafted into His tree, the Tree of Life. The flesh is vanishing away. Hebrews 9 clarifies that it is this tabernacle that is passing away. This tabernacle (your body) is passing from the flesh to the spirit.

Hebrews 9:7, But into the second went the high priest alone once every year, not without blood, which he offered for himself, and for the errors of the people:8 The Holy Ghost this signifying, that the way into the holiest of all was not yet made manifest, <u>while as the first tabernacle was yet standing</u>:9 Which was a figure for the time then present, in which were offered both gifts and sacrifices, that could not make him that did the service perfect, as pertaining to the conscience; 10 Which stood only in meats and drinks, and divers washings, and carnal ordinances, imposed on them until the time of reformation. 11 But <u>Christ being come an high priest of good things to come, by a greater and more perfect tabernacle, not made with hands</u>, that is to say, <u>not of this building</u>; 12 Neither by the blood of goats and calves, but by his own blood he entered in once into the holy place, having obtained eternal redemption for us. 13 For if the blood of bulls and of goats, and the ashes of an heifer sprinkling the unclean, sanctifieth to the purifying of the flesh:14 How much more shall the blood of Christ, who through the eternal Spirit offered himself without spot to God, purge your conscience from dead works to serve the living God? 15 And for this cause he is the mediator of the new testament, that by means of death, for the redemption of the transgressions that were under the first testament, they which are called might receive the promise of eternal inheritance. 16 For where a testament is, there must also of necessity be the death of the testator.

It is the current tabernacle of the Tree of the Knowledge of Good and Evil (the flesh and spirit) that is passing away, to be replaced by a greater and more perfect tabernacle not made with hands, the Tree of Life (spirit). That greater and more perfect tabernacle, the spirit, is not of this building or dual nature. There is no need for the purification of the flesh in that more perfect tabernacle. Remember the concept of a tent or tabernacle is a type of the body in which the life/soul dwells. The new tabernacle is not of the flesh, it is of the spirit only. Yeshua tells us not to worry about the death of our bodies for only God can destroy our spirit.

Matthew 10:28, And fear not them which kill the body, but are not able to kill the soul: but rather fear him which is able to destroy both soul and body in hell.

We need to remember the continuing patterns of the conflict of the flesh and the spirit and how it underlies the reality of the manifest universe. The female must always join with the ascended male, not with another female. That is why all believers (Jew or Gentile) must be grafted into the administrator of resurrection life (Yeshua the Messiah, the manifest Name of YHWH) and having done so, they are all of the Commonwealth of Israel. What do they have in common? The Messiah Yeshua, they are all grafted into the ascended male. This is why the unbelieving mate is sanctified by his/her believing mate. Belief, faith, and trust are from the ascended male.

Who saves us?
- The Torah? No!
- Israel? No.
- Judah? No.
- The manifest Name of YHWH, Yeshua the Messiah? Yes.

It is through this belief on the manifest Name of YHWH, the seed of the woman, the Messiah Yeshua, that our fallen countenance is restored to the image of YHWH. Our duality (flesh and spirit) is made singularity (spirit and resurrected life). We are literally born again when we leave the flesh of these corrupted bodies.

1 Peter 1:19, But with the precious blood of Christ, as of a lamb without blemish and without spot:20 Who verily was foreordained before the foundation of the world, but was manifest in these last times for you, 21 Who by him do believe in God, that raised him up from the dead, and gave him glory; that your faith and hope might be in God. 22 Seeing ye have purified your souls in obeying the truth through the Spirit unto unfeigned love of the brethren, see that ye love one another with a pure heart fervently:23 Being born again, not of corruptible seed, but of incorruptible, by the word of God, which liveth and abideth for ever. 24 For all flesh is as grass, and all the glory of man as the flower of grass. The grass withereth, and the flower thereof falleth away:25 But the word of the Lord endureth for ever. And this is the word which by the Gospel is preached unto you.

What have we learned? We are redeemed by the precious blood of Yeshua the Messiah, the manifest Name of YHWH. By singular faith (unwavering) in Him we believe in God. We are to be born again of incorruptible seed and the corruptible seed (flesh) we currently have will be burned up like grass. This is the Gospel. What seed are you sowing, flesh or spirit?

Galatians 6:7, Be not deceived; God is not mocked: for whatsoever a man soweth, that shall he also reap. 8 For he that soweth to his flesh shall of the flesh reap corruption; but he that soweth to the Spirit shall of the Spirit reap life everlasting. 9 And let us not be weary in well doing: for in due season we shall reap, if we faint not.

If you are a Christian you are mistaken if you think you do not need to keep the Written Torah of Moses. You must accept Yeshua, the manifest Name of YHWH, the resurrected administrator of the resurrected Torah of Moses, and with the Spirit of the Messiah that is reconciled to God, you should do as Malachi instructs and "remember the Law of Moses…with the statutes and judgments".

> Malachi 4:3, And ye shall tread down the wicked; for they shall be ashes under the soles of your feet in the day that I shall do this, saith the Lord of hosts. 4 <u>Remember ye the law of Moses my servant</u>, which I commanded unto him in Horeb for all Israel, with the statutes and judgments. 5 <u>Behold, I will send you Elijah the prophet before the coming of the great and dreadful day of the Lord</u>:6 And he shall turn the heart of the fathers to the children, and the heart of the children to their fathers, lest I come and smite the earth with a curse.

If you are already keeping the written Law of Moses and still have not accepted the new administrator of the Resurrected Covenant, Yeshua the Messiah, then you need to do so. Why? Because otherwise you are still under the old administration of condemnation and death. Through Yeshua you move to the new administration of "grace and abundant mercy" otherwise known as resurrection life.

Take note of the fact that this remembering the Law of Moses is directed to those who fear His name. Believers are defined by fearing the name of the Lord (Malachi 4:2). That name of the Lord is the Messiah Yeshua. So, anyone who thinks they can be a Christian and honoring the manifest Name of the Lord (Matthew 23:39), Yeshua, while refusing to follow His commandments…has a serious theological and biblical quandary to settle.

Knowing this would be an end-time issue, God determined to send an end-time witness to help believers in the Messiah to restore something that needs to be restored. Malachi makes it clear that this event occurs right before the Day of the Lord and that messenger is Elijah coming with the declaration, to believers in the Messiah, to "Remember ye the law of Moses my servant, which I commanded unto him in Horeb for all Israel, with the statutes and judgments…" (Malachi 4:1-5)

26 THE BOOK OF MANIFESTATION AND THE END-TIME BATTLE – ELIJAH VS ANTICHRIST

Yeshua was extremely clear that Elijah would come to restore all things before His return.

> Matthew 17:10, And his disciples asked him, saying, Why then say the scribes that Elias must first come? 11 And Yeshua answered and said unto them, Elias truly shall first come, and restore all things. 12 But I say unto you, That Elias is come already, and they knew him not, but have done unto him whatsoever they listed. Likewise shall also the Son of man suffer of them. 13 Then the disciples understood that he spake unto them of John the Baptist.

Yeshua is clarifying that John fulfilled the Elijah calling and this same Spirit of Elijah would come before the Day of the Lord to fulfill the same ministry, restoration to the Torah of Moses under grace and abundant mercy via the administration of Yeshua the Messiah. We see the commission of those who come in the spirit of Elijah.

> Luke 1:13, But the angel said unto him, Fear not, Zacharias: for thy prayer is heard; and thy wife Elisabeth shall bear thee a son, and thou shalt call his name John. 14 And thou shalt have joy and gladness; and many shall rejoice at his birth. 15 For he shall be great in the sight of the Lord, and shall drink neither wine nor strong drink; and he shall be filled with the Holy Ghost, even from his mother's womb. 16 And many of the children of Israel shall he turn to the Lord their God. 17 And he shall go before him in the spirit and power of Elias (Elijah), to turn the hearts of the fathers to the children, and the disobedient to the wisdom of the just; to make ready a people prepared for the Lord.

This turning of the children to the fathers is talking about the restoration of the future generations being restored to the faith of Abraham, Isaac, and Jacob: The Law of Moses under the administration of grace and mercy via the new administrator, Yeshua the Messiah. Malachi affirms this.

Malachi 4:4, <u>Remember ye the law of Moses my servant</u>, which I commanded unto him in Horeb for all Israel, with the statutes and judgments. 5 Behold, I will send you Elijah the prophet before the coming of the great and dreadful day of the Lord:6 And <u>he shall turn the heart of the fathers to the children, and the heart of the children to their fathers</u>, lest I come and smite the earth with a curse.

The book of Revelation (Manifestation) also affirms this.
- Revelation 12:17, And the dragon was wroth with the woman, and went to make war with the remnant of her seed, <u>which keep the commandments of God, and have the testimony of Yeshua.</u>
- Revelation 14:12, Here is the patience of the saints:<u> here are they that keep the commandments of God, and the faith of Yeshua.</u>

If you have ears to hear, repent and turn to the Lord, Yeshua, and begin to learn about the Written Law of Moses. There is only one way of salvation, Yeshua the Messiah, totally by grace and not by any work or righteousness of your own. Once you have received His sacrifice, learn to walk as He walked and keep His Law.

John 14:15, <u>If ye love me, keep my commandments</u>. 16 And I will pray the Father, and he shall give you another Comforter, that he may abide with you for ever; 17 Even the Spirit of truth; whom the world cannot receive, because it seeth him not, neither knoweth him: but ye know him; for he dwelleth with you, and shall be in you. 18 I will not leave you comfortless: I will come to you. 19 Yet a little while, and the world seeth me no more; but ye see me: because I live, ye shall live also. 20 At that day ye shall know that I am in my Father, and ye in me, and I in you. 21 <u>He that hath my commandments, and keepeth them, he it is that loveth me</u>: and he that loveth me shall be loved of my Father, and <u>I will love him, and will manifest myself to him.</u>

Just as Yeshua, the Prophets, and the Apostles all foretell a great falling away and a man of lawlessness enslaving the people to his mark and the image of the Beast, they also declare that in that time the Spirit of Elijah will oppose the Antichrist with the Holy Spirit and restore the Law of Moses as God intended for His Holy people.
This end-time battle is the flesh vs. the spirit, the mark of the Beast vs. the Mark of God, the Image of the Beast vs. the Image of God, the Law of Moses vs. the Mystery of Iniquity and the Man of Sin.
For millennia people have been watching for this lawless man, all the while

ignoring God's promise to send Elijah to restore the Law of Moses to His people. Erroneous teaching for 2,000 years has led us to the final manifestation of this conflict of light vs darkness. You cannot hope to stand your ground or even determine if you are holding the ground for God or in reality, the Antichrist…without learning about the very Law that God descended to the Earth to reveal to His called-out people.

The Church has deluded itself by the means of inaccurate and unscriptural teaching to believe that its redeemed state is something different from being the "Israel of God". And as such we have a responsibility to find out what Yeshua instructed Moses and all of Israel when he led them in the wilderness.

1 Corinthians 10:4, And did all drink the same spiritual drink: for they drank of that spiritual Rock that followed them: and that Rock was Christ.

It is because of so many unscriptural teachings, doctrines, and holidays, that Christians have sold their birthright of truth so that they might fit in and belong with the other nations. The false paradigm of "law vs. grace" has blinded the eyes of the church of God and we need to do as Yeshua instructs and anoint our eyes with eye salve so that we might behold the truth of our current state (Revelation 3:18). The church has become arrogant in its own conceits, declaring itself more righteous than God. It is committing the same errors that Israel historically committed. What follows next…is judgment and it will begin in our house.

1 Peter 4:7, For the time is come that judgment must begin at the house of God: and if it first begin at us, what shall the end be of them that obey not the gospel of God?

This judgment comes in the form of the Antichrist and lawlessness. All those who love his lies and attach themselves to him will share his fate. Those who claim "once saved…always saved" will find out rather quickly that those who accept the mark and the image of the beast share in his fate.

Revelation 16:2, And the first went, and poured out his vial upon the earth; and there fell a noisome and grievous sore upon the men which had the mark of the beast, and upon them which worshipped his image.

The book of Revelation (Manifestation) is terribly clear that those who worship the beast and his image, by taking his mark…are worshiping a false god. As such they will receive from God those same punishments that are pronounced on the beast. There are many believers that think the church will not be present for these final seven years. Yet the book of Revelation is exceptionally clear that there will be those who hold the testimony of Yeshua and are keeping the Law of Moses…and these same people will be subject to the Antichrist's wrath.

Revelation 12:17, And the dragon was wroth with the woman, and went to make war with the remnant of her seed, which keep the commandments of

God, and have the testimony of Jesus Christ.

The defining characteristics of this group are the defining characteristics of the Body of Christ. To hold that these same believers are not the Body of Christ and not the Church holds no scriptural water.

The defining characteristics of this group are the defining characteristics of the Body of Christ. To hold that these same believers are not the Body of Christ and not the Church is unscriptural.

Revelation 3:14, And unto the angel of the church of the Laodiceans write; These things saith the Amen, the faithful and true witness, the beginning of the creation of God; 15 I know thy works, that thou art neither cold nor hot: I would thou wert cold or hot. 16 <u>So then because thou art lukewarm, and neither cold nor hot, I will spue thee out of my mouth</u>. 17 Because thou sayest, I am rich, and increased with goods, and have need of nothing; and knowest not that thou art wretched, and miserable, and poor, and blind, and naked:18 I counsel thee to buy of me gold tried in the fire, that thou mayest be rich; and white raiment, <u>that thou mayest be clothed, and that the shame of thy nakedness do not appear; and anoint thine eyes with eyesalve, that thou mayest see</u>. 19 As many as I love, I rebuke and chasten: be zealous therefore, and repent. 20 Behold, <u>I stand at the door, and knock</u>: if any man hear my voice, and open the door, I will come in to him, and will sup with him, and he with me. 21 To him that overcometh will I grant to sit with me in my throne, even as I also overcame, and am set down with my Father in his throne.

The church that Yeshua depicts himself as being at the very door knocking and asking to be let in is not ready for Him, not interested in Him, and are essentially spiritually blind. He also indicates they are unclothed and will be spued out of His mouth. All of the identifying marks that indicate redemption is lacking by this end-time church. Yeshua is fulfilling the role of this Elijah ministry pleading with His church to repent and remember the Law of Moses. He is not coming to rapture them away. He is warning them that they are about to get spued out of his mouth into the Great Tribulation. His second coming is prophetically depicted as being near or "at the door", just like Elijah on Passover Eve.

Matthew 24:33, So likewise ye, when ye shall see all these things, know that it is near, <u>even at the doors</u>.

Being at the door would seem to be a marker that Laodicea is the final era of the church and finds itself in apostasy…. needing to repent…not to be raptured, but to keep from being expelled from the Body of Christ.

That being the case only those who do repent are not expelled. Those who are expelled join the Antichrist and his lawless ways. It would strongly appear that "once saved always saved" is unscriptural. If you have bought into this lie, then repent, call out to Yeshua and start reading the Bible for what it actually does say and not for what you want it to say.

The Apostle Paul clearly teaches that those who are "saved" have the need to conform to the Image of the Son of God in order to stay in the body and therefore in the redeemed state.

Romans 8:29, For whom he did foreknow, he also did predestinate to be conformed to the image of his Son, that he might be the firstborn among many brethren.

The truth about the imagery and symbols of the Bible are very important. Ultimately the Son of God being the Image of God restoring our fallen and broken image is the height of the redemption of all things. You will have a choice, conform to the Image of God or conform to the Image of the Beast. Either way you will have to choose and act upon your faith. Your choice will seal your fate.

Romans 12:2, And be not conformed to this world: but be ye transformed by the renewing of your mind, that ye may prove what is that good, and acceptable, and perfect, will of God.

This battle starts in the hearts and minds of man and finally manifests itself in end-time events. Just as Moses had Aaron...Just as Yeshua had John the Baptist...this end time "Elijah" will need you.

Micah 4:2, And many nations shall come, and say, Come, and let us go up to the mountain of the Lord, and to the house of the God of Jacob; and he will teach us of his ways, and we will walk in his paths: for the law shall go forth of Sion, and the word of the Lord from Jerusalem.

Those who profess belief in Christ, yet pretend to think that they can make up their own self-defined law...based on how they feel...all the while attributing their conclusions to "god" are in for a strong bit of correction. The church has been overcome by delusional, self-serving creatures. The repentant need to return to the scriptures and unify them into a collective and cohesive understanding. Yeshua knew that His people would continue to have problems understanding His intentions and their role in the process of redemption. Israel has always had this problem. The same fractal of death and resurrection played out in the Old Testament and is still playing out today in the Body of Christ.

Many pastors, priests, and teachers of the Christian faith have mistakenly assumed that the Church is a separate body from Israel. Israel has and always will be the redeemed state of those who express faith in the Messiah. To assume that those who lived pre-Christ will not be resurrected or did not have the opportunity to express faith in the Lord and as such would not be partakers of the resurrection is to assume a false paradigm that is unscriptural. Those who assume the prophets did not have the indwelling of the Holy Spirit, because it was pre-Pentecost and pre-resurrection, completely misunderstand the scriptures.

When Israel came out of Egypt, God literally met with them in the wilderness and spoke to every one of them. God's manifest presence dwelt with them and led them day by day in the Shekinah Glory. At Christ's resurrection, many of the "Old Testament" saints were raised from the dead as well (Mathew 27:52). The attempt to maintain the inaccurate idea that the Church is separate, new, and different from Israel is unsupportable by the scriptures (Ephesians 2:12, Romans 9:6, Acts 13:23, Romans 11:26, Hebrews 8:8). It is this presumption that the Church is separate from Israel and Judah that has propagated this belief of "law vs. grace". Seeking to be and remain different from Israel, the Church has lost its own scriptures, its true identity, and its measure of truth. In the place of the scriptures and accurate doctrine, the Church has adopted psychology and being "nice", as if these are the true measure of truth and righteousness. Are we so deluded as to think that people of other faiths don't love their own children? Is this the measure of truth and righteousness? Will we hang all that we know on whether a parent loves their child?

Is this the sole measure of truth, whether we are tolerant of deviant and abusive behavior in the name of diversity? Is this the measure of Godliness and truth? Is acceptance of all manner of inappropriate relationships the measure of the "love of Christ"? Is this the measure of truth? Christians have been conned into a constant state of Stockholm Syndrome. They have been convinced that they should reject their own doctrines in the name of Christian love.

The liberal has convinced Christians that they are not being Christian if they do not love and accept others as they are. They have bought into this false image of Christianity that is naïve and unscriptural. The Bible is replete with examples of the faithful of God eschewing evil, rejecting those full of iniquity. It is also filled with the sinful who find company with the called of God because they have fulfilled a Godly requirement, Repentance.

That means they reject their former behavior, recognize and confess the sinfulness of it and pursue after lawful and righteous behavior. Psychology has turned the fruit of the spirit into tolerance and silence and if you fail to conform, then it says the faithful Christian is abusive, evil, and wicked.

The lawful are being made to be unlawful. Just as Christ, the pinnacle of righteousness was made into a lawbreaker so that He could be controlled and killed, people will do the same to those who believe on His name.

Christianity is at a crossroads where they must adhere to truth and be despised for it, or adopt the image of "righteousness" provided by the world and accept the punishments from God that will fall upon those who have joined themselves to the image of the Beast.

Jews also are at a crossroads. There are not several ways of salvation. There is only one way through the new administrator of resurrection life, Yeshua the Messiah. Jews can no longer content themselves with opposing pagan Christianity, who has forsaken God's Law (Law of Moses), and imagine that they are more righteousness than anyone else. The scriptures are clear that the believers in Yeshua should be keeping the Written Law of Moses and that Yeshua, the Apostles, and Paul, all clearly taught this same message.

Those who have a poor understanding of the Law of Moses (Written Torah) have a poor understanding of the Writings of Paul. Jews can no longer sit by and reject Yeshua the Messiah only because Christianity had forsaken the Law. God is calling for the Church and the Jews to remember the Law of Moses. Just as Israel forsook the Law of Moses and needed to be restored by Elijah through his purging Israel of pagan worship, so also the Church is fulfilling this same pattern. Just because Israel falls into iniquity and is called to repentance it does not justify the arguments that the Jews use against Yeshua the Messiah, nor does it make those arguments valid. All the world will be held to account for what it does with the truth of God revealed in nature, to every individual, and through the scriptures.

Jews who cling to the law and reject the lawfully appointed new administrator as was prophetically revealed in Exodus 34 still need to recognize Yeshua as the Messiah.

Matthew 23:39, For I say unto you, Ye shall not see me henceforth, till ye shall say, Blessed is he that cometh in the name of the Lord.

Why must they recognize Him? He is the administrator of the Law of Moses under "grace and mercy".

Exodus 34:5, And the Lord descended in the cloud, and stood with him there, and proclaimed the name of the Lord. 6 And the Lord passed by before him, and proclaimed, The Lord, The Lord God, merciful and gracious, longsuffering, and abundant in goodness and truth, 7 Keeping mercy for thousands, forgiving iniquity and transgression and sin, and that will by no means clear the guilty; visiting the iniquity of the fathers upon the children, and upon the children's children, unto the third and to the fourth generation. 8 And Moses made haste, and bowed his head toward the earth, and worshipped.

Yeshua qualified by the power of "resurrection life". He is the only one to have fulfilled the death and resurrection fractal. The mercy and grace proclaimed at the second giving of the Law comes via His resurrection life.

Hebrews 7:16, Who is made, not after the law of a carnal commandment, but after the power of an endless life.

This endless life comes via YHWH's name and provides the fractal of resurrection and manifestation of fruit.

Exodus 23:21, Beware of him, and obey his voice, provoke him not; for he will not pardon your transgressions: for my name is in him.

Just because Israel is back in the Land, it doesn't mean that they have been forgiven or waived the requirement to recognize Yeshua. Many churches have seemingly approved of Israel without recognizing that they still have the need to accept Yeshua as their Messiah. Israel has been brought to this moment of choice and will be forced by the Antichrist and with the mark of the beast and the image of the beast to make a choice. This could not happen without their first being brought back to the land. Just as Yeshua was brought before the Sanhedrin and forced to acknowledge their authority or be turned over to Pilate for a death sentence, so they also will be brought before the appointed Antichrist to make a choice to either honor and worship the Antichrist or honor and worship the Image of God, the Messiah Yeshua.

2 Corinthians 4:4, In whom the god of this world hath blinded the minds of them which believe not, lest the light of the glorious gospel of Christ, who is the Image of God, should shine unto them.

Jews and Christians are in for a terrible time in the coming years. We should be glad that God has taken such an interest in us to not leave our seed in the hands of those who do not believe in God and do not adhere to truth. This does mean that we will have to fulfill the fractal and pattern of a seed so that our children may inherit truth and righteousness.

Instead of seeking to coexist, you should be seeking God, truth, and righteousness. Millennia of false and unscriptural teaching has blinded Christians to God's expectation that we follow the Law of Moses under the administration of grace and abundant mercy provided by Yeshua the Messiah. He didn't fulfill the Law so that we could make up our own law, He fulfilled the Law in both the fractal of a seed in death and like an ascended and resurrected fruit.

First it brought death and Paul properly called it a "Law of Sin and Death" (Romans 8:2) and by His death and resurrection turned it into the "Law of the Spirit of life"! It wasn't done away, it was changed, just like the believer upon death is changed to resurrection life. The Messiah, the Law, the Believer, and all creation fulfill the same Law first of sin and death, then of resurrection life. The goal of the Christian is not to be free from the Law of Moses, it is to have that Law written on our hearts. The goal is to internalize that very same Law and those very same words.

Hebrews 8:10, For this is the covenant that I will make with the house of Israel after those days, saith the Lord; I will put my laws into their mind, and write them in their hearts: and I will be to them a God, and they shall be to me a people:

Because the Church has said for so many years that they are not Israel, they have ignored the very teachings of the Apostles that instruct them to be obedient to the Torah, the Writings, and the Prophets.

Romans 16:26, But now is made manifest, and by the scriptures of the prophets, according to the commandment of the everlasting God, made known to all nations for the obedience of faith:

The Church needs to wake up and realize the very scriptures that the Apostles told believers to use to validate truthful doctrine are the very scriptures that are labeled the "Old Testament"!

2 Timothy 3:16, All scripture is given by inspiration of God, and is profitable for doctrine, for reproof, for correction, for instruction in righteousness:

It is coming time for a wakeup call. Which side of the "10 virgin" chamber will you wake up on when the Bridegroom comes? Will it be on the side of truth filled with the seed of the Messiah, or will it be on the side of the Antichrist filled with his unlawfulness? Don't think that you will be able to skirt around this choice. God has knowingly brought us to this moment…everyone.

He wants to know if you will stand for the truth or if you will stand for a lie. Will you stand with Elijah returning believers to the Law of Moses or will you stand with the Antichrist and the illusion and deceit of freedom that he promises through his image and through his mark?

Like it or not Christians…this end time choice is about the Law of Moses. Like it or not Jews…this end time choice is about the Image of God, the Messiah Yeshua. Which seed are you going to manifest? Will you seek to save your spirit or your flesh? Within the context of Paul's writing about the ultimate conflict between our fallen image (the flesh) and the spirit we come to a much clearer understanding of the warning that Yeshua provided to His followers.

Luke 17:33, Whosoever shall seek to save his life shall lose it; and whosoever shall lose his life shall preserve it.

Believers are going to be a very small remnant compared to the world population. You will be made to feel bad for disagreeing with so many other people.

Revelation 13:3, And I saw one of his heads as it were wounded to death; and his deadly wound was healed: and all the world wondered after the beast.

The Antichrist's coming is going to be with all kinds of lying wonders and deceitful miracles.

2 Thessalonians 2:8, And then shall that Wicked be revealed, whom the Lord shall consume with the spirit of his mouth, and shall destroy with the brightness of his coming:9 Even him, whose coming is after the working of Satan with all power and signs and lying wonders, 10 And with all deceivableness of unrighteousness in them that perish; because they received not the love of the truth, that they might be saved.

If you are a shallow believer and are looking for signs as the only proof of validity of approval by God, you will be bitterly disappointed.

Revelation 13:12, And he exerciseth all the power of the first beast before him, and causeth the earth and them which dwell therein to worship the first beast, whose deadly wound was healed. 13 And he doeth great wonders, so that he maketh fire come down from heaven on the earth in the sight of men, 14 And deceiveth them that dwell on the earth by the means of those miracles which he had power to do in the sight of the beast; saying to them that dwell on the earth, that they should make an image to the beast, which had the wound by a sword, and did live.

So, if a miracle worker comes, but teaches lawlessness…what will you do? If you haven't read "The Elijah Calling" the first book in the series "Restoring Truth" by Ken Mentell, I would suggest you read it next. If this book has changed your viewpoint for the better, please participate in this outreach by buying a copy of this series for friends and family.

ABOUT THE AUTHOR

Ken Mentell is a believer in Yeshua the Messiah and a follower of the Written Law of Moses.

BOOKS BY KEN MENTELL

THE ELIJAH CALLING
ELIJAH VS ANTICHRIST